Cardiovascular Nursing:
A Comprehensive Guide to Patient Care

By

Leanne H. Fowler, DNP, MBA, AGACNP-BC, CNE

Upon successful completion of this course, continuing education hours will be awarded as follows:

Nurses: 30 Contact Hours*

*Western Schools is accredited as a provider of continuing nursing education by the American Nurses Credentialing Center's Commission on Accreditation.

ABOUT THE AUTHOR

Leanne H. Fowler, DNP, MBA, AGACNP-BC, CNE, is an Adult-Gerontology Acute Care Nurse Practitioner (AGACNP) and Director of the Doctor of Nursing Practice (DNP) – Nurse Practitioner program at Louisiana State University Health New Orleans (LSUH-NO) School of Nursing (SON). She graduated from the University of South Alabama College of Nursing after successfully implementing her DNP project titled, *Preventing Oversedation in the Mechanically Ventilated Critically Ill Adult via a Multiprofessional Implementation of the RASS Tool,* within a 430-bed community hospital. Her DNP concentrated in Nursing Education and AGACNP practice. Dr. Fowler has more than 16 years' experience as a Registered Nurse (RN) with specialty certification as a Critical Care RN. Dr. Fowler has received multiple local and state-wide awards recognizing her expertise in nursing education and critical care nursing. She serves as an active member and is on the board of multiple state and regional nursing and medical organizations in pursuit of the advancement of nursing practice and the profession in general.

> **Leanne H. Fowler** has disclosed that she has no significant financial or other conflicts of interest pertaining to this course book.

ABOUT THE PEER REVIEWER

Andrea K. Robinson, ACNP, is an Adult-Gerontology Acute Care Nurse Practitioner (AGACNP) at Riverside Methodist Hospital in Columbus, Ohio, working in Cardiac Electrophysiology, and she is the Advanced Practice Clinical Coordinator of the Left Atrial Appendage Management Clinic. She has a Bachelor of Science in Business Administration and graduated from the College of Nursing from The Ohio State University. Her Master of Science in Nursing was received from Case Western Reserve University in Cleveland, Ohio. Andrea serves as a Cardiovascular Team Council member of the Ohio Chapter of the American College of Cardiology and is on the Board of Directors for PODEMOS, a nonprofit international medical outreach brigade. She has special interests in stroke risk reduction in atrial fibrillation and preventative medicine in cardiology.

> **Andrea K. Robinson** has disclosed that she has no significant financial or other conflicts of interest pertaining to this course book.

Nurse Planner: Marcie Scott, MSN, RN

> The planner who worked on this continuing education activity has disclosed that she has no significant financial or other conflicts of interest pertaining to this course book.

Copy Editor: Graphic World, Inc.

Indexer: Dianne L. Schneider

ISBN: 978-1-68041-274-1

COURSE INSTRUCTIONS
IMPORTANT: Read these instructions *BEFORE* proceeding!

HOW TO EARN CONTINUING EDUCATION CREDIT

To successfully complete this course you must:
1) Read the entire course
2) Pass the final exam with a score of 75% or higher*
3) Complete the course evaluation

*You have three attempts to pass the exam. If you take the exam online, and fail to receive a passing grade, select "Retake Exam." If you submit the exam by mail or fax and you fail to receive a passing grade, you will be notified by mail and receive an additional answer sheet.

Final exams must be received at Western Schools before the **Complete By** date located at the top of the FasTrax answer sheet enclosed with your course.

Note: The **Complete By** date is either 1 year from the date of purchase, or the expiration date assigned to the course, whichever date comes first.

HOW TO SUBMIT THE FINAL EXAM AND COURSE EVALUATION

ONLINE: BEST OPTION!

For instant grading, regardless of course format purchased, submit your exam online at **www.westernschools.com/my-courses**. Benefits of submitting exam answers online:

➢ Save time and postage
➢ Access grade results instantly and retake the exam immediately, if needed
➢ Identify and review questions answered incorrectly
➢ Access certificate of completion instantly

Note: If you have not yet registered on Western Schools' website, you will need to register and then call customer service at 800-618-1670 to request your courses be made available to you online.

Mail or Fax: To submit your exam and evaluation answers by mail or fax, fill out the FasTrax answer sheet, which is pre-printed with your name, address, and course title. If you are completing more than one course, be sure to record your answers on the correct corresponding answer sheet.

Complete the FasTrax Answer Sheet using blue or black ink only. If you make an error use correction fluid. If the exam has fewer than 100 questions, leave any remaining answer circles blank. Respond to the evaluation questions under the heading "Evaluation," found on the right-hand side of the FasTrax answer sheet. See the FasTrax Exam Grading & Certificate Issue Options enclosed with your course order for further instructions.

CHANGE OF ADDRESS?

Contact our customer service department at 800-618-1670, or customerservice@westernschools.com, if your postal or email address changes prior to completing this course.

WESTERN SCHOOLS GUARANTEES YOUR SATISFACTION

If any continuing education course fails to meet your expectations, or if you are not satisfied for any reason, you may return the course materials for an exchange or a refund (excluding shipping and handling) within 30 days, provided that you have not already received continuing education credit for the course. Software, video, and audio courses must be returned unopened. Textbooks must not be written in or marked up in any other way.

Thank you for using Western Schools to fulfill your continuing education needs!

WESTERN SCHOOLS
P.O. Box 1930, Brockton, MA 02303
800-618-1670 • www.westernschools.com

WESTERN SCHOOLS
COURSE EVALUATION

CARDIOVASCULAR NURSING:
A COMPREHENSIVE GUIDE TO PATIENT CARE

INSTRUCTIONS: Using the scale below, please respond to the following evaluation statements. All responses should be recorded in the right-hand column of the FasTrax answer sheet, in the section marked "Evaluation." Be sure to fill in each corresponding answer circle completely using blue or black ink. Leave any remaining answer circles blank.

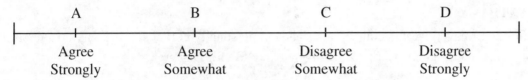

A	B	C	D
Agree Strongly	Agree Somewhat	Disagree Somewhat	Disagree Strongly

OUTCOMES: After completing this course, I am able to:

1. Describe the basic structures of the heart and their physiological functions.

2. Explain the components of cardiac output responsible for hemodynamic alterations.

3. Discuss the impact that epidemiology and behavioral/nonbehavioral risk factors have on the development of cardiovascular disease.

4. Discuss ways pharmacology is used to improve myocardial performance and increase myocardial oxygen supply.

5. Differentiate acute from chronic cardiovascular conditions.

6. Discuss the nursing considerations for chronic cardiovascular disease management throughout the continuum of presentation, diagnosis, and treatment.

7. Discuss the nursing considerations for common acute cardiovascular disease management throughout the continuum of presentation, diagnosis, and treatment.

8. Recognize the impact that cardiovascular conditions have on special populations.

9. Discuss the nursing considerations associated with cardiovascular revascularization therapies and implantable devices.

10. Identify the significance of the comprehensive cardiovascular health history and physical examination.

11. Recognize the significance of collaborative cardiovascular management through an interprofessional team.

COURSE CONTENT

12. The course content was presented in a well-organized and clearly written manner.

13. The course content was presented in a fair, unbiased and balanced manner.

14. The course content presented current developments in the field.

15. The course was relevant to my professional practice or interests.

16. The final examination was at an appropriate level for the content of the course.

17. The course expanded my knowledge and enhanced my skills related to the subject matter.

18. I intend to apply the knowledge and skills I've learned to my practice.

    A. Yes   B. Unsure   C. No   D. Not Applicable

continued on next page

CUSTOMER SERVICE

The following section addresses your experience in interacting with Western Schools. Use the scale below to respond to the statements in this section.

A. Yes   B. No   C. Not Applicable

19. Western Schools staff was responsive to my request for disability accommodations.

20. The Western Schools website was informative and easy to navigate.

21. The process of ordering was easy and efficient.

22. Western Schools staff was knowledgeable and helpful in addressing my questions or problems.

ATTESTATION

23. I certify that I have read the course materials and personally completed the final examination based on the material presented. Mark "A" for Agree and "B" for Disagree.

COURSE RATING

24. My overall rating for this course is

A. Poor   B. Below Average   C. Average   D. Good   E. Excellent

You may be contacted within 3 to 6 months of completing this course to participate in a brief survey to evaluate the impact of this course on your clinical practice and patient/client outcomes.

Note: To provide additional feedback regarding this course and Western Schools services, or to suggest new course topics, use the space provided on the Important Information form found on the back of the FasTrax instruction sheet included with your course.

CONTENTS

Course Evaluation..v

Figures, Tables, and Boxes..xxv

Pretest...xxxi

Introduction...xxxv

    Learning Outcomes xxxv

Chapter 1: Cardiovascular Anatomy and Physiology.......................................1

    Learning Outcome 1

    Chapter Objectives..1

    Introduction...1

    Cardiac Anatomy 1

        Cardiac Chambers..2

        Layers of the Heart...3

        Cardiac Valves...6

    Circulatory System..9

        Arterial System 9

        Capillary System..11

        Venous System...12

        Normal Circulatory Patterns 12

        Circulation Through the Heart 13

    Coronary Circulatory System 15

        Left Coronary Artery System...15

        Right Coronary Artery System 15

        Dominance...16

        Collateral Circulation..16

        Cardiac Veins...17

    Cardiac Physiology 17

        Electrophysiology 17

        Mechanical Physiology 18

        Neurohormonal Regulation..20

    Considerations for Special Populations 23

        Pregnancy...23

        Older Adults...25

    Summary 26

    Exam Questions 27

    References...29

Chapter 2: Principles Of Hemodynamics and Oxygen Delivery **31**

    Learning Outcome 31

    Chapter Objectives...31

    Introduction 31

    Hemodynamic Principles and Ventricular Function...............................31

        Components of Cardiac Output 31

    Oxygen Delivery and Consumption..37

        Oxygen Delivery 37

        Tissue Consumption..38

    Hemodynamic Measurements...39

        Measuring Pressures 39

        Venous Oxygen Saturation Monitoring 41

    Case Study 41

        Questions...42

        Answers...42

    Summary 42

    Exam Questions 43

    References..45

Chapter 3: Epidemiology of Cardiovascular Disease **47**

    Learning Outcome 47

    Chapter Objectives..47

    Introduction 47

    Trends 47

        Global..47

        National...48

    Risk factors 48

        Behavioral...48

        Metabolic 49

        Emerging...50

    Disease Prevention and Health Promotion 50

        Risk Stratification 50

        Primary Versus Secondary Prevention 51

        Health Promotion Initiatives...51

        Nursing Considerations...51

    Summary 52

    Exam Questions 53

    References..55

Chapter 4: Cardiovascular Pharmacotherapeutics 57

  Learning Outcome 57

  Chapter Objectives 57

  Introduction 57

  Cardiovascular Drug Classes 58

    Sympathomimetics 58

    Nonsympathomimetics 60

    Nitrates 61

    Diuretics 63

    Angiotensin-Converting Enzyme Inhibitors 65

    Angiotensin Receptor Blockers 66

    Beta Blockers 67

    Calcium Channel Blockers 68

    Antiarrhythmics 69

    Cardiac Glycoside 71

  Drugs That Affect Coagulation 72

    Coagulation Overview 72

    Thrombolytics and Fibrinolytics 73

    Anticoagulants 75

    Antiplatelets 80

  Applying Pharmacotherapeutics to Hemodynamic Alterations 83

    Pharmacology to Alter Preload 83

    Increasing Preload 83

    Decreasing Preload 83

    Pharmacology to Alter Afterload 83

    Increasing Afterload 83

    Decreasing Afterload 84

    Pharmacology to Alter Contractility 84

    Increasing Contractility 85

    Decreasing Contractility 85

    Pharmacology to Alter Heart Rate 86

    Increasing Heart Rate 86

    Decreasing Heart Rate 86

  Considerations for Special Populations 87

    Pregnancy 87

    Older Adult 87

  Emerging Science 87

    Pharmacogenomics in Cardiovascular Disease 88

Novel Medication..88

Case Study 88

    History of Present Illness 88

    Past Medical History..89

    Physical Exam Findings..89

    Diagnostics Performed..89

    Questions..89

    Answers..89

Summary..90

Exam Questions 91

References..93

Chapter 5: Hypertension and Hyperlipidemia.....................................95

Learning Outcome 95

Chapter Objectives...95

Introduction..95

Hypertension 95

    Causes 95

    Pathophysiology..96

    Epidemiology..97

    Symptoms 97

    Complications 98

    Diagnosis..98

    Treatment Considerations 98

    Collaborative Management..99

Hyperlipidemia 102

    Causes 102

    Pathophysiology..102

    Symptoms 103

    Complications 103

    Diagnosis..103

    Treatment Considerations 103

    Collaborative Management..105

Case Study 111

    History of Present Illness..111

    Past History 111

    Physical Exam Findings..111

    Diagnostics Performed..111

    Questions..111

Answers..111

Summary..112

Exam Questions 115

References..117

Chapter 6: Coronary Heart Disease..**119**

Learning Outcome 119

Chapter Objectives..119

Introduction...119

Pathophysiology of Coronary Heart Disease..119

Angina: The Sign and Symptom of Coronary Heart Disease 121

Features of Angina...122

Stable Angina..122

Unstable Angina..122

Aggravating Factors..122

Complications of Chronic Angina 123

Subpopulations Among Patients With Angina 123

Diagnosis of Coronary Heart Disease...124

Stress Testing..124

Coronary Computed Tomography Angiogram...127

Cardiac Catheterization...127

Treatment Considerations 128

Pharmacological Management...128

Nonpharmacological Treatment Options 130

Long-Term Management 130

Summary..130

Exam Questions 133

References..135

Chapter 7: Cardiomyopathy...**137**

Learning Outcome 137

Chapter Objectives..137

Introduction...137

Dilated Cardiomyopathy 137

Definition 137

Prevalence 137

Causes 137

Pathophysiology..139

Clinical Presentation 139

Physical Examination..139

Diagnosis 139

Medical Therapy 139

Surgical Therapy 140

Patient Outcomes 140

Restrictive Cardiomyopathy 140

Definition 140

Prevalence 140

Causes 140

Pathophysiology 140

Clinical Presentation 141

Physical Examination 141

Diagnosis 141

Medical Therapy 142

Surgical Therapy 142

Outcomes 142

Hypertrophic Cardiomyopathy 142

Definition 142

Prevalence 142

Causes 142

Pathophysiology 143

Clinical Presentation 143

Physical Examination 144

Diagnosis 144

Medical Therapy and Lifestyle Changes 144

Surgical Therapy 144

Outcomes 145

Arrhythmogenic Right Ventricular Cardiomyopathy 145

Definition 145

Prevalence 145

Causes 145

Pathophysiology 145

Clinical Presentation 145

Diagnosis 145

Medical and Surgical Therapy 145

Outcomes 146

Takotsubo Cardiomyopathy 146

Definition 146

Prevalence 146

Causes 146

Pathophysiology 146

Clinical Presentation 147

Physical Examination 147

Diagnosis 147

Medical Therapy 148

Surgical Therapy 148

Outcomes 148

Summary 149

Exam Questions 151

References 153

Chapter 8: Chronic Heart Failure: Pathophysiology, Assessment, and Treatment 155

Learning Outcome 155

Chapter Objectives 155

Introduction 155

Clinical Presentation 156

Etiology 157

Pathophysiology 158

Heart Failure With Reduced Ejection Fraction 158

Heart Failure With Preserved Ejection Fraction 158

Left and Right Ventricular Failure 159

Neurohormonal Responses 160

Assessment of Patients With Heart Failure 164

Initial Evaluation 164

American College of Cardiology/American Heart Association Stages of Heart Failure 165

New York Heart Association Functional Classification 165

Echocardiography 166

Pharmacological Treatment for Heart Failure 166

Angiotensin-Converting Enzyme Inhibitors and Angiotensin II Receptor Blockers 166

Beta Blockers 167

Aldosterone Antagonists 167

Hydralazine and Isosorbide Dinitrate 168

Diuretics 168

Digoxin 168

Contraindicated Medications 168

Nonpharmacological Treatment Strategies for Heart Failure 169

Exercise Training 169

Cardiac Resynchronization Therapy 169

Patient Education 170

    Recognition of Signs and Symptoms 171

    Daily Weights 171

    Medication Adherence 171

    Diet/Sodium Restriction 172

    Physical Activity and Socialization 172

    Follow-Up 172

Case Study 173

    Questions 173

    Answers 173

Summary 174

Exam Questions 175

References 177

Chapter 9: Chronic Heart Failure: Valve Conditions 179

Learning Outcome 179

Chapter Objectives 179

Introduction 179

Mitral Valve 180

    Mitral Valve Stenosis 180

    Mitral Valve Regurgitation 186

Aortic Valve 192

    Aortic Valve Stenosis 192

    Aortic Valve Regurgitation 201

Tricuspid Valve 205

    Tricuspid Valve Regurgitation 205

Summary 208

Exam Questions 209

References 211

Chapter 10: Atrial Fibrillation 213

Learning Outcome 213

Chapter Objectives 213

Introduction 213

Potential Causes 215

Classifications 215

    Atrial Fibrillation Based on Pathophysiology 215

Pathophysiology 217

Symptoms 217

Complications 218

Stroke 218

Hemodynamic Complications...219

Treatment Considerations 219

Rate Control 220

Rhythm Control 221

Antiarrhythmic Medications 221

Cardioversion..224

Use of Pharmacological Agents to Maintain Sinus Rhythm 226

Permanent Pacemaker Insertion..227

Atrial Defibrillators..227

Maze Surgical Procedure 228

Catheter Ablation Techniques...228

Primary Prevention Strategies...229

Treatment for Special Patient Populations..229

Atrial Fibrillation in Acute Myocardial Infarction 229

Atrial Fibrillation With Hypertrophic Cardiomyopathy.................229

Atrial Fibrillation With Wolff-Parkinson-White Syndrome............229

Acute, Hemodynamically Unstable Atrial Fibrillation...................230

Case Study 230

Questions...231

Answers...231

Summary 232

Exam Questions 233

References..235

Chapter 11: Diseases of the Aorta and Peripheral Vasculature........................237

Learning Outcome 237

Chapter Objectives...237

Introduction..237

Aortic Aneurysms 237

Prevalence 239

Causes 240

Pathophysiology...240

Aortic Aneurysm and Dissection 241

Clinical Presentation 242

Physical Examination...242

End Organ Ischemic Injuries 243

Diagnosis...245

Nursing Management 245

Medical Therapy 246

Surgical Therapy 247

Venous Disease 247

Prevalence 248

Causes 248

Pathophysiology 248

Clinical Presentation 249

Physical Examination 249

Diagnosis 250

Nursing Management 250

Medical Therapy 250

Surgical Therapy 251

Outcomes 251

Peripheral Arterial Disease 251

Prevalence 251

Causes 252

Pathophysiology 252

Clinical Presentation 252

Physical Examination 252

Diagnosis 253

Nursing Management 254

Medical Therapy 254

Surgical Therapy 255

Outcomes 255

Case Study 255

Questions 256

Answers 256

Summary 256

Exam Questions 257

References 259

Chapter 12: Implantable Devices for Cardiovascular Disease 261

Learning Outcome 261

Chapter Objectives 261

Introduction 261

Cardiac Pacemakers 262

Review of the Conduction System 262

Indications for Cardiac Pacing 262

Temporary versus Permanent Cardiac Pacemakers 264

Concepts of Permanent Cardiac Pacing 266

Components of a Permanent Cardiac Pacemaker 266

Types of Permanent Cardiac Pacing 268

Cardiac Pacing Modes 269

Pacemaker Insertion 271

Pacemaker Complications 272

Cardiac Resynchronization Therapy 274

Indications 275

Biventricular Pacemaker Insertion 275

Implantable Cardioverter-Defibrillators 276

Indications 276

Functions 276

Implantation 277

Patient Management 277

Pacemaker Postoperative Follow-Up 277

Cardiac Resynchronization Therapy Postoperative Care and Outcomes 279

Implantable Cardioverter-Defibrillator Postoperative Follow-Up 279

Patient Education 280

Pacemaker 280

Cardiac Resynchronization Therapy 281

Implantable Cardioverter-Defibrillator 281

Case Study 283

Questions 283

Answers 283

Summary 284

Exam Questions 285

References 287

Chapter 13: Acute Coronary Syndromes 289

Chapter Objective 289

Learning Outcomes 289

Introduction 289

ST-Segment Elevation Myocardial Infarction 289

Prevalence 290

Causes 290

Pathophysiology 290

Clinical Presentation 291

Physical Examination 292

Diagnosis 292

Primary Treatment Strategy in STEMI 293

Myocardial Locations of STEMIs 295

Key Nursing Care in the Acute Treatment of STEMI 298

Non-ST-Segment Elevation Myocardial Infarction and Unstable Angina 300

Prevalence 300

Causes 300

Pathophysiology 300

Clinical Presentation 300

Physical Examination 300

Diagnosis 300

Primary Treatment Strategies 302

Supportive Medical Therapy Used in All Patients With ACS 303

Oxygen 303

Aspirin 303

Clopidogrel/Prasugrel/Ticagrelor 303

Anticoagulants 303

Nitroglycerin 304

Morphine Sulfate 304

Beta Blockers 304

ACE Inhibitors 305

Complications of Myocardial Infarction 305

Hemodynamic Alterations 305

Ventricular Dysrhythmias 305

Mechanical Complications 306

Ventricular Remodeling 306

Special Considerations 307

Treatment of Cocaine-Induced Chest Pain 307

Variant (Vasospastic or Prinzmetal's) Angina 307

Cardiac Syndrome X 308

Long-Term Management of All Acute Coronary Syndromes 308

Patient Education 309

Cardiac Rehabilitation 311

Psychosocial Issues 313

Case Study 314

Questions 315

Answers 315

Summary 315

Exam Questions 317

References 319

Chapter 14: Acute Heart Failure...**321**

    Learning Outcome 321

    Chapter Objectives..321

    Introduction..321

    Acute Decompensated Heart Failure 321

        Acute Cardiovascular Events Leading to ADHF......................322

        Clinical Presentation 322

        Diagnosis..323

        Treatment Options 324

        Patient Management and Nursing Care 325

    Special Considerations in Heart Failure 325

        Palliative Care and Hospice Referral.......................................326

        Heart Transplantation...326

        Left Ventricular Assist Devices 327

    Summary 327

    Exam Questions 329

    References 331

Chapter 15: Acute Dysrhythmias...**333**

    Learning Outcome 333

    Chapter Objectives...333

    Introduction..333

    Initial Evaluation..333

        Pathophysiology of Dysrhythmias...333

    Tachydysrhythmias...335

        Clinical Approach to Acute Tachydysrhythmias.......................335

        Narrow Complex Tachydysrhythmias 335

        Wide Complex Tachydysrhythmias 340

    Bradydysrythmias 343

        Clinical Management Strategies 344

        Sinus Bradycardia – Symptomatic...344

        Sinus Node Dysfunction 344

        Atrioventricular Block 346

    Cardiac Arrest Dysrhythmias..346

        Ventricular Fibrillation 347

        Pulseless Electrical Activity 347

    Special Populations At Risk for Acute Dysrhythmias......................348

        Patients With Psychiatric Conditions..349

        Patients With Neurological Conditions 349

Patients Who Are Pregnant...350

Patients With Obstructive Sleep Apnea..350

Case Study 350

Questions...351

Answers...351

Summary 352

Exam Questions 353

References...355

Chapter 16: Shock States **357**

Learning Outcome 357

Chapter Objectives...357

Introduction..357

Types of Shock States..357

Obstructive Shock...357

Hypovolemic Shock...359

Distributive Shock 360

Cardiogenic Shock...363

Case Study 364

Questions...365

Answers...365

Summary 365

Exam Questions 367

References...369

Chapter 17: Common Acute Cardiac Emergencies...**371**

Learning Outcome 371

Chapter Objectives...371

Introduction..371

Syncope..371

Causes 371

Presentation...372

Physical Assessment Findings 373

Diagnosis...373

Treatment 373

Nursing Management...374

Hypertensive Emergency 375

Pathophysiology..375

Causes 375

Presentation...375

Physical Assessment Findings 375

Diagnosis 376

Treatment 376

Nursing Management 376

Infectious and Inflammatory Disorders 376

Pericarditis 377

Endocarditis 378

Case Study 380

Questions 380

Answers 380

Summary 381

Exam Questions 383

References 385

Chapter 18: Cardiac Revascularization Therapies **387**

Learning Outcome 387

Chapter Objectives 387

Introduction 387

General Revascularization Strategy Options and Considerations 387

Coronary Artery Bypass Grafting 388

Indications for Coronary Artery Bypass Graft Surgery 389

Contraindications 390

Traditional Coronary Artery Bypass Grafting 390

Graft Material 390

Minimally Invasive Techniques in Cardiac Surgery 395

The Risk for Complications With Coronary Artery Bypass Grafting 396

Anticoagulation and Antiplatelet Therapy Before Surgery 402

Special Populations 402

Postoperative Nursing Care 405

Angina After Coronary Artery Bypass Grafting 407

Percutaneous Coronary Intervention 407

Indications for Percutaneous Coronary Intervention 407

Interventional Revascularization and Adjunct Procedures 409

Advantages of Interventional Treatment 412

Success Rates 412

Complications 413

Special Circumstances 414

Medications Before, During, and After Percutaneous Catheter Intervention 415

Intraprocedure Considerations 416

     Postprocedure Nursing Care 417

    Case Study 420

     Questions.. 420

     Answers 421

    Summary 421

    Exam Questions 423

    References 425

Chapter 19: Cardiovascular History, Health Assessment, and Physical Examination 427

    Learning Outcome 427

    Chapter Objectives 427

    Introduction 427

    Patient Health History: Subjective and Objective Measures 427

     Patient Demographics 428

     History of Present Illness 430

     Medical History 436

     Extracardiac Conditions 436

     Congenital or Childhood History 436

     Hospitalizations... 436

     Special Populations 437

    Risk Stratification for Cardiovascular Disease 438

     Framingham Criteria 438

     $CHADS_2$ Risk Score 438

    Cardiovascular Physical Examination 439

     Comprehensive Cardiovascular Assessment 439

     Cardiovascular-Related Findings in Other Organ Systems 443

     Clinical Manifestations of Cardiovascular Conditions 445

     Acute Coronary Syndrome or Myocardial Infarction.. 445

     Physical Examination Considerations for Special Populations 446

    Case Study 447

     Questions... 447

     Answers 447

    Summary 448

    Exam Questions 449

    References 451

Chapter 20: Collaborative Management: Interprofessional Cardiovascular Team 453

    Learning Outcome 453

    Chapter Objectives 453

    Introduction 453

Core Competencies for Interprofessional Collaborative Practice 453

    Competency Domain 1: Values/Ethics for Interprofessional Practice 454

    Competency Domain 2: Roles/Responsibilities 454

    Competency Domain 3: Interprofessional Communication 454

    Competency Domain 4: Teams and Teamwork 455

Common Roles on the Cardiovascular Healthcare Team 455

    Cardiologist/Physician 455

    Nurse Practitioner 456

    Registered Nurse 456

    Unlicensed Assistive Personnel 456

    Interprofessional Cardiovascular Team Example 457

Summary 457

Exam Questions 459

References 461

Glossary **463**

Index **491**

FIGURES, TABLES, AND BOXES

Chapter 1

Figure 1-1: Heart Placement Within the Thoracic Cavity 2

Figure 1-2: Mediastinal Cardiovascular Structures 3

Figure 1-3: Transverse Section of Ventricular Wall Thickness.....................................4

Figure 1-4: Walls of the Heart 5

Figure 1-5: Heart With Pericardial Sac Opened 7

Figure 1-6: Internal Structures of the Heart..8

Figure 1-7: Chamber Contraction and Valve Function..10

Figure 1-8: Structure of Blood Vessels...11

Figure 1-9: Divisions of Aorta 13

Figure 1-10: Systemic Circulation 14

Figure 1-11: Coronary Arteries..16

Table 1-1: Coronary Artery Supply 17

Figure 1-12: Conduction System of the Heart 18

Table 1-2: Adrenergic Receptor Location and Response 21

Figure 1-13: Heart Displacement in Pregnancy..24

Chapter 2

Figure 2-1: Determinants of Cardiac Output 33

Figure 2-2: HR × SV = CO...34

Table 2-1: Key Definitions Relating to Cardiac Output 34

Figure 2-3: Impact of the Autonomic Nervous System on Heart Rate.............................35

Figure 2-4: Starling's Curve 36

Figure 2-5: Alveolar-Capillary Membrane 38

Figure 2-6: Influencing Factors of Oxyhemoglobin Dissociation 40

Figure 2-7: Pulmonary Artery Pressure Monitoring..41

Chapter 4

Table 4-1: Epinephrine 59

Table 4-2: Norepinephrine 59

Table 4-3: Dopamine 60

Table 4-4: Dobutamine 60

Table 4-5: Phenylephrine (Synthetic Compound) 61

Table 4-6: Calcium Channel Blockers 69

Table 4-7: Thrombolytic and Fibrinolytic Agents 74

Table 4-8: Foods With Moderate to High Content of Vitamin K 77

Table 4-9: Pharmacological Considerations for Increasing Preload 83

Table 4-10: Pharmacological Considerations for Decreasing Preload 84

Table 4-11: Pharmacological Considerations for Increasing Afterload 84

Table 4-12: Pharmacological Considerations for Decreasing Afterload 85

Table 4-13: Pharmacological Considerations for Increasing Contractility (Inotropes) 85

Table 4-14: Pharmacological Considerations for Decreasing Contractility 86

Table 4-15: Pharmacological Considerations for Increasing Heart Rate 86

Table 4-16: Pharmacological Considerations for Decreasing Heart Rate 87

Chapter 5

Table 5-1: Evidence-Based Practice Recommendations for Hypertension Treatment 100

Figure 5-1: Atherosclerosis Progression Secondary to Hyperlipidemia 104

Table 5-2: Effects of Lipid-Lowering Therapy on LDL-C Levels 105

Table 5-3: Effects of Lipid-Lowering Therapy on Triglyceride and HDL-C Levels 106

Box 5-1: Fibrate and Statin Contraindications 109

Box 5-2: HMG-COA Reductase Inhibitor Side Effects 110

Chapter 6

Figure 6-1: Evolution of Atherosclerotic Plaque in Coronary Artery Disease 121

Table 6-1: Common Exercise Stress Test Protocols 125

Chapter 7

Figure 7-1: Types of Cardiomyopathy 138

Figure 7-2: Obstructive Type of Hypertrophic Cardiomyopathy With Septal Wall Thickening 143

Figure 7-3: Takotsubo ("Japanese Octopus Pot") Cardiomyopathy 147

Figure 7-4: Ventriculogram During Systole and Diastole 148

Chapter 8

Figure 8-1: Hypertrophic Left Ventricle in Heart Failure With Preserved Ejection Fraction 159

Table 8-1: Summary Comparison of Heart Failure With Preserved Ejection Fraction
           and Heart Failure With Reduced Ejection Fraction 160

Figure 8-2: Neurohormonal Responses of the Renin-Angiotensin-Aldosterone System
           and Sympathetic Nervous System in Heart Failure 161

Figure 8-3: Vicious Cycle of Neurohormonal Responses and Ventricular Remodeling
           in Heart Failure 162

Table 8-2: Summary of Results of Neurohormonal Stimulation in Heart Failure 163

Figure 8-4: Comparison of Concentric Hypertrophy of Diastolic Dysfunction
           and Eccentric Hypertrophy of Systolic Dysfunction 164

Table 8-3 ACC/AHA Heart Failure Guidelines 166

Table 8-4: New York Heart Association Functional Classifications 166

Chapter 9

Figure 9-1: Normal Mitral Valve 181

Figure 9-2: Mitral Valve Stenosis 182

Table 9-1: Mitral Valve Stenosis Stages 183

Figure 9-3: Normal Functioning Mitral Valve 187

Figure 9-4: Mitral Valve Prolapse 188

Figure 9-5: Ruptured Papillary Muscle 188

Figure 9-6: Aortic Valve Showing the Three Cusps 193

Figure 9-7: Degenerative Aortic Valve Disease 194

Box 9-1: American College of Cardiology/American Heart Association
Recommendations for Aortic Valve Replacement 199

Figure 9-8: Normal Functioning of the Aorta During Systole and Diastole 202

Table 9-2: Peripheral Signs of Chronic Aortic Regurgitation 203

Table 9-3: Aortic Regurgitation Severity 204

Box 9-2: Indications for Tricuspid Regurgitation 208

Chapter 10

Figure 10-1: Normal Sinus-Derived Heartbeat 214

Figure 10-2: Normal Sinus Rhythm 214

Figure 10-3: Atrial Fibrillation 214

Figure 10-4: Mechanisms of Atrial Fibrillation 216

Table 10-1: Antiarrhythmic Classification System and Medications 222

Table 10-2: Antiarrhythmics (by Vaughan Williams Classification) Used in Atrial Fibrillation 222

Figure 10-5: Effect of Class I, III, and IV Antiarrhythmia Agents on Cardiac Action Potential 223

Box 10-1: Drugs Proven Most Effective for Pharmacological Cardioversion of Atrial Fibrillation 226

Box 10-2: Medications Used to Maintain Sinus Rhythm in Patients With Atrial Fibrillation ..226

Table 10-3: Medications Used to Maintain Sinus Rhythm in Special Patient Populations 227

Box 10-3: Medication Options for Rate Control in Atrial Fibrillation With
Wolff-Parkinson-White Syndrome 230

Chapter 11

Figure 11-1: Anatomy of the Aorta 238

Figure 11-2: Aortic Aneurysm Types 239

Figure 11-3: Aortic Aneurysm Classifications 240

Table 11-1: High-Risk Clinical Findings Associated With Aortic Dissection 243

Figure 11-4: Intramural Hematoma Within an Aortic Aneurysm 246

Chapter 12

Figure 12-1: Conduction System of the Heart 262

Box 12-1: Common Indications for Cardiac Pacing 263

Figure 12-2: Temporary Pacing Generators 265

Figure 12-3: Components of a Permanent Dual-Chamber Pacemaker 267

Table 12-1: Pacing Codes 269

Table 12-2: Indications for Cardiac Resynchronization Therapy 275

Chapter 13

Figure 13-1: Continuum of Acute Coronary Syndromes 290

Figure 13-2: Pathogenesis of Acute Coronary Syndrome 291

Table 13-1: Typical and Atypical Presentations of Acute Myocardial Infarction 293

Table 13-2: Indications and Contraindications for Fibrinolytic Reperfusion Therapy 295

Figure 13-3: Substantial ST-Segment Elevation of Inferior Wall Myocardial Infarction 296

Figure 13-4: ST-Segment Elevation of Anterior Septal Myocardial Infarction in Leads V_1 to V_4 297

Figure 13-5: Normal Electrocardiogram 297

Table 13-3: Key Nursing Interventions for ST-Segment Elevated Myocardial Infarction 299

Table 13-4: Summary of Cardiac Biomarkers 302

Table 13-5: Features Associated With High-Risk Acute Coronary Syndrome Patients 302

Chapter 14

Table 14-1: Precipitating Factors for Decompensating Heart Failure 323

Figure 14-1: Impella Ventricular Assist Device 327

Figure 14-2: Long-Term Ventricular Assist Device 328

Chapter 15

Figure 15-1: Conduction Pathways Through the Heart 334

Figure 15-2: Reentry Pathways Through the Heart 336

Figure 15-3: Sinus Tachycardia Electrocardiograph Reading 337

Figure 15-4: Atrioventricular Nodal Reentrant Tachycardia Electrocardiogram Reading 338

Figure 15-5: Accessory Pathway and Electrocardiogram Characteristics With the Atrioventricular
                 Reentrant Tachycardia of Wolff-Parkinson-White Syndrome 339

Figure 15-6: Atrioventricular Nodal Reentrant Tachycardia Compared With Atrioventricular
                 Reentrant Tachycardia 340

Figure 15-7: Focal Atrial Tachycardia in Comparison With Multifocal Atrial Tachycardia
                 Electrocardiogram Readings 341

Figure 15-8: Atrial Flutter With Rapid Ventricular Response Electrocardiogram Readings 342

Figure 15-9: Monomorphic Ventricular Tachycardia Compared With Polymorphic
                 Ventricular Tachycardia Electrocardiogram Reading 343

Figure 15-10: Sinus Bradycardia Electrocardiogram Reading 345

Figure 15-11: Sinus Node Dysfunction Presentations Electrocardiogram Readings 345

Figure 15-12: Mobitz Type II Compared With Complete Atrioventricular Block
                 Electrocardiogram Readings 347

Figure 15-13: Ventricular Fibrillation – Fine Compared With Coarse Electrocardiogram
                 Readings 348

Chapter 16

Table 16-1: Sequential Organ Failure Assessment Score...362

Box 16-1: Quick Sequential Organ Function Assessment (SOFA) Score.................363

Chapter 18

Box 18-1: Indications for Coronary Artery Bypass Graft Surgery.............................389

Figure 18-1: Heart and Lung Bypass Machine..391

Figure 18-2: Heart Cannulation for Cardiopulmonary Bypass...................................392

Figure 18-3: Saphenous Vein Graft Bypassing Coronary Lesion 393

Figure 18-4: Saphenous Vein Graft and Internal Mammary Artery Graft 394

Box 18-2: Strategies to Decrease Sternal Wound Infections.....................................400

Box 18-3: Emergency Coronary Artery Bypass Graft Surgery Recommendations 403

Figure 18-5: Balloon Inflation Causing Plaque Disruption During Percutaneous
Transluminal Coronary Angioplasty..408

Figure 18-6: Coronary Stent Deployment..409

Figure 18-7: Directional Coronary Atherectomy Device 411

Figure 18-8: Rotational Atherectomy 412

Table 18-1: Percutaneous Catheter Intervention Success..413

Table 18-2: Common Vascular Closure Devices and Mechanisms of Action 418

Box 18-4: Sheath Removal Standards to Reduce Bleeding.......................................419

Box 18-5: Cardiovascular Disease Risk Reduction...420

Chapter 19

Table 19-1: Comprehensive Review Of Systems 432

Box 19-1: Grading of Murmurs 443

Chapter 20

Box 20-1: Interprofessional Education and Collaborative Practice Definitions.........455

PRETEST

1. Begin this course by taking the pretest. Circle the answers to the questions on this page, or write the answers on a separate sheet of paper. Do not log answers to the pretest questions on the FasTrax test sheet included with the course.
2. Compare your answers to the pretest key located at the end of the pretest. The pretest key indicates the chapter where the content of that question is discussed. Make note of the questions you missed so that you can focus on those areas as you complete the course.
3. Complete the course by reading the chapters and completing the exam questions at the end of each chapter. Answers to the exam questions should be logged on the FasTrax test sheet included with the course.

Note: Choose the one option that BEST answers each question.

1. Which part of the nervous system allows the body to function under stress?

   a. Autonomic
   b. Parasympathetic
   c. Sympathetic
   d. Cholinergic

2. Which hemodynamic parameter is the amount of blood ejected from the heart in 1 minute?

   a. Contractility
   b. Cardiac output
   c. Preload
   d. Afterload

3. Which cardiovascular risk factor can patients reduce by modifying their dietary behaviors?

   a. Cholesterol
   b. Gender
   c. Race
   d. Smoking

4. Which medication functions by working on the ascending loop of Henle and resulting in a loss of water, hydrogen ions, and electrolytes?

   a. Metolazone
   b. Chlorthalidone
   c. Hydrochlorothiazide
   d. Bumetanide

5. Which condition is most associated with the older adult population?

   a. Mixed dyslipidemia
   b. Isolated systolic hypertension
   c. Diastolic hypertension
   d. Gestational hypertension

6. Which condition occurs with physical exertion or emotional stress and is relieved by rest or sublingual nitroglycerin?

   a. Acute coronary syndrome
   b. Myocardial infarction (MI)
   c. Non-ST-elevated MI
   d. Stable angina

continued on next page

7. Which type of cardiomyopathy is characterized by decreased peak filling and reduced diastolic volume of either or both ventricles with normal or near-normal systolic function and wall thickness?

   ✓ a. Restrictive

   b. Hypertrophic

   c. Arrhythmogenic

   d. Takotsubo

8. Which condition is the most common cause of chronic heart failure?

   a. Cerebral arterial disease

   b. Peripheral arterial disease

   c. Diabetes mellitus

   d. Dilated cardiomyopathy

9. What is a self-care practice is that a primary prevention strategy against developing endocarditis?

   a. Annual health screenings

   b. Daily baths

   ✓ c. Oral hygiene

   d. Sunscreen protection

10. Which condition is a 70-year-old patient with diabetes mellitus, hypertension, and systolic heart failure at high risk for after developing atrial fibrillation?

    ✓ a. Embolic stroke

    b. Heart valve regurgitation

    c. Pulmonary embolus

    d. Cor pulmonale

11. Which condition is most associated with a sudden onset of tearing or ripping chest pain radiating to the back or down the extremities?

    a. Claudication pain

    b. Acute arterial occlusion

    c. Peripheral vascular disease

    ✓ d. Aortic dissection

12. The three routes of temporary cardiac pacing are transcutaneous, transvenous, and

    a. transhepatic.

    ✓ b. epicardial.

    c. myocardial.

    d. intracardiac.

13. Which patient is at a four-fold higher risk for poor outcomes with ST-elevation myocardial infarction when compared with any other population?

    a. A 40-year-old woman who is pregnant

    b. A 75-year-old woman

    c. A 38-year-old man

    ✓ d. A 28-year-old male with cocaine use

14. Which medical therapy is the first-line treatment for acute decompensated heart failure?

    a. Beta blockers

    b. Calcium channel blockers

    ✓ c. Loop diuretics

    d. Nitroglycerin

15. What is the most common tachydysrhythmia?

    ✓ a. Supraventricular tachycardia

    b. Sinus tachycardia

    c. Atrioventricular node reentry tachycardia

    d. Ventricular tachycardia

16. What is the leading cause of cardiogenic shock?

    a. Acute coronary syndrome

    b. Pulmonary hypertension

    c. Atrial fibrillation

    d. Left ventricular failure

17. Which condition is defined as a transient, self-limited loss of consciousness occurring because of decreased cerebral blood flow and usually resulting in a fall?

    a. Cardiogenic shock

    b. Pericarditis

    ✓ c. Syncope

    d. Hypertensive emergency

18. What complication can occur secondary to receiving contrast dye during a percutaneous coronary intervention?

    ✓ a. Nephropathy

    b. Infection

    c. Atrial fibrillation

    d. Acute pain

19. Which pneumonic or acronym is used to facilitate subjective history collection during the patient interview?

    a. CAGE

    b. APETM

    c. OLDCARTS

    d. NSTEMI

20. Which core competency for interprofessional education and collaborative practice focuses on the foundation of mutual respect and trusting interprofessional relationships?

    a. Domain 1: Values/Ethics for Interprofessional Practice

    b. Domain 2: Roles/Responsibilities

    c. Domain 3: Interprofessional Communication

    d. Domain 4: Teams and Teamwork

PRETEST KEY		
1.	C	Chapter 1
2.	B	Chapter 2
3.	A	Chapter 3
4.	D	Chapter 4
5.	B	Chapter 5
6.	D	Chapter 6
7.	A	Chapter 7
8.	D	Chapter 8
9.	C	Chapter 9
10.	A	Chapter 10
11.	D	Chapter 11
12.	B	Chapter 12
13.	B	Chapter 13
14.	C	Chapter 14
15.	B	Chapter 15
16.	D	Chapter 16
17.	C	Chapter 17
18.	A	Chapter 18
19.	C	Chapter 19
20.	A	Chapter 20

INTRODUCTION

LEARNING OUTCOMES

After completing this course, the learner will be able to:

1. Describe the basic structures of the heart and their physiological functions.

2. Explain the components of cardiac output responsible for hemodynamic alterations.

3. Discuss the impact that epidemiology and behavioral/nonbehavioral risk factors have on the development of cardiovascular disease.

4. Discuss ways pharmacology is used to improve myocardial performance and increase myocardial oxygen supply.

5. Differentiate acute from chronic cardiovascular conditions.

6. Discuss the nursing considerations for chronic cardiovascular disease management throughout the continuum of presentation, diagnosis, and treatment.

7. Discuss the nursing considerations for common acute cardiovascular disease management throughout the continuum of presentation, diagnosis, and treatment.

8. Recognize the impact that cardiovascular conditions have on special populations.

9. Discuss the nursing considerations associated with cardiovascular revascularization therapies and implantable devices.

10. Identify the significance of the comprehensive cardiovascular health history and physical examination.

11. Recognize the significance of collaborative cardiovascular management through an interprofessional team.

Cardiovascular disease is responsible for one in every four deaths in the United States in both men and women (Centers for Disease Control and Prevention, 2015). Cardiovascular disease comprises multiple conditions that are primarily the results of atherosclerosis. These conditions are often referred to as atherosclerotic-related cardiovascular disease, which remains the most significant risk factor for hypertension, dyslipidemia, myocardial infarction, and stroke (Anderson, 2016).

Although many advances have recently been made in cardiovascular medicine, they have not been enough to move cardiovascular death from the top of the list. Many people believe that intracoronary stenting and open-heart surgery can solve the problem of heart disease; unfortunately, these procedures resolve only the end result of the problem. Without risk-factor reduction, cardiovascular disease persists. In many cases, before intracoronary stenting and open-heart surgery are treatment options, irreversible damage to the heart occurs, resulting in a decline in cardiac function. Damage to the entire cardiovascular system can also result from processes that do not involve blockage of the coronary arteries, such as the effects of hypertension and heart valve disease (Anderson, 2016).

Because of the prevalence of cardiovascular disease, nurses must be equipped with the knowledge and skills to aid in its reduction. Recognizing patients at risk for cardiovascular disease and taking the initiative to educate patients of the behavioral and nonbehavioral cardiovascular risk factors can enhance other primary prevention strategies aimed to control the prevalence of the disease. In addition to nursing education used as a primary prevention strategy, nurses must also be aware of secondary prevention therapies aimed to minimize the burdens of known disease and complications associated with cardiovascular disease.

This course provides information to support nurses working across all healthcare settings who care for patients at risk for or who already have cardiovascular disease. This course can serve as a reference for nurses working in cardiovascular areas or provide those desiring to work in cardiovascular areas with an introduction to comprehensive cardiovascular care. The curriculum begins with a foundation of cardiovascular anatomy and physiology. When normal cardiovascular functioning is understood, the learner can then move forward to understanding pathophysiology. The content of the chapters on cardiovascular medications and risk factors is referenced throughout the rest of the text as cardiovascular disease processes are discussed. Nursing application points in the clinical setting are highlighted throughout the text to assist in identifying key issues in the care of patients with cardiovascular disease.

Heightened awareness among clinicians and patients is the first step toward impacting this devastating disease. Nurses with comprehensive cardiovascular care knowledge open the door to early recognition and treatment of cardiovascular disease and can initiate introductory conversations of prevention or other lifestyle management. The astute nurse can impact patients' lives through repeated nursing education and interprofessional collaborative care aimed to prevent premature disease and death caused by cardiovascular disease or aimed to contribute to a life that is high quality, long, and healthy.

A note about the terminology used in *Cardiovascular Nursing: A Comprehensive Guide to Patient Care:* Throughout the nursing and healthcare literature, the terms *dysrhythmia* and *arrhythmia* are used interchangeably. This course will adopt the term *dysrhythmia* instead of *arrhythmia,* as the use of the letter a at the beginning of a word (in most accepted medical terminology) signifies the absence of something. Because patients with cardiac rhythm disturbances do in fact have a rhythm, we believe that the word *dysrhythmia* is the more accurate terminology. The term *arrhythmia* was retained when referring to pharmacology and specific classes of medications to represent the continued current verbiage.

References

Anderson, K. M. (2016). *The advanced practice nurse cardiovascular clinician.* New York, NY: Springer Publishing Co.

Centers for Disease Control and Prevention. (2015). *Heart disease facts.* Retrieved from https://www.cdc.gov/heartdisease/facts.htm

CHAPTER 1

CARDIOVASCULAR ANATOMY AND PHYSIOLOGY

LEARNING OUTCOME

After completing this chapter, the learner will be able to identify the anatomical structures and physiological functions of the cardiovascular system.

CHAPTER OBJECTIVES

After completing this chapter, the learner will be able to:

1. Identify the anatomy and physiology of all cardiovascular structures.

2. Differentiate between the electrical and mechanical cardiac physiology.

3. Describe the significance of neurohormonal regulation in cardiac physiology.

4. Identify nursing implications for practice related to the considerations for special populations.

INTRODUCTION

The cardiovascular system is also referred to as the circulatory system, which is composed of a muscular heart and a closed system of vessels (arteries, veins, and capillaries). The purpose of the cardiovascular system is to circulate oxygen- and nutrient-rich blood to all of the tissues of the body. The many structures within

the heart and vessels facilitate the process of tissue perfusion (Patton, Thibodeau, & Douglas, 2012). Cardiovascular anatomy and physiology form an important foundation for understanding all aspects of cardiovascular nursing. A solid physiological basis for the understanding of cardiovascular disease and treatments allows the nurse to link knowledge to practice in a more meaningful way.

CARDIAC ANATOMY

The heart is a muscular, four-chambered organ that resides within the anterior thoracic cavity, between the lungs, and anterior to the aorta, vena cava, esophagus, and vertebral column just behind the sternum in the mediastinal space (see Figure 1-1). The mediastinal space, also referred to as the mediastinum, is the central region of the thoracic cavity. The great vessels (including the aorta, pulmonary artery, inferior vena cava, and superior vena cava) suspend the heart within the mediastinal space just above the diaphragm.

The adult heart is generally approximately the size of a person's clenched fist. The average size and weight varies between male and female individuals but is better predicted by an individual's body weight in the absence of pathologies such as hypertensive hypertrophy. The heart is positioned within the thoracic cavity with

FIGURE 1-1: HEART PLACEMENT WITHIN THE THORACIC CAVITY

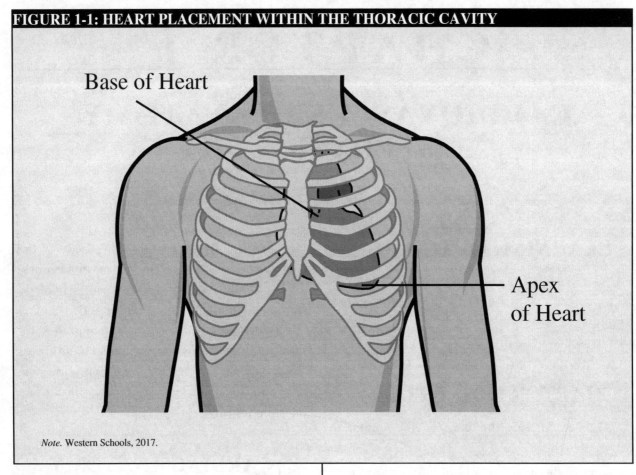

Base of Heart

Apex of Heart

Note. Western Schools, 2017.

its right and left chambers noted in the posterior and anterior planes of the body (see Figure 1-2); for instance, the atria (upper chambers) are positioned posteriorly and the ventricles (lower chambers) are positioned anteriorly. The right ventricle makes up the majority of the anterior and inferior walls of the heart, which are nearest to the chest wall and diaphragm surfaces, respectively. The left ventricle makes up the anterolateral and posterior surfaces of the heart. The apex is the inferior-most distal aspect of the left ventricle and is positioned near the anterior wall at the left midclavicular line between the fourth and fifth intercostal spaces in most adults. The base of the heart consists of both atria, which lie posteriorly juxtaposed to the great vessels and esophagus (Patton et al., 2012).

Cardiac Chambers

The right and left atria are separated by connective tissue called the *interatrial septum.* The right and left atria are low-pressure, thin-walled chambers that receive blood and act as reservoirs. The right atrium receives deoxygenated blood from the venous system via the inferior and superior vena cava, as well as from the coronary sinus (the primary coronary vein). The left atrium receives oxygenated blood from the pulmonary veins after the blood has traveled through the lungs.

The right and left ventricles are the pumping chambers of the heart and receive blood from the atria. The ventricles are separated by the interventricular septum. The right ventricle is a thin-walled (see Figure 1-3), low-pressure pump that receives deoxygenated blood from the right atrium. This ventricle pumps blood

FIGURE 1-2: MEDIASTINAL CARDIOVASCULAR STRUCTURES

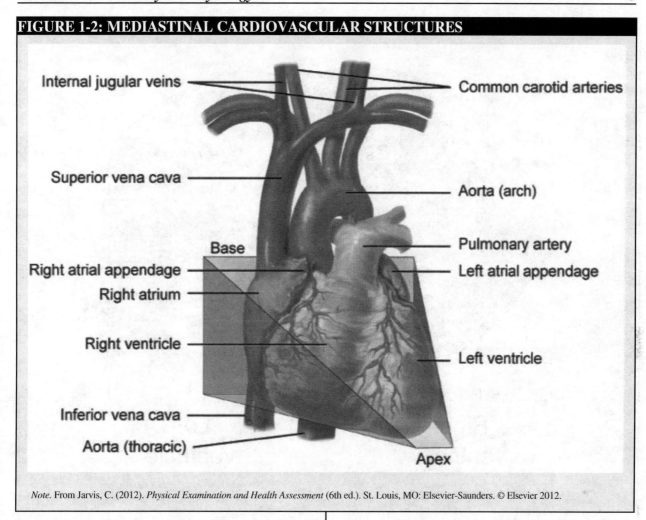

Internal jugular veins

Common carotid arteries

Superior vena cava

Aorta (arch)

Base

Pulmonary artery

Right atrial appendage

Left atrial appendage

Right atrium

Right ventricle

Left ventricle

Inferior vena cava

Aorta (thoracic)

Apex

Note. From Jarvis, C. (2012). *Physical Examination and Health Assessment* (6th ed.). St. Louis, MO: Elsevier-Saunders. © Elsevier 2012.

into the pulmonary artery, which carries the blood to the lungs to exchange carbon dioxide for oxygen. The left ventricle is a thick-walled, high-pressure pump that receives oxygenated blood from the left atrium and pumps blood into the aorta for distribution throughout the circulatory system. In other words, the sole purpose of the muscular heart is to move, or pump, blood to the body's tissues via the vascular system.

NURSING APPLICATION

Because the right ventricular wall is thinner than the left ventricular wall, the right ventricle fails more easily in response to elevated pulmonary pressures (e.g., pulmonary hypertension) than the left ventricle does to elevated systemic pressures (e.g., arterial hypertension). Therefore, patients

can have acute/decompensating right-sided heart failure in the setting of a history of pulmonary hypertension. Assessment findings of right-sided heart failure show that jugular vein distention, hepatomegaly, and dependent edema are seen earlier than in left-sided heart failure.

Layers of the Heart

The three layers of the heart walls are the endocardium (innermost), myocardium (muscular middle layer), and epicardium (outermost). The pericardium is an additional layer surrounding the heart that normally holds a small amount of fluid (see Figure 1-4). Many individuals may also have a layer of adipose tissue along the paths of the coronary vessels called the *epicardial fat.*

FIGURE 1-3: TRANSVERSE SECTION OF VENTRICULAR WALL THICKNESS

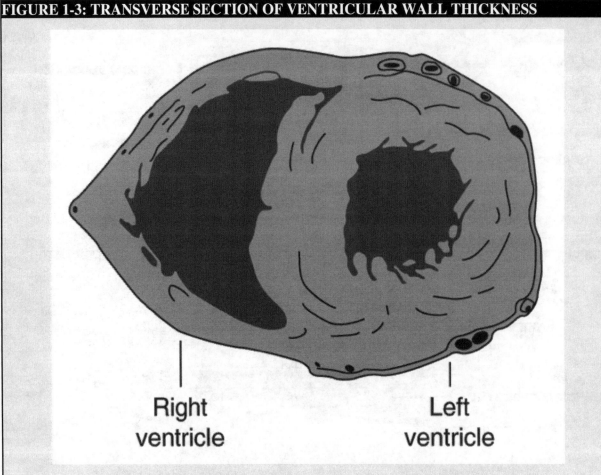

Right
ventricle

Left
ventricle

Note. From Urden, L. D., Stacy, K. M., & Lough, M. E. (2014). *Critical care nursing: Diagnosis and management* (7th ed.). St. Louis, MO: Elsevier/
Mosby. © Elsevier 2014.

Endocardium

The endocardium is a serous membrane that consists of connective tissue, elastic fibers, and a thin layer of epithelial cells that form a smooth surface for the movement of blood and prevention of clot formation. The endocardium is the innermost surface of the heart chambers and continues throughout the innermost layers of the heart creating a closed circulatory system.

NURSING APPLICATION

Inflammation of the endocardium or heart valves is called endocarditis. Endocarditis can affect both native valves and prosthetic valves.

Myocardium

The myocardium is the thick middle layer of the heart. The largest layer of the heart, the myocardium contains cardiac muscle fibers that have the ability to contract and conduct electrical stimuli. The myocardium of the ventricles is thicker than the myocardium of the atria. The left ventricle has the thickest myocardium because of the high pressure in the aorta, which the ventricle must pump against to eject its contents. Compare the difference in muscle thickness between the right and left ventricular myocardium in Figure 1-4. As patients develop myocardial hypertrophy (increased cell size), this layer of the heart becomes larger.

FIGURE 1-4: WALLS OF THE HEART

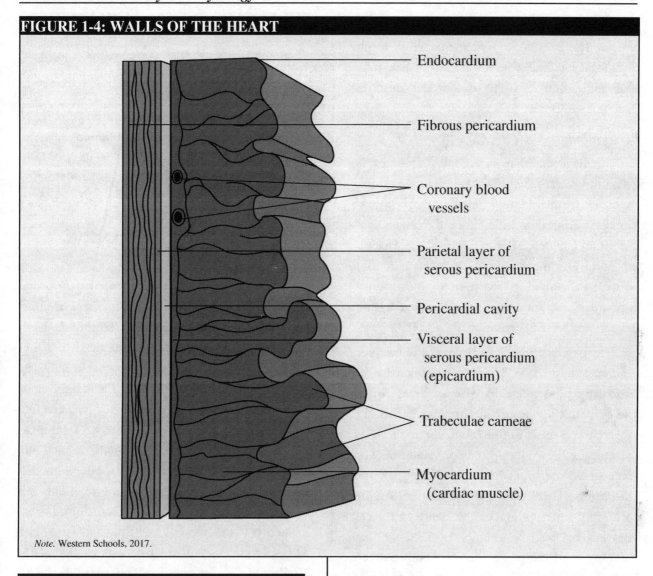

Endocardium

Fibrous pericardium

Coronary blood
vessels

Parietal layer of
serous pericardium

Pericardial cavity

Visceral layer of
serous pericardium
(epicardium)

Trabeculae carneae

Myocardium
(cardiac muscle)

Note. Western Schools, 2017.

NURSING APPLICATION

Damage to the myocardial layer of the heart results in a decreased ability for the heart to contract (pump) and an impaired ability to eject blood from the ventricles. The myocardial layer of the heart can be damaged as a result of a myocardial infarction (MI) or from an inflammatory process (myocarditis). Disease of the myocardium is better known as cardiomyopathy, for which there are multiple etiological considerations that will be discussed in greater detail in Chapter 7.

Epicardium

The epicardium is the smooth outer layer of the heart that contains the network of coronary arteries and veins, the autonomic nerves, the lymphatic system, and fat tissue that is tightly adhered to the heart and base of the great vessels (see Figure 1-4). Coronary blood vessels that supply the myocardium and endocardium with oxygen-rich blood must cross the epicardium before passing through the myocardium and, finally, entering the endocardium. Increased age and obesity increase the amount of fat tissue in the epicardial layer. This fat tissue is also known as *epicardial fat*. Overweight or obese persons may have a large amount of this fat, consequently increasing their risk for coronary artery disease. The presence of increased/excessive epicardial fat facilitates the infiltration of free fatty acids and adipokines into the coronary arteries (Iacobellis & Bianco, 2011).

Pericardium

The thin sac that surrounds the heart is called the *pericardium*. This fibrous sac protects the heart from infection and traumatic injury. The pericardium has little elastic tissue and cannot expand acutely. The majority of the ascending aorta, the main pulmonary artery, all four pulmonary veins, and portions of the inferior and superior vena cavae are contained within the pericardial sac (Loukas et al., 2012).

The pericardium has several layers (see Figures 1-4 and 1-5). The external cover of the pericardium is called the *fibrous pericardium* and is continuous with the external walls of the great vessels. The *parietal pericardium* is the inner lining of the fibrous pericardium. The *visceral pericardium* is another name for the epicardium. This inner lining of the pericardium forms the outer lining of the heart and great vessels. The space between the parietal and visceral layers of the pericardium contains a small amount of lubricating fluid ranging from as little as 10 ml up to 50 ml (Patton et al., 2012). This fluid prevents friction between the epicardium and the fibrous pericardium during each cardiac contraction. However, when the fluid in this space accumulates (pericardial effusion), it can interfere with the ability of the ventricles to fill during diastole, or relaxation, and pump during systole, or contraction. This type of effusion is known as pericardial tamponade (Patton et al., 2012). The amount of fluid that causes tamponade can range from 200 ml up to 2 L (Patton et al., 2012). Pericarditis is inflammation of the pericardium and can contribute to heart dysfunction as well (Loukas et al., 2012).

Cardiac Valves

The four cardiac valves located within the heart are designated as either *atrioventricular (AV) valves* or *semilunar valves* (see Figure 1-6). The valves located between the atria and the ventricles are AV valves. The tricuspid valve is located between the right atrium and right ventricle, and the mitral valve is located between the left atrium and left ventricle. The two semilunar valves are located between the ventricles and the great vessels (Patton et al., 2012). The pulmonic valve is located between the right ventricle and the pulmonary artery, and the aortic valve is located between the left ventricle and the aorta. The sole purpose of cardiac valves is to maintain blood flow in one direction while the heart muscle fulfills its purpose to pump. Together, the heart muscle and valves maintain the concept of *forward flow,* to achieve the mechanical delivery of oxygen and nutrients to all body tissues.

Atrioventricular Valves

The AV valves are anatomically different from the semilunar valves. Papillary muscles project from the inner surface of the ventricle and attach to delicate strands of fibrous material called *chordae tendineae*. The chordae tendineae attach to the valve leaflets (see Figure 1-6). The leaflets form the valve cusps (three cusps for the tricuspid, two for the mitral). The uppermost portions of the valve cusps are joined

FIGURE 1-5: HEART WITH PERICARDIAL SAC OPENED

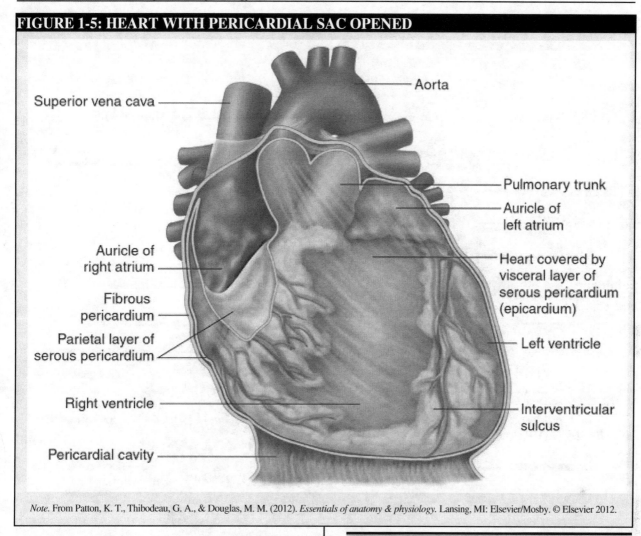

Superior vena cava

Aorta

Pulmonary trunk

Auricle of left atrium

Auricle of right atrium

Heart covered by visceral layer of serous pericardium (epicardium)

Fibrous pericardium

Parietal layer of serous pericardium

Left ventricle

Right ventricle

Pericardial cavity

Interventricular sulcus

Note. From Patton, K. T., Thibodeau, G. A., & Douglas, M. M. (2012). *Essentials of anatomy & physiology.* Lansing, MI: Elsevier/Mosby. © Elsevier 2012.

together by a fibrous ring at the top of the valve, called the *annulus*. The AV valves open passively during diastole, forming a funnel-like shape allowing blood to flow from the atria to the ventricles. At the end of diastole, ventricular pressure increases and forces the valve leaflets to come together and close the valve opening between the atrium and the ventricle. As the ventricle contracts to eject blood, the papillary muscles contract to prevent the valve leaflets from prolapsing into the atrium. As alluded to earlier in the introduction to this *Cardiac Valves* section, the closure of the leaflets prevents the backward flow of blood from the ventricle to the atrium. At the end of systole, when the ventricle relaxes, the AV valves open again and the cycle is repeated.

NURSING APPLICATION

During an acute MI of the left ventricle, the papillary muscle of the mitral valve can become weakened and potentially rupture. If the papillary muscle ruptures, the mitral valve can no longer close properly to maintain unidirectional blood flow. As a result, blood moves backward into the left atrium and pulmonary vasculature during ventricular contraction, causing acute left-sided heart failure and potential pulmonary edema.

Semilunar Valves

Each semilunar valve consists of an annulus and three cusps (see Figure 1-6). The pulmonic and aortic valves have the same structure; how-

FIGURE 1-6: INTERNAL STRUCTURES OF THE HEART

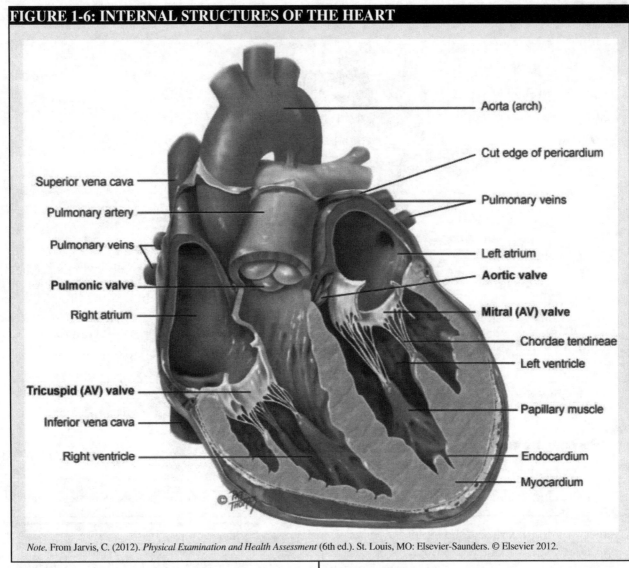

- Aorta (arch)
- Cut edge of pericardium
- Superior vena cava
- Pulmonary artery
- Pulmonary veins
- Pulmonary veins
- **Pulmonic valve**
- Left atrium
- **Aortic valve**
- Right atrium
- **Mitral (AV) valve**
- Chordae tendineae
- Left ventricle
- **Tricuspid (AV) valve**
- Inferior vena cava
- Papillary muscle
- Right ventricle
- Endocardium
- Myocardium

Note. From Jarvis, C. (2012). *Physical Examination and Health Assessment* (6th ed.). St. Louis, MO: Elsevier-Saunders. © Elsevier 2012.

ever, the aortic valve leaflets are heavier and thicker because of the increased pressure system in the left side of the heart. These valves open and close by pressure changes (or pressure gradients) within the heart and the great vessels. A pressure gradient is the movement of air or fluid from a place of higher concentration of pressure to a lower concentration of pressure (Patton et al., 2012). During diastole, the semilunar valves are closed as the ventricles fill with blood from the atria. As the AV valves close and systole begins, the ventricles begin to contract. When the pressure in the ventricles is greater than the pressure on the other side of the semilunar valves, the valves are forced open and blood is ejected out of the ventricles into the great vessels. When ventricular ejection is complete, the pressure in the ventricles is less than the pressure in the great vessels, and the semilunar valves close tightly. Tight closure prevents the backward flow of blood from the great vessels to the ventricles. The cycle then begins again.

NURSING APPLICATION

When auscultating the heart, the first heart sound (S_1), referred to as "lub," is associated with closure of the AV valves. The second heart sound (S_2), referred to as "dub," is associated with closure of the semilunar valves.

These two sounds together form the "lub-dub" heard during cardiac auscultation.

NURSING APPLICATION

S_1 ("lub") represents the beginning of ventricular systole, or contraction, and S_2 ("dub") represents the beginning of ventricular diastole, or relaxation. A murmur heard during auscultation of heart sounds represents turbulent blood flow caused by either valve structural abnormalities or increased blood flow velocity (Griffin, Kapadia, & Rimmerman, 2013).

When cardiac valves function correctly, they permit *forward flow* of blood when open and prevent backward flow of blood when closed. During ventricular systole, the tricuspid and mitral valves close to prevent backward flow of blood from the ventricles into the atria. During ventricular systole, all blood forced from the ventricles during ejection is propelled forward through open pulmonic and aortic valves into the pulmonary and systemic vascular beds. During ventricular diastole, the tricuspid and mitral valves open, allowing filling of the ventricles from the atria. When the pulmonic and aortic valves close properly during ventricular diastole, they prevent the backward flow of blood from the pulmonary and systemic vascular beds into the ventricles (see Figure 1-7).

NURSING APPLICATION

An aortic valve that does not close properly (insufficient) results in a backward flow of blood from the aorta (systemic circulation) into the left ventricle, reducing the stroke volume and cardiac output of the previous contraction. An aortic valve that does not open properly (stenotic) prevents forward flow into the aorta and, if severe, back-

ward flow of blood that has filled the left atria and cannot move into the left ventricle because of residual blood unable to empty during systole. These pathologies will be discussed in greater detail in Chapter 8.

CIRCULATORY SYSTEM

The circulatory system works to achieve forward flow and cardiac output (amount of blood ejected from the heart to the system in 1 minute), for the primary purpose of delivering oxygen and other nutrients to the body at the cellular level. Hemodynamic principles related to the components of stroke volume (amount of blood ejected by the ventricle with each heartbeat) – preload, afterload, and contractility (discussed in greater detail in Chapter 2) – are heavily influenced by the circulatory system. *Preload* is the hemodynamic load (volume of blood in the ventricle) on the myocardial walls (also referred to as degree of stretch) on the myocardial fibers) at the end of diastole. *Afterload* is the amount of pressure the ventricle generates to overcome the resistance created by the arteries and arterioles. *Contractility,* which is significantly impacted by preload, afterload, and the mechanical functional capacity of the myocardium, is the heart muscle's contractile force, or strength (Lough, 2014).

Arterial System

Oxygenated blood leaves the left ventricle and travels to the tissue level via the systemic arterial system. Arteries are made up of elastic tissue that allows them to respond to the high pressures associated with the force of left ventricular contraction. Large arteries also contain smooth muscle.

FIGURE 1-7: CHAMBER CONTRACTION AND VALVE FUNCTION

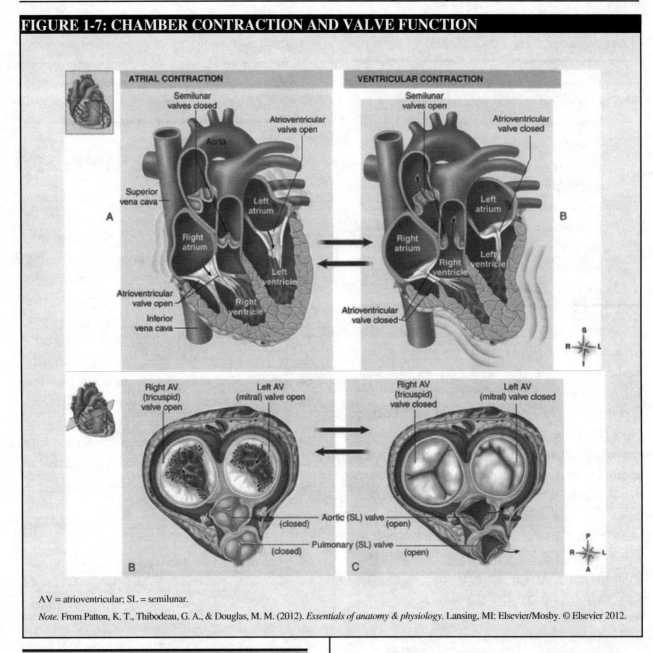

AV = atrioventricular; SL = semilunar.

Note. From Patton, K. T., Thibodeau, G. A., & Douglas, M. M. (2012). *Essentials of anatomy & physiology.* Lansing, MI: Elsevier/Mosby. © Elsevier 2012.

NURSING APPLICATION

When intravenous central nervous system depressants are administered to patients, blood pressure monitoring is appropriate due to arterial smooth muscle relaxation.

All arteries have three layers of tissue surrounding the open lumen (see Figure 1-8). The inner layer, called the *intima,* has a thin lining of endothelium that contains epithelial cells. The intima decreases resistance to flow and minimizes the chance of platelet aggregation (a component of clotting). The *media* (the middle layer) is composed of smooth muscle and elastic connective tissue. The media is responsible for changes in the diameter of the vessel, as needed, to assist with blood pressure control. The fibrous outer layer, called the *adventitia,* is designed to protect the vessel and provide connection to other internal structures. Arteries have the ability to expand or contract in response to the body's cardiac output needs.

FIGURE 1-8: STRUCTURE OF BLOOD VESSELS

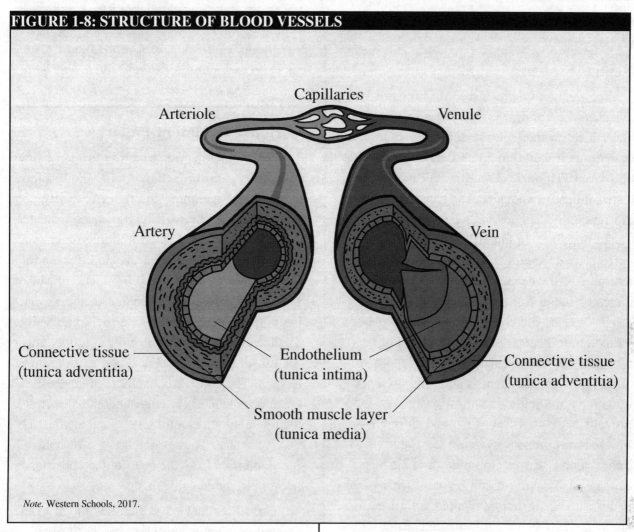

Note. Western Schools, 2017.

The large arteries carry blood from the aorta to the rest of the body. The arteries divide and become smaller as they move away from the aorta. The smallest arteries branch into arterioles. Arterioles connect to the capillary bed. At the arteriole level of the capillary is smooth muscle referred to as the *precapillary sphincter.* The arterioles and the precapillary sphincters regulate blood flow to the capillaries. This regulation of blood flow is primarily determined by the oxygen needs of the tissue through a process called *autoregulation.* When oxygen needs increase, the arterioles dilate. This dilation decreases resistance to flow and results in increased flow to the capillaries (Patton et al., 2012).

Capillary System

When oxygenated blood reaches the capillary level, oxygen and other nutrients are exchanged. Because capillary walls are only one cell thick, gases and nutrients pass through the walls easily. Miles of capillaries are located near almost all body cells. The capillaries contain no smooth muscle; therefore, capillary tone depends on the tone of the vessel just before and after the capillary. Four pressures influence the movement of fluids across capillary membranes: capillary hydrostatic pressure, interstitial hydrostatic pressure, capillary oncotic pressure, and interstitial colloidal oncotic pressure (Patton et al., 2012). After oxygen and nutrients are exchanged for waste products, deoxygenated blood is returned to the right atrium from the capillaries via the venous system.

Venous System

The venous system is a lower-pressure system than the arterial system. Because veins are not subject to the high pressures of the arterial system, their walls are much thinner than those of arteries. Thinner walls allow for much more distensibility, or compliance. At any given time, the venous system generally holds 60% to 80% of the body's total blood volume. The venous system also regulates the amount of blood returning to the heart. Vasoconstriction of veins increases blood flow to the heart by decreasing the amount of blood held in the vascular bed. Vasodilation decreases blood flow to the heart by increasing the vascular bed to hold more volume. The venous system is strongly influenced by gravity and relies on one-way valves to help prevent backward flow of blood through the low-pressure venous system (see Figure 1-8). These venous valves are absent in a small percentage of people and can be damaged by age or by catheter insertion. Venous return is also augmented by contraction of skeletal muscles, which compress veins and help to propel blood forward (returning to the heart).

NURSING APPLICATION

Weakened vein valves cause varicose (dilated) veins. Age, prolonged standing, and pregnancy contribute to varicose veins.

NURSING APPLICATION

In right-sided heart failure, venous valves are important in maintaining the unidirectional flow of blood back to the right side of the heart.

NURSING APPLICATION

Ambulation increases venous return and decreases venous pooling, which contributes to edema and thrombus formation.

Normal Circulatory Patterns

The thoracic aorta, which is located below the aortic arch, branches off to supply blood to the torso, including the thoracic cavity and the lungs. The thoracic aorta arises from the aortic valve and is divided into three segments: ascending aorta, aortic arch, and descending thoracic aorta (see Figure 1-9). The origin of the coronary arteries is located in the ascending aorta, immediately above the aortic valve. The location of the origin of the coronary arteries allows them to receive blood that is rich in oxygen. The aortic arch has three branches: the brachiocephalic artery (right innominate artery), the left common carotid artery, and the left subclavian artery. These branches are responsible for blood flow from the heart to the upper torso, neck, head, brain, and arms.

The abdominal aorta supplies blood to the abdominal organs and the kidneys. At approximately the fourth lumbar vertebra, the abdominal aorta divides into the internal iliac arteries. The structures of the lower trunk, including the reproductive organs and the legs, receive their blood supply from the internal iliac arteries.

The venous system mimics the arterial system in returning blood to the heart. Before entering the heart, the entire venous system enters into either the superior or the inferior vena cava. The superior vena cava receives venous blood returning from the head, neck, upper extremities, and thorax. The inferior vena cava receives blood from below the level of the diaphragm, including the abdomen, pelvis, and lower extremities. The superior and inferior venae cavae empty the returning deoxygenated

FIGURE 1-9: DIVISIONS OF AORTA

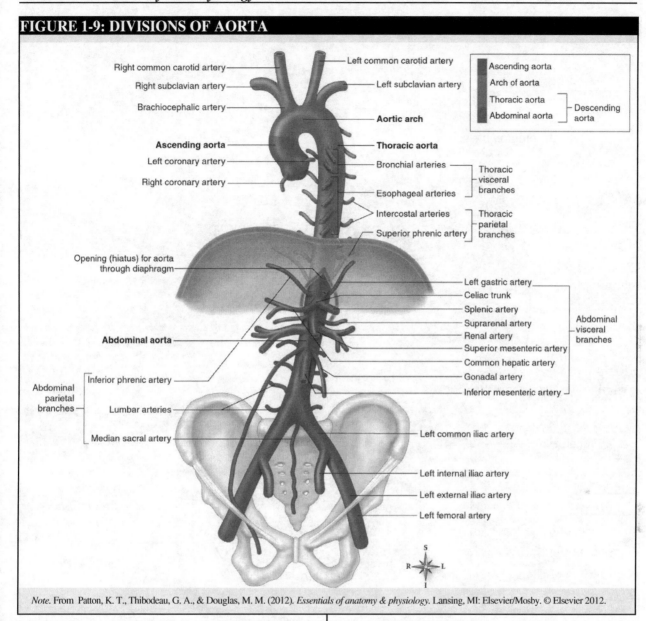

Right common carotid artery
Right subclavian artery
Brachiocephalic artery

Left common carotid artery
Left subclavian artery

Aortic arch

Ascending aorta
Arch of aorta
Thoracic aorta
Abdominal aorta
Descending aorta

Ascending aorta
Left coronary artery
Right coronary artery

Thoracic aorta
Bronchial arteries
Esophageal arteries
Thoracic visceral branches

Intercostal arteries
Superior phrenic artery
Thoracic parietal branches

Opening (hiatus) for aorta through diaphragm

Left gastric artery
Celiac trunk
Splenic artery
Suprarenal artery
Renal artery
Superior mesenteric artery
Common hepatic artery
Gonadal artery
Inferior mesenteric artery
Abdominal visceral branches

Abdominal aorta

Abdominal parietal branches
Inferior phrenic artery
Lumbar arteries
Median sacral artery

Left common iliac artery

Left internal iliac artery
Left external iliac artery
Left femoral artery

Note. From Patton, K. T., Thibodeau, G. A., & Douglas, M. M. (2012). *Essentials of anatomy & physiology.* Lansing, MI: Elsevier/Mosby. © Elsevier 2012.

blood into the right atrium. The coronary veins also drain into the coronary sinus, which then empties directly into the right atrium.

Circulation Through the Heart

When deoxygenated blood is received by the right atrium, it moves to the right ventricle through the tricuspid valve during ventricular diastole (see Figure 1-10). After the right ventricle fills, the tricuspid valve closes and the ventricle contracts and ejects the blood through the open pulmonic valve into the pulmonary artery. The pulmonary artery divides into the right and left pulmonary arteries and carries blood to the pulmonary capillaries, where gas exchange occurs. Blood leaving the right ventricle is low in oxygen and high in carbon dioxide. When gas exchange occurs, oxygen enters the blood and carbon dioxide leaves the blood and is exhaled.

The pulmonary veins return oxygenated blood to the left side of the heart via the left atrium. The blood in the left atrium moves through the open mitral valve into the left ventricle during ventricular diastole. At the end of diastole, the mitral valve closes and the left ventricle contracts, forcing the aortic valve open and ejecting the oxygenated

FIGURE 1-10: SYSTEMIC CIRCULATION

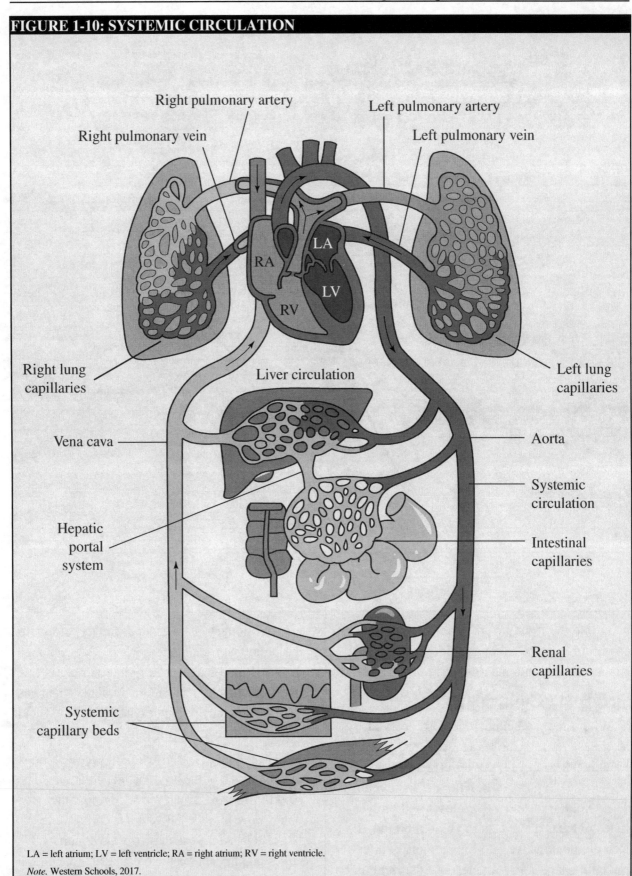

LA = left atrium; LV = left ventricle; RA = right atrium; RV = right ventricle.

Note. Western Schools, 2017.

blood into the aorta for participation in systemic circulation (see Figure 1-10).

CORONARY CIRCULATORY SYSTEM

As stated earlier, the coronary arteries begin in the epicardial layer of the heart. These arteries then travel through the myocardium and, ultimately, to the endocardium to provide oxygen-rich blood to the entire cardiac musculature. During systole, as the heart contracts, blood flow through the coronary arteries is markedly reduced because of compression of the vessels. Therefore, coronary artery perfusion occurs primarily during diastole, when the ventricles are relaxed. Also during diastole, oxygenated blood ejected from the left ventricle to the aorta enters the coronary arteries through two small openings, above the closed aortic valve. These small openings are located in the right and left aortic sinuses. From the openings flow the left and right coronary artery (RCA) systems (see Figure 1-11).

NURSING APPLICATION

Coronary circulation begins with the epicardium and reaches the endocardium last; therefore, myocardial ischemia and infarction begin in the endocardium.

NURSING APPLICATION

A thickened myocardial wall (hypertrophy) results in decreased flow of oxygen-rich blood to the deep myocardium and endocardial layer.

NURSING APPLICATION

Coronary artery perfusion can be compromised if diastole is shortened due to a rapid heart rate.

Left Coronary Artery System

The left main coronary artery, which supplies oxygenated blood to the largest portion of the myocardium, travels a short distance before dividing into the left anterior descending artery (LAD) and left circumflex artery (LCX; see Figure 1-11).

Left Anterior Descending Artery

The LAD supplies oxygenated blood to the anterior wall of the left ventricle, with some perfusion of the right ventricle as well. The septal perforating branches of the LAD supply oxygenated blood to the septum and the bundle branches, whereas the diagonal branches supply oxygenated blood to the anterior left ventricular free wall (see Figure 1-11 and Table 1-1).

Left Circumflex Artery

The LCX supplies oxygenated blood to the lateral wall of the left ventricle and the left atrium. The LCX may also supply oxygenated blood to the inferior wall of the left ventricle in some people. The sinoatrial (SA) node receives oxygenated blood from the nodal branch of the LCX in 45% of the population, and the AV node receives its oxygenated blood from the LCX in 10% of the population (Patton et al., 2012; see Figure 1-11 and Table 1-1).

Right Coronary Artery System

The RCA comes from the right side of the aorta. The RCA supplies oxygenated blood to the right atrium and right ventricle, as well as the inferior and posterior walls of the left ventricle, in most people. The nodal branch of the RCA supplies oxygenated blood to the SA node in 55% of the population, and the AV nodal branch of the RCA supplies oxygenated blood to the AV node in about 90% of the population (Patton et al., 2012). The posterior branch of the left bundle branch system receives oxygenated blood from the RCA and the LAD (see Figure 1-11 and Table 1-1).

FIGURE 1-11: CORONARY ARTERIES

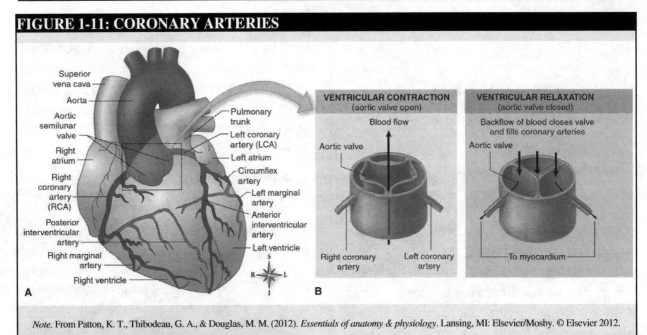

Note. From Patton, K. T., Thibodeau, G. A., & Douglas, M. M. (2012). *Essentials of anatomy & physiology.* Lansing, MI: Elsevier/Mosby. © Elsevier 2012.

TABLE 1-1: CORONARY ARTERY SUPPLY

Coronary Artery	Circulation Supplied to:
Left anterior descending artery	Anterior left ventricle
	Anterior two thirds of septum
	Bundle of His and bundle branches
Left circumflex artery	Left atrium SA node (45% of population)
	AV node (10% of population)
	Lateral left ventricle
	Posterior left ventricle
	Posterior septum (20% of population)
Right coronary artery	Right atrium SA node (55% of population)
	AV node (90% of population)
	Inferior left ventricle
	Posterior septum (80% of population)
	Right ventricle
	Posterior left ventricle
	Left posterior bundle branch

AV = atrioventricular; SA = sinoatrial.

Note. From Western Schools.

Dominance

The term *right* or *left dominance* refers to the vessel (LCX or RCA) from which the posterior descending artery (PDA) arises. In 70% of the population, the PDA arises from the RCA (Patton et al., 2012). In the remainder of the population, the PDA arises from the LCX. The PDA supplies oxygenated blood to the posterior portions of the right and left ventricles, as well as the posterior third of the septum.

Collateral Circulation

Collateral circulation provides communication between the major coronary arteries and their branches. When stenosis of one artery produces a pressure gradient, the collateral vessels can dilate over time and provide a natural bypass for blood flow beyond the stenosis.

The coronary arterioles lie within the myocardium and supply blood to the capillaries. The capillary system is also referred to as the microcirculation. Abnormalities in microcirculation can cause cardiac symptoms in the presence of normal epicardial coronary arteries.

The location of occlusion of a coronary artery provides important information about the structures of the myocardium affected by the occlusion. For example, a total occlusion of the LAD produces a left ventricular anterior wall MI with potential for right and left bundle branch blocks.

Occlusion of the RCA commonly produces various types of bradycardic arrhythmias and heart blocks because the RCA supplies the AV node in approximately 90% of the population and the SA node in approximately 60% of the population (Griffin et al., 2013; Patton et al., 2012).

Cardiac Veins

The cardiac veins drain into the coronary sinus, which empties into the right atrium. In nearly all people, the coronary veins run parallel to the coronary arteries.

CARDIAC PHYSIOLOGY

Electrophysiology

The heart fulfilling its purpose to function as a muscular pump is dependent on the heart's electrical system's stimulus to evoke contraction. The electrical stimulus is also known as impulses or action potentials. The electrical impulses must be coordinated for the heart to pump to contract rhythmically in an effort to maintain forward flow. Coordinated impulses distribute electricity throughout different regions of the myocardium called *conduction pathways* to stimulate the specified region of heart muscle to contract, or pump.

Action Potential

The action potential is a series of events resulting in a change of the electrical charge inside a cell from negative (resting) to positive (stimulated), and back to negative. This change in electrical charge is the result of a difference in the concentration of ions across the cell membrane. The ions primarily responsible for cardiac function are sodium, potassium, and calcium. The cardiac action potential consists of *polarization* (resting state), *depolarization* (stimulation of the cardiac muscle cell), and *repolarization* (return of the cell to a resting state). As depolarization occurs, normal healthy cardiac muscle cells respond with contraction of the muscle. However, depolarization does not guarantee contraction. If a cardiac muscle cell has been damaged, normal contraction might not occur, even when the cell is stimulated. In addition, an abnormal level of sodium, potassium, or calcium can adversely affect the action potential.

Conduction System

Contraction of the chambers of the heart in a coordinated fashion is necessary for normal function of the heart. The cardiac conduction system allows for this systematic approach (see Figure 1-12).

Sinoatrial Node

Stimulation of cardiac muscle cells is normally initiated in a small group of pacemaker cells located in the center of the SA node. The SA node is the natural pacemaker of the heart and sets a heart rate of 60 to 100 beats/min. External nervous system stimulation is not necessary for SA node activity but can impact it. The SA node is located near the coronary sinus and close to the junction of the superior vena cava and the right atrium (Patton et al., 2012). From the SA node, depolarization travels through the right atrial tissue via internodal pathways and through the left atrial tissue via

FIGURE 1-12: CONDUCTION SYSTEM OF THE HEART

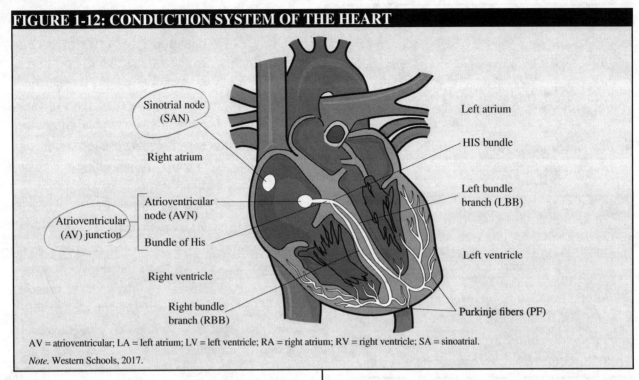

AV = atrioventricular; LA = left atrium; LV = left ventricle; RA = right atrium; RV = right ventricle; SA = sinoatrial.

Note. Western Schools, 2017.

Bachmann bundle. From the internodal pathways, the impulse travels to the AV node.

Atrioventricular Node

The AV node slows conduction from the atria to the ventricles. Conduction is slowed to ensure the ventricles are relaxed at the time of atrial contraction, allowing them to fill completely before contracting. The AV node is located in the right atrium, just above the insertion of the tricuspid valve (Patton et al., 2012).

Atrioventricular Junction

From the AV node, the electrical impulse travels along the *bundle of His.* The AV node and the bundle of His are surrounded by tissue known as the *AV junction.* The AV junction contains pacemaker cells and will initiate a heart rate of 40 to 60 beats/min if no impulse is received from the SA node.

Bundle Branches

The bundle of His divides into the right and left bundle branches. The *right bundle branch* carries the impulse to the right ventricle. The *left bundle branch* divides into the left posterior bundle branch and the left anterior bundle branch. The left posterior bundle branch carries the impulse to the posterior and inferior left ventricle; the left anterior bundle branch carries the impulse to the anterior and superior left ventricle.

Purkinje Fibers

From the bundle branches, the impulse travels to the *Purkinje fibers,* where depolarization is carried through the subendocardial layers of the heart. The *Purkinje network* is also the location of the heart's third group of pacemaker cells. If no impulse is received through the normal conduction patterns, the Purkinje system will initiate a heart rate of 20 to 40 beats/min.

Mechanical Physiology

The electrical function of the heart is the stimulus for the mechanical function of the heart. To fulfill its purpose of delivering oxygen and nutrients to the tissue, the heart's mechanical pump is dependent on multiple factors. In addition to the components of stroke volume (preload, afterload, and contractility), the mechanical function of the heart interplays with a number of physiological responses throughout the cardiac cycle.

The Cardiac Cycle

Systole, contraction of the heart muscle, results in ejection of blood from the chamber. *Diastole,* relaxation of the heart muscle, allows the chamber to fill. Each of the atria and ventricles undergoes systole and diastole. Ventricular filling and influx of blood is normally rapid, lasting only 0.1 second (Patton et al., 2012). The efficiency of the cardiac cycle depends on the health of the cardiac muscle, valves, and conduction system. The heart's conduction system provides the timing of events for atrial and ventricular systole.

Ventricular Diastole

Ventricular diastole begins when ventricular contraction is complete. When the pressure in the pulmonary vascular bed and the aorta exceeds the pressure in the right and left ventricles, the semilunar valves close. Simultaneously, the pressure in the filled atria exceeds the pressure in the nearly empty ventricles and the AV valves (tricuspid and mitral valves) open. When the tricuspid and mitral valves open, a rapid, passive filling of the ventricles occurs as blood moves from the atria through the open valves into the ventricles. Approximately 75% of ventricular filling occurs during this passive filling phase. The remainder of ventricular filling occurs with atrial contraction. This contraction of the atria is also known as *atrial systole.* Atrial systole is commonly referred to as *atrial kick* and contributes as much as 25% of the ventricular volume (Lough, 2014).

NURSING APPLICATION

When a person's heart rhythm converts acutely to atrial fibrillation, he or she loses the atrial kick contribution to left ventricular volume. This loss of atrial kick, which can be as much as 25% of stroke volume, can result in a decrease in stroke volume significant enough to cause a decrease in cardiac output, a decrease in blood pressure, and ultimately, symptoms of decreased perfusion.

Ventricular Systole

After atrial contraction, the pressures in the atria and ventricles equalize, the AV valves partially close, and ventricular systole begins. Ventricular systole has two phases. The first phase is *isovolumic* or *isovolumetric contraction,* so named because the volume of blood in the ventricles does not change during this phase. During isovolumic contraction, the ventricular walls tense and press toward the center of the ventricular cavity. This tensing of the walls increases the pressure in the ventricles. When the pressure in the ventricles exceeds that in the atria, the AV valves close quickly, preventing backward flow of blood into the atria. For ejection of the ventricular contents to occur, the myocardial walls of the ventricles must develop enough pressure to force the semilunar (aortic and pulmonic) valves open. When the pressure in the ventricles exceeds the pressure in the aorta and pulmonary artery, the aortic and pulmonic valves open (Lough, 2014; Patton et al., 2012).

The second phase of systole is *ejection,* during which blood is ejected into the systemic and pulmonary circulation. The semilunar valves close at the end of systole, when the pressure in the arteries exceeds the pressure in the ventricles. Normally, ventricular diastole (ventricular filling) is two times longer than ventricular systole (ventricular emptying).

NURSING APPLICATION

As heart rate increases, ventricular diastolic time shortens, whereas ventricular systolic time essentially stays the same. Therefore, an increased heart rate decreases the time available to fill the ventricles. This decrease in ventricular filling can lead to reduced cardiac output and signs of poor perfusion. Tachycardia, therefore, has the potential to lead to decreased perfusion of end organs.

Contractility

The atria and ventricles have contractile muscle cells called *myocytes.* Without functioning myocytes, the myocardium cannot contract. The remainder of the cardiac cells are either pacemaker cells or cells capable of excitability and conductivity. The adult heart has approximately 19 billion cardiac cells. Millions of cardiac cells are lost with each year of life. If a person lives to 100 years of age, he or she will have lost approximately two thirds of his or her original heart cells. Cardiac muscle cells differ from skeletal muscle cells in that they are shorter, broader, and more interconnected. Intercalated disks form junctions between cardiac muscle cells, allowing them to function as integrated units. The junctions serve as electrical connections, joining muscle fibers in a single unit capable of rapidly conducting an impulse. These connections allow the atria and ventricles to contract almost simultaneously (Lough, 2014; Patton et al., 2012).

Cardiac muscle cells are also more metabolically active, require more energy, and experience more prolonged contractions than do skeletal muscle cells. This prolonged contraction prevents impulses from coming rapidly enough to produce a sustained contraction, thereby preventing cardiac muscle from running low on adenosine triphosphate and becoming fatigued (Patton et al., 2012). The process of myocardial contraction uses the adenosine triphosphate molecules for energy.

The contractile property of the cardiac muscle cell comes from the *myofibril.* Myofibrils consist of repeating units called *sarcomeres* and contain protein units responsible for con-traction. Cardiac muscle fibers contain transverse tubules, also called *T tubules,* which are extensions of the cell membranes. A significant amount of calcium enters the cell through the T tubules from the interstitial fluid surrounding the cells. Without this additional calcium coming through the T tubules, the force of myocardial contraction would be greatly reduced (Patton et al., 2012).

NURSING APPLICATION

The amount of extracellular calcium ions affects the amount of calcium available to enter the cardiac cells via the T tubules. Therefore, low extracellular calcium ions, or a low serum calcium level, can negatively affect the force of myocardial contraction.

Neurohormonal Regulation

Both branches of the *autonomic nervous system* (the sympathetic nervous system and the parasympathetic nervous system) innervate the heart. The *sympathetic nervous system* allows the body to function under stress, and the *parasympathetic nervous system* helps the body conserve and restore resources. Both branches of the autonomic nervous system contribute to regulation of the major components of cardiac output. Because blood pressure is the product of cardiac output and systemic vascular resistance, it is also impacted by the autonomic nervous system.

Sympathetic Nervous System (Adrenergic)

The sympathetic nervous system has two key neurotransmitters, or messengers: epinephrine and norepinephrine. These neurotransmitters, also called *catecholamines,* are released in response to excitation or stress. The excitation or stress can be caused by something as simple as waking up to something as severe as extreme fright. Epinephrine is also called *adrenaline.* The major effects of epinephrine release are increased heart rate, increased stroke volume, increased contractility, increased systolic blood pressure with decreased diastolic blood pressure (resulting in an increase in pulse pressure), and increased blood flow to the extremities. Norepinephrine is also called *noradrenaline.* The major effects of norepinephrine include increased heart rate, increased systolic and diastolic blood pressures, and decreased blood flow to the extremities (Patton et al., 2012). Sympathetic nerve fibers supply the SA node, AV node, and myocardium of the atria and ventricles. When the neurotransmitters are activated by the sympathetic nervous system, the exact effect depends on the specific receptors stimulated (see Table 1-2).

Cardiovascular Receptor Physiology: Adrenergic Receptors

The primary receptors that affect cardiovascular physiology are the alpha, beta, and dopaminergic receptors. As previously mentioned, each receptor is stimulated by neurotransmitters because of endogenous release secondary to the stimulation of the sympathetic nervous system, or they are stimulated by exogenous sources of catecholamines – medications administered. Alpha$_1$ and beta$_2$ stimulation oppose each other in the periphery and oppositely affect systemic vascular resistance. The net result of sympathetic nervous system stimulation on alpha and beta receptors depends on the degree to which each receptor is stimulated. In general, alpha receptors are more sensitive to norepinephrine, and beta receptors are more sensitive to epinephrine (Manaker, 2014).

Beta Receptors

Beta$_1$-adrenergic receptors are located in the heart and, when stimulated, cause an increase in heart rate, conductivity, and contractility. Beta$_2$-adrenergic receptors are located in the lungs and periphery and, when stimulated, cause bronchial and peripheral vasodilation (Manaker, 2014).

Alpha Receptors

Alpha$_1$-adrenergic receptors are located in the vessels of vascular smooth muscle and affect the tone of the small arterioles responsible for determining systemic vascular resistance. Stimulation of alpha receptors results in arterial vasoconstriction and, ultimately, an increase in blood pressure (Manaker, 2014).

Dopaminergic Receptors

The renal, mesenteric, and coronary blood vessels also contain dopaminergic receptors. Stimulation of dopaminergic receptors results in vasodilation (Manaker, 2014).

NURSING APPLICATION

The high sensitivity of beta receptors to epinephrine is the reason epinephrine is used during cardiac resuscitation in patients with pulseless rhythms.

TABLE 1-2: ADRENERGIC RECEPTOR LOCATION AND RESPONSE

Receptor	Location of Receptor	Response to Stimulation
Alpha$_1$	Vascular smooth muscles	Vasoconstriction
Beta$_1$	Sinoatrial node, atrioventricular node, and myocardium	Increased heart rate Increased conduction Increased contractility
Beta$_2$	Vascular and bronchial smooth muscles	Bronchodilation Vasodilation
Dopaminergic	Vascular smooth muscle (renal, coronary, and mesenteric)	Vasodilation

Note. From Western Schools.

Parasympathetic Nervous System (Vagal)

The parasympathetic nervous system innervates the SA node, AV node, AV junction, and myocardium of the atria (Patton et al., 2012). There is minimal parasympathetic innervation of the ventricles. When the parasympathetic nervous system is stimulated, the response is called a *cholinergic,* or *vagal,* response in which a reduction in heart rate can be observed. Acetylcholine is the neurotransmitter that is released when parasympathetic nerve fibers are stimulated. It binds to parasympathetic receptors. Cholinergic receptors are classified into two types: *nicotinic* and *muscarinic* (Dweik, 2015). Parasympathetic receptors located in the heart and smooth muscles are called *muscarinic receptors.* Acetylcholine is the neurotransmitter of this system and stimulates the glands and smooth muscle of the digestive tract. This system also plays a major role in regulating bronchomotor tone (Dweik, 2015).

NURSING APPLICATION

Atropine interferes with the effects of the parasympathetic nervous system. Therefore, atropine will only have an effect on slow heart rates that are the result of parasympathetic stimulation, such as a vagal response. Atropine will not work on heart blocks that occur at a level below the AV node. This is because there are not adequate numbers of parasympathetic fibers below the level of the AV node.

NURSING APPLICATION

Atropine will have no effect in treating slow heart rates after a cardiac transplantation. This is because the transplanted heart lacks innervation by the parasympathetic nervous system (Dweik, 2015).

Stimulation of the parasympathetic nervous system decreases heart rate and slows conduction. It has little effect on the force of ventricular contraction because of the minimal innervation of the parasympathetic nervous system in the ventricles. When the parasympathetic nervous system is stimulated, acetylcholine is released, resulting in a cholinergic, or vagal, response. Acetylcholine directly inhibits the SA node, thus decreasing heart rate. Stimulation of the parasympathetic nervous system also causes vasodilation because of nitric oxide release from the endothelium (Dweik, 2015). Venous vasodilation decreases preload, and arterial vasodilation decreases afterload. Vagal tone is more pronounced during sleeping hours. When blood pressure is elevated, the feedback from the baroreceptors (pressure receptors) causes parasympathetic stimulation, which results in a slower heart rate, decreased force of contraction, and vasodilation. These effects result in lower cardiac output and blood pressure.

NURSING APPLICATION

The activation of the parasympathetic nervous system during an acute hypertensive crisis explains the reflex bradycardia commonly seen in this clinical situation. Conversely, low blood pressure may cause reflex tachycardia.

Baroreceptors

Baroreceptors (also called *pressure receptors* or *mechanoreceptors*) are specialized nerve tissues located in the aortic arch and carotid sinus, which is the origin of the internal carotid artery (Patton et al., 2012). They function as sensors in the nervous system and are sensitive to wall tension within the arterial vessels. An increase or decrease in wall tension and pressure sends signals to the medulla, the vasomotor center in the brainstem, via the *afferent pathways.* The medulla interprets the information it receives from the baroreceptors and transmits information back to the heart and blood vessels via motor nerves called *efferent pathways*. Impulses from this center control the diameter of blood vessels. When blood pressure is increased, baroreceptors recognize the increased wall tension and send a message to inhibit the sympathetic nervous system and stimulate the parasympathetic nervous system. Heart rate slows and veins and arteries dilate throughout the system. These changes result in decreased blood pressure. When blood pressure decreases, wall tension decreases. The opposite effects (increased heart rate and vasoconstriction) occur with stimulation of the sympathetic nervous system (Patton et al., 2012).

NURSING APPLICATION

When the vagal maneuver of carotid massage is performed, baroreceptors in the carotid arteries are stimulated to slow conduction from the SA node through the AV node and, therefore, heart rate is decreased.

Chemoreceptors

The carotid arteries also contain chemoreceptors. These receptors respond to changes in blood chemistry, including arterial oxygen content, arterial carbon dioxide levels, and arterial pH (Patton et al., 2012). As blood pressure lowers to a critical point, the delivery of oxygen also decreases to a critical point. As oxygen delivery decreases, carbon dioxide levels increase. When stimulated by an elevated arterial carbon dioxide level, chemoreceptors send a message to the vasomotor center to stimulate cardiac activity via the sympathetic nervous system. Heart rate increases and vasoconstriction occurs, causing an increase in blood pressure with a resultant increase in oxygenation.

Renin-Angiotensin-Aldosterone System

Renin is released from the kidneys in response to low circulating volume, low cardiac output, or poor kidney perfusion. Activation of the sympathetic nervous system and increased catecholamines stimulate renin release. In response to renin, angiotensin I is converted to angiotensin II in the presence of angiotensin-converting enzyme. Angiotensin-converting enzyme is found in the capillary bed of the lungs and other tissues. The important end results of the renin-angiotensin-aldosterone system (RAAS) are caused by the effects of circulating angiotensin II. Angiotensin II has three primary effects:

1. arterial vasoconstriction,

2. stimulation of thirst, and

3. stimulation of the adrenal cortex to secrete aldosterone (aldosterone increases sodium and water reabsorption).

As the blood vessels constrict and water is reabsorbed and retained, blood pressure increases and perfusion to the body, including the kidneys, improves. This increased perfusion then decreases the production of renin by the kidneys.

NURSING APPLICATION

The end results of stimulation of the RAAS include arterial vasoconstriction and aldosterone secretion. Arterial vasoconstriction increases afterload, and aldosterone secretion increases preload. These effects are clinically important in patients with heart failure who have chronic stimulation of the RAAS.

CONSIDERATIONS FOR SPECIAL POPULATIONS

Pregnancy

During pregnancy, the body experiences significant anatomical and physiological changes to accommodate fetal growth and development. The cardiovascular system undergoes the most dramatic changes of all of the body's organ systems as quickly as the first week of gestation through delivery and until 6 weeks postpartum.

Anatomy Considerations

As the abdominal cavity is filled with the growing uterus, its contents push upward against the diaphragm and ultimately displace the heart (see Figure 1-13). The heart is most often displaced upward and laterally, and it is also rotated forward. Also, as the abdominal cavity's contents increase and progressively get larger during pregnancy, the vena cava is at risk for compression and consequential decreased venous return to the heart when the mother lies in some positions. By the end of gestation, the mother's heart walls thicken and heart mass

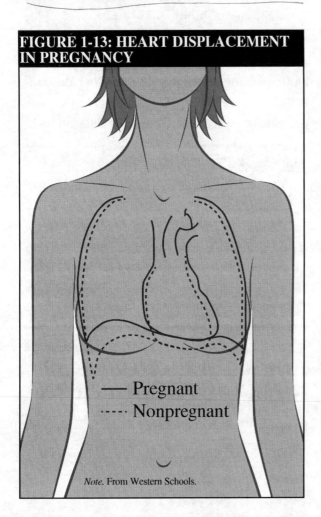

FIGURE 1-13: HEART DISPLACEMENT IN PREGNANCY

—— Pregnant
---- Nonpregnant

Note. From Western Schools.

increases as much as 28% to 52%, respectively, above prepregnancy size and mass. Fortunately, in a normal pregnancy, this remodeling is temporary and the heart returns to its prepregnancy size and mass within the following 6 postpartal months (Yanamandra & Chandraharan, 2012).

Physiology Considerations

The extreme changes that occur during pregnancy occur rapidly and begin in the first week of pregnancy. Increased levels of estrogen and progesterone are associated with skeletal muscle relaxation leading to vasodilation, significant decreases in peripheral vascular resistance, and a decrease in blood pressure. However, with increased metabolic maternal and fetal demands, the heart rate increases progressively to 20% to 25% over the mother's baseline. Despite the altered heart rate and blood pressure parameters, myocardial contractility and ventricular function do not normally change. Other changes the pregnant female encounters include increased vasomotor and sympathetic activity, increased baroreceptor sensitivity, and a weakened response to alpha-adrenergic stimulation (Sanghavi & Rutherford, 2014).

In another effort to meet the increased metabolic maternal and fetal demands, total circulating blood volume, red blood cell production, and red blood cell mass increase. A normal pregnancy is associated with increased erythropoietin production given the mother has normal iron stores and adequate nutrition. Although erythropoiesis increases red blood cell production by 40% during pregnancy, plasma volume increases proportionally more. In the very early weeks of pregnancy, the RAAS is substantially activated. As estrogen levels rise, angiotensinogen production does also, supporting the blood pressure as needed during pregnancy. Vasopressin secretion increases to stimulate drinking as another mechanism to support water retention and blood volume. Increased levels of progesterone provide potent aldosterone antagonism to help maintain adequate serum sodium and potassium levels. Low aldosterone levels during pregnancy are thought to be related to one of the primary causative factors associated with preeclampsia (Sanghavi & Rutherford, 2014).

Older Adults

Cardiovascular disease is the leading cause of death in persons 75 years and older. Although lifestyle choices and pathological factors contribute to cardiovascular disease–related deaths, age-related cardiovascular changes underlie pathophysiological processes. Currently, there are no evidence-based guidelines to apply cardiovascular care to the older adult due to an underrepresentation of older adults in clinical trials. Nevertheless, understanding the fundamental changes that occur with the aging process will improve the care and point-of-care decisions made for the aging adult (Rich et al., 2016).

Anatomy and Physiology Considerations

Anatomical changes to the heart occur with aging. Aging does not account for the overall size increase; however, increases in ventricular wall thickness, cardiac valve thickness and stiffness, and the mass of the heart do occur. There are increases in fat, collagen, elastin, and other cellular changes that contribute to the increased stiffness, decreased contractility, and decreased efficiency in the older adult's heart to meet increased metabolic demands. Increased myocardial stiffness decreases myocardial compliance during the filling phase, thereby limiting the ventricular filling capacity the heart had in its youth. Consequently, a normal age-related reduction in stroke volume occurs in the older adult, contributing to changes in coronary artery perfusion pressures and ventricular remodeling. Some changes in contractility are related to slower release of calcium into the myoplasm during systole. Normal

age-related increases in atrial and ventricular pressures occur as well, causing dilation in the chambers and an increased propensity of atrial arrhythmias further reducing cardiac output. Increased myocardial thickness and chamber dilation (remodeling) impacts the aged conduction pathways of the heart. Other conduction changes occur as a result of the loss of pacemaker and conduction cells with aging. The aging process significantly impacts the electrical and mechanical function of the heart (Boltz, Capezuti, Fulmer, & Zwicker, 2016).

NURSING APPLICATION

The older adult with acute atrial fibrillation with rapid ventricular response does not tolerate the loss of atrial kick as well as the younger adult given the above anatomical and physiological changes. The loss of atrial kick in the older adult reduces cerebral blood flow and increases the risk for syncope and stroke in addition to the increased risk for myocardial ischemia. These are expected age-related changes in the absence of a pathological process. When a pathophysiological process is added to the aged anatomy and physiology, morbidity and mortality rates increase in this population.

Like the heart structures, the vascular system stiffens with age, accounting for an increase in systolic blood pressures. Elasticity of all vessels decreases, making veins overcompliant and apt for the pooling of blood, thereby decreasing the ability of the valves to facilitate forward flow and venous return. Arteries lose elasticity and gain more areas of atherosclerosis. As arterial walls stiffen, baroreceptors lose sensitivity to changes in pressures, thereby reducing the older adult's compensatory mechanisms for hemodynamic changes. Coronary arteries are no different because they become tortuous with localized areas of atherosclerosis as well. Fortunately, the aged adult develops an increased amount of collateral circulation to augment blood flow to the myocardium. In the postmenopausal older adult, the lack of estrogen increases the rate of the aging process in the cardiovascular system (Boltz et al., 2016).

NURSING APPLICATION

Edema and deep vein thrombosis can occur more frequently in the older adult because of normal age-related changes within the cardiovascular system.

SUMMARY

An understanding of basic anatomy and physiology of the heart is essential for all healthcare professionals. The heart is a complex, intricate pump with one purpose: the forward propulsion of blood to perfuse the body. Many anatomical and physiological factors can impact how well the heart fulfills its purpose. Giving special consideration to the changes that occur in pregnant or older adults is necessary to discern appropriate assessments and care. It is the responsibility of all healthcare professionals to apply the fundamentals of anatomy and physiology toward clinical assessments, medication administration, and the impact of all treatments to this intricately designed system.

EXAM QUESTIONS

CHAPTER 1
Questions 1–6

Note: Choose the one option that BEST answers each question.

1. Which cardiac structure is most at risk for failure secondary to sustained elevated intracardiac pressures?

   a. Right atrium
   b. Right ventricle
   c. Left atrium
   d. Left ventricle

2. Which cardiac tissue has delayed conduction to facilitate ventricular filling?

   a. Sinoatrial node
   b. Atrioventricular node
   c. Bundle of His
   d. Purkinje fibers

3. Which electrolyte plays the most important role in myocardial contractility?

   a. Potassium
   b. Sodium
   c. Calcium
   d. Phosphorus

4. Which type of cardiovascular receptor is most sensitive to epinephrine?

   a. Alpha-adrenergic
   b. Beta-adrenergic
   c. Nicotinic
   d. Muscarinic

5. Which physiological mechanism occurs in response to low circulating volume, low cardiac output, or decreased kidney perfusion in an effort to maintain hemodynamic stability?

   a. Baroreceptor stimulation to decrease heart rate
   b. Increased blood pressure stimulating the parasympathetic nervous system
   c. Activation of the renin-angiotensin-aldosterone system (RAAS)
   d. Increased catecholamine excretion to stimulate renin release

6. Which age-related physiological process contributes to the reduced contractility and stroke volume that older adults experience?

   a. Myocardial stiffness
   b. Collagen fiber loss
   c. Adipose fat loss
   d. Ventricular wall thinning

REFERENCES

Boltz, M., Capezuti, E., Fulmer, T., & Zwicker, D. (2016). *Evidence-based geriatric nursing protocols for best practice* (5th ed.). New York, NY: Springer.

Dweik, R. A. (2015). Role of anticholinergic therapy in COPD. *UpToDate.* Retrieved from http://www.uptodate.com/contents/role-of-anticholinergic-therapy-in-copd

Griffin, B. P., Kapadia, S. R., & Rimmerman, C. M. (2013). *Cleveland Clinic Cardiology Board Review* (2nd ed.). Philadelphia, PA: Lippincott Williams & Wilkins.

Iacobellis, G., & Bianco, A. C. (2011). Epicardial adipose tissue: Emerging physiological, pathophysiological, and clinical features. *Trends in Endocrinology and Metabolism, 22*(11), 450-457. doi:10.1016/j.tem.2011.07.003

Lough, M. E. (2014). Cardiovascular anatomy and physiology. In L. D. Urden, K. M. Stacy, & M. E. Lough (Eds.), *Critical care nursing: Diagnosis and management* (7th ed., pp. 200-221). St. Louis, MO: Elsevier/Mosby.

Loukas, M., Walters, A., Boon, J. M., Welch, T. P., Meiring, J. H., & Abrahams, P. H. (2012). Pericardiocentesis: A clinical anatomy review. *Clinical Anatomy, 25*(7), 872-881. doi:10.1002/ca.22032

Manaker, S. (2014). Use of vasopressors and inotropes. *UpToDate.* Retrieved from http://www.uptodate.com/contents/use-of-vasopressors-and-inotropes

Patton, K. T., Thibodeau, G. A., & Douglas, M. M. (2012). *Essentials of anatomy & physiology.* Lansing, MI: Elsevier/Mosby.

Rich, M. W., Chyun, D. A., Skolnick, A. H., Alexander, K. P., Forman, D. E., ... American Heart Association Older Populations Committee of the Council on Clinical Cardiology, Council on Cardiovascular and Stroke Nursing, Council on Cardiovascular Surgery and Anesthesia, and Stroke Council; American College of Cardiology; & American Geriatrics Society. (2016). Knowledge gaps in cardiovascular care of the older adult population: A Scientific Statement from the American Heart Association, American College of Cardiology, and American Geriatrics Society. *Circulation, 133*(21), 2103-2122. doi:10.1161/CIR.0000000000000380

Sanghavi, M., & Rutherford, J. (2014). Cardiovascular management in pregnancy: Cardiovascular physiology of pregnancy. *Circulation, 1*(30), 1003-1008. doi:10.1161/CIRCULATIONAHA.114.009029

Yanamandra, N., & Chandraharan, E. (2012). Anatomical and physiological changes in pregnancy and their implications in clinical practice. In E. Chandraharan & S. Arulkumaran (Eds.), *Obstetric and intrapartum emergencies: A practical guide to management.* Cambridge, England: Cambridge University Press.

CHAPTER 2

PRINCIPLES OF HEMODYNAMICS AND OXYGEN DELIVERY

LEARNING OUTCOME

After completing this chapter, the learner will be able to apply hemodynamic principles to understand the significant role basic cardiovascular anatomy and physiology have on oxygen delivery.

CHAPTER OBJECTIVES

After completing this chapter, the learner will be able to:

1. Identify how alterations in heart rate and stroke volume can negatively affect cardiac output.

2. Identify influencing factors that negatively affect oxygen delivery and tissue consumption.

3. Recognize the significance of hemodynamic pressure monitoring.

INTRODUCTION

Building on the knowledge of the purpose of the anatomical structures and physiology of the heart and blood vessels, the cardiovascular nurse must also understand the significance of changes that can facilitate the success of this system. The term *hemodynamics* captures the physiology and pathophysiology of this system in one word. The term is derived from two words: *heme* means "blood" and *dynamic* means "unstable or change." Thus, hemodynamics captures the many changes this system makes in its effort to facilitate the body's blood volume.

Although there are noninvasive means to assess and evaluate a patient's hemodynamic stability (e.g., noninvasive blood pressure, heart rate, and distal pulse assessments), invasive measures allow the cardiovascular clinician to make more accurate measurements. The cardiovascular nurse must be able to use a variety of tools capable of measuring a patient's hemodynamic status to evaluate the system's effectiveness of oxygen delivery and consumption.

HEMODYNAMIC PRINCIPLES AND VENTRICULAR FUNCTION

Components of Cardiac Output

Cardiac output is the amount of blood ejected from the left ventricle in 1 minute (Urden, Stacy, & Lough, 2014). As simple as the definition of cardiac output is, many changes can occur among the many determinants of cardiac output that can negatively impact oxygen delivery. The cardiovascular nurse must understand the components that make up cardiac output, and if any one of the components is altered, the others must compensate to maintain adequate oxygen delivery.

Cardiac output is generally measured in liters per minute (L/min). The normal range for cardiac output in a healthy adult is approximately 4 to 8 L/min. The more accurate measure of cardiac output is called the *cardiac index,* which incorporates an individual's own body size by using the person's height and weight divided by the person's body surface area. An individual's cardiac output changes throughout the day to meet the varying demands for oxygen delivery during rest or during periods of exertion (Urden et al., 2014).

Adequate cardiac output is attained when the electrical physiology (heart rate) of the heart and the mechanical physiology of the heart (components of stroke volume) cooperate with neurohormonal regulation of the cardiovascular system to meet the body's oxygen demands (see Figure 2-1). Perfusion of the body with oxygenated blood is dependent on cardiac output. Heart rate and stroke volume are the primary determinants of cardiac output as noted in Figures 2-1 and 2-2. Stroke volume has three components: *preload, afterload,* and *contractility.* Changes in heart rate, preload, afterload, or contractility change cardiac output (see Table 2-1). In addition, increasing any one of these factors increases myocardial oxygen demand.

NURSING APPLICATION

Patients with decreased contractility from a previous myocardial infarction have lower ejection fractions and reduced stroke volumes. Patients with low ejection fractions and reduced stroke volume have the potential to exhibit signs of decreased perfusion to the end organs.

Heart Rate

Heart rate is defined as the number of times the heart beats every minute. Normal heart rate in an adult ranges from 60 to 100 beats/min.

The control center of the cardiovascular system lies within the medulla oblongata of the brainstem. This center manipulates heart rate intrinsically via several physiological reflexes that serve as feedback mechanisms to this part of the brain. Such reflexes include the stimulation of baroreceptors, chemoreceptors, right atrial receptors, natriuretic peptides, and the renin-angiotensin-aldosterone system.

In a coordinated effort, the cardiovascular system, autonomic system, and physiological reflexes to changes in blood volume, blood pressures, and specific chemical components within the blood act to maintain an intricate balance for adequate blood flow, oxygenation, and perfusion. During exercise, heart rate naturally increases to meet the increased metabolic needs of the body. Heart rate also decreases as the body's needs decrease, such as during sleep. However, extremely slow heart rates (<40 beats/min) and extremely high heart rates (>150 beats/min) experienced over a prolonged period can negatively affect cardiac output. Rapid heart rates do not allow adequate time for ventricular filling, and slow heart rates do not provide an adequate volume of ejected blood per minute.

Heart rate is greatly influenced by the autonomic nervous system. Parasympathetic nerve fibers (vagus nerves) are concentrated near the sinoatrial and atrioventricular nodes in the atria (see Figure 2-3). Stimulation of vagal nerves produces bradycardia by stimulating the sinoatrial node. Sympathetic nerve fibers follow the path of major coronary arteries beneath the epicardial layer of the heart. Stimulation of these fibers directly augments ventricular function to increase heart rate and contractility (Urden et al., 2014).

Stroke Volume

Stroke volume is the volume of blood ejected by the left ventricle with each beat. Each ventricle holds about 150 ml when full and ejects about

FIGURE 2-1: DETERMINANTS OF CARDIAC OUTPUT

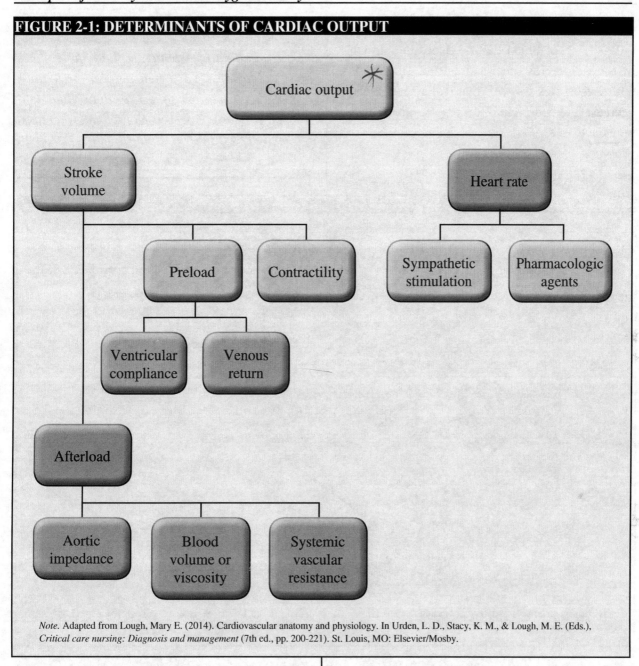

Note. Adapted from Lough, Mary E. (2014). Cardiovascular anatomy and physiology. In Urden, L. D., Stacy, K. M., & Lough, M. E. (Eds.), *Critical care nursing: Diagnosis and management* (7th ed., pp. 200-221). St. Louis, MO: Elsevier/Mosby.

50% to 60% of its volume with each beat (Urden et al., 2014). The percentage of volume ejected with each beat is termed the *ejection fraction.*

Preload

Preload, one of the determinants of stroke volume, is defined as the stretch on the ventricular myocardial fibers at the end of ventricular diastole; it can be used to evaluate volume status. The volume of blood filling the ventricles causes the myocardium to stretch. According to Starling's law (see Figure 2-4), the larger the volume of blood in the ventricle at the end of diastole, the greater the energy of the subsequent contraction (Urden et al., 2014). Therefore, as the filling of the ventricle increases, the strength of the subsequent contraction also increases, resulting in a greater stroke volume.

Venous return to the heart determines the amount of blood entering the ventricles and stretches myocardial fibers. The amount of venous blood returned to the right atrium ultimately enters the right and left ventricles. It is this volume of blood that produces the stretch in the ventricles during diastole. If venous return decreases, as with hypovolemia, preload decreases. When preload decreases, stroke volume decreases.

NURSING APPLICATION

Evaluation of a patient's fluid status gives a clinician a good indication of preload. A patient experiencing extracellular fluid deficit will have a decreased preload, whereas a patient with extracellular fluid overload will have an increased preload.

FIGURE 2-2: HR × SV = CO

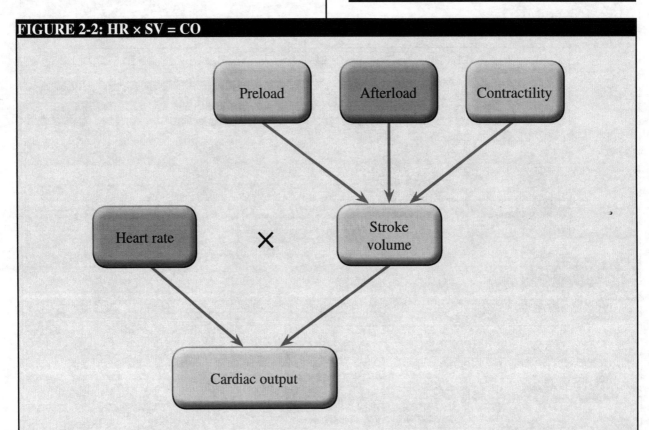

Note. Adapted from Lough, Mary E. (2014). Cardiovascular anatomy and physiology. In Urden, L. D., Stacy, K. M., & Lough, M. E. (Eds.), *Critical care nursing: Diagnosis and management* (7th ed., pp. 200-221). St. Louis, MO: Elsevier/Mosby.

TABLE 2-1: KEY DEFINITIONS RELATING TO CARDIAC OUTPUT	
Cardiac output	Volume of blood ejected by ventricle every minute
	Cardiac output = heart rate × stroke volume
Stroke volume	Volume of blood ejected by ventricle each beat
	Stroke volume = preload + afterload + contractility
Ejection fraction	Percent of volume in ventricle ejected with each beat
Preload	Stretch on the ventricular myocardial fibers at the end of ventricular diastole; determined by the volume in the ventricle at the end of diastole
Afterload	Pressure the ventricle must overcome to eject its contents
Contractility	Ability of the ventricle to pump independent of preload or afterload

Note. From Western Schools.

FIGURE 2-3: IMPACT OF THE AUTONOMIC NERVOUS SYSTEM ON HEART RATE

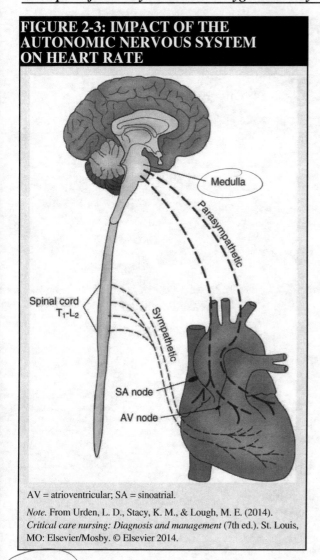

AV = atrioventricular; SA = sinoatrial.

Note. From Urden, L. D., Stacy, K. M., & Lough, M. E. (2014). *Critical care nursing: Diagnosis and management* (7th ed.). St. Louis, MO: Elsevier/Mosby. © Elsevier 2014.

Afterload

Afterload, another component of stroke volume, is the workload or the pressure the ventricle must overcome to eject its contents. Afterload is affected by anatomical structures and physiological changes that may impede the ejection of ventricular contents. These structures and changes include aortic or pulmonic valve function, arterial or pulmonary artery (PA) pressures (vascular resistance), compliance of vascular walls, and diastolic pressure in the great arteries. If the ventricular contents are to be ejected, the pressure in the ventricles must become great enough to force the aortic and pulmonic valves open. A stenotic valve is much more difficult to open due to the abnormalities in the valve. Therefore, aortic or pulmonic stenosis increases afterload.

The overall resistance the left ventricle must pump against, which is termed *systemic vascular resistance,* is primarily determined by the systemic arterioles (Urden et al., 2014). When the arterioles dilate, systemic vascular resistance decreases; when they constrict, systemic vascular resistance increases. Arterioles respond to systemic changes and vasoconstrict or vasodilate depending on the hemodynamic needs of the body. Noncompliant vascular walls (as exist in hypertension) do not relax easily and increase afterload. The vascular resistance the right ventricle must pump against is the pulmonary vascular resistance. It is determined by the PA pressures.

Blood pressure is not equal to systemic vascular resistance. It is a product of cardiac output and systemic vascular resistance. However, blood pressure is a noninvasive method of evaluating systemic vascular resistance. Generally, as diastolic pressure rises, so does systemic vascular resistance.

NURSING APPLICATION

Patients with untreated hypertension have a continuous increase in afterload, resulting in increased left ventricular workload. Sustained increased workload eventually causes the left ventricle to fail. Left ventricular failure, or left-sided heart failure, leads to systolic cardiac dysfunction. The nurse must make the connection that hypertension in the patient with systolic cardiac dysfunction will hasten the patient's demise.

Contractility

The third and final component of the stroke volume equation is contractility. Contractility is the ability of the ventricle to contract independently of preload or afterload. Contractility

FIGURE 2-4: STARLING'S CURVE

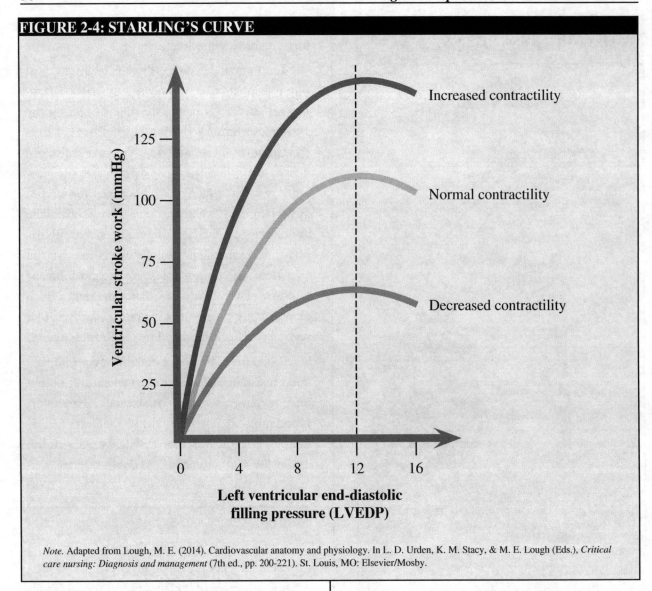

Note. Adapted from Lough, M. E. (2014). Cardiovascular anatomy and physiology. In L. D. Urden, K. M. Stacy, & M. E. Lough (Eds.), *Critical care nursing: Diagnosis and management* (7th ed., pp. 200-221). St. Louis, MO: Elsevier/Mosby.

is referred to as the inotropic state of the myocardium and is a major component of systole. During ventricular contraction, the cardiac muscle shortens (Urden et al., 2014). The extent of myofibril shortening determines the velocity of the ejection of the myocardial contents. Damage to the myocardial muscle cells, as occurs in myocardial infarction, decreases the ability of the myofibrils to shorten and impairs the ability of the ventricle to contract. Overstretch of the myofibrils also results in myofibrils that can no longer shorten effectively.

Additional Factors That Contribute to Cardiac Output

The shape of the left ventricle is designed to provide a contraction that is generally an inward movement. The term *normal muscular synergy* is the inward movement that occurs simultaneously among all walls of the ventricle (Urden et al., 2014). The normally coordinated contraction may become uncoordinated because of a variety of conditions. For example, the ventricle may become damaged because of ischemic heart disease or aneurysms. Abnormalities in conduction, such as bundle branch blocks and ventricular ectopy, can also alter normal contraction patterns. Finally, changes in ventricular size caused by dilation or fibrosis can also alter normal muscular synergy. This *dyssynergy* can result in an increase in the energy needed for contraction and a decrease in cardiac output.

In addition, both ventricles are designed to contract simultaneously. *Ventricular dyssynchrony* occurs when the right and left ventricles do not contract at the same time. This dyssynchrony is commonly demonstrated by a bundle branch block pattern on an electrocardiogram. If the right and left ventricles do not contract in unison, cardiac output and performance are compromised.

NURSING APPLICATION

Dilated cardiomyopathy results from myocardial fibrils that have been overstretched and can no longer shorten normally. Therefore, patients with dilated cardiomyopathy have decreased contractility.

OXYGEN DELIVERY AND CONSUMPTION

Oxygen Delivery

The heart and lungs work together to form the cardiopulmonary circuit. The purpose of the cardiopulmonary circuit is to deliver oxygen to all the tissues of the body. The amount of oxygen delivered to the tissues is determined by three factors: cardiac output, hemoglobin level, and oxygen saturation.

Under normal conditions of arterial blood flow, approximately 1000 ml of oxygen is delivered to the tissues of the body, and the tissues extract approximately 25% of the oxygen delivered to them (Urden et al., 2014). Given approximately 250 ml of oxygen was extracted, venous blood supply generally returns approximately a 75% reserve to the lungs (Urden et al., 2014). If the cardiopulmonary circuit fails to deliver enough oxygen to meet the needs of the tissues, the amount left in the reserve diminishes. The oxygen reserve is measured by assessing the percent of oxygen saturation of venous blood.

The balance of myocardial oxygen supply and demand is key in providing cardiac muscle with the proper amount of oxygen to maintain optimum function. The ability of the myocardium to contract effectively is directly related to the amount of oxygen being supplied to the heart. The myocardium is unique in comparison with other tissues in the body because the left ventricle extracts approximately 75% of the oxygen delivered, as opposed to the 25% extracted by other tissues (Urden et al., 2014). Because there is little oxygen reserve to be used during periods of increased need, the myocardium becomes very dependent on flow from the coronary arteries. The body inherently changes the diameter of the coronary arteries to change the delivery of oxygen. As myocardial oxygen demand increases, the coronary arteries dilate, if able, to deliver more oxygen-rich blood to the myocardium. As myocardial oxygen demand increases, so must the myocardial oxygen supply. Myocardial oxygen demand increases with an increase in any of the four components of cardiac output (heart rate, preload, afterload, or contractility). If myocardial oxygen supply cannot be increased during periods of increased demand, then ischemia occurs.

NURSING APPLICATION

In patients with coronary heart disease, narrowed blood vessels are often unable to dilate enough to provide the necessary oxygen supply to the heart muscle; therefore, angina occurs during periods of increased metabolic demand. The inability to adequately dilate is why stable angina generally occurs with activity and subsides when activity is stopped.

Alveolar Diffusion Capacity

After gaining an understanding of the cardiovascular system's contribution to oxygen delivery, the nurse must consider the alveolar unit's capacity to diffuse oxygen into the blood via the alveolar-capillary membrane (see Figure 2-5). This membrane creates nearly a continuous sheet of blood covering each alveoli. The diameter of each capillary is only big enough to allow a red blood cell to pass through the vessel one at a time. The beauty of this structure is that it allows the red blood cell to touch the walls of the vessel just enough to reduce the amount of plasma that oxygen and carbon dioxide have to diffuse through. Under normal conditions, this alveolar-capillary network is a highly efficient vehicle for gas exchange and, ultimately, maintaining oxygen-rich blood volume.

FIGURE 2-5: ALVEOLAR-CAPILLARY MEMBRANE

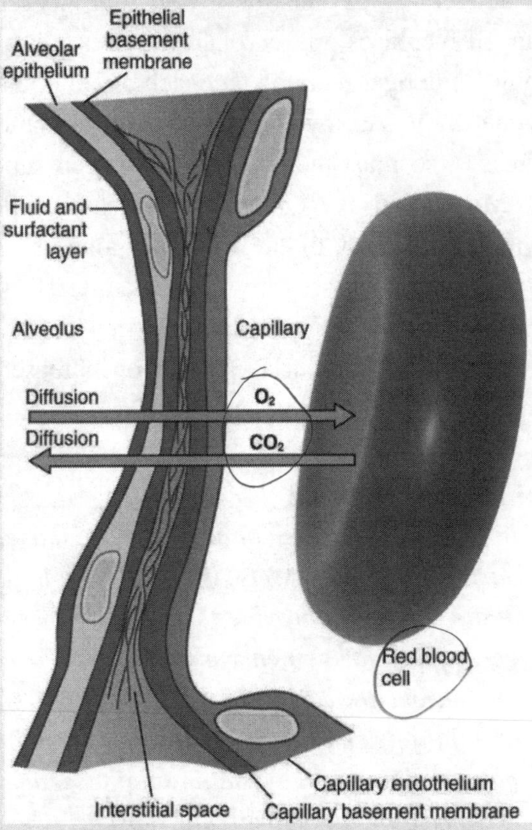

Note. From Patton, K. T., Thibodeau, G. A., & Douglas, M. M. (2012). *Essentials of anatomy & physiology.* Lansing, MI: Elsevier/Mosby. © Elsevier 2012.

NURSING APPLICATION

In the setting of pulmonary edema, the alveolar-capillary membrane is compromised by interstitial edema, which consequently reduces gas exchange and the amount of oxygen in the blood volume.

Hemoglobin

In addition to cardiac output and the capacity of the alveolar-capillary membrane to diffuse oxygen into the blood volume, the oxygen supply of the body's tissues is also dependent on the hemoglobin level and oxygen saturation. Within each red blood cell are approximately 200 to 300 million molecules of hemoglobin (Patton, Thibodeau, & Douglas, 2012). Each hemoglobin molecule has the capacity to chemically bond with four oxygen molecules to form *oxyhemoglobin.* Hemoglobin is the primary transporter of oxygen. Low hemoglobin levels (known as anemia) can exacerbate ischemia in patients with coronary heart disease. If hemoglobin levels become critically low, ischemia can occur, even in patients without coronary heart disease. Oxygen saturation levels also affect the delivery of oxygen to myocardial tissue. Oxygen saturation levels can drop during periods of critical illness. Low oxygen saturation levels are commonly caused by pulmonary conditions that reduce the efficiency of the alveolar-capillary membrane.

Tissue Consumption

The nurse must recognize conditions that increase oxygen demand or increase tissue extraction of oxygen from the arterial blood. For instance, hypermetabolic conditions such as fever, shock, or ischemic conditions (e.g., cerebrovascular accident or acute myocardial infarction) increase the tissues' demand for more oxygen. In physiological states of increased oxygen demand, the cardiovascular system attempts to meet the needs by increasing oxygen delivery via compensatory mechanisms/reflexes (e.g., vasoconstriction or increased contractility) aimed to increase cardiac output.

The nurse must consider the many factors related to alterations in tissue consumption. The primary factor this chapter discusses is associated with those influencing oxyhemoglobin disassociation. Under normal conditions, hemoglobin has a steady and predictable affinity to oxygen. Conditions such as pH imbalances (acidosis or alkalosis), changes in carbon dioxide (hypercapnia/hypocapnia), or extreme temperature abnormalities (hypothermia or fever) alter the relationship and change the affinity hemoglobin has for oxygen. A shift to the right or left on the oxyhemoglobin dissociation curve indicates the oxyhemoglobin relationship has changed (McCance & Huether, 2015; see Figure 2-6). A shift to the left suggests an increased affinity of hemoglobin to oxygen and a decrease in the ability of the body's tissues to extract the oxygen from hemoglobin. A shift to the right indicates a decrease in hemoglobin's affinity to oxygen, thus making it easier for the tissues to extract oxygen.

NURSING APPLICATION

Clinical conditions that cause shifts to the left on the oxyhemoglobin dissociation curve decrease oxygen delivery to body tissues. Thus, with conditions warranting increased oxygen demands, a shift to the right on this curve is preferred.

HEMODYNAMIC MEASUREMENTS

Hemodynamic monitoring involves the use of specific equipment, specialty catheters, and the skills normally displayed by nurses working within critical care environments. Hemodynamic pressures are monitored via invasive techniques of placing catheters within the arteries, veins, or the heart. Invasive monitoring lends to more accurate measurements of cardiovascular pressures than noninvasive means (e.g., noninvasive blood pressure or heart rate). This section will introduce some of the pressures that can be obtained, which will help facilitate the cardiovascular nurse's comprehension of monitoring the components of stroke volume, or the mechanical function of the heart.

Measuring Pressures

Monitoring hemodynamic pressures allows clinicians to evaluate the function of the cardiovascular system continually as needed in critical care units to aid in diagnosis and to evaluate treatments. Alterations in any of the components of stroke volume (preload, afterload, and contractility) can be attained via invasive cardiac pressure monitoring. Systemic vascular resistance (SVR), or afterload, is estimated/calculated by a formula using the mean arterial pressure, central venous pressure (CVP), and cardiac output. Contractility is also estimated by the calculation of a formula including preload measures and SVR. Preload and arterial blood pressure measurements, in contrast, are pressures that can be directly measured via invasive catheters.

Intraarterial Blood Pressure

Invasive blood pressure monitoring is indicated for any condition that compromises cardiac output or fluid volume status. This pressure is most commonly obtained via a catheter cannulating the radial artery. Direct arterial access facilitates accurate measures of systole, diastole, and mean arterial pressures. Another benefit of continual arterial access is the facilitation of frequent collection and monitoring of arterial blood gas measurements.

Central Venous Pressure

CVP reflects filling pressures in the right ventricle, or preload, and is used clinically to assess an individual's overall fluid balance. CVP is most commonly obtained via the distal port of a central venous catheter. Limitations to monitoring CVP occur in clinical conditions that cause increased right atrial pressures (e.g., pulmonary hypertension or right-sided heart failure). Normal right atrial pressure is 2 to 6 mmHg, and normal right ventricular pressure is 15 to 30/0 to 8 mmHg.

Pulmonary Artery Pressures

PA pressures are obtained via a PA catheter cannulated through a central vein, through both

FIGURE 2-6: INFLUENCING FACTORS OF OXYHEMOGLOBIN DISSOCIATION

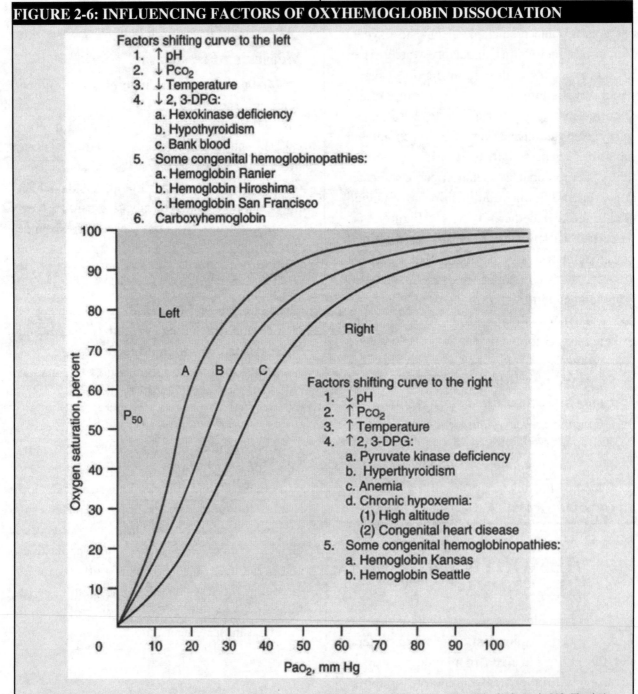

chambers on the right side of the heart, and into the PA, where it rests (see Figure 2-7). Indications for monitoring PA pressures include conditions of hemodynamic instability (e.g., shock or decompensating heart failure) and pulmonary hypertension. Ultimately, PA pressures reflect the dynamics of the pulmonary circulatory system, just as intraarterial pressure monitoring reflects the systemic circulatory system. A normal PA pressure is 15 to 30/8 to 15 mmHg. Pressures created by the volume in the left side of the heart can be obtained by inflating the cuff at the tip of the PA catheter to create an occlusive pressure. The PA occlusive pressure lends the clinician a closer reflection of left ventricular end-diastolic pressure (when the mitral valve is open) to assess the function and volume status of the left ventricle. Normal PA occlusive pressure is 6 to 12 mmHg.

Venous Oxygen Saturation Monitoring

Invasive hemodynamic pressure monitoring allows clinicians to continually monitor venous oxygen saturation for the purpose of evaluating conditions that cause imbalances between oxygen supply and metabolic tissue demand. Considering the cardiovascular system's contribution to oxygen delivery, measuring venous oxygen saturations via invasive hemodynamic monitoring methods provides the clinician with

point-of-care data to identify actual or potential imbalances of oxygen supply and demand that can further compromise the patient (McCance & Huether, 2015).

CASE STUDY

A 72-year-old female goes to the cardiology clinic for intermittent angina chest pain and progressively worsening dyspnea over the last two weeks. She is transported to the emergency department (ED) for urgent evaluation. The patient explains that her chest pain has also been associated with increasing fatigue, exertional dyspnea, and diaphoresis. Also, over the past several days she must rest after short walks around the house and sleep on 3-4 pillows at night to help her breathe. The patient states that last week her symptoms were not as bad and she could go to the grocery store to shop without difficulty. At the ED, the patient's husband reports that his wife has a past medical history of dilated cardiomyopathy and chronic obstructive pulmonary disease. She quit smoking 25 years ago and does not drink alcohol or use illicit drugs. The patient's home medications include a baby aspirin, atorvastatin, carvedilol, losartan, and synthroid. She is compliant with her medication regimen and does not miss

FIGURE 2-7: PLACEMENT OF PULMONARY ARTERY CATHETER

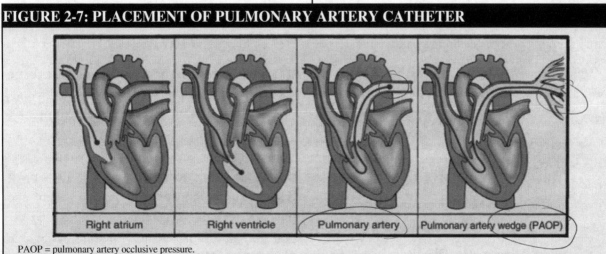

Right atrium | Right ventricle | Pulmonary artery | Pulmonary artery wedge (PAOP)

PAOP = pulmonary artery occlusive pressure.
Note. From Urden, L. D., Stacy, K. M., & Lough, M. E. (2014). *Critical care nursing: Diagnosis and management* (7th ed.). St. Louis, MO: Elsevier/ Mosby. © Elsevier 2014.

doses. She does not know her family history and is retired after teaching for 30 years.

The nurse documents the patient's vital signs as: temperature 97.9 °F; blood pressure 172/100 mmHg; heart rate 109 beats/min; respiratory rate 26 breaths/min; and pulse oximetry on room air 93%. The physical exam findings include a normal color to the skin, which is warm and dry. The patient is awake, alert, and oriented to self, place, time, and situations. She has no neurological deficits, but is generally weak. Upon auscultation of the patient's lungs, the nurse hears bibasilar rales and notes mild use of the patient's accessory muscles. The patient's cardiovascular exam findings include jugular vein distention, a regular heart rate and rhythm, with a S1, S2, and S3 heard. There is no murmur appreciated. Diagnostic studies performed include: a chest radiograph that reveals bilateral interstitial fluid in the lung bases; unremarkable laboratory test results; and a 12-lead EKG showing sinus rhythm, pathological Q waves in the anterior leads, and evidence of left ventricular hypertrophy. The patient is started on supplemental oxygen per nasal cannula. The nurse administers aspirin and intravenous Lasix to the patient and applies transdermal nitroglycerin ointment to her chest. The patient is admitted to the hospital for further evaluation.

Questions

1. Which hemodynamic alteration does the history and physical exam findings indicate?

2. Which interventions were intiated to facilitate oxygen delivery and coronary blood flow?

Answers

1. The patient is experiencing decreased cardiac output most likely associated with decreased contractility and increased afterload and preload. These alterations are consistent with a diagnosis of heart failure.

   The patient's historical data from the last couple of weeks suggest progressively worsening dyspnea, orthopnea, and angina, which is consistent with maintaining forward blood flow with decreasing heart function. The decrease in the patient's heart function may be related to myocardial ischemia and infarction to her heart muscle (evidenced by Q waves on the EKG). The patient's elevated blood pressure is evidence of increased afterload, which is causing increased workload for her weakened heart to maintain forward blood flow. The patient's physical examination findings that are consistent with heart failure include bibasilar crackles, labored respirations, jugular venous distension, and an S3 (ventricular gallop) heart sound.

2. The nurse in the ED administered nitroglycerin and furosemide to facilitate forward flow by reducing the patient's blood pressure and decreasing fluid volume. The nitroglycerin will decrease the patient's preload and afterload by causing vasodilation. The furosemide (Lasix) will decrease the patient's intravascular fluid volume if her renal function is sufficient. By reducing the patient's intravascular volume, the patient's symptoms of heart failure (pulmonary congestion) will hopefully be relieved and her oxygenation will improve. Oxygen therapy is also given to the patient.

SUMMARY

The cardiovascular nurse must have an understanding of hemodynamic principles and factors that influence oxygen delivery. Although invasive hemodynamic pressures or venous oxygen saturation monitoring is performed in the critical care unit, general knowledge of the components of cardiac output and the cardiovascular system's contribution to oxygen delivery is necessary for comprehensive cardiovascular care.

EXAM QUESTIONS

CHAPTER 2
Questions 7–10

Note: Choose the one option that BEST answers each question.

7. What effect does the parasympathetic nervous system have on heart rate?

    a. Myocardial cell excitability

    b. Sinoatrial node stimulation

    c. Purkinje fiber stimulation

    d. Inotropic effect on contractility

8. Which component of stroke volume is a reflection of the patient's volume status and ventricular filling pressures?

    a. Preload

    b. Afterload

    c. Contractility

    d. Heart rate

9. Which condition decreases oxygen delivery to the tissues?

    a. Alkalosis

    b. Hypothermia

    c. Anemia

    d. Hypocapnia

10. Which hemodynamic monitoring system allows the nurse to measure accurate mean arterial pressures?

    a. Intraarterial blood pressure monitoring

    b. Central venous pressure monitoring

    c. Pulmonary artery occlusive pressure monitoring

    d. Systemic vascular resistance monitoring

REFERENCES

Lough, M. E. (2014). Cardiovascular anatomy and physiology. In L. D. Urden, K. M. Stacy, & M. E. Lough (Eds.), *Critical care nursing: Diagnosis and management* (7th ed., pp. 200-221). St. Louis, MO: Elsevier/ Mosby.

McCance, K. L, & Huether, S. E. (2015). *Pathophysiology: The biologic basis for disease in adults and children* (7th ed.). St Louis, MO: Elsevier/Mosby.

Patton, K., Thibodeau, G. A., & Douglas, M. M. (2012). *Essentials of anatomy & physiology.* St. Louis, MO: Elsevier/Mosby.

Urden, L. D., Stacy, K. M., & Lough, M. E. (2014). *Critical care nursing: Diagnosis and management* (7th ed.). St. Louis, MO: Elsevier/Mosby.

CHAPTER 3

EPIDEMIOLOGY OF CARDIOVASCULAR DISEASE

LEARNING OUTCOME

After completing this chapter, the learner will be able to discuss epidemiological factors associated with cardiovascular disease.

CHAPTER OBJECTIVES

After completing this chapter, the learner will be able to:

1. Identify global and national trends of cardiovascular health and disease.

2. Differentiate between modifiable and non-modifiable risk factors for cardiovascular disease.

3. Identify strategies for disease prevention and health promotion.

INTRODUCTION

Cardiovascular disease (CVD) is prevalent in the general population worldwide, affecting adults older than 60 years the most (Wilson, 2016). Despite advances in medicine and the technology aiding advances in medical treatments since 1975, CVD and associated complications remain prevalent and costly across the United States and abroad (Bandosz et al., 2012; Rapsomaniki et al., 2014). Nurses caring for patients with CVD must understand the burden the disease poses to the general population,

identify risk factors for it, and be equipped with the latest health promotion and disease prevention strategies aimed to reduce its prevalence.

TRENDS

Global

Nearly 50% of the general population worldwide is at an overall lifetime risk for CVD by age 30 years (Rapsomaniki et al., 2014). The World Health Organization has found a remarkable increase in CVD among developing countries because of social and economic factors, poorly identified standards of care and cost-effective case management, poor surveillance methods to assess or evaluate epidemiological trends, and poor intercountry, interregional, and global networks (World Health Organization, 2016).

Studies performed on more than 150,000 patients in more than 40 developed countries demonstrate mortality rates are decreasing for coronary heart disease (CHD), whereas mortality rates associated with CVD persist (Nichols, Townsend, Scarborough, & Rayner, 2014). Interestingly, 49 European and Asian countries have nearly a 16-fold higher mortality rate associated with CHD than the United States, with the highest number of deaths being in South Asian regions, but more prevalence of disease in Eastern Europe and Central Asia (Go et al., 2014;

Moran et al., 2014; Ritchey, Wall, Gillespie, George, & Jamal, 2014). Despite trends of reduced mortality rates associated with CHD, as developing countries undergo economic urbanization, industrialization, and globalization, life expectancy is increasing and is exposing more persons to the overall risk factors and lifestyle changes that promote CVD.

National

In the United States, 11.5% of American adults have been diagnosed with CVD. It is the leading cause of death for men and women and for most racial/ethnic groups. The most common type of CVD is CHD (Centers for Disease Control and Prevention, 2016). When drilling down from the global perspective to the national perspective, statistics indicate multiple patterns associated with the prevalence of CVD. For instance, mortality rates vary the most by race/ethnicity and the geographic region of the United States. Geographically, CVD mortality rates are found to be the greatest in the southeastern regions of the country and southern parts of the West Coast (Centers for Disease Control and Prevention, 2016). Trends in morbidity rates of all-cause CVD remain burdensome, and risk factors for all-cause CVD remain "alarmingly high" (Mozaffarian et al., 2016). Trends of mortality rates vary among the types of CVD in the United States. Although mortality rates have been significantly reduced for CHD and stroke in the United States, deaths increased from 2012 through 2014 for persons with heart failure (Ni & Xu, 2015).

RISK FACTORS

Multiple studies conducted worldwide confirm universal risk factors for CVD. Fortunately, the majority of the risk factors that lead to CVD are modifiable, which makes healthy life choices essential for the prevention of CVD. Two studies should be considered when discussing risk factors and prevention of CVD. The INTERHEART study, a landmark study that included patients in 52 participating countries, identified that modifiable factors accounted for more than 90% of the risk for CHD (Yusuf et al., 2004). In 2013, the Lifestyle Work Group, a subcommittee of the American College of Cardiology/American Heart Association Task Force on Practice Guidelines, studied and evaluated modifiable risk factors using evidence on dietary patterns, levels and types of physical activity, and nutritional intake and the role they can play in CVD prevention. This study resulted in guidelines on lifestyle management to reduce cardiovascular risk (Eckel et al., 2014).

Behavioral

The INTERHEART study found nine behavioral, or modifiable, risk factors associated with CVD: smoking, dyslipidemia, hypertension, diabetes, abdominal obesity, psychosocial factors, daily consumption of fruits and vegetables, regular alcohol consumption, and regular physical activity. The American Heart Association (2015b) narrowed the majority of these risk factors into a national campaign called *Life's Simple 7* that encourages all Americans (not only those at risk for or with known CVD) to manage several areas of their health: blood pressure, cholesterol, blood sugar, physical activity or obesity, diet, body weight, and smoking cessation. Patients with any of the earlier risk factors can significantly reduce all causes of CVD by making the earlier everyday lifestyle changes (Ford, Greenlund, & Hong, 2012).

Blood Pressure

Hypertensive heart disease is one of the leading pathophysiological processes responsible for the development of other types of CVD, such as heart failure and cardiomyopathy.

Maintaining a blood pressure lower than 140/90 mmHg is associated with a decreased risk for multiple types of CVD (Ford et al., 2012). Although maintaining a healthy blood pressure can be considered a modifiable risk factor, 20% to 40% of the variation in one's systolic and diastolic blood pressure is due to genetic factors (McCance & Huether, 2015).

Cholesterol

Although cholesterol levels can have genetic influences that contribute to dyslipidemia, modifiable factors are also associated with managing total cholesterol levels less than 140 mg/dL (Ford et al., 2012). When considering the different components of cholesterol, two of them increase a person's risk for disease. Low-density lipoprotein (LDL) is known as "bad cholesterol," and high levels are associated with increased risk for CHD, stroke, and peripheral arterial disease. LDL cholesterol is also known for causing inflammatory effects on the arterial vessel wall. Triglycerides are lipids that at high levels are also associated with increased risk for atherogenic conditions of CVD. Fasting triglyceride levels greater than 150 mg/dL are associated with elevated risks for CVD. Fortunately, the third component of total cholesterol is the high-density lipoprotein (HDL) that is found to exert protective effects against atherosclerotic disease. HDL has been found to promote the efflux of cholesterol from cells and minimize the accumulation of foam cells in the arterial wall, thereby decreasing the risk for atherosclerotic events. *Atherosclerosis* is an insidious pathophysiological process and the leading causative factor for all cases of CHD (Urden, Stacy, & Lough, 2014).

Blood Glucose

Having a fasting blood glucose concentration greater than 126 mg/dL or a hemoglobin A1C greater than 6.4 is associated with damage to the endothelial structures of the cardiovascular system and promotes atherosclerosis. Reducing risks for diabetes includes the prevention or control of the earlier two factors (blood pressure and cholesterol) along with maintaining an ideal body weight for a person's age (Mozaffarian et al., 2015). Individuals at greatest risk for diabetes are persons younger than 45 years who are overweight and have already been diagnosed with hypertension and dyslipidemia (Ford et al., 2012).

Obesity and Physical Activity

Obesity is defined as a body mass index greater than 30 kg/m^2 (Ford et al., 2012) and is one of the leading risk factors for hypertension and diabetes mellitus individually. Although there are findings of genetic factors contributing to obesity, the primary contributing factor is physical inactivity (Ford et al., 2012). Physical inactivity is defined by having a sedentary lifestyle. Physical activity is defined by anything that makes you move your body and burn calories. The American Heart Association recommends a total of 150 minutes of moderate-intensity activity per week or 75 minutes of high-intensity activity per week to increase a person's overall cardiovascular health (American Heart Association, 2015a). Physical activity has been found to decrease blood pressure, increase HDL and lower LDL, and decrease the prevalence of diabetes (Ford et al., 2012).

Metabolic

Age, sex, race/ethnicity, and genetic predispositions for disease (family history) are the metabolic, or nonmodifiable, risk factors for CVD. Minimizing the prevalence of CHD in a person with multiple metabolic risk factors involves closer management of behavioral risk factors that will negatively impact and compound the risk for or severity of CHD (Bandosz et al., 2012).

Age

As a person grows older, atherosclerosis develops at increasing rates. In general, persons 45 years and older are most associated with the initial symptoms of CHD. Increasing physical activity as a person ages reduces his or her relative overall risk for CVD (Urden et al., 2014).

Sex

Men have been found to develop manifestations of CVD approximately 5 to 10 years earlier than women. The prevalence of disease is higher in women 75 years and older. Postmenopausal women have a 3-fold increased risk for CHD compared with premenopausal women. Despite multiple studies demonstrating men having morbidity rates 3-fold higher than women (Ford et al., 2012), women are thought to have more risk for CVD because of higher incidence of diabetes and hypertension (Urden et al., 2014).

Race/Ethnicity

Race and Hispanic origin (ethnicity) are identified separately in epidemiology studies and death certificates because of the lack of data for Hispanics. This means that mortality rates were not inclusive of that group. Non-Hispanic races are generally identified as Whites, Blacks, Asian/Pacific Islanders, American Indians, and Alaskans. Data of deaths for persons of Hispanic origin are to include persons of Hispanic-derived race. Non-Hispanic Blacks and non-Hispanic Whites have the highest rates of death, whereas Alaskan natives or American Indians have the lowest mortality rates from CVD (Ford et al., 2012).

Genetics/Family History

One of the leading initiatives in cardiovascular research related to genetic predispositions for CVD includes the utility of lipoprotein(a) [Lp(a)]. Lp(a) has been linked to the prevalence of premature atherosclerotic CHD and is found in the plasma along with HDL and LDL; however, it is associated with the stimulation of atheroma and clot formation. Testing for Lp(a) is reserved for high-risk patient populations who have a strong family history of premature CVD. Reducing these levels to less than 30 mg/dL is the therapeutic goal and is generally achieved by high doses of nicotinic acid (Urden et al., 2014).

Despite the common belief among the general population that if a person has a family history of diabetes, hypertension, or dyslipidemia, that person will also experience development of those conditions, the genetics only make the person at risk for those conditions. Many patients have reported believing they will develop the disease no matter what and will then require medication to treat the disease. The population must be educated that the genetic risk can be reduced by disease prevention and awareness of their personal behavioral risk factors (Ford et al., 2012).

Emerging

Emerging risk factors in predominantly low- and middle-income countries have been identified as contributing risk factors for CVD. Low birth weight, folate deficiency, and infections are emerging as conditions associated with the prevalence of CVD and may be generalizable to impoverished American populations (World Health Organization, 2016).

HIV is another condition that places persons receiving highly active antiretroviral therapies at risk for CVD. These therapies have increased the longevity of life in the HIV population but exposed them to the common conditions associated with aging, such as CVD (Ford et al., 2012).

DISEASE PREVENTION AND HEALTH PROMOTION

Risk Stratification

The best time for persons to make lifestyle changes is before the onset of disease.

Stratifying an individual's risk for CVD involves the clinician identifying the number of risk factors the person has and appraising for those factors that place the person at greater risk than other factors. For instance, if a person with no known disease has a family history of CVD, smokes cigarettes, and is obese, a clinician would identify tobacco use as the priority risk factor. Prioritizing smoking cessation should not negate the other risk factors, but the clinician should highlight it as a first step toward reducing the overall risk for CVD. Persons with two or more risk factors have the greatest potential to benefit from risk factor reduction.

Primary Versus Secondary Prevention

Interventions aimed to reduce overall CVD risks must be identified in the context of whether the patient has known disease. *Primary prevention* therapies are used for persons without known disease. For persons with a CVD risk profile yet no evidence of disease, such as an acute myocardial infarction, primary prevention therapies such as smoking cessation and weight loss are recommended for preventing or delaying the onset of all types of CVD. *Secondary prevention* therapies are those initiated for the person with symptoms of a known disease. These therapies include prescriptive diets, medications, or any other behavioral change necessary to manage the disease within therapeutic goals or reduce its severity.

Health Promotion Initiatives

The World Health Organization recommends health promotion activities at multiple levels. Laws and regulations must be broad to facilitate a society taking advantage of health promotion activities such as bicycling to work or enjoying tobacco-free environments. Taxation and price policies are other interventions as disincentives to engage in unhealthy behaviors. The promotion of public awareness campaigns is designed to positively influence behaviors and disseminate the benefits of lifestyle changes to at-risk populations. Other more familiar initiatives are community-based interventions aimed to influence specific behaviors such as physical activity, proper nutrition, and alcohol or tobacco cessation. These strategies are a few of many aimed to reduce the prevalence of disease for the betterment of the individual, the community, national health, and the healthcare system (World Health Organization, 2016).

Nursing Considerations

Given CVD is the leading cause of death worldwide, health promotion must be a priority for the cardiovascular nurse. Patient education has been proven to reduce disease prevalence and severity when it is done consistently and through a team approach. The nurse must recognize the appropriateness of patient education on all types of CVD in all healthcare settings. Community education within school-age academic programs is designed as a primary prevention methods to bring awareness to the importance of understanding how proper diets, physical activity routines, and knowing one's family history can reduce the risks for all types of CVD. In primary care settings, nurses can acknowledge the burden CVD places on patients, families, and the healthcare system by making health promotion for CVD risk reduction a theme in the office via multiple approaches such as written educational material, one-on-one counseling, posters, or serial videos (Urden et al., 2014). Those patients in acute care settings may be more difficult to educate in consideration of the severity of illness; however, it does provide a platform for the nurse to use primary and secondary prevention interventions with visiting friends and families. The cardiovascular nurse must center health promotion strategies around patient-centered CVD education specific to the person's identified risk factors.

SUMMARY

C VD persists as the leading cause of death in the United States and abroad. Hypertension, dyslipidemia, and diabetes are well-established risk factors for CVD that can be identified early via screening and health promotion initiatives. More than 90% of all risk factors are modifiable, and those persons with genetic predispositions for disease can delay its onset and decrease its severity. Cardiovascular nurses must be able to acknowledge the epidemiological burden of disease, identify patients' personal risk factors, and apply the appropriate health promotion initiatives consistently to positively impact and combat the prevalence of all types of CVD.

EXAM QUESTIONS

CHAPTER 3
Questions 11–14

Note: Choose the one option that BEST answers each question.

11. The leading cause of death in the United States is

    a. ischemic stroke.
    b. coronary artery disease.
    c. cardiovascular disease.
    d. sudden cardiac death.

12. Which data should be identified as a modifiable CVD risk factor?

    a. Age
    b. Sex
    c. Race/Ethnicity
    d. Cholesterol level

13. Which data should be identified as a nonmodifiable CVD risk factor?

    a. Smoking
    b. Diet
    c. Family history
    d. Physical activity

14. What level of health promotion facilitates persons within a community to enjoy a smoke-free environment?

    a. Laws and regulations
    b. Taxes and price interventions
    c. Public awareness campaigns
    d. Community-based interventions

REFERENCES

American Heart Association. (2015a). *American Heart Association recommendations for physical activity in adults.* Retrieved from http://www.heart.org/HEARTORG/HealthyLiving/PhysicalActivity/FitnessBasics/American-Heart-Association-Recommendations-for-Physical-Activity-in-Adults_UCM_307976_Article.jsp#.V2GDoLsrK70

American Heart Association. (2015b). My life check – life's simple 7. Retrieved from http://www.heart.org/HEARTORG/Conditions/My-Life-Check---Lifes-Simple-7_UCM_471453_Article.jsp#.V2GCnrsrK70

Bandosz, P., O'Flaherty, M., Drygas, W., Rutkowski, M., Koziarek, J., Wyrzykowski, B., ... Capewell, S. (2012). Decline in mortality from coronary heart disease in Poland after socioeconomic transformation: Modelling study. *BMJ, 344,* d8136.

Centers for Disease Control and Prevention. (2016). *Heart disease facts.* Retrieved from http://www.cdc.gov/HeartDisease/facts.htm

Eckel, R. H., Jakicic, J. M., Ard, J. D., de Jesus, J. M., Miller, N. H., Hubbard, V. S., ... Yanovski, S. Z. (2014). 2013 AHA/ACC guideline on lifestyle management to reduce cardiovascular risk: A report of the American College of Cardiology/American Heart Association Task Force on Practice Guidelines. *Journal of the American College of Cardiology, 63*(25_PA). doi:10.1016/j.jacc.2013.11.003

Ford, E. S., Greenlund, K. J., & Hong, Y. (2012). Ideal cardiovascular health and mortality from all causes and diseases of the circulatory system among adults in the United States. *Circulation, 125*(8), 987-995.

Go, A. S., Mozaffarian, D., Roger, V. L., Benjamin, E. J., Berry, J. D., Blaha, M. J., ... Turner, M. B. (2014). Heart disease and stroke statistics – 2014 update: A report from the American Heart Association. *Circulation, 129*(3), e28.

McCance, K. L, & Huether, S. E. (2015). *Pathophysiology: The biologic basis for disease in adults and children* (7th ed.). St Louis, MO: Elsevier/Mosby.

Moran, A. E., Forouzanfar, M. H., Roth, G. A., Mensah, G. A., Ezzati, M., Murray, C. J., & Naghavi, M. (2014). Temporal trends in ischemic heart disease mortality in 21 world regions, 1980 to 2010: The Global Burden of Disease 2010 study. *Circulation, 129*(14), 1483.

Mozaffarian, D., Benjamin, E. J., Go, A. S., Arnett, D. K., Blaha, M. J., Cushman, M., ... Turner, M. B. (2016). Heart disease and stroke statistics – 2015 update: A report from the American Heart Association. *Circulation, 133*(4), e38-e60. doi:10.1161/CIR.0000000000000350

Ni, H., & Xu, J. (2015). Recent trends in heart failure-related mortality: United States, 2000–2014. *NCHS Data Brief.* Retrieved from http://www.cdc.gov/nchs/data/databriefs/db231.htm

Nichols, M., Townsend, N., Scarborough, P., & Rayner, M. (2014). Cardiovascular disease in Europe 2014: Epidemiological update. *European Heart Journal, 35*(42), 2950.

Rapsomaniki, E., Timmis, A., George, J., Pujades-Rodriguez, M., Shah, A. D., Denaxas, S., ... Hemingway, H. (2014). Blood pressure and incidence of twelve cardiovascular diseases: Lifetime risks, healthy life-years lost, and age-specific associations in 1·25 million people. *Lancet, 383*(9932), 1899-1911. doi:10.1016/S0140-6736(14)60685-1

Ritchey, M. D., Wall, H. K., Gillespie, C., George, M. G., & Jamal, A. (2014). Million hearts: Prevalence of leading cardiovascular disease risk factors – United States, 2005-2012. *MMWR Morbidity and Mortality Weekly Report, 63*(21), 462.

Urden, L. D., Stacy, K. M., & Lough, M. E. (2014). *Critical care nursing: Diagnosis and management* (7th ed.). St. Louis, MO: Elsevier/Mosby.

Wilson, P. (2016). Overview of the risk equivalents and established risk factors for cardiovascular disease. *UpToDate*. Retrieved from http://www.uptodate.com/contents/overview-of-the-risk-equivalents-and-established-risk-factors-for-cardiovascular-disease

World Health Organization. (2016). *Cardiovascular disease: Strategic priorities*. Retrieved from http://www.who.int/cardiovascular_diseases/priorities/en/

Yusuf, S., Hawken, S., Ounpuu, S., Dans, T., Avezum, A., Lanas, F., & Lisheng, L. (2004). Effect of potentially modifiable risk factors associated with myocardial infarction in 52 countries (the INTERHEART study): Case-control study. *Lancet, 364*(9438), 937.

CHAPTER 4

CARDIOVASCULAR PHARMACOTHERAPEUTICS

LEARNING OUTCOME

After completing this chapter, the learner will be able to identify how cardiovascular pharmacotherapeutics are used to improve myocardial performance.

CHAPTER OBJECTIVES

After completing this chapter, the learner will be able to:

1. Apply the mechanism of action of sympathomimetics and nonsympathomimetics to appropriate cardiovascular disorders.

2. Discuss the mechanism of action of cardiovascular pharmacotherapeutic agents.

3. Identify indications for the use of cardiovascular pharmacotherapeutic agents and differentiate between medications within classifications.

4. Identify side effects and genetic considerations associated with cardiovascular pharmacotherapeutic agents.

5. Explain nursing considerations for the use of cardiovascular pharmacotherapeutic agents in special populations.

INTRODUCTION

Cardiovascular pharmacology is a complex subject; it grows and changes daily with the addition of each new body of research. This chapter discusses the mechanisms of action, indications/contraindications, and side effects of common cardiovascular pharmacotherapeutic agents and how they affect hemodynamic function. Pharmacotherapeutics specific to the treatment of certain cardiac conditions will be discussed in later chapters.

This chapter is divided into multiple classes of medications. The medications within each class can sometimes overlap with other classes; however, for the purposes of this chapter, each medication is placed in the class of its primary function or mechanism of action. The majority of the medications within each class are more similar than they are different. However, it is important to know that not all of the specific differences between medications within each class are discussed.

The primary goal of cardiovascular pharmacotherapeutic agents is to improve cardiac performance. Most often the specific aim is to improve mechanical function; however, electrical function is often also considered in the selection of appropriate medications. This goal is achieved in a variety of ways, including manipulating the major components of cardiac output and myocardial oxygen demand. In clinical practice, the four components of cardiac output – heart rate, preload, afterload, and contractility – are often manipulated with intravenous agents in emergency situations such as cardiogenic shock, and they are manipulated in chronic disease management with oral medications.

CARDIOVASCULAR DRUG CLASSES

Sympathomimetics

Sympathomimetics are synthetic catecholamines and medications that are used to stimulate the sympathetic nervous system via adrenergic receptors. These medications can be used to increase heart rate, contractility, and afterload.

Mechanism of Action

Different sympathomimetics have different dominant actions, depending on the receptors stimulated.

- Beta-1 receptors are located in the heart. Beta-1 stimulation results in an increase in heart rate and contractility. Specific beta-1 receptor stimulators used to increase contractility include dobutamine (most commonly used sympathomimetic for inotropic purposes), epinephrine, norepinephrine (used primarily as a vasopressor but also has inotropic properties), and dopamine (used primarily as a vasopressor but also has inotropic properties). Beta-1 receptor stimulators used to increase heart rate include epinephrine and dopamine.

- Beta-2 receptors are located in the lungs and peripheral vasculature. Beta-1 stimulation causes bronchial vasodilation and peripheral vasodilation in skeletal muscle.

- Alpha-1 receptors are located in the arterioles. Alpha-1 stimulation causes arteriole vasoconstriction and increases afterload.

Specific alpha-1 receptor stimulators include dopamine, phenylephrine, norepinephrine, and epinephrine.

- Dopaminergic receptors are located in the renal and mesenteric beds. When stimulated, these receptors dilate the renal and mesenteric arteries.

Tables 4-1 to 4-5 detail five of the sympathomimetics that are most commonly used in cardiovascular nursing: epinephrine, norepinephrine, dopamine, dobutamine, and phenylephrine.

Indication

Indications for use of sympathomimetics are dependent on the action desired. The primary indication when using these medications for vasopressor activity is a decrease in the baseline systolic blood pressure by more than 30 mmHg, or a mean arterial pressure less than 60 mmHg (Manaker, 2014). Indication for use of medications with dominant inotropic action is clinical evidence of cardiac failure with evidence of end organ damage. This class of medications is primarily used in different types of shock states to improve cardiac output and tissue perfusion. Hypovolemia should be corrected before administering this class of medication.

Side Effects

All vasopressors and inotropic agents, such as those in this class, should be infused through an appropriately positioned central venous catheter to eliminate the risk for peripheral extravasation. Another side effect to consider is *tachyphylaxis,* the body's responsiveness to the drug decreasing over time. Titrating doses helps to adjust responsiveness to the tachyphylaxis phenomenon and adjust to the patient's clinical condition. A very common side effect of beta-1 agonists is tachycardia. Thus, in the person who is already tachycardic, drug selection to avoid worsening tachycardia is important. The majority of sympathomimetics are also proarrhythmic

TABLE 4-1: EPINEPHRINE	
What receptors are stimulated?	• Beta-1 and beta-2 receptors (at low doses)
	• Alpha-1 receptors (at high doses)
What are the resultant actions?	• Increased contractility (positive inotrope)
	• Increased automaticity
	• Bronchodilation
	• Selective vasoconstriction
When and why is it used?	• Advanced cardiac life support; first-line drug for cardiac standstill
	• Anaphylactic shock
	• Hypotension or profound bradycardia
What are special nursing considerations?	• Instant onset
	• Peak 20 minutes
	• 1 mg intravenously every 3 to 5 minutes during cardiac standstill

Note. Adapted from Gold Standard/Elsevier. (2010). *Clinical pharmacology database.* Retrieved from http://www.clinicalpharmacology.com/?epm=2_1

TABLE 4-2: NOREPINEPHRINE	
What receptors are stimulated?	• Primarily alpha stimulation
	• Some beta-1 receptors
What are the resultant actions?	• Potent vasoconstriction (vasopressor)
	• Some increased contractility (positive inotrope)
When and why is it used?	• Refractory hypotension
	• Shock
	• Used as vasopressor but has inotropic properties
What are special nursing considerations?	• Rapid IV onset
	• Duration 1 to 2 minutes (blood pressure checks every 2 minutes while titrating)
	• Large IV line or central line
	• Phentolamine (alpha blocker) for infiltration of IV site

Note. Adapted from Gold Standard/Elsevier. (2010). *Clinical pharmacology database.* Retrieved from http://www.clinicalpharmacology.com/?epm=2_1

and can evoke life-threatening arrhythmias. An adverse effect of this class of medications could be the increased afterload, or workload, they place on the heart. In cases of heart failure, the vasopressor actions of this class could further weaken the failing myocardium. Finally, alpha- and beta-receptor stimulation can increase myocardial oxygen demand and consumption. These actions do enhance myocardial function but also increase the risk for myocardial ischemia (Manaker, 2014).

Contraindications

Many of the contraindications of the sympathomimetics class of medications are drug specific. For instance, dobutamine is contraindicated in idiopathic hypertrophic subaortic stenosis, and dopamine is not recommended in cardiogenic shock given its common ability to produce dysrhythmias. Patients diagnosed with pheochromocytoma should not receive adrenergic vasopressors during hypotensive periods secondary to the risk for excessive autonomic

TABLE 4-3: DOPAMINE	
What receptors are stimulated?	• Dopaminergic and some beta-1 receptors at low doses • Beta-1 at moderate doses • Pure alpha stimulation at high doses (>10 µg/kg/min)
What are the resultant actions?	• Increased contractility at small and moderate doses • Increased conduction • Vasoconstriction at high doses • Does not treat or prevent renal failure at low doses
When and why is it used?	• Refractory hypotension • Shock
What are special nursing considerations?	• IV onset 1 to 2 minutes • Peak 10 minutes • Maximal effects at 20 µg/kg/min • Large IV line or central line • Phentolamine (alpha blocker) for infiltrate

Note. Adapted from Gold Standard/Elsevier. (2010). *Clinical pharmacology database.* Retrieved from http://www.clinicalpharmacology.com/?epm=2_1

TABLE 4-4: DOBUTAMINE	
What receptors are stimulated?	• Primarily beta-1 • Some alpha-receptor stimulation • Modest beta-2 (more beta-2 than alpha)
What are the resultant actions?	• Increased contractility (positive inotrope) • Increased atrioventricular node conduction • Modest vasoconstriction
When and why is it used?	• As an inotrope with modest afterload reduction
What are special nursing considerations?	• Onset 1 to 2 minutes • Peak 10 minutes • Blood pressure is variable: beta-2 causes vasodilation • Increased cardiac output increases blood pressure

Note. Adapted from Gold Standard/Elsevier. (2010). *Clinical pharmacology database.* Retrieved from http://www.clinicalpharmacology.com/?epm=2_1

stimulation. Patients who are receiving monoamine oxidase inhibitors should not be given high doses of vasopressors secondary to their synergistic effects and potential for exaggerated responses (Dellinger et al., 2013).

Nonsympathomimetics

Nonsympathomimetic medications are also known as nonadrenergic agents. These medications do not stimulate the receptors discussed in the previous section.

Mechanism of Action and Indications

Nonsympathomimetic medications are known for varying actions that are complex and not fully understood. Arginine vasopressin is a nonsympathomimetic medication that can be used as a vasopressor. Because it is an antidiuretic hormone, there is an obvious antidiuretic effect. Although it is a vasoconstrictor, it does allow for regional vasodilation to vital organs. Arginine vasopressin can be used in refractory

TABLE 4-5: PHENYLEPHRINE (SYNTHETIC COMPOUND)	
What receptors are stimulated?	• Direct effect is dominant alpha stimulation • No substantial beta-1 effect at therapeutic doses • Indirect effect: causes release of norepinephrine
What are the resultant actions?	• Potent vasoconstriction (vasopressor)
When and why is it used?	• Refractory hypotension
What are special nursing considerations?	• Rapid IV onset • Duration of action 10 to 15 minutes • Large IV line or central line • Phentolamine (alpha blocker) for infiltration of IV site

Note. Adapted from Gold Standard/Elsevier. (2010). *Clinical pharmacology database.* Retrieved from http://www.clinicalpharmacology.com/?epm=2_1

hypotension not responsive to sympathomimetics. It can help to restore the patient's sensitivity to catecholamines. Exogenous arginine vasopressin is not titrated like other vasopressors; rather, it is administered at a consistent low dose during the course of treatment (Manaker, 2014).

The phosphodiesterase inhibitors (PDEIs) milrinone and inamrinone are nonsympathomimetic medications that are commonly used as inotropes. They create a positive inotropic effect of increasing availability of calcium by inhibiting the degradation of cyclic adenosine monophosphate and thereby increasing contractility. In addition, these inotropic medications simultaneously produce venous and arterial vasodilator effects as a result of their action on vascular and cardiac muscle. Thus, PDEIs have the added benefit of decreasing preload and afterload. PDEIs, like dobutamine, can be used in patients with acute heart failure who need inotropic support, but with fewer dysrhythmic effects. In addition, PDEIs have positive effects on diastolic function (Manaker, 2014).

Side Effects

Side effect profiles are specific to the medication. The side effect profile of vasopressin is related to its actions of fluid retention and vasoconstriction, with the most common negative side effects being abdominal cramping, diar-

rhea, nausea, and angina. Although PDEIs have less potential for dysrhythmias than does dobutamine, patients receiving milrinone must still be closely monitored because of the potential for ventricular dysrhythmias and/or the exacerbation of accelerated ventricular rate in patients with atrial dysrhythmias (Manaker, 2014).

Contraindications

Contraindications are similar to medications in the sympathomimetic class. Nonsympathomimetic medications should be infused via a central venous catheter, and patients should be monitored for tachycardia, dysrhythmias, and ischemic signs and symptoms.

Nitrates

The nitrate class of medications is composed of nitroglycerin, isosorbide, and sodium nitroprusside. The ability of nitrates to positively affect both oxygen supply and demand during acute angina has been found to be effective since the nineteenth century (Woo & Robinson, 2016).

Mechanism of Action

Nitrates act primarily by providing more nitric oxide to the vascular endothelium, causing vasodilation. Nitrates contribute to both sides of the oxygen supply-demand equation equally by dilating capacitance vessels, resulting in decreased systemic resistance (afterload), and by decreasing venous return to the heart (preload). Sodium nitroprusside is known as a more potent arterial vasodilator and afterload reducer, as well as the more potent nitrate in its class. At higher doses of nitroglycerin, arterial vasodilation occurs, consequently decreasing afterload and myocardial workload. Indirect actions are known as reflex responses to decreased arterial pressures perceived by baroreceptors and hormonal mechanisms. The most common reflex response seen with nitrates is tachycardia. However, other reflex responses the clinician must consider include a decrease in platelet aggregation in response to the increase of nitric oxide production. Decreased platelet aggregation in the setting of nitrate use is thought to play a significant role in the reduction of mortality and potentially in the reduction of infarct size (Woo & Robinson, 2016).

Indication

The primary indication for nitrates is angina. However, nitrates such as isosorbide and nitroglycerin paste are commonly used in normotensive heart failure cases to reduce both preload and afterload for the weakened myocardium. Reducing both the amount of volume returning to the weakened heart and the workload it must work against results in decreased myocardial wall tension and an increased transmyocardial gradient. This increased gradient facilitates improved perfusion between the coronary vessels and the subendocardium, thereby increasing myocardial oxygen supply (Woo & Robinson, 2016). Nitroprusside is indicated in hypertensive crisis and other cardiac emergencies, such as acute mitral regurgitation, acute decompensated heart failure, and acute aortic dissection when immediate afterload reduction is needed.

Side Effects

The side effect profile associated with nitrates is related to its vasodilatory effect. Common side effects include orthostatic hypotension, syncope,

flushing, reflex responses such as tachycardia, and headache. Because of its action to cause hypotension, continuous blood pressure monitoring via an arterial line is preferred. Transdermal administration of these medications can cause local hypersensitivity reactions that can be easily resolved by rotating sites. Patients who are taking oral or topical nitrates can develop a tolerance. To prevent this tolerance, allow a nitrate-free period of 8 to 10 hr/day, preferably during the night (Lilley, Collins, & Snyder, 2017). Some patients experience headaches as a result of the vasodilation associated with nitroglycerin.

NURSING APPLICATION

Headaches should be treated immediately because pain increases sympathetic nervous system stimulation and myocardial oxygen demand, potentially worsening ischemia.

Contraindications

Considering the primary action of nitrates is vasodilation, patients with hypotension (systolic blood pressure <90 mmHg, or a mean arterial pressure <60 mmHg), volume depletion, or severe anemia should avoid taking nitrates. Other conditions for which vasodilation would be detrimental are traumatic brain injury and cerebral hemorrhage and closed-angle glaucoma because of the risk for increasing intracranial and intraocular pressures, respectively (Woo & Robinson, 2016). Because nitrates decrease preload, they are also contraindicated in patients with hypertrophic cardiomyopathy, who are dependent on adequate preload to maintain their cardiac output. Nitrates and other vasodilators should also be used with extreme caution in patients with aortic stenosis because these patients have a limited ability to increase cardiac output in response to hypotension. Nitrates are also contraindicated in the acute period after a right ventricular myocardial infarction

(MI) or an inferior MI because these patients are predisposed to significant drops in blood pressure with nitrates. Nitrates can cause some reflex tachycardia; administration with a beta blocker can prevent this side effect. These medications should not be prescribed to patients taking sildenafil (Viagra) or other phosphodiesterase-5 inhibitors because of the risk for profound hypotension secondary to synergistic effects. Despite the risk for thiocyanate toxicity to occur with prolonged administration of sodium nitroprusside, it is not an initial nursing consideration because patients are not at risk unless they have been receiving nitroprusside for several days at high doses or have decreased glomerular filtration rates.

NURSING APPLICATION

Women, in addition to men, should be assessed for taking sildenafil or other phosphodiesterase-5 inhibitors. Both women and men may take sildenafil as it is branded as Viagra for treatment of erectile dysfunction, but also as Revatio for the treatment of pulmonary hypertension.

Diuretics

Diuretics are a class of medications primarily used as first-line agents for heart failure and hypertension to reduce extracellular fluid volume.

Mechanism of Action

Loop Diuretics. Loop diuretics work in the ascending loop of Henle and result in a loss of water, hydrogen ions, and electrolytes (potassium, sodium, and chloride). Loop diuretics result in a greater loss of water and less of a loss of potassium and sodium compared with thiazide diuretics. In addition to promoting loss of total body fluid, loop diuretics also promote venous vasodilation, which further helps in reducing preload.

Loop diuretics have a rapid onset and short duration of action. They are called *high-ceiling diuretics* because additional benefit can be achieved with higher doses. Although they are not effective in treating acute renal failure, loop diuretics may continue to be effective in the presence of renal dysfunction and may be used to remove excess fluid in a fluid overloaded state. Loop diuretics include bumetanide (Bumex), furosemide (Lasix), and torsemide (Demadex).

Thiazide Diuretics. Thiazide diuretics inhibit reabsorption of sodium and chloride in the distal tubule. They have a delayed onset but longer duration of action than loop diuretics. They are also considered less potent than loop diuretics and have decreased effectiveness in the presence of renal dysfunction. Thiazide diuretics are considered low-ceiling diuretics because increased effectiveness is not seen with higher doses. Thiazide diuretics include

- bendrofluazide,
- benzthiazide,
- chlorothiazide,
- chlorthalidone,
- cyclothiazide,
- hydrochlorothiazide,
- hydroflumethiazide,
- indapamide,
- metolazone,
- polythiazide, and
- trichlormethiazide.

Diuretics are theorized to reduce the amount of sodium in the vessel walls, which is thought to be a contributing factor for vasoconstriction. Theoretically, the reduction of sodium within the vessel walls helps to reduce plasma volume and promote a vasodilatory effect.

Aldosterone Antagonists. Aldosterone is a mineralocorticoid hormone released from the adrenal cortex as part of the end result of the action of the renin-angiotensin-aldosterone system. Aldosterone informs the body to hold on to sodium, and therefore water, and to excrete potassium. For this reason, aldosterone antagonists are sometimes referred to as potassium-sparing diuretics. Angiotensin-converting enzyme inhibitors (ACEIs) indirectly affect the release of aldosterone, whereas aldosterone antagonists directly block aldosterone. The end result is a decrease in sodium and water retention and, therefore, a decrease in preload. Two aldosterone antagonists are available: spironolactone and eplerenone. Spironolactone is a nonselective agent that blocks aldosterone and also exhibits an antiandrogenic effect in both men and women (Woo & Robinson, 2016).

Indication

As stated previously, diuretics are used to decrease extracellular volume in heart failure, edematous states, and/or hypertensive states in an effort to decrease peripheral vascular resistance, venous return, and overall total circulating plasma volume. It is this reduction in plasma volume that improves cardiac function and reduces blood pressure. Low-dose spironolactone has been shown to decrease mortality in patients with severe heart failure who are already taking an ACEI (Woo & Robinson, 2016). Diuretics may also be used as adjunctive therapies for ventricular remodeling with calcium channel blockers (CCBs) and ACEIs, or in cases of aldosteronism. Aldosterone is thought to play a very large role in cardiovascular function. Potential effects of aldosterone blockade include (1) minimized release of catecholamines, (2) improved endothelial function, (3) antithrombotic effects, and (4) decreased vascular inflammation and myocardial fibrosis (Nappi & Sieg, 2011).

Side Effects

The most common effect associated with all diuretics is electrolyte imbalance. For instance, in both loop and thiazide diuretics, serum levels of potassium, magnesium, and sodium can be depleted and must be monitored. In contrast, serum calcium levels can be elevated. The adverse effects associated with electrolyte imbalances must be considered with the use of these medications as well (e.g., hypokalemic or hypomagnesemic arrhythmias, or hyponatremic neurological symptoms). In the case of potassium-sparing diuretics, clinicians must monitor for hyperkalemia, especially with concomitant use of ACEIs or angiotensin receptor blockers (ARBs). Thiazides are also most commonly associated with causing hyperuricemia. Other side effects common to all diuretics include glucose intolerance and hypotension. General side effects of thiazide diuretic therapy include (Woo & Robinson, 2016):

Blood chemistry changes, such as

- hypokalemia potassium;
- hyperglycemia (blood sugar);
- hyperuricemia (uric acid):
  - cholesterol,
  - triglycerides, and
  - high-density lipoprotein cholesterol; and
- hypercalcemia.

Other side effects, such as

- dizziness,
- decreased glomerular filtration in kidneys related to hypovolemia,
- impaired glucose tolerance,
- gout, and
- ventricular dysrhythmias (potassium).

The antiandrogenic effect of spironolactone can cause gynecomastia in men, whereas eplerenone specifically does not have this negative side effect (Woo & Robinson, 2016).

Contraindications

Contraindications for diuretics include shock or hypotensive states associated with volume depletion, as well as many acute kidney injury conditions. Diuretics must be used with caution in patients with diabetes, gout, renal calculi, and creatinine clearances less than 25 to 30 ml/min. Older adults are at an increased risk for hypotension and volume depletion leading to orthostasis and falls (Woo & Robinson, 2016).

Angiotensin-Converting Enzyme Inhibitors

ACEIs end with "pril" and include the medications

- benazepril,
- captopril,
- enalapril,
- fosinopril,
- lisinopril,
- quinapril, and
- ramipril.

Mechanism of Action

ACEIs prevent the conversion of angiotensin I to angiotensin II by inhibiting the ACE. Angiotensin II is a potent arterial vasoconstrictor; therefore, ACEIs promote arterial vasodilation by preventing the formation of angiotensin II. This arterial vasodilation reduces afterload.

The formation of angiotensin II also stimulates the release of aldosterone from the adrenals. Aldosterone informs the body to retain sodium, and therefore water, while excreting potassium. Angiotensin II also stimulates the release of arginine vasopressin (antidiuretic hormone), which causes additional vasoconstriction and water reabsorption. When angiotensin II formation is inhibited, the release of aldosterone and vasopressin decreases, and preload and afterload further decrease. Because of the posi-

tive effects of decreasing afterload and preload, ACEIs decrease the workload of the left ventricle. In addition to interfering with the formation of angiotensin II, ACEIs block the breakdown of bradykinin, which directly supports vasodilation.

Indication

ACEIs have positive effects in patients with heart failure. These medications are central to the management of heart failure and are also used after MI. ACEIs can decrease mortality in patients with an ejection fraction less than 40% after an MI by decreasing left ventricular remodeling. In addition, ACEIs are used to treat nephropathy as well as hypertension in patients with diabetes and other high-risk features (Woo & Robinson, 2016). The positive effects of ACEIs commonly take weeks to months to be seen, and these effects include (Opie & Gersh, 2009)

- reduction in left ventricular hypertrophy,
- improvement in endothelial function via increased release of nitric oxide,
- reduction in oxidative stress,
- decrease in inflammatory response,
- promotion of antithrombotic environment via a decrease in fibrinogen, and
- decrease in intraglomerular pressure, glomerular fibrosis, and glomerular protein leak.

Side Effects

The four potential major side effects of ACEIs are hypotension, hyperkalemia, angioedema/chronic cough, and renal dysfunction. These side effects can best be understood by relating the effect to the physiological action of ACEIs:

1. Hypotension is a potential adverse effect caused by the vasodilatory effects of blocking angiotensin II formation.

2. Hyperkalemia (elevated potassium levels) is a potential adverse effect caused by the decreased release of aldosterone from the

adrenals. Aldosterone tells the body to hold on to sodium and to excrete potassium. Because of the risk for hyperkalemia, electrolyte levels and renal function must be monitored carefully during initiation and maintenance of ACEIs.

3. The development of acute angioedema can be a life-threatening complication and is related to the increased circulating levels of bradykinin. A small percentage of patients experience development of a dry, persistent cough related to increased bradykinin, which requires cessation of ACEI treatment.

4. Although ACEIs have an overall renoprotective effect, they can cause adverse renal function in patients with chronic and severe low cardiac output states, those with severe sodium or volume depletion, and those with pre-existing renal disease. These patients have been relying on efferent arteriole vasoconstriction to help support adequate glomerular filtration. The initiation of ACEIs results in efferent arteriole vasodilation. Bilateral renal artery stenosis places the patient at high risk for acute renal dysfunction because afferent arteriole vasodilation is limited and glomerular filtration is dependent on efferent vasoconstriction. A slight increase in creatinine that stabilizes after initiation of an ACEI is not a contraindication for continued administration (Woo & Robinson, 2016).

Contraindications

ACEIs have three absolute contraindications: angioedema, bilateral renal artery stenosis, and pregnancy. Otherwise, other conditions are relative to the severity of illness and treatment regimen. For instance, general contraindications for ACEI administration include (1) systolic blood pressure less than 80 mmHg, (2) elevated serum potassium, and (3) serum creatinine greater than 3 mg/dl (Woo & Robinson, 2016).

Angiotensin Receptor Blockers

ARBs are very similar to ACEIs but use a different pathway to block the conversion to angiotensin II; medication names end with "sartan." Commonly used ARBs include candesartan, irbesartan, telmisartan, eprosartan, losartan, and valsartan.

Mechanism of Action

ARBs directly block angiotensin II after it is formed; therefore, they have similar hemodynamic effects as ACEIs. This section discusses the differences and indications between ARBs and ACEIs. The lack of increased bradykinin levels may decrease the effectiveness of ARBs in the management of heart failure because bradykinin is responsible for additional vasodilator effects that are beneficial in the treatment of heart failure.

Indication

Research comparing the benefits of ACEIs and ARBs is ongoing. However, current heart failure guidelines still recommend ACEIs as the preferred medication for patients with current or prior symptoms and with reduced left ventricular dysfunction. In select patients, ARBs may be used in place of ACEIs as first-line agents.

Current guidelines indicate the use of ARBs when ACEIs are unable to be tolerated because of intractable cough or angioedema. There are other pathways to angiotensin II formation in addition to the ACE pathway. For this reason, both ARB and ACEI use have been found to reduce mortality in acute cardiovascular conditions such as heart failure and MI (Liu et al., 2015). Current guidelines do not indicate the addition of an ARB to patients already taking an ACEI and aldosterone antagonist because of the high risk for hyperkalemia and other adverse effects that may lead to dose reduction.

Side Effects

ARBs do not produce a cough because they do not promote increased bradykinin levels. Although angioedema is less common in patients taking ARBs, some patients will experience development of angioedema with both ACEIs and ARBs. Therefore, great caution must be used in administering an ARB to a patient with a history of angioedema (Woo & Robinson, 2016). Except for the cough, ARBs have side effects and precautions similar to ACEIs, for instance, any effects associated with hypotension (e.g., dizziness or orthostasis).

Contraindications

Contraindications to ARB use are the same as those associated with ACEI use.

Beta Blockers

Beta blockers are also known as adrenergic antagonists.

Mechanism of Action

Beta blockers can block the beta-1 or beta-2 receptors of the sympathetic nervous system. When beta blockers block beta-1 receptors, decreases in heart rate and contractility result; when they block beta-2 receptors, bronchial and peripheral vasoconstriction occur. Therefore, caution should be used when administering beta blockers to patients with restrictive airway disease or peripheral vascular disease.

NURSING APPLICATION

Many patients with cardiac disease have coexisting peripheral vascular disease. If a nonselective blocker is prescribed, the patient may experience an increase in intermittent claudication associated with the peripheral vascular disease. This effect is related to the blockade of beta-2.

Beta blockers decrease myocardial oxygen demand by decreasing contractility and heart rate. They also help increase coronary perfusion by increasing diastolic filling time. Although beta blockers do not cause direct arterial vasodilation, they decrease contractility and heart rate, which decreases cardiac output. A decrease in cardiac output lowers blood pressure. Some beta blockers are cardioselective, meaning they predominantly block beta-1; others are noncardioselective, blocking both beta-1 and beta-2. Beta-1 receptors are also found in the juxtaglomerular apparatus of the kidney. Antagonizing these receptors reduces the release of renin from the kidney, resulting in a reduction of blood pressure (Woo & Robinson, 2016). The blocking of beta-2 is especially problematic for patients with chronic obstructive pulmonary disease because of a passive response of bronchoconstriction when inhibiting with the endogenous adrenergic bronchodilator activity.

Cardioselective beta blockers include

- acebutolol,
- atenolol,
- betaxolol,
- bisoprolol (highly beta-1 selective),
- metoprolol, and
- esmolol (ultra-short-acting).

Noncardioselective beta blockers include

- carvedilol (also has alpha-1 blockade),
- labetalol (also has alpha blockade),
- nadolol,
- penbutolol,
- propranolol,
- timolol, and
- sotalol (also has Class III antiarrhythmic properties).

Indication

Beta blockers are widely prescribed in cardiovascular medicine and are indicated for a number of cardiovascular disorders. Cardiovascular indications for the use of beta blockers include acute MI, angina, aortic dissection, heart failure, hypertension, hypertrophic cardiomyopathy, mitral valve prolapse, digoxin-induced ventricular dysrhythmias, prolonged QT syndrome, supraventricular dysrhythmias, and ventricular dysrhythmias. Beta blockers are included in the practice guidelines for the management of heart failure, stable angina, and acute coronary syndromes. Their use in these disorders will be discussed in more detail in later chapters. When used to treat hypertension, beta blockers prevent reflex tachycardia associated with other vasodilators such as nitroglycerin. Beta blockers are sometimes combined with alpha blockers. Alpha blockers produce vasodilation and are indicated in the treatment of hypertension. Although intraocular hypertension is not a cardiovascular condition, the clinician must be aware of patients receiving ophthalmic beta blockers for the reduction of these pressures.

Side Effects

In the liver, beta blockers can inhibit the process of lipolysis, which is the process responsible for the endogenous reduction of triglycerides and cholesterol and the increase of high-density lipids ("good" cholesterol). Thus, beta blockade can potentiate hyperlipidemic conditions. Beta blockers also inhibit gluconeogenesis and can inhibit the production of insulin. Other effects commonly reported during the use of this class of medication are depression, fatigue, sexual dysfunction, and orthostasis (Woo & Robinson, 2016).

Contraindications

Contraindications to beta-blocker initiation include severe bradycardia, high-degree atrioventricular (AV) block, sick sinus syndrome, and acute decompensated heart failure (Woo & Robinson, 2016). Caution must be exercised when using beta blockers in patients with coexisting depression, asthma, or peripheral vascular disease. Caution is particularly important when using noncardioselective beta blockers in patients with asthma or peripheral vascular disease. Patients with diabetes should exercise caution when taking beta blockers because beta blockers can mask the symptoms of hypoglycemia. Side effects of beta blockers include lethargy, fatigue, insomnia, nightmares, impotence, worsening asthma, and worsening claudication (Woo & Robinson, 2016).

Calcium Channel Blockers

Mechanism of Action

CCBs decrease the flux of calcium across cell membranes. The mechanisms of action of these three potential effects are

- decreased contractility, which blocks inward flow of calcium in phase two of the cardiac action potential and decreases the force of contractions;

- decreased heart rate, which depresses automaticity and velocity and decreases heart rate; and

- decreased afterload, which relaxes vascular smooth muscle.

All CCBs have some common side effects. For example, they all have some degree of inotropic effect; they also reduce coronary and systemic vascular resistance. However, not all CCBs are created equal, and all do not have the same degree of effects. Two subgroups of CCBs further separate their mechanisms of action: dihydropyridines and nondihydropyridines. Nondihydropyridine CCBs include only diltiazem and verapamil, and they are primarily separated from other CCBs because of their ability to reduce AV nodal conduction. This mechanism of action is primarily the reason these medications are drugs of choice for atrial arrhythmias with increased ventricular responses. All other CCBs are considered to fall into the dihydropyridine group. Table 4-6 illustrates the mechanism of action differences between these groups.

Indication

Primary indications for CCBs and specific agents are

* *atrial fibrillation or flutter, paroxysmal supraventricular tachycardia:* nondihydropyridines;

* *angina* (including vasospastic angina): nondihydropyridine with nitrates; *or* dihydropyridine with beta blockers (beta blocker used to prevent reflex tachycardia); and

* *hypertension:* all CCBs can be used.

Additional indications include

* *hypertrophic cardiomyopathy:* nondihydropyridines (avoid dihydropyridines); and

* *treatment and prevention of coronary spasm:* dihydropyridine.

CCBs can be used to decrease heart rate, contractility, and afterload. CCBs are effective in decreasing myocardial oxygen demand. Short- and intermediate-acting dihydropyridine CCBs are not used in the treatment of angina or hypertension because of their questionable safety profiles. Newer generation, longer-acting dihydropyridine CCBs, such as amlodipine, have more coronary vasodilatory properties and are better tolerated in patients with decreased left ventricular dysfunction. Amlodipine, a coronary vasoselective dihydropyridine CCB, is reported to be the best-tolerated CCB in patients with ischemic cardiomyopathy (Woo & Robinson, 2016).

Side Effects

Adverse effects of CCBs include peripheral edema, worsening heart failure, hypotension, and constipation. In addition, nondihydropyridines can cause bradycardia and heart block because of their effect on AV nodal conduction (Woo & Robinson, 2016).

Contraindications

Nifedipine, an older generation dihydropyridine CCB, is contraindicated in unstable angina (UA) because of its predominant peripheral arterial vasodilatory effects. Decompensated heart failure is a contraindication to the administration of CCBs. CCBs are not indicated in the treatment of heart failure because they have a negative inotropic effect and do not have the added benefit of interrupting neurohormonal responses. In patients with heart blocks or bradydysrhythmias, the nondihydropyridines (verapamil and diltiazem) should not be used because of their negative chronotropic effect on the AV node (Woo & Robinson, 2016).

Antiarrhythmics

The cardiovascular clinician must recognize that the use of multiple antiarrhythmics must be the decision of an expert. This is largely due to

TABLE 4-6: CALCIUM CHANNEL BLOCKERS

	Verapamil	Dihydropyridine Calcium Channel Blockers	Diltiazem
Heart rate	↓	↑ (reflex tachycardia)	↓
Atrioventricular nodal conduction	↓	Neutral	↓
Contractility	↓	↓	↓
Arterial vasodilation	↑	↑	↑

Note. From Gold Standard/Elsevier. (2010). *Clinical pharmacology database.* Retrieved from http://www.clinicalpharmacology.com/?epm=2_1

the known fact that this class of cardiovascular medications is also proarrhythmic. Decisions to use many of the drugs in this class of medication are made on an individual basis with consideration of the condition, potential interactions with other drugs being taken, possible adverse responses, and any concurrent clinical problems. Following is a list of antiarrhythmic agents by Vaughan Williams classification.

Class I agents include

- Ia – quinidine, procainamide, and disopyramide;

- Ib – lidocaine, mexiletine, and phenytoin; and

- Ic – flecainide and propafenone.

Class II agents include

- beta blockers – atenolol, sotalol, carvedilol, propranolol, esmolol, and timolol.

Class III agents include

- amiodarone, sotalol, ibutilide, dofetilide, and dronedarone.

Class IV agents include

- nondihydropyridine CCBs – verapamil and diltiazem (Woo & Robinson, 2016).

Mechanism of Action

Class I. Class I antiarrhythmic agents are sodium channel blockers. Within this class are subclasses that perform different actions on the sodium channel. Class Ia drugs lengthen action potential via the sodium channel, whereas Class Ib drugs shorten it, and Class Ic drugs have either no effect or minimally increase the duration of the action potential. These actions mean that Class Ib drugs interact rapidly with sodium channels, whereas Class Ic drugs interact slowly and Class Ia drugs interact intermediately with sodium channels (Woo & Robinson, 2016).

Class II. Class II agents are adrenergic receptor blockers, also known as beta blockers.

Blockade of beta-adrenergic receptors increases the threshold potential and prolongs the effective refractory period, thereby decreasing heart rate and conduction velocity. The other actions of beta blockers discussed in the "Beta Blockers" section apply here as well (Woo & Robinson, 2016).

Class III. The mechanism of action of these antiarrhythmics occurs by potassium channel blockade. Blocking potassium channels results in a decreased rate of the automaticity of ventricular ectopic beats. Class III antiarrhythmics are also known to convert unidirectional blocks to bidirectional blocks in re-entry arrhythmias such as atrial fibrillation (Woo & Robinson, 2016).

Class IV. CCBs make up this class of antiarrhythmic agents and are known as the "slow-channel blockers." These medications increase oxygen supply via vasodilation and afterload reduction while also decreasing heart rate and inotropic activity. The mechanisms of action for CCBs are discussed in more detail in the earlier section "Calcium Channel Blockers" (Woo & Robinson, 2016).

Indication

Indications for the use of any antiarrhythmic agent involve an atrial or ventricular arrhythmia compromising effective cardiac function. The clinician must consider whether the genesis of the arrhythmia is atrial or ventricular because some of these medications (e.g., lidocaine) are effective only with ventricular arrhythmias (Woo & Robinson, 2016).

Side Effects

The most common side effects associated with antiarrhythmic agents are bradycardia, reduced blood pressure, and ectopic heartbeats that can potentiate, or exacerbate, pre-existing arrhythmias. The nurse must also monitor for nausea, vomiting, diarrhea, or constipation, which are most common with Class Ia medications. The effects associated with beta-blocker and CCB therapy also apply (Woo & Robinson, 2016).

Amiodarone has severe effects that are not common to other antiarrhythmic agents; for instance, it is known to cause extrapyramidal syndrome effects, hepatitis, epididymitis, peripheral neuropathy, blue-gray skin tone, and pulmonary fibrosis with cumulative doses or long-term therapy (Woo & Robinson, 2016). Dofetilide and sotalol may cause proarrhythmias, particularly torsades de pointes, because of the effect of the Q-T interval lengthening. For this reason, they are initiated only in a hospital setting with close monitoring (Kumar, 2015).

Contraindications

Because the mechanism of action differs among the subclasses of antiarrhythmics, the precautions and contraindications differ as well. Class Ia medications can inhibit vagal effects and can lead to an increased heart rate and AV conduction. Class Ib agents have the potential to reduce blood pressure because of their negative inotropic effects and should be used with caution in patients with heart failure. Class Ic agents can cause severe exacerbations of arrhythmia in those with pre-existing ventricular tachyarrhythmias or previous MI; thus, they should be used only for patients refractory to less toxic drugs. Class II agents should not be used in patients with bronchospastic disorders like asthma. Class II agents must also be used with caution in patients with diabetes given their potential to inhibit insulin secretion. Some Class III agents can cause hypothyroidism and must be used with caution in those with preexisting thyroid dysfunction. Given the risk for a fatal pulmonary fibrosis with amiodarone, pulmonary function tests may be needed to record a baseline before the initiation of this drug. Class IC agents are contraindicated in patients with ischemic or structural heart disease. Certain Class I and III drugs are contra-

indicated in heart failure. Class IV agents are associated with worsening heart failure and should be avoided in these patients (Woo & Robinson, 2016).

Cardiac Glycoside

Cardiac glycosides are among the oldest known medications still in use and have been used in the treatment of heart failure since 1785 (Woo & Robinson, 2016). Digoxin is the most commonly prescribed medication in this class.

Mechanism of Action

Digoxin has a very complex mechanism of action. It has weak inotropic properties and also some parasympathetic properties. These parasympathetic properties decrease sympathetic outflow and decrease renin production, both of which are particularly beneficial when used in the treatment of heart failure. Cardiac glycosides are known to be strong and highly selective inhibitors of the sodium-potassium-adenosine triphosphatase system, also known as the sodium pump. This is the mechanism that gives the medication its positive inotropic effect. Extracellular potassium decreases the affinity of the enzyme for cardiac glycosides and, as a result, helps to reduce or reverse some of the toxic effects of these drugs (Woo & Robinson, 2016).

Indication

Digoxin is indicated in symptomatic atrial arrhythmias when used concomitantly with CCBs. The medication does not convert the rhythm directly, but it does reduce the heart rate to yield better filling times during diastole and facilitate improved myocardial oxygenation. The drug is also indicated in the treatment of heart failure; however, it is no longer the first-line therapy. Digoxin remains essential in the management of systolic dysfunction (ejection fraction <40%) and an audible S3. The resolution of the S3 is used as evaluation criteria suggesting a positive response to digoxin therapy (Woo & Robinson, 2016).

Side Effects

Gastrointestinal (GI) symptoms are the most common side effects of digoxin; these effects include anorexia, nausea, vomiting, and diarrhea. In older adults, CNS-based effects such as fatigue, disorientation, and hallucinations occur most often.

Digoxin has a narrow therapeutic range, and toxicity can occur even at therapeutic levels. Signs and symptoms of toxicity include nausea, vomiting, headache, confusion, and vision disturbances (e.g., appearance of halos, change in color perception). Low dosages of digoxin (0.125 mg/day) are now used in most patients to avoid toxicity. Interactions occur between digoxin and a variety of medications, including other cardiovascular agents. Some cardiovascular agents reduce the clearance of digoxin and predispose the patient to toxicity. These agents include amiodarone, propafenone, quinidine, felodipine, diltiazem, and verapamil. Other cardiovascular agents, such as nondihydropyridine CCBs, beta blockers, and class III antiarrhythmic agents, can potentiate the action of digoxin (Woo & Robinson, 2016).

Before initiation of digoxin, the patient's electrolyte status should be assessed. Low potassium, low magnesium, and high calcium increase the effect of digoxin. Hypokalemia and hyperkalemia increase the risk for digoxin toxicity. Because digoxin interacts with many other medications, careful assessment of the patient's medication profile is an important nursing intervention (Woo & Robinson, 2016).

Dialysis is not effective in treating digoxin toxicity because of the high tissue-binding property of digoxin. Untreated digoxin-toxicity-induced dysrhythmias can be fatal. Dysrhythmias seen with toxicity usually involve

increased automaticity with impaired conduction, for example, paroxysmal atrial tachycardia with heart block (Woo & Robinson, 2016).

NURSING APPLICATION

Digoxin should be withheld in a patient with any clinical signs of digoxin toxicity, even in the presence of a therapeutic digoxin level, until the patient's clinical condition can be thoroughly discussed with the physician.

Contraindications

Absolute contraindications for digoxin include hypersensitivity to drug components, ventricular fibrillation, acute MI, and myocarditis. Cautious use of this medication must occur with AV block, electrolyte imbalances of potassium, calcium, and magnesium. Patients with idiopathic hypertrophic subaortic stenosis, patients who have hypoxia for any reason, or patients with cor pulmonale should avoid digoxin or be monitored very closely with the use of this medication. Patients with Wolff-Parkinson-White atrial fibrillation should avoid the use of digoxin because it could worsen the arrhythmia. Although the medication has been used for decades in pregnancy without known toxic effects to the fetus, it remains a category C drug and must be used with caution. Older adults are at a greater risk for toxicity if they have low serum levels of albumin, considering digoxin is protein bound. Thus, it must also be used with caution in this population of patients (Woo & Robinson, 2016).

DRUGS THAT AFFECT COAGULATION

Coagulation Overview

The coagulation system has two primary purposes: (1) to protect the integrity of the vessels to prevent harmful bleeding, and (2) to maintain the fluid state of the blood. These two goals must be achieved simultaneously to maintain health. Clotting can be initiated by activation of either the intrinsic pathway or the extrinsic pathway of the clotting cascade. The intrinsic pathway is initiated by vessel injury and direct exposure to collagen. The extrinsic pathway is triggered by the endothelial release of tissue factor. *Tissue factor* is a protein within the subendothelial layer of the vessel released after injury, and it reacts with factor VII to facilitate the formation of a clot. Both pathways initiate the common pathway, through which a fibrin stable clot is produced. In the common pathway three things occur: (1) prothrombin is converted to thrombin, (2) thrombin permits the conversion of fibrinogen to fibrin, and (3) a fibrin stable clot forms. This fibrin stable clot, sometimes called a *red clot,* is the cause of most ST-segment elevation MIs (STEMIs; Patton, Thibodeau, & Douglas, 2012).

Platelets also respond to vessel injury through the processes of adhesion, activation, and aggregation. Platelet aggregation can be large enough to form a platelet plug, a white clot that seals a damaged vessel. This white clot is a primary culprit in UA. In addition to the independent formation of a platelet plug, platelets also release components necessary for the clotting process in the intrinsic pathway and contain a fibrin-stabilizing factor that is important in the final stage of the common pathway, before stable clot formation. Platelets cross-link with fibrinogen via the glycoprotein (GP) IIb/IIIa receptors to form a fibrin mesh, which gives a clot more substance (Patton, Thibodeau, & Douglas, 2012).

Thrombolytics and Fibrinolytics

Two main categories of medications are used to dissolve clots that have already formed: medications that are nonfibrin specific (thrombolytics) and those that are fibrin specific (fibrinolytics). Both types are adminis-

tered intravenously. Table 4-7 lists agents used to dissolve clots during acute STEMIs. For maximum effectiveness and improved patient outcomes, these medications should be administered within 30 minutes of symptom onset (Woo & Robinson, 2016).

Mechanism of Action

Streptokinase was the earliest "clot-busting" medication used to dissolve clots during an acute MI. It is a nonenzyme protein made from hemolytic streptococci that works by combining with circulating plasminogen and forming complexes that catalyze plasmin formation. The resultant increase in circulating plasmin creates a systemic lytic state, dissolving recent clots (Woo & Robinson, 2016).

Anistreplase, also known as anisoylated plasminogen streptokinase activator complex, is an altered form of streptokinase that is prepared in vitro. It converts circulating plasminogen into plasmin and has systemic lytic effects similar to those of streptokinase. Different from streptokinase, anistreplase is able to be given in an intravenous bolus over 2 to 5 minutes (Woo & Robinson, 2016).

Tissue plasminogen activator (t-PA), a fibrin-specific lytic agent, is a serine protease produced by vascular endothelial cells. It is produced for clinical application using recombinant DNA techniques. It has a particular affinity for fibrin; specifically, it activates the plasminogen that is bound to fibrin (Woo & Robinson, 2016).

Alteplase (recombinant t-PA) uses an accelerated dose to achieve more rapid reperfusion. The newer drugs derived from t-PA are reteplase (r-PA), tenecteplase (TNK-t-PA), and lanoteplase (n-PA). These newer agents are designed for bolus dosing to eliminate medication errors associated with the administration of these types of medications. In the GUSTO I Clinical Trial involving both streptokinase and t-PA, there was

TABLE 4-7: THROMBOLYTIC AND FIBRINOLYTIC AGENTS

Type	Actions/Physiological Effects	Agents
Fibrin specific	• Plasminogen activation • Rapid clot lysis • Clot specific	• Tissue plasminogen activators (t-PAs) • Alteplase (recombinant t-PA) • Reteplase (bolus dose recombinant t-PA) • Tenecteplase (single bolus dose recombinant t-PA)
Nonfibrin specific	• Systemic lysis • Slow clot lysis • More prolonged, systemic effect	• Streptokinase • Anistreplase (also known as *anisoylated plasminogen streptokinase activator complex*)

Note. From Western Schools.

an approximate 11.5% to 13.5% rate of error in the administration of these drugs. In the group of patients in which an administration error was made, the mortality at 30 days was higher (Cannon, 2000). For this reason the newer generation fibrinolytic medications have been created to be administered in bolus format, and thus help eliminate potential medication errors.

Indication

t-PA agents have better patency rates compared with streptokinase for ischemic conditions caused by thrombus/clot formation. Early administration of fibrinolytic therapy remains key to improving outcomes, and several clinical trials have demonstrated decreased mortality when fibrinolytic therapy was administered in the prehospital setting (Woo & Robinson, 2016). Prehospital administration of fibrinolytic therapy by paramedics has been found to be complex but suggests the need for more studies, given the apparent potential it has for reduction in mortality rates among patients with STEMI or acute stroke. Studies of paramedics administering these medications have also found that it is necessary in any emergency medical system that there be well-coordinated care and well-trained staff who have the ability to perform and transmit the 12-lead electrocardiogram to a qualified physician trained in STEMI recognition (Jensen et al., 2013).

NURSING APPLICATION

Because thrombolytics and fibrinolytics must be administered within a very short time frame and have specific indications and contraindications, it is important for emergency departments to have clearly written protocols and checklists to guide nurses through the rapid and accurate administration of these medications.

Side Effects

Because it is a foreign protein, streptokinase can cause allergic reactions. The most common signs and symptoms of an allergic reaction include pruritus, urticaria, fever, nausea, flushing, headache, and malaise. In response to receiving streptokinase, patients also produce antistreptokinase antibodies. Allergic response and hypotension can also occur with t-PA and t-PA-related medications. In addition to the allergic or hypersensitivity reactions that some of these medications can cause, they all can cause bleeding. Both r-PA and TNK-t-PA have very short half-lives, and thereby have lower risks of bleeding; the disadvantage is an increased likelihood of reocclusion after administration. TNK-t-PA is a very fibrin-specific medication that causes minimal systemic bleeding (including intracranial bleeding; Woo & Robinson, 2016).

All medications in this group have a very narrow window of therapeutic effect. If dosing is too low, clot lysis does not occur and there is no interruption of the MI. If the dose is too high, systemic bleeding can occur. Bleeding commonly occurs at vascular access sites. However, intracranial bleeding can also occur and have devastating effects. The risk for bleeding is weighed against the potential benefit when making decisions about the administration of these medications.

Contraindications

As one would anticipate, any patient with active bleeding is contraindicated to receive these medications because the risk for fatal hemorrhage is higher than the benefit of treatment. Other contraindications include any recent surgeries (including lumbar puncture), GI bleeding, or neurological injuries (e.g., trauma, stroke). Patients with antibodies to streptokinase may not receive the full benefit of the medication, so it is contraindicated in these patients. Patients with antistreptokinase antibodies include those who have received streptokinase within the last 6 months and those who have had recent streptococcal infection. Because anistreplase contains streptokinase, patients with a severe hypersensitivity to streptokinase should not receive this medication either (Woo & Robinson, 2016).

Anticoagulants

Anticoagulants are another class of medication used to treat thrombotic events associated with cardiovascular disease. In lieu of these drugs dissolving clots as noted in the thrombolytic and fibrinolytic section, anticoagulants interfere with the physiology of clot formation. Anticoagulants have multiple subclasses. The subclasses are discussed separately because of their varying actions and other differences that must be considered.

Mechanism of Action

Heparin. Heparin or unfractionated heparin (UFH) is also known as the commercially produced heparin derived from porcine or bovine tissue. Heparin is an antithrombotic agent but does not lyse existing clots. It works in the intrinsic and common pathways of the clotting cascade to prevent further development of thrombi. In higher doses, heparin also interferes with platelet aggregation. Heparin prevents the conversion of prothrombin to thrombin (factor IIa) by accelerating the action of antithrombin III. Antithrombin III naturally inhibits thrombin. The net result is the neutralization of the clotting capabilities of thrombin. However, heparin does not inactivate fibrin-bound thrombin. Heparin also inactivates clotting factors IXa and Xa. In addition to being an anticoagulant, heparin also indirectly inhibits platelets because thrombin is a potent platelet stimulator.

Heparin binds to plasma proteins, blood cells, and endothelial cells. This nonspecific binding to plasma proteins and endothelial cells limits the bioavailability of the drug at low doses and also contributes to its variable response between patients. Heparin is commonly administered intravenously, using a weight-based protocol to help control anticoagulation response. Heparin can also be administered subcutaneously, and prophylactic doses are generally administered per this route. Weight-based heparin dosing reaches the therapeutic goal more consistently than standard therapy (Woo & Robinson, 2016). It is not absorbed from the gastrointestinal tract, so it cannot be given orally.

The anticoagulation effects of intravenous (IV) heparin are almost instantaneous. Activated partial thromboplastin time (aPTT) is used to monitor the therapeutic effectiveness and safety range of heparin. A baseline aPTT, prothrombin time (PT), International Normalized Ratio (INR), platelet count, hemoglobin level, and hematocrit should be drawn before heparin is started. The goal is to have aPTT at 1.5 times the control. A therapeutic aPTT should be reached within 24 hours of the initiation of therapy. aPTT results should be measured 6 hours after the dose is initiated and again 6 hours after any dose change. After two therapeutic aPTTs have been achieved, measurements can be obtained every 24 hours (Kearon et al., 2016).

Low-Molecular-Weight Heparin. Low-molecular-weight heparin (LMWH) is smaller in size than and is derived from heparin. It works by accelerating the activity of antithrombin III. LMWH has a more potent effect on factor Xa than on factor IIa, although both are inhibited. LMWH produces less inhibition of platelets than does UFH.

LMWH binds less to plasma proteins and endothelial cells than heparin does. It also has a longer half-life, which helps to produce a sustained and more predictable anticoagulation effect. For this reason, clotting times do not need to be monitored as they do with the use of heparin. If needed, antifactor Xa levels can be drawn 4 hours after a subcutaneous dose. At recommended doses, PT and aPTT are not greatly affected. LMWH is administered subcutaneously, either daily or twice a day, depending on the clinical indication (Woo & Robinson, 2016). The following points should be included in patient education for self-administration:

LMWH administration:

- The full length of the half-inch prepackaged needle should be injected.

- The anterolateral or posterolateral walls of the abdomen should be used.

- The skin fold should be held until the needle is fully withdrawn.

- Injection sites should be rotated frequently.

- Injection sites should not be massaged.

Warfarin administration:

- Use an electric shaver.

- Use a soft-bristle toothbrush.

- Wear protective gear while working outside (full shoes and gardening gloves).

- Avoid contact sports.

- Store in a cool, dry place away from light. (It loses its potency when exposed to high heat [Woo & Robinson, 2016].)

Direct Thrombin Inhibitors. Direct thrombin inhibitors have an advantage over heparin because they have the ability to inactivate fibrin-bound thrombin, thereby improving the antithrombotic effect. These medications also bind less to plasma proteins and produce a more reliable anticoagulant effect. Direct thrombin inhibitors include desirudin, bivalirudin, argatroban, and the newest oral formulation, dabigatran.

Factor Xa Inhibitors. Factor Xa inhibitors are a new class of anticoagulant that produces antithrombotic action by neutralizing factor Xa and interrupting the clotting cascade leading to thrombin formation. This class of medications does not inhibit thrombin (factor IIa). Administration is via once-daily subcutaneous injection, and there is no need for laboratory monitoring because bleeding time is not greatly altered. One dose can cover a wide range of body weights. Medications in this class include apixaban, fondaparinux, and rivaroxaban.

Warfarin. Warfarin (Coumadin) is an oral anticoagulant agent. Like heparin, warfarin does not affect existing clots. One of the important actions of warfarin is the inhibition of the synthesis of factor II (prothrombin). Warfarin acts indirectly through the liver by altering the synthesis of other vitamin K-dependent factors in the extrinsic pathway. The vitamin K-dependent factors are left biologically inactive. The medication is also known as a vitamin K antagonist. Vitamin K is essential for the liver to manufacture several clotting factors, including factors II, VII, IX, and X.

There is a lag time of anywhere from 2 to 5 days, most typically 3 to 4 days, to reach a therapeutic level. The reason for this lag time is gradual disappearance of the clotting factors involved. At full therapeutic doses, vitamin K-dependent clotting factors decrease by up to 50%. PT and INR should be monitored to evaluate effectiveness and safety. INR was developed to correct problems with standardization of anticoagulation intensity. INR relates the patient's PT to the intensity of actual coagulation. Hemorrhagic complications of warfarin use have decreased with the use of INR as the standard to monitor PT and guide dosing. Baseline PT and INR should be drawn before initiation of therapy (Kearon et al., 2016).

Dosing usually starts at 5 mg/day. Loading doses are not recommended because time is required to gradually deplete existing clotting factors. Bolus dosing initially may result in excessive anticoagulation after clotting factors are depleted. PT and INR are monitored daily until a therapeutic level is reached. The dosage may need adjustment after 4 to 6 days because of individual sensitivity. After a therapeutic response (INR of 2.0 to 3.0 in most situations) is achieved, PT and INR are usually drawn twice weekly during the first 2 weeks of therapy. They are then drawn on a weekly basis for the remainder of the first 2 months of therapy and are monitored every 4 to 6 weeks on an ongoing basis for the duration of therapy (Kearon et al., 2016).

Patients who are taking warfarin should include this information in their personal identification. Consistency in diet is important, especially with foods that are known to be high in vitamin K. For example, if a patient likes certain foods high in vitamin K, then it is important that his or her diet consistently contain these

foods while warfarin dosing is being adjusted. Sudden or sporadic intake of high-vitamin K foods can alter clotting times. Foods with a moderate to high content of vitamin K are listed in Table 4-8.

Indication

Heparin. Heparin is the anticoagulant of choice for many conditions, including acute MI, pulmonary embolism (PE), and deep vein thrombosis (DVT). In the pathophysiological processes of atherosclerosis and acute coronary syndromes (ACSs), endothelial injury results in thrombi, platelet aggregation, and vasoconstric-

TABLE 4-8: FOODS WITH MODERATE TO HIGH CONTENT OF VITAMIN K

- Brussels sprouts
- Lettuce
- Avocado
- Kale
- Cabbage
- Green tea
- Broccoli
- Green onions
- Liver
- Collard greens
- Cauliflower
- Soybeans
- Mustard greens
- Certain peas
- Soybean oil
- Certain beans
- Parsley
- Turnip greens
- Beet greens
- Dandelion greens
- Spinach (especially when frozen)

Note. Adapted from Woo, T. M., & Robinson, M. V. (2016). *Pharmacotherapeutics for advanced practice nurse prescribers* (4th ed.). Philadelphia, PA: F. A. Davis.

tion. Fibrinogen is ultimately converted to fibrin to produce a fibrin stable clot. The role of heparin in these conditions is to prevent thrombus formation.

Low-Molecular-Weight Heparin. Enoxaparin, a form of LMWH, was first approved by the U.S. Food and Drug Administration (FDA) for DVT prevention in patients undergoing orthopedic surgery. In 1998, enoxaparin received approval for use in the treatment of UA and non-STEMI. Current guidelines indicate the use of a heparin infusion for the patient diagnosed with STEMI who will be undergoing percutaneous intervention (O'Gara et al., 2013). The use of LMWH and heparin continues to be studied in the ACS population undergoing early invasive treatment.

Direct Thrombin Inhibitors. Direct thrombin inhibitors are indicated for the treatment of thrombosis in patients with heparin-induced thrombocytopenia (HIT) and those undergoing percutaneous coronary intervention. Argatroban is a synthetic direct thrombin inhibitor that is indicated for the treatment and prevention of HIT and associated thromboembolic events. Bivalirudin is a synthetic direct thrombin inhibitor that is indicated in ACS for non-STEMI and STEMI. This medication is indicated as an alternative to heparin in all patients, not just patients with, or at risk for, HIT (Kearon et al., 2016).

Dabigatran (Pradaxa) is an oral direct thrombin inhibitor agent and may be used in select patients with atrial fibrillation as an alternative to warfarin. It is also approved for use in DVT/PE treatment and prevention. This new agent is approved for use in nonvalvular atrial fibrillation only in patients with at least one other risk factor for stroke. A therapeutic effect is achieved in 1 hour. The half-life is approximately 13 hours, and for this reason it is dosed twice daily. Dabigatran is out of the system in 1 to 2 days if renal function is normal. Dosing is adjusted to a low dose in patients with renal

dysfunction. Patients who are taking dabigatran do not have to have routine monitoring for clotting times (Kearon et al., 2016).

Factor Xa Inhibitors. Fondaparinux was the first FDA-approved medication in the factor Xa inhibitor class. Fondaparinux is approved for DVT and PE prophylaxis in patients undergoing hip or abdominal surgery. It is also approved for the treatment of DVT or PE in conjunction with warfarin. Fondaparinux is an anticoagulant alternative in patients with non-STEMI. Fondaparinux is not approved as the sole anticoagulant in patients undergoing percutaneous coronary intervention because it does not exhibit potent enough antithrombin activity (Kearon et al., 2016). Novel agents such as apixaban (Eliquis) and rivaroxaban (Xarelto) have also been found to be effective and safe treatments for DVT and PE prophylaxis for patients undergoing orthopedic surgeries, DVT and PE treatment, and as primary stroke prophylaxis with nonvalvular atrial fibrillation (Leung, 2016).

Warfarin. Patients with mechanical prosthetic valves need INRs of 2.5 to 3.5 or 2.0 to 3.0, depending on the location and type of implanted valve. It takes approximately 4 days to return to normal coagulation after warfarin is discontinued. Chronic conditions such as atrial fibrillation, with certain risk factors for stroke, require lifelong therapy. Warfarin reduces the risk for embolic stroke in patients with atrial fibrillation by 65% to 70%. Acute conditions, such as PE and DVT, usually require at least 6 months of therapy. A patient who had an acute MI with a resultant left ventricular thrombus also needs to be on warfarin for at least 6 months (Kearon et al., 2016).

Side Effects

Heparin. In addition to weight, other patient variables affect aPTT. The aPTT response for a given dose of heparin increases with age and decreases in patients who have diabetes and in those who smoke (Woo & Robinson, 2016). Bleeding is an obvious potential complication of heparin administration. Heparin is partially cleared via the kidneys, and increased bleeding can occur in patients with renal dysfunction. The optimal period that heparin can be continued is not yet defined. Most clinical trials involving heparin have continued administration for 2 to 5 days. An aPTT should be drawn with any change in patient condition, and heparin should be immediately discontinued when bleeding is the suspected cause. Patients should have baseline laboratory work drawn before therapy is initiated, including aPTT, PT/INR, complete blood count, and platelets. Hemoglobin level, hematocrit, and platelet count are drawn on a daily basis. Heparin can cause mild to severe thrombocytopenia (platelet count less than 150,000/mm^3). Heparin should be discontinued if platelets fall to less than 100,000/mm^3. The half-life of heparin is very short. If reversal is needed, protamine is the antidote (Kearon et al., 2016).

Mild thrombocytopenia occurs in 10% to 20% of patients, whereas more severe thrombocytopenia occurs in only 1% to 2% of patients. Thrombocytopenia generally occurs 4 to 14 days after initiation of heparin therapy. A rare, but very severe, form of thrombocytopenia, HIT, can occur, resulting in thrombosis. When HIT develops, it is a result of an autoimmune response. These patients should *never* receive heparin, not even the small doses of heparin used in solutions to flush invasive lines (Kearon et al., 2016).

Low-Molecular-Weight Heparin. LMWH is associated with a lower incidence of HIT, but a higher rate of minor bleeding, than is UFH. LMWH is renally cleared, and special dosing is required for patients with chronic renal insufficiency. The half-life of LMWH is much longer than UFH at 4 to 6 hours. Protamine is effective in reversing 60% of the drug (Kearon et al., 2016).

Warfarin. Warfarin is primarily bound to albumin in the blood; very little of it circulates freely. It is, however, the freely circulating amount that produces a therapeutic value. The number of potential drug interactions is high because of the large amount of protein-bound warfarin. Patient education regarding warfarin use is very important, and patient compliance is critical. Patients who are not reliable with medication administration may not be acceptable candidates for warfarin therapy. Patients should be taught to recognize less obvious signs and symptoms of bleeding, such as black, tarry stools. They should also be instructed to report any signs of bleeding, including bleeding gums, epistaxis, and increased bruising. Patients should also be instructed about necessary safety precautions to avoid bleeding (Kearon et al., 2016).

The most common side effect observed with dabigatran is dyspepsia. There have been no reports of HIT with factor Xa inhibitors (Kearon et al., 2016).

Contraindications

All anticoagulants are contraindicated with major active bleeding or if the patient is at high risk for bleeding such as after recent surgery. Uncontrolled hypertension increases the risk for bleeding with these medications as well, so they must be used with caution. Drug-specific considerations are discussed in the following subsections.

Factor Xa Inhibitors. Because of renal clearance, fondaparinux is contraindicated in severe renal dysfunction. Xarelto and apixaban are contraindicated for acute PE if there is hemodynamic instability or requirement of thrombolysis or embolectomy. They are also not to be used in Child-Pugh Class C hepatic impairment. Currently, no agents have been approved by the FDA for their reversal.

Direct Thrombin Inhibitors: Dabigatran is contraindicated in patients with mechanical heart valves or active major bleeding. The FDA has approved a reversal agent for the anticoagulation effect of dabigatran: Idarucizumab can be used for the emergent reversal of dabigatran in patients with life-threatening bleeding or who require emergent surgery (Leung, 2016).

Warfarin. Patients who have malignant hypertension, coagulopathies, or history of bleeding are not candidates for warfarin therapy. Those who abuse alcohol or engage in activities with a high risk for trauma are not candidates either. Many drugs interact with warfarin to alter clotting time. Patients need to be instructed to inform every physician they see, including their dentists, that they are taking warfarin. They also need to be instructed to avoid the use of over-the-counter medications unless approved by a physician. Over-the-counter medications that contain aspirin, ibuprofen, or naproxen should always be avoided by those taking warfarin. Warfarin does cross the placenta and is a known teratogen that can cause birth defects. Women of childbearing age should be counseled about effective birth control and potential risks to the unborn child if pregnancy should occur (Kearon et al., 2016).

Antiplatelets

Antiplatelets are drugs that decrease platelet activity. These drugs do not have a direct effect on the coagulation cascade. Similar to anticoagulants, new antiplatelet medications are emerging. These subclasses are discussed separately in this section.

Mechanism of Action

Glycoprotein IIb/IIIa Inhibitors. The three intravenous GP IIb/IIIa inhibitors currently used include abciximab (ReoPro), eptifibatide (Integrilin), and tirofiban (Aggrastat). All three of these medications interfere with the final pathway of platelet aggregation. They inhibit GP IIb/IIIa receptors, where platelets and fibrinogen bind to form a fibrin mesh. GP IIb/IIIa receptors are abundant on platelet surfaces; there are estimations of 50,000 to 80,000 receptors per platelet (Woo & Robinson, 2016). When platelets are activated, a change occurs in their receptors that increases their affinity to bind to fibrinogen. Fibrinogen links to these receptors and simultaneously binds receptors on two separate platelets. Platelet cross-linking occurs, leading to platelet aggregation. These medications actually occupy the receptors and prevent fibrinogen binding, thereby inhibiting platelet aggregation.

GP IIb/IIIa inhibitors are administered intravenously and may be administered concomitantly with aspirin, clopidogrel, and heparin. UFH is typically used, and doses are reduced when given with GP IIb/IIIa inhibitors because of their effectiveness in blocking thrombin-induced platelet aggregation.

Abciximab (ReoPro) was the first FDA-approved GP IIb/IIIa inhibitor. It has a short half-life, which is balanced by a very strong affinity for receptors. Abciximab can block more than 80% of GP IIb/IIIa receptors. It also blocks other receptors and can produce an anticoagulation effect. Some of its receptor occupation can last for up to 10 days. Platelet aggregation gradually returns to normal 24 to 48 hours after the medication is discontinued. Eptifibatide and tirofiban generally exhibit effects consistent with their plasma levels. Their half-lives are approximately 2 to 3 hours, and platelet aggregation returns to normal within 4 to 8 hours of stopping the medication. When given alone, eptifibatide and tirofiban have no effect on PT or aPTT (Capodanno & Angiolillo, 2013).

Adenosine Diphosphate Inhibitors (P2Y12 inhibitors). Clopidogrel (Plavix) is a thienopyridine derivative that is approved by the FDA for prevention of atherosclerotic events. It inhibits the P2Y12 component of adenosine diphosphate receptors. Adenosine diphosphate activates the GP IIb/IIIa receptors. Clopidogrel irreversibly inhibits the binding of adenosine diphosphate to platelet receptors, and thereby prevents adenosine diphosphate from activating the GP IIb/IIIa receptors. Clopidogrel causes platelet inhibition for the life of the platelet, which is approximately 10 days. Dose-dependent inhibition of platelet aggregation is seen 2 hours after a single oral dose. With repeated daily doses, maximal inhibition of platelet aggregation (up to 60%) occurs in 3 to 7 days. Bleeding time gradually returns to normal approximately 5 days after the drug is discontinued (Capodanno & Angiolillo, 2013).

Prasugrel is a newer agent in the same class as clopidogrel. Prasugrel has been shown to reduce ischemic complications compared with clopidogrel (Capodanno & Angiolillo, 2013). Another newer agent to consider with similar labeling and indications is ticagrelor.

NURSING APPLICATION

Clopidogrel, prasugrel, and ticagrelor are substantially more expensive than aspirin. Because these medications interfere with platelet function and are absolutely crucial in the acute time after percutaneous coronary intervention, it is important for patients to understand the added benefit of these P2Y12 inhibitors to assure compliance. It is also important before discharge to assess for any financial barriers that may limit the patient's ability to comply with treatment. Financial assistance may be available through Partnership for Prescription Assistance (http://www.pparx.org).

Aspirin. Aspirin was first introduced into medicine more than 115 years ago. Since then, it has been widely used for its many therapeutic benefits, including its anti-inflammatory, analgesic, antipyretic, and antithrombotic effects. Aspirin doses ranging from 81 mg to 325 mg are prescribed routinely in most patients with acute and chronic ischemic heart disease (Capodanno & Angiolillo, 2013).

Aspirin works by inhibiting cyclo-oxygenase and inhibiting the synthesis of thromboxane A2. Thromboxane A2 is a potent vasoconstrictor and platelet agonist that is released as a result of vascular injury. Aspirin produces a rapid antiplatelet and vasodilative effect by the immediate inhibition of thromboxane A2 production. Aspirin also inhibits endothelial production of prostaglandin I2. Prostaglandin I2 produces vasodilatation and inhibits platelet aggregation. However, the effects of inhibiting thromboxane A2 dominate over the effects of prostaglandin I2 inhibition. Aspirin appears to affect platelet function for the life of the platelet and results in prolonged bleeding time. Aspirin may also protect low-density lipoprotein cholesterol from the oxidation process and improve endothelial dysfunction. Chewing of aspirin can accelerate absorption into the blood during an acute cardiac event (Capodanno & Angiolillo, 2013).

Indication

Adenosine Diphosphate Inhibitors (P2Y12 inhibitors). Clopidogrel, prasugrel, and ticagrelor are all indicated in the secondary prevention of thrombotic events in patients with UA, non-STEMI, or STEMI managed with percutaneous coronary intervention (Griffin, Kapadia, & Rimmerman, 2013). Historically they have been recommended for at least 12 months with drug-eluding stent or 30 days with bare metal stent to decrease the risk for development of in-stent thrombosis. Longer therapy is sometimes indicated in high-risk patients. Clopidogrel can be used in patients who are allergic to aspirin (Capodanno & Angiolillo, 2013).

Aspirin. Aspirin reduces risk in both primary and secondary prevention of cardiovascular disease and reduces adverse cardiovascular events by an average of 33%. In patients with UA, aspirin decreases short-term and long-term risks for fatal and nonfatal MI. Aspirin is specifically indicated after coronary artery bypass graft surgery for multiple reasons. It prevents early saphenous vein graft closure and is also effective in reducing postoperative MI, stroke, renal failure, and bowel infarction. Aspirin also reduces subsequent mortality. Aspirin must be given within 48 hours of surgery to achieve the maximal benefit of postoperative aspirin use. Aspirin is continued indefinitely postoperatively (Capodanno & Angiolillo, 2013; Woo & Robinson, 2016).

Side Effects

Glycoprotein IIb/IIIa Inhibitors. GP IIb/IIIa inhibitors (such as eptifibatide [Integrilin]) increase the risk for bleeding, which typically occurs at the vascular access site. Platelet count and hemoglobin level should be monitored during the use of GP IIb/IIIa inhibitors. However, thrombocytopenia is not a common complication.

Adenosine Diphosphate Inhibitors (P2Y12 inhibitors). Prasugrel is associated with a higher risk for bleeding in comparison with clopidogrel, particularly in patients with small body size (<60 kg) and in those 75 years of age and older. The usual maintenance dose of prasugrel is 10 mg, but lower doses should be considered in patients with a higher risk for bleeding (Capodanno & Angiolillo, 2013). All P2Y12 inhibitors can cause bleeding, headache, and nausea.

Aspirin. Decreased prostaglandin synthesis with aspirin is responsible for GI side effects such as nausea, ulceration, or bleeding. Aspirin also causes direct irritation of the GI tract.

Enteric-coated aspirin can help minimize this common side effect.

Contraindications

GP IIb/IIIa Inhibitors. GP IIb/IIIa inhibitors are contraindicated when a patient has a history of internal bleeding such as with an intracranial hemorrhage or neoplasm. They should also be avoided with histories of hypersensitivity reactions, stroke, thrombocytopenia, arteriovenous malformation or cerebral aneurysm, severe hypertension, aortic dissection, or acute pericarditis (Woo & Robinson, 2016).

Adenosine Diphosphate Inhibitors (P2Y12 inhibitors). All drugs in this class are contraindicated in patients with hypersensitivity to the active drug or with active bleeding, either gastrointestinal or intracranial. Patients who are taking clopidogrel should avoid the use of omeprazole (Prilosec). When omeprazole is taken with clopidogrel, the ability of clopidogrel to block platelet aggregation is cut in half; this happens because clopidogrel does not become effective until it is metabolized into its active form by the liver enzyme CYP2C19. Omeprazole blocks this enzyme and therefore reduces the effectiveness of clopidogrel. The effectiveness of clopidogrel is also diminished in patients who are poor metabolizers. The reason for poor metabolism in some patients is the genetic differences in the liver enzyme CYP2C19. Tests are available to identify patients who are poor metabolizers. After they are identified, alternate antiplatelet therapy or altered dosing may be indicated. Prasugrel is contraindicated in patients with a history of stroke or transient ischemic attack (Capodanno & Angiolillo, 2013).

Aspirin. Contraindications to aspirin administration include an aspirin allergy, history of GI bleeding, and coagulation disorders.

APPLYING PHARMACO-THERAPEUTICS TO HEMODYNAMIC ALTERATIONS

Hemodynamic alterations are conditions that compromise the maintenance of adequate cardiac output. These conditions can affect one or more of the components of heart rate and stroke volume. Although antiarrhythmics are discussed in an earlier section, the medications addressed in this section are discussed as therapies with direct action on heart rate, preload, afterload, and contractility.

Pharmacology to Alter Preload

Preload is the stretch on the ventricle at the end of diastole. The volume of blood in the ventricle causes this stretch. Optimal preload is necessary for optimal cardiac performance.

Increasing Preload

When preload is too low, cardiac output decreases. Hemorrhagic shock is an example of a clinical situation in which preload drops acutely. Preload is also low when an extracellular fluid deficit exists because of dehydration or when excessive venous vasodilation occurs. When venous vasodilation occurs, blood is pulled away from the heart and preload decreases. The pharmacological options for increasing preload are outlined in Table 4-9.

Decreasing Preload

When preload is too high, a stretch beyond normal physiological limits can cause a decrease in the force of contraction. In addition, increased preload causes an increase in myocardial oxygen demand. Patients with heart failure are at risk for having extracellular fluid overload and may need therapy acutely and on a continual basis to decrease preload. Table 4-10 outlines the pharmacological options for decreasing preload (Manaker, 2014).

Pharmacology to Alter Afterload

Afterload is the resistance that the ventricle must overcome to eject its contents. Systemic vascular resistance measures left ventricular afterload. Systemic vascular resistance also plays a major role in maintaining blood pressure.

Increasing Afterload

An increase in afterload is not a desired effect in patients with heart disease; therefore, medications to increase afterload are given only in emergency situations. For example, medications to increase afterload are indicated when hypotension is unresponsive to fluids or other treatment and blood pressure is dangerously low. Pharmacological options for increasing afterload are listed in Table 4-11. *Vasopressors* is the term given to medications used to increase afterload (Manaker, 2014).

TABLE 4-9: PHARMACOLOGICAL CONSIDERATIONS FOR INCREASING PRELOAD	
Options	Specific Agents/Key Information
1. Administer extracellular fluid expander.	• Isotonic crystalloids, such as 0.9% sodium chloride and lactated Ringer's solution • Colloids, such as albumin, dextran, and hetastarch • Blood or blood products
2. Decrease dose or stop drugs that cause venous vasodilation.	• Nitroglycerin, nesiritide, and morphine sulfate (venous vasodilation pools blood away from the heart and decreases preload)

Note. From Western Schools.

TABLE 4-10: PHARMACOLOGICAL CONSIDERATIONS FOR DECREASING PRELOAD

Options	Specific Agents/Key Information
1. Fluid restriction	• Fluid restriction should be considered (in patients without significant hyponatremia) who demonstrate increased preload that is uncontrolled without sodium restriction or diuretic therapy.
2. Diuretics	• Loop diuretics such as furosemide reduce extracellular circulating volume.
3. Angiotensin-converting enzyme inhibitors (ACEIs)	• ACEIs interfere with the physiological response of the renin-angiotensin-aldosterone system (aldosterone secretion decreases, as do sodium and water retention). • ACEIs end in "pril," such as captopril.
4. Aldosterone antagonists	• Examples include spironolactone and eplerenone. • They directly block aldosterone and decrease sodium and water retention.
5. Venous vasodilators	• Examples include intravenous nitroglycerin, nesiritide, and morphine sulfate (venous vasodilation pools blood away from the heart and decreases preload).

Note. Adapted from Griffin, B. P., Kapadia, S. R., & Rimmerman, C. M. (2013). *Cleveland Clinic cardiology board review* (2nd ed.). Philadelphia, PA: Lippincott Williams & Wilkins.

TABLE 4-11: PHARMACOLOGICAL CONSIDERATIONS FOR INCREASING AFTERLOAD

Options	Specific Agents/Key Information
1. Sympathomimetics to stimulate the alpha receptors of the sympathetic nervous system	• Dopamine (at higher doses) • Norepinephrine • Phenylephrine • Epinephrine (at higher doses)
2. Arginine vasopressin (antidiuretic hormone)	• Vasoconstrictive and antidiuretic effect • Promotes reabsorption of water • Restores catecholamine sensitivity • Use as add-on to another vasopressor to increase efficacy and decrease initial drug choice requirement (not first-line)

Note. Adapted from Dellinger, R. P., Levy, M. M., Rhodes, A., Annane, D., Gerlach, H., Opal, S. M., ... Moreno, R. (2013). Surviving sepsis campaign: International guidelines for management of severe sepsis and septic shock: 2012. *Critical Care Medicine, 41*(2), 580. doi:10.1097/CCM.0b013e31827e83af

Hollenberg, S. M. (2011). Vasoactive drugs in circulatory shock. *American Journal of Respiratory and Critical Care Medicine, 183,* 847. doi:10.1164/rccm.201006-0972CI

Decreasing Afterload

High afterload impedes cardiac output and also increases myocardial oxygen demand. Decreasing afterload is a goal of therapy for all patients with heart failure, left ventricular dysfunction, and hypertension. Table 4-12 lists a variety of pharmacological options used in the reduction of afterload (Liu et al., 2015; Manaker, 2014; Nappi & Sieg, 2011).

Pharmacology to Alter Contractility

Contractility is the actual ability of the ventricle to contract independently of preload or afterload. However, in clinical practice, alterations in preload and afterload have an impact on contractility. In addition, other systemic factors, such as acid-base balance and electrolyte levels, can also affect contractility. Contractility is known to be impaired in cardiac patients who have left ventricular dysfunction and low ejection fractions.

Increasing Contractility

Inotropes are medications that increase contractility (see Table 4-13). Patients who have significant left ventricular dysfunction may need the support of an intravenous inotrope to increase contractility if they are unable to maintain a cardiac output sufficient to meet the demands of the body. Patients in acute cardiogenic shock or patients in end-stage heart failure have known left ventricular dysfunction. Because inotropic agents substantially increase myocardial oxygen demand, it is important to correct problems with preload or afterload before administering an inotropic agent to improve cardiac output (Manaker, 2014).

Decreasing Contractility

Oral medications are commonly prescribed with the intent to decrease contractility and, therefore, decrease myocardial oxygen demand. However, intravenous forms of said medications can be prescribed in acute situations as well. A common indication for these medications is angina. Options for decreasing contractility are listed in Table 4-14 (Manaker, 2014; Woo & Robinson, 2016).

TABLE 4-12: PHARMACOLOGICAL CONSIDERATIONS FOR DECREASING AFTERLOAD

Options	Specific Agents/Key Information
1. Smooth muscle relaxants	• Nitroprusside • Hydralazine
2. Calcium channel blockers	• Dihydropyridine calcium channel blockers (ending in "ine"), such as amlodipine, have strong arterial vasodilator properties
3. Alpha-receptor blockers	• Labetalol (combination alpha and beta blocker) • Prazosin and terazosin
4. Angiotensin-converting enzyme inhibitors	• Interrupt the renin-angiotensin-aldosterone system and limit production of angiotensin II, a potent arterial vasoconstrictor • Medications ending in "pril"
5. Angiotensin II-receptor blockers	• Directly block the effects of angiotensin II • Medications ending in "sartan," such as valsartan
6. Phosphodiesterase inhibitors	• Milrinone (used as an IV inotrope but also has arterial vasodilator properties)

Note. Adapted from Griffin, B. P., Kapadia, S. R., & Rimmerman, C. M. (2013). *Cleveland Clinic cardiology board review* (2nd ed.). Philadelphia, PA: Lippincott Williams & Wilkins.

TABLE 4-13: PHARMACOLOGICAL CONSIDERATIONS FOR INCREASING CONTRACTILITY (INOTROPES)

Options	Specific Agents/Key Information
1. Sympathomimetics that stimulate the beta-1 receptors of the sympathetic nervous system	• Dobutamine (most commonly used because it is a predominant beta-1 stimulator) • Other sympathomimetics may have inotropic properties, even if not used primarily for an inotropic purpose
2. Phosphodiesterase inhibitors	• Milrinone (used as an IV inotrope but also has arterial and venous vasodilator properties)
3. Cardiac glycosides	• Digoxin (weak inotrope and is never used intravenously to support left ventricular dysfunction; exerts weak inotropic properties when given orally)

Note. Adapted from Griffin, B. P., Kapadia, S. R., & Rimmerman, C. M. (2013). *Cleveland Clinic cardiology board review* (2nd ed.). Philadelphia, PA: Lippincott Williams & Wilkins.

Pharmacology to Alter Heart Rate

Cardiac output can be calculated as heart rate multiplied by stroke volume. Increasing heart rate can be an effective strategy for increasing cardiac output. However, if heart rate becomes too rapid, the ventricles do not have time to adequately fill, and cardiac output decreases.

Increasing Heart Rate

In clinical practice, heart rate is only intentionally increased to improve cardiac output when it is less than the normal rate and the patient is symptomatic. If heart rate is normal, it is not increased to a faster rate to increase cardiac output because an increase in heart rate also produces an increase in myocardial oxygen demand. Pharmacological options for increasing heart rate are listed in Table 4-15 (Manaker, 2014).

Decreasing Heart Rate

During a dysrhythmia in which the heart rate is high and the patient is symptomatic, medications can be used to decrease heart rate. Medications that decrease heart rate are also given to patients with normal heart rates when there is a desire to further decrease myocardial oxygen demand. Patients with angina often take medications that reduce their heart rates to decrease myocardial oxygen demand and prevent symptoms. Table 4-16 describes the pharmacological options for decreasing heart rate (Manaker, 2014; Woo & Robinson, 2016).

NURSING APPLICATION

Many oral agents manipulate the components of cardiac output and myocardial oxygen demand. Nurses should consider the hemodynamic impact of oral medications used in chronic conditions as well as the hemodynamic impact of intravenous medications used in acute conditions.

TABLE 4-14: PHARMACOLOGICAL CONSIDERATIONS FOR DECREASING CONTRACTILITY

Options	Specific Agents/Key Information
1. Beta blockers that block the beta-1 receptors of the sympathetic nervous system	• Metoprolol • Carvedilol • "olol" medications
2. Calcium channel blockers	• Metoprolol • Carvedilol [crossed out] *diltiazem* • "olol" medications

Medications that block beta-1 receptors may also have properties that cause beta-2 and alpha-receptor blockade.

Note. From Western Schools.

TABLE 4-15: PHARMACOLOGICAL CONSIDERATIONS FOR INCREASING HEART RATE

Options	Specific Agents/Key Information
1. Parasympatholytics (lysis of the parasympathetic nervous system)	• Atropine (most commonly used pharmacological agent to increase heart rate)
2. Sympathomimetics that stimulate the beta-1 receptors of the sympathetic nervous system	• Epinephrine • Dopamine

Medications that block beta-1 receptors may also have properties that cause beta-2 and alpha-receptor blockade.

Note. From Western Schools.

TABLE 4-16: PHARMACOLOGICAL CONSIDERATIONS FOR DECREASING HEART RATE	
Options	**Specific Agents/Key Information**
1. Beta blockers that block the beta-1 receptors of the sympathetic nervous system	• Metoprolol and carvedilol • "lol" medications • Class II antiarrhythmics[a]
2. Calcium channel blockers	• Diltiazem and verapamil • Class IV antiarrhythmics[a]
3. Cardiac glycosides	• Digoxin
4. Unclassified antiarrhythmics	• Adenosine (slows or stops conduction through the atrioventricular node)
5. Other antiarrhythmics	• Class I and III antiarrhythmics[a] • Used to establish or maintain a normal rhythm and therefore control heart rate

[a]Vaughan Williams classification system.

Note. Adapted from Griffin, B. P., Kapadia, S. R., & Rimmerman, C. M. (2013). *Cleveland Clinic cardiology board review* (2nd ed.). Philadelphia, PA: Lippincott Williams & Wilkins.

CONSIDERATIONS FOR SPECIAL POPULATIONS

Pregnancy

Multiple anatomical and physiological changes occur in the pregnant female. These changes can impact drug absorption and clearance. Some of the physiological changes to consider when prescribing cardiovascular medications to pregnant women include the common conditions associated with pregnancy, such as iron-deficiency anemia, vitamin deficiencies, and changes in her dietary preferences she may not have when not pregnant. These changes can interact or interfere with medications prescribed for cardiovascular conditions during pregnancy (Woo & Robinson, 2016).

Older Adult

One of the primary pharmacological issues in aging is polypharmacy. Prescribing multiple medications for the treatment of multiple medical problems is not always considered to be the best treatment regimen for the older adult. Given the many pharmacokinetic changes that occur with aging, the cliché of "less is more" or "start low and go slow" applies to the use of pharmacological therapies for the older adult population. The aging process involves decreased kidney and liver function, decreased serum albumin levels, and increased total body fat, which can all negatively impact drug absorption, metabolism, and excretion. In addition to the pharmacokinetic changes, the clinician must also consider the pharmacodynamic changes that can occur in older adults. For instance, because of the progressive decline in counterregulatory mechanisms and altered receptor sensitivity associated with aging, older adults are more sensitive to some medications and they are less sensitive to other medications. This means that the clinician's evaluation may find that the older person's response is blunted or exaggerated (Woo & Robinson, 2016).

EMERGING SCIENCE

Pharmacogenomics is the study of how an individual's genes affect that person's response to a drug. As more and more research is performed in this area, explanations for the inferior responses of some drugs are being associated with specific variations of individuals' genes.

Pharmacogenomics in Cardiovascular Disease

Emerging science in pharmacogenomic applications of treatment for cardiovascular disorders surrounds a patient's genetic variations negatively affecting therapeutic responses and dosing. Studies have shown as much as 25% of patients who take clopidogrel have a subtherapeutic antiplatelet response secondary to genetic variations that negatively affects the metabolism of the medication. Warfarin is another medication in which the mechanism of action is altered secondary to the genetic variations of patient. These variations in a patient's genes influence drug dosing, thereby increasing the risks associated with underdosing or overdosing the medication. In the case of clopidogrel, this effect may involve the restenosis of a coronary stent. In the case of the anticoagulant warfarin being underdosed, the risk for thrombotic events increases. Patients found to have not achieved the therapeutic effect of medications like those described earlier should be considered for genetic testing. In some instances, physicians choose to perform genetic testing for gene variations before the start of the medication when in the primary care setting (Cappola & Margulies, 2011).

Novel Medication

While studying other applications of functional genomics in cardiovascular disease, researchers found elevated levels of an inotropic neurohormone called *apelin*. Apelin is an endogenous peptide that is important in the regulation of hypertension-induced pathology such as myocardial hypertrophy and aortic remodeling (Zhong et al., 2015). Apelin is also thought to enhance myocardial insulin resistance during myocardial injury. In many studies

the enhanced insulin resistance is thought to be the mechanism that affords some patients with diabetes to have cardioprotective benefits of their disease, but this remains poorly understood (Zhang et al., 2015). Developmental research to determine the potential of exogenous apelin as a safe and effective novel heart failure and hypertension therapy is ongoing. As new discoveries continue to emerge, expectations for pharmacogenomics applications to cardiovascular conditions will continue to grow and will have a transformational impact on cardiovascular research and practice (Cappola & Margulies, 2011; Woo & Robinson, 2016).

CASE STUDY

History of Present Illness

A 49-year-old male patient, who is accompanied by his wife, presents to the primary care clinic with a report of earlier chest pain, which he felt after shoveling snow that same morning. The patient states the pain was moderate to severe in intensity and was located in the center of his chest with radiation to his jaw and left arm. The patient reports the chest pain lasted about five to ten minutes and was relieved with rest and two nitroglycerin tablets. The patient describes feeling dizzy and very anxious while experiencing the pain. The patient's wife adds that her husband was breathing rapidly and had a pale color during the episode.

Prior to this morning, the patient reports that the only other time he has felt this kind of pain was three years ago. At that time he was diagnosed with stress-induced angina and was prescribed the nitroglycerin tablets, which he has only had to take about two times in the past year. The patient tells the nurse practitioner that he did not report these two episodes to his cardiologist.

Past Medical History

The patient has a medical history of dyslipidemia, hypertension, and exercise-induced asthma. He was prescribed fenofibrate, atenolol, and albuterol to manage these medical problems. The patient and his wife are compliant with a low-cholesterol and low salt diet. The patient admits to a 20 pack year history of smoking, but he is currently weaning himself to a complete tobacco cessation quit date, for which he has planned in two months. He denies using alcohol or illicit drugs, and having any prior surgical history. His mother died while he was a child, but his father is currently 89 years old with a medical history of hypertension, coronary artery disease (CAD), and hypothyroidism. The patient's brother is currently 44 years old with hypertension and CAD as well. The patient also has a sister who is 41 years old with dyslipidemia and hypertension.

Physical Exam Findings

The nurse practitioner records these patient findings upon examination of the patient in the primary care clinic:

- Vital signs: blood pressure 168/90 mm Hg; temperature 37 degrees Celsius; heart rate 94 beats/min; respiratory rate 20 beats/min and irregular; oxygen saturation 95% on room air.

- General observation – The patient is a healthy-appearing, middle-aged male with some shortness of breath noted.

- Lungs – clear bilaterally without wheezing, crackles, or rhonchi appreciated.

- Heart – a palpable apical pulse; S1>S2 at apex; no murmur, gallop, or rubs heard on auscultation.

- Peripheral vasculature – distal pulses are strong bilaterally; no carotid or aortic bruits appreciated; skin is warm and dry.

Diagnostics Performed

A complete blood count, cardiac enzymes, cholesterol panel, and a comprehensive metabolic profile were drawn for the patient. A 12-lead electrocardiogram (EKG) revealed nonspecific ST segment and T-wave abnormalities that are unchanged from a prior EKG performed two years ago.

Questions

1. Which hemodynamic alteration does the nurse suspect by the patient's uncontrolled hypertension? What is the rationale for advising the patient to take nitroglycerin with acute chest pain? What are some side effects of nitroglycerin?

2. Considering the patient's history of asthma, is atenolol an appropriate medication to treat his blood pressure? Is atenolol indicated during the patient's acute episodes of chest pain?

3. Based on the patient's examination findings, does the patient have any other modifiable or nonmodifiable risk factors for CAD?

Answers

1. The patient is experiencing increased afterload to the left ventricle as apparent by his arterial hypertension. Nitroglycerin belongs in the nitrates class of drugs that primarily act by causing vasodilation, which results in decreased afterload and preload to the heart. Therefore, nitroglycerin has the ability to positively affect both oxygen supply and demand during acute periods of chest pain. Tachycardia is a common side effect with nitroglycerin; decreased platelet aggregation is another reflex response seen with the administration of nitroglycerin.

2. Yes. Atenolol is an appropriate drug for the patient because it is a cardioselective beta-blocker, meaning it decreases heart rate and contractility. The patient should

continue taking his atenolol as prescribed during periods of acute chest pain because atenolol acts by blocking beta-1 receptors, ultimately resulting in reduced myocardial oxygen demand by decreasing heart rate and contractility.

3. Yes. The patient's modifiable risk factors include hypertension, hyperlipidemia, and tobacco use. The patient's nonmodifiable risk factor is his family history of heart disease.

SUMMARY

Cardiovascular drugs are commonly used to maximize electrical or mechanical cardiac function. Nurses play a tremendous role in assisting patients with understanding the benefits of their prescribed pharmacological treatment plans, the significance of compliance to the regimen, and the importance of communicating tolerance or intolerance to their medical providers. Patients who truly understand the physiological benefits of therapy can be empowered to participate in decision making and the management of their own care. Nurses must maintain knowledge of current and future trends in cardiovascular pharmacological treatment to comprehensively, safely, and effectively care for patients with related disorders.

EXAM QUESTIONS

CHAPTER 4
Questions 15–25

Note: Choose the one option that BEST answers each question.

15. Which adrenergic receptor can be stimulated to increase heart rate?

    a. Alpha-1
    b. Beta-1
    c. Beta-2
    d. Dopaminergic

16. Which medication is part of the sympathomimetic class?

    a. Norepinephrine
    b. Milrinone
    c. Metoprolol
    d. Diltiazem

17. Which medication is indicated for the patient with heart failure?

    a. Diltiazem
    b. Amlodipine
    c. Isosorbide
    d. Nicardipine

18. Which diuretic is most associated with minimal (if any) potassium loss?

    a. Furosemide
    b. Bumetanide
    c. Spironolactone
    d. Hydrochlorothiazide

19. Which medication inhibits angiotensin-converting enzyme?

    a. Enalapril
    b. Losartan
    c. Metoprolol
    d. Amlodipine

20. The nurse should monitor which laboratory value in a patient taking an angiotensin receptor blocker or an angiotensin-converting enzyme inhibitor with an aldosterone antagonist?

    a. Potassium
    b. Glucose
    c. White blood cell count
    d. Phosphorus

21. Which medication functions as an adrenergic receptor blocker and can decrease heart rate?

    a. Lidocaine
    b. Metoprolol
    c. Verapamil
    d. Flecainide

22. Which medication can be classified as a Class IV antiarrhythmic?

    a. Lidocaine
    b. Metoprolol
    c. Verapamil
    d. Flecainide

23. Which medication is associated with hallucinations and disorientation in the older adult?

    a. Verapamil

    b. Digoxin

    c. Dobutamine

    d. Vasopressin

24. Which medication prevents the conversion of prothrombin to thrombin?

    a. Clopidogrel

    b. Bivalirudin

    c. Warfarin

    d. Heparin

25. The study of how an individual's genes affect that person's response to a drug is known as

    a. Pharmacogenomics

    b. Pharmacoeconomics

    c. Pharmacodynamics

    d. Pharmacokinetics

REFERENCES

Cannon, C. P. (2000). Exploring the issues of appropriate dosing in the treatment of acute myocardial infarction: Potential benefits of bolus fibrinolytic agents. *American Heart Journal, 140*(Suppl. 6), S154-S160.

Capodanno, D., & Angiolillo, D. J. (2013). Management of antiplatelet therapy in patients with coronary artery disease requiring cardiac and noncardiac surgery. *Circulation, 128,* 2785-2798. doi:10.1161/CIRCULATIONAHA.113.003675

Cappola, T. P., & Margulies, K. B. (2011). Genetics primer for the general cardiologist: Functional genomics applied to cardiovascular medicine. *Circulation, 124,* 87-94. doi:10.1161/CIRCULATIONAHA.111.027300

Dellinger, R. P., Levy, M. M., Rhodes, A., Annane, D., Gerlach, H., Opal, S. M., … Moreno, R. (2013). Surviving sepsis campaign: International guidelines for management of severe sepsis and septic shock: 2012. *Critical Care Medicine, 41*(2), 580. doi:10.1097/CCM.0b013e31827e83af

Gold Standard/Elsevier. (2010). *Clinical pharmacology database.* Retrieved from http://www.clinicalpharmacology.com/?epm=2_1

Griffin, B. P., Kapadia, S. R., & Rimmerman, C. M. (2013). *Cleveland Clinic Cardiology Board review* (2nd ed.). Philadelphia, PA: Lippincott Williams & Wilkins.

Hollenberg, S. M. (2011). Vasoactive drugs in circulatory shock. *American Journal of Respiratory and Critical Care Medicine, 183,* 847. doi:10.1164/rccm.201006-0972CI

Jensen, J. L., Walker, M., Denike, D., Matthews, V., Boudreau, C., Hill, W., & Travers, A. (2013). Paramedic myocardial infarction care with fibrinolytics: A process map and hazard analysis. *Prehospital Emergency Care, 17*(4), 429-434. doi:10.3109/10903127.2013.804136

Kearon, C., Akl, E. A., Ornelas, J., Blaivas, A., Jimenez, D., Bounameaux, H., … Moores, L. (2016). Antithrombotic therapy for VTE disease: CHEST guideline and expert panel report. *Chest, 149*(2), 315-352. doi:10.1016/j.chest.2015.11.026

Kumar, K. (2015). Antiarrhythmic drugs to maintain sinus rhythm in patients with atrial fibrillation: Recommendations. *UpToDate.com.* Retrieved from https://www.uptodate.com/contents/antiarrhythmic-drugs-to-maintain-sinus-rhythm-in-patients-with-atrial-fibrillation-recommendations

Leung, L. (2016). Direct oral anticoagulants: Dosing and adverse effects. *UpToDate.com.* Retrieved from https://www.uptodate.com/contents/direct-oral-anticoagulants-dosing-and-adverse-effects

Lilley, L. L., Collins, S. R., & Snyder, J. S. (2017). *Pharmacology and nursing process* (8th ed.). St. Louis, MO: Elsevier.

Liu, J., Masoudi, F. A., Spertus, J. A., Wang, Q., Murugiah, K., Spatz, E. S., … Jiang, L. (2015). Patterns of use of angiotensin-converting enzyme inhibitors/angiotensin receptor blockers among patients with acute myocardial infarction in China from 2001 to 2011: China PEACE-retrospective AMI study. *Journal of the American Heart Association, 4*(2), e001343. doi:10.1161/JAHA.114.001343

Manaker, S. (2014). Use of vasopressors and inotropes. *UpToDate.com*. Retrieved from http://www.uptodate.com/contents/use-of-vasopressors-and-inotropes

Nappi, J. M., & Sieg, A. (2011). Aldosterone and aldosterone receptor antagonists in patients with chronic heart failure. *Vascular Health and Risk Management, 7*, 353-363., doi:10.2147/VHRM.S13779

O'Gara, P. T., Kushner, F. G., Ascheim, D. D., Casey, D. E., Chung, M. K., de Lemos, J. A., … Yancy, C. W. (2013). 2013 ACCF/AHA guideline for the management of ST-elevation myocardial infarction: A report of the American College of Cardiology Foundation/American Heart Association Task Force on Practice Guidelines. *Journal of the American College of Cardiology, 61*(4), e78-e140. doi:10.1016/j.jacc.2012.11.019

Opie, L. H., & Gersh, B. J. (Eds.). (2009). *Drugs for the heart* (7th ed.). Philadelphia, PA: Saunders Elsevier.

Patton, K. T., Thibodeau, G. A., & Douglas, M. M. (2012). *Essentials of anatomy & physiology* (1st ed.). Lansing, MI: Elsevier/Mosby.

Woo, T. M., & Robinson, M. V. (2016). *Pharmacotherapeutics for advanced practice nurse prescribers* (4th ed.). Philadelphia, PA: F. A. Davis.

Zhang, H., Chu, J., Shen, T., Yang, C., Huang, X., Wang, S., … Li, J. (2015). GW26-e0194 apelin ameliorates myocardial insulin resistance and improves myocardial injury in diabetes. *Journal of the American College of Cardiology, 66*(16_S). doi:10.1016/j.jacc.2015.06.1105

Zhong, J., Xu, R., Chen, L., Zhang, Z., Xu, Y., Chang, Q., … Gao, P. (2015). GW26-e2401 enhanced levels of miR-122-5p and let-7b-3p in aortas of spontaneously hypertensive rats associated with downregulated levels of Apelin, miR-1-3p, miR-376b-3p and miR-298-5p. *Journal of the American College of Cardiology, 66*(16_S). doi:10.1016/j.jacc.2015.06.307

CHAPTER 5

HYPERTENSION AND HYPERLIPIDEMIA

LEARNING OUTCOME

After completing this chapter, the learner will be able to describe the nursing management associated with hypertension and hyperlipidemia.

CHAPTER OBJECTIVES

After completing this chapter, the learner will be able to:

1. Identify factors associated with the etiology, pathophysiology, and assessment of patients with hypertension and hyperlipidemia.

2. Utilize knowledge of disease-specific indications in the care of patients with hypertension and hyperlipidemia.

3. Discuss the nursing considerations associated with the collaborative management of patients with hypertension and hyperlipidemia.

4. Discuss the indications and actions for the use of antihypertensives and lipid-lowering agents.

INTRODUCTION

Hypertension and hyperlipidemia, two of the most common diseases, are leading risk factors for cardiovascular events in the United States. Nurses must understand and apply their knowledge of both diseases in the comprehensive management of cardiovascular patients. To provide safe, effective, efficient, timely, and high-quality care to this population, nurses must be able to identify persons at risk for these diseases, or those at risk for complications of these diseases, and clearly communicate those findings to medical providers for a collaborative approach to care. The nurse must also be able to educate patients on the multiple factors that contribute to their disease states and the impact on their health.

HYPERTENSION

Hypertension is one of the most common cardiovascular diseases (CVDs) in the United States. It is a sole major risk factor for stroke, myocardial infarction (MI), vascular disease, and chronic kidney disease (James et al., 2014). The definition of hypertension is systolic blood pressure (SBP) greater than 140 mmHg or diastolic blood pressure (DBP) greater than 90 mmHg. In addition, patients who are being treated for elevated blood pressure are considered to have hypertension even when their blood pressures are at goal (James et al., 2014).

Causes

Despite decades of research, the etiology of most hypertensive cases is still largely unknown. What is known is there are direct or primary causes and secondary causes of hypertension. Primary, or essential, hypertension accounts for 90% to 95% of all adult cases and develops because of environmental or genetic causes. The genetic components of diabetes, obesity, and heart disease are factors that contribute to the causes of primary hypertension. Research focusing on hypertension and the linkage to the role of genetics and gene-targeted medications has not demonstrated a positive impact on the disease process of hypertension (Madhur, Riaz, Dreisbach, & Harrison, 2014).

Coexisting risk factors are also associated with essential hypertension, including hyperlipidemia, diabetes, and obesity. Although the majority of hypertension in adults is essential, healthcare providers should always assess for identifiable causes of secondary hypertension. An unidentified secondary cause is often the reason for resistant hypertension.

Secondary hypertension, defined as hypertension caused by an underlying or secondary cause, can develop from multiple sources. Renal causes include polycystic kidney disease, chronic kidney disease, urinary tract obstruction, or a renin-producing tumor. Vascular causes include coarctation of aorta, vasculitis, or collagen vascular disease. Endocrine causes are related to exogenous or endogenous hormonal imbalances such as the administration of steroids. Oral contraceptives are another common endocrine-related cause of secondary hypertension. Drugs or toxins that can cause secondary hypertension include alcohol, cocaine, decongestants, nicotine, and others. Obstructive sleep apnea is another cause or risk factor for secondary hypertension (Madhur et al., 2014).

Pathophysiology

The pathogenesis of hypertension is multifactorial with consideration of the multiple modulators of blood pressure. For instance, there are neurohormonal mediators; vascular reactivity, elasticity, and caliber; circulating blood volume and viscosity; and cardiac output components that all influence blood pressure in an effort to maintain adequate perfusion to all tissues. Although many specifics remain unknown about the pathogenesis of hypertension, researchers report findings in both humans and animals that primary hypertension is greatly associated with immunological factors. These studies revealed that hypertension is strongly associated with renal infiltration of immune cells, and immunological treatment was found to reduce blood pressure. The theory suggests T-lymphocyte activation stimulates the sympathetic nervous system, thereby contributing to the pathogenesis of primary hypertension. There is still much left to be proven, however (Guzik et al., 2007; Harrison et al., 2011; Madhur et al., 2010).

In addition to the theory of an immunological influence to the pathogenesis of hypertension, it is widely accepted that primary hypertension is the result of a complex interaction between environmental factors and genetics, and that combined effect causes renal and vascular dysfunction. These changes increase the vascular tone and blood volume and are mediated by the sympathetic nervous system, renin-angiotensin-aldosterone system, and natriuretic peptides. Inflammation and insulin resistance are also implicated in essential hypertension (Huether & McCance, 2017). The result leads to

- excessive salt and water retention from impaired ability of the kidneys to excrete sodium and water;

- dysfunction of the autonomic nervous system with increased sympathetic nervous system stimulation and higher levels of circulating norepinephrine, resulting in increased vasoconstriction;

- impaired endothelial dysfunction with decreased production of nitric oxide; and

- dysfunction of the renin-angiotensin-aldosterone system (Huether & McCance, 2017).

Epidemiology

Considering the prevalence of hypertension and many unknown pathophysiological factors, the nurse must recognize the prevalence of the disease's characteristics. Black individuals have the highest prevalence of hypertension globally and, on average, have been seen to develop the disease at younger ages than their White, Hispanic/Latino, Asian, and American Indian counterparts (James et al., 2014; Mozaffarian et al., 2015). This population also has higher complication rates of stroke and end-stage kidney disease in comparison with other populations with hypertension. In the United States, the White population was found to have hypertension and its associated complications, such as (but not limited to) coronary artery disease (CAD), cardiomyopathy, heart failure, and chronic kidney disease, later in life as an older adult (Mozaffarian et al., 2015). Men were predominantly found to have higher rates of hypertension until the age of 45 years, when the rates became more equal between men and women. However, obese women older than 45 years who use oral contraceptives have a 2- to 3-fold higher risk than women of the same age who do not take oral contraceptives (Madhur et al., 2014; Mozaffarian et al., 2015).

For people younger than 50 years, DBP is very important. As a person ages, however, SBP becomes a more important indicator of cardiovascular risk. In people older than 50 years, an SBP greater than 140 mmHg is a more important indicator of cardiovascular risk than is diastolic hypertension (Mozaffarian et al., 2015). Whereas SBP continues to rise with age, DBP begins to decline at 60 years of age. This rise in SBP with associated decrease in DBP results in a widening

of the pulse pressure. There is also an increased risk for cardiovascular events associated with a widened pulse pressure (Griffin, Kapadia, & Rimmerman, 2013; Guzik et al., 2007).

NURSING APPLICATION

The coronary arteries are perfused during diastole, so it is important to maintain an adequate DBP.

Symptoms

Hypertension is largely asymptomatic. Many patients go undiagnosed for years before symptoms develop. Thus, the nurse must consider epidemiology and apply knowledge of the factors that place patients at higher risk for this often "silent" disease. Risk factors for all-cause CVD were discussed in Chapter 3. Risk factors specific to hypertension are not much different. Obtaining a thorough history is necessary to capture the person's lifestyle comprehensively. For instance, the nurse must inquire about use of over-the-counter medications that may contain ephedrine, the use of oral contraceptives, and the use or abuse of alcohol, tobacco, or illicit drugs. The nurse must calculate body mass index to identify obesity and inquire about the person's activity level, dietary habits, and psychosocial stressors. These factors are significant in the stratification of risks and primary prevention of hypertension.

When the patient is symptomatic due to uncontrolled and accelerated hypertension, the patient often reports headache, vision changes (e.g., blurriness, floaters), light-headedness or dizziness, and sometimes extreme symptoms such as chest pain, palpitations, or strokelike symptoms (e.g., numbness and tingling, weakness, facial droop). The nurse must recognize that these extreme symptoms may be late findings of a hypertensive emergency and are indicative of end organ damage. Hypertensive emergencies are discussed in Chapter 17.

Complications

Goals of hypertension management include the prevention of damage (evidence of injury such as an elevated troponin or creatinine) to target organs.

- *Heart:* Hypertension is associated with the development of left ventricular hypertrophy, CAD, MI, and heart failure.

- *Brain:* Hypertension increases the risk for transient ischemic attacks and ischemic or hemorrhagic stroke. Malignant hypertension can also cause cerebral encephalopathy when blood pressure is so high that the brain can no longer maintain autoregulation.

- *Kidneys:* Hypertension causes nephropathy through the production of atherosclerotic renal lesions. Chronic renal disease causes hypertension, and hypertension accelerates the progression of chronic renal disease to end-stage disease.

- *Peripheral arteries:* Hypertension produces vascular damage that impairs endothelial vasodilatation and accelerates atherosclerosis in the peripheral arteries as well as in the coronary and cerebral arteries.

- *Eyes:* Vessel damage to the retina caused by hypertension is called *hypertensive retinopathy* (James et al., 2014).

Diagnosis

The diagnosis of hypertension requires a series of blood pressure readings and a comprehensive health history. Traditionally, hypertension was diagnosed when the patient had three office visits with blood pressures greater than normal. Although this method still has some utility, the Institute for Clinical Systems Improvement (2014) provides other guidelines for the diagnosis of hypertension as well. For instance, ambulatory blood pressure monitoring is used to monitor daily blood pressure over a 24- to 48-hour period. The ambulatory blood pressure monitoring method measures the person's blood pressure every 20 to 30 minutes while awake and while asleep. This method provides the clinician with a 24-hour trend of blood pressure readings to establish the percentage of elevated readings, overall blood pressure load, and extent of blood pressure fall during sleep. There is usually a 10% to 20% drop in blood pressure during sleep. Patients found to have a 24-hour blood pressure greater than 135/85 are found to have a 2-fold higher risk for having a cardiovascular event than do those with normal pressures. Indications for using the ambulatory blood pressure monitoring diagnostic method are discrepancies of blood pressure readings reported outside of the office visit, labile readings, or poorly controlled pressures (Institute for Clinical Systems Improvement, 2014).

Diagnosis of secondary hypertension is dependent on the identification of the primary problem such as pheochromocytoma, serotonin syndrome, coarctation of the aorta, use of over-the-counter or illicit drugs, among others. Diagnosis is also dependent on advanced diagnostic differentiation skills and a thorough health history employed by the advanced practitioner or physician.

Treatment Considerations

Given the multitude of potential contributing factors to hypertension, treatment considerations can be complex. Treatments must consider age of the patient, stage or severity of hypertension, and any comorbidities that accompany the disease. The clinician must recognize that guidelines are created and published by a panel of experts after the synthesis of available studies is complete. Understanding that there may be multiple limitations associated with the studies and multiple research questions not yet studied will allow the clinician to merely consider the guidelines as recommendations in the collaborative approach for treatment.

Evidence-Based Guidelines

Multiple national organizations are focusing on the appropriate treatment of hypertension. Many of these organizations combine their efforts to publish joint statements or guidelines recommending the best treatments for hypertension in an effort to standardize care. However, some of the groups focus on specific populations such as persons with diabetes or those with coronary heart disease. Although the nurse does not determine the medical treatment plan, the nurse must understand the treatment goals and necessary lifestyle modification education for patients with hypertension and those with comorbidities in addition to hypertension. A summary of hypertension treatment recommendations denoting the differences in treatment for those with specific comorbidities appears in Table 5-1.

Blood Pressure Targets/Goals

Goals of treatment are determined in consideration of the patient's age, lifestyle, and accompanying diseases of chronic kidney disease, diabetes, heart failure, or previous history of CAD, MI, or stroke. Table 5-1 differentiates goals set for patients with the varying factors discussed earlier in this chapter.

Considerations for Special Populations

Pregnancy

Hypertension is the most common medical problem experienced during pregnancy. Hypertensive disorders during pregnancy are classified into four categories: (1) chronic hypertension, (2) preeclampsia-eclampsia, (3) preeclampsia superimposed on chronic hypertension, and (4) gestational hypertension (transient and formerly known as pregnancy-induced hypertension).

Older Adults

Isolated systolic hypertension is defined as an SBP greater than 160 mmHg with a normal DBP. Isolated systolic hypertension increases the risk for nonfatal MI and cardiovascular death in low-risk patients and the general population. Isolated systolic hypertension accounts for most cases of hypertension in older adults. Systolic hypertension is often more difficult to control than diastolic hypertension. Because antihypertensive medication is used to bring down SBP, there is concern that the DBP may drop too low in those with isolated systolic hypertension, especially in the elderly population (Boltz & Capezuti, 2016).

Older adults can show substantial benefits when hypertension is adequately treated. Systolic pressure, rather than diastolic pressure, is a better predictor of events among this group of patients. *Pseudohypertension* is increased blood pressure resulting from the incompressibility of blood vessels that happens in older adults because of excessive vascular stiffness. For this reason, thiazide diuretics are the preferred first-line treatment of hypertension in older adults. Long-acting dihydropyridine calcium channel blockers (e.g., amlodipine) can also be used (Boltz & Capezuti, 2016).

Collaborative Management

Nonpharmacological Treatment

Four lifestyle interventions remain the mainstay of nonpharmacological treatment to delay or prevent the onset of hypertension:

1. weight reduction,
2. increased physical activity,
3. sodium reduction, and
4. the DASH (Dietary Approaches to Stop Hypertension) diet.

Weight reduction is the most effective lifestyle modification. Weight reduction can reduce

TABLE 5-1: EVIDENCE-BASED PRACTICE RECOMMENDATIONS FOR HYPERTENSION TREATMENT

Guideline	Population	Goal BP, mmHg	Initial Drug Treatment
JNC-8 (2014)	General: age >60 years	<150/90	Non-Black: thiazide-type diuretic, ACEI, ARB, or CCB
	General: age <60 years	<140/90	
	Diabetes: age >18 years	<140/90	Black: thiazide-type diuretic or CCB
	CKD: age >18 years	<140/90	ACEI or ARB
2015 AHA/ ACC/ASH Statement	>80 years	<150/90	
	CAD with ACS, HF	<140/90	BB, *plus* ACEI or ARB *if* DM, CKD, or LV dysfunction, *plus* thiazide/thiazide-like diuretic (If BB contraindicated, nondihydropyridine CCB substituted in absence of LV dysfunction.)
	CAD post-MI, CVA/ TIA, CAD, PAD, AAA	<130/80	BB, *plus* ACEI or ARB, *plus* aldosterone antagonist if HF or DM, *plus* loop diuretic if HF (If BB contraindicated, nondihydropyridine CCB substituted in absence of LV dysfunction.)
ADA Guideline (2015)	DM	Age >60 years: BP <140/90	BP >120/80 – therapeutic lifestyle changes
		Age <60 years: BP <130/80	BP >140/90 – TLC, *plus* ACEI or ARB If multidrug therapy needed, *plus* thiazide diuretic

BP = blood pressure; JNC-8 = eighth Joint National Committee; CKD = chronic kidney disease; ACEI = angiotensin-converting enzyme inhibitor; ARB = angiotensin receptor blocker; CCB = calcium channel blocker; AHA = American Heart Association; ACC = American College of Cardiology; ASH = American Society of Hypertension; CAD = coronary artery disease; ACS = acute coronary syndrome; HF = heart failure; BB = beta blocker; DM = diabetes mellitus; LV = left ventricular; MI = myocardial infarction; CVA = cardiovascular accident; TIA = transient ischemic attack; PAD = peripheral artery disease; AAA = Abdominal Aortic Aneurysm; ADA = American Diabetes Association; TLC = Therapeutic Lifestyle Changes.

Note. Adapted from American Diabetes Association. (2015). Cardiovascular disease and risk management. *Diabetes Care, 38*(1), S49-S57. doi:10.2337/dc15-S011

James, P. A., Oparil, S., Carter, B. L., Cushman, W. C., Dennison-Himmelfarb, C., Handler, J., ... Ortiz, E. (2014). 2014 Evidence-based guideline for the management of high blood pressure in adults: Report from the panel members appointed to the eighth Joint National Committee (JNC 8). *JAMA, 311*(5), 507-520. doi:10.1001/jama.2013.28442

Rosendorff, C., Lackland, D. T., Aronow, W. S., Blumenthal, R. S., de Lemos, J. A., Findeis, L., Gore, J. M., ... White, W. B. (2015). Treatment of hypertension in patients with coronary artery disease: A scientific statement from the American Heart Association, American College of Cardiology, and American Society of Hypertension. *Hypertension, 65,* 1372-1407. doi:10.1161/HYP.0000000000000018

blood pressure by 5 to 20 mmHg per 5 lb of weight loss. For effective blood pressure management, patients should engage in physical activity almost every day for 30 to 45 minutes (James et al., 2014).

Some individuals are salt sensitive and others are not; therefore, sodium reduction affects blood pressure for some patients and not others. All patients with high blood pressure should evaluate the effects of a sodium-restricted diet.

NURSING APPLICATION

It is important for patients with hypertension to understand that 75% of sodium intake comes from processed food, not from added salt.

After weight loss, the DASH diet is the second most effective lifestyle intervention. The DASH diet manipulates potassium, calcium, and magnesium, whereas holding sodium constant. Low calcium consumption is associated with hypertension, and high potassium consumption is associated with lower blood pressure in people with hypertension.

The DASH diet is high in fruits, vegetables, and low-fat dairy products. It is low in saturated fat and total fat, and rich in potassium and calcium. This diet has been found to reduce both SBP and DBP by as much as 8 to 14 mmHg (James et al., 2014). Unlike weight reduction, smoking cessation has not been shown to directly decrease blood pressure, although there are numerous other cardiovascular benefits.

Pharmacological Treatment

Pharmacological treatment of blood pressure has been shown to protect against stroke, coronary events, heart failure, and progression of renal disease and to reduce all-cause mortality. Specific agents recommended for specified indications are also noted in Table 5-1. The nurse must recognize when the patient is on recommended therapies, whether the therapies are effective, and whether the patient is tolerating the treatment. The nurse is often the first line of communication to the medical provider who can alter the medical plan of care. Those nursing actions demonstrate collaborative management, high-quality care, and patient advocacy.

The medication classes recommended for treatment were discussed in great detail in Chapter 4, and this chapter further discusses the rationales for the treatment of hypertension with these drugs.

Thiazide and Thiazide-Type Diuretics

Multiple highly appraised studies support the use of thiazides for the treatment of hypertension and report them being highly effective in reducing blood pressure and preventing cerebrovascular events. The concern of thiazides contributing to hyperglycemia, and thus new-onset diabetes mellitus, was found not to be valid (Rosendorff et al., 2015).

Beta Blockers

Beta-blocker administration remains the effective standard of care for hypertension in patients with angina and previous MI and left ventricular dysfunction. Specifically, carvedilol, metoprolol succinate, and bisoprolol were shown to improve outcomes in patients with heart failure (Rosendorff et al., 2015).

Angiotensin-Converting Enzyme Inhibitors

Angiotensin-converting enzyme inhibitors (ACEIs) are recommended for all patients after MI. They have been proven to improve heart failure and slow progression of chronic kidney disease (renal protective). When combined with thiazide diuretics, they have been proven to reduce the incidence of stroke. Ramipril demonstrated reductions of morbidity and all-cause mortality in individuals with known CAD and hypertension. Studies conducted worldwide (e.g., HOPE, EUROPA, and PEACE trials) have consistently reported improved outcomes with the treatment of ACEIs in patients with hypertension and known CAD (Rosendorff et al., 2015).

Angiotensin Receptor Blockers

Similar to the effectiveness of ACEIs, angiotensin receptor blockers (ARBs) have demonstrated similar, not equal, results. ARBs have been found to be somewhat inferior to ACEIs; however, in the setting of ACEI intolerance, ARBs do demonstrate a reduction in morbidity and mortality in these patients. Research questions surrounded the benefit of combining ACEIs and ARBs; however, no statistically significant difference between them has been found for cardiovascular events (Rosendorff et al., 2015).

Aldosterone Antagonists

Aldosterone antagonists (spironolactone and eplerenone) were found to lower blood pressure and have a protective effect in patients with chronic heart failure when used alone or in combination with other antihypertensive agents (Rosendorff et al., 2015).

Calcium Channel Blockers

Drugs in the calcium channel blocker class of antihypertensives are recommended as alternatives to beta blockers for blood pressure reduction in patients with CAD because their results toward the prevention of heart failure were more effective than beta blockers. Calcium channel blockers should be avoided in patients with heart failure. Although they have no proven benefit for the prevention of heart failure, dihydropyridine calcium channel blockers yield equivalent and sometimes superior results in blood pressure reduction in comparison with beta blockers, ACEIs, and thiazides (Rosendorff et al., 2015).

HYPERLIPIDEMIA

Hyperlipidemia, also known as dyslipidemia, is defined as abnormal levels of serum lipoproteins. The term *lipoprotein* refers to triglycerides, cholesterol, phospholipids, and lipids bound to carrier proteins. Hyperlipidemia is the leading cause of atherosclerosis and CAD in the United States and involves abnormalities of one or more serum lipoproteins (Huether & McCance, 2017; Mozaffarian et al., 2015). The term is broad and nonspecific because it can involve hypercholesteremia, familial hypercholesterolemia, and/or hypertriglyceridemia.

Causes

A diet rich in saturated fats is the leading cause of hyperlipidemia. However, many individuals have a genetic predisposition for this disorder. Primary, or familial, hyperlipidemia results from genetic defects that cause abnormal lipid-metabolizing enzymes and abnormal cellular receptors. Secondary causes include other systemic disorders such as diabetes, hypothyroidism, pancreatitis, and renal nephrosis.

Certain medications are also known to be causative factors for hyperlipidemia; these include antiretrovirals, glucocorticoids, interferons, and diuretics (Huether & McCance, 2017).

Pathophysiology

Lipid metabolism is complex. It involves the packaging of dietary fat into particles known as chylomicrons in the small intestine. These particles are necessary for the absorption of fat and function by transporting dietary lipids from the intestine to the liver and peripheral cells. These particles are the least dense lipoproteins and mostly contain triglycerides. An elevated triglyceride level is greater than 150 mg/dl. Triglycerides can normally be removed, stored by adipose tissue, or used by muscle as an energy source. The chylomicron remnants are mostly made of cholesterol and then are taken up by the liver. The liver then produces several lipoproteins via a series of chemical reactions. These lipoproteins are known as very low-density lipoproteins (VLDLs), low-density lipoproteins (LDLs), or high-density lipoproteins (HDLs).

"Bad cholesterol," or LDL, is normally responsible for the delivery of cholesterol to the tissues. However, increased serum LDL levels are associated with increased risk for CAD. Serum LDL levels are normally controlled by receptors in the liver that bind with LDL to limit the liver's synthesis of it. However, high dietary intake of cholesterol and saturated fats and dysfunction of LDL receptors in the liver result in high LDL levels in the blood, migration of LDL into the vessel wall, oxidative stress, and phagocytosis, which are the key steps in the pathogenesis of *atherosclerosis*. Elevated (≥70 mg/dl) levels of LDL also cause endothelial injury, inflammation, and immune responses associated with atherogenesis (Huether & McCance, 2017).

When "good cholesterol," or HDL, is at adequate serum levels, it plays an important role in preventing atherosclerotic disease by returning excess cholesterol from the tissues to the liver for processing or elimination via bile. HDL also participates in endothelial repair and the reduction of thrombosis formation. Exercise, weight loss, fish oil consumption, and moderate alcohol use (1 to 2 drinks/day) are associated with modest increases in HDL levels (Huether & McCance, 2017).

Symptoms

The manifestations associated with hyperlipidemia are any suggestive of inadequate blood flow to tissues. These include signs of ischemia, such as chest pain or claudication pains. The pathogenesis of hyperlipidemia alone does not produce symptoms until it has progressed enough into atherosclerotic lesions, or fibrous plaques, that interfere with vascular blood flow (see Figure 5-1). Fibrous plaque is formed within the smooth muscle cells near the region of the endothelial injury. In that area, collagen is produced by the injured cells, calcifies, protrudes into the vessel lumen, and obstructs blood flow to distal tissues (especially during exercise), thereby causing symptoms of tissue ischemia.

Complications

Complications of hyperlipidemia are related to the atherosclerotic conditions of the blood vessels interfering with adequate blood flow to the tissues. The most common disease associated with hyperlipidemia is CAD. CAD is the leading cause of myocardial ischemia and is a major risk factor for death in the United States. Other diseases that occur secondary to tissue ischemia are cerebrovascular disease, chronic kidney disease, and peripheral vascular disease, to name a few (Huether & McCance, 2017; Mozaffarian et al., 2015).

Diagnosis

Medical providers make the hyperlipidemia diagnosis based on the measurement of a serum lipid panel such as triglycerides, HDL, and LDL. Familial hyperlipidemia is determined by advanced lipid testing in addition to the lipid panel. When these levels are greater than levels most associated with CVD, a lipid metabolism disorder is diagnosed, risks for CVD are determined, and the most appropriate therapy is then considered.

Treatment Considerations

Treatment considerations are aimed to reduce a patient's risk for CVD or a cardiovascular event. Guidelines recommend categorizing patients into four groups of primary and secondary prevention patients. Depending on the patient category, medical providers will choose therapies in consideration of which "intensity" of statin therapy to initiate to achieve reductions in the serum LDL cholesterol level (Stone et al., 2013).

Pregnancy

Pregnancy is a condition that can increase LDL and triglyceride levels. Re-evaluation and the consideration of treatment is determined via CVD risk stratification and safety factors associated with pharmacological agents. This treatment must be guided by the obstetric specialist (Stone et al., 2013).

Aged Adults

National guidelines do not make treatment recommendations based on gender; however, age is considered given the increased risk for CAD with aging (Stone et al., 2013). Adults older than 75 years have the greatest potential for overall CVD risk reduction and therapy.

FIGURE 5-1: ATHEROSCLEROSIS PROGRESSION SECONDARY TO HYPERLIPIDEMIA

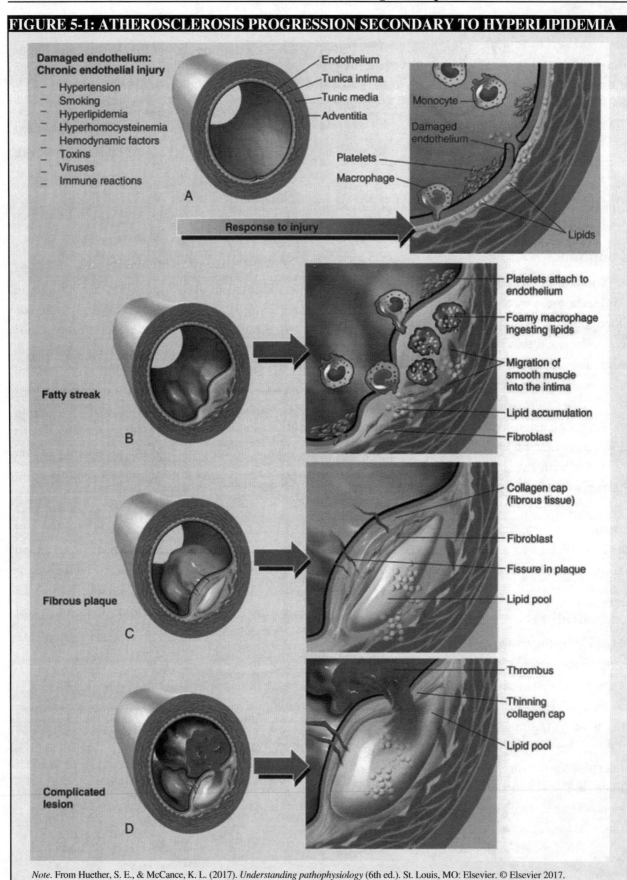

Note. From Huether, S. E., & McCance, K. L. (2017). *Understanding pathophysiology* (6th ed.). St. Louis, MO: Elsevier. © Elsevier 2017.

Collaborative Management

Nonpharmacological Treatment

Lifestyle modification is the foundational risk reduction strategy for hyperlipidemia and CVD in general. Adhering to a heart-healthy diet, regular exercise, avoidance of tobacco products, and maintenance of a healthy weight are crucial to health promotion and atherosclerotic CVD risk reduction (Stone et al., 2013).

Pharmacological Treatment

Low-Density Lipoprotein Cholesterol

A 1% reduction in total cholesterol reduces the incidence of cardiac events by 2%. In addition, a 1% increase in HDL reduces the risk by 2% to 4%. Therefore, reduction of LDL is a primary goal in the management of coronary heart disease. In the presence of established CAD, lipid-lowering therapy should be prescribed with even mild elevations of LDL. The effects of various groups of medications on LDL levels are outlined in Table 5-2 (Stone et al., 2013).

Of the available lipid-lowering drugs, the HMG-coenzyme A(HMG-CoA) reductase inhibitors (statins) are the most potent for reducing LDL. Other agents that substantially lower LDL are bile acid resins and nicotinic acid. All three of these drug classes have a dose-dependent effect on LDL (Stone et al., 2013).

The effect of fibrates on LDL is different. Fibrates primarily decrease triglycerides and, therefore, indirectly increase HDL. Among the fibrates, fenofibrate has a greater effect on LDL and triglyceride reduction than clofibrate or gemfibrozil (Stone et al., 2013).

Triglycerides and High-Density Lipoprotein Cholesterol

The most effective agents for improving triglyceride and HDL levels are nicotinic acid (niacin) and the fibrates. Nicotinic acid has a dose-dependent effect; however, side effects may prevent patients from taking a sufficient dose. Fibrates have a fixed-dose effect and do not have the irritating side effects associated with nicotinic acid. Statins, especially simvastatin and atorvastatin, also lower triglycerides and increase HDL. Bile acid resins increase HDL but may also increase triglycerides. Bile acid sequestrants may actually cause a transient compensatory increase in triglyceride levels. Concomitant use of fenofibrate and a low- or moderate-intensity statin can be considered to reduce triglycerides greater than 500 mg/dl. However, the use of gemfibrozil should not be started with statin therapies because of an increased risk for muscle symptoms and rhabdomyolysis (Stone et al., 2013). Table 5-3 details the effects of lipid-lowering medications on triglyceride and HDL cholesterol levels.

TABLE 5-2: EFFECTS OF LIPID-LOWERING THERAPY ON LDL-C LEVELS

Class of Medications	Reduction
HMG-CoA reductase inhibitors (statins)	18% to 60%
Bile acid sequestrants	15% to 30%
Nicotinic acid	15% to 30%
Fibrates	5% to 20%
Intestinal absorption inhibitors	18%

Note. Adapted from Berra, K. A., & Fair, J. M. (2010). Lipid management and cardiovascular disease. In S. L. Woods, E. S. S. Froelicher, S. U. Motzer, & E. J. Bridges (Eds.), *Cardiac nursing* (6th ed., pp. 823-841). Philadelphia, PA: Lippincott Williams & Wilkins.

NURSING APPLICATION

Educating patients on the expected quantifiable improvements in lipid levels associated with drug therapy allows patients to actively participate in decision making about when to add drug therapy to healthy dietary changes.

TABLE 5-3: EFFECTS OF LIPID-LOWERING THERAPY ON TRIGLYCERIDE AND HDL-C LEVELS

Class of Medications	HDL-C	Triglycerides
Nicotinic acid	↑ 15% to 35%	↓ 20% to 50%
Fibrates	↑ 10% to 20%	↓ 20% to 50%
HMG-CoA reductase inhibitors (statins)	↑ 5% to 15%	↓ 7% to 37%
Bile acid sequestrants	↑ 3% to 5%	Does not decrease, may even increase
Intestinal absorption inhibitors	↑ 1%	↓ 8%

Note. Adapted from Berra, K. A., & Fair, J. M. (2010). Lipid management and cardiovascular disease. In S. L. Woods, E. S. S. Froelicher, S. U. Motzer, & E. J. Bridges (Eds.), *Cardiac nursing* (6th ed., pp. 823-841). Philadelphia, PA: Lippincott Williams & Wilkins.

Bile Acid Sequestrants (Resins)

Bile acid sequestrants, also called *resins,* include cholestyramine (Questran), colestipol (Colestid), and colesevelam (Welchol). These drugs combine with bile acids in the intestine and form an insoluble complex that is excreted in feces. The low level of bile acids provides feedback to the hepatic circulation to stimulate the production of more bile acids. Because cholesterol is used in the production of bile acids, the liver is also stimulated to produce more cholesterol. Cholesterol, specifically the oxidation of cholesterol from LDL, is a major precursor for the formation of bile acids. The body breaks down cholesterol to make bile acids and then compensates by increasing LDL receptors to remove LDL from circulation. Although the liver is stimulated to produce more cholesterol, this new cholesterol is used to produce more bile acids. A net decrease in total cholesterol and LDL results. Bile acid sequestrants have minimal effects on HDL and can actually increase triglyceride levels (Stone et al., 2013).

NURSING APPLICATION

Bile acid sequestrants should be taken with the largest meal of the day because intestinal bile acids are greatest at this time.

The cholesterol-lowering effects of resins usually begin in 24 to 48 hours, and peak effects are achieved within a 2- to 4-week time period.

Colesevelam is approved for use with statins and produces a synergistic effect.

Side effects of bile acid sequestrants include gastrointestinal (GI) distress and constipation. Constipation is the most common and troublesome side effect. Bile acid sequestrants can bind with other substances (including other medications) in addition to binding to bile acids. Because of this binding potential, bile acid sequestrants interfere with the absorption of fat-soluble vitamins (A, D, and K). It may also accelerate their clearance and lower their effective plasma levels (Stone et al., 2013).

NURSING APPLICATION

Because of their binding property, bile acid sequestrants should not be taken at the same time as other medications. Advise patients to take other medications 1 hour before or 4 hours after taking bile acid sequestrants.

The use of these medications is contraindicated in patients with biliary obstruction or abnormal intestinal function. Because bile acid sequestrants can increase triglyceride levels, they are also contraindicated in patients with elevated triglycerides. The powder forms of bile acid sequestrants should be mixed with fluids. Bile acid resins are insoluble and form a gritty solution. This may not be pleasing to some patients and can affect compliance with the therapeutic regimen. Tablets should not be cut, chewed, or crushed because they are designed to break down in the GI tract. Colestipol is not absorbed and therefore has less toxic potential, making it safer for use in children and pregnant women. Bile acid sequestrants have the potential to decrease the absorption of several medications, including digoxin, warfarin, thiazide diuretics, and thyroxin, and also impair the absorption of vitamin K (Stone et al., 2013).

Nicotinic Acid (Niacin)

Also called niacin, nicotinic acid is a B complex vitamin. Because niacin is used in the enrichment of refined flour, niacin deficiency is rare in the United States. Dietary requirements for niacin can be met by the intake of either nicotinic acid or nicotinamide. As vitamins, both of these substances have identical functions. However, as pharmacological agents, they are very different. In addition to being a vitamin, niacin has additional dose-related pharmacological effects not seen with nicotinamide (Stone et al., 2013).

Niacin may cause a release of histamine or prostacyclin that is responsible for vasodilatation and the classic "flush" associated with niacin use. The dilation of the cutaneous blood vessels increases blood flow to the face, neck, and chest. This vasodilatation can also produce pruritus, headaches, or other pain. Histamine can also increase gastric acid secretion, increasing the likelihood of GI side effects. Niacin was the first lipid-lowering agent shown to decrease mortality in patients with MI (Stone et al., 2013).

Nicotinic acid-related agents include Niacor, Slo-Niacin, and Niaspan. Decreased VLDL cholesterol production is one of the primary actions of niacin. One explanation for this result is that niacin decreases the lipolysis of triglycerides in adipose tissue, thereby reducing the transport of free fatty acids to the liver and decreasing hepatic triglyceride synthesis. Decreased triglyceride synthesis results in a reduction of VLDL

production. Lowered LDL cholesterol can be a result of decreased VLDL production; alternatively, niacin may promote increased clearance of LDL precursors. Niacin also raises HDL levels through a mechanism that is not fully understood but is related to increased levels of apolipoprotein A-I and lipoprotein A-I and a decrease in levels of apolipoprotein B. Women may have better results than men when taking niacin at the same dose (Stone et al., 2013).

Side effects of niacin include flushing, GI distress, hyperglycemia, gout, and liver toxicity. Flushing and dyspepsia are likely to limit adherence to therapy. Flushing usually subsides within 2 weeks on a stable dose. When given 30 minutes before niacin, aspirin (325 mg) may also blunt the flushing response (Berra & Fair, 2010). Niacin should be administered with food to minimize GI side effects.

Fibrates

Fibrates are also called *fibric acid agents* and include clofibrate (Atromid-S), fenofibrate (Tricor), and gemfibrozil (Lopid). The mechanism of action for these medications is complex and not fully understood; however, they stimulate lipoprotein lipase activity, which increases catabolism and clearance of triglycerides. They also decrease hepatic triglyceride production. In addition, they may decrease cholesterol synthesis, increase the mobilization of cholesterol from tissues, enhance the removal of cholesterol from the liver, and increase cholesterol excretion in feces. They decrease VLDL synthesis and significantly reduce triglycerides. Fibrates raise HDL levels (Stone et al., 2013).

Fibrates are the drug of choice for increased LDL and hypertriglyceridemia. They are also the first-line medications to reduce the risk for pancreatitis in patients with very high levels of triglycerides (Stone et al., 2013). Fibrates decrease triglycerides by 25% to 50% and increase HDL in the presence of hypertriglyceridemia. However, they have variable effects on LDL. Despite this, fibrates, particularly fenofibrate, may increase the production of larger, less dense LDL particles, helping to promote LDL metabolism and reduce the number of smaller, more dense particles associated with atherosclerosis. Fenofibrate also reduces lipoprotein (a) and serum fibrinogen, which is an independent risk factor for thrombosis. Serum triglyceride levels begin to fall within 2 to 5 days, with maximal effects achieved within 3 weeks, allowing for close evaluation of treatment in patients (Stone et al., 2013).

Side effects of fibrates include dyspepsia, rash, alopecia, fatigue, headache, impotence, anemia, myositis flulike syndrome, cholelithiasis, and abnormal liver function test results. Because fibrates are excreted through the kidneys, they are contraindicated in patients with severe renal disease. They are also contraindicated in patients with hepatic disease or preexisting gallbladder disease (Stone et al., 2013).

Combining a fibrate with a statin raises safety concerns because of the potential for myopathy and overt rhabdomyolysis. One fibrate (fenofibrate), however, does not interfere with the catabolism of statins as mentioned earlier. Again, concomitant use of gemfibrozil with a statin increases the risk for rhabdomyolysis and is therefore contraindicated. However, almost all reports of such adverse effects have occurred in situations in which the drug combination should have been avoided. Box 5-1 lists situations for which fibrates and statins should not be combined (Stone et al., 2013).

HMG-CoA Reductase Inhibitors

HMG-CoA reductase inhibitors, also known as statins, have been widely studied in various clinical trials. The landmark Scandinavian Simvastatin Survival Study (Pedersen et al., 1994) showed that simvastatin for secondary prevention not only reduced lipid levels but also reduced future coronary events and overall mortality. Primary prevention studies have shown that statins reduce the need for coronary revascularization and reduce the risk for coronary mortality and morbidity. All medications in this group have been shown to reduce the risk for CVD in clinical trials. Statins are recommended as first-line agents because of their proven predictable results, overall safety profile, and ability to be well tolerated by most patients. Statins may have effects other than lipid lowering that play a role in their cardiovascular protective abilities. Some of these proposed additional benefits include improving endothelial function, contributing to an antithrombotic environment, and inhibiting inflammatory response. The Jupiter Trial, for example, showed a reduction in cardiovascular events in patients taking rosuvastatin who had normal LDL cholesterol levels but high levels of high-sensitivity C-reactive protein (Ridker et al., 2008). Examples of HMG-CoA reductase inhibitors include lovastatin (Mevacor), simvastatin (Zocor), pravastatin (Pravachol), fluvastatin (Lescol), atorvastatin (Lipitor), and rosuvastatin (Crestor; Stone et al., 2013).

Lovastatin and simvastatin are administered in an inactive form and require hydrolysis to be activated. The mechanism of action of statins involves the inhibition of HMG-CoA reductase, which catalyzes an early step in cholesterol synthesis. These inhibitors reduce the quantity of mevalonic acid, a precursor to cholesterol. Cholesterol levels in liver cells are reduced, and the body responds with increased hepatic uptake of LDL from the circulation. The result is a decrease in total cholesterol, LDL, triglycerides, and apolipoprotein B. Some statins also increase HDL (Stone et al., 2013).

BOX 5-1: FIBRATE AND STATIN CONTRAINDICATIONS

Fibrate and statin relative contraindications include

- high dosages of statins, particularly simvastatin 80 mg/day or atorvastatin 80 mg/day;

- patients with renal insufficiency (fibrates are renally excreted and plasma levels are increased in patients with renal insufficiency, thereby increasing the risk for drug-drug interactions);

- patients taking any agent that interferes with clearance of statins (e.g., the immunosuppressive agent tacrolimus has this effect); and

- patients older than 70 years because of general increased problems with renal and hepatic function.

Note. Adapted from Berra, K. A., & Fair, J. M. (2010). Lipid management and cardiovascular disease. In S. L. Woods, E. S. S. Froelicher, S. U. Motzer, & E. J. Bridges (Eds.), *Cardiac nursing* (6th ed., pp. 823–841). Philadelphia, PA: Lippincott Williams & Wilkins.

The effect of HMG-CoA reductase inhibitors is dose dependent. The most active time for cholesterol biosynthesis is during the very early morning hours. For this reason, it is generally recommended to give statins late in the evening, before bedtime. However, not all medications in this group are clinically affected by the administration time. For example, the effects of atorvastatin on LDL reduction are not affected by the time of day it is administered and better fit into the patient's routine of taking other medications. Higher doses of the most potent statins are generally needed to decrease triglyceride levels (Stone et al., 2013).

Atorvastatin at the maximal dose has the greatest LDL-lowering effect of all the HMG-CoA reductase inhibitors. Atorvastatin has a longer half-life and greater hepatic selectivity than the other HMG-CoA reductase inhibitors, which might explain its greater LDL-lowering ability. At maximal doses, LDL can be lowered by 60%. Clinical benefits of atorvastatin have been seen in patients with acute coronary syndrome, patients at high risk for hypertension, and patients with type 2 diabetes (Stone et al., 2013).

Fluvastatin has some properties that differ from other medications in its class. For example, it has a short half-life, is highly bound to proteins, and does not cross the blood-brain barrier. Some researchers claim that fluvastatin is less likely than other HMG-CoA reductase inhibitors to cause systemic side effects (Stone et al., 2013).

Side effects of HMG-CoA reductase inhibitors range in their severity from minor to serious (see Box 5-2). Although there is a small risk for these serious side effects, special precautions are important to assure patient safety. Statins are contraindicated in patients with acute or chronic liver disease. Liver function studies should be assessed at baseline, after 12 weeks of therapy, and every 6 months thereafter. A baseline creatinine kinase should be assessed to aid, if needed, in the future diagnosis of myopathy. Patients must be instructed to immediately report to their prescribing medical provider all signs and symptoms related to the potential serious side effects noted in Box 5-2 (Stone et al., 2013).

Statins can be combined with nicotinic acid, bile acid sequestrants, and even fibrates if necessary. Caution must be used, however, if combining with fibrates because of the increased risk for rhabdomyolysis. Predisposing factors to the development of myopathy and potential rhabdomyolysis include the coadministration of statins with certain other medications, including fibrates, niacin, cyclosporine, erythromycin, and azole antifungal agents. Combination of a

BOX 5-2: HMG-COA REDUCTASE INHIBITOR SIDE EFFECTS

Minor effects include

- headache,
- gastrointestinal effects, and
- potential worsening of cataracts.

Serious effects include

- myopathy (ranges in presentation), for example,
  - myalgia and fatigue,
  - objective myopathy, or
  - rhabdomyolysis;
- hepatic failure;
- decreased or brown urine;
- fever blistering or loosening of the skin;
- skin rash or itching; and
- yellowing of the skin or eyes.

Note. Adapted from Berra, K. A., & Fair, J. M. (2010). Lipid management and cardiovascular disease. In S. L. Woods, E. S. S. Froelicher, S. U. Motzer, & E. J. Bridges (Eds.), *Cardiac nursing* (6th ed., pp. 823-841). Philadelphia, PA: Lippincott Williams & Wilkins.

statin with a fibrate is the most acknowledged combination for increasing the risk for rhabdomyolysis (Stone et al., 2013). Specific factors to consider when combining a statin with a fibrate were discussed in the sections about fibrate therapy and considerations for lowering triglycerides and HDL.

Grapefruit juice contains an agent that slows the activity of the liver enzyme that metabolizes some of the agents in this class, particularly simvastatin and atorvastatin. Therefore, grapefruit juice consumption can increase the expected drug levels of a given dose and increase the risk for rhabdomyolysis. Patients should be instructed not to consume large quantities of grapefruit juice when taking these drugs (Stone et al., 2013).

NURSING APPLICATION

Coadministration of certain medications with HMG-CoA reductase inhibitors can cause rhabdomyolysis. Instruct patients to report all medications they are taking to each prescribing physician.

Intestinal Absorption Inhibitors

Intestinal absorption inhibitors are another class of lipid-lowering medications. These medications can be used alone or in combination with HMG-CoA reductase inhibitors. Ezetimibe blocks the absorption of cholesterol in the small intestine and therefore decreases the delivery of intestinal cholesterol to the liver. This results in a decrease of cholesterol stores in the liver and a subsequent increase in blood clearance of cholesterol (Stone et al., 2013).

PCSK9 Inhibitors

PCSK9 inhibitors are the newest class of lipid-lowering medications. Observation studies first identified that the naturally occurring loss of function of polymorphisms resulting in PCSK9 underexpression could lead to LDL lowering. This occurs by blocking the PCSK9, which increases the availability of LDL-R to remove LDL cholesterol from the blood. In 2015, the FDA approved the first two PCSK9 inhibitors, alirocumab and evolocumab. They are currently indicated as an adjunct to diet and maximally tolerated statin therapy for adults who are not at their LDL goal or who have familial hypercholesterolemia (U.S. Food and Drug Administration 2015a; U.S. Food and Drug Administration 2015b).

CASE STUDY

History of Present Illness

A 49-year-old male patient, who is accompanied by his wife, presents to the primary care clinic with a report of recent chest pain, which he felt after shoveling snow three days ago. The patient states the pain was moderate to severe in intensity and was located in the center of his chest with radiation to his jaw and left arm. The patient reports the chest pain lasted about five to ten minutes and was relieved with rest and two nitroglycerin tablets. The patient describes feeling dizzy and very anxious while experiencing the pain. The patient's wife adds that her husband was breathing rapidly and had a pale color during the episode.

Prior to this most recent episode of chest pain, the patient reports that the only other time he has felt this kind of pain was three years ago. At that time he was diagnosed with stress-induced angina and was prescribed the nitroglycerin tablets, which he has only had to take about two times in the past year. The patient tells the nurse practitioner that he did not report these two episodes to his cardiologist.

Past History

The patient has a medical history of hyperlipidemia and hypertension. He was prescribed fenofibrate and atenolol to manage these medical problems. The patient and his wife are compliant with a low-cholesterol and low salt diet. The patient admits to a 20 pack year history of smoking, but he is currently weaning himself to a complete tobacco cessation quit date, for which he has planned in two months. He denies using alcohol or illicit drugs, and having any prior surgical history. His mother died while he was a child, but his father is currently 89 years old with a medical history of hypertension, coronary artery disease (CAD), and hypothyroidism. The patient's brother is currently 44 years old with hypertension and CAD as well. The patient also has a sister who is 41 years old with dyslipidemia and hypertension.

Physical Exam Findings

The nurse practitioner records these patient findings upon examination of the patient in the primary care clinic:

- Vital signs: blood pressure 168/90 mm Hg; temperature 37 degrees Celsius; heart rate 80 beats/min; respiratory rate 20 beats/min and regular; oxygen saturation 95% on room air.

- General observation – The patient is a healthy-appearing, middle-aged male with no apparent distress noted.

- Lungs – clear bilaterally without wheezing, crackles, or rhonchi appreciated.

- Heart – a palpable apical pulse; S1>S2 at apex; no murmur, gallop, or rubs heard on auscultation.

- Peripheral vasculature – distal pulses are strong bilaterally; no carotid or aortic bruits appreciated; skin is warm and dry.

Diagnostics Performed

A complete blood count, cardiac enzymes, cholesterol panel, and a comprehensive metabolic profile were drawn for the patient. All laboratory results were unremarkable, except the total cholesterol level was 220 mg/dL (HDL 35, LDL 130, and triglycerides 320 mg/dL). A 12-lead electrocardiogram (EKG) revealed nonspecific ST segment and T-wave abnormalities that are unchanged from a prior EKG performed two years ago.

Questions

1. Is the patient's hypertension controlled or uncontrolled?

2. Is the patient's hyperlipidemia being treated optimally?

3. Which lifestyle modifications does the nurse review with the patient?

Answers

1. The patient's hypertension is uncontrolled. Assuming his blood pressure was taken appropriately, his resting blood pressure should not be this high for his medical history and age. The patient should be advised to return for followup monitoring of his blood pressure, or perhaps ambulatory blood pressure monitoring may be discussed as a potential followup action. If subsequent blood pressure monitoring continues to show elevated readings, then adding a second agent, such as an angiotensin-converting enzyme inhibitor (ACEI), should be considered for the patient.

2. The patient's hyperlipidemia is not being treated optimally. Assuming his lipid profile was collected after fasting for the appropriate time, the patient's triglyceride and HDL levels are not optimal for reducing future cardiovascular risks, especially given his family history of CAD. Fenofibrates are useful in lowering triglycerides and indirectly raising HDL; however, the results are ineffective at the time of this visit. The clinician should inquire more closely about the foods the patient is eating before discussing either an increase in his fibrate dose or the addition of a statin.

3. Specific dietary instructions the patient should be following include eating both a low-fat and low-cholesterol diet. The nurse should also reinforce the importance of limiting saturated fat, trans fat, and cholesterol in the diet. The nurse should encourage the patient to follow all dietary recommendations made by the patient's provider or dietitian. The nurse can

encourage the patient to eat these foods, which are low in cholesterol (U.S. Department of Health and Human Services, 2005):

- fruits,
- vegetables,
- whole grains,
- low-fat or non-fat dairy products,
- fish,
- poultry without the skin, and
- lean meats (in moderate amounts).

The nurse should also reinforce the importance of limiting saturated fat, trans fat, and cholesterol in the diet. The nurse should encourage the patient to follow all dietary recommendations made by the patient's provider or dietitian. The nurse should also discuss following all exercise recommendations and taking all medications as prescribed, including what to do if the patient misses a dose. The nurse can praise the patient for his plan to stop smoking, and follow up with him to check on his progress with quitting.

SUMMARY

Many of the medications discussed in this chapter are administered indefinitely, or patients will be prescribed and maintained on these medications for their lifetime. These medications will need to be administered to patients throughout the continuum of health care. Nurses in all settings play an important role in patient education and assessment of therapeutic and adverse effects. Nurses in the cardiovascular setting play a critical role in the accurate administration of potentially dangerous medications, such as IV anticoagulant and antiplatelet therapies. Nurses in the emergency department setting also may play a role in administration of potentially life-saving therapies involving thrombolytic and fibrinolytic agents. The agents that increase myocardial oxygen supply play a major role in the reduction of risk for CVD and the mortality associated with it.

EXAM QUESTIONS

CHAPTER 5
Questions 26–30

Note: Choose the one option that BEST answers each question.

26. Which pathophysiological factor is thought to be most associated with primary hypertension?

    a. T-lymphocyte involvement
    b. Low-density lipoprotein oxidation
    c. Hepatic metabolism of lipoproteins
    d. Familial hypercholesterolemia

27. Which medication is recommended as a renal-protective treatment for patients with hypertension?

    a. Metoprolol
    b. Amlodipine
    c. Ramipril
    d. Diltiazem

28. Which condition is most related to the atherosclerosis associated with coronary artery disease?

    a. Hypertension
    b. Hyperlipidemia
    c. Myocardial infarction
    d. Claudication pains

29. Which special population of patients is most at risk for hyperlipidemia and would benefit the most from risk reduction therapy?

    a. Young women
    b. Young men
    c. Pregnant females
    d. Aged adults

30. Which class of medications is most effective in lowering low-density lipoprotein?

    a. Bile acid sequestrants
    b. Nicotinic acid
    c. Fibrates
    d. HMG-coenzyme A reductase inhibitors

REFERENCES

American Diabetes Association. (2015). Cardiovascular disease and risk management. *Diabetes Care, 38*(1), S49-S57. doi:10.2337/dc15-S011

Berra, K. A., & Fair, J. M. (2010). Lipid management and cardiovascular disease. In S. L. Woods, E. S. S. Froelicher, S. U. Motzer, & E. J. Bridges (Eds.), *Cardiac nursing* (6th ed., pp. 823-841). Philadelphia, PA: Lippincott Williams & Wilkins.

Boltz, M., & Capezuti, E. (2016). *Evidence-based geriatric nursing protocols for best practice.* New York, NY: Springer.

Griffin, B. P., Kapadia, S. R., & Rimmerman, C. M. (2013). *Cleveland Clinic Cardiology Board review* (2nd ed.). Philadelphia, PA: Lippincott Williams & Wilkins.

Guzik, T. J., Hoch, N. E., Brown, K. A., McCann, L. A., Rahman, A., Dikalov, S., ... Harrison, D. G. (2007). Role of the T cell in the genesis of angiotensin II induced hypertension and vascular dysfunction. *Journal Experimental Medicine, 204*(10), 2449-2460.

Harrison, D. G., Guzik, T. J., Lob, H. E., Madhur, M., Marvar, P. J., Salim, T., ... Weyand, C. (2011). Inflammation, immunity, and hypertension. *Hypertension, 57*(2), 132-140. doi: 10.1161/HYPERTENSIONAHA.110.163576

Huether, S. E., & McCance, K. L. (2017). *Understanding pathophysiology* (6th ed.). St. Louis, MO: Elsevier.

Institute for Clinical Systems Improvement. (2014). *Healthcare guideline: Hypertension diagnosis and treatment.* Bloomington, MN: Institute for Clinical Systems Improvement.

James, P. A., Oparil, S., Carter, B. L., Cushman, W. C., Dennison-Himmelfarb, C., Handler, J., ... Ortiz, E. (2014). 2014 Evidence-based guideline for the management of high blood pressure in adults: Report from the panel members appointed to the eighth Joint National Committee (JNC 8). *JAMA, 311*(5), 507-520. doi:10.1001/jama.2013.284427

Madhur, M. S., Lob, H. E., McCann, L. A., Iwakura, Y., Blinder, Y., Guzik, T. J., & Harrison, D. G. (2010). Interleukin 17 promotes angiotensin II-induced hypertension and vascular dysfunction. *Hypertension,* 55(2), 500-507. doi:10.1161/HYPERTENSIONAHA.109.145094

Madhur, M. S., Riaz, K., Dreisbach, A. W., & Harrison, D. G. (2014). Hypertension. The Medscape from WebMD Journal of Medicine. Retrieved from http://emedicine.medscape.com/article/241381-overview

Mozaffarian, D., Benjamin, E. J., Go, A. S., Arnett, D. K., Blaha, M. J., Cushman, M., ... Turner, M. B. (2015). Heart disease and stroke statistics – 2015 update: A report from the American Heart Association. *Circulation, 132.* doi:10.1161/CIR.0000000000000350

Pedersen, T. R., Kjekshus, J., Berg, K., Haghfelt, T., Faergemn, O., Thorgeirsson, G., ... Wedel, H. (1994). Randomised trial of cholesterol lowering in 4444 patients with coronary heart disease: The Scandinavian Simvastatin Survival Study (4S). *The Lancet, 344,* 1383-1389. doi:10.1016/S0140-6736(94)90566-5

Ridker, P. M., Danielson, E., Fonseca, F. A., Genest, J., Gotto, A. M., Kastelein, J. J., ... Glynn, R. J. (2008). Rosuvastatin to prevent vascular events in men and women with elevated C-reactive protein. *New England Journal of Medicine, 359*(21), 2195-2207. Retrieved from http://www.nejm.org/doi/full/10.1056/NEJMoa0807646

Rosendorff, C., Lackland, D. T., Aronow, W. S., Blumenthal, R. S., de Lemos, J. A., Findeis, L., Gore, J. M., ... White, W. B. (2015). Treatment of hypertension in patients with coronary artery disease: A scientific statement from the American Heart Association, American College of Cardiology, and American Society of Hypertension. *Hypertension, 65,* 1372-1407. doi:10.1161/HYP.0000000000000018

Stone, N. J., Robinson, J., Lichtenstein, A. H., Merz, C. N. B., Blum, C. B., Eckel, R. H., ... Wilson, P. W. F. (2013). 2013 ACC/AHA guideline on the treatment of blood cholesterol to reduce atherosclerotic cardiovascular risk in adults. *Circulation, 129*(25 Suppl. 2), S1-S45. doi:10.1161/01.cir.0000437738.63853.7a

U.S. Department of Health and Human Services. (2005). *Your guide to lowering your cholesterol with TLC.* Retrieved from https://www.nhlbi.nih.gov/files/docs/public/heart/chol_tlc.pdf

U.S. Food and Drug Administration. (2015a). *FDA approves Praluent to treat certain patients with high cholesterol.* Retrieved from http://www.fda.gov/NewsEvents/Newsroom/Press Announcements/ucm455883.htm

U.S. Food and Drug Administration. (2015b). *FDA approves Repatha to treat certain patients with high cholesterol.* Retrieved from http://www.fda.gov/NewsEvents/Newsroom/Press Announcements/ucm460082.htm

CHAPTER 6

CORONARY HEART DISEASE

LEARNING OUTCOME

After completing this chapter, the learner will be able to identify pathophysiological processes associated with coronary heart disease and angina.

CHAPTER OBJECTIVES

After completing this chapter, the learner will be able to:

1. Summarize the pathophysiological processes involved in patients with coronary heart disease.

2. Differentiate between features of stable and unstable angina.

3. Discuss the nursing considerations of specific populations of patients with coronary heart disease and angina.

4. Select diagnostic testing appropriate for the management of patients with suspected coronary heart disease.

5. Describe treatment options and nursing care for patients with coronary heart disease.

INTRODUCTION

Coronary heart disease (CHD) is the most common type of heart disease worldwide and is responsible for more than 370,000 deaths in the United States annually (Xu, Murphy, Kochanek, & Bastian, 2016). Nurses must be able to apply knowledge of the pathophysiological processes of this disease to their care of patients' dietary, genetic, and lifestyle factors. Nurses must also be able to identify a variety of patient presentations that occur secondary to CHD.

PATHOPHYSIOLOGY OF CORONARY HEART DISEASE

The development of CHD begins in adolescence and continues throughout life. CHD, also known as coronary artery disease (CAD), is the presence of atherosclerosis or atherosclerotic plaque in the coronary arteries. CHD is considered a chronic condition but can lead to acute cardiac events. Cardiovascular risk factors (discussed in Chapter 3) accelerate the process. Atherosclerosis involves the deposit of lipids, calcium, fibrin, and other cellular substances within the lining of the arteries. This deposit initiates a progressive inflammatory response in an effort to heal the endothelium. As atherosclerotic plaque progresses, the lumen of the coronary artery can become narrowed and blood flow can be impaired. Reduced blood flow can lead to ischemia (a lack of oxygen to the myocardium). The end result of this inflammatory process is the production of a fibrous atherosclerotic plaque that can partially or totally occlude blood flow. Prolonged ischemia can result in injury and, ultimately, necrosis of myocardial tissue (Huether & McCance, 2017).

Although atherosclerosis begins early in life, it may not produce clinical symptoms for several decades. The first step in the development of atherosclerotic plaque is the accumulation of intimal macrophage foam cells that are rich in lipids. As time progresses, smooth muscle cells become more involved as they accumulate intracellular lipids, and fatty streaks form between the endothelium and the intima of the artery. In this early developmental phase, the inflammatory process is activated and immune cells, such as T lymphocytes and mast cells, begin to invade the lesion. As progression continues, extracellular lipids are deposited among the layers of smooth muscle cells. These deposits begin to destroy the integrity of intimal smooth muscle cells and harden (Huether & McCance, 2017).

As the lesion matures into one of clinical significance, an extracellular lipid core develops; this is sometimes called an *atheroma*. Calcium deposits may be contained within the lipid core. At this stage, foam cells also die and contribute their necrotic components to the growth of the lipid core. The lipid core thickens the artery wall, usually at the external edge, but does not greatly narrow the lumen. Eventually, fibrous tissue (mainly collagen) forms a fibrous cap that covers the lipid core. This lesion is sometimes referred to as a *fibrous atheroma* because of the accumulation of the fibrous connective tissue within the intima. These lesions cause more noticeable vessel narrowing and are clinically significant because they are prone to ulcerations and sudden rupture. Microscopic ulcerations of the vulnerable plaque initiate plaque rupture in most coronary events. Both mechanical and inflammatory vascular changes affect the vulnerability of plaque (Huether & McCance, 2017).

The release of enzymes from immune response cells contributes to the vulnerability of rupture by weakening the collagen matrix of the fibrous cap. When plaque ruptures, the core of the lipid is exposed to circulating blood. This exposure results in platelet adherence, activation, and aggregation, then subsequent activation of the coagulation pathway, with resultant thrombus formation. After rupture, reparative cells respond and incorporate existing thrombi into the expanding lesion. New fibrous tissue is formed to repair the lesion, causing further narrowing of the lumen of the vessel. At this stage in the atherosclerosis process, the tunica media and tunica adventitia are also affected by the inflammatory response (Huether & McCance, 2017).

Stable plaques have thick fibrous caps that separate the lipid core from the endothelium. Stable plaques are less complicated than vulnerable plaques and tend to have smooth outlines. More vulnerable plaques have thinner caps. Both mechanical features and inflammatory responses affect the vulnerability of a lesion. The role of the inflammatory response in acute coronary syndromes (ACSs) has been the focus in identifying risk factors that are able to measure levels of risk for vascular inflammation. Biomarkers for this inflammation include high-sensitivity C-reactive protein, fibrinogen, homocysteine, lipoprotein A, serum amyloid A, and interleukin-6 (Huether & McCance, 2017).

Rupture of a coronary plaque produces an acute coronary event and increases the short-term risk for cardiac death or nonfatal myocardial infarction (MI). It is important to know that most vulnerable plaques identified during cardiac catheterization (angiography) are not found in tightly stenotic vessels. Patients can have plaque in the coronary arteries that does not cause lumen stenosis. This plaque can be visualized using intracoronary ultrasound. It is this plaque that is usually most vulnerable and the cause of ACSs. In most patients, MI results from atheromas producing less than 50% narrowing of the vessel lumen. Plaques that cause greater than 75% stenosis and angina are usually more stable plaques and less likely to rupture (Huether & McCance, 2017). Figure 6-1 compares features of vulnerable and stable plaques.

Because vulnerable plaque typically does not produce symptomatic stenotic disease, stress testing has a limited ability to detect vulnerable plaque. Vulnerable plaque may not be visible as a stenotic lesion but may be visualized using intracoronary ultrasound cardiac catheterization.

NURSING APPLICATION

When a patient with CHD risk factors has a cardiac catheterization that shows minimal stenotic disease, it is important for the nurse to understand that this patient may still have a substantial plaque burden and be at high risk for vulnerable plaque rupture. Nurses must incorporate aggressive risk factor modification for such patients, just as they do for patients with stenotic disease. Patients with significant risk factors are at the highest risk for progressive atherosclerosis. For this reason, all patients with risk factors should be aggressively treated with risk-reduction strategies, regardless of the results of diagnostic tests.

ANGINA: THE SIGN AND SYMPTOM OF CORONARY HEART DISEASE

Patients with CHD experience symptoms caused by an imbalance between oxygen supply and demand. Angina pectoris is the clinical symptom that results from decreased blood flow to the myocardium. Angina usually occurs in patients with CHD involving 70% or more stenosis in at least one major proximal epicardial coronary artery. Decreased blood flow results in ischemia, or a temporary lack of oxygen to the heart muscle. Although typically caused by CHD, angina can also be caused by other cardiac conditions, such as coronary artery spasm, valvular heart disease, uncontrolled hypertension, and hypertrophic cardiomyopathy.

Most patients describe angina as a sensation of pressure, tightness, heaviness, burning, or squeezing. This sensation can be felt behind

FIGURE 6-1: EVOLUTION OF ATHEROSCLEROTIC PLAQUE IN CORONARY ARTERY DISEASE

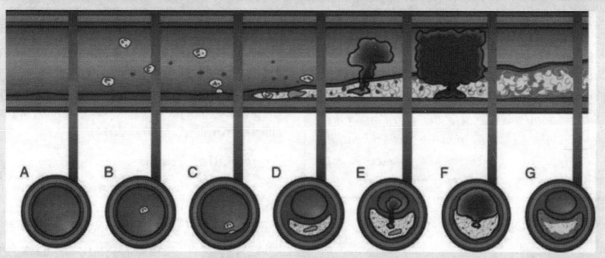

Note. From Urden, L. D., Stacy, K. M., & Lough, M. E. (2014). *Critical care nursing: Diagnosis and management* (7th ed.). St. Louis, MO: Elsevier/Mosby. © Elsevier 2014.

the sternum and in the upper back, shoulder, arm, jaw, or epigastric area. Angina is rarely described as a sharp or stabbing pain, and it should not worsen with changes in position or respiration. Anginal pain usually does not occur in the middle to lower abdomen and does not usually radiate to the lower extremities. The duration of angina is typically defined in minutes, as opposed to seconds or hours. Some patients do not experience any of the symptoms previously described. Instead, they may experience dyspnea, nausea, palpitations, or diaphoresis, alone or in combination. These additional symptoms also may be accompanied by discomfort of the chest, back, shoulder, arm, or jaw. Some patients with acute MI have had preceding angina (Huether & McCance, 2017).

When assessing a patient with angina, the nurse should ask the following questions regarding symptoms.

- What is the quality of discomfort (e.g., pressure, squeezing, or heaviness)?

- Where is the discomfort located? Does it radiate? If so, where?

- When did the discomfort start, and how long did it last?

- Were any actions performed or sensations felt before the start of the discomfort?

- What lessens or relieves the discomfort? What makes it worse?

NURSING APPLICATION

It is important to use the word discomfort when assessing patients with potential angina. Many patients with dyspnea or chest pressure deny the presence of pain.

FEATURES OF ANGINA

Angina pectoris can be classified as stable or unstable, and its presentation ranges from stable angina to acute MI. Within this presentation spectrum, the clinician must be able to differentiate stable angina from the angina associated with ACSs. The term ACS is used to describe the presentation of CHD in the form of unstable angina, non-ST-segment elevation MI, or ST-segment elevation MI (Amsterdam et al., 2014).

Stable Angina

Stable angina pectoris typically occurs with physical exertion or emotional stress and is relieved by rest or sublingual nitroglycerin. Angina is considered stable when its pattern is predictable over several weeks. To be considered predictable, angina should be triggered by the same amount of physical or emotional stress and should be easily relieved by rest or sublingual nitroglycerin (Amsterdam et al., 2014).

Unstable Angina

Angina is considered unstable when it occurs with minimal exertion or when an increased dose of nitroglycerin is required to achieve relief. Acute angina during rest is also considered unstable angina. Any angina that increases in severity or is very severe on first presentation is considered unstable. Unstable angina is caused by an unstable or ruptured plaque that causes abrupt closure of a coronary artery. It is treated very differently from stable angina. Treatment for unstable angina will be discussed later in this chapter (Amsterdam et al., 2014).

Aggravating Factors

Patients with CHD experience symptoms caused by an imbalance between oxygen supply and demand. Certain conditions can upset the balance between myocardial oxygen supply and demand. Conditions that can increase myocardial oxygen demand include hyperthermia, hypertension, tachycardia, and conditions that produce overstimulation of the sympathetic nervous system, such as cocaine use and hyperthyroidism. Certain coexisting cardiac conditions can also increase myocardial oxygen demand and reduce supply, including aortic stenosis and hypertrophic cardiomyopathy. Noncardiac conditions that decrease the delivery of oxygen to tissues can also exacerbate angina. These include conditions associated with a decreased hemoglobin level (such as gastrointestinal bleeding) or conditions that decrease oxygen saturation levels (such as exacerbations of chronic lung disease).

Complications of Chronic Angina

The extent of ischemia and its impact on left ventricular function determine the outcomes in patients with angina. Complications of ischemia include mitral regurgitation or left ventricular thrombi development, which is the result of left ventricular dilation and dysfunction.

Subpopulations Among Patients With Angina

Angina in Women

The presentation of angina in women is often different from the presentation in men. The most common presentation of CAD in women is atypical and typical angina, as opposed to men, who typically show an initial presentation of MI or sudden cardiac death; however, the female presentation of angina as a symptom of CAD often goes undiagnosed because women are more likely to present with chest pain accompanied by atypical features (Griffin, Kapadia, & Rimmerman, 2013).

Coronary spasm, mitral valve prolapse, and microvascular disease are more likely to be the causes of symptoms in women. Women presenting with anginal symptoms who proceed to cardiac catheterization have less documented stenotic disease of major epicardial coronary arteries. Women are also more likely to have unstable angina (associated with an unstable or ruptured plaque) than acute MIs, as mentioned in the earlier *Unstable Angina* subsection (Amsterdam et al., 2014). Women are also older than men on presentation with ACSs and have a higher incidence of complications, including the development of heart failure. Substernal chest pressure that radiates to the arm or jaw is less common in women than in men. Women may describe more generalized epigastric discomfort or present with less specific complaints, such as dyspnea or fatigue (Huether & McCance, 2017).

Many women, and even some healthcare providers, do not acknowledge heart disease as a major health risk for women. For this reason, many women delay seeking health care when they experience symptoms and may attribute their symptoms to other noncardiac causes (Amsterdam et al., 2014; Mehta et al., 2016). Although heart disease kills more women than all cancers combined, many women still consider breast cancer and other forms of cancer as their primary health risk (Mehta et al., 2016).

NURSING APPLICATION

Women presenting with symptoms of discomfort from their nose to their navel should be evaluated for the presence of CHD. Women should be educated about the risk and specific manifestation of CHD in their gender.

Before menopause, women appear to have a protective mechanism in place against CHD. However, after menopause, the risk for CHD in women begins to approach that of men, but they lag behind men in their presentation of CHD by about 10 years. The protective effect of the premenopausal state has led to the study of hormone replacement therapy as a strategy to reduce the risk for heart disease in women. However, no strong evidence proves that this benefit reduces the incidence of CHD in post-menopausal women, so it is not recommended (Boardman et al., 2015).

Angina in Older Adults

Among older adults, angina is commonly described with more generalized symptoms, such as weakness, dyspnea, and confusion. These symptoms are often attributed to the aging process, and they may be the reason that a diagnosis of angina is overlooked. Older adults also face special challenges in the medical management of angina. In many cases, these patients have multiple health and pharmacological factors that impact the effects of cardiovascular drugs, such as multiple comorbidities and polypharmaceutical treatments. In addition, many medications need to be prescribed at lower starting doses. Older adults are particularly sensitive to drugs with a hypotensive response (Amsterdam et al., 2014).

Angina in People With Diabetes

Autonomic dysfunction occurs in about one third of patients with diabetes and can affect the symptoms they experience with angina and ACSs. Patients with diabetes may be less likely to experience pain. Patients with diabetes have more severe multivessel disease and also have higher rates of complications after acute cardiac events (Amsterdam et al., 2014).

DIAGNOSIS OF CORONARY HEART DISEASE

Initial diagnosis of CHD involves a thorough history and physical examination. Laboratory studies, cardiac imaging studies, 12-lead electrocardiogram (ECG) testing, stress testing, and cardiac catheterization may be used as additional diagnostic tools. Assessment information also includes the presence of cardiovascular risk factors and a history of CHD, cerebrovascular disease, or peripheral vascular disease, which increases the likelihood that the presentation of symptoms is related to myocardial ischemia (Huether & McCance, 2017).

The 12-lead ECG can be normal in many patients with chronic stable angina; therefore, a normal ECG does not exclude CHD. However, an abnormal ECG showing signs of left ventricular hypertrophy, Q waves, or ST-segment depression or the presence of a cardiac dysrhythmia increases the likelihood that CHD is the cause of the symptoms (Huether & McCance, 2017).

In addition to a 12-lead ECG, initial assessment parameters for evaluating a patient for CHD include blood pressure, ankle-brachial index, and laboratory testing, including hemoglobin level and hematocrit to rule out anemia, a fasting blood sugar level to rule out diabetes, and a fasting lipid profile to assess for hyperlipidemia (Amsterdam et al., 2014).

When a patient presents with potential symptoms of angina, other cardiac and non-cardiac conditions should be considered. Pulmonary disorders, gastrointestinal disorders, chest wall pain, and, sometimes, psychiatric conditions can manifest in symptoms similar to those of angina (Huether & McCance, 2017).

Stress Testing

Stress testing, with or without myocardial imaging, is a common tool used in the diagnosis of CHD. Stress testing can be done using exercise or chemicals. Treadmills or bicycles are used for exercise stress tests. Certain patients are not candidates for exercise stress testing without accompanying myocardial imaging because the ECG alone may not provide adequate diagnostic information. These patients include those with left bundle branch block, greater than 1 mm ST-segment depression at rest, paced ventricular rhythm, or Wolff-Parkinson-White syndrome (Fletcher et al., 2013). Other absolute contraindications to exercise stress testing include hemodynamically significant arrhythmias, symptomatic heart failure, severe aortic stenosis, acute pulmonary embolus, myocarditis, and acute aortic dissection (Griffin et al., 2013).

When patients exercise, myocardial oxygen demand increases and coronary arteries dilate in response to this increased demand. In a patient with CHD, the coronary arteries are not able to adequately dilate to meet the needs of the increased myocardial oxygen demand, and abnormalities occur on the 12-lead ECG or associated imaging studies. The most common protocol for exercise stress testing is the Bruce protocol. Table 6-1 describes the key features of the Bruce and modified Bruce protocols (Bashore, Granger, Jackson, & Patel, 2016).

Four pharmacological agents are used in chemical stress testing: dobutamine, dipyridamole, adenosine, and regadenoson. Dipyridamole, adenosine, and regadenoson cause coronary microvascular dilatation similar to the coronary artery vasodilation that occurs with exercise. The coronary vasodilation caused by these three medications is related to interaction with the adenosine A2a receptor, which is responsible for coronary vasodilation. In addition to stimulation of this adenosine receptor, dipyridamole and adenosine are nonselective adenosine receptor stimulators and also stimulate the A1, A2b, and A3 receptors. Stimulation of these other receptors is what causes the unwanted side effect of atrioventricular block (A1 receptor) and bronchospasm (A2b and A3 receptors). Because of the vasodilation effect, all three medications commonly cause chest pain because vasodilation pulls blood away from compromised areas of the myocardium. Another common side effect caused by vasodilation is flushing. Because of the risk for bronchospasm, any patient with reactive airway disease or active wheezing before stress testing is not a candidate for dipyridamole or adenosine. Because of the selectivity to the A2a receptor, regadenoson has a lower incidence of the side effects of atrioventricular block or bronchoconstriction (Bashore et al., 2016). Another advantage of regadenoson over dipyridamole and adenosine is that it can be given via a rapid 10-second infusion and does not need to be weight based. Dipyridamole and adenosine are weight-based infusions given over 4 minutes.

TABLE 6-1: COMMON EXERCISE STRESS TEST PROTOCOLS

Type of Protocol	Stage 1 Starting Point	Key Features
Bruce protocol	1.7 mph 10% grade 5 METs	• Stage 2: 2.5 mph, 12% grade, 7 METs • Stage 3: 3.4 mph, 14% grade, 9 METs • There are a maximum of 10 potential stages • 3-minute stages to allow for achievement of steady state • in MET level between stages is more pronounced than in other protocols
Modified Bruce protocol[a]	1.7 mph 0 grade	• Two warm-up stages of 3 minutes each • Second stage: 1.7 mph and 5% grade • Third stage corresponds to stage 1 of standard Bruce protocol

[a]Used in elderly patients and those with decreased exercise capacity because of cardiac function.

MET = metabolic equivalent; mph = miles per hour.

Note. Adapted from Bashore, T., Granger, C. B., Jackson, K. P., & Patel, M. R. (2016). Heart disease. In M. Papadakis (Ed.), *CURRENT medical diagnosis and treatment 2016* (pp. 321-434). New York, NY: McGraw-Hill Education.

Aminophylline can be given as an antidote to all three medications but is seldom needed with adenosine because of its short half-life or with regadenoson because of its limited side effects (Amsterdam et al., 2014).

NURSING APPLICATION

Patients scheduled for chemical stress testing involving adenosine or dipyridamole should be assessed for the presence of lung disease and wheezing before the test. Patients who are currently taking aminophylline-containing medications should not undergo chemical stress testing involving dipyridamole, adenosine, or regadenoson because aminophylline counteracts the medications being administered for the stress test.

Dobutamine works differently from the other three agents. Dobutamine stress testing more closely mimics exercise stress testing. During a dobutamine stress test, high-dose dobutamine is used to increase contractility and heart rate, thereby increasing myocardial oxygen demand. In response to this increased myocardial oxygen demand, the coronary arteries dilate. They do not, however, dilate to the extent they do with agents that produce more direct coronary vasodilation. A potential side effect of dobutamine that is not present with dipyridamole, adenosine, or regadenoson is cardiac tachydysrhythmias (Bashore et al., 2016).

Exercise or chemical stress testing is combined with pretest cardiac imaging, such as cardiac echocardiography or radionuclide imaging; pretest and posttest cardiac images are compared. CHD is suspected when echocardiography images show a new wall motion abnormality after exercise or after the administration of high-dose dobutamine. Echocardiography is not used as the imaging modality with dipyridamole, adenosine, or regadenoson stress testing. When radionuclide imaging is used, the peak stress images are compared with the resting images. An area of relative hypoperfusion on the peak stress images is suspicious for CHD (Amsterdam et al., 2014).

All pharmacological stress testing is done in conjunction with myocardial imaging. The imaging portion of a stress test provides information about the extent, severity, and location of ischemia, whereas the exercise portion of a stress test (excluding dipyridamole and adenosine testing) can provide prognostic information. One example of prognostic information obtained from exercise stress testing is the heart rate recovery score. This score is calculated by taking the heart rate at peak exercise and subtracting the heart rate at 1 to 2 minutes after exercise. An abnormal score at 1 minute is considered to be 12 to 22 beats/min. Other studies used the value calculated at 2 minutes and considered an abnormal score to be 22 to 42 beats/min. A low score is considered to be less than 8 beats/min and is associated with a high risk for death. A score of 8 to 12 beats/min is considered an intermediate risk. When patients are able to exercise on a treadmill for 6 to 12 minutes, exercise stress testing is generally performed instead of chemical stress testing. Patients on beta blockers who are scheduled to undergo exercise stress testing should have these medications held for approximately 48 hours before testing. If these medications are not held, an adequate heart rate may be difficult to achieve. Exercise stress testing is less sensitive in women than in men (Fletcher et al., 2013).

Absolute contraindications to stress testing in high-risk patients include any conditions that increase oxygen demand (or consumption) and have the potential to decrease oxygen supply. These conditions include acute MI less than or equal to 2 days old, acute myocarditis or pericarditis, acute pulmonary embolism, acute aortic dissection, symptomatic heart failure, severe aortic stenosis, symptomatic dysrhythmias, and high-risk unstable angina (Fletcher et al., 2013).

Coronary Computed Tomography Angiogram

Coronary computed tomography angiogram (CCTA) can be used to assess for calcium deposits or soft fatty plaque in coronary arteries. This test is a contrasted computed tomography study concentrated on visualizing the coronary arteries and degree of plaque within them. Use of this technology in the diagnosis of CAD is rapidly evolving. The procedure involves the administration of an iodine-based contrast agent, and the patient does receive an exposure to radiation. As the technology evolves and technique improves, radiation doses are being lowered. The administration of an intravenous beta blocker can be used to slow the heart rate and capture better images; however, patients with high heart rates can be imaged using dual-score computed tomography if beta blockade is contraindicated or undesired. Although CCTA is less invasive than cardiac catheterization, the latter remains the gold standard in the diagnosis of CAD. Currently, the use of a 64-slice CCTA demonstrates high diagnostic reliability in patients suspected to have CAD. In the past many challenges existed and inconsistencies were found when using CCTA as a diagnostic tool for CAD; however, the majority of those tests were using 4- and 16-slice CCTA technology that was proven less reliable for a diagnosis (Sun, Choo, & Ng, 2012). Other limitations in the accuracy of CCTA include resting heart rate greater than 60 to 70 beats/min, irregular heart rhythms, inability to hold a breath for 5 seconds, severe coronary calcifications and presence of coronary stents, or small-caliber vessels less than 1.5 mm. Relative contraindications include patients at high risk for contrast nephropathy or serum creatinine levels greater than 2.0 mg/dl (Gerber & Manning, 2015).

Cardiac Catheterization

Cardiac catheterization, or angiography, is currently the gold standard for determining the presence, location, and extent of obstructive CHD. Cardiac catheterization is an invasive procedure with rare but serious risks for adverse outcomes, including stroke, MI, and death. For this reason, patients are carefully chosen and must meet certain criteria. The American Heart Association and American College of Cardiology have very specific recommendations for appropriate indications for cardiac catheterization. Candidates for cardiac catheterization include patients with a suspected acute coronary syndrome, suspected or known CAD, high-risk findings during ECG stress testing or stress testing with cardiac imaging, or CCTA lesions found to cause 50% or greater obstruction. Other indications for cardiac catheterization include patients being medically managed or patients with persistent ischemic symptoms postrevascularization (Patel et al., 2012).

In addition to determining the location and severity of lesions, cardiac catheterization can evaluate intracardiac pressures and left ventricular function. Cardiac catheterization is also done to evaluate patients with possible vasospastic angina who have chest pain at rest. Provocative testing can be done in the cardiac catheterization laboratory using ergonovine maleate. If needed, intracoronary vasodilators can be given to treat the induced spasm.

Patients can receive diagnostic cardiac catheterization and return home the same day if no further treatment is done. Cardiac catheterization is performed by inserting a catheter through the femoral or radial artery and guiding it to the heart. If femoral or radial artery access cannot be used, then brachial access can be used. Care of the insertion site (usually the groin or wrist) after the procedure is a major nursing focus. A period of bed rest in an observation unit is indicated after the procedure for femoral access. The amount of bed rest required before discharge depends on the type of closure used for the femoral artery insertion site. If the manual pressure method of sheath removal is used, then the patient typically remains on bed rest for 4 to 8 hours. If a closure device is used, then a much shorter period of bed rest and an earlier discharge are possible. For radial access sites, a transradial pressure band will be applied and will be slowly loosened over 1 to 3 hours. Nursing care after cardiac catheterization involves frequent assessment of the insertion site for external bleeding and hematoma development. Distal pulses are also assessed to assure adequate circulation (Levine et al., 2015).

NURSING APPLICATION

The development of bleeding or a hematoma at the insertion site is treated by applying firm manual pressure. Patients and families must be instructed to activate their Emergency Medical Services and apply firm manual pressure to the site if bleeding occurs after discharge.

TREATMENT CONSIDERATIONS

Stable patients who are diagnosed with greater than 70% stenosis during cardiac catheterization have three primary treatment options: medical treatment, primary (percutaneous) coronary intervention (PCI), or coronary artery bypass grafting (Amsterdam et al., 2014; Levine et al., 2015). PCI most often includes balloon angioplasty with either a bare metal or drug-eluting stent. Lifestyle modification and aggressive risk factor reduction are included in all three treatment arms. The goal of medical treatment for CHD is to improve quality of life by reducing symptoms and preventing compli-

cations including disease progression, MI, and death. Treatment decisions should be a collaboration between the medical provider and the patient in an effort to stop disease progression, increase the patient's quality of life, and reduce the risk for death (Patel et al., 2012).

Pharmacological Management

Treatment of angina usually begins with medical therapy. Medical management of patients with CHD includes lifestyle and dietary modifications and the use of multiple combinations of medications, most commonly including antiplatelets, antianginal therapy, lipid-lowering agents, and antianginals (cardiovascular pharmacological therapies are discussed further in Chapter 4).

Antiplatelet Therapy

Antiplatelet therapy is prescribed for all patients without contraindications for the medication. Aspirin is the primary antiplatelet agent used for patients with known CHD or those with symptoms suggestive of CHD. For patients with known CHD, peripheral vascular disease, or stroke, aspirin in doses from 75 to 325 mg has been shown to reduce the risk for MI, stroke, and vascular death (Capodanno & Angiolillo, 2013).

Clopidogrel was found to be more effective than aspirin in reducing the risk for MI, stroke, and death in patients with atherosclerotic vascular disease, but there is a dramatic cost difference between aspirin and clopidogrel. Affordability prevents clopidogrel from being more widely used as a primary antiplatelet agent. However, clopidogrel is used as an alternative for patients who are sensitive to aspirin. Prasugrel, a newer antiplatelet agent, is not indicated in the treatment of stable angina. It is indicated to prevent thromboembolic complications in patients with ACSs who are treated with PCI (Capodanno & Angiolillo, 2013).

Antianginal Agents

Patients with CHD are also prescribed antianginal agents. These agents include beta blockers, nitrates, and calcium channel blockers. The goals of antianginal therapy are to reduce symptoms and improve activity tolerance, thereby improving quality of life.

Beta Blockers

Beta blockers are the first-line agents in the treatment of stable angina. Beta blockers are very effective in controlling angina brought on by physical exertion. The initial target heart rate goal is 55 to 60 beats/min at rest for patients with stable angina. Resting heart rate may need to be lowered if angina cannot be controlled. Patients can experience side effects with beta blockers that limit dosing, and beta blockers are not used to treat vasospastic angina. Beta blockers are the one class of antianginal medications with survival benefits in specific groups of patients, such as those patients who have had a recent MI (Woo & Robinson, 2016).

Nitrates

Nitrates improve exercise tolerance and prolong the time to onset of angina. For nitrates to remain effective, patients need to have an 8- to 10-hour nitrate-free period each day. Headache is the most common side effect of nitrate use. Headaches usually subside over time in patients taking long-acting nitrates. Patients with a history of angina should always carry sublingual nitroglycerin (Amsterdam et al., 2014).

NURSING APPLICATION

Headaches associated with nitroglycerin administration should be treated because pain activates the sympathetic nervous system, which increases myocardial oxygen demand and, potentially, myocardial ischemia.

Calcium Channel Blockers

Calcium channel blockers or long-acting nitrates are used as first-line agents for vasospastic angina because they are direct coronary vasodilators. These medications can also be added to beta-blocker therapy when angina is not controlled. Calcium channel blockers must be used with caution in patients with impaired systolic left ventricular dysfunction (heart failure). Amlodipine and felodipine (newer dihydropyridine calcium channel blockers) are more selective coronary artery vasodilators and are better tolerated than other calcium channel blockers in patients with left ventricular dysfunction (Amsterdam et al., 2014).

Ranolazine

Ranolazine is used in combination with other antianginal agents including amlodipine, beta blockers, and nitrates. The exact mechanism of action is not fully understood, but it is thought that ranolazine works on the cardiac ion channels to reduce the amount of intracellular sodium. Increased intracellular sodium can result in an increase in intracellular calcium due to the sodium-calcium exchange pump. By lowering intracellular sodium, ranolazine can reduce intracellular calcium overload and improve ventricular function. Because of this effect, ranolazine can also prevent dysrhythmias induced by ischemia. Unlike other antianginal agents, the effects of ranolazine are not dependent on changes in heart rate or blood pressure. Ranolazine is not used as a first-line antianginal medication because of its ability to potentially prolong the QT interval. It should not be used in patients with hepatic cirrhosis or other liver disorders and is contraindicated with the consumption of grapefruit juice. Renal function should be monitored when taking this medication, and patients older than 75 years must be monitored closely because of an increased incidence of adverse reactions in this population (Woo & Robinson, 2016).

Nonpharmacological Treatment Options

PCI and coronary artery bypass grafting are the two nonpharmacological treatment options for patients with CHD. These two forms of cardiac revascularization are discussed, along with transmyocardial revascularization, in Chapter 18.

Counterpulsation therapy, also known as therapy via an intra-aortic balloon pump, is another acute, temporary, nonpharmacological treatment option used for patients with refractory, or unresponsive, angina on maximal medical therapy and/or those who are not candidates for revascularization. The intra-aortic balloon pump provides mechanical support for the oxygen-deprived or failing heart. The use of the device involves the placement of a catheter, most commonly via the femoral artery, into the descending aorta just below the subclavian artery. The distal tip of the catheter contains a 30- to 40-cc balloon that inflates during diastole and deflates during systole of each cardiac cycle. During inflation, in the diastolic phase, the balloon displaces oxygenated blood retrograde (above the balloon into the aortic arch and ascending aorta), perfusing the coronary arteries during diastole; it also displaces oxygenated blood antegrade to the system. The diastolic perfusion of the displaced blood flow supplies the myocardium with twice the delivery of oxygen it would normally receive. During deflation, the amount of blood displaced in the aorta during inflation is now "empty," causing a negative pressure and reducing the afterload the heart must pump against. This afterload reduction decreases the workload of the failing heart, thereby decreasing oxygen consumption (Urden, Stacy, & Lough, 2015).

Long-Term Management

For patients with stable angina, it is important to evaluate the effectiveness of risk factor reduction with each follow-up visit. An assessment of the patient's anginal symptoms, functional capacity, and tolerance to medications is also important. The patient should know to report worsening angina or rest angina. Follow-up office visits are usually scheduled every 4 to 6 months during the first year after initiation of antianginal therapy. Long-term follow-up is generally based on the patient's other existing medical conditions but should occur at least annually. Patients with conditions that exacerbate angina (e.g., heart failure or atrial fibrillation with rapid ventricular responses) require more frequent follow-up. Follow-up visits can be alternated between the primary care provider and the cardiologist (Amsterdam et al., 2014). To facilitate the continuity of care and clarity of the patient's medication regimen, communication between the specialist and primary care provider is crucial for the patient's safety.

NURSING APPLICATION

Patients who alternate follow-up visits between a cardiologist, a primary care physician, and perhaps another specialist need to be instructed on the importance of always carrying a current medication list to alert all involved physicians of any medication changes between office visits.

SUMMARY

Nurses who specialize in the care of patients with cardiac conditions have made a tremendous impact on patient outcomes. From the original focus of dysrhythmia detection and treatment, to hemodynamic monitoring and aggressive intervention for all aspects of the disease process, cardiac nurses continue to play an important role in improving patient outcomes.

CHD is a chronic, progressive, and systemic process. The systemic disease – not just the symptomatic stenosis – must be treated.

Medical advances in the treatment of CHD offer hope in altering the course of disease progression. Nurses in all settings care for patients with cardiovascular disease at some stage on the continuum. Nursing knowledge linked to clinical practice can make a difference in the care of patients with CHD.

EXAM QUESTIONS

CHAPTER 6
Questions 31–35

Note: Choose the one option that BEST answers each question.

31. Which pathophysiological process is associated with the reduction of blood flow in arteries and is responsible for coronary heart disease?

    a. Baroreceptor stimulation
    b. Atherosclerosis
    c. Angina
    d. Parasympathetic response

32. Which characteristics are suggestive of unstable angina?

    a. Sharp, intermittent intrascapular pain
    b. Acute pain expected with certain types of exertion
    c. Acute chest, neck, jaw, or shoulder pain that occurs at rest
    d. Acute pain predictably occurring with emotional stress

33. Which acute coronary syndrome do women experience more often than men?

    a. ST-elevation myocardial infarction
    b. Non-ST-elevation myocardial infarction
    c. Stable angina
    d. Unstable angina

34. What is the gold standard procedure to definitively diagnose the presence, location, and severity of coronary heart disease?

    a. Stress testing with nuclear imaging
    b. Cardiac revascularization
    c. Cardiac catheterization
    d. Coronary computed tomography

35. Which information should the nurse share with the patient regarding his or her long-term management of coronary heart disease?

    a. "Notify your cardiologist of worsening angina or angina during rest."
    b. "Double your aspirin dose if you have forgotten to take it."
    c. "Report your blood pressure and heart rate before taking medications each day."
    d. "You can stop dietary modifications as long as you take your medication."

REFERENCES

Amsterdam, E. A., Wenger, N. K., Brindis, R. G., Casey, D. E., Ganiats, T. G., Holmes, D. R., ... Zieman, S. J. (2014). 2014 AHA/ACC guideline for the management of patients with non–ST-elevation acute coronary syndromes: A report of the American College of Cardiology/American Heart Association Task Force on Practice Guidelines. *Circulation, 130,* e344-e426. doi:10.1161/CIR.0000000000000134

Bashore, T., Granger, C. B., Jackson, K. P., & Patel, M. R. (2016). Heart Disease. In M. Papadakis (Ed.), *CURRENT medical diagnosis and treatment 2016* (pp. 321-434). New York, NY: McGraw-Hill Education.

Boardman, H. M. P., Hartley, L., Eisinga, A., Main, C., Roque I Figuis, M., Bonfill, C. X., ... Knight, B. (2015). Hormone therapy for preventing cardiovascular disease in postmenopausal women. *Cochrane Database of Systematic Reviews, 3,* CD002229. doi:10.1002/14651858.CD002229.pub4

Capodanno, D., & Angiolillo, D. J. (2013). Management of antiplatelet therapy in patients with coronary artery disease requiring cardiac and noncardiac surgery. *Circulation, 128,* 2785-2798. doi:10.1161/CIRCULATIONAHA.113.003675

Fletcher, G. F., Ades, P. A., Kligfield, P., Arena, R., Balady, Bittner, V. A., ... Williams, M. A. (2013). Exercise standards for testing and training: A scientific statement from the American Heart Association. *Circulation, 128*(8), 873. doi:10.1161/CIR.0b013e31829b5b44

Gerber, T. C., & Manning, W. J. (2015). Noninvasive coronary imaging with cardiac computed tomography and cardiovascular magnetic resonance. *UpToDate.* Retrieved from http://www.uptodate.com/contents/noninvasive-coronary-imaging-with-cardiac-computed-tomography-and-cardiovascular-magnetic-resonance

Griffin, B. P., Kapadia, S. R., & Rimmerman, C. M. (2013). *Cleveland Clinic cardiology board review* (2nd ed.). Philadelphia, PA: Lippincott Williams & Wilkins.

Huether, S. E., & McCance, K. L. (2017). *Understanding pathophysiology* (6th ed.). St. Louis, MO: Elsevier.

Levine, G. N., Bates, E. R., Blankenship, J. C., Bailey, S. R., Bittl, J. A., Cercek, B., ... Ting, H. H. (2015). 2015 ACC/AHA/SCAI focused update on primary percutaneous coronary intervention for patients with ST-elevation myocardial infarction: An update of the 2011 ACCF/AHA/SCAI guideline for percutaneous coronary intervention and the 2013 ACCF/AHA guideline for the management of ST-elevation myocardial infarction: A report of the American College of Cardiology/American Heart Association task force on clinical practice guidelines and the Society for Cardiovascular Angiography and Interventions. *Circulation, 133,* 1135-1147. doi:10.1161/CIR.0000000000000336

Mehta, L. S., Beckie, T. M., DeVon, H. A., Grines, C. L., Krumholz, H. M., Johnson, M. N., ... Wenger, N. K. (2016). Acute myocardial infarction in women: A scientific statement from the American Heart Association. *Circulation, 133,* 916-947. doi:10.1161/CIR.0000000000000351

Patel, M. R., Bailey, S. R., Bonow, R. O., Chambers, C. E., Chan, P. S., Dehmer, G. J., ... Ward, R. P. (2012). ACCF/SCAI/AATS/ AHA/ASE/ASNC/HFSA/HRS/SCCM/ SCCT/SCMR/STS 2012 appropriate use criteria for diagnostic catheterization. *Journal of the American College of Cardiology, 59*(22), 1995-2027. doi:10.1016/j.jacc.2012.03.003

Scruth, E., & Haynes, A. (2015). Cardiovascular disorders. In L. D. Urden, K. M. Stacy, & M. E. Lough (Eds.), *Critical care nursing: Diagnosis and management* (7th ed., pp. 200-221). St. Louis, MO: Elsevier/Mosby.

Sun, Z., Choo, G. H., & Ng, K. H. (2012). Coronary CT angiography: Current status and continuing challenges. *British Journal of Radiology, 85*(1013), 495-510. doi:10.1259/bjr/15296170

Urden, L., Stacy, K., & Lough, M. (2015). *Critical care nursing* (7th ed.). St. Louis, MO: Elsevier/Mosby.

Woo, T. M., & Robinson, M. V. (2016). *Pharmacotherapeutics for advanced practice nurse prescribers* (4th ed.). Philadelphia, PA: F. A. Davis.

Xu, J., Murphy, S. L., Kochanek, K. D., & Bastian, B. A. (2016). Deaths: Final data 2013. *National Vital Statistics Reports, 64*(2). Retrieved from http://www.cdc.gov/ nchs/data/nvsr/nvsr64/nvsr64_02.pdf

CHAPTER 7

CARDIOMYOPATHY

LEARNING OUTCOME

After completing this chapter, the learner will be able to describe the pathophysiology and current therapeutic strategies for patients with cardiomyopathies.

CHAPTER OBJECTIVES

After completing this chapter, the learner will be able to:

1. Differentiate among the types of cardiomyopathy.

2. Identify the causative factors for cardiomyopathy.

3. Describe clinical presentations of patients with cardiomyopathy.

4. Summarize medical and surgical therapies and lifestyle changes used for the treatment of cardiomyopathy.

INTRODUCTION

Cardiomyopathies are disorders known to primarily affect the myocardium. The nurse must recognize that myocardial dysfunction significantly impacts all of the mechanical components of stroke volume, thereby negatively affecting cardiac output. A variety of cardiomyopathies are associated with different causative factors. This chapter presents the most common cardiomyopathies to assist the cardio-vascular nurse in caring for patients with these conditions (see Figure 7-1).

DILATED CARDIOMYOPATHY

Definition

Dilated cardiomyopathy (DCM) is characterized by global, or diffuse, systolic dysfunction, increased intracardiac volume, increased ventricular chamber size with normal ventricular wall thickness, and heart failure with a reduced ejection fraction (Huether & McCance, 2017).

Prevalence

In the United States, DCM is one of the most common causes of heart failure found among adults during autopsy. It commonly occurs in the third or fourth decade of life with a survival rate of less than 50% at 10 years from the diagnosis. Fortunately, with adequate supportive care, survival rates improve. Women are associated with peripartum incidences of DCM, which may be reversible in up to 50% of this population. However, DCM is found to return with subsequent pregnancies (Lakdawala, Stevenson, & Loscalzo, 2015).

Causes

DCM can be classified by causes into three categories: (1) familial, (2) primary without family history, or (3) secondary. It is most commonly the result of ischemic heart disease, valvular disease, diabetes, renal failure, alcohol or drug toxicity, peripartum complications, or infection. Approximately two thirds of patients have no known family history of DCM, and roughly 15% of DCM cases are secondary to chronic.

Chronic myocarditis is most often caused by viruses (e.g., coxsackievirus, adenovirus, parvovirus, and HIV) that lead to scarring and heart failure (Lakdawala et al., 2015). There is also a strong correlation of DCM with genetic or

FIGURE 7-1: TYPES OF CARDIOMYOPATHY

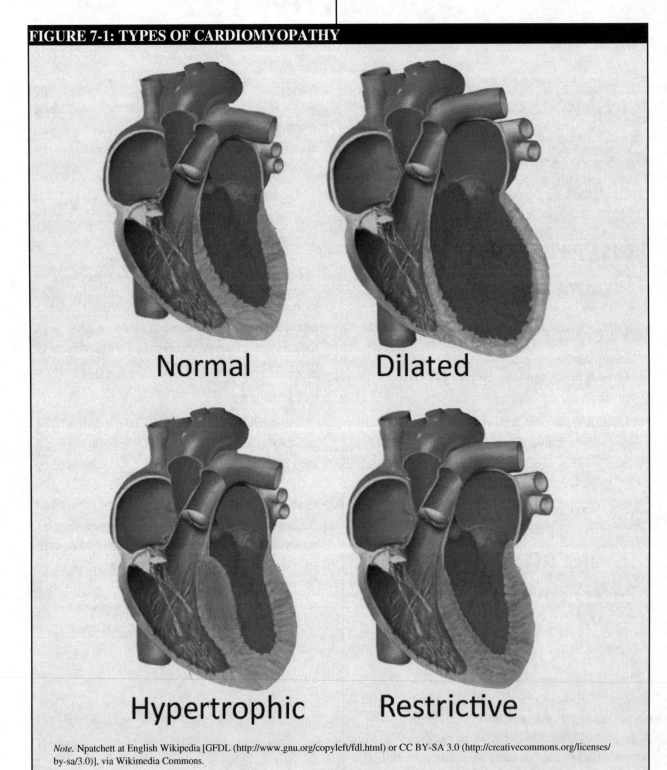

Normal   Dilated

Hypertrophic   Restrictive

Note. Npatchett at English Wikipedia [GFDL (http://www.gnu.org/copyleft/fdl.html) or CC BY-SA 3.0 (http://creativecommons.org/licenses/by-sa/3.0)], via Wikimedia Commons.

inherited disorders such as muscular dystrophy (Huether & McCance, 2017).

Pathophysiology

The pathology of DCM is a progressive, diffuse, and usually irreversible disease eventually leading to heart failure with reduced ejection fraction (formerly known as "systolic heart failure"). Biopsies of endomyocardial tissue have findings ranging from minimum to marked variation in myofiber size. Common histological features include myofiber loss to varying degrees and interstitial fibrosis. The process of this pathophysiology is dependent on the etiology (Huether & McCance, 2017). The myocardium loses elasticity and succumbs to the intracardiac pressures, becoming hypercompliant to increased ventricular size more than atrial chamber size. Contractility is further impaired with volume overload.

Autosomal dominant forms of DCM are most often associated with mutations in genes encoding cytoskeletal proteins within the sarcomere, nuclear membrane, and intercalated disc. In addition to DCM findings, these patients also have an atrioventricular block. Another genetic finding in patients with DCM is the X-linked gene responsible for Emery-Dreifuss muscular dystrophy. Those patients diagnosed with Emery-Dreifuss muscular dystrophy are also more likely to have hemochromatosis and elevated serum creatinine kinase levels, thereby complicating the pathophysiology and presentation of DCM (Huether & McCance, 2017).

Clinical Presentation

Persons with DCM usually report dyspnea that progressively worsens upon exertion, fatigue, and pedal edema (Huether & McCance, 2017).

Physical Examination

Findings most common during the physical examination include a displaced apical impulse, a S3 gallop, peripheral edema, jugular vein distention, and rales upon lung auscultation (Huether & McCance, 2017).

Diagnosis

Cardiac imaging assists in the diagnosis of DCM. An echocardiogram and a chest radiograph are the most common modalities used to make a diagnosis (Huether & McCance, 2017). The hallmark finding is left ventricular dilation greater than 4 cm, which is generally found by autopsy. In patients with four-chamber dilation with ventricular chamber size greater than atrial size, diagnosis is made on clinical findings. In patients with atrial fibrillation, larger atrial dilation is seen. Endomyocardial biopsy can also be performed to make a specific diagnosis; however, biopsy is positively diagnostic of amyloidosis in only approximately 25% of the patients. This is because histological features of DCM are nonspecific, making this disease a microscopic diagnosis of exclusion. Negative findings are important to the diagnostic plan because they can rule out rare causes of DCM. Lack of inflammation, amyloids, iron, granulomas, or myocyte necrosis excludes the rarest forms of DCM. Occasionally, biopsy may reveal fibrofatty changes suggesting arrhythmogenic right ventricular cardiomyopathy (ARVC) (Lakdawala et al., 2015).

Medical Therapy

Treatments for DCM primarily aim to reduce blood volume, increase contractility, and reverse the underlying disorder, if possible. Blood volume reduction is done using diuretics to eliminate blood volume and preload. Nitrates can also be utilized to reduce preload by vasodilation (Huether & McCance, 2017). Common medications used in treating many cardiomyopathies include beta blockers and angiotensin-converting enzyme inhibitors.

Surgical Therapy

The only curative therapy for severe cases of DCM is heart transplantation. Heart transplantation remains the treatment of choice for irreversible disease. Cardiac revascularization is done in an effort to stop the progression of DCM related to ischemic heart disease secondary to coronary artery disease (Huether & McCance, 2017).

Patient Outcomes

The survival rate of DCM is less than 50%. However, supportive care was found to increase survival rates by 5 to 10 years. Ventricular tachyarrhythmias occur most often in patients with higher survival rates, and they are often treated with antiarrhythmics and automated implantable cardioverter-defibrillator placement (Mozaffarian et al., 2015).

RESTRICTIVE CARDIOMYOPATHY

Definition

Restrictive cardiomyopathy (RCM) is a myocardial disease characterized by restrictive filling and reduced diastolic volume of either or both ventricles with normal or near-normal systolic function and wall thickness. This definition is to have distinction from constrictive pericarditis, a similar but often reversible condition that is curable by surgical intervention (Amaki et al., 2015).

Prevalence

RCM is rare and the least common among clinically recognized cardiomyopathies. It is diagnosed mainly in the United States, but some of its subtypes are most commonly found in certain populations in other countries. For instance, obliterative RCM is most commonly found in children and young adults in tropical and sub-tropical areas of Africa, and it accounts for approximately one quarter of the deaths in this area (Mozaffarian et al., 2015).

Causes

Characterized by restrictive filling and increased diastolic pressure of one or both ventricles maintaining normal to near-normal systolic function and myocardial thickness, RCM occurs idiopathically (as primary RCM) or as a cardiac manifestation of systemic disease. Systemic diseases such as lymphoma, sarcoidosis, scleroderma, amyloidosis, and hemochromatosis may contribute to the development of secondary RCM. The causes can be categorized into four broad groups: (1) idiopathic, (2) infiltrative, (3) treatment induced, and (4) malignancy (Lakdawala et al., 2015).

Pathophysiology

The descriptor *restrictive* speaks to the pathophysiology of RCM. The myocardium progressively develops into noncompliant, rigid, stiff muscle. The rigidity of the myocardium impedes, or limits, ventricular filling, thereby raising diastolic pressures during the diastolic phase. Because of the progressive nature of this disease, persistently high diastolic pressure leads to right-sided heart failure and systemic venous congestion. Diastolic stiffness ultimately leads to decreased cardiac output; consequently, eventually, this disease progresses to heart failure and dysrhythmias that cause death. Systolic function and myocardial wall thickness remain normal in the early stages of the disease (Huether & McCance, 2017).

Idiopathic RCM maintains the common characteristics of progressive myocardial fibrosis and diastolic dysfunction; however, it is found to have nonspecific histopathological changes.

Obliterative RCM is rare and is secondary to end-stage eosinophilic syndromes. This disease involves an intracavitary thrombus filling the left ventricular apex, thereby impeding ventricular filling. The fibrosis of the endocardium also extends to the atrioventricular valves, causing mild-to-moderate valve regurgitation.

When RCM occurs in the setting of amyloidosis, the myocardium is then infiltrated with intracellular accumulation of amyloid protein composition in sufficient amounts to impair the function of the organ. Myeloma-related amyloidosis occurs as diffuse deposits of myeloma protein fibrils throughout the myocardium, causing RCM and creating a firm and rubbery consistency that prevents collapsibility of the heart during autopsy (Huether & McCance, 2017).

Radiation-induced RCM is a complication of radiotherapy that becomes more evident several years after treatment. Differentiating RCM from constrictive pericarditis is vital to the treatment and prognosis of the patient (Huether & McCance, 2017).

Clinical Presentation

The patient's presentation is very similar to that of left- or right-sided heart failure. Patients may report feeling tired, generally weak, and fatigued. Patients may also report associated symptoms such as syncope, orthostatic hypotension, and thromboembolic complications, such as a pulmonary embolism, and may experience chest pain. There is a high risk for systemic emboli in patients who present with atrial fibrillation as well as symptoms of RCM. Infiltrative types of RCM are commonly associated with conduction disturbances, whereas amyloid-related RCM is not. It is important that the nurse recognize that a patient history of radiation therapy, heart transplantation, chemotherapy, or a systemic disease can be significant for the diagnostic plan (Lakdawala et al., 2015).

Physical Examination

For the general examination, the patient presenting with symptoms of RCM may be dyspneic, have hepatomegaly, have pitting lower-extremity edema, and report being more comfortable in the sitting position because of fluid in the abdomen and lungs. Weight loss, jugular vein distention, and cardiac cachexia are also common in most types of RCM.

The cardiovascular examination for RCM is characterized by an S3 heart sound (except in amyloidosis) and mitral/tricuspid murmurs. The respiratory examination will commonly have findings related to bilateral pleural effusions. Large effusions are common in amyloid-related RCM.

NURSING APPLICATION

Rales are not common with RCM due to right-sided heart failure and low left-sided stroke volume and cardiac output. Fluid overload findings are systemic – hepatomegaly, venous congestion, jugular vein distention, among others.

Nurses should consider an amyloid-related illness when findings of easy bruising, periorbital purpura, macroglossia, carpal tunnel syndrome, painful and firm palpation of an enlarged liver, and other systemic findings are present.

Cardiovascular clinicians may be able to discern a Kussmaul sign while performing the physical examination. A Kussmaul sign is found when the jugular venous pulse either does not fall or rises with inspiration. Kussmaul sign is not found with RCM because the pulse volume is decreased due to a reduced stroke volume and cardiac output (Lakdawala et al., 2015).

Diagnosis

Identifying the underlying cause is vital in stagnating or slowing the progression of RCM. Echocardiogram is useful in visualizing and measuring heart wall thickness, chamber size, and intracardiac pressures. The findings of the echocardiogram usually indicate whether biopsy is needed. Myocardial biopsy is necessary to accomplish the identification of the underlying origin and aim treatments toward the applicable cause (Lakdawala et al., 2015).

Medical Therapy

Like DCM, RCM has no specific curative treatments. Supportive therapies are aimed at treating specific causes that have had some success, for example, corticosteroids for sarcoidosis, chemotherapy for amyloidosis, or phlebotomy and chelation for hemochromatosis. Some mainstays of medical treatment, such as diuretics, vasodilators, angiotensin-converting enzyme inhibitors, and anticoagulation as indicated, are almost always used to treat heart failure-related disease processes in patients with RCM (Yancy et al., 2013).

Surgical Therapy

Surgical therapies consider the etiology (if it can be identified) of RCM but maintain limited options. For instance, heart or heart–liver transplantation is thought to afford many patients with longer lives, but this is not guaranteed for some causes. In some patients, permanent pacing or left ventricular assist devices are considered as therapeutic options (Yancy et al., 2013). It is important for the nurse to recognize that these options are mostly supportive and not curative. The nurse must educate the patients and their families of these factors.

Outcomes

Prognosis of RCM is greatly dependent on its etiology and pathology. Unfortunately, when RCM is treated, the outcome is often unsatisfactory. Adults have poor prognoses with prolonged courses of heart failure and complications such as cardiac cirrhosis and thromboembolism. The prognosis for children diagnosed with RCM-related heart failure is especially poor, with short periods of time before death. Patients unable to receive cardiac transplantation as a treatment option usually die of low cardiac output failure (Mozaffarian et al., 2015).

HYPERTROPHIC CARDIOMYOPATHY

Definition

Hypertrophic cardiomyopathy (HCM) is characteristically known for a thickening of the myocardium. There are two major categories of HCM: (1) hypertrophic obstructive cardiomyopathy, and (2) hypertensive or valvular HCM. These categories will be discussed in greater detail in the following subsections.

Prevalence

The overall prevalence rate of HCM in the United States is approximately 0.2% of the population. However, morphological evidence of disease is found in echocardiographic screenings of approximately 25% of first-degree relatives of those with HCM. HCM is only slightly more common in males than females, and given the genetic pattern of autosomal dominance, there is no sex predilection. HCM is usually found in females at younger ages, but in general is most common in the third decade of life (Mozaffarian et al., 2015).

Causes

Primary HCM is caused by an autosomal dominant genetic mutation leading to septal thickening and hypertrophic obstructive cardiomyopathy. Secondary HCM is most commonly caused by uncontrolled hypertension or valve dysfunction (most often aortic stenosis; Huether & McCance, 2017).

Pathophysiology

Primary HCM is one of the most common genetic cardiac conditions. This type is characterized by thickening of the septal wall (shown in Figure 7-2) secondary to a mutation in the cardiac sarcomere protein gene most frequently transmitted as an autosomal dominant trait. Because of this thickening, the left ventricular outflow tract is compromised, especially with increased heart rates. This obstruction decreases intravascular volumes and places the patient at high risk for ventricular arrhythmias and sudden death (Huether & McCance, 2017).

The most common types of HCM are those secondary to hypertension and valvular disease.

Secondary HCM occurs because of increased resistance to ventricular ejection. This is most often seen in patients with uncontrolled hypertension or aortic valve stenosis. The muscle thickens because of hypertrophy of myocytes in an effort to compensate for the increased myocardial workload. Long-term dysfunction of the myocytes develops when these causes persist, leading first to diastolic dysfunction and later to systolic dysfunction (Huether & McCance, 2017).

Clinical Presentation

Patients with HCM have varying presentations and range from being asymptomatic in some patients to sudden cardiac death in others. Patients with HCM may have the following symptoms:

FIGURE 7-2: OBSTRUCTIVE TYPE OF HYPERTROPHIC CARDIOMYOPATHY WITH SEPTAL WALL THICKENING

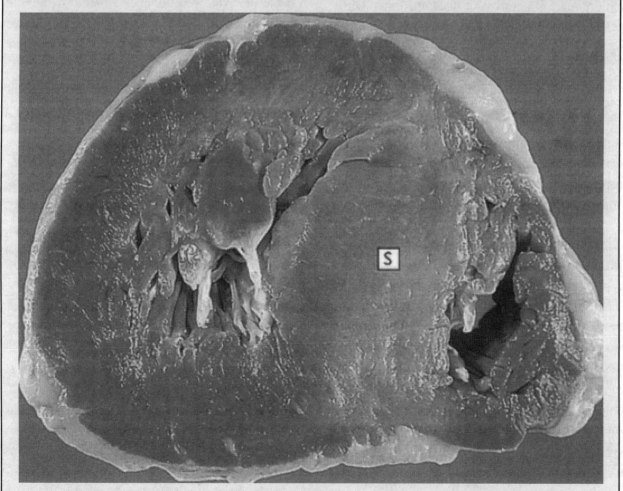

Note. From Huether, S. E., & McCance, K. L. (2017). *Understanding pathophysiology* (6th ed.). St. Louis, MO: Elsevier. © Elsevier 2017.

angina, dizziness, syncope or presyncope, dyspnea at all times or dyspnea on exertion, orthopnea, and palpitations. Of these symptoms, dyspnea is the most common complaint associated with this disease (Yancy et al., 2013).

Physical Examination

The physical examination of a patient with HCM may reveal an abnormally forceful, enlarged double apical impulse that is displaced laterally on palpation, a paradoxically split S2, a jugular venous pulse, and a double carotid arterial pulse. Murmurs may include a systolic ejection crescendo-decrescendo murmur, holo-systolic murmur at the apex and axilla of mitral regurgitation, or a diastolic decrescendo murmur of aortic regurgitation. Extra heart sounds, most commonly an S4 in adults and an S3 in children, are suggestive of decompensated congestive heart failure (Lakdawala et al., 2015).

Diagnosis

Diagnosis of HCM is confirmed with echocardiogram and cardiac catheterization. Left ventricular hypertrophy, left atrial enlargement, septal hypertrophy, abnormal systolic anterior leaflet motion of the mitral valve, mitral valve prolapse or regurgitation, and decreased mid-aortic flow are some of the common findings per those diagnostics. Genetic testing is not yet widely available but is expected to be in the future. Chest radiographs reveal an enlarged cardiac silhouette. Electrocardiographic studies most commonly reveal ST-T wave abnormalities and indications of left ventricular hypertrophy. Other electrocardiographic findings associated with HCM include atrial enlargement, abnormal and prominent Q waves in the anterior precordial and lateral leads, short P-R intervals with QRS pre-excitation, and atrial fibrillation, which is a poor prognostic sign (Yancy et al., 2013).

Medical Therapy and Lifestyle Changes

Therapies are aimed to reduce ventricular contractility while increasing ventricular volume, compliance, and outflow tract dimensions. Medications accomplishing these goals are mostly beta blockers and calcium channel blockers. Alternative therapies include antiarrhythmics such as diltiazem, amiodarone, or disopyramide. Antitussives are sometimes administered to prevent coughing (Yancy et al., 2013). A stepwise approach to uncontrolled hypertension in primary and secondary HCM has been proven effective (Argulian et al., 2013).

If possible, avoidance of inotropes, nitrates, and sympathomimetic amines is important in these patients. Diuretics should also be used with caution in patients with obstructive HCM because of the risk for exacerbating decreased intravascular volume. Digitalis is contraindicated in patients with HCM unless they are found to have refractory atrial fibrillation.

Lifestyle modifications are as important as pharmacological therapies when considering the pathophysiology of HCM types. Total abstinence from highly strenuous activity such as competitive athletics, shoveling snow, and lifting very heavy objects is vital due to the risk for arrhythmogenic sudden cardiac death. There are no specific diet recommendations; however, excessive weight gain should be avoided (Yancy et al., 2013).

Surgical Therapy

HCM has a variety of surgical options. The invasive therapies include septal reduction therapy, septal myomectomy, alcohol septal ablation, catheter septal ablation, implantable cardioverter-defibrillator, heart transplantation, and surgical therapies for atrial fibrillation. Indications are related to the patient's symptoms and are specific to the type of HCM diagnosed (Yancy et al., 2013).

Outcomes

Mortality rates for patients with HCM have significantly improved over the last 40 years. Because some patients are asymptomatic until their first symptom of sudden cardiac death, early identification of patients with this disease is crucial to preventing this outcome. Sudden cardiac death is thought to be associated with vigorous exertion or competitive sports. Screening first-degree relatives before the onset of symptoms is often beneficial in identifying risk factors for HCM. Patients with a myriad of arrhythmias are at the highest risk for sudden death (Mozaffarian et al., 2015; Yancy et al., 2013).

ARRHYTHMOGENIC RIGHT VENTRICULAR CARDIOMYOPATHY

Definition

Arrhythmogenic right ventricular cardiomyopathy (ARVC), sometimes referred to as arrhythmogenic right ventricular dysplasia, is a primary disease of the heart muscle resulting in fibrofatty replacement of the right ventricle and the subepicardial region of the left ventricle (Huether & McCance, 2017).

Prevalence

ARVC may represent approximately 2% to 5% of the sudden cardiac deaths of young adults, with higher incidence in exertional deaths. ARVC is most common among males younger than 40 years. It is extremely uncommon in children younger than 10 years (Mozaffarian et al., 2015).

Causes

ARVC is suspected to be secondary to an inflammatory process modulated by genetic influences in desmosome-related proteins. Autopsy findings are suggestive of this disease progressing from events of myocarditis to ARVC; however, more research is needed to confirm this (Huether & McCance, 2017).

Pathophysiology

Although its name refers to the right ventricle, this heart muscle disease has biventricular involvement. Inflammatory changes, or infiltrates, typically occur within the subepicardial region and relate more to fibrosis than to fatty infiltrates. These changes are thought to start in the right ventricle and progress to the left ventricle. Because of the progressive nature of the disease, intractable arrhythmias and heart failure often develop in patients with ARVC. ARVC can also cause sudden death (Huether & McCance, 2017).

Clinical Presentation

Primary symptoms of ARVC are related to arrhythmias and conduction disturbances. Unfortunately, the disease is often asymptomatic until syncope or sudden death occurs (Huether & McCance, 2017).

Diagnosis

Diagnosis is most often made by autopsy. However, if ARVC is suspected early enough, a diagnosis can be made by biopsy or magnetic resonance imaging. In cases of ARVC, biopsy may reveal adipose tissue deposits within the anterior wall of the right ventricle toward the apex. The diffuse loss of desmosomal proteins via immunohistochemical evaluation is suggestive of a diagnosis of ARVC (Yancy et al., 2013).

Medical and Surgical Therapy

Due to the natural history of this disease and delayed diagnosis, therapies for ARVC are empiric and supportive. These may include beta blockers or antiarrhythmics for the suppression of arrhythmias, standard therapies for heart failure as indicated, and the potential prevention of sudden cardiac death by implantation of an implantable cardioverter-defibrillator for those with risk factors (Yancy et al., 2013).

Outcomes

Athletes experience sudden death secondary to ARVC more than the nonathletic adult. The prognosis for persons diagnosed with ARVC with left ventricular involvement is poor. The nurse must recognize the significance in obtaining a comprehensive history for persons with risk factors in an effort to prevent sudden cardiac death (Mozaffarian et al., 2015).

TAKOTSUBO CARDIOMYOPATHY

Definition

Unlike the other cardiomyopathies discussed in this chapter, takotsubo cardiomyopathy (TCM) is an acute and transient cardiac syndrome (not disease) involving akinesis of the apex of the left ventricle. It mimics acute coronary syndromes (ACSs).

CLINICAL APPLICATION

The apex is known as the point of maximum impulse and is the strongest region of the left ventricle. If this region no longer contracts (akinetic), cardiac output is acutely compromised and the patient may experience acute decompensating left ventricular heart failure.

The word *takotsubo* is Japanese and translates to "octopus pot." The syndrome was first described in Japan and was named TCM because of the heart's resemblance to the shape of an octopus pot (see Figure 7-3).

Prevalence

TCM is most common in postmenopausal women (Sharkey, Lesser, & Maron, 2011). Approximately 2.2% of patients diagnosed with ACS were subsequently diagnosed with TCM. TCM seems to occur more in the afternoon versus ACS, which occurs more in the early morning. Patients with TCM are most commonly Asian females (57.2%), with Caucasian females (40%) being the second most prevalent group. Interestingly, a systematic review found that patients with TCM had a lower incidence of traditional cardiac risk factors like hypertension, hyperlipidemia, diabetes, smoking, or positive family histories of heart disease than patients with CHD without TCM (Pilgrim & Wyss, 2008).

Causes

Specific causes for TCM are unknown; however, it is highly correlated with emotionally or physically stressful events (e.g., job loss, dissolution of a marriage, motor vehicle crash, relationship conflict, and death of a loved one). It is thought that stressors stimulate excessive release of adrenaline and the heart muscle succumbs to this by taking the shape of a Japanese octopus pot (Sharkey et al., 2011).

Pathophysiology

Theories surrounding the pathophysiology of TCM question whether it is caused by multivessel coronary artery spasm, impaired cardiac microvascular function, impaired myocardial fatty acid metabolism, ACS with reperfusion injury, or endogenous catecholamine-induced myocardial stunning. Given the normal myocardium at rest and with aerobic activity meets approximately 90% of its energy needs from fatty acid metabolism, myocardial ischemic events can suppress this pathway, causing the muscle to largely utilize glucose instead. Biopsy findings of patients with TCM have revealed reversible focal myocytolysis, mono-

FIGURE 7-3: TAKOTSUBO ("JAPANESE OCTOPUS POT") CARDIOMYOPATHY

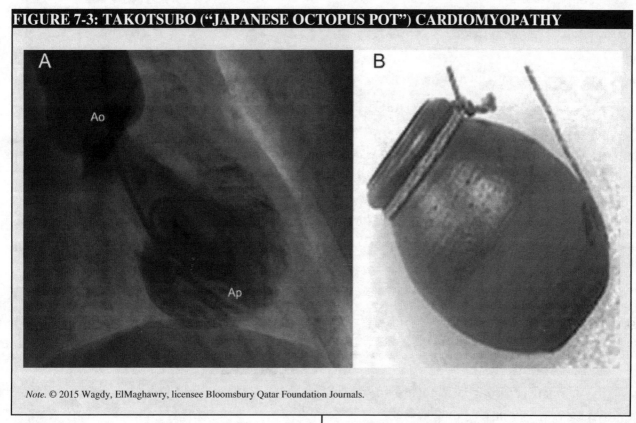

nuclear infiltrates, and contract band necrosis. These findings were reproduced in rats as well (Huether & McCance, 2017).

Clinical Presentation

Clinical presentations of TCM are very similar to those of ACS. Common patient presentations include reports of chest pain, ST-segment elevation on 12-lead ECG, and cardiac enzyme elevation consistent with myocardial infarction. However, when the patient undergoes cardiac catheterization, left ventricular ballooning is present with no significant obstructive coronary artery disease. A thorough health history has most often revealed recent emotional or physical stress in the minutes to hours preceding the patient's presentation to acute medical providers. Health histories may not reveal traditional cardiac risk factors (Yancy et al., 2013).

Physical Examination

Findings during the physical examination are mostly nonspecific. In severe cases, findings similar to those with acute left-sided heart failure may be present (e.g., dyspnea, rales, murmur, or extra heart sound). Murmurs and rales should be recognized as late findings (Yancy et al., 2013).

Diagnosis

Diagnosis is generally made in the cardiac catheterization laboratory with cardiac imaging. Despite ST-elevation on the 12-lead electrocardiogram and elevated cardiac enzymes being present, cardiac angiography does not reveal obstructive lesions. Furthermore, the ventriculogram performed during angiogram reveals the octopus pot shape during systole and normal shape during diastole (see Figure 7-4). During systole, the octopus pot shape is characteristically known for having a narrow opening (narrow left ventricular outflow tract) and round bottom (apical ballooning; Yancy et al., 2013).

Cardiac magnetic resonance imaging is increasingly being used to differentiate TCM

FIGURE 7-4: VENTRICULOGRAM DURING SYSTOLE AND DIASTOLE

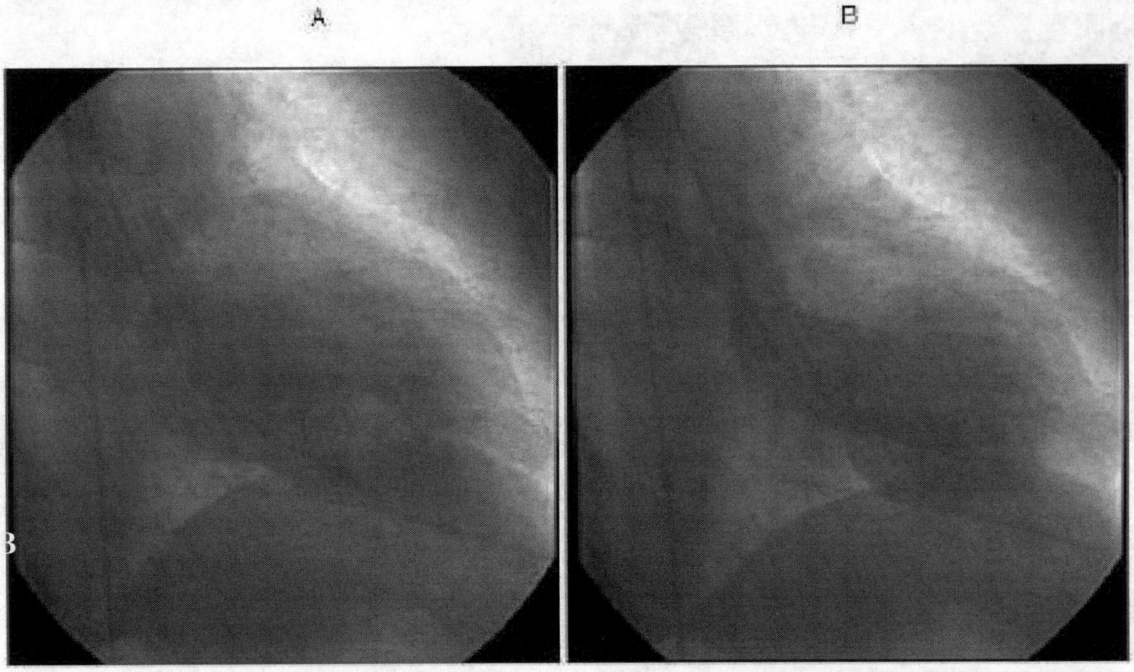

(A) Normal ventricular shape in diastole.

(B) Octopus pot shape during systole.

Note. ©2010 Beydoun et al; licensee BioMed Central Ltd.

from myocarditis and myocardial infarction. This is still usually performed after cardiac angiography given the necessity to exclude obstructive coronary artery disease (Yancy et al., 2013).

Medical Therapy

Fortunately, with timely recognition and supportive therapies, the syndrome is typically reversible. Medications used to promote recovery of the ventricular function are most commonly used, such as beta blockers in combination with angiotensin-converting enzyme inhibitors. Anticoagulants are prescribed for prophylactic means aimed to avoid thromboembolic complications. In severe cases, vasopressors may be indicated to increase cardiac output. Diuretics are also prescribed as needed for severe cases causing heart failure and pulmonary edema (Sharkey et al., 2011).

Surgical Therapy

Surgical interventions are rarely indicated but may include the use of an intra-aortic balloon pump to decrease the workload on the transiently weakened heart and promote increased oxygen delivery to the recovering myocardium and other tissues.

Outcomes

Fortunately, recovery from TCM is usually rapid and complete. The "stunned" heart muscle gradually regains function (contraction). The course of recovery is generally complete in 3 to 7 days, at which time all medications and other therapies are discontinued and baseline heart function has returned. Recurrent episodes of TCM occur in approximately 5% in patients; for this reason, some clinicians will continue beta-blocker or combination alpha- and beta-blocker therapy indefinitely, with a lack of other contra-indications (Sharkey et al., 2011).

SUMMARY

Cardiomyopathies account for many primary and secondary cardiac muscle diseases, disabilities, and death. The cardiovascular nurse must recognize the significance of the role of obtaining comprehensive health histories, performing prudent physical assessments, communicating concerning findings to the medical provider, and recognizing safety considerations for medical and surgical therapies. The nurse's role in advocating and educating patients with cardiomyopathies and their families is important. Appropriate patient education can prevent sudden cardiac death associated with many of these heart muscle diseases.

EXAM QUESTIONS

CHAPTER 7
Questions 36–42

Note: Choose the one option that BEST answers each question.

36. Which type of cardiomyopathy is most associated with systolic dysfunction?

    a. Restrictive cardiomyopathy

    b. Dilated cardiomyopathy

    c. Arrhythmogenic right ventricular cardiomyopathy

    d. Hypertrophic cardiomyopathy

37. Which type of cardiomyopathy is the most common cardiomyopathy in the United States?

    a. Restrictive cardiomyopathy

    b. Dilated cardiomyopathy

    c. Arrhythmogenic right ventricular cardiomyopathy

    d. Hypertrophic cardiomyopathy

38. Which type of cardiomyopathy is most associated with diastolic dysfunction?

    a. Restrictive cardiomyopathy

    b. Dilated cardiomyopathy

    c. Arrhythmogenic right ventricular cardiomyopathy

    d. Takotsubo cardiomyopathy

39. Patients are instructed to avoid strenuous activity to prevent sudden cardiac death from increased left ventricular outflow obstruction with which type of cardiomyopathy?

    a. Restrictive cardiomyopathy

    b. Dilated cardiomyopathy

    c. Arrhythmogenic right ventricular cardiomyopathy

    d. Hypertrophic cardiomyopathy

40. Which type of cardiomyopathy is most associated with inflammatory changes of the right ventricle and the subepicardial area of the left ventricle in young adults?

    a. Restrictive cardiomyopathy

    b. Dilated cardiomyopathy

    c. Arrhythmogenic right ventricular cardiomyopathy

    d. Hypertrophic cardiomyopathy

41. Which type of cardiomyopathy is caused by acute emotional or physiological stress and adrenaline surges?

    a. Restrictive cardiomyopathy

    b. Dilated cardiomyopathy

    c. Hypertrophic cardiomyopathy

    d. Takotsubo cardiomyopathy

continued on next page

42. Medications that are commonly used in combination for the treatment of heart failure to facilitate recovery of the ventricle include angiotensin-converting enzyme inhibitors and

    a. beta blockers.

    b. calcium channel blockers.

    c. nitrates.

    d. nonsteroidal anti-inflammatory agents.

REFERENCES

Amaki, M., Savino, J., Ain, D. L., Sanz, J., Pedrizzetti, G., Kulkami, H., … Sengupta, P. P. (2015). Diagnostic concordance of echocardiography and cardiac magnetic resonance-based tissue tracking for differentiating constrictive pericarditis from restrictive cardiomyopathy. *Circulation Cardiovascular Imaging, 7*(5), 819-827. doi:10.1161/CIRCIMAGING.114.002103

Argulian, E., Messerli, F. H., Aziz, E. F., Winson, G., Agarwal, V., Kaddaha, F., … Sherrid, M. V. (2013). Antihypertensive therapy in hypertrophic cardiomyopathy. *American Journal of Cardiology, 111*(7), 1040-1045. doi:10.1016/j.amjcard.2012.12.026

Huether, S. E., & McCance, K. L. (2017). *Understanding pathophysiology* (6th ed.). St. Louis, MO: Elsevier.

Lakdawala, N. K., Stevenson, L. W., & Loscalzo, J. (2015). Cardiomyopathy and myocarditis. In D. Kasper, A. Fauci, S. Hauser, D. Longo, J. Jameson, & J. Loscalzo (Eds.), *Harrison's principles of internal medicine* (19th ed.). New York, NY: McGraw-Hill.

Mozaffarian, D., Benjamin, E. J., Go, A. S., Arnett, D. K., Blaha, M. J., Cushman, M., … Turner, M. B. (2015). Heart disease and stroke statistics – 2015 update: A report from the American Heart Association. *Circulation, 131*(4), e29-e322. doi:10.1161/CIR.0000000000000350

Pilgrim, T. M., & Wyss, T. R. (2008). Takotsubo cardiomyopathy or transient left ventricular apical ballooning syndrome: A systematic review. *Int J Cardiol, 124*(3), 283-92. doi:10.1016/j.ijcard.2007.07.002

Sharkey, S. W., Lesser, J. R., & Maron, B. J. (2011). Takotsubo (stress) cardiomyopathy. *Circulation, 124,* e460-e462. doi:10.1161/CIRCULATIONAHA.111.052662

Tomich, E. B. (2015). Takotsubo cardiomyopathy. *Medscape.* Retrieved from http://emedicine.medscape.com/article/1513631-overview

Yancy, C. W., Jessup, M., Bozkurt, B., Butler, J., Casey, D. E., Drazner, M. H., … Wilkoff, B. L. (2013). 2013 ACCF/AHA Guideline for the management of heart failure a report of the American College of Cardiology Foundation/American Heart Association task force on practice guidelines. *Circulation, 128,* e240-e327. doi:10.1161/CIR.0b013e31829e8776

CHAPTER 8

CHRONIC HEART FAILURE: PATHOPHYSIOLOGY, ASSESSMENT, AND TREATMENT

LEARNING OUTCOME

After completing this chapter, the learner will be able to describe nursing interventions for the management of patients with chronic heart failure.

CHAPTER OBJECTIVES

After completing this chapter, the learner will be able to:

1. Describe the clinical presentation and etiology of chronic heart failure.

2. Identify pathophysiological characteristics of chronic heart failure.

3. Apply nursing assessment strategies for patients with or at risk for chronic heart failure.

4. Summarize appropriate treatments and the goals of treatment for patients with chronic heart failure.

INTRODUCTION

Understanding chronic heart failure management is very important in cardiovascular nursing. According to statistics published in 2013, approximately 5.1 million people in the United States live with heart failure. After being diagnosed with heart failure, approximately half of these patients die within 5 years of being diagnosed (Go et al., 2013).

Epidemiological studies have shown that the incidence of heart failure has generally remained stable over the past four decades. However, the older adult population has an increasingly higher prevalence of heart failure than other populations. Due to the aging population and the number of older adults surviving illness, the prevalence of heart failure is projected to increase. Disparities across ethnic populations also have been identified. White females have the lowest prevalence of heart failure, and Black males have the highest prevalence of heart failure and also greater 5-year mortality rates than White individuals (Yancy et al., 2013). The cardiovascular nurse must be knowledgeable of these factors and apply them in the comprehensive management of patients with chronic heart failure.

Heart failure is a complex clinical syndrome that can result from any cardiac disorder that impairs the ability of the ventricle to either fill properly or eject optimally. Because patients can present without signs and symptoms of decompensation in chronic heart failure, the term "heart failure" is recommended for use in lieu of "congestive heart failure." Because heart failure is a myriad of signs and symptoms resulting from a number of cardiac impairments, it is not synonymous with "cardiomyopathy" (heart muscle disease) or "left ventricular dysfunction" (localized impairment of the heart) (Yancy et al., 2013).

The term *heart failure with reduced ejection fraction* (HFrEF) is a condition that was formerly known as *systolic heart failure*. Patients diagnosed with HFrEF have an ejection fraction (percent of blood the ventricle ejects per beat relative to the total amount of blood in the ventricle) less than 40%. Notably, patients in this subset of heart failure often also have accompanying diastolic dysfunction that the prior term ("systolic heart failure") did not account for. Survival rates in patients with the HFrEF classification are much lower than in those patients described as having heart failure with preserved ejection fraction (HFpEF) classifications (Yancy et al., 2013).

HFpEF is a condition that was formerly known as *diastolic heart failure*. Patients diagnosed with HFpEF have an ejection fraction from 40% to 71%. The term *HFpEF* is recommended because of the varying degrees of diastolic function associated with this subgroup and the difficulty in making the diagnosis because of multiple other noncardiac causes of symptoms suggestive of heart failure. The different subclassifications for this group of patients are

- heart failure with preserved ejection fraction (HFpEF);
- borderline, if the ejection fraction is 40% to 41% (HFpEF, borderline); and
- improved, if the ejection fraction was formerly reduced but is now greater than 40% (HFpEF, improved).

Patients with HFpEF (improved) should be identified as unique from the chronic preserved ejection fraction group because they are clinically distinct due to the previous left ventricular

systolic dysfunction, and research is currently being done to investigate further management of these patients (Yancy et al., 2013). For the purpose of this chapter, only general HFpEF will be referenced, not the subgroups.

CLINICAL PRESENTATION

Heart failure has a significant negative impact on health-related quality of life (HRQOL) in the areas of physical functioning and vitality. A significant predictor of rehospitalization and mortality is patients whose HRQOL does not demonstrate improvement after discharge. Population differences include women, who have been found to have poorer HRQOL than men, and Mexican Hispanics, who report better HRQOL than other ethnic groups in the United States (Yancy et al., 2013).

Most patients with heart failure present with decreased exercise tolerance caused by dyspnea or fatigue. Because these presenting symptoms are nonspecific, many patients are not readily diagnosed with heart failure. These symptoms are sometimes attributed to deconditioning associated with the aging process. Many patients with heart failure also have coexisting conditions (such as pulmonary disease) that contribute to exercise intolerance. These coexisting conditions make differential diagnosis challenging. Furthermore, symptom assessment is more difficult in older patients. Many older adults do not experience exertional dyspnea because they have developed more sedentary lifestyles to accommodate their decreased functional capacity.

NURSING APPLICATION

When assessing for exertional dyspnea, remember to do so within the context of the patient's activity level. The nurse must ask the patient about dyspnea with exertion and must also assess the degree to which the patient has been exerting himself or herself. A patient who sits in a chair for the majority of the day may not present with the same complaint of dyspnea on exertion as a patient attempting to complete activities of daily living.

Patients may also present with *extracellular fluid (*ECF) overload, manifested as peripheral edema or abdominal swelling. Anorexia commonly accompanies abdominal swelling. Additional findings during a physical examination that indicate fluid overload are the presence of a third heart sound (S3) and jugular venous distention. Patients with pulmonary congestion present with dyspnea on exertion, orthopnea, and paroxysmal nocturnal dyspnea. Pulmonary congestion usually occurs when the left ventricle rapidly fails. However, some patients with left ventricular end-stage heart failure have no signs of pulmonary congestion. Regardless of initial presentation, progressive changes in symptoms over time are common to most patients with heart failure. The end result is a pathological state in which the heart is unable to pump enough oxygenated blood to meet the body's metabolic needs (Yancy et al., 2013).

NURSING APPLICATION

When assessing for a third heart sound, the nurse listens at the fifth intercostal space, left midclavicular line, with the bell of the stethoscope. A normal S1 and S2 sound like "lub dub." When the third heart sound is added, it will sound like "lub dub da."

In summary, the hallmark manifestations of heart failure include (1) varying degrees of dyspnea and fatigue, both of which may affect exercise tolerance; and/or (2) ECF retention, causing dependent peripheral edema and some-

times pulmonary congestion. Patients may have only one of the two manifestations of heart failure at any given time, reinforcing why the term "heart failure" is more accurate than "congestive heart failure." Notably, with either dyspnea and fatigue or ECF retention, the patient's functional capacity and quality of life are negatively impacted (Yancy et al., 2013).

Important risk factors for heart failure include any that are associated with an increased propensity for structural heart disease. For instance, hypertension is one of the single most important risk factors to control in an effort to prevent or stagnate the progression of heart failure. The incidence of heart failure is greater in patients with higher blood pressures for long durations and in older adults. Diabetes mellitus is another factor that markedly increases the risk for heart failure in patients without structural heart disease. In addition, because obesity and insulin resistance are strongly correlated with diabetes, these factors become risk factors for heart failure as well. Atherosclerotic disease anywhere in the body (e.g., coronary arteries, cerebral arteries, or peripheral arteries) is known to contribute to the likelihood for development of heart failure secondary to ischemic disease. Appropriately treating hypertension, dyslipidemia, atherosclerosis, and diabetes mellitus can significantly reduce the risk for development of heart failure (Yancy et al., 2013). Nurses must be vigilant in seeking opportunities to reinforce appropriate management of these risk factors to aid in the reduction of heart failure and improve the HRQOL of patients.

ETIOLOGY

A variety of cardiac disorders and cardiac structural abnormalities can cause heart failure. Dilated cardiomyopathy (DCM), a heterogeneous group of heart muscle diseases, is the most common cause of chronic heart failure (Yancy et al. 2013). As noted in Chapter 7, which discusses DCM, hypertension remains the primary risk factor contributing to both DCM and heart failure. Other causes of heart failure include other types of cardiomyopathies, valvular disease, thyroid disease, growth hormone deficiency and acromegaly, viral infection, alcohol abuse, cocaine abuse, pregnancy, inflammatory disorders, and idiopathic causes (Yancy et al., 2013).

When a patient presents with heart failure syndrome, the following questions can help determine the cause (Anderson, 2016):

- Does the patient have a history of ischemic heart disease or associated risk factors, such as diabetes, hypertension, hyperlipidemia, or peripheral vascular disease?

- Does the patient have a history of or clinical evidence of valvular heart disease?

- Has the patient been exposed to chest irradiation or had any exposure to cardiotoxic agents?

- Does the patient's lifestyle involve any illicit drug or excessive alcohol use?

- Does the patient have a family history of idiopathic cardiomyopathy or unexplained sudden cardiac death?

- Is there any suspicion of noncardiac causes, such as

   ◦ hyperthyroidism,

   ◦ infectious process,

   ◦ collagen vascular disorder, or

   ◦ pheochromocytoma?

PATHOPHYSIOLOGY

Heart failure is a progressive disorder resulting in decreased mechanical function of the heart (Yancy et al., 2013). During this progression, ventricular dysfunction begins with an initial insult to the myocardium. Even without further identifiable insults, ventricular dysfunction continues to progress.

As mentioned in the previous sections, left ventricular dysfunction in heart failure is described as reduced (ejection fraction < 40%) to preserved (ejection fraction between 40% and 71%). Patients can also have a reduced ejection fraction with diastolic dysfunction. Patients with combined systolic and diastolic dysfunction have a poorer prognosis and are more difficult to treat than those with isolated systolic or diastolic dysfunction (Yancy et al., 2013).

Heart Failure With Reduced Ejection Fraction

With substantial dilation of the ventricle, reduced wall motion occurs and the heart is unable to contract effectively. As a result, the patient's ejection fraction decreases. A normal ejection fraction is greater than or equal to 55% (Huether & McCance, 2017).

Patients with HFrEF can have low cardiac output. As a result of structural changes in the left ventricle, left ventricular end-diastolic volume (preload) increases and can lead to pulmonary congestion. Dilated cardiomyopathy (ischemic or idiopathic) is a common cause of HFrEF. *Cardiomyopathy* should not be used interchangeably with *systolic heart failure.* Cardiomyopathy is a structural disorder associated with the development of heart failure, whereas heart failure is a clinical syndrome characterized by the presentation of certain symptoms (Huether & McCance, 2017; Yancy et al., 2013).

Heart Failure With Preserved Ejection Fraction

In patients classified with HFpEF, the ventricle is not dilated and the ejection fraction primarily remains within normal limits. However, the ventricle has impaired relaxation and does not fill properly. This class of heart failure is most associated with left ventricular hypertrophy (including hypertrophic cardiomyopathy). The aging process negatively affects the elastic properties of the heart, resulting in varying degrees of myocardial stiffening interfering with the diastolic (filling phase) function of the heart. In particular, older women are at high risk for HFpEF. Ischemic heart disease and restrictive or hypertrophic cardiomyopathy can also cause HFpEF. These conditions are also associated with the ventricle becoming stiff or noncompliant. A noncompliant ventricle is unable to completely relax during diastole, thereby impairing filling (see Figure 8-1). In some cases the ejection fraction is elevated to levels of 70% to 75%. This elevation in ejection fraction occurs because there is no contractile deficit in HFpEF. In this classification of heart failure, the total volume in the ventricle at the end of diastole may actually be less than normal filling volume because of the stiffness and noncompliance of the left ventricle. Therefore, ejection of 70% of volume does not truly result in a greater cardiac output (Huether & McCance, 2017).

In HFpEF, end-diastolic pressures are elevated; however, volumes remain low to normal. To increase diastolic filling, the pressure in the left atria increases. When increased left atrial pressure rises above the pressure in the pulmonary capillaries, pulmonary edema can result. Patients with HFpEF commonly become symptomatic with exertion when the heart rate is increased. When the heart rate is increased, ventricular filling time is reduced. Increased levels of circulating catecholamines also increase heart rate and inevitably make this type of heart failure worse (Huether & McCance, 2017). Table 8-1 summarizes the comparison between HFrEF and HFpEF.

FIGURE 8-1: HYPERTROPHIC LEFT VENTRICLE IN HEART FAILURE WITH PRESERVED EJECTION FRACTION

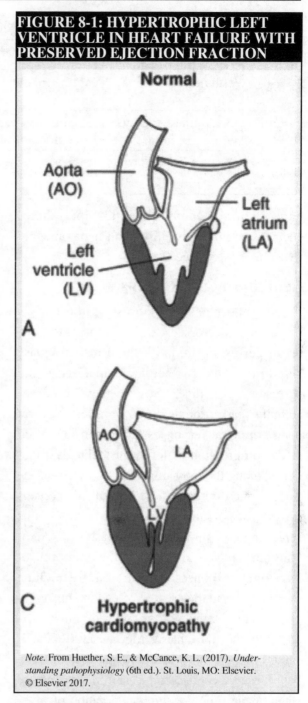

Note. From Huether, S. E., & McCance, K. L. (2017). *Understanding pathophysiology* (6th ed.). St. Louis, MO: Elsevier. © Elsevier 2017.

Left and Right Ventricular Failure

The left and right ventricles are part of a closed circulatory system. Right ventricular failure is most often the result of prolonged left ventricular failure. Isolated right ventricular failure can occur with right ventricular myocardial infarction, pulmonary hypertension, or chronic severe tricuspid regurgitation. Signs of right ventricular heart failure include weight

TABLE 8-1: SUMMARY COMPARISON OF HEART FAILURE WITH PRESERVED EJECTION FRACTION AND HEART FAILURE WITH REDUCED EJECTION FRACTION

HFrEF	Two thirds of patients with heart failure	Decreased left ventricular contractility and ejection fraction	Most common cause is coronary heart disease resulting in myocardial infarction or chronic ischemia
HFpEF	One third of patients with heart failure	Impaired left ventricular relaxation and abnormal filling	Usually related to chronic hypertension or ischemic heart disease

Note. Adapted from Yancy, C. W., Jessup, M., Bozkurt, B., Butler, J., Casey, D. E., Drazner, M. H., ... Wilkoff, B. L. (2013). 2013 ACCF/AHA guideline for the management of heart failure: A report of the American College of Cardiology Foundation/American Heart Association Task Force on Practice Guidelines. *Circulation, 128,* e240-e327. doi:10.1161/CIR.0b013e31829e8776

gain, jugular venous distention, peripheral edema, abdominal swelling, and hepatomegaly (Huether & McCance, 2017).

Neurohormonal Responses

Neurohormonal responses are the body's response to decreased cardiac output and poor organ perfusion. Initially, these responses are helpful in improving cardiac output and organ perfusion. Over time, however, these responses actually lead to clinical deterioration. Several neurohormonal responses have been identified in the progression of left ventricular dysfunction. Among the most important and well-understood of these responses are sympathetic nervous system (SNS) stimulation and activation of the renin-angiotensin-aldosterone system (RAAS; Huether & McCance, 2017). Other neurohormonal responses to heart failure include increased circulating levels of endothelin, vasopressin (also known as *antidiuretic hormone*), and cytokines (Huether & McCance, 2017). The same compensatory mechanisms that initially help preserve cardiac output and blood pressure actually cause progressive deterioration of myocardial function in the long term.

Sympathetic Nervous System Stimulation

One of the first responses to a failing left ventricle, prompting a decrease in cardiac output and blood pressure, is the activation of the SNS. The fall in blood pressure activates baroreceptors and vasomotor regulatory centers in the medulla. The result is an increased level of circulating catecholamines, which stimulate alpha- and beta-adrenergic receptors to increase heart rate, peripheral vasoconstriction (increase afterload), and contractility. Over time in chronic heart failure, beta receptors become less able to respond to circulating catecholamines. This decreased response to circulating catecholamines is called *beta-receptor down-regulation* and is an attempt to protect the failing heart from chronic overstimulation of the SNS. Beta-receptor down-regulation contributes to the exercise intolerance associated with heart failure. Chronic stimulation of the SNS also accelerates the ventricular remodeling process (Huether & McCance, 2017).

Increased heart rate, afterload, and contractility help maintain cardiac output and blood pressure, but also have the negative effect of increasing myocardial oxygen demand. Over time, this increased stimulation of the SNS can worsen ischemia and can cause cardiac dysrhythmias and sudden cardiac death. Circulating catecholamines and angiotensin II cause an increase in cellular calcium, which contributes to the development of cardiac dysrhythmias in heart failure. In addition, overactivation of the SNS causes direct adverse effects on the structure and function of the heart. These cardiotoxic properties are responsible for the beta-receptor down-regulation seen with chronic heart failure (Huether & McCance, 2017).

Renin-Angiotensin-Aldosterone System

Activation of the RAAS is another compensatory neurohormonal response to a failing heart. The RAAS is activated as the kidneys respond to decreased renal perfusion. It is also activated by an increase in SNS stimulation. When the RAAS is activated, circulating levels of renin, angiotensin II, and aldosterone increase. Angiotensin II is a potent vasoconstrictor; thus, systemic vascular resistance and afterload increase. Aldosterone is a mineralocorticoid responsible for sodium and water retention. When sodium is retained by the body, so is water; therefore, preload increases. Enhanced preload increases end-diastolic volume in the ventricles, which further dilates the ventricles and enhances the ventricular remodeling process. If the left ventricle becomes overstretched, contractility is depressed (Huether & McCance, 2017). Figure 8-2 summarizes the neurohormonal responses of the SNS and RAAS.

Vasopressin and Endothelin

In chronic heart failure, angiotensin II and osmotic stimuli produce increased vasopressin release, thereby causing a reabsorption of water and additional vasoconstriction. Levels of endothelin (an endogenous hormonal vasoconstrictor) are elevated in heart failure in response to angiotensin II, vasopressin, and circulating catecholamines (Huether & McCance, 2017).

NURSING APPLICATION

Current treatment for heart failure involves inhibition of neurohormonal systems with beta blockers and angiotensin-converting enzyme (ACE) inhibitors. Patients typically do not understand the neurohormonal blockade associated with these medications or the importance they play in stopping disease progression. If patients think that these medications are only used to treat hypertension and that their blood pressures are normal, then they may be less compliant with therapy because they do not fully understand its impact.

FIGURE 8-2: NEUROHORMONAL RESPONSES OF THE RENIN-ANGIOTENSIN-ALDOSTERONE SYSTEM AND SYMPATHETIC NERVOUS SYSTEM IN HEART FAILURE

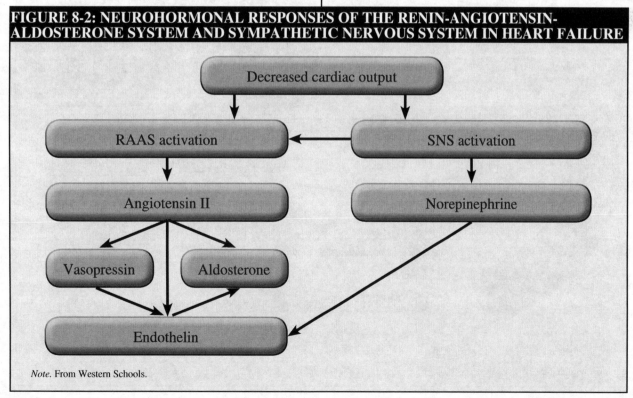

Note. From Western Schools.

Inflammatory Response

Cytokine levels are also elevated in heart failure, producing local and systemic inflammatory responses. Local inflammatory responses occur early in the course of the disease; systemic responses occur later in the course. Cytokines, neurohormones, mechanical stress, and certain physiological conditions can promote cell growth (hypertrophy) and cell death (apoptosis) often seen in the ventricular remodeling process (Huether & McCance, 2017). Figure 8-3 shows the vicious cycle of heart failure caused by uninterrupted neurohormonal responses.

Positive Neurohormonal Response

The release of the hormones atrial natriuretic peptide and brain natriuretic peptide from cardiac myocytes is the one beneficial neurohormonal response in heart failure. These hormones have the positive effect of systemic and pulmonary vasodilation, and also enhance sodium and water excretion in the setting of adequate kidney function.

Other neurohormonal responses work to counteract the vasoconstrictive effects of the SNS and RAAS stimulation. However, the vasoconstrictive effects of neurohormonal activation commonly overpower these counterefforts. Table 8-2 summarizes the results of neurohormonal responses to heart failure (Huether & McCance, 2017).

Left Ventricular Remodeling

Left ventricular remodeling is another response to the initial left ventricular injury. Remodeling is a process of pathological growth, whereby the ventricles hypertrophy and then dilate. Ventricular remodeling occurs as a result of myocyte hypertrophy in response to either pressure overload or volume overload in the ventricles. When pressure overload occurs, the myocytes

FIGURE 8-3: VICIOUS CYCLE OF NEUROHORMONAL RESPONSES AND VENTRICULAR REMODELING IN HEART FAILURE

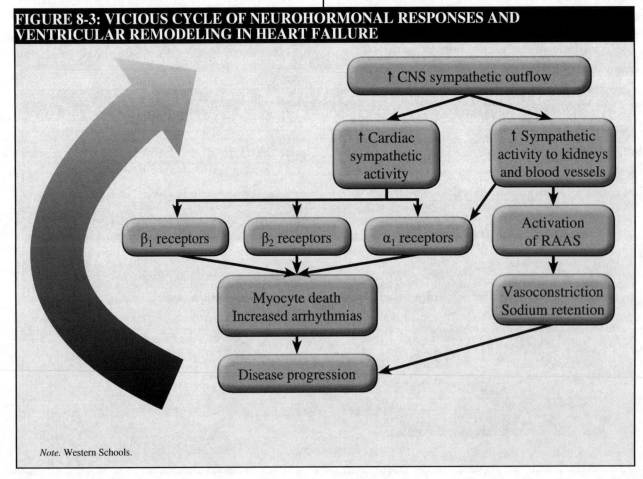

Note. Western Schools.

TABLE 8-2: SUMMARY OF RESULTS OF NEUROHORMONAL STIMULATION IN HEART FAILURE	
SNS	• Stimulation of RAAS and endothelin • Vasoconstriction (increased afterload), increased heart rate, increased contractility • Aggravation of ischemia • Potentiation of dysrhythmias • Acceleration of ventricular remodeling • Direct toxicity to cardiac myocytes
RAAS	• Arterial vasoconstriction from angiotensin II • Stimulation of vasopressin and endothelin • Sodium and water retention from increased aldosterone • Endothelial dysfunction from increased aldosterone • Organ fibrosis from increased aldosterone
Vasopressin	• Reabsorption of water • Vasoconstriction
Endothelin	• Vasoconstriction • Fluid retention • Increased contractility • Hypertrophy
Cytokines	• Proinflammatory response • Contribution to apoptosis (programmed cell death) • Contribution to cardiac cachexia (systemic inflammatory response)
Natriuretic peptides[a]	• Systemic and pulmonary vasodilatation • Increased sodium and water excretion • Suppression of other neurohormones
Nitric oxide[a], bradykinin[a]	• Arterial smooth muscle relaxation and vasodilation, some prostaglandins[a]

[a]Neurohormonal response with positive benefit in heart failure.

SNS = sympathetic nervous system; RAAS = renin-angiotensin-aldosterone system.

Note. Adapted from Huether, S. E., & McCance, K. L. (2017). Understanding pathophysiology (6th ed.). St. Louis, MO: Elsevier.

thicken and concentric hypertrophy results. When volume overload occurs, the myocytes elongate and eccentric hypertrophy results (Huether & McCance, 2017). Figure 8-4 compares the concentric hypertrophy of diastolic heart failure with the eccentric hypertrophy of systolic heart failure. Remember that patients can have coexisting systolic and diastolic dysfunction.

The process of ventricular remodeling is very complex at the cellular level. Concentric hypertrophy causes left ventricular wall thickening and leads to an increased risk for subendocardial ischemia. Eccentric hypertrophy and eventual dilation can cause regurgitation (backward flow through) of the mitral valve and elevated left atrial pressures. These effects accelerate the remodeling process (Huether & McCance, 2017).

Another component of ventricular remodeling includes necrosis and apoptosis of cardiac myocytes. Necrosis (accidental cell death) occurs in response to deprivation of oxygen. Apoptosis (programmed cell death) is stimulated by several factors, including angiotensin II, cytokines, and cellular injury from hypoxia. Myocyte loss in either form can facilitate slippage of myocytes. In response to slippage, a reparative fibrosis occurs that makes the ventricle stiffer (Huether & McCance, 2017).

FIGURE 8-4: COMPARISON OF CONCENTRIC HYPERTROPHY OF DIASTOLIC DYSFUNCTION AND ECCENTRIC HYPERTROPHY OF SYSTOLIC DYSFUNCTION

Hypertrophic cardiomyopathy

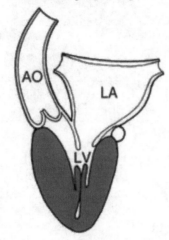

A. Concentric Hypertrophy

Dilated cardiomyopathy

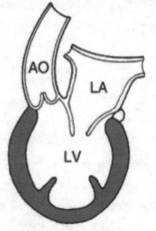

B. Eccentric Hypertrophy

AO = aorta; LA = left atrium; LV = left ventricle.

Note. From Huether, S. E., & McCance, K. L. (2017). *Understanding pathophysiology* (6th ed.). St. Louis, MO: Elsevier. © Elsevier 2017.

The process of ventricular remodeling is complicated by other physiological responses beyond the scope of this chapter. However, the cardiovascular nurse should understand that remodeling is enhanced by the prolonged activation of the SNS, RAAS, and other neurohormonal responses, including endothelin production. In addition to norepinephrine, other substances produced in response to these neurohormonal responses may have direct cardiotoxic effects (Huether & McCance, 2017).

ASSESSMENT OF PATIENTS WITH HEART FAILURE

Initial Evaluation

Recommendations from the American College of Cardiology (ACC) and American Heart Association (AHA) guidelines for the management of heart failure include

- a thorough history and physical examination to identify cardiac and noncardiac conditions that contribute to the development and acceleration of heart failure;

- an initial and ongoing assessment of functional capacity, based on the patient's ability to perform routine activities of daily living;

- an initial and ongoing assessment of fluid volume status;

- an initial electrocardiogram and chest radiograph;

- an initial two-dimensional echocardiogram with Doppler to assess the function of the left ventricle; and

- an initial evaluation of laboratory tests, including complete blood count, electrolytes, blood urea nitrogen, creatinine, blood glucose, thyroid-stimulating hormone, liver function studies, and urinalysis.

(Yancey et al., 2013)

Because of the high association between ischemic heart disease and heart failure, most patients with chest pain of unknown etiology presenting with the clinical syndrome of heart failure also undergo cardiac catheterization (Yancy et al., 2013).

American College of Cardiology/ American Heart Association Stages of Heart Failure

The 2013 ACC/AHA Heart Failure Guidelines organized treatment strategies based on the "stage" or classification of heart failure (Yancy et al., 2013). Nurses can use this classification system (see Table 8-3) to identify severity of heart failure to help guide patient management.

New York Heart Association Functional Classification

The New York Heart Association (NYHA) classification (see Table 8-4) is the most commonly used system to assess functional capacity. The NYHA classification system is based on the patient's activity levels and related symptoms at the time of evaluation. The patient may move up and down the scale based on his or her current health status. When evaluating the staging system, the first two stages (I and II) are actually void of any evidence of heart failure. However, these two stages provide the key to long-term prevention, because therapies in these stages are focused on preventing the development of left ventricular remodeling and, ultimately, heart failure. Stages III and IV focus on therapies for patients with signs and symptoms of heart failure. Treating patients appropriately in stages I and II would hopefully eliminate the movement of patients to stages III and IV. Patients generally only progress on the NYHA scale from minimal limitations toward worsening functional status. Thus, as the patient progresses toward the most severe stages, the NYHA classification is used by clinicians as an independent risk factor for mortality (Yancy et al., 2013).

NURSING APPLICATION

Medications are provided to patients either for a mortality benefit or for symptom relief. When administering medications to a patient, nurses evaluate why the patient is receiving that particular medication. This helps the nurse provide better education for the patient. For example, in ACC/AHA stage B heart failure, beta blockers and ACE inhibitors are indicated for patients with low ejection fractions when no other symptoms of heart failure exist. In this stage, the medications are used for their long-term mortality benefit.

The NYHA classification system does have limitations of use because of the subjectivity involved in the assessment process. In addition, NYHA functional capacity class assessment does not always progress in a systematic way. Patients can move between classes throughout the progression of the disease. NYHA classifications do not correspond to the ACC/AHA stages of heart failure progression but can be used as an alternative (Yancy et al., 2013).

NURSING APPLICATION

Because patients commonly decrease their activity levels to adjust to declining functional capacity, it is important to ask specific questions regarding the level of activity the patient is able to tolerate. For example, ask, "Is there any leisure activity you are no longer able to do that you wish you still could do?" An additional inquiry to assess activity level is, "Tell me what you do on a typical day."

Echocardiography

Two-dimensional echocardiography with Doppler flow studies is the most frequently used diagnostic test in evaluating patients with the clinical syndrome of heart failure. A noninvasive, cost-effective diagnostic tool, the echocardiogram

TABLE 8-3 ACC/AHA HEART FAILURE GUIDELINES

	Stage	Objective Assessment	Example
AT RISK FOR HEART FAILURE	A	No objective evidence of cardiovascular disease. No symptoms and no limitation in ordinary physical activity.	Patients with: • hypertension • atheroscierotic disease • diabetes mellitus • obesity • metabolic syndrome *OR* Patients • using cardiotoxins • with family history of cardiomyopathy
	B	Objective evidence of minimal cardio-vascular disease. Mild symptoms and slight limitation during ordinary activity. Comfortable at rest.	Patients with: • previous MI • LV remodeling, including LVH and low EF • Asymptomatic valvular disease
HEART FAILURE	C	Objective evidence of moderately severe cardiovascular disease. Marked limitation in activity due to symptoms, even during less-than-ordinary activity. Comfortable only at rest.	Patients with: • Known structural heart disease and • HF signs and symptoms
	D	Objective evidence of severe cardiovascular disease. Severe limitations. Experiences symptoms even while at rest.	Patients with: • Marked HF symptoms at rest • Recurrent hospitalizations despite GDMT

EF, ejection fraction; GDMT, guideline-directed medical therapy; HF, heart failure; LV, left ventricular; LVH, left ventricular hypertrophy; MI, myocardial infarction.

Note. Adapted from: American Heart Association. (2016). *Classes of heart failure.* Retrieved from http://www.heart.org/HEARTORG/Conditions/HeartFailure/AboutHeartFailure/Classes-of-Heart-Failure_UCM_306328_Article.jsp#.WDRcTlLru00

Yancy, C. W., Jessup, M., Bozkurt, B., Butler, J., Casey, D. E., Drazner, M. H., ... Wilkoff, B. L. (2013). 2013 ACCF/AHA guideline for the management of heart failure: A report of the American College of Cardiology Foundation/American Heart Association Task Force on Practice Guidelines. *Circulation, 128,* e240-e327. doi:10.1161/CIR.0b013e31829e8776

TABLE 8-4: NEW YORK HEART ASSOCIATION FUNCTIONAL CLASSIFICATIONS

Class I	Class II	Class III	Class IV
Cardiac disease with no resulting limitation on physical activity	Cardiac disease with slight limitation on physical activity	Cardiac disease with marked limitation on physical activity	Cardiac disease resulting in inability to carry out any physical activity without discomfort
Ordinary activity free from fatigue, palpitations, dyspnea, and anginal pain	Comfortable at rest but ordinary activity results in fatigue, palpitations, dyspnea, or anginal pain	Comfortable at rest but less-than-ordinary activity results in fatigue, palpitations, dyspnea, or anginal pain	Possible symptoms of cardiac insufficiency at rest

Note. Adapted from Yancy, C. W., Jessup, M., Bozkurt, B., Butler, J., Casey, D. E., Drazner, M. H., ... Wilkoff, B. L. (2013). 2013 ACCF/AHA guideline for the management of heart failure: A report of the American College of Cardiology Foundation/American Heart Association Task Force on Practice Guidelines. *Circulation, 128,* e240-e327. doi:10.1161/CIR.0b013e31829e8776

can identify the type of ventricular dysfunction and measure the ejection fraction. When HFrEF is identified, the echocardiogram can assist in determining the cause. Regional wall-motion abnormalities indicate ischemic heart disease as the cause, whereas global dysfunction indicates a nonischemic origin. An echocardiogram can also identify other causes of heart failure, such as valvular or pericardial disease. Although an echocardiogram can provide essential information regarding the possible cause of heart failure, it cannot identify the exact cause. A follow-up myocardial biopsy may be warranted to facilitate making a diagnosis (Yancy et al., 2013).

PHARMACOLOGICAL TREATMENT FOR HEART FAILURE

Angiotensin-Converting Enzyme Inhibitors and Angiotensin II Receptor Blockers

ACE inhibitors are indicated in HFrEF and have a positive impact in heart failure by interfering with the ventricular remodeling process, stagnation of disease progression, and risk reduction for death (Yancy et al., 2013). ACE inhibitors also improve symptoms and contribute to a sense of well-being. Benefits are seen in all stages of heart failure, although it may take several weeks to months for the effects to be seen. There is a proven morbidity and mortality benefit with ACE and angiotensin II receptor blockers (ARBs) in HFrEF.

ACE inhibitors remain the first choice for interruption of the RAAS in chronic heart failure and should be given to all patients with current or prior symptoms of heart failure who have a reduced ejection fraction. ARBs (an alternative to ACE inhibitors) directly block angiotensin II. ARBs are indicated in patients who cannot tolerate ACE inhibitors because of cough or angioedema. Current heart failure guidelines recommend against the routine combined use of ACE inhibitors and ARBs (Yancy et al., 2013).

Beta Blockers

Beta blockers are indicated in HFrEF as well and are used to reduce mortality and block the neurohormonal responses of chronic SNS stimulation (Yancy et al., 2013, 2016). Multiple studies have found a mortality benefit in patients treated with beta blockers. Beta blockers have several beneficial effects, including favorably affecting ventricular remodeling and apoptosis. Beta blockers can decrease dysrhythmias and ischemia by decreasing heart rate and contractility, thereby decreasing myocardial oxygen consumption. Beta blockers are indicated in heart failure stages B, C, and D.

Beta blockers are initiated in low doses and slowly titrate upward. Beta blockers are not initiated when the patient is in fluid overload or a decompensated state. However, patients who show signs of decompensation after a maintenance dose of beta-blocker therapy has been administered generally do not have beta-blocker therapy discontinued.

NURSING APPLICATION

When chronic oral therapy with ACE inhibitors and beta blockers has been established, these agents should generally be continued if the patient needs to be hospitalized for an acute exacerbation. An exception would be in a patient who is hemodynamically unstable during his or her acute exacerbation (Yancy et al., 2013).

Aldosterone Antagonists

An aldosterone antagonist, such as spironolactone or eplerenone, can be beneficial in patients with HFrEF who experience symptoms at rest. Adding these agents to existing HFrEF drug regimens has demonstrated benefit in a select group of patients with preserved renal function (creatinine < 2.5 mg/dl). Use of these agents in combination with ACE inhibitors or ARBs must be done carefully to avoid life-threatening hyperkalemia. Current guidelines also recommend against the use of these agents with combined ACE inhibitors and ARB regimens (ACE inhibitor + ARB + aldosterone antagonist; Yancy et al., 2013, 2016).

Novel Heart Failure Therapies

New therapies proven to be comparable with current medical and device therapies for heart failure are the introduction of an angiotensin receptor-neprilysin inhibitor (ARNI) and sinoatrial node modulator (Yancy et al., 2016).

The new ARNI therapy is a medication combination of an ARB (valsartan) with an inhibitor of neprilysin (sacubitril). Neprilysin is an enzyme that degrades bradykinin, adrenomedullin, natriuretic peptides, and other vasoactive peptides. This medication is recommended in patients with symptomatic HFrEF in lieu of an ACE inhibitor or ARB used in conjunction with beta blockers and aldosterone antagonists to reduce morbidity and mortality. New studies revealed a significant reduction in cardiovascular-related deaths and heart failure hospitalizations when using this medication in comparison to using enalapril, an ACE inhibitor, alone. For this reason, an ARNI is also recommended to replace a well-tolerated ACE inhibitor or ARB regimen to further reduce morbidity and mortality in patients with NYHA class II or III HFrEF. Clinicians must be aware of the risk for hypotension, renal insufficiency, and angioedema with ARNI therapy. Also, ARNI should not be used in conjunction with other ACE inhibitors or within 36 hours of the last dose of an ACE inhibitor. ARNI should also be avoided in patients with a prior history of angioedema (Yancy et al., 2016).

Ivabradine is a sinoatrial node modulator, which is a new medication that functions by selectively inhibiting a specific current in the sinoatrial node to reduce heart rate. Ivabradine is recommended to decrease hospitalizations for patients in NYHA class II to III HFrEF who are in sinus rhythm with a resting heart rate greater than 70 beats per minute and being treated with the maximum tolerated dose for beta blockers (Yancy et al., 2016).

Hydralazine and Isosorbide Dinitrate

A combination of hydralazine and isosorbide dinitrate should be added to the treatment regimen for African Americans with moderate-to-severe symptoms of heart failure on optimal treatment with beta blockers, ACE inhibitors, and diuretics. This should also be done for patients with current or prior symptomatic HFrEF who cannot tolerate ACE inhibitor or ARB therapy, hypotension, or renal insufficiency (Yancy et al., 2013). Unfortunately, despite its benefits, treatment adherence can be poor because of the large number of pills required to maintain therapeutic doses. Frequent adverse effects also include headache, dizziness, and gastrointestinal symptoms interfering with medical compliance.

Diuretics

Diuretics are added to the treatment regimen for HFrEF in patients with evidence of fluid retention, unless contraindicated. Loop diuretics are preferred because of their work at the loop of Henle to increase sodium and water excretion. However, thiazide diuretics may also be considered for hypertensive patients (Yancy et al., 2013). After fluid overload has been resolved, diuretics are usually continued to maintain fluid volume status. Few patients with heart failure are able to maintain optimal ECF balance without the use of a diuretic.

Diuretics improve symptoms more rapidly than any other drug and can also increase cardiac function and improve exercise tolerance. Optimal use of diuretics is also key to the effectiveness of ACE inhibitor and beta-blocker therapies. ACE inhibitor therapy is less effective and patients are less likely to tolerate beta-blocker therapy if the diuretic dose is too low and ECF overload is present. The risks for hypotension and renal insufficiency are increased with ACE inhibitor use if the diuretic dose is too high. The primary risks of treatment with diuretics include electrolyte imbalances and fluid depletion (Yancy et al., 2013).

Digoxin

Digoxin is a weak inotropic agent but has benefits in HFrEF associated with persistent symptoms. The benefits digoxin offers are likely the result of its effects of reducing sympathetic outflow and suppressing renin secretion. Digoxin can improve symptoms and decrease the rate of hospitalization but has not been proven to reduce mortality in this population. A dosage of 0.125 mg/day (lower than once thought necessary to be effective) is recommended for most patients (Yancy et al., 2013).

Contraindicated Medications

Although ACE inhibitors, ARBs, beta blockers, diuretics, and digoxin are used in the treatment of heart failure, certain medications should be avoided in patients with heart failure. Many antiarrhythmics are poorly tolerated in patients with heart failure because of their proarrhythmic and cardiodepressant effects. Amiodarone and dofetilide are the only antiarrhythmics to have neutral effects on survival in patients with heart failure (Yancy et al., 2013). Calcium channel blockers, with the exception of amlodipine, adversely affect survival in patients with HFrEF. Amlodipine has a neutral effect in heart failure and can be used if needed to treat coexisting angina or hypertension; however, amlodipine should be closely monitored because it can cause peripheral edema in some patients. Certain antidiabetic medications should

be avoided as well. For instance, use of metformin (Glucophage) places the patient in heart failure at a higher risk for lactic acidosis. In addition, thiazolidinediones such as pioglitazone (Actos) can exacerbate heart failure because of its adverse effects of worsening dyspnea, increased weight gain, and edema in NYHA class III or IV heart failure (Yancy et al., 2013).

Patients with heart failure should also be instructed to avoid the use of nonsteroidal anti-inflammatory drugs, which can cause sodium retention and peripheral vasoconstriction. These medications diminish the efficacy of diuretics and ACE inhibitors while enhancing the likelihood of toxic renal effects. Interestingly, although inotropic medications can be used as a bridging therapy for acute episodes of decompensating heart failure, long-term inotropic therapy is deemed potentially harmful for the patient with HFrEF except if intended for the palliative management of patients with end-stage disease (Yancy et al., 2013).

NONPHARMACOLOGICAL TREATMENT STRATEGIES FOR HEART FAILURE

Exercise Training

Controlled trials have shown exercise training, in addition to medical therapies, can improve symptoms, quality of life, and exercise capacity in patients with heart failure. Exercise training in patients with heart failure is best accomplished in a formally structured program, such as cardiac rehabilitation. Studies show that many of the hemodynamic abnormalities associated with chronic heart failure improve with exercise training. The physiological benefits of exercise training for patients with chronic heart failure occur in skeletal muscle as opposed to in the heart itself (Anderson, 2016).

Cardiac Resynchronization Therapy

Cardiac resynchronization therapy is indicated in patients with moderate-to-severe heart failure and those with wide QRS complexes who are symptomatic despite optimal medical therapy. Prolongation of the QRS interval is associated with worse outcomes (Yancy et al., 2013). In resynchronization therapy, a biventricular pacemaker is placed with leads in both the right and the left ventricles. A lead is also implanted in the right atrium, if the patient does not have permanent atrial fibrillation, to allow for atrial pacing. Resynchronization is common in heart failure because approximately one third of patients with a low ejection fraction and NYHA class III or IV heart failure have bundle branch block that causes the right and left ventricles to depolarize at different times. When this occurs, the walls of the right and left ventricles do not contract simultaneously. This causes dyssynchrony, which decreases myocardial function and cardiac output. Resynchronization therapy with a biventricular pacemaker allows the right and left ventricles to contract simultaneously, thereby improving cardiac performance, exercise tolerance, quality of life, and mortality. An increase in the 6-minute walk distance, reduction in multiple medication regimens, and reduction of hospital readmissions are evident in the first 3 months of resynchronization therapy in some patients. The evidence is strongest in patients who are in sinus rhythm, because they benefit the most from biventricular pacing, as well as patients with QRS duration greater than 150 ms and patients with NYHA class II and III symptoms (Yancy et al., 2013).

NURSING APPLICATION

Cardiac resynchronization therapy is a therapeutic treatment that is very useful for patients in heart failure. These devices are placed to address dyssynchrony, rather than heart rate issues. With this in mind, nurses know that therapy is delivered when ventricular pacing occurs. If there is no ventricular pacing, then there is no synchrony between the right and the left bundles. It is important to differentiate between this patient population and the patient population with pacemakers implanted to maintain normal heart rates.

PATIENT EDUCATION

Heart failure is the final path for many cardiac disorders. Heart failure care is complex and involves continuity across the continuum of care. Research shows that careful monitoring and follow-up make a difference. Nurses play an important role in the monitoring and following up of patients with heart failure. Nurses also contribute substantially to patient and family education. Teaching the patient and family self-management strategies is key in the effective management of heart failure, especially during the transition between inpatient and outpatient settings. Addressing healthcare literacy is key to effectively teach self-management strategies to this patient population. Through discharge education, postdischarge telephone follow-up, and nurse-led heart failure clinics, nurses are making a difference in the management of heart failure. Patients are integral to the management of heart failure, and nurses can positively impact self-management of this disease process by teaching self-care strategies and incorporating self-management into patients' care plans (Yancy et al., 2013).

Discharge instructions must reinforce the following six specific areas of care (Anderson, 2016):

1. recognition and response to signs and symptoms of worsening heart failure,

2. daily weight monitoring,

3. discharge medications (with an emphasis on adherence, persistence, and dose adjustment based on individual follow-up parameters),

4. diet/sodium restriction compliance,

5. activity level (limitations and progressive increases), and

6. follow-up appointment compliance and communication with office nursing/medical personnel.

NURSING APPLICATION

Healthcare illiteracy can exist in the presence of literacy. Even patients who are able to read may not be able to adequately understand the complexities of instructions and language used in health care. Several strategies can be initiated to improve health literacy (Anderson, 2016).

* *Create a trusting relationship.*

* *Provide instructions slowly.*

* *Use commonly understood words, rather than medical terminology.*

* *Focus on practical information about self-care, rather than details about pathophysiology.*

* *Ask patients to teach back what they have learned.*

Additional resource information on this very important topic of health literacy can be found in the healthcare literacy fact sheets that are available for download at the Center for Health Care Strategies, Inc. website (http://www.chcs.org/?s=health+literacy).

Recognition of Signs and Symptoms

Patients need to understand how to recognize the signs and symptoms of worsening heart failure. Recognizing changes in activity tolerance is key. As activity intolerance is decreasing, heart failure symptoms may be increasing. Some patients and families find it helpful to keep an activity diary as an objective record of their activities and tolerance.

Daily Weights

Daily weights can be the most sensitive indicator in assessing ECF status. It is important to remind patients to weigh themselves at the same time of day, wearing a similar amount of clothing and no shoes, for the most accurate trend. A scale with large numbers for visibility is important for older adult patients. Some patients require family assistance to weigh themselves because they cannot independently step onto and off of a scale. Scales with grab bars are beneficial, but because of their cost, they may not be a practical option for all patients.

Nurses should instruct patients to keep a chart of daily weights and take the chart with them to their physician office visits. Patients should also be instructed to report any gain of 3 pounds in 2 days or any gain of greater than 3 pounds in 1 week (Yancy et al., 2013). Some hospitals have programs that allow patients to call in and report their weights each day to a nurse or a computer system. Patients with weight gain and patients who do not call in are identified for further follow-up.

NURSING APPLICATION

Asking about the presence of a working scale at home is a key nursing intervention. Patients should be aware that the monitoring of their daily weights is not for the evaluation of adipose tissue, but for the evaluation of fluid retention. It is important for patients to report their weight gain even if they do not have any other symptoms, because it can be an early indicator of volume overload.

Medication Adherence

Medication adherence is critical to the effective management of heart failure. Patients are more compliant when they fully understand the benefits of therapy. It is important to make sure the patient understands the benefits of therapy, including those medications that may not improve symptoms but improve long-term mortality. Patients with heart failure are on multiple medications, which can cause a variety of compliance issues. A careful assessment of any financial concerns regarding prescribed medications is also important. Nurses should discuss any financial concerns with physicians so that every effort can be made to prescribe the most cost-effective, yet appropriate, medication regimen. Social services should be consulted to assure patients receive all available healthcare support services. Home health care can be invaluable in assessing the home environment and evaluating medication compliance and understanding in that setting (Anderson, 2016).

Physical limitations that affect adherence include poor vision and poor dexterity. The nurse should assess each patient's ability to read the small print on labels, open vials, and divide pills (if necessary). The nurse should also instruct the patient to report any perceived side effects to his or her physician before stopping any medications. Because of the risk for significant renal impairment when taking nonsteroidal anti-inflammatory drugs with diuretic and ACE inhibitor therapy, nurses should instruct patients to avoid the combined use of these medications (Anderson, 2016; Yancy et al., 2013).

Patients should always carry with them a complete list of medications and their doses, especially to every physician office visit. Nurses can facilitate this practice by providing a comprehensive, legible list of medications with a current date printed on a wallet card. Nurses should review all admission and discharge medications to ensure the necessary medications are ordered and different physicians did not inadvertently order two medications in the same drug classification (Anderson, 2016).

Diet/Sodium Restriction

Patients with heart failure also need information regarding adherence to a moderate, sodium-restricted diet. In the presence of a sodium restriction, diuretic therapy is more effective and is associated with better patient outcomes (Yancy et al., 2013). In many cases, patients do not realize the hidden sodium content in processed foods. Because many foods contain high amounts of sodium, patients and their caregivers must learn how to read food labels. Patients with heart failure should limit their sodium intake to 2 to 3 g/day, unless ordered otherwise. Fresh foods are the best choice for low sodium content. Frozen foods typically contain less sodium than do canned foods.

NURSING APPLICATION

Many patients understand not to use the salt shaker but do not understand how to read a food label. Instruct patients to look for the sodium content in foods when reading labels. Also instruct patients to look for portion size to determine the amount of sodium in each serving. Keeping a diary of daily sodium intake may be helpful for some patients in tracking their sodium consumption.

Physical Activity and Socialization

Physical activity should be promoted in all patients with heart failure to prevent deconditioning. Most patients benefit from exercise training in a formal cardiac rehabilitation program. Participation in this type of program also provides interaction with other people and the opportunity for a healthcare provider to assess the patient at regular intervals.

Patients with heart failure are at risk for isolation and depression if they have limited activity tolerance. Many hospitals and communities have support groups for patients and families living with heart failure. Nurses should carefully assess support systems and opportunities for socialization in patients who are homebound.

Follow-Up

Close physician or advanced practice nurse follow-up care is critical to the successful management of heart failure. Patients need to understand the importance of keeping all scheduled appointments, even when they are feeling well. Many medications are titrated to optimal doses on an outpatient basis. Nurses need to identify any barriers to keeping office appointments, such as lack of transportation or conflicting work schedules of family members. Additional resources for patient education can be found at the Heart Failure Society of America website (http://www.hfsa.org).

NURSING APPLICATION

There are many reasons for nonadherence in the patient with heart failure. It is essential that the nurse listens carefully to the patient and asks specific questions to fully appreciate the patient's understanding of discharge instructions. Asking the simple question, "Do you have any questions?" does not ascertain the patient's understanding of the instructions. A more appropriate question might be framed in a manner that demonstrates understanding, such as, "What are you going to do if your weight increases 3 pounds over 2 days?"

CASE STUDY

Grace is a 68-year-old female patient who presents to the emergency department. She explains, "I just had to come back to the hospital because I cannot breathe or catch my breath." She also reports, "I have to sleep in my recliner, and I am tired just trying to get up to use the bathroom."

Grace has a medical history of type 2 diabetes and HFrEF. She was discharged from the same hospital 2 weeks ago with a diagnosis of exacerbation of heart failure. The triage nurse in the emergency department notices that Grace's feet and legs are severely swollen. When the triage nurse questions Grace about her diet, Grace describes strictly following the fluid and salt restriction orders from her prior discharge. However, Grace reports gaining 1 to 2 pounds every day after her discharge.

The nurse further questions Grace about her typical daily intake of foods. Grace denies using canned foods, but admits to sometimes eating frozen food because she tires easily when standing to cook. Grace also reports enjoying fresh fruits and vegetables.

The nurse confirms that Grace has been compliant with her home medication regimen, which includes

- furosemide (Lasix), 40 mg, orally, once a day;
- potassium chloride, 20 mEq, orally, once a day;
- pioglitazone (Actos), 500 mg, orally, twice a day; and
- enalapril (Vasotec), 5 mg, orally, twice a day.

Grace is admitted to the telemetry unit in the hospital. Her cardiologist orders the following changes to her medication regimen.

- Continue enalapril, 5 mg, orally, twice a day.
- Administer Lasix, 80 mg, IV push now, then continue at 40 mg, IV, twice a day.
- Continue potassium chloride, 20 mEq, orally, once a day with use of the following sliding scale, as needed:
  - serum K^+ 3.5 to 4.0 mEq/L – 20 mEq, orally, once a day;
  - serum K^+ 3.0 to 3.4 mEq/L – 40 mEq, orally, once a day; or
  - serum K^+ < 3.0 mEq/L – notify the physician.

- REPLACE Actos with glipizide (Glucotrol), 10 mg, orally, once each morning.

- ADD carvedilol (Coreg), 3.125 mg, orally, every 12 hr.

Questions

1. Which medication in Grace's previous daily regimen may have contributed to her weight gain?

2. Which teaching point about weight gain to patients with heart failure could have prevented Grace from waiting 2 weeks before seeking medical attention?

3. How do ACE inhibitors, such as enalapril, work to reduce heart failure?

Answers

1. Pioglitazone (Actos) can exacerbate heart failure because of its adverse effects of worsening dyspnea and increasing weight gain and edema in patients in NYHA class III or IV heart failure (Yancy et al., 2013).

2. Patients with heart failure need to be instructed about self-monitoring for weight gain. Patients should be instructed to report any weight gain of 3 lb in 2 days or any weight gain greater than 3 lb in 1 week (Yancy et al., 2013). Some hospitals have programs that allow patients to call in and report their weights each day to a nurse or a computer system. Patients with weight gain and patients who do not call in are identified for further follow-up action by a nurse.

3. Angiotensin-converting enzyme (ACE) inhibitors are indicated in HFrEF because of their positive effects of interfering with the ventricular remodeling process, stagnating the disease progression, and reducing the risk of death (Yancy et al. 2013). ACE inhibitors also improve symptoms and contribute to the patient's sense of well-being. Benefits are seen in all stages of heart fail-ure, although it may take several weeks to months for the effects to be seen.

SUMMARY

Heart failure is a complex clinical syndrome of cardiac dysfunction in which nurses play a vital role in helping patients to manage their condition. Applying their knowledge of the causative factors and pathophysiological mechanisms of heart failure, nurses are able to recognize its clinical presentations. Nurses also make prudent assessments and communicate their physical and behavioral findings to the interdisciplinary team for comprehensive and collaborative management of the patient to maximize clinical outcomes. The role of nurses in providing heart failure education to the patient with heart failure and family members is crucial to helping maintain stability of the disease and avoid hospital readmissions. Nurses implement heart failure prevention strategies and education for patients who are at risk for heart failure, including patients with existing coronary heart disease who have not yet experienced development of heart failure. Lifestyle or behavioral factors such as diet, tobacco use, medication adherence, and physical activity must be reinforced as priority interventions for the management of heart failure. Pharmacological therapies can reduce the progression of heart failure and risk for death, but these medical benefits are strengthened with compliance to lifestyle recommendations. The nurse's understanding of the many facets of heart failure management is vital to patients' continued care needs and health.

EXAM QUESTIONS

CHAPTER 8
Questions 43–46

Note: Choose the one option that BEST answers each question.

43. Which symptoms are most associated with heart failure?

    a. Palpitations with syncope or near syncope

    b. Chest pain with palpitations or diaphoresis

    c. Generalized weakness and diaphoresis

    d. Dyspnea and fatigue or dependent edema

44. Which neurohormonal responses in heart failure lead to clinical deterioration over time?

    a. Activation of the liver to release glycogen stores

    b. Increased production of cholesterol to make more needed hormones

    c. Activation of the sympathetic nervous system and renin-angiotensin-aldosterone system

    d. Increased production of hemoglobin to increase oxygen capacity

45. Which test is recommended in the initial evaluation of a patient with suspected heart failure?

    a. Electrocardiogram

    b. Three-dimensional echocardiogram

    c. Creatine phosphokinase test

    d. 24-Hour urine collection

46. Which is a true statement concerning the use of diuretics in heart failure?

    a. Diuretics have common life-threatening side effects and are used only in severe decompensated heart failure.

    b. Diuretics are used in patients with heart failure who have past and present signs of fluid overload.

    c. Diuretics are used for patients with heart failure because they reduce mortality.

    d. Diuretics should only be used in patients with heart failure who cannot tolerate ACE inhibitors.

REFERENCES

Anderson, K. M. (2016). *The advanced practice nurse cardiovascular clinician.* New York, NY: Springer.

Colucci, W. S. (2004). Heart failure. In E. Braunwald (Ed.), *Essential atlas of heart diseases* (2nd ed., pp. 105-142). Philadelphia, PA: Current Medicine, Inc.

Go, A. S., Mozaffarian, D., Roger, V. L., Benjamin, E. J., Berry, J. D., Borden, W. B., ...Turner, M. B. (2013). Heart disease and stroke statistics – 2013 update: A report from the American Heart Association. *Circulation, 127,* e6-e245. doi:10.1161/CIR.0b013e31828124ad

Huether, S. E., & McCance, K. L. (2017). *Understanding pathophysiology* (6th ed.). St. Louis, MO: Elsevier.

Yancy, C. W., Jessup, M., Bozkurt, B., Butler, J., Casey, D. E., Drazner, M. H., ... Wilkoff, B. L. (2013). 2013 ACCF/AHA guideline for the management of heart failure: A report of the American College of Cardiology Foundation/American Heart Association Task Force on Practice Guidelines. *Circulation, 128,* e240-e327. doi:10.1161/CIR.0b013e31829e8776

Yancy, C. W., Jessup, M., Bozkurt, B., Butler, J., Casey, D. E., Colvin, M. M., ... Westlake, C. (2016). 2016 ACC/AHA/HFSA focused update on new pharmacological therapy for heart failure: An update of the 2013 ACCF/AHA guideline for the management of heart failure: A report of the American College of Cardiology/American Heart Association Task Force on Clinical Practice Guidelines and the Heart Failure Society of America. *Circulation, 134*(13), e282-e293. doi:10.1161/CIR.0000000000000435

CHAPTER 9

CHRONIC HEART FAILURE: VALVE CONDITIONS

LEARNING OUTCOME

After completing this chapter, the learner will be able to describe the nurse's role in the collaborative management of patients with chronic heart failure secondary to valvular disorders.

CHAPTER OBJECTIVES

After completing this chapter, the learner will be able to:

1. Recognize patient presentation and assessment findings indicative of heart failure that is secondary to mitral, aortic, or tricuspid valvular dysfunction.

2. Discuss collaborative management of patients with heart failure that is secondary to mitral, aortic, or tricuspid valvular dysfunction.

3. Describe medical and surgical treatment interventions for patients with heart failure that is secondary to mitral, aortic, or tricuspid valvular dysfunction.

INTRODUCTION

Valvular heart disease is the dysfunction of intracardiac valves that interferes with the maintenance of forward blood flow through the heart. Valvular heart disease can lead to heart failure because of an accumulation of blood volume overstretching the myocardium of the affected heart chambers. The overstretching of the heart impairs contractility and, if it is chronic, leads to heart failure. Hemodynamic alterations can be related to these structural defects, placing the patient at risk for volume overload and leading to the syndrome of heart failure (Nishimura et al., 2014).

Valve dysfunction can interfere with the forward flow of blood movement through the heart in varying degrees because of stenosis (hardening of the valve) or regurgitation (prolapse or the partial closing of the valve). Valvular stenosis is defined as the constriction or narrowing of the valve orifice, causing an impedance of blood flow forward. Stenosis also increases the workload of the cardiac chamber most proximal to the diseased valve. The pressure within the affected chamber then rises in an attempt to overcome resistance and empty itself into the following chamber. This process poses greater exertion by the myocardium and leads to hypertrophy (Huether & McCance, 2017).

Any valve in the heart can be affected by stenosis; however, the mitral and aortic valves on the left side of the heart are most often affected. The impedance of blood flow on the left side of the heart can lead to increased intraventricular or intraatrial pressures and subsequent congestion throughout the pulmonary vasculature. Ultimately, cardiac output and systemic perfusion are compromised.

Regurgitant blood flow through valves is the undesired directional movement of blood in the heart; this occurs secondary to valves improperly closing during different phases of the cardiac cycle. This type of dysfunction primarily occurs with the mitral, aortic, or tricuspid valves (Nishimura et al., 2014).

MITRAL VALVE

The mitral valve is the gateway between the left atrium and the left ventricle. The mitral valve opens passively during the beginning of diastole, allowing blood to flow passively from the atrium to the ventricle. At the end of diastole, the atrium contracts (atrial kick) and sends an additional volume to the ventricle. As the pressure in the ventricle increases, the mitral valve begins to close. Isovolumic contraction begins and further pressure in the ventricle builds, forcing the mitral valve to snap shut. The papillary muscles contract, preventing the mitral valve leaflets from prolapsing into the left atrium during systole. The closed mitral valve forms a tight seal to assure that the blood being ejected from the ventricle flows forward through the aortic valve and not backward into the left atrium. When ventricular ejection is complete and the pressure in the left ventricle becomes lower than the pressure in the left atrium, the mitral valve opens and the cycle begins again (see Figure 9-1). Proper function of the valve allows blood to move from the atrium to the ventricle. Normal function of the mitral valve plays a key role in the volume of blood in the left ventricle before ejection. This volume is essential for systemic perfusion. A dysfunctional mitral valve can alter left ventricular preload and, consequently, perfusion (Huether & McCance, 2017).

Mitral Valve Stenosis

Definition

Mitral valve stenosis occurs when the mitral valve no longer opens normally, causing an obstruction of blood flow from the left atrium to the left ventricle (see Figure 9-2).

Causes

The number one cause of mitral stenosis is rheumatic fever (Huether & McCance, 2017; Nishimura et al., 2014). As the incidence of rheumatic fever decreases in the United States, so does the incidence of mitral stenosis. Congenital mitral stenosis, atrial myxoma, systemic lupus erythematosus, and bacterial endocarditis can also contribute to the development of mitral stenosis, but these causes are rare (Huether & McCance, 2017). Mitral stenosis is twice as common in women as it is in men. Many patients with rheumatic mitral stenosis have no recollection of having had rheumatic fever (American Heart Association, 2016).

Pathophysiology

Fibrosis and calcification of the valve leaflets develop in the rheumatic mitral valve. The valve commissures fuse together, and the chordae tendineae thicken and shorten. The combination of some or all of these changes results in a valve orifice that is much smaller than normal. The normal mitral valve area is 4 cm^2 to 5 cm^2 (Nishimura et al., 2014). As the valve opening becomes smaller, passive blood flow is more difficult from the atrium to the ventricle. Because the ventricle depends on diastolic filling to maintain stroke volume, left atrial pressure must rise in an attempt to maintain normal flow across the valve. This increase in left atrial pressure is transferred back to the pulmonary vascular bed, as pulmonary pressure subsequently increases. As the obstruction worsens, the chronic increase in left atrial pressure results

FIGURE 9-1: NORMAL MITRAL VALVE

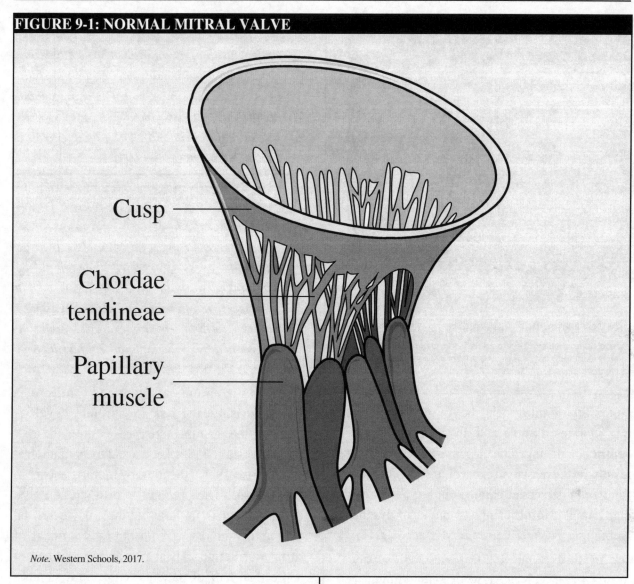

Cusp

Chordae
tendineae

Papillary
muscle

Note. Western Schools, 2017.

in pulmonary hypertension and, ultimately, right ventricular failure. The left atrium dilates and hypertrophies in response to the increased pressure and volume, and it becomes increasingly more difficult to empty the atrium. The enlarged left atrium puts the patient at risk for the development of thrombi in the atrium (Huether & McCance, 2017).

Clinical Presentation

The development of symptoms could begin as long as 20 to 40 years after the development of rheumatic fever. After the onset of initial symptoms, another 10 years may pass before symptoms occur that change the patient's life-style. Symptoms that occur with activity usually appear when the valve area has narrowed to less than 2.5 cm². Symptoms that occur at rest usually appear when the valve orifice is less than 1.5 cm² (Nishimura et al., 2014). When symptoms begin, they develop slowly and patients make adjustments in activity levels to compensate for the changes, often without being aware they are doing so. Dyspnea with exertion, with no symptoms at rest, is the most common initial finding. Conditions that increase heart rate, such as pregnancy, new-onset atrial fibrillation, hyperthyroidism, or fever, commonly result in symptoms that may alert the clinician to the

FIGURE 9-2: MITRAL VALVE STENOSIS

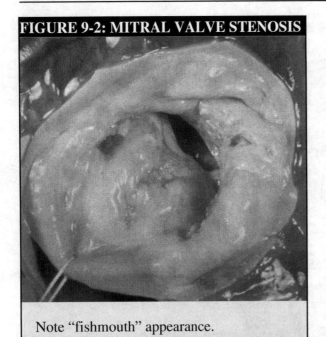

Note "fishmouth" appearance.

Note. Science Source®. Science Source® is a registered trademark of Photo Researchers, Inc. Images and Text Copyright © 2017 Photo Researchers, Inc. All Rights Reserved.

possibility of mitral stenosis. An increased heart rate shortens diastole and, therefore, decreases ventricular filling time. Decreased filling time results in decreased stroke volume, which contributes to decreased cardiac output. When cardiac output is insufficient, symptoms of dyspnea and fatigue occur (Huether & McCance, 2017).

As valve dysfunction increases and the valve orifice decreases, symptoms increase. Pulmonary symptoms such as orthopnea and paroxysmal nocturnal dyspnea develop. With the development of severe mitral stenosis (valve orifice less than 1 cm^2), the patient develops dyspnea at rest and is essentially confined to a bed or a chair as the complications of pulmonary hypertension worsen. Cough and hemoptysis develop as the disease progresses. Ultimately, the failure of the cardiovascular system affects the right side of the heart, and signs of right ventricular failure appear (Huether & McCance, 2017).

NURSING APPLICATION

Patients with severe mitral stenosis may experience acute pulmonary edema with exercise because the narrowed mitral opening cannot handle the increased blood flow produced by the normal increase in heart rate and venous return that occurs with exercise.

NURSING APPLICATION

Even though patients with mild-to-moderate mitral stenosis should be counseled to avoid unusually stressful exercise, they should be encouraged to maintain a low-level aerobic exercise program to maintain cardiovascular fitness. The limits of this exercise should be determined by individual patient tolerance.

With the atrium enlarging and cardiac output decreasing, the risk for thrombi development in the atrium increases, as does the risk for embolization. Stroke, caused by an embolus, is often the first indication of mitral stenosis in many cases. The probability of a stroke exists if the patient is in sinus rhythm; however, the probability increases with the development of atrial fibrillation. Atrial fibrillation is noted in more than half of patients with mitral stenosis because of atrial enlargement (Nishimura et al., 2014). Atrial fibrillation is discussed in more detail in Chapter 10.

NURSING APPLICATION

Patients with mitral stenosis are dependent on atrial contraction for a large portion of ventricular filling because stenosis slows the passive filling of the ventricle from the atrium. Therefore, the development of atrial fibrillation in patients with mitral stenosis can quickly result in symptoms of decreased perfusion because atrial contraction is lost with the onset of atrial fibrillation.

Physical Examination

On cardiac auscultation, the first heart sound (S1, or "lub") is louder than normal unless the valve is heavily calcified; then the sound is diminished. The second heart sound (S2, or "dub") is associated with closure of the aortic and pulmonic valves. At the same time, the mitral and tricuspid valves open. The opening of a stenotic mitral valve results in a sound that may be heard immediately after the second heart sound. This sound is called an opening snap and is best heard at the cardiac apex (fifth intercostal space, at the midclavicular line) with the diaphragm of the stethoscope. At the same location, a low-pitched rumbling diastolic murmur can be heard with the bell of the stethoscope. The murmur occurs during ventricular diastole and can be heard after the second heart sound and before the first heart sound. The more severe the disease process, the longer the murmur lasts throughout diastole. The murmur is best heard with the patient lying on the left side or during exercise. Patients may also present with signs of right ventricular failure, including crackles, jugular venous distension, hepatomegaly, and peripheral edema. Mitral facies is a pinkish purple discoloration of the cheeks that is common in patients with severe mitral stenosis (Anderson, 2016).

NURSING APPLICATION

Diastolic murmurs are often difficult to hear because of their low pitch. It is important to listen carefully in a quiet room. It may take 5 to 10 seconds to recognize a lower-grade diastolic murmur. The murmur of mitral stenosis is best heard with the bell of the stethoscope placed lightly over the apex of the heart (fifth intercostal space, left midclavicular line).

Diagnosis and Management

Echocardiogram. Echocardiography is the method of choice for diagnosing mitral stenosis. With echocardiography, the mitral valve orifice can be measured to assist in the determination of stenosis severity (see Table 9-1). Valve motion, leaflet thickness, and calcification can also be evaluated with echocardiography. In addition to an evaluation of the valve itself, left atrial size and pulmonary artery pressures are measured. Patients with mitral stenosis may also benefit from transesophageal echocardiography to detect valve vegetation or thrombi in the left atrium (Nishimura et al., 2014).

TABLE 9-1: MITRAL VALVE STENOSIS STAGES	
> 1.5 cm^2	Mild
1.0 to 1.5 cm^2	Moderate
< 1.0 cm^2	Severe

Note. From Nishimura, R. A., Otto, C. M., Bonow, R. O., Carabello, B. A., Erwin, J. P., Guyton, R. A., ... Thomas, J. D.; American College of Cardiology/American Heart Association Task Force on Practice Guidelines. (2014). 2014 AHA/ACC guideline for the management of patients with valvular heart disease: A report of the American College of Cardiology/American Heart Association Task Force on Practice Guidelines. *Journal of the American College of Cardiology, 63*(22), e57-e185. doi:10.1016/j.jacc.2014.02.536

Cardiac Catheterization. If valve replacement is needed, cardiac catheterization allows for assessing the need for coronary artery revascularization. During cardiac catheterization, left atrial pressure can be measured to assist in the evaluation of the progression of the valve disease. However, cardiac catheterization is not as useful as echocardiography in determining the severity of the stenosis (Nishimura et al., 2014).

Chest X-ray Film. The presence of signs of mitral stenosis on chest x-ray film depends on the extent of the disease. As the disease progresses and pulmonary hypertension develops, the pulmonary arteries are more visible on the x-ray film. An elevation of the left mainstem bronchus, with left atrial enlargement, also may be noted. Signs of pulmonary edema are noted if the patient is in a volume overload state (Nishimura et al., 2014).

Electrocardiogram. The electrocardiogram (ECG) demonstrates signs of left atrial enlargement with abnormal P waves (wide, notched P waves in lead II). If right ventricular hypertrophy is present, a QRS axis shift to the right may be visible. These ECG changes are neither sensitive nor specific to mitral stenosis and always require other testing for confirmation.

The ECG may also show atrial fibrillation. New-onset atrial fibrillation is a treatable rhythm that can be identified by comparing the patient's current ECG with previous ECGs (Nishimura et al., 2014).

NURSING APPLICATION

Clinicians should be particularly alert for the development of atrial fibrillation because the incidence of stroke is higher with this rhythm. Many patients are unaware of the development of an irregularly irregular heart rhythm, but astute practitioners can recognize the changes of atrial fibrillation and begin appropriate treatment.

Medical Therapy

Rhythm Control. Medical management is of limited use in patients with normal sinus rhythm who are asymptomatic. When symptoms begin, treatment is directed to alleviation of symptoms. Atrial fibrillation commonly occurs in patients with mitral stenosis who are symptomatic (January et al., 2014). Calcium channel blockers (diltiazem and verapamil), beta blockers, or digoxin can be useful in the treatment of atrial fibrillation to maintain a ventricular rate of less than 100 beats/min because these medications slow conduction through the atrioventricular node. Because atrial fibrillation is poorly tolerated, it is reasonable to attempt to return the patient to normal sinus rhythm with cardioversion, either electrical or chemical (with medications). Continued use of antiarrhythmics after successful cardioversion to sinus rhythm has proven to be helpful in maintaining a normal rhythm (January et al., 2014).

Anticoagulation. Anticoagulation is necessary for patients with mitral stenosis and either paroxysmal or persistent atrial fibrillation. The benefits of anticoagulation in patients with mitral stenosis and normal sinus rhythm are controversial in the literature. Patients with mitral stenosis and normal sinus rhythm who have a history of left atrial thrombus or embolic events have experienced some benefits on anticoagulation. Currently, anticoagulant therapy is recommended in patients with mitral stenosis and atrial fibrillation or patients with mitral stenosis and prior embolic events. Patients with atrial fibrillation and mitral stenosis are considered to have valvular atrial fibrillation, and the only currently approved anticoagulant is a vitamin K antagonist (warfarin) or heparin (Nishimura et al., 2014).

Beta Blockers. By decreasing contractility, beta blockers can help decrease ventricular pressure and improve filling from the atria. A decreased heart rate can benefit patients who are experiencing symptoms from high heart rates during activity. The decrease in heart rate provides a longer diastolic time, resulting in better diastolic filling of the ventricle and emptying of the atrium. Beta blockers may also help to control fast ventricular rates in atrial fibrillation (January et al., 2014; Nishimura et al., 2014).

Diuretics. Diuretics and sodium restrictions provide symptomatic support for patients who experience symptoms of extracellular fluid (ECF) overload. These measures reduce volume and, ultimately, venous return to the heart (preload).

Physical Activity and Exercise. Patients with more than mild mitral stenosis should be advised to avoid the stress of strenuous physical activity and exercise. The increase of heart rate decreases the diastolic filling time and will decrease the movement of blood from the left atrium to the left ventricle. Patients with mitral stenosis (especially moderate to severe) should be instructed to seek medical attention if they have a sudden onset of shortness of breath. Acute pulmonary edema can occur suddenly in these patients, especially with the onset of rapid atrial fibrillation (Anderson, 2016).

Endocarditis Prophylaxis. It is important to discuss good oral hygiene practices as a primary strategy for the prevention of endocarditis. However, the prophylactic use of antibiotics for patients with native valve disease is not recommended (Nishimura et al., 2014).

Surgical Interventions

When the valve area becomes less than 1.5 cm^2, most patients with mitral stenosis begin to experience symptoms at rest and report that their lifestyle is affected. When these symptoms occur, surgical options should be considered (Nishimura et al., 2014).

Percutaneous Mitral Balloon Commissurotomy. As stenosis develops, the commissures (points where valve leaflets come together) begin to fuse together. During percutaneous mitral balloon commissurotomy, commissures are cut apart to allow for increased movement of the leaflets. This procedure is beneficial to patients with pliable leaflets that have no calcification. Mitral commissurotomy can be performed as a closed heart repair or an open heart repair. If the patient is symptomatic with severe mitral stenosis but has no other indications for cardiac surgery, the percutaneous method is preferred. If a patient is asymptomatic but has very severe mitral stenosis, this approach can also be considered. However, open-heart repair is becoming the preferred method because the surgeon can visualize the valve and remove calcium deposits and left atrial clots as needed (Nishimura et al., 2014). Open mitral commissurotomy involves an open-heart procedure requiring the use of cardiac bypass.

Mitral Valve Replacement. Patients with extensive calcification and mitral regurgitation, in addition to stenosis and pulmonary hypertension, are candidates for mitral valve replacement. The material (metal or biological tissue) the valve is replaced with determines the long-term maintenance regimen. Although general mortality rates are not different between the two types of valves, the duration of the grafted valve's function and postoperative treatment regimen vary. For instance, a mechanical valve replacement is made of metal and will require lifelong anticoagulation therapy to avoid thrombus formation or embolization, or both. However, a benefit of receiving a mechanical valve is its duration of therapy being more than 20 years after surgical replacement. Valve replacement with a bioprosthetic, or tissue, material does not require anticoagulation therapy if the patient maintains a sinus rhythm postoperatively. However, approximately 10 years after valve replacement, the grafted tissue begins to deteriorate and requires replacement within the next 5 to 10 years (Nishimura et al., 2014).

Outcomes Management

As cardiovascular technology and skill continue to advance, patients undergoing valvotomy and open-heart commissurotomy continue to experience excellent short- and long-term results (Nishimura et al., 2014). Patients who have the correct valve anatomy should undergo percutaneous mitral balloon commissurotomy to avoid the risks associated with bypass surgery. The risk for surgery increases with age but remains fairly low. Patients begin to experience an improvement in symptoms as soon as the valve is replaced or repaired. There is gradual regression of the pulmonary hypertension over time. An echocardiogram should be completed no sooner than 72 hours after the procedure. Patients should follow up yearly with a physical examination, chest x-ray, and ECG. Further echocardiograms are indicated only if symptoms recur (Nishimura et al., 2014).

After valve replacement (with either a tissue or a mechanical valve), all patients are at high risk for endocarditis and do benefit from endocarditis prophylaxis before dental procedures (Nishimura et al., 2014). Patients with a mechanical valve will be placed on lifelong warfarin therapy. Those with a tissue or bioprosthetic valve may be placed on warfarin for 3 months postoperatively and then switched to lifelong aspirin therapy. Thus, risks for bleeding or complications related to bleeding must be considered for the patient who received a mechanical valve.

Mitral Valve Regurgitation

Definition

Mitral valve regurgitation (insufficiency or incompetence) occurs when a backward flow of blood occurs from the left ventricle to the left atrium during ventricular systole. This backward flow of blood is caused by inadequate closure of the mitral valve.

Causes

Mitral valve prolapse is the most common valve dysfunction in the United States and most common secondary cause of mitral regurgitation (Huether & McCance, 2017). However, not all patients with mitral valve prolapse have mitral regurgitation. Mitral valve prolapse is a billowing of one or both of the mitral valve leaflets into the left atrium during ventricular systole, with or without regurgitation. Young women are most commonly affected by mitral valve prolapse. Mitral valve prolapse can be famil-

ial and passed from generation to generation. Patients with Marfan's syndrome and other connective tissue diseases also have an increased prevalence of mitral valve prolapse. In addition to mitral valve prolapse, rheumatic heart disease, bacterial endocarditis, ischemic heart disease, left ventricular dilation, and hypertrophic cardiomyopathy are some of the primary causes of mitral regurgitation (Huether & McCance, 2017; Nishimura et al., 2014).

Mitral valve prolapse occurs when changes in the valve leaflets and chordae tendineae result in lengthening of the chordae tendineae. Normally, the papillary muscle contracts during ventricular systole. This contraction applies pressure to the chordae tendineae. As contraction occurs, the chordae tendineae pull on the valve leaflets to prevent them from prolapsing into the atria as the force of ventricular contraction and ejection pushes against the leaflets (see Figure 9-3). In mitral valve prolapse, the lengthened chordae tendineae cannot keep the valve leaflet in its proper place, and the valve leaflets are forced into the left atrial chamber (see Figure 9-4). Mitral valve prolapse occurring in young, otherwise healthy women may cause either no regurgitation or only mild mitral regurgitation, with little effect on the heart (Huether & McCance, 2017).

In rheumatic heart disease, the valve leaflets become fibrotic and shorten. Inflammation of the valve from the disease process may also lead to calcification. When marked calcification occurs, the leaflets become very stiff and remain in a fixed, open position.

Myocardial infarction can result in impairment or rupture of a papillary muscle. When the myocardial wall becomes damaged, attachment of the papillary muscle to that ventricular wall can become impaired. As the heart pumps, the papillary muscle continues to contract. With each contraction of the papillary

FIGURE 9-3: NORMAL FUNCTIONING MITRAL VALVE

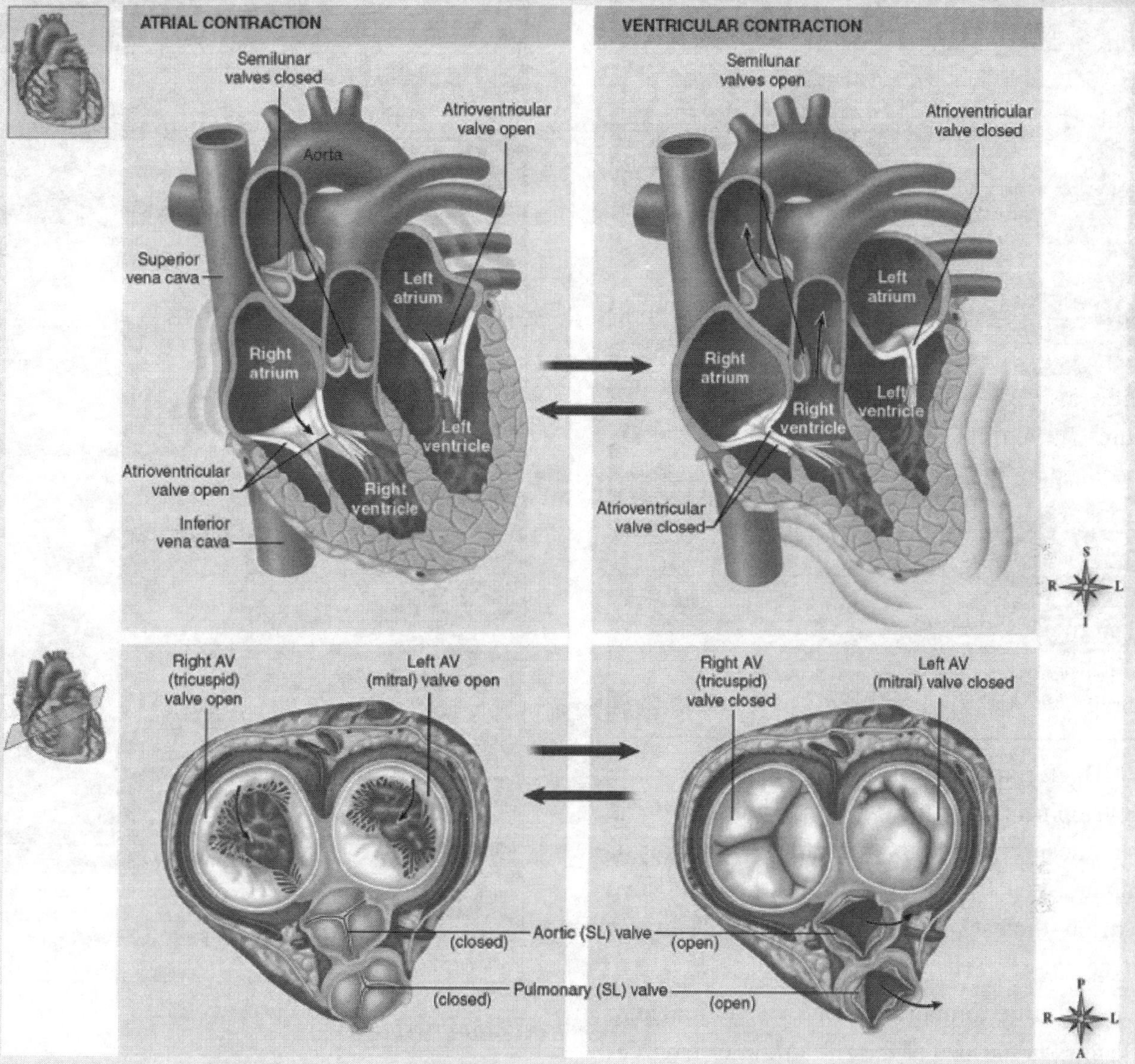

(**A**) The valve leaflets are widely open in ventricular diastole. (**B**) The valve leaflets close during ventricular systole. (**C**) The mitral valve annulus and cusps form a funnel-like structure when the mitral valve is open.

Note. From Patton, K. T., Thibodeau, G. A., & Douglas, M. M. (2012). *Essentials of anatomy & physiology.* Lansing, MI: Elsevier/Mosby. © Elsevier 2012.

muscle, the attachment to the ventricle can weaken. If enough damage to the myocardial wall or papillary muscle has occurred, the papillary muscle can disconnect from the ventricular wall (see Figure 9-5). This results in an acute mitral regurgitation state, and emergency measures are necessary to prevent death (Huether & McCance, 2017; Nishimura et al., 2014).

NURSING APPLICATION

Inferior wall myocardial infarctions greatly increase the risk for acute papillary muscle ruptures. Papillary muscle ruptures generally do not occur at the onset of the infarct but may develop 48 to 72 hours later.

FIGURE 9-4: MITRAL VALVE PROLAPSE

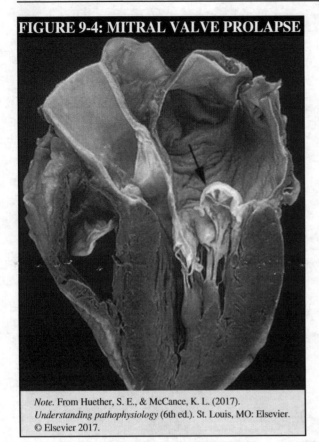

Note. From Huether, S. E., & McCance, K. L. (2017).
Understanding pathophysiology (6th ed.). St. Louis, MO: Elsevier.
© Elsevier 2017.

Bacterial invasion of the heart, with the development of endocarditis, can cause chordae tendineae or papillary muscle dysfunction or rupture. Vegetation can also develop on the valve leaflets themselves, disrupting their ability to close properly (Huether & McCance, 2017).

Without damage to the valve leaflets, changes in the size of the left atrium or left ventricle can affect the mitral valve annulus. Dilation of the left ventricle or left atrium can stretch the mitral annulus, preventing the leaflets from closing properly (Huether & McCance, 2017).

Mitral valve regurgitation has a variety of causes, but the pathophysiological results are the same no matter what the cause. Rather, it is the development of regurgitation, be it acute or chronic, that changes the clinical picture. Therefore, the clinical presentations of chronic and acute mitral regurgitation are discussed separately below (Huether & McCance, 2017).

FIGURE 9-5: RUPTURED PAPILLARY MUSCLE

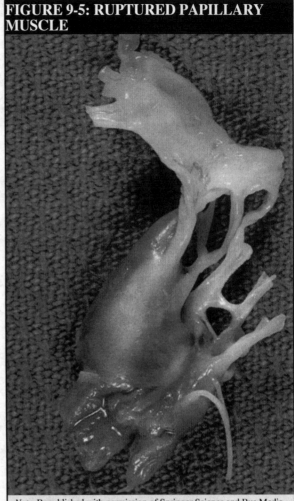

Note. Republished with permission of Springer Science and Bus Media B V. From Butany, J., & Gotlieb, A. (2000). In E. Braunwald and B. M. McManus (Eds.), *Atlas of cardiovascular pathology for the clinician.* Current Medicine.

Pathophysiology

During ventricular systole, the contracting left ventricle forces blood forward through the aortic valve. In the presence of mitral regurgitation, some of that forward blood flow is diverted retrograde (backward) through the dysfunctional mitral valve. This retrograde flow decreases the normal stroke volume (forward flow) by the percentage of blood that is diverted backward. As the left atrium continues to fill normally from the pulmonary system, the volume of blood returning through the abnormal mitral valve increases the normal volume of blood in the left atrium. This acute increase in left atrial volume results in an increase in pressure in the left atrium. The left atrium responds to this increased volume and pressure by dilating. If this dilation is not adequate to handle the increased volume and pressure, the effects are transferred backward to the pulmonary system and pulmonary hypertension develops (Huether & McCance, 2017).

Because the left atrium has a larger volume, the left ventricle ultimately receives this larger volume from the atrium during diastole. The ventricle adjusts to this increased volume by enlarging. Additionally, left ventricular contractions actually may become stronger for a period of time. The purpose of these changes (increase in left ventricular filling and increase in contraction) is to compensate for the volume of blood that is returned to the atrium with each beat. As ejection occurs, normal stroke volume is ejected forward with the additional volume being returned to the left atrium through the regurgitant valve. This compensatory mechanism functions well for many years, until the myocardial fibers have been stretched beyond their physical limitations and systolic ventricular dysfunction occurs (Huether & McCance, 2017).

Clinical Presentation

Patients with chronic mitral regurgitation may remain asymptomatic for many years. As symptoms develop, the patient most frequently reports fatigue and dyspnea, initially on exertion. These symptoms progress to include paroxysmal nocturnal dyspnea, orthopnea, and even palpitations from atrial fibrillation. In many cases, the initial diagnosis of mitral regurgitation is made when patients present with new-onset atrial fibrillation. The early expression of mitral valve prolapse may include symptoms of tachycardia, orthostatic hypotension, or panic attacks (Huether & McCance, 2017).

NURSING APPLICATION

Patients with mitral valve prolapse should avoid caffeine and other stimulants because they can increase the incidence of tachycardia and anxiety attacks.

Physical Examination

The classic murmur of mitral regurgitation is a systolic, blowing, high-pitched murmur that is best heard at the apex of the heart with the diaphragm of the stethoscope. Occasionally, due to the leaflet that is prolapsed, the murmur is louder at the aortic area (second intercostal space, right sternal border). The murmur generally radiates to the axillae but may also be heard over the spine, again depending on the leaflet that is defective. In addition to the murmur, an extra heart sound (S3) is audible due to the increased left ventricular volume (Huether & McCance, 2017).

Increased heart rate is noted in patients with atrial fibrillation or heart failure. As stroke volume decreases, pulse pressure narrows and the carotid pulse volume may decrease. The apical impulse, normally at the apex, becomes displaced due to dilation of the left ventricle. If the patient is in heart failure, assessment findings may include increased respiratory rate with audible crackles. If left ventricular failure has progressed enough to reflect failure on the right side of the heart, then jugular venous distension, hepatomegaly, and edema will be present.

NURSING APPLICATION

When assessing for an S3, listen at the fifth intercostal space, left midclavicular line with the bell of the stethoscope. Normal S1 and S2 sound like "lub dub." When the S3 is added, it will sound like "lub dub da" or like the rhythm of the statement "I Believe."

Diagnosis and Management

Echocardiogram. Echocardiography is the recommended standard for assessment of mitral valve disease. An echocardiogram can determine left ventricular and left atrial volumes, left atrial ejection fraction, and an approximation of the severity of regurgitation. The cause of the mitral regurgitation is commonly determined during this study. The severity of the disease process is identified as *mild* (1+), *moderate* (2+), or *severe* (3 to 4+). Echocardiography is a baseline study that can be used for many years to monitor the progression of the disease (Nishimura et al., 2014; Yancy et al., 2013).

Cardiac Catheterization. Cardiac catheterization is necessary to determine the presence of coronary artery disease in patients facing mitral valve surgery. Ventricular function and ejection fraction can be assessed, as well as pulmonary pressures. However, echocardiography remains the gold standard for this diagnosis (Nishimura et al., 2014).

Chest X-ray Film. An enlarged left atrium and left ventricle are noted on chest x-ray film. If pulmonary hypertension has developed, right ventricular and pulmonary artery enlargement are also present. Patients in a volume overload state will show signs of pulmonary edema (Nishimura et al., 2014).

Electrocardiogram. The 12-lead ECG shows evidence of left atrial hypertrophy with abnormal P waves (wide, notched P waves in lead II). Left ventricular hypertrophy is also demonstrated by large QRS complexes with associated ST-segment abnormalities. Atrial fibrillation or ectopic beats may be noted. These ECG changes are neither sensitive nor specific to mitral regurgitation and always require other testing for confirmation (Nishimura et al., 2014).

Medical Therapy

For patients with normal ventricular function who are asymptomatic, no treatment has been found to decrease the progression of the disease process. When patients have been diagnosed with mitral valve regurgitation, they should be monitored on a regular basis. For instance, an initial echocardiogram and yearly physical examinations are recommended for patients with mild mitral regurgitation, no symptoms, and no evidence of left ventricular dysfunction or enlargement. Patients should be instructed to report any signs of physical deterioration to their physicians. When symptoms develop, an annual or biannual echocardiogram should be completed if moderate or severe mitral regurgitation is present. Chronic mitral regurgitation typically develops as a result of left ventricular dysfunction. As symptoms dictate, guideline-directed medical therapy with beta blockers, angiotensin-converting enzyme (ACE) inhibitors, and diuretics is recommended (Nishimura et al., 2014).

NURSING APPLICATION

Regular follow-up for patients with mitral regurgitation becomes important in determining the correct timing for valve replacement. Appropriate timing of replacement can prevent irreversible ventricular damage.

Rhythm Control. Digoxin and beta blockers can provide ventricular rate control for atrial fibrillation secondary to mitral valve regurgitation. Attempting to return the patient to a regular rhythm with cardioversion, either electrical or chemical, is reasonable if the guidelines regarding anticoagulation are followed (Nishimura et al., 2014).

Anticoagulation. Anticoagulation therapy is warranted to prevent stroke when atrial fibrillation occurs secondary to mitral valve regurgitation.

Fluid Volume Control. If the patient exhibits signs of heart failure, a low-sodium diet and fluid restriction may be beneficial. However, liberal salt and water intake can benefit patients with mitral valve prolapse who are experiencing orthostatic hypotension. In the patient with heart failure with reduced ejection fraction (HFrEF), diuretics can be added to medical therapy to optimize fluid management (Nishimura et al., 2014).

Angiotensin-Converting Enzyme Inhibitors. If patients are not surgical candidates because of increased risk or a desire not to have surgery, vasodilators, especially ACE inhibitors, have been found to be helpful in decreasing regurgitation. ACE inhibitors decrease afterload and preload. The decrease in afterload decreases the resistance to ejection, thereby decreasing regurgitation and allowing blood to move forward. There is no definitive evidence that ACE inhibitors provide any benefit in the patient with mitral regurgitation who does not have symptoms.

Physical Activity and Exercise. Physical activity is not restricted in the patient with asymptomatic mitral regurgitation, a normal left ventricle and atrium, and no signs of pulmonary hypertension.

Endocarditis Prophylaxis. As with mitral stenosis, prophylactic use of antibiotics for patients with native valve disease is not recommended. However, in the setting of surgical valve repair, prophylactic antibiotic treatment is recommended before dental procedures (Nishimura et al., 2014).

Surgical Interventions

Surgical interventions are certainly considered for patients who are severely symptomatic despite medical therapies and for symptomatic patients who also need other cardiac surgical interventions such as bypass grafting. When the patient has indications for other cardiac surgical interventions, the valve repair or replacement and second indicated cardiac surgery can be done concomitantly. If surgical intervention occurs before marked damage, the ventricle can be preserved and pulmonary hypertension should improve. As the severity of left ventricular dysfunction increases, so does operative mortality. Therefore, patients with mild-to-moderate mitral regurgitation who have no symptoms and an ejection fraction less than 60% are also candidates for surgery (Nishimura et al., 2014).

The mitral valve can either be replaced or repaired. The mitral valve is a very complex structure, but preservation of as much of that structure as possible results in improved long-term outcomes (Nishimura et al., 2014). Repair is more difficult because, in many cases, structures other than the leaflets require repair. Mitral valve repair surgeries take longer than mitral valve replacement and result in longer cardiopulmonary bypass time. Repaired valves offer patients who are not in atrial fibrillation the opportunity to avoid anticoagulants, and they also prevent the need for future replacements (Nishimura et al., 2014).

If valve replacement is required, the chordae tendineae and papillary muscles may be left in place and attached to the new valve. Mechanical valves are preferred over bioprosthetic valves for their longevity; however, lifelong anticoagulation is required. Bioprosthetic valves may be appropriate for patients who need to avoid anticoagulation (Nishimura et al., 2014).

Outcomes Management

Patients who have developed mitral regurgitation because of myocardial ischemia or infarction have a poorer prognosis than others with mitral regurgitation secondary to global left ventricular dysfunction from the myocardial infarction (Nishimura et al., 2014). As noted with aortic valve disease, when the native valve has been replaced with either a tissue or a mechanical valve, the risk for endocarditis increases, and these patients do benefit from endocarditis prophylaxis with antibiotics before dental procedures (Nishimura et al., 2014). Patients with mechanical valves will be placed on lifelong warfarin therapy. Those with tissue or bioprosthetic valves may be placed on warfarin for 3 months postoperatively and then switched to lifelong aspirin therapy. The literature demonstrates a higher risk for thromboembolism in patients with mechanical mitral valves. For this reason, international normalized ratios in such patients are maintained at higher levels (2.5 to 3.5) than for patients with mechanical heart valves in other locations.

AORTIC VALVE

The aortic valve is the gateway to the circulatory system of the body. The normal aortic valve consists of an annulus and three cusps (see Figure 9-6). The aortic valve functions by pressure changes in the left ventricle and the aorta. During diastole, the aortic valve is closed while the left ventricle fills with blood from the left atrium. As the left ventricle fills, the pressure in the left ventricle rises. When the pressure in the left ventricle becomes greater than the pressure in the left atrium, the mitral valve closes between the left atrium and left ventricle, ending diastole. The left ventricle begins to contract as systole begins. When the pressure in the left ventricle is greater than the pressure on the other side of the aortic valve, the valve is forced open and blood is ejected out of the left ventricle into the aorta. After ejection is complete, the pressure in the left ventricle becomes less than the pressure in the aorta and the aortic valve snaps shut. The aortic valve closes tightly to prevent the backflow of blood from the aorta to the left ventricle, and the cycle begins again. Proper functioning of the valve allows blood to flow from the left ventricle to the aorta and

prevents backflow. Valve dysfunction occurs when the valve does not open properly or close completely. Normal aortic valve function is essential for normal cardiac output. Impedance of forward flow of blood, or backflow of blood that should be moving forward, can greatly affect cardiac output. Blood flow from the left ventricle to the aorta is key in delivering the required oxygenated blood to the body (Huether & McCance, 2017).

Aortic Valve Stenosis

Definition

Aortic stenosis exists when there is obstruction of flow at the level of the aortic valve. Opening of the aortic valve leaflets is usually restricted.

Causes

Aortic valve stenosis is classified as congenital or acquired. Congenital valve disease occurs when an abnormal number of valve cusps (unicuspid or bicuspid) are present. Fusion of one or more of the commissures is most commonly found in this congenital disease (Huether & McCance, 2017). It is the most common cause of aortic stenosis in patients younger than 75 years, but uncommonly results in severe aortic stenosis before this age (Mozaffarian et al., 2016).

Acquired aortic stenosis, caused by rheumatic heart disease or degenerative calcification, accounts for most symptom-producing aortic stenosis in patients older than 75 years (Mozaffarian et al., 2016). Aortic disease secondary to rheumatic heart disease is almost always accompanied by mitral valve disease. Aortic stenosis without the presence of mitral valve disease is generally considered nonrheumatic in origin. The U.S. incidence of rheumatic aortic valve disease has decreased appreciably with the decrease in the incidence of rheumatic heart disease in the United States (Nishimura et al., 2014).

FIGURE 9-6: AORTIC VALVE SHOWING THE THREE CUSPS

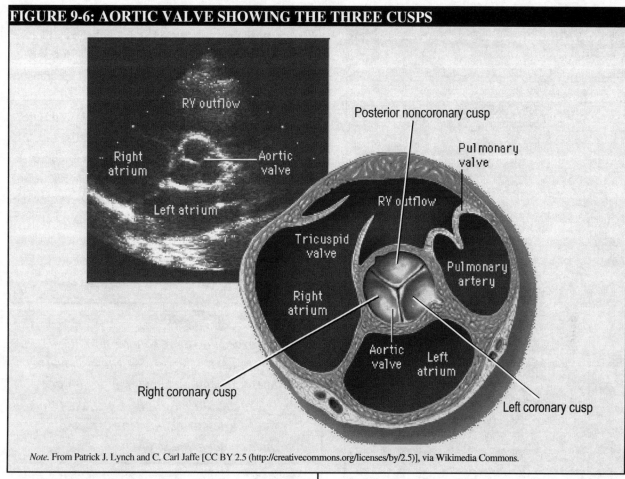

Note. From Patrick J. Lynch and C. Carl Jaffe [CC BY 2.5 (http://creativecommons.org/licenses/by/2.5)], via Wikimedia Commons.

The most common cause of aortic stenosis in adults is related to degenerative calcification secondary to the aging process. Degenerative calcification is a disease process that involves lipid accumulation, inflammation, and calcification of the valve leaflets (Nishimura et al., 2014). As the disease progresses, the valve leaflets retract and stiffen (Huether & McCance, 2017) and the leaflets become noncompliant (see Figure 9-7). Aortic stenosis resulting from degenerative calcification has been associated with male gender more than female, elevated lipoprotein and elevated low-density lipoprotein cholesterol levels, hypertension, smoking, diabetes, elevated serum calcium levels, and elevated serum creatinine levels (Huether & McCance, 2017).

Pathophysiology

The primary process that occurs with rheumatic heart disease is progressive fibrosis of the valve leaflets with fusion of the commissures (points where the valve leaflets connect) and, occasionally, calcification. In senile degenerative calcification, the valve leaflets thicken and develop calcified nodules that restrict their movement, resulting in valve leaflets that do not open easily or fully (see Figure 9-7).

As the aortic valve opening narrows because of the damaged valve leaflets, blood flow through the valve becomes turbulent and less efficient. The left ventricle must work harder to eject blood across the stiff, noncompliant valve. As valve compliance decreases, afterload increases. Afterload is the pressure the left ventricle must overcome to eject blood. In an effort to compensate for the increase in after-

FIGURE 9-7: DEGENERATIVE AORTIC VALVE DISEASE

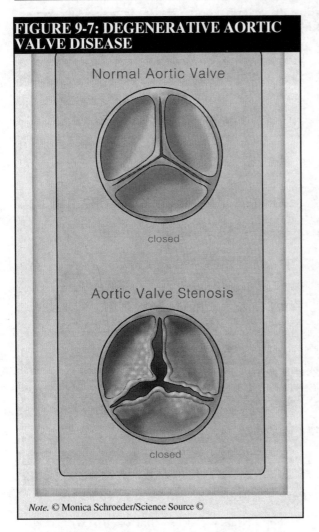

Normal Aortic Valve

closed

Aortic Valve Stenosis

closed

Note. © Monica Schroeder/Science Source ©

load, the left ventricular wall mass (myocardial wall thickness) increases in size, resulting in progressive concentric left ventricular hypertrophy. Concentric hypertrophy is characterized by increasing left ventricular wall mass with no increase in ventricular chamber size. In fact, the increasing muscle mass may begin to encroach on the chamber and actually decrease the size of the intraventricular chamber.

As the left ventricular wall becomes thicker, an associated decrease occurs in the ability of the ventricular wall to expand normally during ventricular filling. Referred to as diastolic dysfunction, this inability to expand results in decreased ventricle filling during diastole. With less volume entering the ventricle, there is less volume available for ejection during systole. The ventricle

normally ejects 50% to 60% of its contents with each beat. Now, however, the thickened myocardium compensates with a stronger contraction and ejects a larger percentage of the decreased volume, thereby maintaining good cardiac output. As the disease progresses, the left ventricle's attempt to compensate ultimately fails and left ventricular contractile function begins to decrease. This decrease in contractile function results in decreased stroke volume, leaving the ventricle with an excess volume at the end of each contraction. This overload is transferred to the left atrium, and ultimately the lungs, as initial heart failure symptoms present (Huether & McCance, 2017).

NURSING APPLICATION

Intravascular fluid balance in patients with severe aortic stenosis is critical because the left ventricular chamber is no longer able to expand during filling. Complete filling of the ventricular chamber is essential to produce an adequate stroke volume.

NURSING APPLICATION

The development of atrial fibrillation results in the loss of atrial kick, which results in a decrease in ventricular preload (ventricular filling) and an associated decrease in stroke volume.

Clinical Presentation

As the obstruction to flow from the left ventricle continues to increase, the left ventricular mass also increases. This ability to compensate can last many years before symptoms appear. Symptoms generally begin to appear when the valve opening is one-third to one-fourth of its normal size (Nishimura et al., 2014). When symptoms appear, mortality rates increase greatly. After the onset of symptoms, heart failure is present and progressively worsens. The average mortality rate for patients without surgical correction is 2 to 3 years in comparison with greater than 10 years for patients who received surgical intervention (Mozaffarian et al., 2016). As the valve opening becomes narrower, or the obstruction to flow becomes greater, a trio of classic symptoms occurs: angina pectoris, syncope, and heart failure (Huether & McCance, 2017).

Angina. Increased left ventricular wall mass (hypertrophy) increases left ventricular myocardial oxygen demand. While the patient is at rest, blood supply may be adequate to meet the body's needs. However, with stress or exercise, the increased myocardial oxygen demand of the thickened ventricular wall can no longer be met, resulting in angina. Commonly, angina during exercise is the first presenting symptom in aortic stenosis. Angina can, of course, be caused by coronary heart disease (CHD) in addition to increased wall mass. Many patients with aortic stenosis presenting with angina also have CHD (Huether & McCance, 2017).

NURSING APPLICATION

Patients with little or no significant CHD may still have angina as a result of a thickened myocardial wall. These patients benefit from the same measures that increase oxygen supply to the myocardium, such as supplemental oxygen and adequate hemoglobin levels.

Syncope. During exercise, total systemic vascular resistance (ventricular afterload) normally decreases to allow for a better flow of blood out of the ventricle. This decrease in systemic vascular resistance results in decreased blood pressure. The normal compensatory mechanism of the heart is to increase cardiac output to compensate for decreased pressure. This system keeps blood pressure in a normal range and allows patients to tolerate exercise while providing the body with an increased flow of oxygenated blood. However, with a narrowed valve opening, it is essentially impossible to increase cardiac output because the restriction of the valve does not allow for increased blood flow. Patients with severe aortic stenosis experience decreased blood pressure during exercise, resulting in light-headedness, dizziness, and blackout spells. In patients with aortic stenosis, exercise may also cause ventricular or atrial dysrhythmias, resulting in syncopal episodes (Huether & McCance, 2017).

NURSING APPLICATION

Patients should be reminded not to make any sudden position moves. They should be taught to move from a lying position to a standing position slowly and to be aware that exercise may result in syncope.

NURSING APPLICATION

Patients with mild aortic stenosis are not restricted in activity levels or exercise. Patients with moderate aortic stenosis should avoid strenuous activities and competitive sports. Patients with severe aortic stenosis should be advised to limit their activities to low levels.

Heart Failure. Patients with severe aortic stenosis typically develop heart failure with preserved ejection fraction (HFpEF) first and, ultimately, heart failure with reduced ejection fraction (HFrEF). Left ventricular hypertrophy results in diastolic dysfunction as the thick-walled ventricle becomes noncompliant and loses its ability to expand during filling. This inability to expand decreases the amount of blood that can enter the left ventricle from the left atrium and results in a backflow of blood into the left atrium. The subsequent overload in the left atrium is transferred back to the pulmonary veins and pulmonary edema results.

Additionally, over time, the hypertrophy that has been compensating for the increased after-load causes the myofibrils to stretch beyond the point of returning to a normal state. The ability of the ventricle to contract decreases, and ejection fraction begins to decline (HFrEF). This decrease in ejection fraction again results in a state of ECF overload because the ventricle is unable to empty properly. The patient experiences dyspnea on exertion, orthopnea, and paroxysmal nocturnal dyspnea, as well as other signs of volume over-load (Yancy et al., 2013).

Physical Examination

A stenotic aortic valve may produce a mur-mur before causing any noteworthy hemody-namic changes. The systolic ejection murmur of aortic stenosis is best heard over the sec-ond intercostal space, left of the sternal border. The murmur is described as a medium-pitched murmur heard equally well with the bell or the diaphragm of the stethoscope (Huether & McCance, 2017). It is described as rough and may become harsh as stenosis worsens. The murmur radiates to the right shoulder and both carotid arteries. In older adults with calcific aor-tic stenosis, the murmur may also radiate to the apex (fifth intercostal space, left midclavicular line), resulting in a misinterpretation of mitral regurgitation. The intensity of the murmur does not correspond with the severity of the stenosis. As aortic stenosis increases in severity, the mur-mur actually decreases in intensity (Huether & McCance, 2017).

In addition to the murmur and normal first and second heart sounds (S1 and S2, or "lub" and "dub," respectively), a fourth heart sound (S4) may be audible just before the S1. As left ventricular mass increases, the compliance of the ventricle decreases along with the ven-tricle's ability to expand during diastolic filling. With this decrease in compliance, the S4 can be heard late in ventricular diastole, when the atrial

kick ejects blood into the already full ventricle. When aortic stenosis is advanced and systolic failure occurs, a third heart sound (S3) can also be heard (Huether & McCance, 2017).

A normal carotid pulse is sharp and quick. As aortic stenosis worsens, it becomes more dif-ficult for the left ventricle to quickly push the valve open. As the valve slowly opens, the rush of blood through the valve is delayed, resulting in a decrease in the sharpness of the upstroke of the carotid pulse (Huether & McCance, 2017).

Diagnosis and Management

The best method of screening for valvular heart disease is through cardiac auscultation. The murmur of aortic stenosis is usually rec-ognized long before the patient presents with symptoms. Whereas some systolic murmurs may result from conditions other than aortic stenosis, an echocardiogram is a useful tool in determining the presence of valvular heart dis-ease after a murmur is identified.

Echocardiography. The echocardiogram is the primary tool used to confirm the diagnosis of aortic stenosis and quantify its severity. During echocardiography, the pressure gradient differ-ence from one side of the valve to the other can be assessed. As valve stenosis worsens, the pres-sure gradient increases. In addition, the aortic valve area is calculated. Normal valve area ranges from 3 to 4 cm^2. It is not until the valve area is approximately one-fourth of the normal size that any changes in flow occur. A valve area of less than 1.0 cm^2 indicates severe stenosis and should prompt close evaluation of the need for surgical intervention (Nishimura et al., 2014). A pressure gradient over the aortic valve is also assessed by echocardiography. Once the pressure gradient exceeds 40 mmHg, the patient's condition is con-sidered severe. Left ventricular mass, valve leaflet mobility, and systolic and diastolic function can also be assessed using echocardiography.

Cardiac Stress Testing. Exercise stress testing is contraindicated in the symptomatic patient with aortic stenosis because of the high risk for complications (Nishimura et al., 2014). In the patient without symptoms, exercise stress testing may be used to elicit symptoms of aortic stenosis to determine the severity. Typically, a low-dose dobutamine infusion is used during cardiac stress testing. Patients with asymptomatic aortic stenosis undergoing exercise stress testing should be observed carefully for symptoms of severe aortic valve disease, especially for signs of syncope.

Cardiac Catheterization. Patients with symptomatic aortic stenosis require cardiac catheterization to determine the extent, if any, of CHD. If valve replacement is questionable, the presence of treatable CHD answers the question and moves the patient toward surgery. A valve area of less than 0.8 cm2 on cardiac catheterization, indicating critical aortic valve stenosis, is associated with increased mortality rates and supports a decision for surgical valve replacement (Nishimura et al., 2014).

Electrocardiogram. An ECG demonstrates an increased QRS voltage with associated ST-segment and T-wave abnormalities when the patient has aortic stenosis. The increased QRS voltage is due to the increase in myocardial mass. Atrial abnormalities (demonstrated by abnormal P waves) indicate atrial enlargement. These ECG changes are neither sensitive nor specific to aortic stenosis and always require other testing for confirmation (Nishimura et al., 2014).

Chest X-ray Film. On chest x-ray film, the heart with stenosis usually appears normal in size. The shape, however, demonstrates a rounded left ventricular border, representing concentric hypertrophy. The aortic shadow may become enlarged and, occasionally, calcification of the valve is visible on the lateral view (Nishimura et al., 2014).

NURSING APPLICATION

Any clinician in any practice environment should assess for cardiac murmurs. Murmur detection is the key to early recognition of valvular heart disease. When the patient is aware of the presence of valvular heart disease, routine follow-up can be established to assure the successful long-term treatment of the disease process.

Medical Therapy

No current medical treatment strategies demonstrate a slowing of the disease progression with calcific aortic stenosis. Statins therapy was found to have no benefit in reducing the progression of aortic stenosis or contributing to improved survival rates (Nishimura et al., 2014). Medical treatment beyond occasional rate control with atrial fibrillation is rarely needed early in the disease process. Medication temporarily resolves heart failure; however, if the valve is not replaced, failure worsens and death remains the end result.

Diuretics. Patient with hypertension should be treated according to guidelines, with careful attention to use of diuretics if the left ventricle chamber is small (James et al., 2014; Rosendorff et al., 2015). Even small decreases in left ventricular volume can reduce cardiac output, which may worsen symptoms in severe aortic stenosis (Nishimura et al., 2014).

NURSING APPLICATION

Severe aortic stenosis complicates the treatment of heart failure and often eliminates the patient as a surgical candidate, which leaves the patient with limited treatment options. Referral of the patient and family to palliative care is important so that they receive as much psychosocial support and options for symptom management as possible.

Angiotensin-Converting Enzyme Inhibitors. Although indicated for heart failure, angiotensin-converting enzyme (ACE) inhibitors are contraindicated in patients with severe aortic stenosis. ACE inhibitors decrease systemic vascular resistance, thereby decreasing cardiac output and blood pressure (Nishimura et al., 2014). The normal response to this change is an increase in heart rate to compensate for the decrease in blood pressure. A stenotic valve prevents large volumes of blood from being forced through, resulting in an inability to increase cardiac output. Hypotension develops, and syncope or other ischemic complications could ultimately result.

Nitroglycerin. Nitrates should be used with caution in patients with severe disease. It is important to remember that low-dose nitroglycerin decreases preload. With the hypertrophy that has developed, preload is already decreased because of the inability of the ventricle to expand during filling. Any further loss of filling would result in a decrease in stroke volume. Nitroglycerin at high doses could further complicate the issue by causing a decrease in systemic vascular resistance similar to the effects of ACE inhibitors. However, in the critical care setting with invasive hemodynamic monitoring, cautious use of vasodilators can have some benefit to the patient with severe disease (Nishimura et al., 2014).

Beta Blockers. Beta blockers are beneficial to the patient with concurrent CHD and hypertension. However, relative contraindications exist in severe aortic stenosis because beta blockers inhibit the normal adrenergic response that has been occurring to compensate for decreased cardiac output (increased heart rate and contractility) and lessen the ability of the ventricle to overcome the pressure gradient that has developed (Nishimura et al., 2014).

NURSING APPLICATION

Vasodilators and other medications that can cause hypotension must be used with great caution in patients with severe aortic stenosis because aortic stenosis is a mechanical obstruction that results in a fixed cardiac output and inability of the heart to compensate for hypotension. However, in a patient with significant hypertension, these medications may be used to lower blood pressure and reduce left ventricular afterload.

Routine Follow-up. The patient without symptoms should be educated on the importance of routine follow-up with the healthcare team. Periodic echocardiograms, along with physical assessments, allow the physician to monitor the progression of valvular stenosis. The nurse should educate the patient and family to report any signs or symptoms of angina, heart failure, or syncope, which would indicate the presence of severe or worsening aortic stenosis.

Physical Activity and Exercise. Physical activity and exercise is not restricted in the patient with asymptomatic aortic stenosis. Patients with moderate-to-severe aortic stenosis should not participate in competitive sports. When in doubt about the ability to exercise, an exercise stress test can be performed to assess activity tolerance.

Endocarditis Prophylaxis. The prophylactic use of antibiotics for patients with native valve disease is not recommended for the patient with aortic stenosis of any severity. The maintenance of optimal oral health and hygiene has been shown to reduce the incidence of endocarditis and bacteremia from daily activities. However, prophylactic antibiotic therapy has been shown to reduce the incidence of endocarditis in patient status post-aortic valve replacement (Nishimura et al., 2014).

Surgical Interventions

When symptoms appear, the need for surgical repair becomes imminent because the risk for sudden death increases as well. Surgical outcomes improve with early detection. Therefore, close follow-up of patients with aortic stenosis is warranted to facilitate an early decision to treat when symptoms begin (Nishimura et al., 2014). Several surgical options are available after the patient becomes symptomatic. Early symptoms of severe aortic stenosis are typically dyspnea on exertion and decreased exercise tolerance. The triad of heart failure, angina, and syncope occurs in later stages, so close monitoring of early symptoms can prompt earlier intervention (Nishimura et al., 2014).

Percutaneous Balloon Valvuloplasty. A balloon inflated in the valve orifice can be used to fracture calcium deposits in the leaflets and stretch the aortic annulus. This procedure is considered palliative or as a bridge to surgical or transcatheter aortic valve replacement, and should be reserved for patients who are not immediate surgical candidates but are seeking relief from symptoms. Studies show this approach is inferior to repair or replacement done by the open-heart surgical technique (Nishimura et al., 2014). Before the procedure, patients should be evaluated for aortic regurgitation. Aortic regurgitation is an expected postoperative result after valvuloplasty. The procedure should not be performed if the patient has 2+ or greater aortic valve regurgitation.

Aortic Valve Replacement. Surgery to replace the valve is the treatment of choice in most symptomatic adults with aortic stenosis who are not at high or prohibitive surgical risk (see Box 9-1). There has been no demonstrated benefit from surgery for patients with mild-to-moderate aortic stenosis who do not have symptoms. Therefore, surgery is not indicated until symptoms appear. However, mortality rates and morbidity rates

---

BOX 9-1: AMERICAN COLLEGE OF CARDIOLOGY/AMERICAN HEART ASSOCIATION RECOMMENDATIONS FOR AORTIC VALVE REPLACEMENT

- Patients with severe aortic stenosis who are symptomatic

- Patients with severe aortic stenosis (with or without symptoms) undergoing coronary artery bypass surgery

- Patients with severe aortic stenosis (with or without symptoms) undergoing surgery on the aorta or other heart valves

- Patients with severe aortic stenosis (without symptoms) and one of the following:
  - Left ventricular systolic dysfunction (ejection fraction < 50%)
  - Abnormal response to exercise
  - High likelihood of rapid disease progression
  - Extremely severe aortic stenosis (valve areas < 0.6 cm^2, mean gradient > 60 mmHg, jet velocity > 5.0 m/s) when operative mortality is expected to be 1% or less

Note. Adapted from Nishimura, R. A., Otto, C. M., Bonow, R. O., Carabello, B. A., Erwin, J. P., Guyton, R. A., … Thomas, J. D.; American College of Cardiology/American Heart Association Task Force on Practice Guidelines. (2014). 2014 AHA/ACC guideline for the management of patients with valvular heart disease: A report of the American College of Cardiology/American Heart Association Task Force on Practice Guidelines. *Journal of the American College of Cardiology, 63*(22), e57-e185. doi:10.1016/j.jacc.2014.02.536

---

decrease after replacement surgery in asymptomatic patients with severe aortic stenosis noted on echocardiogram (Nishimura et al., 2014).

Before surgery, the mitral valve is also evaluated because, quite frequently, mitral regurgitation also exists and mitral valve replacement may also be necessary. Cardiac catheterization should also be performed to determine the need for coronary artery bypass surgery. A preoperative assessment of left ventricular function determines the degree of systolic or diastolic dysfunction, or both. Surgical mortality risk is lowest in those with normal left ventricular function and increases as systolic function decreases (Nishimura et al., 2014).

NURSING APPLICATION

Patients with aortic valve disease should be aware of signs of decompensation. With early recognition, the appropriate treatment can take place before any systolic dysfunction occurs.

The type of valve prosthesis used is determined by the anticipated life span of the patient and the patient's ability to tolerate anticoagulants. Mechanical valves have better durability than tissue valves that come from human or pig donors (bioprosthetics), but they require lifelong anticoagulation with warfarin, whereas tissue valves usually require only aspirin daily with no additional anticoagulant. Mechanical valves are generally best suited for young patients with no contraindications to anticoagulation. However, young women who plan on becoming pregnant should have tissue valves because the utilization of anticoagulation during pregnancy increases fetal mortality (Nishimura et al., 2014). Older adult patients with a life expectancy less than that of the tissue valve (7 to 10 years) are better suited for tissue valves and can avoid the need for anticoagulation and its associated complications.

Some centers also perform the Ross procedure, which involves placing a patient's pulmonic valve in the aortic valve position and placing a tissue valve in the pulmonic valve location. It has been noted that tissue valves last longer in the lower-pressure right heart and the need for anticoagulation is avoided. This approach has advantages and disadvantages. Although there are some advantages in children

as valves grow with the child, overall in adults, the deterioration of the tissue valve offsets the potential advantages (Nishimura et al., 2014).

Transcatheter/Transapical Aortic Valve Replacement. Because the prevalence of aortic valve stenosis will most likely increase as the population ages, increasing efforts are being made to develop treatments that will allow patients to avoid open-heart surgical procedures. Unlike traditional valve replacement, transcatheter aortic valve replacement does not require the removal of the native valve. A bioprosthetic valve is attached to a stent. The stent is expanded at the site of the native valve with the stent holding the new valve in place. There are several approaches with minimally invasive aortic valve replacement. The transcatheter approach either utilizes the aortic artery directly to the aortic valve or reaches the aortic valve through the femoral vein with a puncture through the septum. The transapical approach requires a small, left-sided incision at approximately the location of the sixth intercostal space, with a small puncture of the left ventricle to reach the aortic valve. Studies of this method demonstrate that the benefits are inferior to those achieved with the open-heart approach to replacement, and the latter involves higher thrombotic and stroke risks and slightly higher mortality rates (Nishimura et al., 2014).

Outcomes Management

After successful aortic valve replacement, decreased left ventricular systolic pressure and decreased afterload result in improved ejection fraction and increased cardiac output. Left ventricular hypertrophy actually regresses, with most of that regression occurring in the first year but continuing to improve for up to 10 years, and gradually improving systolic function. However, diastolic function most likely never returns to normal because of the increase in collagen content in the myocardial tissue (Nishimura et al., 2014). After the damaged valve has been replaced with either a tissue or a mechanical valve, the risk for endocarditis increases, and patients with prosthetic valves do benefit from endocarditis prophylaxis with antibiotics prior to dental procedures (Nishimura et al., 2014). As mentioned earlier, mechanical valves require lifelong warfarin therapy, whereas bioprosthetic valves require warfarin therapy for 3 months after surgery and then lifelong aspirin therapy.

Aortic Valve Regurgitation

Definition

Aortic valve regurgitation occurs when the valve cusps do not close tightly and blood is allowed to travel retrograde, or backward, through the valve during ventricular systole. A variety of processes can affect the valve cusps, the aortic root, or both, resulting in aortic regurgitation (see Figure 9-6).

Causes

Aortic regurgitation can be classified as acute or chronic. Symptoms depend on the severity and rapidity of onset. With the decreased incidence of rheumatic valve disease in the United States, chronic nonrheumatic causes now account for the majority of isolated cases of aortic regurgitation. Causes of nonrheumatic valve disease include congenital bicuspid valve demise, systemic hypertension, myxomatous degeneration, infective endocarditis, and connective tissue diseases, as well as calcifications that affect the valve's cusps. Many patients with chronic aortic regurgitation have processes that affect the aortic root, including Marfan's syndrome, aortic dissection, inflammatory diseases, collagen vascular disease, and syphilitic aortitis (Huether & McCance, 2017). Acute aortic regurgitation is seen with trauma, acute bacterial endocarditis, and acute aortic dissection (Nishimura et al., 2014). Because the presentation of acute aortic regurgitation is entirely different from that of

chronic aortic regurgitation, the two are discussed separately.

Pathophysiology of Aortic Regurgitation

Normally, as the ventricle ejects blood through the aortic valve, the aorta expands to accept the volume. When the pressure in the ventricle becomes less than the pressure in the aorta, the aortic valve closes. The aorta relaxes, and blood is dispersed to the area of least resistance. The expansion and relaxation of the aorta are known as the elastic and recoil properties of the aorta. With a competent aortic valve, blood moves forward. The closed valve stops blood from moving backward toward the aortic valve (see Figure 9-8).

In patients with aortic regurgitation, blood enters the left ventricle normally from the left atrium. Blood also enters the left ventricle from the aorta because the valve does not close properly, and backflow occurs from the aorta through the aortic valve into the left ventricle. This results in a larger-than-normal volume in the left ventricle. To compensate, the left ventricular chamber size increases gradually to allow for the additional volume. The left ventricular wall thickness also increases gradually to help maintain normal wall stress. The enlarged left ventricular chamber maintains a normal or near-normal preload, and the increase in wall thickness helps to increase stroke volume. This increased stroke volume is necessary because a portion of the blood ejected to the aorta with each beat returns to the left ventricle during ventricular diastole through the regurgitant valve. If the ventricle can eject a larger-than-normal volume with each beat, the cardiac output needs should be met. While maintaining preload, normal wall stress, and contractility, ejection fraction remains the same. This phase of the disease process is considered the chronic compensatory phase and lasts for many years or even decades. As with aortic stenosis, patients

FIGURE 9-8: NORMAL FUNCTIONING OF THE AORTA DURING SYSTOLE AND DIASTOLE

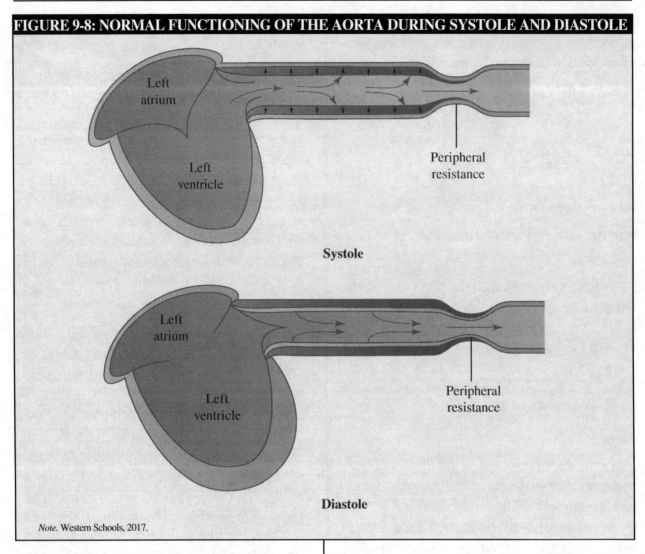

Note. Western Schools, 2017.

remain asymptomatic for years with very low morbidity (Huether & McCance, 2017).

Eventually, however, the compensatory mechanisms begin to fail and the enlarged heart begins to show signs of decompensation. As dilation of the left ventricle continues, contractility eventually decreases because the myocardium has been overstretched. Left ventricular ejection fraction also decreases, resulting in decreased cardiac output (systolic dysfunction). As ejection fraction decreases, left ventricular volume (preload) increases because of the inability of the ventricles to empty appropriately. In addition, afterload increases to compensate for decreased cardiac output. Heart rate also increases to compensate for the decrease in cardiac output; how-

ever, this increased rate is often ineffective. After decades without any difficulties, patients begin to experience symptoms of ECF overload (Huether & McCance, 2017).

Clinical Presentation

Although patients commonly remain asymptomatic for years, the initial symptoms noted most frequently are exertional dyspnea and fatigue caused by the failing left ventricle. As the disease progresses, paroxysmal nocturnal dyspnea and orthopnea with pulmonary edema can also develop. Angina can result from an inability of the coronary arteries to supply the volume of oxygenated blood needed for the increased myocardial mass. Patients with aortic regurgitation commonly experience ischemia without associated CHD. The incidence of concurrent CHD with aortic regurgitation is less common than with aortic stenosis (Huether & McCance, 2017).

Physical Examination

A variety of signs can lead a healthcare professional toward a diagnosis of aortic regurgitation. A diastolic murmur, displaced left ventricular impulse, wide pulse pressure, and specific peripheral findings are characteristic signs of chronic aortic regurgitation (see Table 9-2). The characteristic murmur of aortic regurgitation is a soft, diastolic murmur best heard at the third intercostal space to the left of the sternum. The murmur is loudest at end expiration and is better recognized with the patient sitting and leaning forward. If the patient has aortic root disease (Marfan's syndrome), then the murmur is best heard to the right of the sternum (Anderson, 2016). Occasionally, the murmur is described as a diastolic rumble heard best at the apex; in this case, it is referred to as an Austin Flint murmur (Zoghbi & Crawford, 2009). The apical impulse (normally at the apex of the heart) is displaced leftward and downward because of the hypertrophy and is forceful because of increased stroke volume.

As regurgitation progresses, diastolic blood pressure decreases, resulting in a widened pulse pressure (difference between the systolic and diastolic pressure). Diastolic blood pressure decreases as more blood is returned to the left ventricle; it is generally less than 60 mmHg. In addition, systolic pressure increases as a result of increased stroke volume. Pulse pressure is commonly greater than 50 mmHg (Huether & McCance, 2017). The same physiological changes that are responsible for widened pulse pressure also result in a variety of peripheral signs that have been associated with chronic aortic regurgitation (see Table 9-2).

NURSING APPLICATION

If the Korotkoff sound is heard down to zero when auscultating a blood pressure for a patient with aortic regurgitation, note the point at which muffling of the Korotkoff sound occurs. This point correlates with the patient's diastolic pressure (Anderson, 2016).

Diagnosis and Management

Echocardiography. When the characteristic signs of aortic regurgitation are detected, echocardiography is again the test of choice to confirm the diagnosis. During echocardiography, an assessment can be made of the severity of regurgitation, morphology of the valve, left ventricular size and function, and the aortic root. The severity of regurgitation is determined by a variety of methods and calculations. Generally, the severity of regurgitation is expressed as a number from 1 (mild) to 4 (severe) (see Table 9-3; Nishimura et al., 2014).

TABLE 9-2: PERIPHERAL SIGNS OF CHRONIC AORTIC REGURGITATION	
Sign	**Description**
Water-hammer pulse (Corrigan's pulse)	A rapid rise and collapse of the pulse upon palpation of the peripheral pulse
de Musset's sign	Bobbing of the head with each heartbeat
Traube's sign (pistol shot sounds)	Booming systolic and diastolic sounds heard over the femoral artery
Duroziez's sign	Systolic bruit heard over the femoral artery when compressed proximally and diastolic murmur heard over the femoral artery when compressed distally

Note. Adapted from Huether, S. E., & McCance, K. L. (2017). *Understanding pathophysiology* (6th ed.). St. Louis, MO: Elsevier.

TABLE 9-3: AORTIC REGURGITATION SEVERITY

1+	Mild aortic regurgitation
2+	Moderate aortic regurgitation
3+	Moderately severe aortic regurgitation
4+	Severe aortic regurgitation

Note. From Nishimura, R. A., Otto, C. M., Bonow, R. O., Carabello, B. A., Erwin, J. P., Guyton, R. A., ... Thomas, J. D.; American College of Cardiology/American Heart Association Task Force on Practice Guidelines. (2014). 2014 AHA/ACC guideline for the management of patients with valvular heart disease: A report of the American College of Cardiology/American Heart Association Task Force on Practice Guidelines. *Journal of the American College of Cardiology, 63*(22), e57-e185. doi:10.1016/j.jacc.2014.02.536

Cardiac Catheterization. Cardiac catheterization should be completed in patients with symptomatic aortic regurgitation who are having aortic valve replacement surgery to determine the extent, if any, of CHD. As with aortic stenosis, if valve replacement is questionable, the presence of treatable CHD can answer the question and move the patient toward surgery. Cardiac catheterization is also indicated to assess the severity of regurgitation and the extent of left ventricular function if noninvasive tests are inconclusive (Nishimura et al., 2014).

Chest X-ray Film. A chest x-ray film shows left ventricular hypertrophy (enlarged heart) and pulmonary congestion, as would be expected in a patient with heart failure (Nishimura et al., 2014; Yancy et al., 2013).

Electrocardiogram. A 12-lead ECG demonstrates the increased QRS voltage that is seen with left ventricular hypertrophy. These ECG changes are neither sensitive nor specific to aortic regurgitation and always require other testing for confirmation (Nishimura et al., 2014).

Stress Test. Stress testing can be useful in patients with mild symptoms but is not indicated in the patient who is symptomatic. The test provides an evaluation of exercise tolerance, with an assessment of both symptomatic response and hemodynamic effects. This test assists in determining the need for surgical intervention in the patient who is asymptomatic (Nishimura et al., 2014).

Routine Follow-up. The patient who is asymptomatic should understand the importance of routine follow-up with the physician. Periodic echocardiograms, along with a physical assessment, allow the physician to monitor the progression of the valvular regurgitation. The patient should be aware of the signs and symptoms that indicate severe aortic regurgitation.

Physical Activity and Exercise. Physical activity is not restricted in the patient with asymptomatic aortic regurgitation. Patients with moderate aortic regurgitation who are asymptomatic may be able to participate in competitive sports. When in doubt about the ability to exercise, an exercise stress test can be performed to evaluate activity tolerance.

Medical Therapy

Patients may remain asymptomatic for many years. If patients with mild aortic regurgitation remain asymptomatic and have normal left ventricular function, no medication is necessary. The medical treatment of aortic regurgitation is accomplished with different drug classes that promote vasodilation.

Vasodilator Therapy. The vasodilating mechanism of action overlaps across multiple classes of medications. The medications with vasodilatory action (preferably calcium channel blockers (e.g., dihydropyridine) ACE inhibitors, or angiotensin II receptor blockers) are helpful in reducing blood pressure and improving forward movement of cardiac output in symptomatic patients with chronic aortic regurgitation. However, these medications are not routinely recommended to asymptomatic patients because they have not been proven to have any benefit.

Beta-Blocker Therapy. Beta blockers are not as highly recommended for their vasodilatory action but are still reasonable to use because the effect of heart rate reduction contributes to higher stroke volumes, thereby increasing systolic pressures. Again, beta blockers are only indicated in symptomatic patients (Nishimura et al., 2014).

Endocarditis Prophylaxis. Antibiotic prophylaxis is not recommended for patients with native valve disease but has the benefit of reducing morbidity and mortality in the postsurgical repair population before dental procedures (Nishimura et al., 2014).

Surgical Interventions

Because mortality with valve replacement worsens as ejection fraction worsens, careful assessment of left ventricular function is essential. Patients with chronic aortic regurgitation should have regular follow-up serial testing. When patients experience development of left ventricular dysfunction, with or without symptoms, with an ejection fraction less than 50%, valve replacement surgery is recommended to decrease overall mortality and reduce surgery-related mortality risks. As the severity of left ventricular dysfunction increases, so does the mortality rate with surgery; therefore, early intervention is indicated (Nishimura et al., 2014).

Surgical options for replacement of the aortic valve in patients with aortic regurgitation are the same as those for aortic stenosis. Older adults commonly have aortic stenosis and CHD in addition to aortic regurgitation. The determination for surgery should be based on quality of life and not longevity, thus making symptom relief the most important guide in making the decision for aortic valve replacement.

Outcomes Management

Left ventricular function generally improves for up to 2 years after surgery, with a minimal decline (if any) in ventricular hypertrophy. These results vary depending on the preoperative condition of the left ventricle. An echocardiogram should be performed shortly after surgery. If the initial echocardiogram shows improvement, then serial echocardiograms are not necessary. Patients who continue to demonstrate signs of heart failure secondary to valve dysfunction should be treated with ACE inhibitors, as is standard for all patients with heart failure. After valve replacement with either a tissue or a mechanical valve, all patients are at high risk for endocarditis and do benefit from endocarditis prophylaxis before dental procedures. Patients with mechanical valves are placed on lifelong warfarin therapy. Those with tissue or bioprosthetic valves may be placed on warfarin for 3 months postoperatively and then switched to lifelong aspirin therapy (Nishimura et al., 2014).

TRICUSPID VALVE

Similar to the mitral valve, the tricuspid valve directs blood flow between the atria and the ventricle of the right heart. Dysfunction of this valve is not commonly detected, or involved with physiological consequences, unless there is severe disease (Nishimura et al., 2014). Nevertheless, tricuspid valvular disease can still negatively impact the patient with chronic heart failure. Tricuspid valve regurgitation occurs most often in patients with tricuspid valve dysfunction (Nishimura et al., 2014).

Tricuspid Valve Regurgitation

Definition

Tricuspid valve regurgitation occurs with annular dilation and leaflet tethering in the setting of right ventricular remodeling that occurs in response to volume overload and increased intracardiac pressures (Nishimura et al., 2014).

Causes

Tricuspid valve regurgitation is far more common than stenosis and can be caused by congenital defects, rheumatic heart disease, endocarditis, or trauma (termed functional tricuspid regurgitation). However, primary tricuspid regurgitation can manifest in trace-to-mild degrees of regurgitation in individuals with anatomically normal valves for unknown reasons (Nishimura et al., 2014).

Pathophysiology

Tricuspid valve incompetence leads to volume overload in the right atrium and ventricle, thereby increasing the patient's propensity for atrial arrhythmias (such as atrial fibrillation) and right-sided heart failure.

Clinical Presentation

Mild to moderate tricuspid regurgitation is most often asymptomatic. Patients with severe tricuspid regurgitation present with signs and symptoms like those with right heart failure. When the patients are symptomatic, their degree of regurgitation fits into the stage IV category of heart failure and they have a poor prognosis despite their age. Symptoms of severe tricuspid regurgitation include fatigue, abdominal fullness, edema, palpitations, atrial fibrillation, elevated right atrial pressures, and progressive hepatic dysfunction (Nishimura et al., 2014).

Physical Examination

Mild to moderate tricuspid regurgitation is most often undetectable on the physical examination. Advanced tricuspid regurgitation produces signs similar to right heart failure such as a systolic murmur (heard at the lower left sternal border) that increases in intensity with inspiration. Other physical examination findings often indicative of severe tricuspid regurgitation include a pulsatile liver edge, a jugular venous pulse, ascites, and edema (Nishimura et al., 2014).

Diagnosis and Management

Transthoracic echocardiogram (TTE) distinguishes primary from functional tricuspid regurgitation. TTE is used to measure the relationship between the valve's annular diameter and regurgitant volume to diagnose functional tricuspid regurgitation. A diastolic diameter > 40 mm indicates significant annular dilation and the risk for progressive tricuspid regurgitation. In cases with right ventricular remodeling, the valve leaflet tethering height and area also contribute to functional tricuspid regurgitation (Nishimura et al., 2014).

Right ventriculography also aids in the evaluation and diagnosis of tricuspid regurgitation. Cardiac output and pulmonary vascular resistance is measured to assess the severity of tricuspid regurgitation. Exercise testing is also considered to assess the capacity for activity for a patient with severe tricuspid regurgitations who has no to minimal symptoms at baseline (Nishimura et al., 2014).

Fluid Volume Status. Several serial physical assessment parameters are compared to determine ECF volume status, including the patient's weight; the amount of jugular venous distention; edema of the legs, abdomen, sacral area, or scrotum; and/or the presence of organ congestion (hepatomegaly or rales).

A reliable sign of ECF overload is jugular venous distention in the absence of chronic conditions that cause distention (right-heart failure; Huether and McCance, 2017). Most patients with peripheral edema also have ECF overload; however, peripheral edema also has noncardiac causes, making the finding of peripheral edema less specific to heart failure. Most patients with compensated chronic heart failure do not have audible rales or crackles in their lung fields on physical examination. Rales or crackles are generally a sign of acute heart failure. Therefore, the absence of pulmonary rales should not be considered an adequate measure of optimal fluid volume status. Short-term assessment of ECF volume status is best measured by a change in daily weight.

NURSING APPLICATION

Patients should be instructed to weigh themselves daily first thing in the morning, after urinating, and before eating. They should be instructed to use the same scale and wear the same amount of clothing. A weight gain of more than 2 pounds in 24 hours or more than 3 pounds in a week should be reported to the physician. Keep in mind that 1 pound of weight = 1 pint of fluid. (This particular application is related to patient education and patient self-care. Patients weigh themselves in pounds at home, so that is why patients are instructed in pounds).

Many physicians have patients adjust their diuretic doses at home based on daily weights. With the assessment of daily weights and appropriate intervention, ECF volume can be managed on an outpatient basis and many hospital admissions can be avoided.

Laboratory Values. Routine measurement of brain natriuretic peptide, cardiac biomarkers, electrolytes, and renal function is important in the patient with heart failure due to chronic valve conditions. Many of these levels become altered because of the disease process, progression, and/or treatment. Monitoring potassium levels is particularly important in patients with heart failure because diuretics can cause hypokalemia. Many patients with heart failure are also on digoxin (which requires monitoring of digoxin levels), and hypokalemia increases the risk for digoxin toxicity. In contrast, other medications used in the treatment of heart failure, such as ACE inhibitors, angiotensin II receptor blockers, and aldosterone antagonists, can predispose patients to hyperkalemia. Patients taking loop diuretics who experience the expected side effect of hypokalemia and who also take one or more medications that can predispose patients to hyperkalemia are unlikely to be prescribed potassium supplements.

Thyroid levels should be assessed because hyperthyroidism and hypothyroidism can contribute to heart failure. Other biomarkers emerging in heart failure research include measures reflecting inflammation, oxidative stress, neurohormonal disarray, and myocardial remodeling. Further research is warranted in identifying the reliability, cost-effectiveness, and utility of these markers (Yancy et al., 2013).

Medical Therapy

Because of the necessity to maintain preload to the left side of the heart, treatment for right-sided valve dysfunction is not usually indicated. Symptom management is initiated as needed and is similar to that used in other incompetent valve treatment regimens and in heart failure (see Fluid Volume Status and Laboratory Values sections above.) (Huether & McCance, 2017). When medical therapies for tricuspid regurgitation are needed, they are aimed at reducing pulmonary afterload by treating pulmonary hypertension and managing systemic hypertension. Both effects lead to facilitating right ventricular cardiac output and oxygen delivery to tissues.

In severe tricuspid regurgitation, diuretics can be used cautiously to reduce volume overload. Loop diuretics are recommended with aldosterone added (especially if the patient has hepatic congestion), if needed. Diuretics must be monitored closely in these patients due to the risk of reducing too much volume and causing a low-flow syndrome.

Surgical Interventions

The risks and benefits of surgical interventions aimed to repair or replace the tricuspid valve must be considered carefully in patients with irreversible pulmonary hypertension or systolic dysfunction of the right ventricle because of the chance of worsened right ventricular failure after surgery. Tricuspid valve repair is preferable to valve replacement because of the lower ischemic time the patient undergoes during surgery. When replacement is necessary, the type of valve used for replacement is individualized with consideration to the patient's risk of thrombosis and need for anticoagulation. Studies revealed there was no difference in mortality rates between mechanical or bioprosthetic (tissue) valves (Nishimura et al., 2014). Indications for surgical intervention are listed in Box 9-2.

BOX 9-2: INDICATIONS FOR TRICUSPID REGURGITATION

- Mild to moderate functional tricuspid regurgitation with evidence of right heart failure or annular dilation > 40 mm in diameter

- Symptomatic patients who are unresponsive to medical therapy

- Reoperation can be considered for isolated tricuspid valve dysfunction in patients with right ventricular dysfunction but without severe pulmonary hypertension.

Note. Adapted from Nishimura, R. A., Otto, C. M., Bonow, R. O., Carabello, B. A., Erwin, J. P., Guyton, R. A., ... Thomas, J. D.; American College of Cardiology/American Heart Association Task Force on Practice Guidelines. (2014). 2014 AHA/ACC guideline for the management of patients with valvular heart disease: A report of the American College of Cardiology/American Heart Association Task Force on Practice Guidelines. *Journal of the American College of Cardiology, 63*(22), e57-e185. doi:10.1016/j.jacc.2014.02.536

Outcomes Management

Patients with mild to moderate tricuspid regurgitation often remain asymptomatic; however, approximately 25% may progress to have reduced long-term function and survival if left uncorrected (Nishimura et al., 2014). Outcomes in patients with tricuspid repair or replacement during surgical repair of left-sided valves is preferred over reoperation for tricuspid repair after left-sided surgery. Reoperation is associated with a perioperative mortality rate of 10% to 25% (Nishimura et al., 2014).

SUMMARY

Valvular dysfunction negatively impacts patients with chronic heart failure and can significantly contribute to decompensation. Nurses must recognize and differentiate the patient presentations and clinical assessment findings common to mitral, aortic, and tricuspid valve dysfunction. Although these patients have chronic dysfunction, it is necessary to recognize hemodynamic changes in this population for early evaluation of the patient and their regular medications in an effort to make the necessary adjustments, provide a higher level of care, or prevent acute decompensation. Nurses must also be able to describe the medical and surgical treatment options associated with each valve dysfunction in order to understand the patient's needs, to perform post-intervention evaluations (medical or surgical), and to provide support to the patient and family with supplemental education. Gaining knowledge in valve dysfunctions' effect on chronic heart failure allows the nurse to significantly improve patient outcomes.

EXAM QUESTIONS

CHAPTER 9
Questions 47–51

Note: Choose the one option that BEST answers each question.

47. What is the most common cause of mitral stenosis?

    a. Heart failure

    b. Rheumatic fever

    c. Myocardial infarction

    d. Mitral incompetence

48. When a patient with mitral stenosis is diagnosed with atrial fibrillation, the nurse anticipates administering

    a. endocarditis prophylaxis.

    b. angiotensin-converting enzyme (ACE) inhibitors.

    c. vasodilator therapy.

    d. anticoagulation therapy.

49. Which valvular dysfunction involves retrograde blood flow into the left atrium?

    a. Mitral regurgitation

    b. Mitral stenosis

    c. Aortic regurgitation

    d. Aortic stenosis

50. Which physical assessment finding is associated with aortic valve stenosis?

    a. Diastolic murmur heard at apex

    b. Opening snap at apex

    c. Systolic murmur radiating to right shoulder

    d. Systolic murmur radiating to left lateral chest wall

51. Which intervention helps to reduce mortality rates in the patient with aortic regurgitation?

    a. ACE inhibitors

    b. Cardiac catheterization

    c. Valve replacement surgery

    d. Echocardiography

REFERENCES

American Heart Association. (2016). *Problem: Mitral valve stenosis.* Retrieved from http://www.heart.org/HEARTORG/Conditions/More/HeartValveProblemsandDisease/Problem-Mitral-Valve-Stenosis_UCM_450370_Article.jsp#.V2gKKk1wVjo

Anderson, K. M. (2016). *The advanced practice nurse cardiovascular clinician.* New York, NY: Springer.

Butany, J., & Gotlieb, A. (2000). In E. Braunwald & B. M. McManus (Eds.), *Atlas of cardiovascular pathology for the clinician.* Current Medicine.

Darovic, G. O. (2002). *Hemodynamic monitoring: Invasive and noninvasive clinical application* (3rd ed.). Philadelphia, PA: Elsevier/Saunders.

Huether, S. E., & McCance, K. L. (2017). *Understanding pathophysiology* (6th ed.). St. Louis, MO: Elsevier.

James, P. A., Oparil, S., Carter, B. L., Cushman, W. C., Dennison-Himmelfarb, C., Handler, J. ... Ortiz, E. (2014). 2014 evidence-based guideline for the management of high blood pressure in adults: Report from the panel members appointed to the Eighth Joint National Committee (JNC 8). *JAMA, 311*(5), 507-520. doi:10.1001/jama.2013.284427

January, C. T., Wann, L. S., Alpert, J. S., Calkins, H., Cigarroa, J. E., Cleveland, J. C., ... Yancy, C. W.; ACC/AHA Task Force Members. (2014). 2014 AHA/ACC/HRS guideline for the management of patients with atrial fibrillation: Executive summary: A report of the American College of Cardiology/American Heart Association Task Force on Practice Guidelines and the Heart Rhythm Society. *Circulation, 130*(23), 2071. doi:10.1161/CIR.0000000000000040

Lough, M. E. (2014). Cardiovascular anatomy and physiology. In L. D. Urden, K. M. Stacy, & M. E. Lough (Eds.), *Critical care nursing: Diagnosis and management* (7th ed., pp. 200-221). St. Louis, MO: Elsevier/Mosby.

Mozaffarian, D., Benjamin, E. J., Go, A. S., Arnett, D. K., Blaha, M. J., Cushman, M., ... Turner M. B.; American Heart Association Statistics Committee; Stroke Statistics Subcommittee. (2016). Heart disease and stroke statistics – 2015 update: A report from the American Heart Association. *Circulation, 133*(4), e38-e360. doi:10.1161/CIR.0000000000000350

Nishimura, R. A., Otto, C. M., Bonow, R. O., Carabello, B. A., Erwin, J. P., Guyton, R. A., ... Thomas, J. D.; American College of Cardiology/American Heart Association Task Force on Practice Guidelines. (2014). 2014 AHA/ACC guideline for the management of patients with valvular heart disease: A report of the American College of Cardiology/American Heart Association Task Force on Practice Guidelines. *Journal of the American College of Cardiology, 63*(22), e57-e185. doi:10.1016/j.jacc.2014.02.536

Rosendorff, C., Lackland, D. T., Allison, M., Aronow, W. S., Black, H. R., Blumenthal, R. S., ... White, W. B. (2015). Treatment of hypertension in patients with coronary artery disease: A scientific statement from the American Heart Association, American College of Cardiology, and American Society of Hypertension. *Hypertension, 65,* 1372-1407. doi: 10.1161/HYP.0000000000000018

Virmani, R., Burke, A., & Farb, A. (1997). In E. Branwald & S. H. Rahimtoola (Eds.), *Atlas of heart diseases: Valvular heart disease.* Current Medicine.

Yancy, C. W., Jessup, M., Bozkurt, B., Butler, J., Casey, D. E., Drazner, M. H., ... Wilkoff, B. L. (2013). 2013 ACCF/AHA guideline for the management of heart failure: A report of the American College of Cardiology Foundation/American Heart Association Task Force on Practice Guidelines. *Circulation, 128,* e240-e327. doi:10.1161/CIR.0b013e31829e8776

Zoghbi, W. A., & Crawford, M. H. (2009). Aortic regurgitation. In M. H. Crawford (Ed.), *Current diagnosis and treatment in cardiology* (3rd ed., pp. 95-105). New York, NY: McGraw-Hill.

CHAPTER 10

ATRIAL FIBRILLATION

LEARNING OUTCOME

After completing this chapter, the learner will be able to discuss the implications and current management strategies of atrial fibrillation.

CHAPTER OBJECTIVES

After completing this chapter, the learner will be able to:

1. Discuss the potential causes of atrial fibrillation.

2. Differentiate among idiopathic, paroxysmal, persistent, and permanent atrial fibrillation.

3. Relate pathophysiological and etiological factors of atrial fibrillation to nursing assessment and management.

4. Describe appropriate treatments for atrial fibrillation, including rhythm control, rate control, and newer options.

INTRODUCTION

Atrial fibrillation is rapid, chaotic activity of the atria, resulting in the deterioration of atrial mechanical activity. This rapid, unorganized atrial activity produces irregular atrial fibrillation waves with an atrial rate greater than 350 beats/min. Atrial fibrillation is the most common of all sustained cardiac dysrhythmias. The prevalence of atrial fibrillation increases as the population ages; in the United States, atrial fibrillation affects approximately 2.7 million people annually (American Heart Association, 2016).

In a normal rhythm, the sinoatrial node acts as the heart's pacemaker. The electrical impulse then travels through the right and left atria, depolarizing both atria before it reaches the atrioventricular (AV) node. After conduction passes through the AV node, it passes down both bundle branches to the Purkinje fibers, depolarizing both ventricles. On an electrocardiogram (ECG), sinus rhythm is identified by a P wave, representing atrial depolarization, followed by a QRS complex, representing ventricular depolarization. Figure 10-1 shows a normal sinus beat. Figure 10-2 shows consecutive sinus beats, or a regular sinus rhythm. In atrial fibrillation, the P wave on the ECG is replaced with atrial fibrillation waves (see Figure 10-3).

Atrial fibrillation has variable ventricular conduction, resulting in an irregularly irregular ventricular rhythm (also shown in Figure 10-3). In atrial fibrillation, the AV node is bombarded with atrial depolarization waves and, when AV nodal conduction is intact, a very rapid ventricular response rate can result. A slow ventricular response in the presence of untreated atrial fibrillation is a sign of an underlying conduction abnormality.

NURSING APPLICATION

It is important to remember that atrial fibrillation is not the only cause of an irregular rhythm, so an irregular pulse alone cannot be used to diagnose atrial fibrillation. Also, a patient in atrial fibrillation with an

FIGURE 10-1: NORMAL SINUS-DERIVED HEARTBEAT

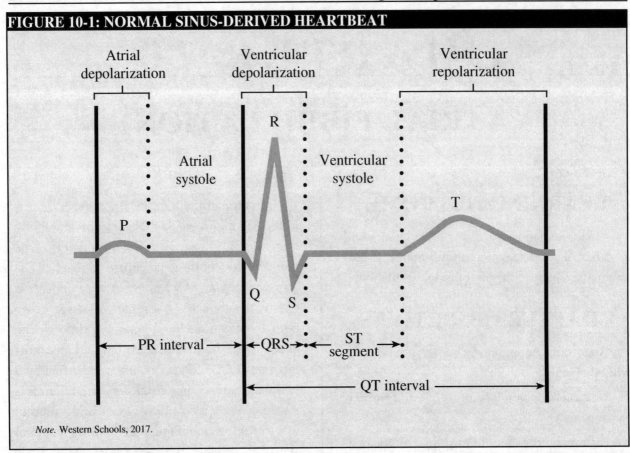

Note. Western Schools, 2017.

FIGURE 10-2: NORMAL SINUS RHYTHM

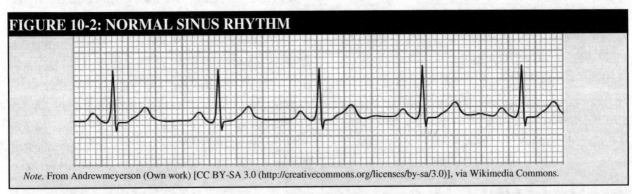

Note. From Andrewmeyerson (Own work) [CC BY-SA 3.0 (http://creativecommons.org/licenses/by-sa/3.0)], via Wikimedia Commons.

FIGURE 10-3: ATRIAL FIBRILLATION

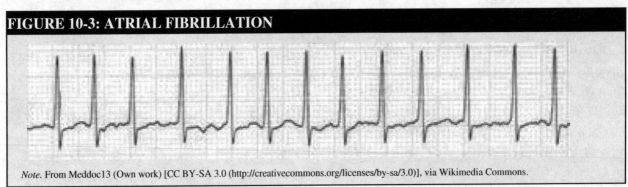

Note. From Meddoc13 (Own work) [CC BY-SA 3.0 (http://creativecommons.org/licenses/by-sa/3.0)], via Wikimedia Commons.

implanted pacemaker may have a regular ventricular response and therefore a regular pulse; however, atrial fibrillation remains the underlying rhythm.

An ECG reading in at least one lead is necessary to confirm the presence of atrial fibrillation waves for proper diagnosis of atrial fibrillation.

POTENTIAL CAUSES

Atrial fibrillation has many acute and transient noncardiopulmonary causes, including surgery, hyperthyroidism, electrocution, drug use, and alcohol use (see Figure 10-4). Acute cardiopulmonary causes include pulmonary embolism, chronic obstructive pulmonary disease, obstructive sleep apnea, myocardial infarction (MI), myocarditis, pericarditis, and cardiac or thoracic surgery (Wadke, 2013). Exercise or emotional stressors can also trigger atrial fibrillation.

The incidence of atrial fibrillation increases with age, and atrial fibrillation is commonly associated with chronic cardiovascular conditions, including mitral valve stenosis, hypertension, heart failure, cardiomyopathy, coronary heart disease, and Wolff-Parkinson-White (WPW) syndrome (Wadke, 2013). Lung pathology in chronic lung disease is also a common cause of atrial fibrillation because increased pulmonary pressures cause an increase in right ventricular work and right ventricular enlargement. Eventually, the right atrium is also affected, increasing the risk for atrial dysrhythmias.

CLASSIFICATIONS

Atrial fibrillation can be classified by more than one method. The first classification involves determining its onset: Note whether this is a first occurrence (single episode) of atrial fibrillation or whether it is recurrent (two or more episodes) atrial fibrillation. Atrial fibrillation can also be classified by its duration as paroxysmal, persistent, long-standing persistent, or permanent (January et al., 2014).

- *Paroxysmal atrial fibrillation:* This type of atrial fibrillation comes on spontaneously and terminates spontaneously, or with intervention. To be classified as paroxysmal, atrial fibrillation cannot last longer than 7 days, and it usually lasts less than 24 hours.

- *Persistent atrial fibrillation:* Persistent atrial fibrillation lasts longer than 7 days.

- *Long-standing persistent atrial fibrillation:* This type of atrial fibrillation persists for longer than 12 months.

- *Permanent atrial fibrillation:* Permanent atrial fibrillation is accepted as permanent by both the patient and the clinician, and a decision is made not to pursue any further attempts to restore sinus rhythm. This term describes a therapeutic attitude rather than a pathophysiological attribute of the arrhythmia.

Notably, both paroxysmal and persistent atrial fibrillation can be seen in first-time presentations. They can also both be recurrent.

Atrial Fibrillation Based on Pathophysiology

The current state of knowledge and understanding of atrial fibrillation is continuously evolving. Diagnosing the rhythm's underlying pathophysiology is useful for attempting to understand the cause of atrial fibrillation and choose treatment regimens.

Nonvalvular Atrial Fibrillation

Nonvalvular atrial fibrillation refers to atrial fibrillation in patients without rheumatic heart (mitral valve stenosis) disease, a mechanical or bioprosthetic valve, or a history of mitral valve repair. Differentiating whether atrial fibrillation is valvular related or classified as nonvalvular related

FIGURE 10-4: MECHANISMS OF ATRIAL FIBRILLATION

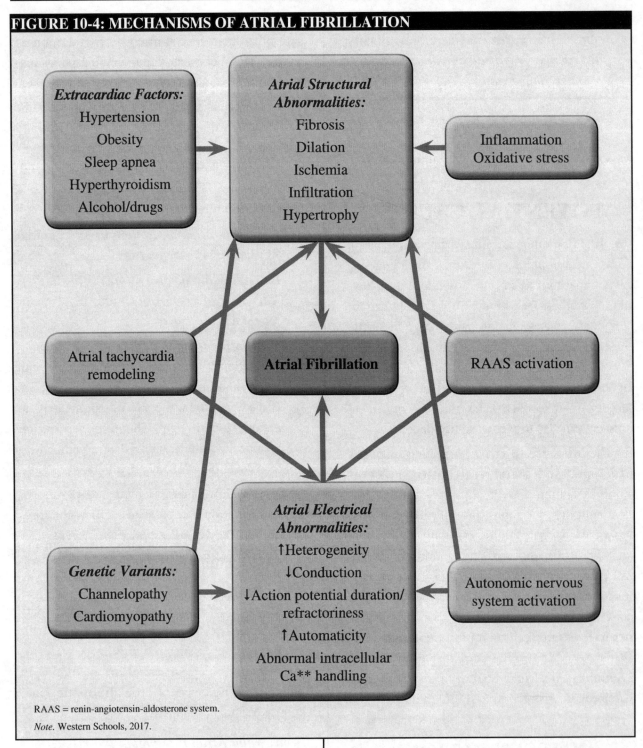

RAAS = renin-angiotensin-aldosterone system.

Note. Western Schools, 2017.

is necessary for the selection of appropriate treatments, especially decisions regarding choice of anticoagulation (Huether & McCance, 2017).

Neurogenic Atrial Fibrillation

Neurogenic atrial fibrillation accounts for atrial fibrillation in a small number of patients.

In these patients, either increased vagal tone or increased adrenergic tone triggers the onset of atrial fibrillation (Huether & McCance, 2017).

Idiopathic Atrial Fibrillation

Some patients with atrial fibrillation have normal cardiac and pulmonary function and no known predisposing causes. This type of atrial fibrillation is known as idiopathic atrial fibrillation because it has not been found to be caused by any pathophysiology. Patients with this type of atrial fibrillation are also younger than 60 years and are not hypertensive (Wyse et al., 2014).

PATHOPHYSIOLOGY

Structural abnormalities, atrial electrical abnormalities, and extracardiac factors can all contribute to atrial fibrillation because of the promotion of abnormal impulse formation or propagation. Specific mechanisms of the pathophysiological processes are largely not well understood but are most often connected to the structural changes that occur within the atria (January et al., 2014).

Atrial fibrillation can start with a premature atrial contraction, which is an ectopic beat (beat beginning outside the sinoatrial node). This premature atrial contraction is usually the source of paroxysmal atrial fibrillation. Premature atrial beats are usually caused by trigger beats coming from one or more of the superior pulmonary veins located near the junction of the left atrium. These trigger beats occur because of enhanced automaticity of the tissue. Other sources for ectopic beats triggering paroxysmal atrial fibrillation include the right atrium and, less commonly, the superior vena cava or coronary sinus (Huether & McCance, 2017).

Structural disease of the atria is usually responsible for maintaining atrial fibrillation, such as that which occurs in persistent and permanent atrial fibrillation. The existence of atrial fibrillation contributes to the development of the structural damage of the atria, with the end result being atrial scarring, fibrosis, and myopathy. Various pathological processes are thought to be involved in the development of these structural changes, including ischemia,

inflammation, fatty infiltration, atrial hypertrophy, and progressive atrial dilation (January et al., 2014). Atrial hypertrophy and progressive atrial dilation can be either a cause or a consequence of atrial fibrillation. Pathological changes such as fibrosis of the atria occurring with aging may explain the increased incidence of atrial fibrillation in the older adult population (Huether & McCance, 2017). In patients with structural disease of the atria, a reentrant mechanism, rather than a focal ectopic mechanism, is usually responsible for the maintenance of atrial fibrillation. Reentrant mechanisms in atrial fibrillation can involve many microcircuits, or pathways to the atrioventricular (AV) node, and are often the reason it is refractory to antiarrhythmic treatments. These reentrant pathways make cardioversion to sinus rhythm more difficult because of the electrophysiological structural remodeling that occurs over time. This remodeling involves fibrosis of the reentrant microcircuits, thereby contributing to a persistent arrhythmia being refractory to cardioversion (Kasper et al., 2015).

SYMPTOMS

Symptoms of atrial fibrillation are commonly related to the fast ventricular rate. In some patients who are asymptomatic, the dysrhythmia is discovered during episodic healthcare-related visits. The duration of the episode of atrial fibrillation also affects the symptoms. If the ventricular rate is controlled and the patient is still symptomatic, symptoms are typically related to loss of the atrial kick (decrease in cardiac output). Patients who already have decreased ventricular function experience more symptoms from loss of the atrial kick than do those with normal left ventricular function. Common symptoms of atrial fibrillation include palpitations, dyspnea, fatigue, weakness, light-headedness, diaphoresis, and chest pain. Patients in atrial fibrillation may also experience polyuria caused by the increased release of atrial natriuretic peptide from overstimulation and overstretch of the atria (Wynn et al., 2014).

Many patients with atrial fibrillation are asymptomatic. These patients are at risk for development of tachycardia-induced cardiomyopathy from poor ventricular rate control. These patients may also present for the first time with more serious complications, such as stroke or heart failure (Anderson, 2016).

NURSING APPLICATION

Patients who present with symptoms of stroke or transient ischemic attack should be assessed for the presence of asymptomatic, undiagnosed atrial fibrillation.

When patients experience hemodynamic compromise caused by atrial fibrillation, more serious symptoms, such as syncope and pulmonary edema, can occur. Syncope is a rare symptom and usually indicates additional underlying pathology compromising cardiac output, such as aortic valve stenosis or hypertrophic obstructive cardiomyopathy (Anderson, 2016).

COMPLICATIONS

Atrial fibrillation is rarely immediately life-threatening, but it may cause long-term complications. The two major complications associated with atrial fibrillation are an increased risk for thromboembolic events, particularly stroke, and hemodynamic compromise.

Stroke

Patients with atrial fibrillation are at an increased risk for thromboembolism due to potential thrombus formation in the left atrium and left atrial appendage. Embolization of a thrombus in the left atrium or left atrial append-

age can cause stroke. Patients in atrial fibrillation may also have other independent risk factors for stroke. Those patients at highest risk are those with other comorbidities or risk factors such as congestive heart failure, hypertension, previous thromboembolism, stroke or transient ischemic attack, diabetes mellitus, peripheral vascular disease, and/or age older than 65 years (January et al., 2014).

Patients in atrial fibrillation who are younger than 60 years and have no existing cardiac or pulmonary disease (idiopathic atrial fibrillation) are at the lowest risk for stroke. Patients with atrial fibrillation with rheumatic heart disease have an even higher risk for stroke than those with nonvalvular heart disease (Wyse et al., 2014).

In patients with atrial fibrillation, thrombi most commonly form in the left atrial appendage and are the source of clots in stroke (Anderson et al., 2013). In atrial fibrillation, the velocity of blood flow through the left atrium and left atrial appendage is decreased. This decrease in velocity increases the risk for thrombus formation. Atrial fibrillation is commonly diagnosed for the first time in patients presenting with new thrombotic stroke. Prevention of thrombotic complications is a major goal in the treatment of atrial fibrillation.

Patients with a diagnosis of nonvalvular atrial fibrillation and a CHA_2DS_2-VASc score of 2 or greater are recommended to receive anticoagulation therapy to decrease the risk for stroke. The CHA_2DS_2-VASc risk score is a tool used to predict the patient's risk for a thromboembolic event (e.g., ischemic stroke; January et al., 2014). Anticoagulation has been shown to substantially reduce the risk for stroke in patients with atrial fibrillation, but it has risks for bleeding in certain patients, and those patients should be treated with caution (January et al., 2014). Dabigatran (an oral direct thrombin inhibitor) is another option for anticoagulation to reduce stroke risk in select patients with nonvalvular atrial fibrillation. Antiplatelet therapy alone, such as aspirin or clopidogrel, is not generally used for stroke prevention in patients with atrial fibrillation. In certain young patients with idiopathic atrial fibrillation and no other stroke risk factors, antiplatelet therapy is recommended (January et al., 2014).

All patients older than 65 years with atrial fibrillation should receive anticoagulation therapy with warfarin unless contraindicated per current guidelines (January et al., 2014). Although warfarin therapy is proven to prevent stroke, older adult patients have an increased risk for bleeding complications from warfarin and are likely to receive other anticoagulants if their risk scores are low. Aspirin therapy is considered in older patients who have contraindications to warfarin therapy (Anderson et al., 2013).

In patients receiving oral anticoagulation for stroke prevention, the international normalized ratio (INR) should be between 2 and 3 (January et al., 2014). If a patient needs anticoagulation for another reason, such as a prosthetic valve, the INR may need to be higher. The INR is checked at least weekly during the initiation phase. After the INR is therapeutic and stable, it can be reassessed monthly. Aspirin is used only in low-risk patients or as an alternative for patients with contraindications to oral anticoagulation therapy. Patients in atrial flutter have the same antithrombotic prevention strategies as those in atrial fibrillation (Anderson et al., 2013).

Hemodynamic Complications

Hemodynamic complications of atrial fibrillation are associated with rapid ventricular rate, irregular ventricular response, and loss of atrial contraction (kick). Atrial fibrillation can cause a loss in cardiac output of up to 20% because atrial contraction is lost. People become more dependent on the atrial kick with age. Loss of the atrial kick can lead to increased left atrial pressure, which, in turn, can lead to increased pulmonary pressure. The irregularity of the R-R interval (irregularity of the QRS complexes) within the cardiac rhythm also adversely affects hemodynamic performance (Anderson, 2016).

Some patients with atrial fibrillation are at high risk for experiencing a substantial decrease in cardiac output. These patients have conditions that impair diastolic filling at baseline, including mitral stenosis, hypertrophic cardiomyopathy (HCM), restrictive cardiomyopathy, and hypertension with diastolic dysfunction (Anderson et al., 2013).

Another long-term complication of atrial fibrillation is the development of ventricular dilated cardiomyopathy from an accelerated ventricular rate. This complication is also called *tachycardia-induced cardiomyopathy*. Control of ventricular rate can lead to complete or partial reversal of this complication (Anderson et al., 2013; January et al., 2014).

TREATMENT CONSIDERATIONS

If a patient presents with an initial episode of paroxysmal (self-terminating) atrial fibrillation, no additional treatment may be needed. If paroxysmal atrial fibrillation is recurrent and the patient is symptomatic, then antidysrhythmic therapy may be prescribed to keep the patient in sinus rhythm or to limit the number of episodes. If the patient has continued paroxysmal episodes, then rate-control medication and antithrombotic medication may also be given (Anderson et al., 2013).

The overall goal of treatment in atrial fibrillation is to reduce symptoms, reduce the duration and frequency of episodes, and reduce the risk for stroke. Treatment strategies for rate control achieve these goals more than rhythm control. Rhythm-control treatments are aimed for and are more successful in the patient experiencing new-onset (<48 hours) atrial fibrillation than in patients with persistent or permanent atrial fibrillation. Because findings of two large clinical trials (AFFIRM and RACE) found an all-cause reduction in mortality with rate-control therapies and increased complications with rhythm-control therapies, guidelines do not recommend rhythm-control therapy for patients with recurrent, persistent, or permanent atrial fibrillation (Van Gelder et al., 2002; Wyse et al., 2002).

When patients first present with persistent atrial fibrillation, a decision must be made between these two treatment arms. The maintenance of sinus rhythm generally requires the long-term use of antiarrhythmic pharmacology, so the benefits of sinus rhythm have to be weighed against the adverse or toxic effects of antiarrhythmic medications. For this reason, rate control may be considered acceptable in patients who are not symptomatic. If symptoms of atrial fibrillation are present with effective rate control, then cardioversion is attempted (Anderson et al., 2013).

Rate Control

It is very important to control the ventricular rate in atrial fibrillation to avoid the development of tachycardia-induced cardiomyopathy. Ventricular rate is considered controlled when it is less than 80 beats/min at rest in the symptomatic patient or less than 110 beats/min at rest in the asymptomatic patient (January et al., 2014). Rate control is accomplished by medications that slow conduction through the AV node, including beta blockers, nondihydropyridine calcium channel blockers (verapamil and diltiazem), and digoxin. Nondihydropyridine calcium channel blockers and beta blockers are the most commonly used medications for rate control in atrial fibrillation. In patients with heart failure, digoxin or amiodarone can be used to control ventricular rate, and nondihydropyridine calcium channel

blockers should be avoided. In patients with the presence of an accessory pathway (Wolff-Parkinson-White [WPW] syndrome), special considerations must be taken when using medications to slow ventricular rate (Anderson et al., 2013; January et al., 2014). These considerations are discussed at the end of this chapter.

Patients with paroxysmal atrial fibrillation who receive rate-control medications may experience sinus bradycardia or heart block as a complication when they are in a normal sinus rhythm. Other patients may develop too slow of a ventricular response and become symptomatic, even while in atrial fibrillation. These patients may require insertion of a permanent pacemaker to maintain a minimum ventricular rate (which prevents sinus bradycardia and heart block) while on sufficient doses of medications to control the ventricular rate (Anderson et al., 2013).

If medication therapy does not adequately control ventricular rate, the AV node can be ablated. AV node ablation results in complete heart block and requires the placement of a permanent pacemaker. Although this strategy can be helpful in preventing tachycardia-induced cardiomyopathy, it has potential downsides. Because atrial fibrillation remains the underlying rhythm, the patient needs continued anticoagulation therapy. With ablation of the AV node, permanent loss of AV synchrony occurs and the patient has continued pacemaker dependence (Anderson et al., 2013).

Many patients who have experienced at least one unsuccessful attempt to restore and maintain their rhythm to sinus rhythm (rhythm control) are left in atrial fibrillation with appropriate rate control and continuous antithrombotic therapy.

NURSING APPLICATION

Diltiazem is commonly used for rate control in patients with atrial fibrillation and rapid ven-

tricular response. It is important to remember that in decompensated heart failure, diltiazem should not be the drug of choice for ventricular rate control because it may worsen the patient's hemodynamic status.

Rhythm Control

Potential benefits of restoring sinus rhythm include prevention of thrombus formation, prevention of atrial myopathy, and relief of the patient's symptoms. When a patient presents for the first time with persistent atrial fibrillation and the decision is made to restore and maintain sinus rhythm, cardioversion (electrical or pharmacological) is performed. A patient who has been in atrial fibrillation for longer than 48 hours will need special considerations to prevent an embolic complication of the cardioversion. For the first cardioversion, antiarrhythmics are generally not used unless the patient has been in atrial fibrillation for longer than 3 months (January et al., 2014).

If the first cardioversion is unsuccessful, or if there is early recurrence of atrial fibrillation, repeat electrical cardioversion with antiarrhythmic drug therapy is performed. The use of antiarrhythmic drug therapy with electrical cardioversion increases the long-term success. However, all antiarrhythmic medications, including those used for pharmacological cardioversion and those used to maintain sinus rhythm, have the potential for toxic side effects (January et al., 2014).

Antiarrhythmic Medications

Antiarrhythmic agents that are used in the treatment of atrial fibrillation are assessed by their classifications and also by their roles in the pharmacological cardioversion of atrial fibrillation and the maintenance of sinus rhythm. According to the Vaughan Williams classification system, antiarrhythmic drugs can be grouped into four classifications that are related to their basic mechanisms of action (see Table 10-1). For instance, Class I medications are considered to be strong antiarrhythmic agents and sodium channel (also known as the fast channel) blockade. Class I medications can be subcategorized further by their effect on repolarization. Class I subcategories include Ia, Ib, and Ic. Class II, III, and IV medications function by beta blockade, potassium channel blockage, or calcium channel blockade, respectively (Urden, Stacy, & Lough, 2015).

Class II medications are beta blockers, and class IV medications are calcium channel blockers. These medications have been discussed in more detail in Chapter 4. Their role in the treatment of atrial fibrillation is primarily that of rate control by slowing conduction through the AV node (Anderson et al., 2013). Beta blockers may also be used to help maintain sinus rhythm in idiopathic atrial fibrillation and prevent recurrence of atrial fibrillation caused by adrenergic stimulation. Beta blockers work by blocking the sympathetic nervous system and are the only group of medications in this classification system that does not affect the cardiac action potential (Anderson et al., 2013).

Class I antiarrhythmic agents are sometimes called *sodium channel blockers* because they work in the fast sodium channel of the cardiac action potential. Class I agents have three distinct subgroups: Class Ia, Ib, and Ic. Class III agents are sometimes called *potassium channel blockers* because they work by blocking the influx of potassium during the cardiac action potential. Both Class I and Class III antiarrhythmic medications have serious potential adverse effects and, therefore, require careful nursing assessment and patient education (Anderson et al., 2013). Table 10-2 outlines antiarrhythmics used in the management of atrial fibrillation.

TABLE 10-1: ANTIARRHYTHMIC CLASSIFICATION SYSTEM AND MEDICATIONS

Class	Mechanism	Medications	Treatment Goal
I	Sodium-channel blockade	Ia – Quinidine, procainamide, disopyramide Ib – Lidocaine, tocainide, mexiletine Ic – Flecainide, encainide, propafenone	Rhythm conversion/control
II	Beta-blockade	Ia – Quinidine, procainamide, disopyramide Ib – Lidocaine, tocainide, mexiletine Ic – Flecainide, encainide, propafenone	Rate control
III	Potassium-channel blockade	Amiodarone, ibutilide, sotalol, dofetilide, dronedarone	Rhythm conversion/control
IV	Calcium-channel blockade	Diltiazem, verapamil	Rate control

Note. From Urden, L. D., Stacy, K. M., & Lough, M. E. (2015). *Critical care nursing diagnosis and management* (7th ed.). St. Louis, MO: Elsevier/Mosby.

TABLE 10-2: ANTIARRHYTHMICS (BY VAUGHAN WILLIAMS CLASSIFICATION) USED IN ATRIAL FIBRILLATION

Class	Specific Medications	Purpose of Medication	Major Cardiac Adverse Effects
Class Ia	Disopyramide	Rhythm control	Torsades de pointes, heart failure
	Procainamide	Rhythm control	Torsades de pointes
	Quinidine	Rhythm control	Torsades de pointes
Class Ib	Not used in atrial fibrillation		
Class Ic	Flecainide	Rhythm control	Ventricular tachycardia, heart failure, atrial flutter with 1:1 AV conduction
	Propafenone	Rhythm control	Ventricular tachycardia, heart failure, atrial flutter with 1:1 AV conduction
Class II	Beta blockers	Rate control	Bradycardia, hypotension
Class III	Amiodaronea	Rhythm control	Hypotension, bradycardia, Torsades de pointes (rare), extracardiac organ toxicity
	Dronedaronea	Rhythm control	Torsades de pointes
	Dofetilide	Rhythm control	Torsades de pointes, QT prolongation
	Ibutilide	Rhythm control	Torsades de pointes, QT prolongation
	Sotalola (also contains beta blocker)	Rhythm control	Torsades de pointes, QT prolongation, heart failure, beta-blocker side effects
Class IV	Calcium channel blockers	Rate control	Bradycardia, hypotension

aAdditional rate-control component.

AV = atrioventricular.

Note. Adapted from Fuster, V., Rydén, L. E., Cannom, D. S., Crijns, H. J., Curtis, A. B., Ellenbogen, K. A., ... Wann, L. S. (2011). 2011 ACCF/AHA/HRS focused updates incorporated into the ACC/AHA/ESC 2006 guidelines for the management of patients with atrial fibrillation: A report of the American College of Cardiology Foundation/American Heart Association Task Force on Practice Guidelines. *Circulation, 123*(10), e269-e367. doi:10.1161/CIR.0b013e318214876d

One of the dangerous adverse effects of the Class I and III medications used in the treatment of atrial fibrillation is the development of ventricular dysrhythmias, such as torsades de pointes, polymorphic or monomorphic ventricular tachycardia, or ventricular fibrillation. Medications with this potential are called *proarrhythmic* (Anderson et al., 2013). Figure 10-5 illustrates the effects of Class I and III antiarrhythmic agents on the cardiac action potential.

Torsades de pointes is a particular type of ventricular dysrhythmia that can occur in the presence of a long QT interval. The QT interval is measured from the beginning of the QRS complex to the end of the T wave. Figure 10-1 points out the QT interval in a normal beat. Class Ia and III agents place the patient at particular risk for torsades de pointes because of their potential for increasing the QT interval. Class Ia agents delay depolarization and prolong the QRS, whereas class III agents delay repolarization and prolong the T wave. Both actions have the end result of prolonging the QT interval.

For this reason, some of these medications, particularly Class III agents, are initiated in a hospital setting, where the patient's cardiac rhythm can be monitored. For example, dofetilide is only to be initiated in an inpatient hospital setting. The Class IC medications also have atrial proarrhythmic effects and can potentially promote conversion of the atrial dysrhythmia to atrial flutter with a fast 1:1 AV conduction. For example, flecainide and propafenone have the potential to induce atrial flutter when they are used for the pharmacological cardioversion of atrial fibrillation (Fuster et al., 2011). Because of the high side-effect profile of all antiarrhythmic medications, any reversible causes of atrial fibrillation should be eliminated before medications are initiated (Anderson, 2016).

Amiodarone is a class III antiarrhythmic with unique considerations. Although effective, it has the potential to cause the development of extracardiac organ toxicity, including thyroid dysfunction, polyneuropathy, and liver and pulmonary toxicity. One of the most dangerous

FIGURE 10-5: EFFECT OF CLASS I, III, AND IV ANTIARRHYTHMIA AGENTS ON CARDIAC ACTION POTENTIAL

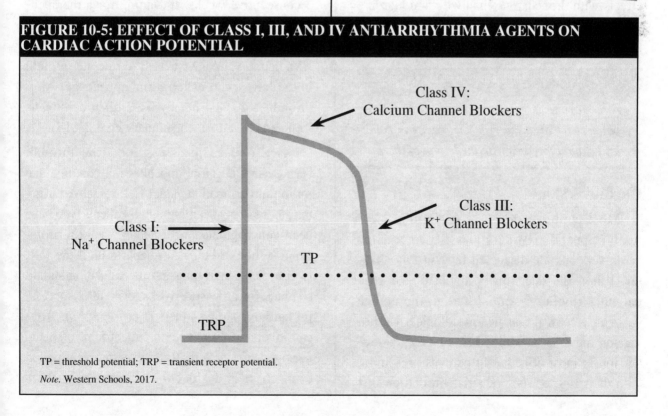

TP = threshold potential; TRP = transient receptor potential.

Note. Western Schools, 2017.

side effects is a potentially lethal interstitial pneumonitis that results in irreversible pulmonary fibrosis. Patients taking amiodarone should have a baseline pulmonary function study and chest radiographs every 3 to 6 months. Liver function studies are also monitored on a regular basis. Because the toxic effects are cumulative and dose related, the use of amiodarone is reserved for carefully selected patients who are not suited for other treatments. Patients who take amiodarone should receive the lowest effective dose (January et al., 2014).

Patients with heart failure are sensitive to the proarrhythmic effects of drugs; therefore, not all antiarrhythmic drugs are safe in patients with heart failure. Amiodarone is a safer medication in the presence of heart failure or considerable left ventricular hypertrophy because, although it does increase the QT interval, it rarely causes torsades de pointes. Dronedarone, a newer class III antiarrhythmic, is used to decrease hospitalizations in patients with atrial fibrillation. There are fewer extracardiac side effects with dronedarone than with amiodarone, yet it should not be used in the setting of heart failure (January et al., 2014).

NURSING APPLICATION

Amiodarone is generally not used in young patients because the risk for toxicity is cumulative and increases with the length of therapy.

Cardioversion

Most cardioversions are performed electively. Special considerations for emergency cardioversions are discussed later in this chapter. When the decision is made to restore a patient's rhythm to sinus rhythm, the choice between electrical and pharmacological cardioversion must be made. Pharmacological cardioversion is most effective in patients presenting with their first episode of atrial fibrillation that

has lasted no more than 7 days. Whether pharmacological or electrical cardioversion is chosen, the patient's heart rate should be controlled before elective cardioversion. Patients who are in atrial fibrillation longer than 48 hours require anticoagulation and a transesophageal echocardiogram (TEE) to evaluate for left atrial appendage thrombus before cardioversion to decrease the risk for stroke. If a patient presents with atrial fibrillation with an onset of less than 48 hours, then the decision to anticoagulate before cardioversion is based on the patient's other risk factors for thrombus formation (Anderson et al., 2013).

The risk for thrombotic stroke is the same for electrical and pharmacological cardioversion. However, the toxicities associated with antiarrhythmic drugs must be considered in deciding the method of cardioversion (January et al., 2014). Two approaches to anticoagulation can be taken before cardioversion. Patients can be started on warfarin and then wait until the INR is between 2 and 3 for a minimum of 3 consecutive weeks. If waiting for a therapeutic INR for this period of time is not desirable, patients can receive anticoagulation therapy with heparin and have a TEE to rule out thrombi in the left atrium or left atrial appendage. After thrombi are ruled out by TEE, then cardioversion can be performed (January et al., 2014).

TEE is used to assess for atrial thrombi because the left atrial appendage, a common site for thrombi formation, is not well visualized using transthoracic echocardiography. Patients who have been anticoagulated with heparin before cardioversion should remain on heparin until the INR is in a therapeutic range. Anticoagulation should continue for at least 4 weeks, even after successful cardioversion (Anderson et al., 2013). After cardioversion (spontaneous, electrical, or pharmacological), the left atrium experiences a period of mechanical dysfunction (stunning) that lasts for several weeks. Thrombi can still form during this period of mechanical dysfunction, and emboli can be released when mechanical function returns to normal (Fuster et al., 2011). Patients need to continue on anticoagulation for a minimum of 4 weeks after cardioversion to prevent thrombus formation. Even patients with no thrombi on TEE before cardioversion have the possibility of developing thrombi and emboli after cardioversion.

Direct Current Cardioversion

In direct current cardioversion (DCCV), the electrical shock is synchronized with the intrinsic activity of the heart. DCCV is different from the delivery of a desynchronized shock (defibrillation) in the treatment of pulseless ventricular tachycardia or ventricular fibrillation. Most cardioversions are performed with the two paddles or electrode patches placed in the anterior (sternum) and posterior (left scapular area) positions. Defibrillators using a biphasic waveform require lower levels of energy, fewer shocks, and result in better outcomes. Therefore, cardioversion with biphasic waveform is the current standard for cardioversion (Fuster et al., 2011). DCCV is performed with the use of short-acting anesthetic agents or with agents to induce conscious sedation; therefore, the patient must be given nothing by mouth before the procedure (Fuster et al., 2011). Personnel skilled in airway management must be present, and the patient should be monitored with a cardiac monitor and pulse oximetry. Emergency equipment must be readily available, including oxygen, suction, intubation supplies, and other emergency medications and equipment. Standard hospital policies are followed, as with all patients receiving anesthesia or conscious sedation. Short-term cardiac dysrhythmias are a potential complication of cardioversion. Patients are placed on a cardiac monitor for a period of time specified by their cardiologist, who gives consideration of the patient's comorbidities and risks for dysrhythmias. Patients with hypokalemia or digoxin toxicity are at increased risk for development of serious ventricular dysrhythmias after cardioversion. Electrolyte abnormalities should be corrected before cardioversion (Anderson et al., 2013).

NURSING APPLICATION

Potassium levels and digoxin levels (for patients on digoxin) should be assessed before elective cardioversion.

The initial success rate of cardioversion is much higher than the long-term success rate. If the patient has an early relapse into atrial fibrillation, then repeat cardioversion using preprocedure antiarrhythmic drug therapy can help reduce the rate of recurrent atrial fibrillation. Patients with permanent pacemakers or implantable cardioverter-defibrillators can be safely cardioverted out of atrial fibrillation. The paddles should be placed away from the device to avoid damage, and the device is interrogated before and after the procedure to assure correct functioning (Anderson et al., 2013).

Pharmacological Cardioversion

The advantage of pharmacological cardioversion over DCCV is that there is no need for sedation of the patient. In addition, some patients are not comfortable with DCCV and prefer pharmacological cardioversion. Medications proven effective in pharmacological cardioversion are listed in Box 10-1. Not all of these medications are approved for or are labeled for this use in the United States (Fuster et al., 2011). Other antiarrhythmic agents can be used to maintain sinus rhythm after successful cardioversion has occurred.

BOX 10-1: DRUGS PROVEN MOST EFFECTIVE FOR PHARMACOLOGICAL CARDIOVERSION OF ATRIAL FIBRILLATION

- Dofetilide
- Flecainide
- Ibutilide
- Propafenone

All of these drugs have Class I recommendations for the cardioversion of atrial fibrillation with a duration of less than or equal to 7 days. Dofetilide also has a Class I recommendation for the cardioversion of atrial fibrillation with a duration longer than 7 days.

Note. Adapted from Fuster, V., Rydén, L. E., Cannom, D. S., Crijns, H. J., Curtis, A. B., Ellenbogen, K. A., ... Wann, L. S. (2011). 2011 ACCF/AHA/HRS focused updates incorporated into the ACC/AHA/ESC 2006 guidelines for the management of patients with atrial fibrillation: A report of the American College of Cardiology Foundation/American Heart Association Task Force on Practice Guidelines. *Circulation, 123*(10), e269-e367. doi:10.1161/CIR.0b013e318214876d

Use of Pharmacological Agents to Maintain Sinus Rhythm

Pharmacology is used to maintain sinus rhythm in patients with recurrent paroxysmal atrial fibrillation or in patients who still have persistent atrial fibrillation after cardioversion. Because of the chronic nature of atrial fibrillation, most patients are likely to have a recurrence if not treated with antiarrhythmic therapy. Patients who are older, have been in atrial fibrillation longer, and who have underlying heart disease are at risk for increased recurrent episodes. Even with antiarrhythmic therapy, many patients experience a relapse. A relapse does not necessarily indicate treatment failure. Antiarrhythmic therapy that controls the frequency and severity of occurrences may be considered a success (January et al., 2014).

Before antiarrhythmic drug therapy is used to maintain sinus rhythm, it is important to identify and treat any reversible causes. Because of potential toxic side effects, antiarrhythmic therapy is typically not used in treating the first episode of atrial fibrillation or in treating infrequent episodes of paroxysmal atrial fibrillation that produce tolerable symptoms. Box 10-2 lists medications used to maintain sinus rhythm (January et al., 2014).

BOX 10-2: MEDICATIONS USED TO MAINTAIN SINUS RHYTHM IN PATIENTS WITH ATRIAL FIBRILLATION

- Dofetilide
- Amiodarone
- Disopyramide
- Dofetilide
- Flecainide
- Procainamide
- Propafenone
- Quinidine
- Sotalol

Note. Adapted from Fuster, V., Rydén, L. E., Cannom, D. S., Crijns, H. J., Curtis, A. B., Ellenbogen, K. A., ... Wann, L. S. (2011). 2011 ACCF/AHA/HRS focused updates incorporated into the ACC/AHA/ESC 2006 guidelines for the management of patients with atrial fibrillation: A report of the American College of Cardiology Foundation/American Heart Association Task Force on Practice Guidelines. *Circulation, 123*(10), e269-e367. doi:10.1161/CIR.0b013e318214876d

Table 10-3 lists first-line medications for maintenance of sinus rhythm in special patient populations. Second- and third-line agents are not discussed. All medication decisions are based on individual patient characteristics. In addition, if a single drug therapy fails, combination therapy may be used (January et al., 2014).

TABLE 10-3: MEDICATIONS USED TO MAINTAIN SINUS RHYTHM IN SPECIAL PATIENT POPULATIONS

Special Patient Populations	Medications Used to Maintain Sinus Rhythm
Idiopathic atrial fibrillation	Flecainide Propafenone Sotalol Beta blockers
Neurogenic atrial fibrillation	Disopyramide or flecainide (for vagal induced) Beta blockers or sotalol (for adrenergic induced)
Atrial fibrillation in heart failure	Amiodarone (less proarrhythmic effects) Dofetilide
Atrial fibrillation in coronary heart disease	Sotalol (beta-blocking properties) Amiodarone Dofetilide Dronedarone
Atrial fibrillation in hypertensive heart disease with left ventricular hypertrophy and septal wall thickness >1.5 cm	Amiodarone (with significant hypertrophy) Dronedarone

Note. Adapted from Fuster, V., Rydén, L. E., Cannom, D. S., Crijns, H. J., Curtis, A. B., Ellenbogen, K. A., … Wann, L. S. (2011). 2011 ACCF/AHA/HRS focused updates incorporated into the ACC/AHA/ESC 2006 guidelines for the management of patients with atrial fibrillation: A report of the American College of Cardiology Foundation/American Heart Association Task Force on Practice Guidelines. *Circulation, 123*(10), e269-e367. doi:10.1161/CIR.0b013e318214876d

Permanent Pacemaker Insertion

Permanent pacemaker insertion is required after any complete ablation (scarring of conduction pathways within the atria) of the AV node. Implantation of a permanent pacemaker may also be used in conjunction with more aggressive medication administration for rate control. Pacemakers inserted in patients with atrial fibrillation have mode-switching capability to change modes when the patient enters into atrial fibrillation. The purpose of a mode-switching pacemaker is to avoid a rapid pacing response to the sensing of rapid atrial activity. Ventricular pacing during atrial fibrillation can also provide symptomatic relief by providing a regular ventricular response (Anderson et al., 2013).

In patients who receive permanent pacemakers for reasons other than atrial fibrillation, atrial pacing (as opposed to ventricular pacing) has reduced the occurrence of atrial fibrillation (Fuster et al., 2011). Atrial pacing was thus thought to be a potential primary strategy for atrial fibrillation prevention. Atrial pacing, however, has not been proven to prevent the development of atrial fibrillation when used as a primary strategy. Pacemaker devices can also be programmed to perform overdrive pacing in response to episodes of atrial fibrillation. The goal of this therapy is to override the atrial fibrillation with a paced rhythm (Anderson, 2016).

Atrial Defibrillators

Atrial defibrillators are approved for the treatment of atrial fibrillation but are not widely used. Unlike with implantable cardioverter-defibrillators, which shock patients out of life-threatening ventricular dysrhythmias, most patients are not willing to receive a cardioversion shock for non-life-threatening atrial fibrillation. Attempts have been made to find a shock waveform that can successfully cardiovert atrial fibrillation and be tolerated by a conscious patient. Limitations of this technology still prevent it from being frequently used (Anderson, 2016).

Maze Surgical Procedure

The Maze surgical procedure is commonly performed in patients with symptomatic atrial fibrillation who are already undergoing open-heart surgery for another reason. The Maze procedure involves making a series of incisions in the atria using radiofrequency or some other form of energy. Incisions are made to block reentrant pathways within the atrial tissue and to channel conduction in a more normal fashion. The barriers created by the incisions limit the amount of myocardium available to sustain the reentrant circuits. The pulmonary veins can also be electrically isolated during the Maze procedure. The addition of the Maze procedure to another open-heart surgical procedure increases the risk for complications associated with cardiothoracic surgery (e.g., bleeding, stroke, among others). Because the procedure is so invasive, it is seldom done as a stand-alone surgery. However, if the Maze procedure is performed alone, the complications are similar to other cardiothoracic procedures involving a median sternotomy and cardiopulmonary bypass. Therefore, the benefit of having the Maze procedure performed in conjunction with a second needed cardiothoracic surgery (such as valve replacement or bypass grafting) may be greater than any potential risks. Less invasive techniques not requiring a sternotomy are being developed to make this procedure a more attractive option in the treatment of atrial fibrillation (Anderson, 2016; Mozaffarian et al., 2015).

Catheter Ablation Techniques

Initial catheter ablation techniques in atrial fibrillation used radiofrequency ablation to create linear scars in the atria and mimic the surgical Maze procedure. The next phase in catheter ablation involved targeting foci within or near the pulmonary veins that were often responsible for triggering atrial fibrillation. This technique has evolved from targeting individual foci to doing a circumferential isolation of the entire musculature surrounding the pulmonary veins. Subsequent research has shown that triggering foci can originate in multiple areas throughout the right and left atrium. Active research continues in the area of ablation for atrial fibrillation, including techniques such as the use of complex fractionated ECGs to determine the target sites for ablation (Mozaffarian et al., 2015).

Atrioventricular Node Ablation

Ablation of the AV node does not cure atrial fibrillation, but rather it permanently prevents any rapid ventricular response. Patients who require AV nodal ablation because of uncontrolled rapid ventricular response also need permanent pacemaker implantation (Anderson, 2016).

Percutaneous left atrial appendage transcatheter occlusion is performed to prevent thromboembolic stroke in patients with non-valvular atrial fibrillation as an alternative to oral anticoagulation therapy. Patient selection includes patients at high risk for stroke who will tolerate dual-antiplatelet therapy postprocedure and/or who may have had complicated treatment courses with oral anticoagulant therapy. Contraindications include patients with low stroke risk scores, patients with valvular heart disease, or patients with an atrial septal defect. This procedure is done in a cardiac catheterization laboratory or during cardiothoracic surgery. Right cardiac catheterization is done with a transseptal puncture. An occlusive device is placed in the left atrial appendage to prevent embolization of a thrombus (De Backer et al., 2014). If patients do not meet selection criteria, the atrial appendage can also be sutured during open-heart surgery in patients with a history of atrial fibrillation. The goals are to prevent embolization of a thrombus from the left atrial appendage into systemic circulation and to avoid the complications and monitoring requirements of warfarin. Postprocedure considerations include verifying there is no device embolization via TEE before discharge and again at 45 days after the procedure (De Backer et al., 2014). Results of the WATCHMAN trial found that dual-antiplatelet therapy for 6 months postprocedure followed by aspirin as monotherapy indefinitely was adequate as an antithrombotic regimen (Plicht et al., 2013).

Primary Prevention Strategies

Research regarding the primary prevention of atrial fibrillation is ongoing and complex because prevention is heavily dependent on comorbidities of the patient (Menezes et al., 2013). Studies have found the use of angiotensin-converting enzyme inhibitors and angiotensin receptor blockers is effective in the primary prevention of atrial fibrillation in some patients with end-stage kidney disease (Lin et al., 2015). Although it has been shown in studies that the use of atrial pacing decreases the incidence of atrial fibrillation, there is no evidence to support the use of permanent pacing for the primary prevention of atrial fibrillation if there are no other indications for a pacemaker (January et al., 2014).

TREATMENT FOR SPECIAL PATIENT POPULATIONS

Atrial Fibrillation in Acute Myocardial Infarction

Atrial fibrillation can be a complication of an acute MI. If a patient experiences atrial fibrillation as a complication of acute MI, then the patient is at higher risk for other adverse outcomes (January et al., 2014). Immediate cardioversion is recommended with concomitant treatment with intravenous beta blockers to slow the heart rate if acute heart failure and significant left ventricular dysfunction are absent. Intravenous digoxin or amiodarone can also be used to slow the heart rate. Class IC antiarrhythmics are contraindicated in acute MI. Anticoagulation with warfarin is also recommended for those patients who are not contraindicated by a CHA2DS2-VASc score greater than 2 (January et al., 2014).

Atrial Fibrillation With Hypertrophic Cardiomyopathy

Atrial fibrillation is a common complication of HCM. Patients with HCM are also among the patients who are most dependent on the atrial kick to maintain adequate cardiac output. These patients can experience considerable loss of cardiac output and potential syncope with the development of atrial fibrillation. Disopyramide and amiodarone, combined with a beta blocker or a nondihydropyridine calcium channel blocker, are the two preferred antiarrhythmic regimens for maintaining sinus rhythm. Catheter ablation can be beneficial if antiarrhythmics are not tolerated or efficacious. Anticoagulation is also recommended for patients independent of their CHA2DS2-VASc scores (January et al., 2014).

Atrial Fibrillation With Wolff-Parkinson-White Syndrome

Patients with WPW syndrome have an accessory pathway that connects the atria to the ventricles. During atrial fibrillation, conduction from the rapidly firing atria can travel over the accessory pathway and cause a faster ventricular response than conduction through the AV node. If this rapidly conducted atrial fibrillation is treated with the typical agents that slow conduction over the AV node, there is an increased conduction over the accessory pathway. The ventricular response may be so rapid that the rhythm can deteriorate to ventricular fibrillation. Long-term treatment involves ablation of the accessory pathway. If the patient is hemodynamically unstable, then electrical cardioversion is indicated. For patients with WPW syndrome who are in atrial fibrillation and are hemodynamically stable but have a wide QRS on the ECG, intravenous procainamide or ibutilide is recommended to restore sinus rhythm. If the patient is hemodynamically stable with a narrow QRS, then intravenous medications that slow conduction over the accessory pathway may be considered for rate control (January et al., 2014). These medications are listed in Box 10-3. Notably, amiodarone, adenosine, and non-dihydropyridine calcium channel blockers can be potentially harmful.

BOX 10-3: MEDICATION OPTIONS FOR RATE CONTROL IN ATRIAL FIBRILLATION WITH WOLFF-PARKINSON-WHITE SYNDROME

- Procainamide

- Disopyramide

- Ibutilide

- Amiodarone

Note. Adapted from Fuster, V., Rydén, L. E., Cannom, D. S., Crijns, H. J., Curtis, A. B., Ellenbogen, K. A., … Wann, L. S. (2011). 2011 ACCF/AHA/HRS focused updates incorporated into the ACC/AHA/ESC 2006 guidelines for the management of patients with atrial fibrillation: A report of the American College of Cardiology Foundation/American Heart Association Task Force on Practice Guidelines. *Circulation, 123*(10), e269-e367. doi:10.1161/CIR.0b013e318214876d

NURSING APPLICATION

It is important to know the history of WPW syndrome in patients with atrial fibrillation. If an accessory pathway is present, patients are at risk for a rapid ventricular response. Patients in atrial fibrillation with known WPW syndrome are treated differently from those without WPW syndrome. Medications

that slow conduction through the AV node (including adenosine, amiodarone, calcium channel blockers, and digoxin) are not indicated in the treatment of atrial fibrillation in the presence of WPW syndrome.

Acute, Hemodynamically Unstable Atrial Fibrillation

Patients with new-onset atrial fibrillation (less than 48 hours in duration) and rapid ventricular rates who are hemodynamically unstable need emergency electrical cardioversion. Patients should be given unfractionated heparin, low-molecular-weight heparin, factor XA, or direct thrombin inhibitors (new oral anticoagulants) before cardioversion. Immediate cardioversion should also be performed in situations in which rate control in atrial fibrillation cannot be achieved with pharmacological treatment, including in the presence of acute MI or angina, symptomatic hypotension, and heart failure.

Rate control is always the first goal in atrial fibrillation with rapid ventricular response. When rate control cannot be achieved through pharmacotherapy, the patient is at risk for becoming hemodynamically unstable, and electrical cardioversion should be considered. Studies of DCCV in the emergency department for this group of patients with atrial fibrillation demonstrate decreased mortality (January et al., 2014).

CASE STUDY

Bob is a 72-year-old male patient who visits his cardiologist for occasional "spells" of palpitations when he gets into bed to sleep at night. He reports this occurring almost every day the past week and feels it is getting worse. The nurse in the cardiology office obtains a 12-lead ECG, which shows that Bob is in atrial fibrillation with a heart rate of 84 beats/min. Bob denies syncope, chest pain, dyspnea, or other complaints. He has noticed left calf pain. Bob reports no fever, chills, or recent illnesses while the nurse is updating his health history.

His medical history includes glaucoma and mild dyslipidemia. Bob controls his dyslipidemia by modifying his diet. Bob states that he has never had a surgery. He does not know his family history and only takes a daily dose of vitamin D and baby aspirin for home medications. He has never smoked tobacco or used illicit drugs. He is now abstinent from alcohol use and only drank socially when he was younger. His daughter feels he has been more forgetful and occasionally seems to slur his words when speaking. Bob's vital signs and physical examination findings are as follows:

Vital signs:	Temp 97.8°F, BP 144/76 mmHg, HR 84 bpm, RR 22 breaths/min, SpO$_2$ 95% on room air
Constitutional:	Nontoxic, in no acute distress, nonanxious
HEENT:	Anicteric, no conjunctivitis, PERRL, pink and moist mucous membranes, no oral lesions, thrush, or exudate
Neck:	Supple, nontender, no masses appreciated, jugular venous distension present, left carotid bruit present, no lymphadenopathy
Lungs:	Clear to auscultation bilaterally, anteriorly, and posteriorly
Heart:	Regularly irregular, no murmurs, gallops, or rubs
Abdomen:	Nondistended, obese, decreased bowel sounds, no bruits, nontender, soft, no pulsatile masses or palpable organ borders
Extremities:	Left lower extremity with non-pitting swelling and tenderness upon palpation of the calf. No tenderness, swelling, redness noted to the right lower extremity. All distal pulses are palpable equally

Questions

1. What initial treatments are most appropriate for Bob's new diagnosis of atrial fibrillation?

2. Given his symptoms, for which complication should Bob be evaluated?

Answers

1. The overall goal of treatment in atrial fibrillation is to reduce symptoms, reduce the duration and frequency of episodes, and reduce the risk for stroke. Because Bob has reported symptoms lasting longer than 48 hours, treatment of the dysrhythmia should be aimed at rate control, an all-cause reduction in mortality, and avoidance of increased complications with rhythm-control therapies. If symptoms of atrial fibrillation are present with effective rate control, then cardioversion may be considered. For the prevention of stroke, the patient's risk for stroke should be calculated using the CHA2DS2-VASc tool. If his score is greater than 2 on this tool, anticoagulant therapy should be considered with further consideration to his risk for bleeding.

2. Given Bob's report of leg pain, his daughter's concern of confusion and slurred speech, and the cardiologist's examination findings of a left carotid bruit and left lower-extremity pain and swelling, the patient may have experienced a thromboembolic complication (e.g., deep vein thrombosis and stroke). The cardiologist further evaluates Bob to confirm these possible diagnoses by ordering ultrasound imaging of the affected extremity and carotids, as well as brain imaging.

SUMMARY

Atrial fibrillation is a common, chronic cardiac dysrhythmia with no current definitive cure. It can be caused by or can complicate many other cardiac disorders. Patients with atrial fibrillation are at risk for acute decompensation from rapid ventricular response and are also at risk for long-term hemodynamic and thromboembolic complications. The increased risk for stroke is one of the most life-threatening complications. Long-term anticoagulation is required in patients with atrial fibrillation with a CHA_2DS_2-VASc score of 2 or more to reduce the risk for stroke.

Rate control is an important aspect of treatment for all patients with atrial fibrillation. Patients who are symptomatic also have the option of rhythm control through pharmacological or electrical cardioversion. Most patients require ongoing antiarrhythmic medications to maintain sinus rhythm. Future improvements in ablative techniques may offer more definitive treatment to a larger number of patients with atrial fibrillation, including those who have previously been categorized as having permanent atrial fibrillation.

Nurses outside the cardiac arena are likely to care for patients with atrial fibrillation and play a crucial role in the management of these patients. Assessment of the initial and ongoing rhythm, symptoms, hemodynamic status (blood pressure and heart rate), and potential complications are key nursing considerations. Patient education regarding compliance with anticoagulation and antithrombotic medication is critical to the patient in persistent or permanent atrial fibrillation to prevent devastating thromboembolic complications.

EXAM QUESTIONS

CHAPTER 10
Questions 52–55

Note: Choose the one option that BEST answers each question.

52. Which condition is a potential cause of atrial fibrillation?

    a. Obstructive sleep apnea
    b. Osteoarthritis
    c. Hyperglycemia
    d. Varicose veins

53. Which type of atrial fibrillation is likely to occur in a healthy 40-year-old patient?

    a. Idiopathic atrial fibrillation
    b. Nonvalvular atrial fibrillation
    c. Neurogenic atrial fibrillation
    d. Permanent atrial fibrillation

54. Which rate-control medication does the nurse anticipate administering to a patient with atrial fibrillation and a rapid ventricular response?

    a. Flecainide
    b. Procainamide
    c. Verapamil
    d. Warfarin

55. Which treatment for atrial fibrillation involves creating linear scars in the atria?

    a. Direct current cardioversion
    b. Permanent pacemaker placement
    c. Atrial defibrillator placement
    d. Catheter ablation

REFERENCES

American Heart Association. (2016). *What is atrial fibrillation?* Retrieved from http://www.heart.org/HEARTORG/Conditions/Arrhythmia/AboutArrhythmia/What-is-Atrial-Fibrillation-AFib-or-AF_UCM_423748_Article.jsp#.V2L8Zk1wVjo

Anderson, J. L., Halperin, J. L., Wann, L. S., Curtis, A. B., Ellenbogen, K. A., Estes, N. A., ... Tracy, C. M. (2013). Management of patients with atrial fibrillation (compilation of 2006 ACCF/AHA/ESC and 2011 ACCF/AHA/HRS recommendations): A report of the American College of Cardiology/American Heart Association Task Force on Practice Guidelines. *Journal of the American College of Cardiology, 61*(18), 1935-1944. doi:10.1016/j.jacc.2013.02.001

Anderson, K. M. (2016). *The advanced practice nurse cardiovascular clinician.* New York, NY: Springer Publishing Co.

De Backer, O., Arnous, S., Ihlemann, N., Vejlstrup, N., Jorgensen, E., Pehrson, S., ... Franzen, O. W. (2014). Percutaneous left atrial appendage occlusion for stroke prevention in atrial fibrillation: An update. *Open Heart, 1*(1), e000020. doi:10.1136/openhrt-2013-000020

Fuster, V., Rydén, L. E., Cannom, D. S., Crijns, H. J., Curtis, A. B., Ellenbogen, K. A., ... Wann, L. S. (2011). 2011 ACCF/AHA/HRS focused updates incorporated into the ACC/AHA/ESC 2006 guidelines for the management of patients with atrial fibrillation: A report of the American College of Cardiology Foundation/American Heart Association Task Force on Practice Guidelines. *Circulation, 123*(10), e269-e367. doi:10.1161/CIR.0b013e318214876d

Huether, S. E., & McCance, K. L. (2017). *Understanding pathophysiology* (6th ed.). St. Louis, MO: Elsevier.

January, C. T., Wann, L. S., Alpert, J. S., Calkins, H., Cigarroa, J. E., Cleveland, J. C., ... Yancy, C. W. (2014). 2014 AHA/ACC/HRS guideline for the management of patients with atrial fibrillation: Executive summary: A report of the American College of Cardiology/American Heart Association Task Force on Practice Guidelines and the Heart Rhythm Society. *Circulation, 130*(23), 2071. doi:10.1161/CIR.0000000000000040

Kasper, D., Fauci, A., Hauser, S., Longo, D., Jameson, J., & Loscalzo, J. (2015). *Harrison's principles of internal medicine* (Vol. 1 and 2, 19th ed.). New York, NY: McGraw-Hill.

Lin, T. T., Yang, Y. H., Liao, M. T., Tsai, C. T., Hwang, J. J., Chiang, F. T., … Lin, L. Y. (2015). Primary prevention of atrial fibrillation with angiotensin-converting enzyme inhibitors and angiotensin receptor blockers in patients with end-stage renal disease undergoing dialysis. *Kidney International, 88*(2), 378-385. doi:10.1038/ki.2015.96

Menezes, A. R., Lavie, C. J., DiNicolantonio, J. J., O'Keefe, J., Morin, D. P., Khatib, S., & Milani, R. V. (2013). Atrial fibrillation in the 21st century: A current understanding of risk factors and primary prevention strategies. *Mayo Clinic Proceedings, 88*(4), 394-409. doi:10.1016/j.mayocp.2013.01.022

Mozaffarian, D., Benjamin, E. J., Go, A. S., Arnett, D. K., Blaha, M. J., Cushman, M., … Turner MB (2015). Heart disease and stroke statistics – 2015 update: A report from the American Heart Association. *Circulation.* doi: 10.1161/CIR.0000000000000350

Plicht, B., Konorza, T. F., Kahlert, P., Al-Rashid, F., Kaelsch, H., Jánosi, R. A. … Erbel, R. (2013). Risk factors for thrombus formation on the Amplatzer Cardiac Plug after left atrial appendage occlusion. *JACC: Cardiovascular Interventions, 6*(6), 606-613. doi:10.1016/j.jcin.2013.02.014

Urden, L. D., Stacy, K. M., & Lough, M. E. (2015). *Critical care nursing diagnosis and management* (7th ed.). St. Louis, MO: Elsevier/Mosby.

Van Gelder, I. C., Hagens, V. E., Bosker, H. A., Kingma, J. H., Kamp, O., Kingma, T., … Crijns, H. J. (2002). A comparison of rate control and rhythm control in patients with recurrent persistent atrial fibrillation. *New England Journal of Medicine, 347*(23), 1834-1840. doi:10.1056/NEJMoa021375

Wadke, R. (2013). Atrial fibrillation. *Disease-a-Month, 59*(3), 67-73. doi:10.1016/j.disamonth.2012.12.002

Wynn, G. J., Todd, D. M., Webber, M., Bonnett, L., McShane, J., Kirchhof, P., & Gupta, D. (2014). The European Heart Rhythm Association symptom classification for atrial fibrillation: Validation and improvement through a simple modification. *Europace, 16*(7), 965-972. doi:10.1093/europace/eut395

Wyse, D. G., Van Gelder, I. C., Ellinor, P. T., Go, A. S., Kalman, J. M., Narayan, S. M., … Rienstra, M. (2014). Lone atrial fibrillation: Does it exist? *Journal of the American College of Cardiology, 63*(17), 1715. doi:10.1016/j.jacc.2014.01.023

Wyse, D. G., Waldo, A. L., DiMarco, J. P., Domanski, M. J., Rosenberg, Y., Schron, E. B., … Corley, S. D.; Atrial Fibrillation Follow-up Investigation of Rhythm Management (AFFIRM) Investigators. (2002). A comparison of rate control and rhythm control in patients with atrial fibrillation. *New England Journal of Medicine, 347*(23), 1825-1833. doi:10.1056/NEJMoa021328

CHAPTER 11

DISEASES OF THE AORTA AND PERIPHERAL VASCULATURE

LEARNING OUTCOME

After completing this chapter, the learner will be able to describe the nursing management associated with patients diagnosed with diseases of the aorta and peripheral vasculature.

CHAPTER OBJECTIVES

After completing this chapter, the learner will be able to:

1. Identify pathophysiological factors associated with the development of diseases of the aorta or the peripheral vasculature.

2. Discuss nursing management of patients with diseases of the aorta or the peripheral vasculature.

3. Identify effective medical treatment for patients with diseases of the aorta or the peripheral vasculature.

4. Differentiate between the clinical presentation of peripheral arterial disease and chronic venous disease.

INTRODUCTION

Diseases of the aorta and peripheral vasculature present costly burdens to the health of millions of Americans (Mozaffarian et al., 2015). The appropriate management of these patients is often complex and requires multiple

strategies for treatment and prevention of further disease development. The cardiovascular nurse must be able to comprehensively recognize the factors involved in the pathogenesis of these diseases, apply that knowledge accordingly, recognize and differentiate between acute and chronic presentations of these diseases, and facilitate patient management and treatment for these diseases. Although there are many diseases of the aorta and peripheral vasculature, this chapter will discuss the most common ones: aortic aneurysm, chronic venous disease, and peripheral arterial disease.

AORTIC ANEURYSMS

The aorta is the large central artery that delivers blood and oxygen to the body. It starts after the aortic valve and ends at the bifurcation of the iliac arteries (see Figure 11-1). An *aneurysm* is a local dilation or outpouching of a vessel wall or of a ventricular wall of the heart (Huether & McCance, 2017). This section will focus on aneurysms that occur in the aorta.

A *true aneurysm* involves all three layers of the artery wall and is described as a weakening of the vessel. The dilation or outpouching of the weakened area develops because of the arterial blood pressure pushing against this area of low wall tension. Large vessels, such as the aorta, must have vascular walls with the capacity, or tension, to withstand the internal

FIGURE 11-1: ANATOMY OF THE AORTA

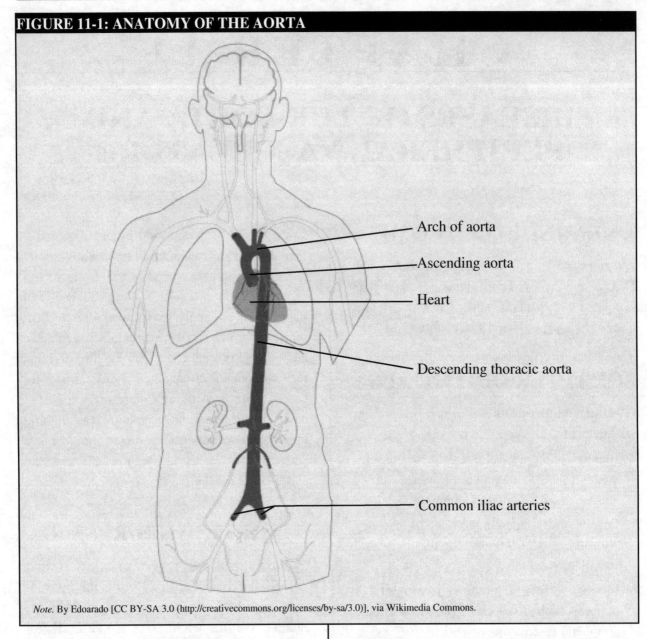

Arch of aorta

Ascending aorta

Heart

Descending thoracic aorta

Common iliac arteries

Note. By Edoarado [CC BY-SA 3.0 (http://creativecommons.org/licenses/by-sa/3.0)], via Wikimedia Commons.

pressures generated by blood flow. Arteries have thicker vessel walls to support directing high-pressure blood flow. These thicker walls result in increased wall tension. The majority of true aneurysms develop circumferentially and are described as *fusiform* (see Figure 11-2). Aneurysms that do not develop around the full radius of the vessel and develop a spherical shape are described as *saccular* aneurysms (Huether & McCance, 2017).

False aneurysms involve the collection of blood within the vessel walls, or hematoma, communicating with the intravascular space (see Figure 11-2). These aneurysms are most often caused by a leak between a vascular graft and a natural artery at the site of anastomosis. False aneurysms can also be caused by cannulation of the vessel wall during invasive procedures and were formerly known as pseudoaneurysms. False aneurysms are generally iatrogenic (i.e., caused by medical examination or treatment; Huether & McCance, 2017).

True aneurysms most commonly occur in the thoracic or abdominal aorta. There are

FIGURE 11-2: AORTIC ANEURYSMS

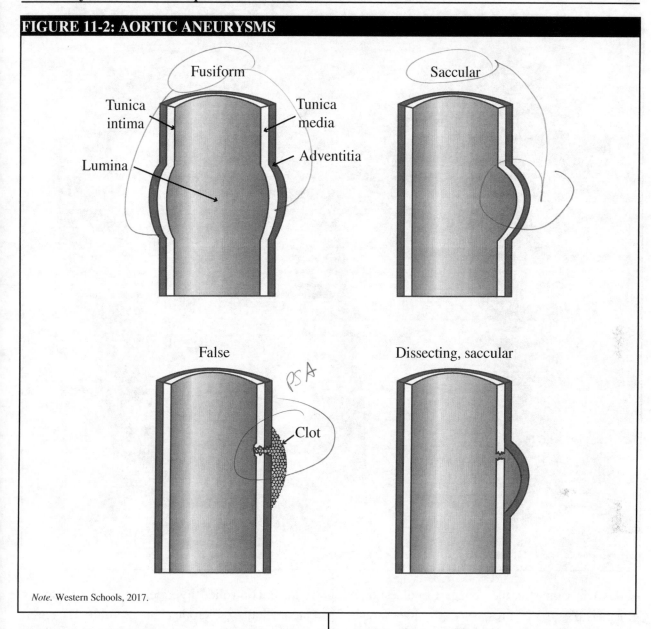

Note. Western Schools, 2017.

multiple classification systems based on the location of the aneurysm and/or type of aneurysmal dissection (separation of vessel wall layers) (Hiratzka et al., 2010). The DeBakey and Stanford classifications are the most commonly used and refer to aneurysmal dissections (illustrated in Figure 11-3). These classifications will be referred to throughout the remainder of this chapter (Hiratzka et al., 2010).

Prevalence

Aortic aneurysm is a major primary cause of death within the United States, but mortality rates have trended downward over the last few years. Aortic aneurysm was the primary cause for more than 17,215 deaths in the year 2009 and 9,863 deaths in 2014 (Centers for Disease Control and Prevention, 2015; Go et al., 2013). Thoracic aortic aneurysms occur less frequently than AAAs but are more deadly (Mozaffarian et al., 2015). The prevalence of AAA is higher in men than in women. The prevalence rate of AAA ranging from 2.9 to 4.9 cm in diameter in men between 45 and 54 years of age is 1.3%, and it increases to 12.5% for men between 75 and 84 years of age. In comparison, the prevalence rate

FIGURE 11-3: AORTIC ANEURYSM CLASSIFICATIONS

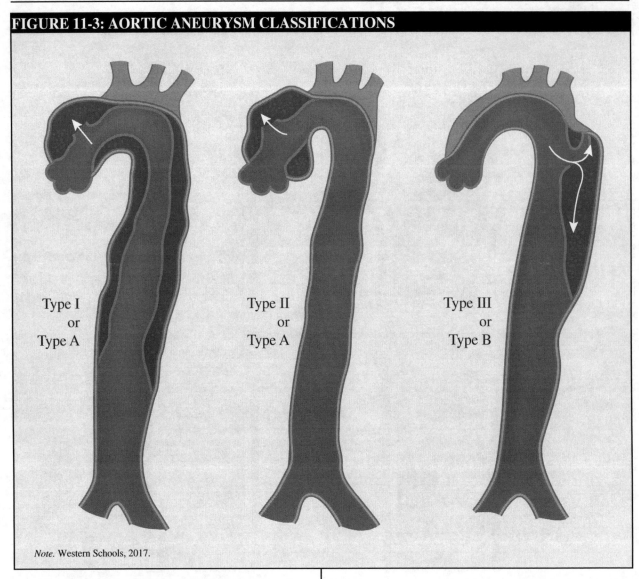

Type I
or
Type A

Type II
or
Type A

Type III
or
Type B

Note. Western Schools, 2017.

of AAA in women in the youngest to oldest age groups is 0% to 5.2%, respectively (Mozaffarian et al., 2015). Growth rates of AAAs were found to average 2.21 mm per year independent of age and sex. However, these rates are higher in smokers (by 0.33 mm/year) and lower in individuals with diabetes (by 0.52 mm/year). Rupture rates are higher in smokers and women despite the lower prevalence of AAA in women.

Causes

The majority of patients diagnosed with aortic aneurysm have a history of systemic hypertension, which places the aorta under the condition of persistent high stress (especially with uncontrolled hypertension). Other causes include atherosclerotic changes within the aorta, blunt trauma, Marfan's syndrome (connective tissue disorder), syphilis or other infections involving the arterial walls, pregnancy, or a penetrating injury or dissection (Huether & McCance, 2017; Scruth & Haynes, 2014). Behavioral, or modifiable, factors associated with increased risk for aortic aneurysm development include diet and smoking (Huether & McCance, 2017; Mozaffarian et al., 2015).

Pathophysiology

The outpouching or ballooning of the vessel wall can occur at any location along the aorta secondary to a weakened area of the layers of the vessel and increased pressures within the intravascular space further decreasing wall tension. According to the *law of Laplace,* the pressure required to inflate a sphere is equal to twice the surface tension divided by the radius of the sphere ($p = 2T/r$). This means the blood pressure must be greater than the wall tension of the aorta to maintain lumen patency. When the wall tension is less than adequate, the blood pressure within the localized area of weakened vessel causes an aneurysm to form. This process is most often gradual over a period of years; however, specific risk factors such as smoking, infections, or genetic conditions can accelerate the growth of an aneurysm (Huether & McCance, 2017).

Aortic Aneurysm and Dissection

Aortic dissection involves the aneurysm perforating and separating the layers of the aortic vessel walls and allowing blood to accumulate into that space to form a false lumen via a tear within the intima (see Figures 11-2 and 11-3). The location of the dissection is directly connected to the patient's risk for death or disabling morbidity. For instance, patients with ascending thoracic aneurysm and dissection are at high risk for tamponade and subsequent cardiogenic shock, myocardial infarction, and/or stroke that lead to imminent death or significant disabilities. Patients with thoracic aortic dissections have a higher mortality rate than those with AAA dissections. AAA dissections are associated with higher complication rates such as mesenteric ischemia, acute kidney injury and chronic kidney disease (CKD), limb ischemia, and refractory pain despite endovascular or other surgical repair (Mozaffarian et al., 2015). Rupture, or dissection, of AAAs is most commonly associated with those aneurysms larger than 5 cm and is significantly more common in women than in men (18% versus 12%, respectively; Mohler, 2016). Higher postoperative repair mortality rates are associated with those patients who experience preoperative hypotension, shock, and signs of poor organ perfusion (Moll et al., 2011).

The DeBakey and Stanford systems classify aortic dissections into different subtypes. The DeBakey classification system divides aortic dissections into three main categories based on the origin of the intimal tear and extent of the dissection.

- Type I dissection originates in the ascending aorta propagating distally to include at least the aortic arch or a portion of the descending aorta.

- Type II dissection originates and is confined to the ascending aorta.

- Type III thoracic aortic dissection has two subtypes.

  1. Type IIIa is limited to the descending thoracic aorta.

  2. Type IIIb extends beyond the level of the diaphragm into the abdominal cavity.

(Hiratzka et al., 2010)

The Stanford classification system is organized into two types distinguished by whether the dissection involves the ascending aorta, without considering the point of origin of the intimal tear.

- Type A dissections involve the ascending aorta.

- Type B dissections may involve the aortic arch but do not include the ascending aorta.

(Hiratzka et al., 2010)

Abdominal aortic aneurysms (AAA) are not classified but are referred to in terms of their proximity to the vessels branching from the aorta (e.g., gastric artery, mesenteric artery, or renal artery). All aneurysms have the potential for fatal hemodynamic instability because a significant portion of cardiac output accumulates within the false lumen in lieu of the intravascular spaces responsible for the perfusion of the body's organs and tissues (Huether & McCance, 2017; Scruth & Haynes, 2014).

An aortic dissection is a surgical emergency regardless of whether it involves the thoracic aorta or the abdominal aorta (Anderson et al., 2013). Depending on the progression of the dissection, the false lumen can thrombose over time and the thrombosed false lumen can provide some degree of stability for an unpredictable period of time. This type of dissection is known as an intramural hematoma (Hiratzka et al., 2010).

NURSING APPLICATION

The location of the aneurysm is important to apply toward the analysis of physical examination findings and toward anticipating the patient's treatment plan. For instance, all patients with aneurysms involving the ascending aorta are surgical candidates but also have the highest risk for mortality (Hiratzka et al., 2010). Distinguishing thoracic from abdominal aneurysms helps to guide patient assessment and treatment planning.

Clinical Presentation

The existence of an aortic aneurysm is not always obvious before it reaches the point of dissection. Clinical presentations are dependent on the location and size of the aneurysm. Aortic aneurysms less than 4 cm are not commonly associated with patient complaints (Scruth & Haynes, 2014). Thoracic aneurysms most often cause the patient to present with or complain of central anterior chest pain or midscapular back pain described as a burning, ripping, or tearing sensation (Hiratzka et al., 2010). Other complaints include dysphagia (difficulty swallowing), dyspnea, ischemic symptoms in any of the extremities, neurological deficits, and mental sta-

tus changes. Abdominal aneurysms can cause the patient to present with or report a slow-growing pulsatile abdominal mass; thoracic, abdominal, or lower back pain radiating down the back, abdomen, or legs; constipation; or signs and symptoms of neurovascular compromise to the lower extremities (e.g., pain, numbness, tingling, paresis, or cold skin temperature). Complaints of the sudden onset of tearing or ripping chest pain radiating down the back or down to the extremities are most commonly associated with aortic dissection (Huether & McCance, 2017; Scruth & Haynes, 2014).

When collecting a family history, the nurse should identify whether any relatives died of sudden cardiac death. A paternal history of sudden death around the age of 45 years may suggest acute aortic dissection as a possible causative factor. Histories that reveal relatives with Marfan's syndrome or other connective tissue disorders should also be considered when determining whether patients are at risk for aortic aneurysm or dissection (Hiratzka et al., 2010).

Physical Examination

During a routine examination, in the supine position, the deep palpation of a pulsatile mass left of the midline within the epigastric to upper umbilical region can indicate an AAA. Thoracic aneurysms are often found on examination of the chest radiograph, incidentally manifesting as abnormally shaped vascular pedicles or widened mediastinal spaces. Other physical examination findings associated with aortic aneurysms include decreased capillary refills, cool skin, and signs of neurovascular compromise of distal extremities. Aortic dissection is associated with hemodynamic instability that can initially present as hypertension and progress to hypotension with a widening pulse pressure. Other examination findings with acute dissection of the aorta include fleeting peripheral pulses, peripheral ischemic signs (e.g., mottled skin or pallor), and a new aortic regurgitation murmur (Huether & McCance, 2017; Lough, 2014; Scruth & Haynes, 2014). The presence of limb ischemia is highly associated with end organ ischemia (Hiratzka et al., 2010). High-risk findings that should be acknowledged as red flag findings include those listed in Table 11-1.

End Organ Ischemic Injuries

Ischemic injuries to the body's tissues and organs can occur as perfusion deficits or postobstructive arterial thrombosis causing intravascular lumen compression secondary to dissection. Such injuries can affect any tissue within the body, but most commonly affect the neurological, cardiovascular, pulmonary, digestive, and renal systems. Thoracic aneurysm cause the most ischemic injuries and, therefore, are the leading cause of aortic aneurysm-related deaths (Hiratzka et al., 2010; Huether & McCance, 2017).

Cardiac Complications

The heart is the organ most commonly affected by ascending aortic aneurysmal dissections. Clinical manifestations of cardiac complications secondary to thoracic aortic dissection can present differently. For instance, acute aortic regurgitation occurs most commonly (41% to 76%) because of aortic root dilation impeding adequate valve closure and manifesting as a new diastolic murmur that may or may not be associated with secondary hemodynamic compromise or shock (Hiratzka et al., 2010).

Other cardiac complications include myocardial ischemia or infarction, or both, secondary to decreased intravascular cardiac output. Clinical manifestations of these complications are indistinguishable from those of acute coronary syndromes (see more detailed discussion in Chapter 13).

TABLE 11-1: HIGH-RISK CLINICAL FINDINGS ASSOCIATED WITH AORTIC DISSECTION

High-Risk Features	Clinical Findings
Historical features	• Connective tissue disorders (e.g., Marfan's syndrome, Turner's syndrome, Loeys-Dietz syndrome) • Gene mutations *FBN1, TGFBR1, TGFBR2, ACTA2,* and *MYH11* • Familial history of aortic dissection or sudden cardiac death before age 50 years • Known aortic valve disease • Recent aortic intravascular procedure (e.g., coronary angiogram or intervention) • Known aortic aneurysm • Syncope
Pain features in the chest, back, or abdomen	• Abrupt or sudden onset • Severe intensity • Ripping, tearing, stabbing, or sharp quality
Physical examination features	• Pulse deficit • Systolic blood pressure limb differential ≥20 mmHg • Focal neurological deficit • New aortic regurgitation murmur • Palpable, pulsatile abdominal mass within the epigastric to supraumbilical regions

Note. From Western Schools.

Heart failure and shock are other cardiac complications associated with a dissected thoracic aneurysm that could be secondary to the development of aortic valve insufficiency, acute myocardial infarction, or cardiac tamponade. Clinical manifestations may include symptoms of angina and signs of shock (cardiogenic or hypovolemic).

Cardiac tamponade is diagnosed in 8% to 10% of patients with aortic dissection and a pericardial effusion caused by the accumulation of blood into false aneurysmal lumen draining blood into the pericardial sac per gravity (Hiratzka et al., 2010). This complication is an ominous predictor of poor outcomes and the leading cause of mortality in patients diagnosed with ascending aortic dissections. Clinical manifestations of cardiac tamponade include hypotension, narrowing pulse pressure, and pulse deficit, as well as evidence of systemic neurovascular compromise or ischemia, such as mental status changes, cool distal extremities, or mottled skin (Hiratzka et al., 2010; Huether & McCance, 2017).

Syncope is another well-known thoracic aortic dissection-related complication, occurring in approximately 13% of patients, secondary to tamponade, decreased cardiac output, or arrhythmias occurring as a result of myocardial ischemia (Hiratzka et al., 2010).

NURSING APPLICATION

Hemodynamic considerations must be anticipated in the patient with aortic dissection. Nurses may need to take blood pressure readings in both arms and both legs to identify the highest central blood pressure (Hiratzka et al., 2010). The nurse must also be prepared for hemodynamic monitoring and should prepare the monitoring equipment (e.g., setting up the bedside monitor, priming pressure tubing, and preparing to assist the medical provider in line placement).

Neurological Complications

Neurological complications occur with all types of aortic dissections on a spectrum of severity. For instance, ascending aortic dissections propagate central neurological deficits, whereas AAAs may have localized deficits at the level of the spinal nerve injured or distal tissue (e.g., legs or feet). Such neurological injuries can result from hypotension, malperfusion, thromboembolism, or nerve compression. The most common neurological complications are ischemic stroke (predominantly within the right cerebral hemisphere) and ischemic neuropathy (described as limb pain or paresis), which occur in 53% and 37% of patients with aortic dissection, respectively (Hiratzka et al., 2010). Another less common (1% to 3%) neurological complication that can occur with thoracic aortic dissections is paraplegia secondary to malperfusion of the thoracic spinal cord (Hiratzka et al., 2010).

Pulmonary Complications

The most common pulmonary system complication is a pleural effusion, which occurs in approximately 16% of patients with thoracic aortic dissections (Hiratzka et al., 2010). Small pleural effusions are usually exudative and found to be associated with an inflammatory response. Large effusions were more associated with the result of blood leaking from the aorta into the pleural space. Other dissection-related complications involve pulmonary artery compression secondary to intramural thrombosis or blood accumulation. Over time, pulmonary artery compression develops into an aortopulmonary fistula, most often manifesting as dyspnea and least often (in 1% to 3% of patients) manifesting as hemoptysis (Hiratzka et al., 2010).

Gastrointestinal Complications

Mesenteric ischemia is the most common gastrointestinal complication associated with aortic dissections. Mesenteric ischemia is also the most common cause of death in the patient with descending aortic dissections (Hiratzka et al., 2010). Clinical manifestations of mesenteric ischemia can include nonspecific abdominal pain that is out of proportion to physical examination findings and serum markers for bowel ischemia, such as elevated lactic acid, lipase, amylase, or liver enzymes (Scruth & Haynes, 2014).

Gastrointestinal bleeding is rare but can occur as the result of a massive mesenteric infarction or aortoesophageal fistula. Dissection-related gastrointestinal bleeding is associated with significant hemodynamic instability, shock, and poor prognosis (Hiratzka et al., 2010).

Diagnosis

Diagnostic decision making should be guided by the stratification of risk factors for aortic dissection with specific questioning of the high-risk features listed in Table 11-1. Evaluation by serum laboratory markers is non-specific and has little utility in risk stratifica-tion or diagnosis of an aneurysm or dissection. However, identifying those patients who are at low, intermediate, and high risk for dissection is key in determining the extent to which diag-nostic tests should be performed. For instance, those patients with low-to-intermediate risk should be screened by evaluation of a 12-lead electrocardiogram for ST elevation or other ischemic changes, and the evaluation of a chest radiograph (in the anterior, posterior, or lateral view) can identify the presence of mediastinal changes or aortic dilation. These tests are not definitive diagnostic tools but are less invasive and less costly for the screening of aneurysms.

Computed tomography (CT) with intrave-nous contrast performed of the chest, abdomen, and pelvis is the best test to diagnose, locate, and measure the size of an aortic aneurysm from the aortic root to the iliac bifurcation (Hiratzka et al., 2010). The invasive procedure of an aortogram

performed in the cardiac catheterization labora-tory is another definitive diagnostic test. A trans-thoracic or transesophageal echocardiogram can also visualize and measure the size of an aneu-rysm, yet it is limited to user technique and the patient's body habitus (thin-framed versus obese; Hiratzka et al., 2010; Huether & McCance, 2017; Scruth & Haynes, 2014). In the patient with a suspected emergent dissection, a CT scan (pref-erably contrast enhanced) of the chest, abdomen, and pelvis should be performed and not delayed by other tests, such as negative chest radiographs or serum studies, to facilitate timely surgical repair and optimal patient outcome (Hiratzka et al., 2010).

An intramural hematoma may be identified by a contrasted CT study (see Figure 11-4). This finding can differ depending on the age of the hematoma and whether the intimal tear is sealed off and no longer leaking blood into the false lumen. This finding is most common in the older adult and is associated with an acute aortic aneurysm syndrome, but not necessar-ily acute dissection. An intramural hematoma can entirely resolve on its own spontaneously or convert to a classic dissection, indicating the need for surgical repair (Hiratzka et al., 2010).

Nursing Management

The medical management of small aneu-rysms or nonsurgical aneurysms involves decreasing the patient's risk factors for dissection as much as possible. This treatment plan involves strict blood pressure control, lipid profile optimi-zation, and smoking cessation. Patients should be taught lifestyle modifications such as moderate medical provider-approved exercise, changes in diet, and smoking cessation. Patients must be educated and informed that smoking has been linked to a doubling of the growth rate of tho-racic aneurysms (Hiratzka et al., 2010; Moll et al., 2011).

FIGURE 11-4: INTRAMURAL HEMATOMA WITHIN AN AORTIC ANEURYSM

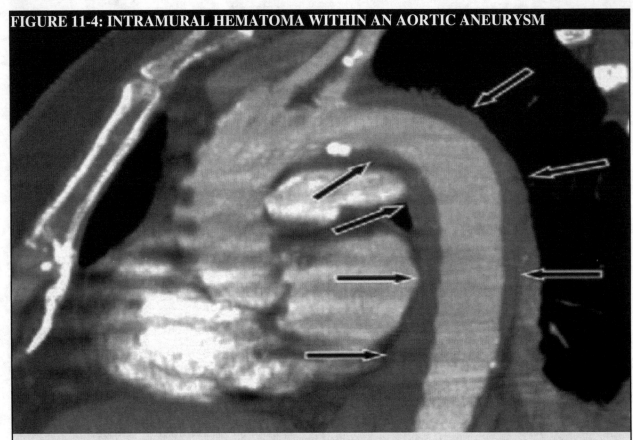

Arrows denote the intramural collection of blood that is not communicating with the intravascular contrasted blood.

Note. From Hiratzka, L. F., Bakris, G. L., Beckman, J. A., Bersin, R. M., Carr, V. F., Casey, D. E., ... Williams, D. M. (2010). 2010 ACCF/AHA/AATS/ACR/ASA/SCA/SCAI/SIR/STS/SVM guidelines for the diagnosis and management of patients with thoracic aortic disease. *Journal of the American College of Cardiology, 55*(14), e27-e129. doi:10.1016/j.jacc.2010.02.015. © Elsevier 2010.

Medical Therapy

Antihypertensive therapy aims to maintain a goal blood pressure less than 140/90 mmHg in patients without diabetes and 130/80 mmHg in patients with diabetes and CKD to reduce the risk for stroke, acute myocardial infarction, heart failure, and cardiovascular death. Medications such as beta blockers and angiotensin-converting enzyme (ACE) inhibitors should be used for blood pressure control (Hiratzka et al., 2010; Moll et al., 2011).

Dyslipidemia therapy aims to reduce the low-density lipoprotein (LDL) cholesterol level to less than 70 mg/dl. Most patients require statin therapy to accomplish this goal. Reducing the LDL cholesterol level with statin therapy is associated with delaying atherogenesis; however, there is not enough research to determine the direct effect on aneurysm growth rates (Hiratzka et al., 2010; Moll et al., 2011).

Initial treatment for acute aortic dissection is aimed at decreasing aortic wall stress by controlling the heart rate and blood pressure with intravenous beta-adrenergic blockers titrated to a target heart rate of 60 beats/min. If beta-blocking agents are contraindicated, intravenous nondihydropyridine calcium-channel-blocking agents should be used for rate control. If the blood pressure remains greater than 120 mmHg when the heart rate is reduced to the desired goal, ACE inhibitors should be administered intravenously to further reduce blood pressure and maintain end organ perfusion. Beta-blocking agents should be administered with caution in the patient with a new aortic regurgitation murmur because the medications will inhibit the compensatory tachycardia response and negatively affect cardiac output. Vasodilators should be avoided in acute dissections because of their association with reflex tachycardia, which can propagate further expansion of the dissection (Hiratzka et al., 2010; Scruth & Haynes, 2014).

Pain control is important in the management of stable and dissecting aneurysms secondary to the sympathetic response associated with increased pain. Uncontrolled pain increases this stress response, thereby increasing the patient's heart rate and blood pressure.

Surgical Therapy

For AAAs, surgical consultation is recommended for female patients whose aneurysms are 4.5 cm or greater and for male patients whose aneurysms are 5.0 to 5.5 cm (Moll et al., 2011). Consultation is also recommended in all patients with an ascending aortic aneurysm because of the risk for postoperative complications, including sudden death, and mortality rates. Otherwise, consultation for a surgical evaluation of other thoracic aneurysms with a diameter of 5.5 cm or greater or a growth rate of 0.5 cm per year is recommended. Patients with genetic mutations predisposing them to aneurysms or connective tissue disorders should be evaluated for surgical repair of smaller aneurysms (4.2 to 4.4 cm in diameter). Patients undergoing aortic valve repair with an aortic root diameter greater than 4.5 cm should be considered for concomitant aortic root repair or replacement to prevent ascending dissections (Hiratzka et al., 2010).

Surgical consultation should be initiated before any medical intervention in the patient with acute aortic dissection. Dissection of an ascending aortic aneurysm has the highest risk for life-threatening complications and should be evaluated by the surgeon urgently to reduce the overall-cause mortality in this patient (Hiratzka et al., 2010). Dissection of the descending aorta could be managed medically as long as no life-threatening complications (e.g., malperfusion syndrome, dissection progression, or inability to control blood pressure) develop (Hiratzka et al., 2010; Moll et al., 2011).

Surgical therapies are dependent on the location and size of the aortic dissection. For instance, a partial aortic root dissection can be treated by resuspending the aortic valve. However, dissection of any other part of the ascending aorta requires resection of the affected vessel and replacement with a graft (Hiratzka et al., 2010). Abdominal aneurysmal dissections are often repaired by endovascular grafting similar to the procedure of a coronary stent placement. However, the location and size of the dissection determines this as well. If endovascular grafting cannot be performed, a vascular or general surgeon performs extravascular grafting (Moll et al., 2011). An intramural hematoma is treated the same as a dissection (Hiratzka et al., 2010; Scruth & Haynes, 2014).

VENOUS DISEASE

Chronic venous disease (CVD) manifests clinically along a spectrum of primary and secondary venous conditions related to chronic venous insufficiency (CVI). For instance, varicose veins, venous valvular incompetence, and thrombus formation within veins all fall along this spectrum. *Chronic venous insufficiency* is defined as inadequate venous return over a long period (greater than 3 to 6 months) that causes persistent ambulatory venous hypertension resulting in multiple venous pathologies such as edema, leg pain, and ulcerations (Eberhardt & Raffetto, 2014). For the purposes of this chapter, CVD and CVI will be used interchangeably.

Prevalence

Approximately 2.5 million people in the United States are diagnosed with CVI, and within this group the incidence increases with age. An estimated 20% of these patients experience development of venous ulcers, which contributes to a significant socioeconomic burden on patients and the healthcare system in general. Following the development of venous ulcers, disability, overall quality of life, and prognosis for recovery are all poor (Eberhardt & Raffetto, 2014).

Causes

Etiological classifications were established to standardize the reporting, diagnosis, and treatment of CVD. The Clinical, Etiology, Anatomic, Pathophysiology (CEAP) classification system provides the opportunity to objectively and uniformly approach the patient with CVD. The CEAP classifications are based on seven categories and whether symptoms are clinically absent or present. The etiological classification distinguishes among congenital (e.g., Klippel-Trenaunay or Parkes Weber syndromes), primary, or secondary causes for CVD. Primary CVD is often of uncertain etiology, whereas secondary CVD occurs as a consequence of a known condition. The anatomic classification identifies the location of dysfunction. For instance, a vein within the superficial venous system may have incompetent valves leading to CVI. The pathophysiological classification describes the underlying pathological mechanism causing the CVD. For instance, venous obstruction explains the cause of CVI (Eberhardt & Raffetto, 2014).

Causes of CVI are most commonly related to progressive atherosclerotic disease. However, other etiological factors include varicose veins (congenital and acquired); valvular incompetence; and inflammatory, infectious, or obstructive conditions such as deep vein thrombosis (DVT) or thrombophlebitis. Although venous valvular incompetence and obstructive causative factors significantly contribute to these mechanisms, dysfunction of the calf muscle pump (contraction of calf muscles during ambulation facilitating venous return) is the primary problem contributing to CVI in the adult older than 70 years (Eberhardt & Raffetto, 2014).

Pathophysiology

Dysfunction of the valves within superficial veins leads to retrograde blood flow, known as *reflux,* resulting in increased hydrostatic venous pressures. Over time, overdistention of these vessels manifests as varicose veins and progresses to edema and ulcerations. Valve failure within deep veins such as the communicating perforator also leads to increased hydrostatic pressures and venous hypertension. Insufficiency within deep veins results in retrograde blood flow back into the superficial venous system and its associated complications (Eberhardt & Raffetto, 2014).

Obstruction to the outflow of venous blood can also cause increased venous pressures, leading to secondary muscle pump dysfunction and CVI. The most common type of obstructive venous disease is DVT. Poor recovery of DVTs associated with postthrombotic venous obstruction is highly associated with venous ulceration development and more rapid progression of CVD. Primary dysfunction of the muscle pump is rare and is associated with neuromuscular conditions or muscle-wasting syndromes. Muscle pump dysfunction results in the ineffective emptying of the venous system, severe reflux, and ultimately a secondary obstructive flow within the venous system in the lower extremities. The hemodynamic changes within the venous vasculature of the lower extremities are transmitted into the microcirculation, resulting in the development of venous microangiopathy (Eberhardt & Raffetto, 2014).

Microangiopathy accounts for the elongation, dilation, and tortuosity of the capillary beds. Other microvascular changes include the thickening of capillary basement membranes with increased collagen and elastic fibers and endothelial damage with widening of interendothelial spaces, resulting in increased capillary permeability and pericapillary edema. Secondary to the prolonged or chronic increased hydrostatic venous pressure and increased capillary permeability, the fluid extravasated into the interstitial space contains plasma proteins, white blood cells, and red blood cells. Biologists postulate the hyperpigmentation of the skin occurs secondary to hemosiderin depositions and chronic eczematous inflammatory cutaneous changes (Huether & McCance, 2017). The ulcerations associated with CVD develop because of the breakdown of subcutaneous tissues produced by increased intracompartmental (or interstitial) fluid volume and pressure. Fibrosis develops in the dermis and subcutaneous fat (called *lipodermatosclerosis*) in the late stages of CVD. The persistent high intracompartmental pressures progress to the obstruction of lymph fluid draining into the venous system, thereby contributing to lymphedema (Eberhardt & Raffetto, 2014).

Clinical Presentation

Patient complaints surrounding CVD describe a progressive, insidious onset of symptoms ranging from esthetic worries about their varicose veins and "spider veins" to more serious concerns about their swelling, nonhealing ulcers, and chronic pain. In the early stages of CVD, patients may describe localized areas of telangiectases or reticular veins. As CVD progresses, complaints related to cutaneous changes (e.g., induration, discolorations, swelling, or slow-healing wounds) and discom-

fort (e.g., leg heaviness, swelling, and pain) increase. As the severity of CVD progresses, patients also report experiencing recurrent episodes of chronic wound infections, thrombophlebitis, cellulitis, and dermatitis (inflammatory changes associated with chronic edematous skin; Eberhardt & Raffetto, 2014).

Physical Examination

The most common physical examination findings in most patients with CVD include telangiectases, reticular veins, and varicose veins. As the disease progresses, interstitial edema accumulates within the perimalleolar region bilaterally and extends up the leg as dependent fluid accumulates. Prolonged standing worsens this finding.

NURSING APPLICATION

Patients with CVD must be instructed to avoid prolonged standing positions or to use compression stockings if standing is recommended.

Hyperpigmentation of the skin develops over time as well. Traumatic injuries to patients with CVD heal poorly and can develop into ulcers. Because of the chronic venous congestion, ulcerations can spontaneously develop without trauma. Venous ulcers most commonly develop in the medial malleolar regions. Palpating the skin may reveal indurated areas, old epithelialized wounds or scars, and concomitant eczematous and lipodermatosclerotic areas (Eberhardt & Raffetto, 2014).

Complications associated with CVD include thrombophlebitis, cellulitis, wound infections, and dermatitis. Physical examination findings associated with these CVD complications are no different from their primary manifestations. For instance, thrombophlebitis can reveal red streaks along the vein with palpable cords that are inflamed, localized swelling, and tenderness to touch. Cellulitis presents as a unilateral localized area of swelling and erythema that is warm to the touch and tender, often secondary to the patient's own skin flora. The dermatitis associated with CVD can be multifactorial and can manifest as localized patches of eczematous areas of skin; bilateral, circumferential erythema; swelling; and diffuse tenderness (Anderson, 2016; Eberhardt & Raffetto, 2014).

Diagnosis

As guided by the CEAP tool, diagnosis is primarily made from clinical findings. However, a few diagnostic tests have some utility in confirming the clinical diagnosis of CVD. For instance, venous duplex imaging is the most common noninvasive technique used to confirm a CVD diagnosis. The direction of blood flow and valve competence are examined utilizing ultrasound and a variety of sonographic maneuvers. The test measures reflux times with the superficial and deep veins. Reflux times greater than 0.5 and 1.0 second in the superficial and deep veins, respectively, indicate venous insufficiency. A longer duration of reflux is indicative of greater severity of the disease. Other noninvasive diagnostic techniques rarely used to confirm CVD diagnosis include air plethysmography and photoplethysmography. Advances in utilizing noninvasive CT and magnetic resonance venography for CVD diagnosis are being researched. CT and magnetic resonance venography are already being used to identify, evaluate, and landmark complex venous anatomy before interventions are performed (Eberhardt & Raffetto, 2014).

Invasive modalities on the path to replacing venous duplex imaging include contrast venography. Contrast venography involves injection of contrast into the dorsum of the foot to visualize the blood flow traveling toward the head or injection of contrast proximally while the patient is in a semivertical position on a tilt table to visualize blood flow toward the foot. This test evaluates the severity of reflux to identify the amount of venous reconstruction necessary for improved patient outcomes. Intravascular ultrasound is another example of an invasive diagnostic test for CVD. The gold standard for assessing the hemodynamics of CVD is ambulatory venous pressure monitoring (Eberhardt & Raffetto, 2014). These pressures are measured in the upright posture at rest and after exercise.

Nursing Management

Compression stockings are the first-line therapy for and the mainstay of conservative medical management for the patient with CVD. Stockings generating 30 to 40 mmHg of compression result in a significant improvement in pain, swelling, skin hyperpigmentation, activity, and overall well-being if compliance with wearing them is 70% to 80%. Other measures aim to reduce symptoms and prevent progression of the disease. Maintaining an ideal body weight has demonstrated improvement in manifestations of CVI; thus, obesity prevention or weight reduction is recommended. Skin and wound care using topical moisturizers is important to maintain skin health and prevent fissuring and skin breakdown. With consideration to calf muscle pump dysfunction being associated with high rates of CVI, daily structured calf muscle exercises were found to improve calf muscle pump function. Therefore, supplementing CVD therapies with a prescribed, daily, and structured calf exercise regimen may benefit these patients (Eberhardt & Raffetto, 2014).

Medical Therapy

Four groups of pharmacological therapies for CVD – coumarins, flavonoids, saponosides, and plant extracts – are being used and evaluated in European countries, but they are not approved for use in the United States. These drugs have venoactive properties thought to improve vascular tone and capillary permeability. Their exact mechanisms of action are still not largely known. Other medications such as aspirin and pentoxifylline administered with the use of compression therapy are being studied to evaluate their possible benefits of improved wound healing and patient comfort. However, these therapies have not been approved by the U.S. Food and Drug Administration for this indication while more research is being conducted (Eberhardt & Raffetto, 2014).

Surgical Therapy

Surgical interventions range from laser therapies to sclerose varicosities, ablation of incompetent valves, or obstruction relief to improve venous outflow to invasive measures of valve reconstruction, resection of affected vein segments, and the ligation of perforator veins contributing to focal high pressures within superficial veins at the site of an ulcer. Regardless of the surgical approach to treatment of CVD, the goal is to eliminate the cause or reduce the amount of increased venous pressures and the progression of the syndromes associated with CVD. Invasive therapies are usually reserved for severe cases with unsatisfactory response to conservative treatments (Eberhardt & Raffetto, 2014).

Outcomes

The majority of patients with CVD experience mild or early manifestations of the syndromes that do not progress to the late, severe presentations. Conservative treatments applied to patients with mild or early CVD syndromes such as varicose veins are inadequate in limiting disease progress. Varicose veins treated with any form of laser therapy are associated with better outcomes and less frequent recurrence than those treated with conservative modalities. Patients with progressive or severe CVD in which venous stasis ulcers have developed are associated with poor outcomes such as repeated infections, higher incidence of DVT,

and disability. Compliance with the application of compression stockings in severe cases of CVD demonstrates better outcomes than some invasive treatments because of the ability of the stockings to apply opposing pressure to the lower extremities and facilitate venous return (Eberhardt & Raffetto, 2014).

PERIPHERAL ARTERIAL DISEASE

*P*eripheral arterial disease (PAD) is the narrowing of peripheral arteries to the legs, stomach, arms, and head (American Heart Association, 2014). PAD is a chronic atherosclerotic condition with a significant risk for developing into an acute occlusive problem, potentially resulting in permanent ischemic injury without intervention. In contrast with many cases of severe venous disease, occlusive PAD (the severe form of PAD) requires hospital and sometimes critical care admission to treat an acute thrombotic occlusion most commonly involving the arteries of the lower extremities (Scruth & Haynes, 2014).

Prevalence

PAD is the leading cause worldwide of peripheral limb ischemia, which compromises ambulation. In the United States, the disease affects less than 4% of patients younger than 40 years and approximately 22% of patients older than 70 years (Ryjewski, 2016; Scruth & Haynes, 2014). Approximately 8.5 million Americans older than 40 years have PAD, and the annual incidence rate in the United States is 2.76%. The disease has the highest prevalence observed among older adults, non-Hispanic African Americans, and women. However, the prevalence of PAD is significantly higher in active smokers than individuals who have never smoked and in patients with persistent, uncontrolled hypertension (Ryjewski, 2016).

Causes

The process of atherosclerosis causes PAD. The most common conditions that are known to contribute to atherogenesis and are highly associated with PAD are diabetes, hypertension, dyslipidemia, and smoking. Persistently uncontrolled hypertension is thought to increase the risk for PAD 4-fold. Smokers were found to have more than a 2-fold increase of PAD development in comparison with patients who never smoked (Ryjewski, 2016).

Pathophysiology

The pathogenesis of PAD is associated with the development and growth of atherosclerotic plaque within arterial walls in response to endothelial injury of the intima. Initial endothelial insults are thought to be caused by excess LDLs or very low density lipoproteins within the bloodstream. Inflammatory responses to repeated endothelial injuries lead to atheroma formations that calcify over time. The calcified plaque growth progresses to flow-limiting stenotic lesions within the vessel, resulting in impaired blood flow to tissues distal to this site. When plaque growth exceeds 50% the diameter of the vessel, the ability of the artery to vasodilate under conditions of increased metabolic demand (i.e., ambulation or physical exertion) is inadequate (Ryjewski, 2016).

Rupture or ulceration of the atherosclerotic plaque produces embolic debris downstream. Plaque rupture activates inflammatory mediators, platelets, and clotting factors to the surface of the break and the embolized debris. Thrombus formation leads to a partial or complete occlusive crisis and subsequent tissue ischemia. As a result of the lack of adequate oxygen, muscles distal to the occlusion fatigue very quickly with exertion, causing acute ischemic pain that is sometimes relieved with rest and elevation of legs from a dependent position, which is slightly lower than or equal to the level of the heart (Ryjewski, 2016).

Clinical Presentation

Asymptomatic

The early and more benign stages of PAD are grossly asymptomatic. However, PAD can also be asymptomatic in later stages in patients with neuropathic disease that prevents the sensation of the pain produced by ischemia. Other factors associated with the patient presenting with PAD include a personal history of diabetes, hypertension, dyslipidemia, CKD, sedentary lifestyle, and tobacco use. A comprehensive health history should inquire about any difficulty walking, ischemic pain, and/or poorly healing wounds. These historical factors and the presence of PAD in a first-order relative are especially important to ask any patient older than 50 years who has atherosclerotic disease (Anderson et al., 2013).

Claudication and Critical Limb Ischemia

The classic clinical features that patients with PAD present with are intermittent claudication (IC) and its more severe form of critical limb ischemia (CLI). *Claudication* is acute pain associated with muscle ischemia. Patients report the inability to tolerate walking the same distances days or weeks before the onset of claudication pain. These pains are generally indicative of occlusive, or partially occlusive, PAD. Other complaints include pallor of the affected extremity, cool skin, numbness, tingling, paresis, and with late findings of occlusive PAD, darkened or dusky toes (Ryjewski, 2016).

Physical Examination

Examination of the patient with PAD should involve a comprehensive peripheral neurovascular assessment. The inspection and palpation for symmetrical findings is key. Patients presenting with acute limb ischemia demonstrate hallmark signs known as the "6 Ps": pain, pulselessness, paresthesias, pallor, paralysis, and polarity or poikilothermia. *Poikilothermia* is a later addition to the 6 Ps that involves the affected extremity assuming the temperature of its environment. When pulselessness is found in the patient, the clinician must recognize that there is arterial occlusion and that this finding is a surgical emergency (Anderson, 2016).

Patients with asymptomatic PAD may still present with signs of decreased perfusion to the distal extremities. For instance, the affected extremity may have less hair distribution, be cooler to touch than the other extremity, show sensory deficits, and have weaker distal pulses (distal from the level of the occlusion) than the other extremity. Asymmetric findings such as those mentioned earlier should provide clues to the clinician for PAD. Other findings associated with chronic PAD ischemia include hair loss, thickened toenails, stasis dermatitis, gangrenous lesions, chronic ulcers, and *rubor* (a reddened color of lower extremities; Anderson, 2016).

Diagnosis

Ankle-Brachial and Toe-Brachial Indexes

Measuring the ankle-brachial index (ABI) is the most effective, objective, cost-effective, and noninvasive test used to diagnose PAD in patients 65 years and older (Anderson, 2016). The resting ABI should be used in all patients suspected to have PAD with one or more of the following findings: age 65 years or older with exertional leg symptoms or nonhealing wounds, or age 50 years and older with a history of smoking or diabetes and exertional leg symptoms (Anderson et al., 2013). A normal resting ABI is 0.91 to 1.30. In asymptomatic patients suspected of having PAD, the resting ABI can be normal, but exercise ABI measurements should also be taken to identify claudication or limb ischemia. Exercise treadmill tests measure preexercise and postexercise ABI values to differentiate arterial claudication from nonarterial claudication, known as *pseudoclaudication.*

Clinicians can also use exercise tests to determine functional capacity, exercise limitations, and safety of exercise (Anderson, 2013).

In patients with an ABI greater than 1.30 but no other clinical evidence of atherosclerosis, a toe-brachial index or pulse volume recording measurement can be useful to diagnose lower-extremity PAD. The ABI should be recorded as noncompressible values if greater than 1.40, normal values if 1.0 to 1.40, borderline if 0.91 to 0.99, and abnormal if 0.90 or less. Noncompressible findings when measuring the ABI are unreliable and are often found in patients with diabetes or severe atherosclerosis. Thus, other diagnostic testing must be performed.

Other Diagnostic Tests for Peripheral Arterial Disease

ABI tests can be used to diagnose claudication and PAD, but they do not diagnose anatomic location or the degree of stenosis. A duplex ultrasound test is used to identify the location and severity of stenosis and is a noninvasive and cost-effective approach for regular surveillance of stenotic lesions before and after surgical intervention. The location and severity of disease guides selection of candidates for surgical intervention. CT angiography and magnetic resonance angiography are also noninvasive methods of visualizing the location and severity of stenosis. Similar to the gold standard for CAD, angiography performed in the cardiac catheterization laboratory is the gold standard for acute occlusive PAD because of the opportunity to intervene after visualization. The limitation to imaging studies not performed by ultrasound is the necessity to use contrast dye. Contrast studies must consider kidney function and hypersensitivities to contrast dye. Patients with existing hypersensitivities to contrast dye or known kidney disease should be premedicated with the appropriate therapies, such as intravenous hydration, diphenhydramine, steroids, and/or acetaminophen.

Patients who undergo angiography per catheter should be re-evaluated no later than 2 weeks after the procedure to assess for complications such as worsened disease secondary to plaque rupture, late hypersensitivity reactions, or deterioration in kidney function (Anderson et al., 2013).

Nursing Management

Cardiovascular risk-reduction strategies are used to reduce the risk for acute events in all patients with risk for atherosclerotic disease or those suspected to have PAD. Medical treatments include interventions that focus on management of behavioral (modifiable) and biological risk factors. Smoking cessation counseling and other forms of tobacco cessation counseling should occur with every visit and should include a quit plan involving pharmacological and nonpharmacological strategies. Diet counseling aimed toward lowering LDL cholesterol and hyperglycemia is also necessary for patients with dyslipidemia.

Medical Therapy

Pharmacological therapies are used to manage thrombotic risks, hypertension, and dyslipidemia (Anderson et al., 2013).

Antithrombotic Drugs

Antiplatelet medications are recommended in patients with PAD to reduce the risk for MI, ischemic stroke, or cardiovascular death. A daily aspirin dose of 75 to 325 mg or a daily clopidogrel dose of 75 mg is found to be a safe and effective treatment for asymptomatic patients with an ABI less than or equal to 0.9 or patients with symptomatic lower-extremity PAD, IC, or CLI. Combination therapy with aspirin and clopidogrel is recommended for patients with PAD perceived to be at high risk for cardiovascular death who are not at an increased risk for bleeding. Studies found that warfarin demonstrated no benefit in reducing the risk for cardiovascular death and increased the risk for major bleeding (Anderson et al., 2013).

Antihypertensive Drugs

All patients with PAD should maintain a blood pressure less than 140/90 mmHg, and those with diabetes or kidney disease should maintain a blood pressure less than 130/80 mmHg. Maintaining blood pressures less than the goal reduces the risk for MI, stroke, heart failure, and cardiovascular death. Beta blockers and ACE inhibitors are recommended medications to treat hypertension in patients with PAD (Anderson et al., 2013).

Lipid-Lowering Drugs

All patients with PAD should maintain LDL cholesterol levels less than 100 mg/dl, and those at very high risk for ischemic events should maintain LDL levels less than 70 mg/dl. Statin medications are recommended as first-line agents to reduce LDL. A fibric acid derivative is recommended for patients with PAD with low high-density lipoprotein cholesterol, normal LDL, and elevated triglycerides (Anderson et al., 2013).

Diabetes Therapies

Patients with PAD and diabetes have increased risk for injury to the feet and lower extremities. In addition to maintaining a hemoglobin A1c less than 7%, proper foot care is important in preventing wounds and promoting healing in existing wounds (Anderson et al., 2013).

Claudication Therapies

All patients with PAD and claudication can benefit from supervised exercise training for a minimum of 30 to 45 minutes at least three times per week. Supervised exercise training is recommended as an initial treatment of IC for a minimum of 12 weeks. Pharmacological therapies for IC include cilostazol and pentoxifylline to improve symptoms and walking distance for patients. Cilostazol is the first-line therapy, and pentoxifylline is recommended as an alternative or second-line therapy. Other studies examining the effectiveness of medical therapies such as l-arginine, ginkgo biloba, vasodilator prostaglandins (beraprost and iloprost), vitamin E, or propionyl-l-carnitine to improve symptoms and walking distance were not well supported by the evidence-based outcomes in PAD research (Anderson et al., 2013).

Surgical Therapy

Invasive interventions are indicated in patients with life-disabling symptomatic PAD when there is a reasonable likelihood of symptomatic improvement and there has been an inadequate response to medical or exercise therapy. Endovascular procedures of angioplasty and stenting may be recommended in arterial stenosis greater than 50% the diameter of the vessel or flow-limiting dissection, depending on the location of the stenosis. Endovascular procedures are not recommended for patients with severe ischemic PAD and an ABI less than 0.4 in the absence of clinical symptoms of CLI. Catheter-based thrombolysis can be performed in patients with acute limb ischemia (Anderson et al., 2013).

Bypass grafting procedures utilizing autogenous veins (when possible) or synthetic grafts are indicated for patients with disabling symptomatic PAD who are not endovascular repair candidates. Endarterectomy is often performed within the affected vessel before bypass grafting is done. Bypass grafting is also recommended in patients who have had acute limb ischemia for more than 14 days. Surgical interventions are not recommended for the patient with severe ischemic PAD and an ABI of 0.4 or less (Anderson et al., 2013).

Outcomes

Patients with PAD progress to CLI at unpredictable rates without lifestyle changes or medical or surgical interventions. Studies comparing medical and surgical therapies against one another demonstrated supervised exercise was superior to endovascular stenting when measuring treadmill walking distance in patients with PAD. However, optimal medical care alone was inferior when compared with the exercise and stent groups. Despite many improved outcomes in hospitalized patients with PAD after surgical intervention, women had higher in-hospital mortality rates regardless of disease severity or the procedure performed. In patients whose disease required major lower-extremity amputation, the mortality rate was 48.3% at 1 year (Anderson et al., 2013).

CASE STUDY

A 68-year-old man presents to the emergency department with sudden-onset back pain while working on his truck. He describes the pain as first an intense burning sensation in the middle of his back between his shoulder blades. He reported sitting down for a few minutes and thought it was getting better. However, when attempting to walk back into his home, the pain returned in his back and moved to the center of his chest and became more severe. His wife says he complained of his left leg hurting during this time and was sweating more than when he was working on the truck. The patient added how it felt as though his left leg was going numb on him and was very heavy. His vital signs on arrival were a temperature of 97.9°F, blood pressure of 110/90 mmHg, heart rate of 108 beats/min, and respiratory rate of 32 breaths/min. His medical history includes hypertension, nonocclusive coronary artery disease, heart failure with a preserved ejection fraction, sleep apnea, and depression. His surgical history includes an appendectomy and internal fixation of the right femur after a motor vehicle crash 20 years ago. The patient's home medications include a baby aspirin, benazepril, carvedilol, lovastatin, and fluoxetine daily. The patient's social history includes smoking less than one pack per day currently, but an average of a pack and a half for more than 30 years. He drinks beers daily and whiskey on the weekends. He has never used illicit drugs. His father is deceased and had a history of hypertension, heart failure, chronic obstructive pulmonary disease, and stroke. His mother is deceased and had a history of diabetes and stroke. He has two brothers with hypertension and one brother had a heart attack at 48 years old.

Physical examination findings were unremarkable. The patient's emergency department evaluation included laboratory results that were unremarkable except for a mild anemia and a CT scan of the chest and abdomen revealing a 6.2-cm saccular descending thoracic aneurysm and dissection extending to the abdominal aorta.

Questions

1. What assessment findings and medical history are congruent with the diagnosis of a thoracic aneurysm and dissection?

2. What interventions should be included in the patient's plan of care when receiving the report of the CT scan?

Answers

1. Complaints of the sudden onset of tearing or ripping chest pain radiating down to the back or down the extremities are most commonly associated with aortic dissection. Thoracic aneurysms most often cause the patient to present with or complain of central anterior chest pain or midscapular back pain described as a burning, ripping, or tearing sensation. Abdominal aneurysms can cause the patient to complain of pain radiating down the back, abdomen, or legs. The patient's medical history is significant for hypertension, nonocclusive CAD, and tobacco abuse, which are both significant risk factors for aortic aneurysm and dissection.

His family history is indicative of atherosclerotic disease, which also places him at risk for the same conditions.

2. An emergency surgical evaluation and preparing for hospitalization and/or surgery should be a priority. Blood pressure control with a beta blocker is another priority; however, this patient's blood pressure is acceptable. The patient's pain should be managed, and evaluation for ischemic injury to other organs or extremities should be performed.

SUMMARY

Diseases of the aorta and peripheral vasculature can have disabling effects on the quality of life of patients and their families. Knowledge of the often complex conditions affecting these patients is essential for providing them with comprehensive nursing care. Nurses can significantly help to improve outcomes in these patients with competent cardiovascular care of these diseases.

EXAM QUESTIONS

CHAPTER 11
Questions 56–59

Note: Choose the one option that BEST answers each question.

56. Which intravenous medication is appropriate initial treatment for patients with acute aortic dissection to control heart rate and blood pressure?

    a. Beta-blocking agents
    b. Calcium channel blocking agents
    c. Angiotensin-converting enzyme inhibitors
    d. Vasodilators

57. Which pathophysiological factor contributes to chronic venous disease?

    a. Endothelial injury
    b. Calcified plaque growth
    c. Increased hydrostatic pressures
    d. Excess low density lipoproteins

58. Which clinical finding is associated with acute limb ischemia in the patient with peripheral arterial disease?

    a. Medial malleolar ulcers
    b. Poikilothermia
    c. Varicose veins
    d. Perimalleolar edema

59. Which management goal is appropriate for a patient with diabetes and peripheral arterial disease?

    a. Blood pressure less than 130/80 mmHg
    b. Hemoglobin A1c greater than 7%
    c. Low-density lipoproteins greater than 100 mg/dl
    d. Blood pressure less than 140/90 mmHg

REFERENCES

American Heart Association. (2014). *About peripheral artery disease (PAD)*. Retrieved from http://www.heart.org/HEARTORG/Conditions/More/PeripheralArteryDisease/About-Peripheral-Artery-Disease-PAD_UCM_301301_Article.jsp#.V3yc6_krLIU

Anderson, J. L., Halperin, J. L., DeMets, D., Guyton, R. A., Hochman, J. S., Kovacs, R. J., ... Shen, W. K. (2013). Management of patients with peripheral artery disease (Compilation of 2005 and 2011 ACCF/AHA guideline recommendations): A report of the American College of Cardiology Foundation/American Heart Association Task Force on Practice Guidelines. *Journal of the American College of Cardiology, 61*(14),1555-1570. doi:10.1016/j.jacc.2013.01.004

Anderson, K. M. (2016). The comprehensive cardiovascular physical examination. In K. M. Anderson (Ed.), *The advanced practice nurse cardiovascular clinician*. New York, NY: Springer.

Centers for Disease Control and Prevention. (2015). *Underlying cause of death 1999-2013 on CDC WONDER Online Database*. Retrieved from http://www.cdc.gov/dhdsp/data_statistics/fact_sheets/fs_aortic_aneurysm.htm

Eberhardt, R. T., & Raffetto, J. D. (2014). Chronic venous insufficiency. *Circulation, 130*, 333-346. doi:10.1161/CIRCULATIONAHA.113.006898

Go, A. S., Mozaffarian, D., Roger, V. L., Benjamin, E. J., Berry, J. D., Borden, W. B., ... Turner, M. B. (2013). Heart disease and stroke statistics – 2013 update: A report from the American Heart Association. *Circulation, 127*(1), e6-e245. doi:10.1161/CIR.0b013e31828124ad

Hiratzka, L. F., Bakris, G. L., Beckman, J. A., Bersin, R. M., Carr, V. F., Casey, D. E., ... Williams, D. M. (2010). 2010 ACCF/AHA/AATS/ACR/ASA/SCA/SCAI/SIR/STS/SVM guidelines for the diagnosis and management of patients with thoracic aortic disease. *Journal of the American College of Cardiology, 55*(14), e27-e129. doi:10.1016/j.jacc.2010.02.015

Huether, S. E., & McCance, K. L. (2017). *Understanding pathophysiology* (6th ed.). St. Louis, MO: Elsevier.

Lough, M. E. (2014). Cardiovascular anatomy and physiology. In L. D. Urden, K. M. Stacy, & M. E. Lough (Eds.), *Critical care nursing: Diagnosis and management* (7th ed., pp. 200-221). St. Louis, MO: Elsevier/Mosby.

Mohler, E. R. (2016). Patient information: Abdominal aortic aneurysms (beyond the basics). *UpToDate*. Retrieved from http://www.uptodate.com/contents/abdominal-aortic-aneurysm-beyond-the-basics

Moll, F. L., Powell, J. T., Fraedrich, G., Verzini, F., Haulon, S., Waltham, M., ... Ricco, J. B. (2011). Management of abdominal aortic aneurysms clinical practice guidelines for the European Society of Vascular Surgery. *European Journal of Vascular and Endovascular Surgery, 41*(S1), S1-S58. doi:10.1016/j.ejvs.2010.09.011

Mozaffarian, D., Benjamin, E. J., Go, A. S., Arnett, D. K., Blaha, M. J., Cushman, M., ... Turner, M. B. (2015). Heart disease and stroke statistics – 2015 update: A report from the American Heart Association. *Circulation, 131,* e29-e322. doi:10.1161/CIR.0000000000000152

Patton, K. T., Thibodeau, G. A., & Douglas, M. M. (2012). *Essentials of anatomy & physiology* (1st ed.). Lansing, MI: Elsevier/Mosby.

Ryjewski, C. (2016). Peripheral arterial disease. In K. M. Anderson (Ed.), *The advanced practice nurse cardiovascular clinician.* New York, NY: Springer.

Scruth, E., & Haynes, A. (2014). Cardiovascular disorders. In L. D. Urden, K. M. Stacy, & M. E. Lough (Eds.), *Critical care nursing: Diagnosis and management* (7th ed., pp. 338-441). St. Louis, MO: Elsevier/Mosby.

CHAPTER 12

IMPLANTABLE DEVICES FOR CARDIOVASCULAR DISEASE

LEARNING OUTCOME

After completing this chapter, the learner will be able to describe the indications for cardiac pacemakers and defibrillators, and the effects of these devices on a patient.

CHAPTER OBJECTIVES

After completing this chapter, the learner will be able to:

1. Describe the indications for implantable cardiac devices.

2. Identify the complications associated with implanted cardiac devices.

3. Explain the functions of a cardiac pacemaker and an implantable cardioverter-defibrillator.

4. Summarize collaborative management for patients who require implanted cardiac devices.

5. Select appropriate patient education for therapies that involve implanted cardiac devices.

INTRODUCTION

Physicians have been experimenting with electrical stimulation of muscles for many years. In 1788 in London, Charles Kite wrote a paper titled "An Essay Upon the Recovery of the Apparently Dead," in which he described how he used electrical stimulation to the heart to revive a 3-year-old child (Nelson, 1993). Many devices have been developed over the years in an attempt to stimulate the electrical system of the heart. In the mid-1950s, the first pacemakers were used (Nelson, 1993). Initially, a small wire was placed in the heart. The wire was then connected to an external pacemaker that was the size of a microwave oven. The patient could travel only as far as the power cord could stretch. However, this drawback was desirable to the alternative, which was death. In 1957, the first battery-powered pacemaker was developed. This device (still an external device) was small enough to be strapped to the patient (Nelson, 1993).

Since 1957, the science of cardiac pacing has grown and changed dramatically. As of 2010, the number of pacemakers implanted annually was about 370,000 (Mozaffarian et al., 2016). Technology has advanced from a device that was external and the size of a microwave oven to a device that is totally implantable and the size of a half dollar. In addition, the field of electrophysiology has become a specialty of its own. However, the search for a device that mimics the heart's natural electrical system continues. For healthcare professionals, the implants have become more complex and intricate. For patients, the implantation procedure and the impact of the device on their quality of life have become less obtrusive. Cardiovascular nurses must understand the utility and potential complications of such devices in patients with cardiovascular disease.

CARDIAC PACEMAKERS

As previously stated, cardiac pacemakers have evolved over the past 50 years from large external devices to small implantable devices placed within a pocket created in the chest wall. Pacemakers can be inserted on a temporary or permanent basis to support and enhance the electrical and mechanical functions of the heart (Dirks & Waters, 2014). Nurses must apply the fundamentals of cardiac anatomy and physiology to their knowledge of pacemaker indications, available routes of pacing, complications of pacing, and necessary pacing education for patients and families to facilitate desirable clinical outcomes.

Review of the Conduction System

To understand how cardiac pacemakers work, one must understand the cardiac conduction system (see Figure 12-1). The sinoatrial (SA) node is the natural pacemaker of the heart, and it normally fires at a rate between 60 and 100 beats/min. Electricity is conducted from the SA node to the atrioventricular (AV) node via intermodal pathways within the atrial chambers of the heart. Conduction is slowed down at the AV node to assure that the ventricles are relaxed at the time of

atrial contraction and have time to fill completely before contracting. From the AV node, the electrical impulse travels along the bundle of His. The bundle of His divides into the right and left bundle branches and conducts impulses through each ventricle. From the ventricles, the impulse travels to the Purkinje fibers, where the depolarization is carried through to the endocardial layers of the heart (Patton, Thibodeau, & Douglas, 2012). A detailed review of cardiac electrophysiology is provided in Chapter 1.

Indications for Cardiac Pacing

As pacemakers continue to improve, the indications for cardiac pacing continue to change. The decision to insert a pacemaker draws the attention of the medical community and the insurance industry because these devices, especially implantable defibrillators, can be expensive, so their necessity is carefully scrutinized. Nevertheless, research studies demonstrate improved quality of life and prevention of sudden death with the appropriate use of pacemakers and implanted defibrillators (Gillis et al., 2012; National Institute for Health and Care Excellence, 2014; Yancy et al., 2013).

FIGURE 12-1: CONDUCTION SYSTEM OF THE HEART

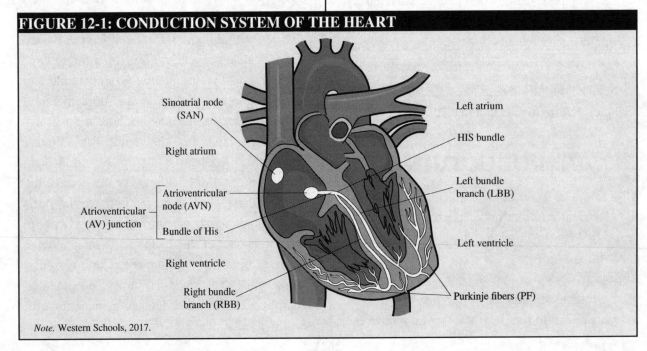

Note. Western Schools, 2017.

Practitioners should make decisions based on individual patient needs. Indications for permanent cardiac pacemaker insertion can be complex because of the need to consider many variables. In this text, we review the most common indications for cardiac pacemaker insertion (see Box 12-1).

BOX 12-1: COMMON INDICATIONS FOR CARDIAC PACING[a]

- Sinoatrial node dysfunction
- Atrioventricular node disease
- Hypersensitive carotid sinus syndrome
- Neurocardiogenic syncope
- Long QT syndrome
- Hypertrophic cardiomyopathy

[a]This is a greatly abbreviated listing of the complex indications for pacemakers.

Note. Adapted from Gillis, A. M., Russo, A. M., Ellenbogen, K. A., Swerdlow, C. D., Olshansky, B., Al-Khatib, S. M., … Shen, W.-K. (2012). HRS/ACCF expert consensus statement on pacemaker device and mode selection. *Journal of the American College of Cardiology, 60*(7), 682-703. doi:10.1016/j.jacc.2012.06.011

Sinoatrial Node Dysfunction

When the SA node fails, a variety of dysrhythmias may result. SA node dysfunction is also referred to as sick sinus syndrome. These dysrhythmias include bradycardia (slow heartbeat), sinus arrest (no heartbeat), SA block (no impulse initiated in the SA node), and tachy-brady syndrome (very fast heart rates alternating with very slow heart rates). Patients with SA node dysfunction experience very slow heart rates and are commonly symptomatic. They may actually have a pause in the heartbeat and experience momentary dizziness (Dirks & Waters, 2014). All of these dysrhythmias may occur intermittently, and 24-hour monitoring is very helpful in documenting rhythm irregularities and helping the clinician determine whether pacing is indicated (Gillis et al., 2012).

SA node dysfunction may also be demonstrated as chronotropic incompetence. During exercise, heart rate increases as a normal response to meet the body's increased needs. This rate increase is referred to as a chronotropic response. In some patients with SA node dysfunction, this response is no longer present, resulting in symptoms of activity intolerance related to inadequate increase in heart rate to meet the body's exertional demand. Although this response is essential for exercise, it is also important for any increase in activity (Dirks & Waters, 2014).

Atrioventricular Block

The most common reason for pacemaker implantation is heart block, or AV block (Gillis et al., 2012). In AV block, something in the conduction system prevents the impulse from traveling normally from the SA node through the AV node to the ventricles. There are several types of AV block (this is discussed further in Chapter 15). Patients are generally unaware of first-degree block; second-degree block can cause symptoms; and high-grade (or advanced) blocks and third-degree heart blocks most often result in symptoms, ranging from dizziness to complete unresponsiveness. Any type of AV block with symptomatic bradycardia is an indication for cardiac pacing. If patients do not have symptoms but have documented heart rates of less than 40 beats/min, they also are candidates for cardiac pacing (Gillis et al., 2012).

Occasionally, aggressive disease treatment with medications may result in AV blocks and low heart rates. Because many of the medications that lower heart rates or cause heart blocks are important to the patient's welfare, the benefits of a pacemaker being implanted outweigh the risks of stopping the medication (Gillis et al., 2012). Finally, any patient with third-degree AV block is a candidate for pacing, even when no symptoms are present. Studies show that placing pacemakers in patients with third-degree AV block, with or without symptoms, can decrease mortality rates (Gillis et al., 2012).

Bifascicular Block

Other candidates for pacemakers are those with bifascicular blocks, or bundle branch blocks. The right bundle branch has one fascicle, and the left bundle branch has two fascicles: the anterior and posterior fascicles. One or more of these fascicles can become blocked. When the right bundle branch and one of the left bundle branch fascicles become blocked, the patient has a bifascicular block. Many people with bundle branch blocks do not require cardiac pacemakers; however, those with other concurrent conditions (e.g., patients who also have an intermittent third-degree AV block or type II second-degree AV block) do require pacing (Gillis et al., 2012). The bundle branches supply the impulse to the ventricles. If the right fascicle and both fascicles of the left bundle branch become blocked, no message is sent to the ventricles to contract. Thus, some patients are at high risk for death, and permanent pacing has been shown to reduce mortality rates for this population (Gillis et al., 2012).

Neurocardiogenic Syncope

Syncope (brief, self-limited loss of consciousness) occurring as a result of an exaggerated reflex in response to carotid sinus stimulation is defined as neurocardiogenic syncope (Gillis et al., 2012). This form of syncope is also known as hypersensitive carotid sinus syndrome. The hypersensitivity results from

- a cardioinhibitory response – excessive parasympathetic tone – and/or

- a vasodepressor response – inhibition of sympathetic discharge.

All other causes of syncope should be ruled out before implanting a permanent pacemaker (Gillis et al., 2012).

Symptoms resulting from the cardioinhibitory mechanism of neurogenic syncope involve the slowing of the sinus rate with a prolonged PR interval or even a complete or high-grade AV block. Symptoms resulting from the vasodepressor mechanism of neurocardiogenic syncope involve vasodilation or hypotension independent of the changes occurring in heart rate (Gillis et al., 2012). Unfortunately, these symptoms are not reproducible clinically as with types of syncope in which symptoms can be reproduced by a clinician performing carotid massage. However, in patients experiencing recurrent neurocardiogenic syncope, the placement of pacemakers overwhelmingly reduced the occurrence rate to approximately 9% (Gillis et al., 2012).

Temporary versus Permanent Cardiac Pacemakers

Temporary cardiac pacing is utilized in acute care settings for urgent, symptomatic conditions secondary to electrophysiological dysfunction (e.g., acute myocardial infarction or drug toxicity). The three routes of temporary pacing are

- transcutaneous (via electroconductive pads that can be connected to a defibrillator for pacing energy),

- transvenous (a pacing wire inserted via the vena cava into the patient's heart connected to an external pacing generator for energy), or

- epicardial (pacing wires connected to the epicardial layer of the heart during surgery and also connected to an external pacing generator for energy).

If the cause of the slow rhythm is determined to be a permanent electrophysiological dysfunction, a permanent pacemaker is implanted (Dirks & Waters, 2014). Figure 12-2 illustrates external pulsing generators.

FIGURE 12-2: TEMPORARY PACING GENERATORS

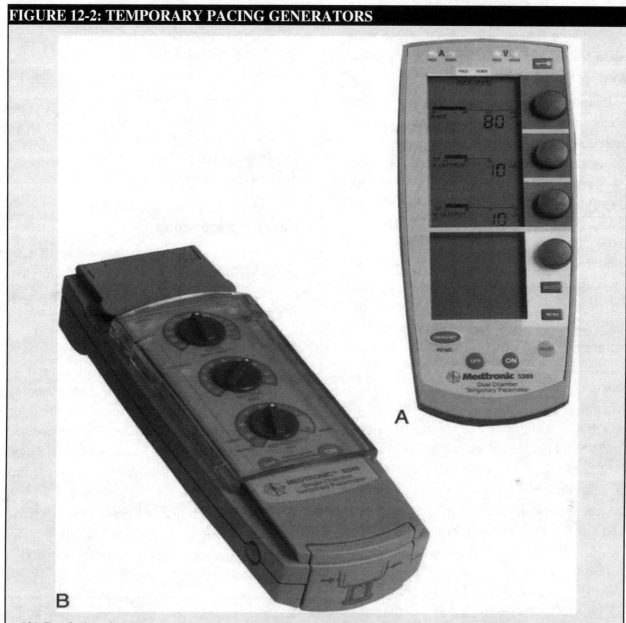

(**A**) Dual-chamber generator to pace atria and ventricles. (**B**) Single-chamber generator to pace ventricles only.

Note. From Urden, L. D., Stacy, K. M., & Lough, M. E. (2014). *Critical care nursing: Diagnosis and management* (7th ed.). St. Louis, MO: Elsevier/ Mosby. © Elsevier 2014.

Although temporary pacing is considered a life-saving intervention, it has multiple limitations and requires the cardiovascular clinician to be skilled at maintaining pacing capture for the best patient outcomes. For instance, transcutaneous pacing involves repeated microshocks through the patient's chest wall and can be very painful to the patient. Furthermore, each patient's chest wall has variable levels of transthoracic impedance secondary to body composition of muscle, fat (e.g., obesity), and air (e.g., barreled chest of the patient with chronic obstructive pulmonary disease). The amount of muscle, fat, or air contributes to the amount of energy (joules) that is necessary for the external pacing generator to gain capture. Increased energy use in transthoracic patients equals increased pain and is often intolerable to patients without concurrent medication administration of analgesics and sedatives (Dirks & Waters, 2014).

The limitations associated with transvenous or epicardial pacing are less than those of transcutaneous pacing, however, and involve the ability of the pacing wires to maintain direct contact with the heart. Epicardial pacing wires are often sewn in and maintain contact well unless they are pulled off unintentionally with patient movement or the patient inadvertently pulls the wires. Transvenous pacing wires are screwed into the endocardial layer of the heart muscle during placement and can be dislodged secondary to patient movement, inadvertent pulling on the external wires, or by anything that increases intrathoracic pressures (e.g., coughing, sneezing, or mechanical ventilation). When endocardial wires become dislodged, the now free-floating wire can irritate the ventricles' conductive pathways and evoke ventricular arrhythmias (e.g., ventricular tachycardia). In some situations, the patient can be placed in the left lateral lying position to allow gravity to facilitate the wire making contact with the heart muscle until further intervention can be performed (Dirks & Waters, 2014). Cardiovascular clinicians must be skilled in the use of temporary pacing to optimize patient outcomes and bridge the patient to electrophysiological recovery or implantation of a permanent pacemaker.

Concepts of Permanent Cardiac Pacing

As discussed in Chapter 1, the action potential is a series of events resulting in a change of the electrical charge inside the cell from negative (resting) to positive (stimulated) and back to negative. This action potential consists of depolarization (stimulation of cardiac muscle cells) and repolarization (return of cells to their resting state). Depolarization is conducted in a systematic method through the electrical system of the heart, as described earlier in this chapter. As depolarization occurs, healthy cardiac muscle cells respond by contracting the muscle. Patients who require permanent pacemakers usually no longer have a dependable systematic method for sending electrical messages to the cardiac muscle. Rather, the implanted pacemaker takes over and stimulates the cardiac muscles to contract.

Components of a Permanent Cardiac Pacemaker

The standard cardiac pacemaker that is implanted to regulate heartbeat includes the pacemaker generator and the pacing wires with an electrode (see Figure 12-3).

Pacemaker Generator

The pacemaker generator is also referred to as the pacemaker battery or pulse generator. It usually consists of a lithium battery and the electrical microcircuitry necessary for the cardiac pacemaker to function. The pacemaker generator is usually placed in a subcutaneous pocket in the chest wall. The preferred site is the within the left shoulder of a right-handed person and the right shoulder of a left-handed person. The battery is the only part of a pacemaker system that is typically removed and replaced (Dirks & Waters, 2014).

NURSING APPLICATION

It is important to take the patient's lifestyle into consideration before pacemaker insertion. For example, if a patient is a hunter and uses a rifle, the pacemaker generator should be placed in the shoulder that is not used when aiming the gun.

Pacemaker Lead

The pacemaker lead is an insulated wire that is connected to the pacemaker battery. For a ventricular pacemaker, the lead is threaded

FIGURE 12-3: COMPONENTS OF A PERMANENT DUAL-CHAMBER PACEMAKER

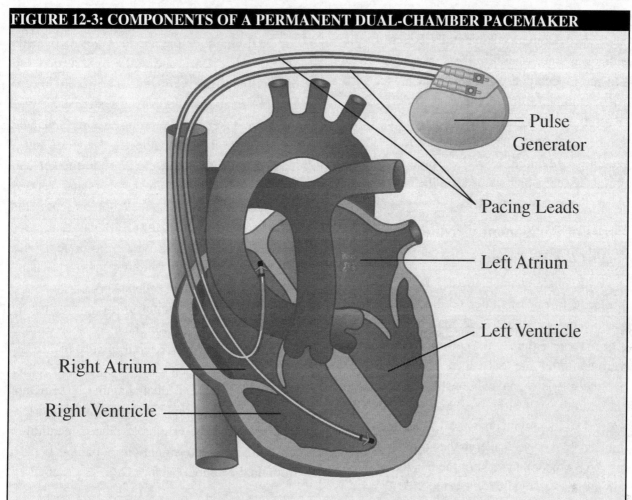

Pulse Generator

Pacing Leads

Left Atrium

Left Ventricle

Right Atrium

Right Ventricle

The pulse generator and leads are shown. This is a dual-chamber pacemaker with an electrode in the right atrium and an electrode in the right ventricle.

Note. Western Schools, 2017.

through a vein to the superior vena cava and into the right atrium, then through the tricuspid valve and into the right ventricle. The end of the lead wire is left in contact with the wall of the right ventricle. The lead contains a conducting wire that carries the impulse from the pacemaker battery to the wall of the heart. It is insulated to protect against fracture. If the lead fractures, the electrical stimulus no longer reaches the heart and the pacemaker fails. A new lead is then placed, and the old lead is disconnected from the battery, but usually left in place. When pacemaker batteries are replaced, the leads are routinely left in place. It is not unusual to leave a nonfunctioning lead in place,

disconnect it from the generator, ground the wire with cap, and simply add a new functional lead beside it. Removal of a lead may result in a tear in the myocardial wall (Dirks & Waters, 2014). If a lead does need to be removed – for example, if it becomes infected – this should be done only by a physician who is well trained in lead removal (Gillis et al., 2012).

Pacemaker Electrode

At the end of the lead is an electrode. The electrode is the device that delivers the electrical stimulus to the cardiac wall. The ability of the electrode to have good contact with healthy cardiac tissue is critical. Many types of "fixation" devices are available to assist with a good connection. Some leads naturally adhere to the wall over time, whereas others can be screwed into the myocardial wall. Different devices are utilized depending on the ease or difficulty of establishing a good connection. Over time, the electrode at the end of the lead in the heart becomes epithelialized and covered over with fibrous tissue, which helps keep the electrode in place (Dirks & Waters, 2014).

Types of Permanent Cardiac Pacing

Single-Chamber Pacing

With single-chamber pacemakers, one lead is placed in one chamber of the heart. When pacemakers were first developed, a single lead was placed in the right ventricle. Thus, these were and often are still called *right ventricular pacemakers*. Now, an additional lead can also be placed in the right atrium, for example, when the SA node does not fire on its own. If an impulse is initiated by the pacemaker in the atrium (simulating the SA node), the rest of the conduction system responds normally (Gillis et al., 2012).

Right ventricular pacemakers are programmed to stimulate the right ventricle if no other stimulus is received by the ventricle within a preset timeframe. This system completely ignores atrial activity, resulting in loss of atrial kick. Atrial kick contributes 25% of cardiac output. Over time, patients with single-chamber right ventricular pacemakers developed what was referred to as "pacemaker syndrome," primarily as a result of the loss of atrial kick. As a result of the negative effects (or less-than-optimal effects) of single-chamber right ventricular pacemakers, researchers strived to develop a pacemaker that better mimicked the normal activities of the heart, thereby leading to the development of dual-chamber pacemakers (Dirks & Waters, 2014; Gillis et al., 2012).

Dual-Chamber Pacing

Dual-chamber pacing involves two leads placed in the heart, one in the right atrium and one in the right ventricle (shown in Figure 12-3). A dual-chamber pacing system is the typical pacemaker configuration that is implanted today. With a lead in the right atrium and a lead in the right ventricle, the pacemaker can sense the activity in both chambers and respond to activity that is present or not present. This configuration mimics the heart's normal conduction system and provides the patient with better overall cardiac output (Dirks & Waters, 2014). Dual-chamber pacemakers can increase a patient's cardiac output up to approximately 40% (Gillis et al., 2012). The increase in cardiac output also improves overall quality of life for these patients. When patients present for pacer battery replacement, dual-chamber systems are recommended to replace single-chamber pacemakers that were originally placed, pending a cardiologist's determination of patient benefit from dual-chamber pacing (Gillis et al., 2012).

Biventricular Pacemakers

Biventricular pacemakers, also known as cardiac resynchronization therapy (CRT), is a newer technology that has been developed (see later discussion in Cardiac Resynchronization Therapy section).

Leadless Right Ventricular Pacing

A recent novel approach to permanent pacing involves the use of the smallest pacing device developed to date and approved by the Food and Drug Administration (Medtronic, 2016; Reynolds et al., 2016). The device, named Micra, is the size of a large multivitamin and is placed in the right ventricle percutaneously via the femoral vein. This device was created to avoid the need of a pacemaker pocket in the chest wall and the cannulation of the transvenous lead. Early nonrandomized, single-study group trials indicate the new device has equivalent efficacy and safety outcomes and superior complication rates in comparison to pacemakers with leads. Future research is needed to conduct head to head, randomized comparison studies to other devices (Reynolds et al. 2016).

Cardiac Pacing Modes

Once implanted, cardiac pacemakers are programmed to function in a manner that is determined by a cardiologist to be best for patients on an individual basis. Today, pacemakers can be programmed noninvasively and painlessly in a cardiologist's office. These devices can be reprogrammed and changed as the patient's needs dictate (Dirks & Waters, 2014).

The Pacer Code

When referring to a pacemaker and its function, a series of letters are used to assist healthcare professionals in determining how the pacemaker should function. An international system of codes was established for identifying pacemaker functioning (Gillis et al., 2012). The first four letters of this code are consistently used to identify pacing modes, whereas the fifth one is not yet consistently used (see Table 12-1). The fifth letter reflects the capability of newer devices to sense from different sites within the chamber where the lead is implanted. Discussion of the fifth letter of the code is beyond the scope of this course.

VVI Pacing Mode

The original pacemakers were ventricular pacemakers only and were designated as VVI pacemakers. Some patients continue to have pacemakers programmed in the VVI mode. In the VVI mode, the first position indicates the chamber paced and that the pacemaker electrode in the right ventricle can pace the right ventricle if necessary. The second position indicates that the electrode in the right ventricle senses the patient's own electrical activity in the ventricle. The third position indicates that, on sensing normal activity in the ventricle, the pacer will not fire (inhibits pacing activity). If there is no normal activity from the heart, the pacemaker will fire. The most common reason for the VVI mode is atrial fibrillation. In atrial fibrillation, communication between the atrium and the ventricle is not normal, and there is little ability to set up a communication system with a dual-chamber pacemaker. It is becoming more common that patients with a dual-chamber pacemaker in atrial fibrillation have a pacer mode of DDI. This is a more technologically complex configuration that is beyond the scope of this text, but it is mentioned because it is one of the many configurations. A few patients still have old single-chamber pacemakers that were placed many years ago and only function in VVI mode (Dirks & Waters, 2014).

TABLE 12-1: PACING CODES

Position I	Position II	Position III	Position IV	Position V
Chamber(s) paced	Chamber(s) sensed	Response to sensing	Rate modulation	Multisite pacing
O = none	O = none	O = none	O = none	O = none
A = atrium	A = atrium	T = triggered	R = rate modulation	A = atrium
V = ventricle	V = ventricle	I = inhibited		V = ventricle
D = dual (A+V)	D = dual (A+V)	D = dual (T+I)		D = dual (A+V)

Note. Adapted from Dirks, J., & Waters, J. (2014). Cardiovascular therapeutic management. In L. D. Urden, K. M. Stacy, & M. E. Lough (Eds.), *Critical care nursing: Diagnosis and management* (7th ed., pp. 200-221). St. Louis, MO: Elsevier/Mosby.

DDD Pacing Mode

The most common pacemaker configuration is the DDD mode. When the pacemaker is programmed for DDD, an electrode in the right atrium and one in the right ventricle are both used for the pacing mode. The DDD mode is commonly referred to as AV sequential pacing. The D in the first position indicates that the electrode in the atrium and the electrode in the ventricle are programmed to pace the atrium and the ventricle if there is no normal electrical activity. The D in the second position indicates that the device can sense any normal electrical activity (depolarization) in the atrium or ventricle. The D in the third and final position refers to the pacemaker's response as it senses the activity of the heart. The best situation in most patients is to allow the heart to function as normally as possible and utilize the pacemaker only if the heart is unable to function. Therefore, the atrial electrode is set up to allow a preset period for the atrium to contract naturally. If normal contraction occurs, the atrial electrode is inhibited and does not fire. The atrial electrode then sends a message (trigger) to the ventricular electrode. The message to the ventricular electrode is the same as if a message was coming through the AV node to the ventricles via the bundle branches. This message sets up another cycle. The ventricular electrode, although triggered by the atrial system, waits a preset amount of time for the patient's own system to function, causing the ventricle to contract. If natural contraction occurs, then the ventricular electrode senses this, is inhibited, and does not fire. Then the cycle repeats itself in the atrium. Anytime that the atrium or ventricle does not depolarize naturally, the pacemaker sends an impulse to that part of the heart (Dirks & Waters, 2014).

Rate Responsiveness

The fourth position noted with pacemaker modes is an R. This stands for rate responsiveness. The body's natural ability to increase heart rate in response to physiological needs is called a *chronotropic response* and, as previously mentioned, does not always function as needed. Rate responsiveness provides the chronotropic response when the patient's body does not. A pacemaker with rate-responsive pacing increases the pacemaker rate based on the physiological needs of the body. A wide variety of methods are available for detecting the physiological needs of the body. Motion sensors and minute ventilation sensors are the most common methods of determining chronotropic needs. With the setting of rate variability, the patient will have an upper rate and a lower rate programmed. These will be the fastest and the slowest rates that the pacemaker will fire (Dirks & Waters, 2014).

NURSING APPLICATION

Patients who have rate modulation programmed in their pacemakers may have a wide variability of heart rates when pacing, depending on their physiological needs.

Other Pacemaker Modes

Multiple combinations can be programmed into pacemakers. Pacemaker systems have become very complex, and a physician trained in the complex physiology of cardiac pacing is required to configure the pacemaker functions to best meet the physiological needs of the patient. Those needs may change as the patient changes, and the pacemaker is reprogrammed to meet those needs.

Paradigm Shift in Permanent Pacing

With advances in technology and knowledge, technology that was once straightforward has become quite complex. Dual-chamber pacemakers were developed in an attempt to mimic the normal AV conduction pattern that was missing with single-chamber ventricular pacemakers. Literature demonstrates an increased incidence of heart failure hospitalization and new-onset atrial fibrillation with continuous right ventricular pacing (Gillis et al., 2012). This is most likely occurring because right ventricular pacing creates a pattern of left bundle branch block and dyssynchrony between the right and left ventricle. With this in mind, pacemaker programming has become quite sophisticated in an attempt to minimize right ventricular pacing. The goal today with pacemaker programming is to allow the patient's native conduction system to predominate over the pacemaker. Atrial pacing is not related to the deleterious effects, only ventricular pacing. The less right ventricular pacing that occurs, the better for the patient, as long as the patient's own rhythm provides adequate perfusion and the patient is without symptoms. The newer programming modes (which are not discussed in this chapter) make it much more difficult for the untrained practitioner to determine appropriate pacemaker function during bedside cardiac monitoring (Dirks & Waters, 2014).

NURSING APPLICATION

It is important to understand the reason the patient has a pacemaker, because dual-chamber pacemakers are programmed differently than biventricular pacemakers (discussed later in this chapter). When questioning whether the pacemaker is functioning normally on a rhythm strip, always assess the patient. The patient's stability should be the first concern. A stable patient allows time for further evaluation of the pacemaker.

Pacemaker Insertion

Previously inserted in the operating room by a thoracic surgeon, permanent pacemakers are now commonly inserted in cardiac catheterization or electrophysiology laboratories by cardiologists who specialize in the field of electrophysiology. The procedure itself is conducted in a room with the same physical requirements as an operating room. Patients are usually awake during the procedure, with light sedation and analgesics to keep them comfortable. A local anesthetic is used at the site of insertion. A small incision, 2 to 3 inches in length, is made for pacemaker generator insertion in the left or right shoulder area, over the location of the subclavian vein. The leads are fed through the subclavian vein into the heart and connected to the pacemaker generator. The pacemaker is programmed and tested. When accurate pacing is assured, the incision is closed. The procedure is relatively quick, usually less than 2 hours. If a patient is having only a generator or battery replaced, even less time is required because the leads remain in place. The old incision is opened, and the old generator is disconnected from the old leads and removed. The new generator is connected to the old leads and inserted into the pocket. The pacemaker is programmed and, when functioning is confirmed, the incision is closed (Dirks & Waters, 2014). As stated earlier, if a new lead is required, the old lead is usually left in place to avoid the possibility of a myocardial tear or bleeding that can be associated with removal of a lead.

Patients may go to a recovery room after pacemaker placement, but they most often return to a nursing unit that has cardiac monitoring capabilities. With routine new pacemaker insertion, the patient is often hospitalized overnight. If only the generator has been replaced, the procedure is typically done on an outpatient basis. It is important that the leads remain at the location of placement in the operating room. Over time, fibrous tissue grows around the electrode and keeps the lead in place. The patient initially has some limitation of movement (e.g., affected arm immobilizer or sling) until there is assurance that the lead is secure. Specifically, patients should avoid raising their arm above their head on the side where the pacemaker was inserted for approximately 2 weeks after implantation to prevent lead dislodgement from the endocardium. These restrictions are only for when a new lead has been implanted – not for generator replacement only. The patient is also instructed to limit the movement of the affected shoulder and not to lie on the affected side for the first 12 to 24 hours (Dirks & Waters, 2014).

As with any surgical procedure, it is not uncommon for patients to experience discomfort at the site for the first several days. Generally, over-the-counter pain relief medications ease the discomfort, and discomfort should lessen as the wound heals. The incision may also be discolored. The incision is often closed with internal sutures that do not require removal. If external sutures are used, they are removed in 7 to 10 days. The site should be kept dry for 5 to 7 days, and many clinicians order prophylactic topical antibiotic ointment administration daily (Dirks & Waters, 2012).

After discharge, most activity is resumed quickly, with full recovery in 2 weeks. During the next couple of months, depending on the physician's treatment preference, the patient should avoid heavy pushing, pulling, and lifting (10 pounds) with the arm and shoulder where the pacemaker is placed. The patient should be reminded that he or she can use the arm on the affected side during this restricted period, within the guidelines of the restriction. Driving is also limited for a period of 1 to 4 weeks, again according to the physician's preference (Dirks & Waters, 2014).

NURSING APPLICATION

Limiting movement of the arm on the affected side is important in the immediate postoperative period when a new pacemaker lead has been implanted. The simple activity of using the elbows to move from a cart to the bed can dislodge some leads.

Pacemaker Complications

Pneumothorax

Pacemaker implantation is not without complications. During the procedure, the physician may puncture the lung while attempting to obtain vein access. A punctured lung may not initially be evident, and all pacemaker implant patients should have a postprocedure chest X-ray to assess for pneumothorax. Respiratory distress during or after the procedure should raise the suspicion of pneumothorax. Treatment of pneumothorax depends on the size and symptoms. In more severe cases, insertion of a chest tube is required (Dirks & Waters, 2014).

Hemothorax

Bleeding into the thoracic cavity may also occur if an artery is nicked or lacerated by a needle during the procedure. If this occurs, pressure can be applied and the situation will resolve. If the artery penetration is large, a hemothorax may result and surgical repair of the artery is required (Dirks & Waters, 2012).

Myocardial Perforation

During lead placement, the lead can perforate the heart wall. The right ventricle is at greatest risk for this complication given its muscle thickness is at least two to three times less than that of the left ventricle (Patton et al., 2012). The lead can go through the heart wall to another chamber or, in the worst case, may traverse the entire heart wall to the pericardium. A full-thickness perforation can occur when myocardial tissue is old, steroid therapy has been used, or there was recent infarction (especially of the right ventricular wall or septum). Cardiac tamponade (bleeding into the pericardial sac) can occur quickly and would require urgent or emergent pericardiocentesis to remove the fluid from the pericardial sac or surgery to repair the damage. Perforation of the tissue may occur without this severe complication in healthier cardiac muscle tissue. Patients who are taking anticoagulants will have their medications held by their physician for a prescribed amount of time before and after the procedure to limit excessive bleeding (Dirks & Waters, 2014).

Infection

Pacemaker-site infections can occur in the early postoperative stage or months to years after implantation. *Staphylococcal* species is the most prevalent infecting organism (Hussein et al., 2016). Patients with diabetes mellitus and patients who develop postoperative hematomas have a higher incidence of pacemaker-site infections (Hussein et al., 2016). Bacteria can adhere to the pacing generator and pacing leads, and create a protective *biofilm* around itself that inhibits the antiseptic or bactericidal effects of most antibiotics (Sandoe et al., 2015). It is thought that the presence of a bacterial biofilm is the cause of increased antibiotic resistance among implanted cardiac device infections (Hussein et al., 2016).

When an infection is noted, intravenous antibiotic therapy should be initiated. Determination of the extent of infection is crucial to adequate treatment and whether the infection will extend to the pacing generator, pacing leads, or the individual's cardiac structures (e.g., valves or myocardium). Clinicians must recognize that *Staphylococcal* species have an affinity to implanted devices within the body and have the capability of developing a biofilm around its vegetations. When the components of the device are also infected, they must be removed while treatment with intravenous antibiotics continues. After device removal, surveillance blood cultures are collected for evidence of the bacteria no longer being present. When blood cultures are negative for bacterial growth, device replacement is considered. The new pacemaker system is usually placed in a new location to reduce the potential for reinfection of the new system (Hussein et al., 2016; Sandoe et al., 2015).

Twiddler's Syndrome

Twiddler's syndrome is rare but often results from a patient manipulating the pacer generator under the skin. The "twiddler" actually turns the device over and over and over again under the skin. As the device is turned, the leads twist to the point of actual damage to the lead. Usually, the damage is discovered after the pacemaker fails to function properly, and it often causes lethal arrhythmias. The twisted wires are readily seen on chest X-ray film. Surgical intervention is required to open the incision and replace the leads. It is only shortly after the implantation of a device that one can turn it over. Over time, the device becomes attached to its surroundings, making twiddling difficult. Fixating the leads in place has been found to prevent the occurrence of twiddling (Mandal, Pande, & Kahali, 2012).

NURSING APPLICATION

Instruct patients to ignore the urge to touch their pacemaker in the early, postoperative setting to avoid the possibility of twiddler's syndrome and infection.

Other Complications

Other pacemaker complications include pacemaker generator migration, which involves actual movement of the pacemaker generator from its original location to a new location in the chest wall. This migration may be of little consequence if there is no malfunction of the pacemaker due to lead displacement or if there is no patient discomfort at the new location of the device. The pacemaker may also erode through the skin, usually because of pressure on the site. Early recognition of pressure on the pacemaker generator by tight skin allows the physician to intervene before the skin is penetrated. After the skin is penetrated, the entire system is considered contaminated and requires replacement (Hussein et al., 2016).

Pacemaker lead migration can also occur. Generator migration can subsequently cause pacing leads to withdraw from their implanted sites or progress through their implanted sites, leading to perforation of the myocardium. Alternatively, pacing leads can migrate without generator migration. Because of the turbulence of blood flow, leads can become disconnected from the generator or from the heart wall. Consequently, this leads to device dysfunction. When pacing leads disconnect from the heart wall, they are then free floating in the chamber. Free-floating pacing leads often repeatedly agitate the ventricular endocardium, causing lethal ventricular arrhythmias. Lead migration can usually be identified by chest radiograph and requires prompt attention. Sometimes the leads can just be screwed back into place; however, there are times when the leads must be replaced. Because of the risk for perforating the heart wall, leads that are not functioning properly and that spontaneously disconnect from the generator are capped, left in place, and new leads are placed and connected to the generator (Hussein et al., 2016).

NURSING APPLICATION

Car seatbelts may irritate a pacemaker site in some patients. Suggest to the patient use of a thick, soft fabric (lamb's wool) around the seatbelt strap to provide a soft surface at the site of the pacemaker.

CARDIAC RESYNCHRONIZATION THERAPY

Cardiac resynchronization therapy (CRT) is a nonpharmacological treatment strategy for heart failure. As heart failure progresses to worsened systolic ventricular function, electromechanical dysfunction or dyssynchrony occurs. Electromechanical dyssynchrony occurs because of delayed electrical conduction throughout the ventricle and consequently a delayed mechanical response of contraction. This dyssynchrony occurs most often with left bundle branch block (Tracy et al., 2012). These patients have decreased ejection fraction, decreased cardiac output, an increase in myocardial oxygen consumption, and an increase in signs and symptoms of cardiopulmonary congestion. In addition, QRS duration wider than 120 ms (normal is ≤100 ms) on an electrocardiogram (ECG) is associated with increased mortality in patients with an ejection fraction less than 20% to 35% (Tracy et al., 2012). In left bundle branch block, the right ventricle contracts first, followed by the left ventricle. Generally, the lateral wall of the left ventricle is the last wall to contract in left bundle branch block. CRT is a therapy aimed at eliminating the dyssynchrony and involves the utilization of a pacemaker lead in both the right and the left ventricle to resynchronize the ventricles. Thus, this therapy is also referred to as "biventricular pacing" (Anderson, 2015).

NURSING APPLICATION

It is important to remember that CRT is a therapeutic treatment used in heart failure. These devices are not placed because of heart rate issues. With this in mind, when ventricular pacing occurs, therapy is delivered. If there is no ventricular pacing, then there is no synchrony between the right and left bundle. It is important to differentiate this patient population from the patient population with pacemakers implanted to maintain normal heart rates.

Indications

CRT is costly; therefore, the guidelines for device implantation are strict. Currently, the U.S. Food and Drug Administration has approved CRT for a specific group of patients (see Table 12-2). This population includes patients who are symptomatic on full goal-directed medical therapy for heart failure with New York Heart Association Class II, III, or IV. In addition, patients must meet strict criteria for ejection fraction, left ventricular size, QRS duration, and cardiac rhythm (Tracy et al., 2012).

Biventricular Pacemaker Insertion

Like other pacemakers, the biventricular pacemaker generator is placed in a pocket in the chest wall. Pacemaker leads are placed in the right atrium and right ventricle in the normal method. A third lead is attached to the left ventricle in the location of the left lateral ven-

tricular wall. The right atrial and ventricular leads are placed inside the chambers, whereas the left ventricular lead is threaded through the coronary sinus and into the left ventricular cardiac vein. This approach results in a lead that is pacing from the outer surface of the heart. The left lateral wall placement of the lead is effective because the left lateral wall of the left ventricle is the part of the heart that contracts last. Implantation of this lead may be difficult because the ventricle is typically quite dilated. Occasionally, the lead cannot be placed percutaneously and must be placed in the operating room through a surgical incision in the chest wall (Dirks & Waters, 2014).

After the leads are in place, the goal of therapy is to have both ventricular pacemaker leads stimulating the respective ventricles at the same time; this is achieved through extensive device programming. Many patients who are candidates for biventricular pacing are also candidates for implantable cardioverter-defibrillators (ICDs). If an ICD is indicated, it can be placed at the same time as the biventricular pacing leads (Dirks & Waters, 2014).

TABLE 12-2: INDICATIONS FOR CARDIAC RESYNCHRONIZATION THERAPY

Parameter	Clinical Findings[a]
NYHA functional class	Class II, III, or IV
Ejection fraction	≤ 35% (Class I)
	≤ 30% (Class IIb)
QRS duration	≥ 150 ms (Class I recommendation)
	≥ 120-149 ms (Class IIa recommendation)
Left ventricular size	Diameter at end of diastole > 55 mm
Cardiac rhythm with left bundle branch block	Sinus rhythm (Class I)
	Atrial fibrillation, rate controlled (Class IIa)

[a]Clinical findings are not used in isolation for medical decision making. This table identifies only the parameters of the clinical findings. Guideline recommendations must be reviewed for specific details to guide medical decision making.

NYHA = New York Heart Association.

Note. Adapted from Tracy, C. M., Epstein, A. E., Darbar, D., DiMarco, J. P., Dunbar, S. B., Estes, N. A. M., ... Varosy, P. D. (2012). 2012 ACCF/AHA/HRS focused update of the 2008 guidelines for device-based therapy of cardiac rhythm abnormalities. *Journal of the American College of Cardiology, 60*(14), 1297-1313. doi:10.1016/j.jacc.2012.07.009

IMPLANTABLE CARDIOVERTER-DEFIBRILLATORS

Since the early 1980s, ICDs have been used to improve outcomes for patients with advanced cardiac disease, and the technology for ICDs has grown dramatically. The initial devices were large and bulky, requiring thoracic surgery for implantation. The generators were implanted in the abdomen, with patches applied to the heart. Contemporary devices are similar to the size of a pacemaker and are implanted in the same location as permanent pacemakers (Priori et al., 2015; Yancy et al., 2013).

Indications

Initially, ICDs were indicated for patients who survived resuscitated cardiac arrest caused by ventricular tachycardia or ventricular fibrillation. Therefore, ICDs were deemed secondary prevention devices (Dirks & Waters, 2014). As ICD device technology improved over the years, indications have expanded to be a primary prevention strategy for patients experiencing tachydysrhythmias who are at risk for sudden cardiac death (Yancy et al., 2013).

Functions

Like pacemakers, ICDs are multiprogrammable, with a large variety of technical options for treating dysrhythmias. The ultimate goal of therapy is to avoid the dysrhythmias completely. Appropriate administration of antiarrhythmic medications is aimed to control the dysrhythmias and prevent ICD interventions. Amiodarone, especially with the adjunctive use of beta blockers, has been shown to reduce the firing of ICDs (Priori et al., 2015).

NURSING APPLICATION

Patients with ICD should be instructed to continue taking their medications. ICDs do not eliminate the development of dysrhythmias; they only terminate the dysrhythmias once they have occurred. Antiarrhythmic medications control the development of dysrhythmias.

NURSING APPLICATION

Patients with ICD who have not demonstrated any dysrhythmias are therefore not on antiarrhythmic medications. These patients are at high risk for the development of a dysrhythmia but will not be prescribed any medication until they have demonstrated evidence of a dysrhythmia.

The ICD generator includes technology for permanent cardiac pacing and cardiac defibrillation. The device is programmed to sense ventricular tachycardia through a variety of sophisticated methods that are programmed to the patient's needs when the device is implanted. The method for termination of the dysrhythmia is determined after testing the device after implantation and before wound closure (Dirks & Waters, 2014).

Antitachycardia Pacing

Antitachycardia pacing is also referred to as overdrive pacing and is one way the device can terminate a tachydysrhythmia. When a rapid dysrhythmia is detected, the pacemaker paces at a rate higher than the patient's rate in an attempt to override the rapid rhythm. This method has proven to be an effective method to control some ventricular tachycardias and occurs without the patient experiencing a shock. However, patient sensitivity to feeling pacing varies. Some patients do and others do not notice when overdrive pacing is occurring (Dirks & Waters, 2014).

Defibrillation

Defibrillation is utilized as needed to terminate dysrhythmias. The shock administered can be either a cardioversion shock or a full defibrillation shock. The cardioversion shock uses less energy than the defibrillation shock. If the cardioversion shock is programmed into the device as a therapy, it is attempted before the defibrillation shock. If cardioversion does not terminate the dysrhythmia, a defibrillation shock is administered. The administration of a shock to the heart is not as strong as those seen with external defibrillators. However, they are most definitely felt by patients and are painful. The lowest amount of energy needed to terminate the dysrhythmia is determined when the device is implanted. The shock administered should be strong enough to take control of the heart and eliminate the dysrhythmia as the controlling rhythm (Priori et al., 2015).

Implantation

An electrophysiologist who is trained in ICD insertion should implant the device. Occasionally, an ICD is placed in the operating room by a heart surgeon in conjunction with open-heart surgery. The defibrillator is located on the lead that is placed in the right ventricle. The pacemaker functions as a normal pacemaker. In many cases, the pacemaker is needed only after a shock is delivered and a brief pause in the patient's own rhythm occurs as the heart resets itself after the shock. During implantation of the device, the patient is awake. However, after implantation, it is necessary to test the device to assure that it will fire. During this portion of the procedure, conscious sedation or anesthesia is utilized to protect the patient from discomfort associated with defibrillation. The electrophysiologist programs the device to the most effective settings. After the procedure, the patient is returned to a recovery room or a nursing unit capable of cardiac monitoring. Patients are commonly discharged the next day if no complications occur and ventricular dysrhythmias are under control (Dirks & Waters, 2014).

The subcutaneous ICD (SICD) is a technology developed over the last decade and approved for use by the FDA in 2012 (Food & Drug Administration, 2015). This technology is leadless and consists of a device generator and defibrillation lead placed under the skin under the left breast beside the sternum. This technology avoids transvenous cannulation of leads and the necessity of a generator pocket within the chest wall (as with the traditional permanent pacemaker with leads). In comparison to the traditional ICD devices, the advantages of not having leads dwelling within the central veins and the potential necessity for extraction. Disadvantages include the size being larger than the traditional device due to a larger battery and the necessity for higher amplitude of energy for the shock to transmit through the transthoracic wall and cavity to the myocardium. Generally speaking, the SICD provides a safe alternative option for life-threatening rhythm termination therapy in patients who are ICD candidates but must be studied further in larger populations to determine its overall benefit in comparison to traditional devices (Chang, Doshi, & Saxon, 2014).

PATIENT MANAGEMENT

Pacemaker Postoperative Follow-up

Patients with new implants will have individualized, predetermined follow-up appointments. As technology continues to advance, follow-up appointments will not always be in-office visits because most devices used for implantation for more than 10 years have telephone-monitoring capabilities (Tracy et al., 2012). Transtelephonic monitoring allows cardiology office clinicians to access device history and real-time data to evaluate its function. This capability is especially important to patients who live in rural areas, those with limited means of transportation, and those who have restricted mobility. A follow-up office appointment allows the physician or nurse practitioner to observe the insertion site, perform a physical examination, and also access pacemaker data to evaluate its function.

Transtelephonic Monitoring

Pacemaker function should be assessed at regular intervals determined by the physician, but is also assessed for episodic events requiring device interrogation. Patients with pacemakers are given transmitting devices that allow them to transmit the needed information. There is usually a prescheduled time for the patient to make the phone call to the office. When the call is made, the patient is given instructions on how to transmit. This transmission involves utilizing the phone with the transmitting device over the pacemaker. Devices implanted before 2008 provided office clinicians with a transmittal in the form of an ECG. The ECG allowed the physician to determine whether the pacemaker was functioning normally and determined battery life. Contemporary devices allow for full transtelephonic interrogation of the devices, providing office clinicians with device history and real-time data including wireless telemetry and shock impedance (Tracy et al., 2012). After the information is received by the physician, the "appointment" is over; the physician will review the information and then call the patient to communicate whether there are any concerns regarding pacemaker function.

Many patients can successfully transmit over the phone without any difficulty. Some patients may require help from a second person. It is usually during the first office visit after insertion that transmission instructions are reviewed and an assessment of the patient's ability to use this method is made.

The evolution of pacemaker capabilities (e.g., overdrive pacing, biventricular pacing, and archiving data) drives the demand for high-powered batteries to sustain them. Contemporary pacing generators are powered by lithium anode batteries for this reason and have an average life span ranging from 7 to 10 years (Mond & Freitag, 2014). Pacemaker batteries have a "staged" level of functioning resulting in a loss in full charge. Thus, the battery functions at full level of voltage for a period of time and then loses voltage. When the battery approaches about 90% depletion, it reaches the elective replacement interval (ERI). This is the change detected during telephonic transmission. The patient is notified of this finding and is informed a replacement will be necessary in the near future. Battery replacement is not an emergent situation, but it should be done soon after ERI is reached. The procedure is usually scheduled as an outpatient procedure (Anderson, 2015).

NURSING APPLICATION

It is important to assure patients that by completing pacemaker checks over the phone and following up with the physician according to the scheduled timeframes, there will be plenty of warning regarding battery ERI. Patients who are not well informed about battery ERI and battery replacement may think that they will die when the battery is depleted.

NURSING APPLICATION

If the patient does not follow up as scheduled by the physician, he or she may miss the ERI warning. When the battery reaches "end of life," the battery needs to be replaced immediately in those patients who rely on the pacemaker on a regular basis.

Pacemaker Reprogramming

Occasionally, the original settings on a pacemaker may require adjustment to better meet the physiological needs of the patient or to optimize the pacemaker function and preserve the battery. Changes to the device's settings are most often completed during an office visit for close patient monitoring. Pacemakers have multiple parameters that can be adjusted at any time. Reprogramming a pacemaker involves placing a programmer device over the pacing generator. The size and shape of the device varies from one manufacturer to another, but most devices are no larger than the size of a man's hand. The programmer is handheld and connected to a computer. When it is over the pacemaker, the programmer transmits information from the pacer to the computer. Once the information is obtained, the physician can make adjustments on the computer that are transmitted back to the pacemaker. After all of the necessary changes have been made, the reprogramming is over. Reprogramming is a painless, short procedure that should result in improved functioning of the pacemaker (Anderson, 2015).

Cardiac Resynchronization Therapy Postoperative Care and Outcomes

Postoperative care for CRTs differs little from that of patients with standard pacemakers. However, patients with CRT are likely to require more frequent in-office follow-up, because their pacemakers are adjusted and reprogrammed more often to best meet their physiological needs (Anderson, 2015). Overall, patients benefit from reduced morbidity and mortality after CRT. Patients who receive CRT with ICD placement have greater benefits than those who received CRT with permanent pacemaker placement (Tracy et al., 2012).

Implantable Cardioverter-Defibrillator Postoperative Follow-up

Postoperative care for ICDs is similar to the postoperative care necessary for patients with pacemakers. However, patients with ICDs are generally restricted from driving for a longer period. These limitations vary somewhat by physician. The goal is to prevent the possibility of developing a dysrhythmia that incapacitates the driver while behind the wheel. Many patients find adherence to this restriction very difficult (Dirks & Waters, 2014).

Office Visits

Follow-up visits after ICD implantation may occur more frequently than with permanent pacemaker insertion. Patients may have office visits rather than phone transmissions, because electrophysiologists want to assess the function of the device and evaluate the patient's response. However, most manufacturers have remote device interrogation capabilities, decreasing the need for frequent office visits. This remote monitoring is accomplished through radiofrequency transmission via a telephone system similar to remote monitoring of permanent pacemakers. These remote monitoring systems also have the ability to notify the electrophysiologist's office if the device fires or if the device is inadvertently deactivated. In the office, with a programmer similar to the one used for pacemakers, electrophysiologists can determine the number of therapies that have been delivered by the device, including the success of the therapy. During this time, the battery level is also checked. Battery life depends on the frequency of the therapy, as well as the energy utilized with those therapies. As with pacemakers, it is predetermined when battery ERI is reached, so replacement of the battery can be scheduled. These pacemaker checks are essential in maintaining good function of the ICD (Dirks & Waters, 2014).

Magnet Function With an Implantable Cardioverter-Defibrillator

A magnet placed over the pulse generator in a normal pacemaker causes the pacemaker to pace without sensing any of the heart's normal activity. An ICD does not function in the same manner. A magnet placed over an ICD disables the device while the magnet is in place. When the magnet is moved away from the device, the device should function in the normal manner. All device companies have specific functionality, and each device may function with some differences. It is important for healthcare workers to be aware that a magnet over an ICD disables the device and no treatment will occur if dysrhythmias develop. The best practice is not to use magnets near these devices unless instructed to do so by a qualified physician (Dirks & Waters, 2014).

PATIENT EDUCATION

Pacemaker

As pacemakers become more sophisticated, restrictions for the patient decrease. However, patients should be informed of specific care instructions after pacemaker insertion. Because of the complexities in the function of permanent pacemakers, patient education should be focused on priority information regarding safety, prevention of infection, and follow-up. As with all patient education, healthcare literacy must be considered when planning educational interventions (Urden, Stacy, & Lough, 2014).

The following patient education information about pacemakers is adapted from the American Heart Association (2014):

- Every patient should receive a pacemaker card identifying the type of pacemaker, leads, and date of insertion and carry it in his or her wallet.

- Patients should always inform physicians and dentists that they have pacemakers before receiving care. Dental equipment should not negatively affect pacemakers, and routine antibiotic prophylaxis is not recommended.

- A pacemaker may trigger airport metal detectors, but the metal detectors will not harm the pacemaker. Even so, patients should not linger around metal detectors. Patients should inform security personnel of their pacemakers and ask them not to hold metal detectors near their pacemakers longer than necessary. Having the pacemaker identification card on hand is expected by security personnel.

- Patients with pacemakers should not undergo magnetic resonance imaging (MRI) because it can damage the pacemaker, unless the patient has an MRI conditional device. The magnet in the MRI will cause the pacemaker to pace asynchronously, without regard for the patient's own rhythm. In some instances, some reprogramming may be done to allow for MRI. However, this is limited to very specific instances. Current studies are investigating the viability of MRI utilizing shielding materials in patients with pacemakers. Other radiology procedures have not been shown to affect pacemakers. In patients who have the newer MRI conditional devices, they should follow the manufacturer's guidelines because most require a 6-week waiting period after implant before undergoing MRI.

- Radiation equipment used for treating cancer can damage pacemakers. Patients with pacemakers should not have radiation treatments until arrangements have been made with the physicians managing the pacemakers. The pacemaker should be shielded as much as possible because as radiation dosing increases, so does the risk to the pacemaker. In some situations, the pacemaker may be moved to another location in the body to avoid direct radiation. The pacemaker should be checked after each radiation treatment. If the patient is pacemaker dependent (fully dependent on the pacemaker for a heart rate), a temporary pacemaker may be inserted during treatment to assure there is no loss of heart rate. The temporary pacemaker battery can be placed away from the body and shielded during the procedure.

- Power-generating equipment, arc welding equipment, and powerful magnets (such as those found in some medical equipment and motors) can inhibit a pacemaker from functioning properly. Patients should avoid being near this type of equipment. If a patient becomes dizzy around questionable equipment (such as a power station) or while working on a running engine, he or she should back away from the equipment and the pacemaker should resume normal functioning.

- After the initial recovery period (determined by the physician), no restrictions to arm movement are necessary.

- Patients should report any dizziness or syncope to their physicians. If they are able to learn to take their own pulses, they can be instructed to measure the pulse rate daily and notify their physicians if it is slower than the programmed low rate on their pacemakers. This may be difficult for some patients. The best indicator for patients with pacemakers is how they are feeling.

- Patients should be reminded of the importance of keeping appointments – both in-person appointments and telephonic monitoring – for routine pacemaker assessment.

Cardiac Resynchronization Therapy

The standard education that was reviewed for traditional pacemaker insertion is the same for CRT because it is pacemaker technology. It is important for patients with CRT to realize that this therapy does not eliminate the need for continued medical therapy. In fact, medications used for mortality benefit (angiotensin-converting enzyme inhibitors and beta blockers) may actually be increased to higher therapeutic levels than the patient was able to tolerate without biventricular pacing. In addition, patient symptoms of heart failure may improve; consequently, medication use for symptom relief may be decreased (diuretics; Yancy et al., 2013).

Implantable Cardioverter-Defibrillator

Emotional Impact

Patient education for the recipient of an ICD involves technical and emotional aspects of care. Implantation of an ICD is generally emotionally difficult because the patient realizes that his or her life may depend on the device. The emotional impact extends beyond the patient to the family. There is a fear of death, as well as a fear that the device may not function. In addition, patients may also experience fear and anxiety related to the anticipation of an actual shock. Patients have reported sleeplessness because of this fear and anxiety. Families may also become overprotective because they worry about the device. Thorough patient education and support is essential to help patients and families understand the device. If an ICD support group is available, the patient and the patient's significant other should be encouraged to attend.

Device Activation Education

As stated earlier, the goal of therapy is to have a medication regimen that prevents dysrhythmias from occurring. However, dysrhythmias may occur, so the patient and family should be aware of the proper response. Physicians may vary in their preference regarding notification of a shock, but the following list provides basic information regarding patient response to device activation (Anderson, 2015):

1. All patients with ICDs should have a well-thought-out plan for obtaining emergency medical assistance. Close family and friends should be aware of the plan in the event that the device does not work properly. Close family and friends should be trained in cardiopulmonary resuscitation (CPR).

2. Patients describe the feeling of a full defibrillation shock as being "kicked in the chest." A cardioversion shock is less intense. The patient should not notice normal cardiac pacing, but may notice antitachycardia pacing.

3. Family and friends should be aware they are in no danger if they come in contact with the patient when the defibrillator discharges.

4. When a shock occurs, the patient should notify the physician who is handling monitoring of the ICD that the shock occurred. The physician does not need to be called immediately, but should be notified when his or her office opens. The physician needs to be aware of device firing so adjustments can be made as needed.

5. If the device fires multiple times and the patient returns to normal (awake and appropriate), the physician should be called immediately.

6. If the device continues to fire without success, someone should call the emergency medical system and begin CPR if the patient becomes unconscious.

7. If at any time the ICD fires and the patient does not return to normal (awake and appropriate) after the shock, even if only one shock was delivered, the patient should be taken to the nearest emergency department via the emergency medical system.

Note. These are general recommendations. Each electrophysiologist has specific instructions based on the patient's indications for the device and the specific device that was implanted.

Electromagnetic Interference

On rare occasions (less than 1% per patient per year), electromagnetic interference may cause an ICD to fire or may disable it (Priori et al., 2015). All precautions noted with pacemakers apply to ICDs. It is important for patients to notify security personnel of ICDs. Patients should not allow handheld metal detector wands to be held over the device for more than a few seconds. These contain magnets that can disable the device if left in place too long. As with permanent pacemakers, patients should carry the manufacturer's device identification card (Anderson, 2015).

ICDs present an additional set of concerns for the patient undergoing surgery or procedures such as endoscopy with polyp removal. The patient should make sure those involved with the procedure are well aware that he or she has an ICD. Special precautions are necessary that are beyond the scope of this discussion.

Other Educational Considerations

The surgical complications, postoperative considerations, and patient education discussed for permanent pacemakers also apply to patients with an ICD or CRT because these devices also have pacemaker technology.

NURSING APPLICATION

Many patients meeting criteria for CRT also meet criteria for an ICD. It is important to know what therapy your patient has implanted. If the patient has CRT with an ICD, it is often referred to as a CRT-D pacemaker.

CASE STUDY

A 67-year-old male patient presents to the emergency department (ED) reporting chest pain off and on for the past week in the center of his chest. The patient describes taking sublingual nitroglycerin multiple times this week to help the pain, but it continues to return. He also reports feeling weaker and more tired than usual. His wife reminds him of experiencing palpitations for the last few days as well.

The patient denies having fever, syncope, abdominal pain, nausea, or vomiting. He has a medical history of nonvalvular atrial fibrillation with rate control, dyslipidemia, hypertension, and angina pectoris. He had an angiogram performed 3 years ago revealing stable coronary artery lesions in the distal left anterior descending and inferior vessels. The patient's surgical history includes three left knee surgeries over the last 15 years and a tonsillectomy as a child. His daily home medications include atorvastatin, a baby aspirin, apixaban, metoprolol, and lisinopril. His mother and sister are alive and have hypertension. He does not know his father's medical history. He quit smoking cigarettes 20 years ago and cigars 10 years ago. He drinks one to two beers daily and has never used illicit drugs.

A 12-lead ECG was performed and revealed atrial fibrillation with a rate of 48 beats/min. Laboratory results were collected and were unremarkable for major abnormalities warranting medical intervention. The emergency department physician consults the patient's cardiologist, who recommends pacemaker placement to allow for rhythm-control therapy. A dual-chamber, or DDDR, permanent pacemaker is placed, and amiodarone is added to the patient's medication regimen.

The patient recovered in the hospital overnight and was discharged home the next day. During the patient's follow-up cardiology appointment, he reports feeling better with no recurrence of his previous symptoms.

Questions

1. What do the DDDR codes for the patient's new pacemaker mean?

2. Which patient education after pacemaker placement does the nurse provide to the patient at discharge?

Answers

1. The D in the first position indicates that the electrode in the atrium and the electrode in the ventricle are programmed to pace the atrium and the ventricle if there is no normal electrical activity from the patient's heart. The D in the second position indicates that the device can sense any normal electrical activity (depolarization) in the atrium or ventricle. The D in the third position refers to the pacemaker's response as it senses the activity of the heart. The R in the fourth position stands for rate responsiveness.

2. The patient is instructed to avoid raising the affected arm above the head for approximately 2 weeks after implantation to prevent lead dislodgement from the endocardium. The patient is also advised to limit the movement of the affected shoulder and not to lie on the affected side for the first 12 to 24 hours. A pacemaker identification card is given to the patient, and he is instructed to carry it with him at all times in his wallet.

The patient is also instructed to avoid undergoing MRI because it can damage the pacemaker. Patients should report any dizziness or syncope to his physician. In addition, the patient is instructed to take his own pulse so that he can measure his pulse rate daily and notify the clinician if it is slower than the programmed low rate on his pacemaker. The patient is also instructed about the importance to keep all scheduled follow-up office visits.

SUMMARY

The use and development of implantable cardiac devices has grown dramatically over the past half century. With these developments, patient outcomes continue to improve. Cardiovascular nurses must utilize their fundamental knowledge of cardiovascular anatomy and physiology to patient indications for implantable cardiac devices. Understanding the indications and functions of these devices will not only improve patient care, but also improve patient education about self-care and particular medications or treatments. As new research findings continue to lead the direction of treatment for advanced cardiac disease, the nurse must also prevent (if possible) and identify complications associated with implanted cardiac devices. Proper patient management and education will help ensure the devices function as intended.

EXAM QUESTIONS

CHAPTER 12
Questions 60–66

Note: Choose the one option that BEST answers each question.

60. Which finding is an indication for a permanent pacemaker?

    a. Sinoatrial node dysfunction
    b. Nonrefractory atrial flutter
    c. Left bundle branch block
    d. New York Heart Association Class I heart failure

61. Which condition is described as a self-limited loss of consciousness and is an indication for an implanted cardiac device?

    a. Cerebrovascular infarct
    b. Recurrent neurocardiogenic syncope
    c. Myocardial infarction
    d. Paroxysmal tachydysrhythmia

62. What pacemaker complication is associated with the patient turning the pacing generator and subsequently twisting the pacing leads?

    a. Pneumothorax
    b. Vegetative infection
    c. Myocardial perforation
    d. Twiddler's syndrome

63. Which implanted cardiac device is associated with pacing both ventricles simultaneously?

    a. A permanent pacemaker
    b. An implantable cardioverter-defibrillator
    c. A biventricular pacemaker
    d. A transvenous pacemaker

64. For which implanted device can follow-up evaluations usually be performed over the phone after the first in-person evaluation?

    a. A permanent pacemaker
    b. An epicardial pacemaker
    c. A transcutaneous pacemaker
    d. A transvenous pacemaker

65. Which implanted cardiac device can be disabled by a magnet?

    a. Single-chamber pacemaker
    b. Implantable cardioverter-defibrillator
    c. Biventricular pacemaker
    d. Dual-chamber pacemaker

66. A patient who has just received an implantable cardioverter-defibrillator (ICD) is preparing for discharge. Which of these statements should the nurse make as part of the necessary patient education?

    a. "Notify the physician immediately when the ICD fires one time."
    b. "Patients can usually feel when overdrive pacing occurs."
    c. "Be sure to keep all in-office appointments."
    d. "Your family is not expected to know CPR."

REFERENCES

American Heart Association. (2014). *Living with your pacemaker*. Retrieved from http://www.heart.org/HEARTORG/Conditions/Arrhythmia/PreventionTreatment ofArrhythmia/Living-With-Your-Pacemaker _UCM_305290_Article.jsp#.V_rWzfkrLIU

Anderson, K. M. (Ed.). (2015). *The advanced practice nurse cardiovascular clinician*. New York, NY: Springer Publishing.

Chang, P. M., Doshi, R., & Saxon, L. A. (2014). Subcutaneous implantable carioverter-defibrillator. *Circulation, 129,* e644-646. doi: 10.1161/CIRCULATIONAHA.113.006645

Dirks, J., & Waters, J. (2014). Cardiovascular therapeutic management. In L. D. Urden, K. M. Stacy, & M. E. Lough (Eds.), *Critical care nursing: Diagnosis and management* (7th ed., pp. 200-221). St. Louis, MO: Elsevier/Mosby.

Food & Drug Administration. (2015). *Subcutaneous implantable defibrillator (S-ICD) system – P110042*. Retrieved from http:// www.fda.gov/MedicalDevices/Products andMedicalProcedures/DeviceApprovals andClearances/Recently-ApprovedDevices/ ucm326541.htm

Gillis, A. M., Russo, A. M., Ellenbogen, K. A., Swerdlow, C. D., Olshansky, B., Al-Khatib, S. M., ... Shen, W.-K. (2012). HRS/ACCF expert consensus statement on pacemaker device and mode selection. *Journal of the American College of Cardiology, 60*(7), 682-703. doi:10.1016/j.jacc.2012.06.011

Hussein, A. A., Baghdy, Y., Wazni, O. M., Brunner, M. P., Kabbach, G., Shao, M., ... Tarakji, K. G. (2016). Microbiology of cardiac implantable electronic device infections. *JACCCEP, 2*(4), 498-505. doi:10.1016/j. jacep.2016.01.019

Mandal, S., Pande, A., & Kahali, D. (2012). A rare case of very early pacemaker Twiddler's syndrome. *Heart Views, 13*(3), 114-115. doi:10.4103/1995-705X.102157

Medtronic. (2016). *FDA Approves the world's smallest pacemaker*. Retrieved from http:// www.medtronic.com/us-en/about/news/ micra-fda-approval.html

Mond, H. G., & Freitag, G. (2014). The cardiac implantable electronic device power source: Evolution and revolution. *Pacing Clinical Electrophysiology, 37*(12), 1728-1745. doi:10.1111/pace.12526

Mozaffarian, D., Benjamin, E. J, Alan, S. G., Arnett, D. K., Blaha, M. J., Cushman, M., ... Turner, M. B. (2016). Heart disease and stroke statistics – 2016 update: A report from the American Heart Association. *Cirulation, 134*(21), e1-e323. doi: 10.1161/ CIR.0000000000000350

National Institute for Health and Care Excellence. (2014). *Dual-chamber pacemakers for symptomatic bradycardia due to sick sinus syndrome without atrioventricular block (part review of technology appraisal guidance 88)*. Retrieved from https://www. guideline.gov/summaries/summary/48878?

Nelson, G. D. (1993). Historical perspectives: A brief history of cardiac pacing. *Texas Heart Institute Journal, 20*(1), 12-18. Retrieved from http://www.ncbi.nlm.nih.gov/pmc/articles/PMC325046/pdf/thij00040-0032.pdf

Patton, K. T., Thibodeau, G. A., & Douglas, M. M. (2012). *Essentials of anatomy & physiology* (1st ed.). Lansing, MI: Elsevier/Mosby.

Priori, S. G., Blomstrom-Lundqvist, C., Mazzanti, A., Blom, N., Borggrefe, M., Camm, J., ... Van Veldhuisen, D. J. (2015). 2015 ESC guidelines for the management of patients with ventricular arrhythmias and the prevention of sudden cardiac death. *European Heart Journal, 36*(41), 2793-2867. doi:10.1093/eurheartj/ehv316

Reynolds, D., Duray, G. Z., Omar, R., Soejima, K., Neuzil, P., Zhang, S., ... Ritter, P. (2016). A leadless intracardiac transcatheter pacing system. *The New England Journal of Medicine, 374,* 533-541. doi: 10.1056/NEJMoa1511643

Sandoe, J. A. T., Barlow, G., Chambers, J. B., Gammage, M., Guleri, A., Howard, P., ... Watkin, R. (2015). Guidelines for the diagnosis, prevention and management of implantable cardiac electronic device infection. Report of a joint working party project on behalf of the British Society for Antimicrobial Chemotherapy, British Heart Rhythm Society, British Cardiovascular Society, British Heart Valve Society and British Society for Echocardiography. *Journal of Antimicrobial Chemotherapy, 70,* 325-359. doi:10.1093/jac/dku383

Tracy, C. M., Epstein, A. E., Darbar, D., DiMarco, J. P., Dunbar, S. B., Estes, N. A. M., ... Varosy, P. D. (2012). 2012 ACCF/AHA/HRS focused update of the 2008 guidelines for device-based therapy of cardiac rhythm abnormalities. *Journal of the American College of Cardiology, 60*(14), 1297-1313. doi:10.1016/j.jacc.2012.07.009

Urden, L. D., Stacy, K. M., & Lough, M. E. (2014). *Critical care nursing diagnosis and management* (7th ed.). St. Louis, MO: Elsevier/Mosby.

Yancy, C. W., Jessup, M., Bozkurt, B., Butler, J., Casey, D. E., Drazner, M. H., ... Wilkoff, B. L. (2013). 2013 ACCF/AHA guideline for the management of heart failure: A report of the American College of Cardiology Foundation/American Heart Association Task Force on Practice Guidelines. *Circulation, 128,* e240-e327. doi:10.1161/CIR.0b013e31829e8776

CHAPTER 13

ACUTE CORONARY SYNDROMES

CHAPTER OBJECTIVE

After completing this chapter, the learner will be able to discuss the comprehensive nursing management of acute coronary syndromes.

LEARNING OUTCOMES

After completing this chapter, the learner will be able to:

1. Apply knowledge of the pathophysiology and clinical presentations of acute coronary syndromes to the appropriate nursing care.

2. Define the different characteristics of acute coronary syndromes.

3. Identify appropriate treatments for acute coronary syndromes.

4. Describe the nurse's role in aggressive risk factor management and patient education in the comprehensive management of acute coronary syndromes.

INTRODUCTION

Within the United States, acute coronary syndrome (ACS) affects more than 780,000 persons each year and is one of the most common hospital diagnoses in the nation. The median age at ACS presentation is 68 years, and the male-to-female ratio is approximately 3:2 (Amsterdam et al., 2014). The term ACS refers to three acute cardiac conditions involving myocardial ischemia. As illustrated in Figure 13-1,

an ACS can include presentations of unstable angina (UA), non-ST-segment elevated myocardial infarction (NSTEMI), and ST-segment elevated myocardial infarction (STEMI). Decisions about medical and interventional treatments are determined by specific findings noted upon patient presentation with ACS. These presentations guide the subclassification of ACS into the three categories according to the presence or absence of ST-segment elevation on the presenting electrocardiogram (ECG) and abnormal elevation of myocardial biomarkers (e.g., troponins; Mozaffarian et al., 2016). The cardiovascular nurse must differentiate between stable angina and ACS presentations and, when the presentations suggest ACS, recognize the urgency for treatment aimed at preserving myocardial cell life and muscle function.

NURSING APPLICATION

All patients should be taught the importance of immediately seeking medical attention for any symptoms suggesting a "heart attack." Patients need to understand the physiological importance of early treatment in preserving myocardial function.

ST-SEGMENT ELEVATION MYOCARDIAL INFARCTION

A STEMI is a presentation of ACS and represents acute myocardial infarction (AMI).

FIGURE 13-1: CONTINUUM OF ACUTE CORONARY SYNDROMES

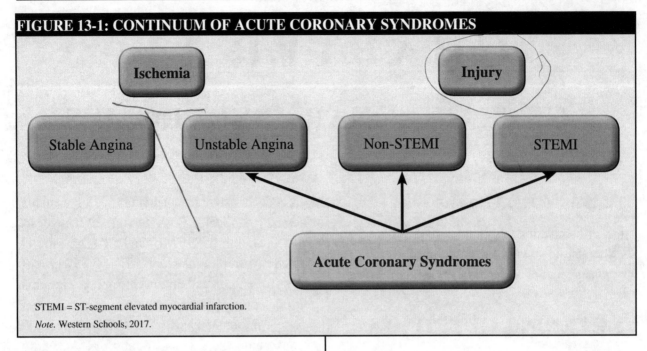

STEMI = ST-segment elevated myocardial infarction.

Note. Western Schools, 2017.

As noted in Figure 13-1, not all categories of ACS involve AMI. STEMI is an emergent cardiac condition that requires rapid intervention aimed at preserving myocardial cell life and muscle function. This clinical syndrome is characterized by persistent electrocardiographic ST elevation and subsequent release of biomarkers of myocardial necrosis.

Prevalence

Despite studies indicating a decline in the incidence of STEMIs, this type of AMI remains burdensome in the United States and worldwide. Approximately 25% to 40% of all patients in the United States diagnosed with ACS or AMI present with STEMI (Mozaffarian et al., 2016; O'Gara et al., 2013). Men have a higher incidence of STEMI than women. Patients with diabetes represent approximately 23% of all STEMI patients and have been found to have poorer outcomes (O'Gara et al., 2013). Patients older than 70 years have a 4-fold greater risk for poor outcomes with STEMI compared with any other population (O'Gara et al., 2013). As a result of improved methods and systems of care for this population, the incidence of disease and death continues to improve.

Causes

STEMI is caused by thrombosis of a coronary vessel secondary to the rupture of plaque. The rupture of plaque can occur spontaneously or be provoked by vasospasm or intravascular catheter manipulation. Injury to the vulnerable plaque is facilitated by hypertension, tobacco smoking, and continued lipid accumulation. In rare occasions, STEMI occurs as a result of complete occlusion of the vessel caused by coronary emboli (Antman & Loscalzo, 2017).

Pathophysiology

STEMI occurs with abrupt onset of complete thrombotic vessel occlusion that is most often caused by the rupturing of unstable vulnerable plaque (or atheroma) within the coronary artery (see Figure 13-2). When vulnerable plaque ruptures, its contents are exposed to the blood, initiating inflammatory mechanisms favorable for thrombogenesis. Thrombogenesis involves the release of multiple chemicals and the activation of platelets responsible for containing the foreign matter entering the blood (lipid core). A platelet-rich thrombus forms at the site of injury, blocking blood flow and causing an ischemic injury to

FIGURE 13-2: PATHOGENESIS OF ACUTE CORONARY SYNDROME

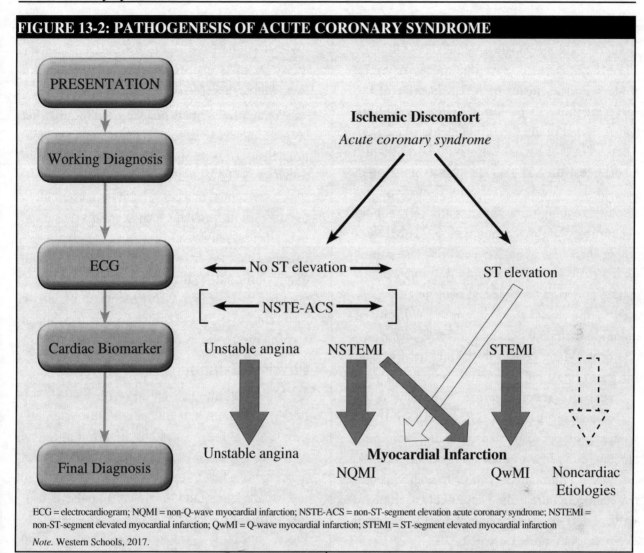

ECG = electrocardiogram; NQMI = non-Q-wave myocardial infarction; NSTE-ACS = non-ST-segment elevation acute coronary syndrome; NSTEMI = non-ST-segment elevated myocardial infarction; QwMI = Q-wave myocardial infarction; STEMI = ST-segment elevated myocardial infarction

Note. Western Schools, 2017.

myocardial cells. Vulnerable plaque is characterized by a thin fibrous cap separating the rich lipid core from the blood (Antman & Loscalzo, 2017).

Initially, the endocardial layer of heart tissue is the first to become ischemic and begin to die. As ischemia continues and the injury extends, the myocardium (or subendocardium) is affected. If STEMI is left untreated and continues to progress, the injury can extend toward the epicardium, affecting the full thickness of the myocardium. A full-thickness MI is commonly referred to as a transmural MI.

Because of the development of collateral circulation over time, a gradually growing coronary artery stenosis does not typically precipitate STEMI. Patients with chronic ischemic heart disease have collateral circulation providing protection during the occlusion of a coronary vessel. Collateral vessels are those that connect major branches of coronary arteries. As luminal narrowing gradually occurs, pressure changes promote the development and use of these collateral vessels to supply oxygen to ischemic areas. New capillaries can grow in response to ischemia. Younger patients without collateral circulation are more vulnerable to extensive damage from an occluded coronary artery.

Clinical Presentation

In up to half of STEMI cases, vigorous physical exertion (e.g., physical exercise, emotional stress, or medical illness) was the precipitating factor (O'Gara et al., 2013). Although STEMI can occur at any time of day or night, studies find a cluster of STEMIs seen in the early morning a few hours after awakening (Mozaffarian et al., 2016; O'Gara et al., 2013). Acute pain is the most common clinical feature associated with STEMI. The pain is most often described as severe in intensity, heavy, squeezing, or crushing, and occasionally as stabbing or burning. Pain associated with a STEMI lasts longer than that of angina pectoris. The pain is typically located in the central anterior chest and/or epigastric region and occasionally radiates to the arms. Less common locations of radiation include the abdomen, back, lower jaw, and neck. Many people mistake epigastric pain for gastrointestinal discomfort associated with indigestion. Accompanying symptoms often include generalized weakness (especially in women), diaphoresis, nausea and/or vomiting, anxiety, or a sense of impending doom. STEMI-associated pain, unlike pain from angina pectoris, can occur at rest and is not likely to improve with rest if its onset occurred with physical exertion (Antman & Loscalzo, 2017).

Women often have atypical presentations of ACS for reasons that are not fully understood. Women were less likely than men to present with chest pain but have more of the associated symptoms. Women younger than 45 years were more likely than other groups to present without chest pain. Women often present with angina-equivalent symptoms such as dyspnea, weakness, unusual fatigue, and indigestion. Women have also been found to report pain in the upper back, arm, neck, and jaw more often than their male counterparts. Unlike men, women are more likely to have more high-risk presentations without centralized chest pain (Mehta et al., 2016). Studies report that, although women were more likely to present with nonobstruc-

tive coronary heart disease (CHD), 40% of the women studied with nonobstructive coronary artery stenosis had evidence of plaque disruption (Mehta et al., 2016).

Women described nuanced symptoms that seemed initially to pass, then recur, and then build in intensity over passing days. Atypical presentations for STEMI and other ACS presentations pose grave consequences related to delayed identification of the problem such as misdiagnosis and delayed revascularization. Consequently, atypical presentations in women are associated with disproportionately higher AMI mortality rates (Antman & Loscalzo, 2017; Mehta et al., 2016). See Table 13-1 for the comparison of typical and atypical presentations of AMI.

Physical Examination

Most patients presenting with STEMI are notably anxious and restless. Pallor, clamminess, and cool skin of the distal extremities can result from the decrease in cardiac output. Upon auscultation, heart sounds over the precordium are usually quiet, and the apical impulse is usually difficult to palpate. When heart sounds are heard, murmurs, extra sounds (S3 and S4), and splitting sounds can be present. A pericardial friction rub may be heard in patients with transmural STEMI because of associated pericarditis. Vital signs can reflect lower-than-baseline systolic pressures or hypotension, and the heart rate can be tachycardic (common with anterior MIs) or bradycardic (common with inferior MIs; Antman & Loscalzo, 2017).

Diagnosis

The first diagnostic test for finding STEMI is the 12-lead ECG. When the 12-lead ECG finds ST elevation, other diagnostic tests such as myocardial biomarkers are delayed until after intervention is initiated to reduce the risk for further myocardial cell death (O'Gara et al., 2013). STEMI is further defined by new ST

TABLE 13-1: TYPICAL AND ATYPICAL PRESENTATIONS OF ACUTE MYOCARDIAL INFARCTION

Typical Symptoms	Atypical Symptoms

• Chest pain and/or discomfort (i.e., heavy, crushing, pressure, tightness, squeezing)
• Radiating pain to jaw, neck, shoulders, arm, and/or back
• Epigastric pain
• Associated symptoms of
  ◦ dyspnea
  ◦ nausea
  ◦ vomiting
  ◦ light-headedness
  ◦ diaphoresis
	• Chest pain (i.e., sharp, pleuritic, burning, aching, soreness, reproducible)
	• Upper back pain
	• Epigastric pain or indigestion
	• Flu-like symptoms
	• Associated symptoms of
	  ◦ unusual fatigue
	  ◦ unusual dyspnea
	  ◦ dizziness
	  ◦ generalized scared and/or anxious feeling
	  ◦ generalized weakness
	  ◦ palpitations

Note. From Western Schools.

elevation at the J point in at least two contiguous leads of 2 mm or greater in men or 1.5 mm or greater in women in leads V2 to V3 and/or 1 mm or greater in other contiguous chest or limb leads (in the absence of left ventricular hypertrophy or left bundle branch block [LBBB]). New or presumably new LBBB can also be considered a STEMI equivalent but is rare. Because LBBB STEMI-equivalent presentations are rare and may interfere with ST-elevation analysis, the finding of a new LBBB should not be considered a STEMI equivalent without other findings suggestive of AMI (O'Gara et al., 2013).

If the 12-lead ECG is not definitive for STEMI, such as in the case of LBBB, the cardiac troponin serum biomarker is used (O'Gara et al., 2013). An acutely elevated serum troponin level greater than 1.0 ng/ml is considered diagnostic for myocardial necrosis and ACS (Anderson, 2016). Patients with acute or late-stage chronic kidney disease, end-stage kidney disease, or chronic heart failure can have chronically elevated troponin levels, but they are not normally greater than 1.0 ng/ml (Anderson, 2016).

Primary Treatment Strategy in STEMI

Reperfusion is the primary treatment strategy in STEMI because the underlying pathophysiology is a fibrin-stable clot. Reperfusion is defined as the restoration of oxygen to ischemic tissue. Patients with STEMI need to receive reperfusion therapy as quickly as possible (O'Gara et al., 2013). Adjunctive supportive pharmacological treatment is also administered while the patient is prepared for reperfusion therapy, but the administration of supportive pharmacological therapy should not delay the time to reperfusion. Pharmacological therapies are discussed later in this chapter.

Two methods of reperfusion are available: fibrinolysis (administration of fibrinolytics) and percutaneous coronary intervention (PCI). If a patient is receiving a fibrinolytic, the drug should be administered within 30 minutes of arrival in the emergency department or on first contact with the paramedics. If a patient is receiving PCI (dilation and/or stent placement within the area of vessel occlusion), balloon inflation should occur within 90 minutes of arrival in the emergency department or at first contact with the paramedics.

PCI is the preferred method of reperfusion if patients can be promptly treated within the 90-minute time frame by an experienced operator in an experienced cardiac catheterization laboratory. Fibrinolysis is the preferred method of reperfusion when there is a delay to PCI or when PCI is not an option. If any contraindications to fibrinolytic therapy exist, the patient should be transferred directly to a facility capable of performing PCI. PCI is also the preferred option for safety reasons if the onset of symptoms is longer than 3 hours, if the diagnosis of STEMI is uncertain, or if the patient is in shock or has severe congestive heart failure. A planned facilitated PCI (after administration of a fibrinolytic) is an option for reperfusion in select patients, including those for whom PCI is not available within 90 minutes, as long as the risk for bleeding is not high. A thorough history and physical examination are required to determine potential high-risk features for bleeding, such as the use of anticoagulants, a history of peptic ulcers, and uncontrolled hypertension. If facilitated PCI will be performed, a full dose of fibrinolytic therapy is not used (O'Gara et al., 2013).

Criteria for Reperfusion

In addition to patients with ST-segment elevation on a 12-lead ECG, patients with a new (or presumably new) LBBB and those with evidence of posterior wall MI may also be candidates for immediate reperfusion therapy. An initial ECG should be completed within 10 minutes of arrival to the hospital if it was not already completed en route by Emergency Medical Services (EMS). If the initial ECG is not diagnostic of ST-segment elevation and the patient remains symptomatic, then serial ECGs should be done at 5- to 10-minute intervals until a diagnosis is made or until symptoms resolve. Imaging studies such as echocardiogra-

phy can also be done in the emergency department to identify wall motion abnormalities if the patient's symptoms suggest acute MI but the ECG is not clearly demonstrating ST-segment elevation (O'Gara et al., 2013).

ST-segment elevation may be difficult to determine in the presence of LBBB because a normal degree of ST-segment elevation already exists with LBBB. In posterior wall MI, ST-segment elevation does not show on a standard 12-lead ECG, but an echocardiogram may show poor function of the posterior wall, helping to confirm the diagnosis. A transmural posterior wall AMI may demonstrate 12-lead ECG changes of ST-segment depression in at least two precordial leads (V1-V4; O'Gara et al., 2013).

Fibrinolytic Therapy

As noted in Table 13-2, the administration of fibrinolytics has specific indications and contraindications (O'Gara et al., 2013). Several fibrinolytic agents are available and were discussed in more detail in Chapter 4.

Intracranial hemorrhage is a potential complication of fibrinolytic therapy, so any patient with STEMI at substantial risk for intracranial hemorrhage should be treated with PCI rather than fibrinolytic therapy (O'Gara et al., 2013). Any change in neurological status within 24 hours of administration of a fibrinolytic is considered an intracranial hemorrhage until proven otherwise. All fibrinolytic, anticoagulation, and antiplatelet therapies should be immediately discontinued when a change in neurological status occurs until intracranial hemorrhage is ruled out. Signs of successful reperfusion with fibrinolytics include relief of presenting symptoms, reduction of at least 50% of initial ST-segment elevation on repeat ECG, and hemodynamic and electrical stability.

TABLE 13-2: INDICATIONS AND CONTRAINDICATIONS FOR FIBRINOLYTIC REPERFUSION THERAPY

Indications	Contraindications
• Symptom onset within 12 hours of administration (ideally within 3 hours) • ST-segment elevation >1 mm in two leads evaluating the same wall of the myocardium or the presence of a new left bundle branch block • ECG and other findings consistent with a true isolated posterior wall MI	• Prior intracranial hemorrhage • Known structural cerebrovascular lesion • Malignant intracranial neoplasm • Significant closed head injury within the last 3 months • Ischemic stroke within the last 3 months (unless within the last 3 hours) • Suspected aortic dissection • Active bleeding or bleeding diathesis (excluding menses) • Symptoms older than 24 hours • ST-segment depression (unless indicative of a true posterior wall MI)

ECG = electrocardiogram; MI = myocardial infarction.

Note. Adapted from O'Gara, P. T., Kushner, F. G., Ascheim, D. D., Casey, D. E., Chung, M. K., de Lemos, J. A., … Zhao, D. X. (2013). 2013 ACCF/ AHA guideline for the management of ST-elevation myocardial infarction: A report of the American College of Cardiology Foundation/American Heart Association Task Force on practice guidelines. *Journal of the American College of Cardiology, 61*(4), e78-e140. doi:10.1016/j.jacc.2012.11.019

NURSING APPLICATION

The pain of aortic dissection can mimic the pain of MI. ECG changes associated with pericarditis can also mimic the ECG changes seen in acute MI. It is key in both of these circumstances to differentiate these diagnoses from acute MI because treatment with fibrinolytic therapy could be devastating in either case.

Multiple highly appraised research studies noted in the 2013 STEMI guidelines have demonstrated the safety and feasibility of prehospital fibrinolytic therapy administration by trained EMS personnel. However, this service is not used in most communities within the United States. Within rural communities where prehospital treatment could provide the most benefit, the resources to adequately train the paramedics or purchase the necessary equipment may not be available. Therefore, these effective treatments are not being provided to the populations most

vulnerable to cardiovascular death (O'Gara et al., 2013).

Myocardial Locations of STEMIs

On a 12-lead ECG, inferior wall MIs show ST-segment elevation in the inferior leads: leads II, III, and aVF. Figure 13-3 shows a 12-lead ECG representation of an inferior wall MI. The inferior wall of the left ventricle is fed by the right coronary artery (RCA); therefore, occlusion of the RCA is suspected in patients with inferior wall MIs. Inferior wall MIs are sometimes associated with additional involvement of the posterior wall of the left ventricle or the right ventricle. A right-sided ECG using right-sided chest leads should be performed with all patients with inferior wall MIs to assess for involvement of the right ventricle (O'Gara et al., 2013). Patients with right ventricular involvement are treated differently, as discussed later in this chapter. The more proximal the occlusion of the RCA, the greater the amount of myocardium involved in the infarction.

FIGURE 13-3: SUBSTANTIAL ST-SEGMENT ELEVATION OF INFERIOR WALL MYOCARDIAL INFARCTION

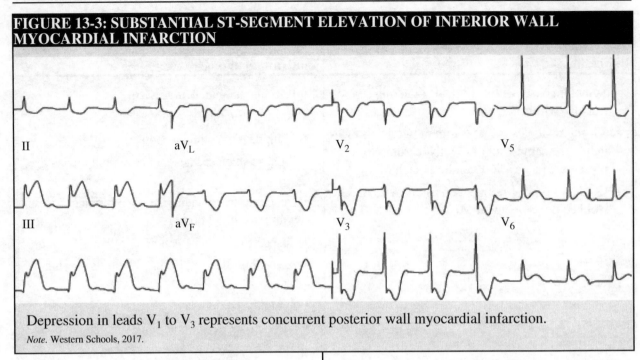

Depression in leads V_1 to V_3 represents concurrent posterior wall myocardial infarction.

Note. Western Schools, 2017.

Because the RCA also feeds the sinoatrial and atrioventricular (AV) nodes in the majority of people, bradycardia and first- and second-degree heart block are common complications of inferior wall MI. Patients with inferior wall MIs have increased parasympathetic activity associated with bradycardia, nausea, and vomiting. Patients with inferior-posterior MIs are also at risk for the development of papillary muscle rupture resulting in acute mitral regurgitation, potentially causing acute heart failure and an emergent situation (O'Gara et al., 2013).

NURSING APPLICATION

First- or second-degree heart block seen in inferior MI usually does not progress to complete heart block because the bundle of His and bundle branches are not fed by the RCA.

Anterior Wall Myocardial Infarction

The left anterior descending artery (LAD) supplies blood to the anterior portion of the septum and the anterior wall of the left ventricle. An occlusion of the LAD produces an infarct of the anterior wall of the left ventricle, producing ST-segment elevation in leads V3 and V4 on a 12-lead ECG. If the lesion is proximal and the septum is involved, ST-segment elevation occurs in leads V1 through V4. Figure 13-4 shows a 12-lead ECG representation of an anterior septal MI. Both Figures 13-3 and 13-4 can be compared with the normal ECG in Figure 13-5.

Because the bundle branches of the conduction system run through the septum, patients with occlusion of the LAD are at risk for the development of bundle branch blocks and complete heart blocks. Patients with septal infarcts are also at risk for ventricular septal rupture. Patients with anterior wall MIs have a worse prognosis than those with inferior wall MIs because of the high risk for profound left ventricular dysfunction, leading to heart failure and cardiogenic shock (O'Gara et al., 2013).

NURSING APPLICATION

The assessment of a new holosystolic murmur in an unstable patient with an anteroseptal MI can indicate a ventricular septal rupture. This condition is a medical emergency that requires emergency surgery to repair the rupture.

FIGURE 13-4: ST-SEGMENT ELEVATION OF ANTERIOR SEPTAL MYOCARDIAL INFARCTION IN LEADS V₁ TO V₄

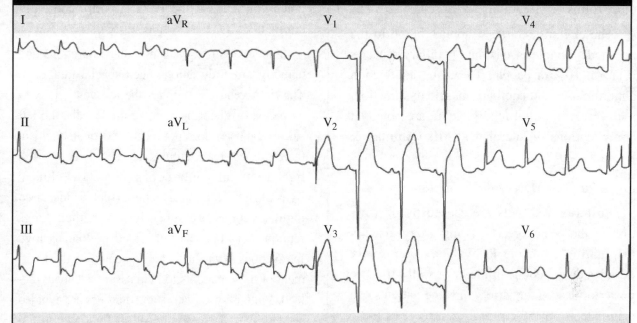

ST-segment elevation of anteroseptal and lateral wall myocardial infarction. Note the ST-segment elevation in leads V_1 to V_5, I, and aV_L.
Note. Western Schools, 2017.

FIGURE 13-5: NORMAL ELECTROCARDIOGRAM

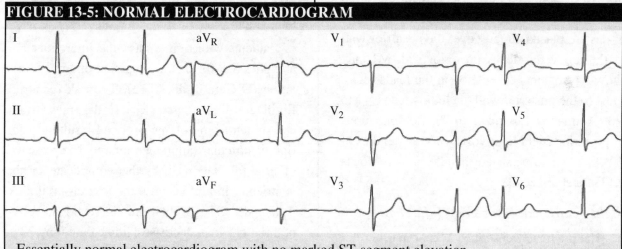

Essentially normal electrocardiogram with no marked ST-segment elevation.
Note. Western Schools, 2017.

Lateral Wall Myocardial Infarction

The circumflex artery, off the left main coronary artery, supplies blood to the lateral wall of the left ventricle. Other coronary branches also supply blood to portions of the lateral wall. On a 12-lead ECG, leads I and aVL (high lateral leads) and leads V5 and V6 (low lateral leads) face the lateral wall of the myocardium. The portion of the myocardium supplied by the circumflex artery is less represented on a 12-lead ECG than the myocardium supplied by the RCA or LAD. For this reason, occlusions of the circumflex artery may be less visible on a 12-lead ECG than occlusions of the LAD and RCA. A large portion of the myocardium is supplied by the circumflex artery, and a stand-alone lateral wall MI should be treated as aggressively as other forms of MI (Antman & Loscalzo, 2017).

The circumflex artery supplies blood to the AV node, bundle of His, and papillary muscles in about 10% of people. Therefore, conduction abnormalities and papillary muscle dysfunction, with resultant mitral regurgitation, are potential complications of lateral wall MIs (Antman & Loscalzo, 2017).

Posterior Wall Myocardial Infarction

Posterior wall MIs are caused by obstruction of the posterior descending artery, usually originating from the RCA. They commonly occur in conjunction with inferior wall MIs. The posterior descending artery in some patients can originate from the circumflex artery; in these patients, a posterior MI may occur in conjunction with lateral wall MI. A true isolated posterior MI does not produce ST-segment elevation on a standard 12-lead ECG because no electrodes are placed directly over the posterior wall of the left ventricle. A posterior wall MI may show ST-segment depression in the leads reciprocal to the posterior wall, including leads V1 to V3 (Antman & Loscalzo, 2017). Complications of posterior wall MIs involve varying degrees of AV blocks and persistent bundle branch blocks (O'Gara et al., 2013).

Right Ventricular Myocardial Infarction

The previously described MIs primarily refer to infarctions of the left ventricle. Infarction of the right ventricle occurs in a third to half of inferior wall MIs and poses a great threat for acute right-sided heart failure. Right ventricular MI is associated with an increased mortality risk. In most people, the marginal branch of the RCA feeds the right ventricle; therefore, an occlusion proximal to this branch infarcts the right ventricle. An ECG with right precordial leads should be done on all patients with inferior MIs to assess for the presence of a right ventricular infarct. ST-segment elevation can be seen in the right precordial leads if the ECG is performed early during the MI (O'Gara et al., 2013).

Patients with right ventricular infarctions and hemodynamic alterations need special treatment. The right ventricle supplies the left ventricle with its preload. When the right ventricle fails, the left side of the heart does not receive adequate preload; therefore, cardiac output decreases. Patients with right ventricular infarctions may show clinical signs of right-sided heart failure (such as increased jugular venous pressure); however, their lungs remain clear because left-sided preload is low. Intravenous (IV) fluids are indicated in the treatment of these patients to help assure adequate preload. Venous vasodilators and diuretics are avoided because they decrease preload. If fluid administration is ineffective in supplying adequate preload to the left side of the heart, inotropic medications such as dobutamine may be needed to support the failing right ventricle (O'Gara et al., 2013).

Patients with right ventricular infarctions are at higher risk for the development of atrial fibrillation (O'Gara et al., 2013). The risk for atrial fibrillation is increased because the right atrium can stretch from volume overload resulting from right ventricular failure and infarct. The presence of atrial fibrillation can further complicate a right ventricular infarct because the loss of atrial kick further decreases right ventricular preload. Loss of atrial kick can decrease cardiac output by 20% to 25% (January et al., 2014). Patients who have hemodynamic instability require emergency cardioversion.

Key Nursing Care in the Acute Treatment of STEMI

Patients with STEMI are initially admitted to a coronary care or critical care unit. Key coronary care nursing interventions in the care of patients with STEMI are listed in Table 13-3. When hemo-

TABLE 13-3: KEY NURSING INTERVENTIONS FOR ST-SEGMENT ELEVATED MYOCARDIAL INFARCTION

- On admission, assure full-dose (325 mg) aspirin was administered in the prehospital setting or emergency department.

- Evaluate anginal symptoms to confirm that they are improved or resolved.

- Assess that response to beta-blocker therapy is adequate to control heart rate and dysrhythmias without causing hypotension.

- Assess for the presence of angina and the need for additional antianginal medications.

- Reassess oxygen saturation after 6 hours of supplemental oxygen and discontinue if saturation is more than 90%.

- Administer anxiolytics as needed to reduce anxiety.

- Assess heart sounds for new holosystolic murmurs.

- Restrict activity for at least the first 12 hours and then begin a step-by-step approach to activity progression (phase I cardiac rehabilitation exercises).

- Utilize cardiac monitoring and ST-segment monitoring to assess for recurrent ischemia and the presence of dysrhythmias.

- Insulin therapy may be used to achieve blood glucose levels less than 180 mg/dl in patients with STEMI. Care should be taken to avoid hypoglycemia.

- Observe for signs of left ventricular dysfunction, including hypotension or clinical signs of heart failure.

- Include the family. Family visits do not have a negative impact on vital signs or cardiac rhythm.

Note. Adapted from Anderson, K. M. (2016). The advanced practice nurse cardiovascular clinician. New York, NY: Springer Publishing.

O'Gara, P. T., Kushner, F. G., Ascheim, D. D., Casey, D. E., Chung, M. K., de Lemos, J. A., ... Zhao, D. X. (2013). 2013 ACCF/AHA guideline for the management of ST-elevation myocardial infarction: A report of the American College of Cardiology Foundation/American Heart Association Task Force on Practice Guidelines. *Journal of the American College of Cardiology, 61*(4), e78-e140. doi:10.1016/j.jacc.2012.11.019

dynamic stability is achieved, patients can be transferred to a step-down or progressive care unit. With successful reperfusion, some patients can be transferred to a step-down unit within 24 hours.

NURSING APPLICATION

In patients for whom there is concern for the development of hypotension, treatments with proven mortality benefits, such as beta-blocker and angiotensin-converting enzyme (ACE) inhibitor administration, need to take priority over the administration of IV nitroglycerin in the management of continuing ischemia.

NURSING APPLICATION

Control of pain and anxiety is key for patient comfort and also to reduce myocardial oxygen demand. Pain and anxiety activate the sympathetic nervous system and increase myocardial oxygen demand.

NON-ST-SEGMENT ELEVATION MYOCARDIAL INFARCTION AND UNSTABLE ANGINA

Because of the similarity in the presentations of UA and NSTEMI, they are often grouped together, whereas a STEMI presentation markedly stands apart. UA and NSTEMI are closely related in pathogenesis and clinical presentation. The primary difference between the two is severity of myocardial injury (Anderson, 2016).

Except in patients with true posterior AMIs, NSTEMI is characterized by the absence of persistent ST-elevation on the 12-lead ECG with acutely elevated biomarkers. In contrast, the same clinical features with the absence of acutely elevated biomarkers indicate UA (Amsterdam et al., 2014).

Prevalence

In the United States, approximately 70% of all ACS cases are diagnosed as NSTEMI or UA (Cannon & Braumwald, 2017). Although the overall incidence of ACS is higher in men than in women, the incidence of non-ST-elevated related ACS (NSTE-ACS) is higher in women (Cannon & Braumwald, 2017). Patients with NSTE-ACS were found to have more comorbidities than those with STEMI (Amsterdam et al., 2014).

Causes

Partial occlusion of the coronary artery by a thrombus is the cause of NSTE-ACS. Partial occlusion most often occurs because of the rupturing of unstable vulnerable plaque (or atheroma) within the coronary artery (see Figure 13-2). Vasospasm of the artery is another cause that contributes to the potential partial occlusion of the vessel.

Pathophysiology

In contrast with the pathophysiology of STEMI, NSTEMI and UA most often result from a ruptured plaque causing a partially occluded vessel. The partial occlusion is directly caused by incomplete thrombosis. This incomplete thrombosis is often referred to as a soft clot or platelet plug. The process of thrombogenesis is similar to that in the pathophysiology of a STEMI (Antman & Loscalzo, 2017).

Clinical Presentation

Patients often describe substernal chest pain or epigastric pain radiating to the left arm, left shoulder, and/or neck, similar to that of typical STEMI presentations. Anginal equivalents are also similar to those of STEMI presentations such as dyspnea, epigastric discomfort, nausea, or weakness, which women report more often than symptoms of chest pain (Anderson, 2016; O'Gara et al., 2013).

Physical Examination

Physical examination findings resemble those found in patients with stable angina (discussed in Chapter 6) and may be unremarkable. However, with NSTEMI, if a large area of the myocardium is injured, physical findings of diaphoresis, pale and cool skin, extra heart sounds, basilar rales, and hemodynamic instability can be observed as in STEMI.

Diagnosis

An NSTEMI cannot be differentiated from UA at the time of presentation because the 12-lead ECG findings, such as ST-segment depression and T-wave inversion, may be similar. In UA, these ECG changes are usually more transient; in NSTEMI, they are usually more persistent. Any transient ST-segment or T-wave change more than 0.5 mm during a symptomatic episode occurring at rest is a sign of ischemia related to CHD. Patients in this category are at an increased risk for recurrent ischemia, MI, and death within the first 2 months after the acute event (Amsterdam et al., 2014).

NURSING APPLICATION

A change of 0.5 mm in an ST segment is a subtle change. Therefore, clinicians must be skilled to detect even the most subtle changes to recognize injury or ischemia on the 12-lead ECG.

NURSING APPLICATION

It is important for the nurse to recognize that, although the patient with an NSTEMI may not receive urgent reperfusion or have an ECG as impressive as that of the patient with a STEMI, the risk for complications and death is high after an NSTEMI, and treatment with evidence-based practice recommendations is important to reduce complications in this group of patients.

Cardiac biomarkers are released into the blood when necrosis occurs as a result of membrane rupture of the myocytes. Cardiac biomarkers used in the evaluation of ACSs include myoglobin, creatinine kinase (CK), creatinine kinase-MB (CK-MB), and troponins I and T. Myoglobin is useful as a cardiac biomarker because increased blood levels can be detected within 2 hours after myocardial damage. Although it is a very sensitive biomarker, it is not specific to myocardial damage. CK is an enzyme present in the heart, brain, and skeletal muscle, so elevations of CK in the blood are not specific to myocardial damage either. CK-MB measurements are helpful in identifying myocardial damage because the level of CK-MB in the blood is normally very low, but it rapidly rises in the presence of myocardial damage and is more specific to the heart (Amsterdam et al., 2014).

Troponins I and T are found only in cardiac muscle and are the most sensitive biomarkers for myocardial damage. Because troponin levels remain elevated for a long period, with a gradual return to normal, they are beneficial in diagnosis of patients presenting late after symptom onset. Troponin levels are capable of diagnosing small amounts of myocardial necrosis not measured by rises in CK-MB levels. Elevated cardiac troponin levels identify myocardial necrosis but do not specifically identify ischemia or infarction as the cause of necrosis. A positive troponin level in the presence of ECG changes that are consistent with injury or ischemia confirms the diagnosis of myocardial infarction. An elevated troponin level after a PCI procedure is also consistent with a myocardial infarction. Cardiac troponins I and T are generally considered equal in their diagnostic values, except in patients with renal dysfunction, who may have a nonspecific elevation in cardiac troponin T that is not related to myocardial injury. In patients with renal dysfunction, cardiac troponin I is more specific for myocardial injury than cardiac troponin T and is therefore the preferred cardiac biomarker in this population (O'Gara et al., 2013).

Alternative markers and combinations of markers to assess cardiac risk continue to be investigated. B-type natriuretic peptide or N-terminal pro-B-type natriuretic peptide are two markers known to add additional prognostic value in the patient's overall risk assessment. In addition, there are newer methods of assessing for changes in troponin levels while the levels are still within the normal range. Other new methods involve assessing the delta values, which allows for the detection of changes before the troponin levels are expected to rise to more than normal (O'Gara et al., 2013). Table 13-4 summarizes the cardiac biomarkers.

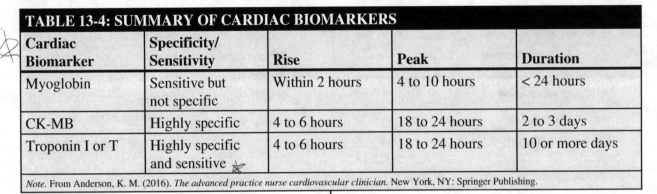

TABLE 13-4: SUMMARY OF CARDIAC BIOMARKERS				
Cardiac Biomarker	**Specificity/ Sensitivity**	**Rise**	**Peak**	**Duration**
Myoglobin	Sensitive but not specific	Within 2 hours	4 to 10 hours	< 24 hours
CK-MB	Highly specific	4 to 6 hours	18 to 24 hours	2 to 3 days
Troponin I or T	Highly specific and sensitive	4 to 6 hours	18 to 24 hours	10 or more days

Note. From Anderson, K. M. (2016). *The advanced practice nurse cardiovascular clinician.* New York, NY: Springer Publishing.

Primary Treatment Strategies

Because the underlying pathophysiology of NSTEMI and UA is a soft clot or platelet plug, the primary treatment strategy is focused heavily on antiplatelet therapy. In addition to aspirin, clopidogrel and glycoprotein IIb/IIIa inhibitors are used as antiplatelet therapy. Anticoagulation therapy (e.g., heparin or low-molecular-weight heparin) is also required in conjunction with antiplatelet therapy in these patients.

In addition to a focus on antiplatelet therapy, treatment of patients with UA and NSTEMI involves a decision between an early invasive strategy or an initial conservative strategy. The early invasive treatment arm involves cardiac catheterization and revascularization within the first 4 to 24 hours of admission. The potential advantage of an early invasive strategy is that approximately 60% to 70% of patients will be able to have a PCI to the culprit lesion. Approximately 20% of patients will be identified as having left main coronary artery disease (CAD) or triple vessel disease with left ventricular dysfunction (Amsterdam et al., 2014). The remainder of patients will not have significant obstructive CAD (O'Gara et al., 2013). Early invasive treatment is recommended for high-risk patients but can also be used in other patient groups. Because of the potential higher rate of complications in women who have PCI, an early invasive strategy is not recommended for women who present with low-risk features (Mehta et al.,

2016). Features associated with high-risk patients are listed in Table 13-5.

The specifics of antiplatelet and anticoagulation therapy are driven by the invasive or conservative strategy, as well as the patient's risk status. A loading dose of clopidogrel, ticagrelor, or prasugrel, administered as soon as possible, is recommended for all patients receiving either initial invasive or conservative treatment. When patients are receiving an early invasive strategy, clopidogrel is to be administered before angi-

TABLE 13-5: FEATURES ASSOCIATED WITH HIGH-RISK ACUTE CORONARY SYNDROME PATIENTS
• Recent percutaneous coronary intervention or history of coronary artery bypass grafting
• Recurrent ischemia
• Depressed left ventricular function or clinical signs of heart failure
• Sustained ventricular dysrhythmias or hemodynamic instability
• Significant ST-segment changes on a 12-lead electrocardiogram or high-risk findings on other noninvasive testing
• Positive troponins

Note. Adapted from O'Gara, P. T., Kushner, F. G., Ascheim, D. D., Casey, D. E., Chung, M. K., de Lemos, J. A., … Zhao, D. X. (2013). 2013 ACCF/AHA guideline for the management of ST-elevation myocardial infarction: A report of the American College of Cardiology Foundation/American Heart Association Task Force on Practice Guidelines. *Journal of the American College of Cardiology, 61*(4), e78-e140. doi:10.1016/j.jacc.2012.11.019

ography. If prasugrel is used, it is not adminis-tered until the time of the procedure. High-risk patients receiving an early invasive strategy should receive a glycoprotein IIb/IIIa inhibitor. The addition of glycoprotein IIb/IIIa inhibi-tors may also be considered in patients who are being managed conservatively. The choice of anticoagulant to be used in NSTEMI is depen-dent on patient risk (including risk of bleeding), treatment strategy, hospital and/or physician preferences, and duration of therapy, includ-ing the concern for development of heparin-induced thrombocytopenia. Four potential types of anticoagulants can be used in patients with NSTEMI or UA: unfractionated heparin, low-molecular-weight heparin, factor Xa inhibitors, and direct thrombin inhibitors. Specifics related to antiplatelet and anticoagulant medications are discussed in Chapter 4.

SUPPORTIVE MEDICAL THERAPY USED IN ALL PATIENTS WITH ACS

All patients with ACS, including STEMI, NSTEMI, and UA, will receive supportive medical management in addition to their pri-mary treatment strategies.

Oxygen

Oxygen is appropriate for patients with an arterial oxygen saturation less than 90%, respi-ratory distress, or other high-risk symptoms of hypoxemia. No benefit has been shown for the use of oxygen in patients with adequate arterial oxygen saturation. Unnecessary use of oxy-gen may increase coronary vascular resistance (O'Gara et al., 2013).

Aspirin

Initial treatment of all patients presenting with ACSs includes administering aspirin imme-diately on patient' arrival, if not already taken at home or given by EMS. Nonenteric-coated aspirin, in the dose range of 162 to 325 mg, should be chewed by the patient (O'Gara et al., 2013). A targeted history and physical examina-tion should be completed, focusing on the goal of early reperfusion for patients with STEMI. Special attention should be paid to contraindi-cations to fibrinolytic therapy and assessment of possible myocardial mimics, such as aortic dissection (pain mimic) and pericarditis (ECG mimic). Focus on prehospital care of patients with STEMI is increasing, including the training of Advanced Life Support providers to identify STEMI on a 12-lead ECG and complete a reper-fusion checklist before arrival in the hospital.

Clopidogrel/Prasugrel/Ticagrelor

As discussed previously, additional anti-platelet therapy with clopidogrel, ticagrelor, or prasugrel is a primary strategy in the treat-ment of NSTEMI and UA (Amsterdam, 2014). Clopidogrel or prasugrel is also used in the treatment of patients with STEMI, regardless of whether they receive reperfusion (O'Gara et al., 2013). Specifics regarding administration are dependent on the type of immediate reperfusion strategy, as well as any additional revasculariza-tion procedures. Antiplatelet therapy specific to revascularization procedures is discussed in Chapter 6.

Anticoagulants

Anticoagulant therapy is a key component in patients with STEMI, NSTEMI, and UA. Four types of anticoagulants are used in patients with ACS: unfractionated heparin, low-molec-ular-weight heparin, direct thrombin inhibitors, and factor Xa inhibitors. The decision regard-ing which anticoagulant to use can be quite complex, taking into account many different factors. Patients with STEMI who have PCI as their reperfusion strategy will have anticoagula-tion as part of their PCI procedure. Patients with

STEMI who receive fibrinolytic therapy as their reperfusion strategy should receive an anticoagulant for a minimum of 48 hours and ideally for the duration of the hospital stay up to 8 days. Patients with NSTEMI or UA will also receive anticoagulation with either an early invasive or early conservative treatment strategy. The factor Xa inhibitor fondaparinux cannot be used as the sole anticoagulant in patients undergoing PCI in any setting because of the higher risk for catheter-associated thrombosis. Fondaparinux is most commonly used in patients with NSTEMI being managed conservatively who have a higher risk for bleeding (O'Gara et al., 2013).

Nitroglycerin

Sublingual nitroglycerin and high-dose IV nitroglycerin dilate arteries and veins. Up to three doses of sublingual nitroglycerin, 0.4 mg, can be given every 5 minutes. If ischemic discomfort continues after sublingual nitroglycerin and beta-blocker administration, an IV nitroglycerin drip can be started at 10 µg/min and titrated in increments of 10 µg every 3 to 5 minutes until symptoms are relieved or until the patient's blood pressure does not allow further titration. The effective dose range is 5 to 100 µg/min, but doses of 200 µg/min have been used. In addition to managing ischemic symptoms, IV nitroglycerin can be used in treating patients who are hypertensive or who have signs of pulmonary congestion (O'Gara et al., 2013).

Nitroglycerin should not be used in patients who are hypotensive, bradycardic, or tachycardic; those who have taken sildenafil within 24 hours or tadalafil within 48 hours; or those with right ventricular infarct or right-sided heart failure. If blood pressure is a limiting factor or other contraindications exist, beta blockers should be given priority administration over nitrates (O'Gara et al., 2013).

Morphine Sulfate

Morphine sulfate is the pain reliever of choice for ischemic cardiac pain associated with STEMI (O'Gara et al., 2013). The initial dose is usually 2 to 4 mg IV. Morphine can be repeated at 5-minute intervals in increments of 2 to 8 mg. In patients with NSTEMI or UA, morphine is typically given in doses of 1 to 5 mg when ischemic symptoms are not responsive to sublingual nitroglycerin and beta-blocker therapy. Morphine is a preload reducer that also reduces anxiety and limits activity of the sympathetic nervous system (O'Gara et al., 2013).

Beta Blockers

Oral beta blockers should be administered within 24 hours in patients with STEMI, NSTEMI, or UA if no contraindications exist. Beta blockers may also be given IV initially in patients with STEMI who present with hypertension. IV beta blockers should be used with caution in those patients presenting with NSTEMI or UA. Although beta blockers can reduce the incidence of reinfarction and ventricular fibrillation during the inpatient stay, they can also potentiate the incidence of cardiogenic shock. Beta blockers are contraindicated in patients with low cardiac output, those who show signs of heart failure, and those identified as high risk for cardiogenic shock (as in the patient with an anterior AMI). Relative contraindications for beta blockers include advanced first-degree AV block, second- or-third degree AV block, active asthma, or reactive airway disease (O'Gara et al., 2013).

ACE Inhibitors

ACE inhibitors are given within the first 24 hours of an acute MI (STEMI or NSTEMI) in patients with most of the following characteristics: anterior wall MI, presence of pulmonary congestion, left ventricular ejection fraction less than 40%, hypertension, diabetes, and chronic kidney disease. Contraindications such as acute kidney injury or a history of hypersensitivity must be considered before administration (O'Gara et al., 2013).

COMPLICATIONS OF MYOCARDIAL INFARCTION

Hemodynamic Alterations

When myocardial function is impaired as a result of MI, stroke volume decreases. To compensate for decreased stroke volume, heart rate increases. If myocardial function is impaired to the point that adequate stroke volume cannot be maintained, diastolic filling pressures increase and pulmonary edema results.

NURSING APPLICATION

Tachycardia is a poor prognostic sign in the presence of an acute MI because it is a compensatory mechanism for decreasing stroke volume caused by a failing left ventricle.

Hemodynamic alterations depend on the size and location of the infarction. A large MI affecting more than 40% of the myocardium can result in circulatory collapse and cardiogenic shock (O'Gara et al., 2013). The prognosis of patients in cardiac shock remains very poor unless successful revascularization can occur in a timely fashion. Long-term hemodynamic alterations from left ventricular dysfunction result in chronic heart failure. With current reperfusion technology, many patients with MIs are left with no clinical evidence of left ventricular dysfunction.

Ventricular Dysrhythmias

Ventricular fibrillation is a major cause of preventable death in the early period after MI. Many episodes of prehospital sudden death are caused by untreated ventricular fibrillation. During MI, dysrhythmias are caused by ischemia to the electrical conduction system, catecholamine release, and electrolyte imbalances. Hypokalemia and hypomagnesemia increase the risk for ventricular fibrillation. Routine magnesium sulfate is not administered in STEMI; however, any magnesium deficiency should be corrected. Any episodes of torsades de pointes (a specific type of ventricular tachycardia associated with a prolonged QT interval) should be treated with IV magnesium sulfate.

NURSING APPLICATION

Any patient presenting with signs of MI needs to be connected to a cardiac monitor immediately and observed in an area with trained personnel who have immediate access to a defibrillator and other emergency cardiac equipment and medications.

Mechanical Complications

Septal Rupture

Septal rupture is most common with a large anteroseptal infarction and most commonly occurs 3 to 7 days after an infarct (O'Gara et al., 2013). The patient experiences sudden and severe left ventricular failure. Blood is shunted from the left side of the heart back to the right side through the ruptured area. This shunting of blood results in poor systemic perfusion. The rupture also produces a very loud holosystolic murmur. Emergency measures to reduce afterload are indicated while the patient is prepared for surgical repair.

Papillary Muscle Dysfunction or Rupture

Papillary muscle dysfunction and rupture can result in acute mitral valve regurgitation secondary to an inferior-posterior wall MI anytime within the first week after infarction (O'Gara et al., 2013). As with septal ruptures, emergency measures to reduce afterload are indicated while preparing the patient for emergency surgery.

Pericarditis

Pericarditis, caused by inflammation of the pericardial sac, can occur immediately after an MI or several weeks later. When pericarditis occurs several weeks after an infarction, it is called *Dressler's syndrome*. When it occurs acutely, it is usually caused by a transmural infarct extending to the epicardium and causing an inflammatory response. Pain associated with pericarditis is sharp and severe. It is worse with inspiration and is relieved by leaning forward. A pericardial friction rub may be heard during auscultation of the heart. As with many complications of MI, the incidence of pericarditis has decreased significantly because of early reperfusion therapy (O'Gara et al., 2013).

Left Ventricular Aneurysm

Left ventricular aneurysm is a potential complication of MI. Ventricular aneurysms are classified as true or false, based on whether they are associated with myocardial rupture. A ventricular aneurysm classified as a true aneurysm is a local outpouching of the ventricular wall that results in dysfunction of that portion of the left ventricle. One danger of a true ventricular aneurysm is that the bulging area can house an unpredictably sized thrombus, which can later embolize, resulting in any variety of embolic cardiovascular conditions (e.g., stroke, AMI, or mesenteric or renal artery occlusion). Another potential complication of a true aneurysm is that it can become the source of ventricular arrhythmias. Aneurysms classified as true aneurysms, however, are not likely to rupture. True aneurysms are most associated with anterolateral and apical MI (O'Gara et al., 2013).

An aneurysm is classed as a false aneurysm or pseudoaneurysm when there is actual rupture into the pericardial sac. Adhesions in the pericardial sac contain the rupture. This type of aneurysm is most often associated with infarction to the thinner portion of the left ventricle, the posterior lateral wall. This type of aneurysm needs to be closely monitored for an increase in size, which requires immediate surgical repair to prevent further bleeding (O'Gara et al., 2013).

Ventricular Remodeling

During an AMI, cellular edema potentiates an inflammatory response, leading to the recruitment of stem cells and tissue regeneration. Catecholamines are also released from myocardial cells during the acute phase of injury, increasing the risk for dysrhythmias during this vulnerable time.

NURSING APPLICATION

Beta blockers are particularly important in suppressing cardiac dysrhythmias in ischemic tissue because they suppress catecholamine release.

Initially, damaged tissue is bruised and cyanotic. During this period, the cardiac biomarkers are released. By the second or third day, white blood cells begin to invade the necrotic tissue. Scavenger cells release enzymes to break down necrotic tissue. The necrotic wall can become very thin during this phase, and cardiac rupture is most likely to occur at this time. By the second week, a weak collagen matrix has formed, but the myocardium is still vulnerable to reinjury. By the third week, scar formation has started, and at 6 weeks, the necrotic area is completely replaced with scar tissue. Although this scar tissue is very strong, it does not contribute to the contractile function of the myocardium (Antman & Loscalzo, 2017; O'Gara et al., 2013).

In addition to postinfarction changes in necrotic tissue, the noninfarcted surrounding areas can also be affected. Surviving myocytes hypertrophy in an attempt to compensate for damaged tissue. Excessive noncontractile collagen is present in the newly hypertrophied myocardium, leading to a stiff and noncompliant ventricle that is unable to fill properly during the cardiac cycle. As a result, cardiac output is impaired (Antman & Loscalzo, 2017).

SPECIAL CONSIDERATIONS

Treatment of Cocaine-Induced Chest Pain

Cocaine use evokes sympathetic nervous system activation and direct stimulation of vascular smooth muscle, resulting in spasm and vasoconstriction. Cocaine also promotes platelet aggregation and thrombus formation. Chronic cocaine use accelerates the process of atherosclerosis. Cocaine-induced ischemic chest discomfort cannot be distinguished from UA or NSTEMI caused by CHD. Cocaine use has become widespread, so this etiology of symptoms and ECG changes must be considered. Nitroglycerin or calcium channel blockers are used to treat cocaine-induced chest pain. If ST-segment elevation is present, then calcium channel blockers are administered IV. If ST-segment elevation does not resolve with medical treatment, then reperfusion with PCI is indicated. After successful medical treatment, it is recommended that patients with cocaine-induced chest pain and ECG changes be observed for up to 24 hours (McCord et al., 2008).

Variant (Vasospastic or Prinzmetal's) Angina

Variant angina is caused by spasm of the coronary arteries. This type of angina usually occurs spontaneously but can also be triggered by exercise, hyperventilation, and cold. The only known associated risk factor for variant angina is smoking (Amsterdam et al., 2014). Patients can have long asymptomatic periods between episodes. The pathophysiology of variant angina is not fully understood. One possible explanation is that endothelial dysfunction causes an imbalance between local vasodilative and local vasoconstrictive factors.

Transient ST-segment elevation usually occurs with variant angina but usually does not result in MI if the spasm occurs in a nonstenotic vessel. However, if the patient has spasms in vessels that are already stenosed, AMI can occur as a STEMI or NSTEMI presentation. This type of angina is treated with nitroglycerin and calcium channel blockers (O'Gara et al., 2013).

Cardiac Syndrome X

Cardiac syndrome X, a condition in which the patient has anginal symptoms and ECG or stress testing, has identified objective evidence of ischemia, but no obstructive CAD is found on cardiac catheterization. This syndrome occurs in women more often than in men. One possible explanation involves microvascular dysfunction. In some patients who have severe symptoms, an abnormal pain perception is also thought to be involved. Exercise and statin therapy can be used to improve endothelial function. Risk factor reduction is appropriate because some patients will later present with MI. Antianginal medications are used to control symptoms. In severe cases refractory to medications, transcutaneous electrical nerve stimulation or spinal cord stimulation has been used for pain control (O'Gara et al., 2013).

LONG-TERM MANAGEMENT OF ALL ACUTE CORONARY SYNDROMES

After an acute event, most patients resume a medical management course similar to patients with stable angina. Patients who have experienced an ACS continue a daily dose of aspirin indefinitely. The long-term maintenance dosage of aspirin is generally 81 to 162 mg daily (Amsterdam et al., 2014). Clopidogrel, ticagrelor, or prasugrel use is appropriate if the patient is unable to take aspirin. Clopidogrel, ticagrelor, or prasugrel is usually continued for 1 year in all patients with STEMI or NSTEMI, regardless of revascularization, and choice of drug depends on clinical strategy (Amsterdam et al., 2014; O'Gara et al., 2013).

Beta blockers are initiated within 24 hours in all patients with ACS (if there are no con-traindications) and continued indefinitely after discharge. ACE inhibitors are given within the first 24 hours to patients meeting specific criteria and are continued indefinitely. An angiotensin II receptor blocker may be used as an alternative for patients unable to tolerate ACE inhibitors. Beta blockers and ACE inhibitors help alter ventricular remodeling that occurs after MI. Aldosterone antagonists are given after MI to patients with ejection fractions of 40% or less, those who have clinical heart failure, and those who have diabetes. Aldosterone antagonists are added to existing therapy for patients who are already on ACE inhibitor therapy. Aldosterone antagonists cannot be added to therapy for patients with renal dysfunction or hyperkalemia. Discharge medications also include a lipid-lowering agent (preferably a statin) that should be initiated 24 to 96 hours after admission of the patient diagnosed with ACS (O'Gara et al., 2013).

Discharge medical management includes three main objectives:

1. Improve prognosis.

   - Aspirin

   - Clopidogrel (or prasugrel or ticagrelor)

   - Beta blockers

   - Lipid-lowering drugs (statins)

   - ACE inhibitors or angiotensin II receptor blockers

   - Aldosterone antagonists

2. Control ischemia (if revascularization is not done or if above medications are not effective).

   - Beta blockers (increased doses)

   - Nitrates (all patients should be given sublingual nitroglycerin)

   - Calcium channel blockers

3. Provide secondary prevention through risk factor reduction.

- Smoking cessation
- Reduction of hyperlipidemia
- Hypertension control
- Diabetes control
- Weight management
- Increased physical activity
- Annual influenza vaccine

(Eckel et al., 2013; O'Gara et al., 2013)

Patients should not take nonsteroidal anti-inflammatory drugs (NSAIDs) for pain after STEMI or NSTEMI because of their association with increased risk for complications, including hypertension, reinfarction, heart failure, myocardial rupture, and mortality (O'Gara et al., 2013). Acetaminophen, small doses of narcotic, or nonacetylated salicylates are recommended as pain relievers over NSAIDs. If not effective, a nonselective cyclooxygenase-2 NSAID such as naproxen may be used outside of the acute phase of ACS. Selective cyclooxygenase-2 NSAIDs are contraindicated in ACS because of an increased risk for reinfarction, hypertension, cardiac rupture, and death (O'Gara et al., 2013).

Patient Education

Medical Follow-up

Patients who have experienced ACS should be instructed on the importance of physician follow-up. High-risk patients should be seen within 2 weeks after discharge and low-risk patients within 6 weeks. The patient should be instructed to notify the physician anytime there is a change in condition, such as a change in activity tolerance or perceived medication side effects.

Risk Factor Reduction

A major focus of patient education for any patient with CHD is secondary prevention by aggressive reduction of cardiac risk factors to reduce the risk for future events (discussed in detail in Chapter 3). Primary risk factor reduction includes smoking cessation; dietary restrictions of fat, cholesterol, and sodium; and hypertension and dyslipidemia control (Eckel et al., 2013).

Recognition of Signs and Symptoms and Emergency Response

Another focus is the recognition of and response to symptoms of an acute coronary event such as dyspnea, fatigue, and angina. Patients should know how to activate the EMS and where the nearest hospital with 24-hour cardiac care is located. Patients should be instructed on the indications for use of sublingual nitroglycerin or nitroglycerin spray, and should be instructed to activate the EMS if symptoms do not improve after 5 minutes or after one dose of sublingual nitroglycerin. The goal in earlier activation of the EMS is to reduce the time to reperfusion. Patients with signs and symptoms of ACS should also be instructed to chew aspirin (162 to 325 mg, if not already taken) while awaiting the arrival of EMS (Amsterdam et al., 2014; O'Gara et al., 2013). It is important to instruct patients that they should never drive themselves or let a family member drive them to the hospital if they think they are having a heart attack. It is important to be transported by trained emergency personnel who can respond immediately to any complications.

Patients with a history of stable angina should be instructed to rest with the onset of angina and to take up to three sublingual nitroglycerin tablets. Patients should notify the EMS if pain persists after the use of three sublingual nitroglycerin tablets. Family members who are appropriate candidates may be given resources to learn about cardiopulmonary resuscitation and the use of automated external defibrillators.

NURSING APPLICATION

It is important to understand the patient's potential need for sublingual nitroglycerin when giving discharge instructions. Patients who have no known CHD or who have been successfully revascularized should not need to take sublingual nitroglycerin. However, should these patients have chest pain, they should activate the EMS if substantial relief has not occurred after one sublingual nitroglycerin tablet. In contrast, a patient with chronic stable angina may expect occasional bouts of angina that require treatment with up to three sublingual nitroglycerin tablets.

Medication Adherence

Patients with chronic cardiac disease are commonly prescribed multiple medications, and the risk for noncompliance is high. Noncompliance with medications is associated with increased adverse outcomes in patients with cardiac conditions. Patient education regarding prescribed medications is a key intervention for nurses, pharmacists, dietitians, and other members of the interdisciplinary team. Education occurs before discharge and continues in the office and cardiac rehabilitation settings. Patients who have had revascularization and are experiencing improvements in symptoms might not understand the importance of continued medical treatment. Those patients with fixed or low incomes might also have financial concerns regarding their medication regimens.

Activity

Patients should be instructed on special postdischarge activity restrictions on activities such as driving, weightlifting, and sexual activity. These decisions are usually individualized based on the patient's clinical condition. Driving regulations may also vary between states. In most cases, a patient with an uncomplicated hospital course can drive about 1 week after discharge pending physician approval (Amsterdam et al., 2014). The patient may be uncomfortable asking about resuming sexual relationships, so instructions regarding sexual activity should be included as a routine part of all discharge instructions. A patient with a history of angina during sexual relationships may be instructed by the physician to take nitroglycerin before engaging in sexual activities.

Daily walking is the exercise of choice after an acute cardiac event. After the initial recovery period, stable patients should walk a minimum of 30 minutes daily. Patients should walk at least 3 to 4 days per week, but preferably every day. The daily walking regimen should be supplemented by an increase in activities of daily living. Special considerations for the initial recovery period are discussed later in this chapter. All patients with STEMI should be referred to formal, comprehensive, multidisciplinary cardiac rehabilitation programs. All patients with ACS who are at moderate to high risk and have multiple risk factors should also be referred to formal cardiac rehabilitation programs, where supervised exercise and continued patient education can be provided. Additional information about exercise and cardiac rehabilitation is provided in the next section (Amsterdam et al., 2014).

Anxiety and Stress

Anxiety is common during and immediately after the acute phase of a cardiac event (Anderson, 2016). Nurses can assist in reducing anxiety by helping the patient gain accurate perceptions of the recovery process. Teaching the patient about relaxation techniques and methods of worry control can help reduce anxiety. An example of a worry-control technique is to schedule 5-minute periods twice a day to worry. At other times of the day, worries are set aside. Nurses can use the expertise of clinical nurse specialists to develop a comprehensive plan of care that includes the psychosocial needs of the cardiac patient.

Teaching Principles

The key to effective patient education is to individualize the approach, based on the patient's preferred method of learning, and take advantage of every patient encounter. Nurses should be prepared to utilize all teachable moments. Many patients are afraid or have anxiety or depression after an acute cardiac event. Patients must be allowed to express concerns and have questions answered before they are able to accept new information. Patient and family education is a very important tool in relieving stress when the patient and family are ready to receive information. If the patient and family are not ready, providing information can actually increase stress. Patients should be active participants in the education process. Adult patients need to be in control of their learning; therefore, it is critical to assess the patient's readiness and desire for information (Anderson, 2016).

In many cases, sharing scientific information about the value of the treatment or risk factor plan increases motivation. Patients who are engaged should be encouraged to seek out additional information and resources from the library or on the Internet. Family, as defined by the patient, should be included in education. When providing patient education, it is helpful to individualize the information to the patient. For example, discuss the patient's individual risk factors, type of ACS, area of infarction, and specific ejection fraction. This allows the patient to assimilate and take ownership of the information being provided.

Effective patient education requires a great deal of time and is often neglected. However, the rewards of effective patient education can be tremendous. Patients can benefit in the form of improved physical functioning and quality of life and, possibly, improved survival from increased adherence to the medical regimen.

Cardiac Rehabilitation

Exercise in the Early Recovery Period

Initiation of activity early in the recovery period after an acute cardiac event is important to increase functional capacity, decrease or alleviate anginal symptoms, reduce disability, and improve overall quality of life (O'Gara et al., 2013). Patients also develop altered distribution of body fluids with bed rest and can develop orthostatic intolerance. The goal of rehabilitation in the early recovery period is to counteract the negative effects of deconditioning. Complications after an acute event are not increased with early activity progression in stable patients. Phase I cardiac rehabilitation exercises are initiated in a patient after an MI as soon as the patient is medically stable and after evaluation for orthostatic hypotension. Phase I exercises usually begin on day 1 or 2 after an acute AMI, depending on the size of the MI. Cardiac rehabilitation is typically initiated on postoperative day 1 for patients with coronary artery bypass grafting. The development of thrombophlebitis or another complicating illness may also restrict the patient's ability to begin exercise (Anderson, 2016).

In the early recovery period, patients should walk for 5 to 10 minutes at a time. Only nonresistive range-of-motion exercises should be performed because resistive exercises increase afterload and, therefore, the workload of the ventricles. The majority of patients begin with a 1.5 to 2.0 metabolic equivalent (MET) level of exercise (e.g., using a bedside commode, transferring to a chair, feeding self, or washing face and hands), progressing to 2 to 3 METs of activity (e.g., sitting up longer, walking to bathroom, or showering). The goal is for patients to be at a level of activity equivalent with activities of daily living by the time of discharge. With shorter hospital stays, the steps involved in inpatient rehabilitation programs have been modified to allow for more rapid progression. During early recovery, an increase of 20 beats/min above resting heart rate, or a heart rate more than 110 beats/min, may be used as a guideline for assessment of activity intolerance. These signs demonstrate an inappropriate chronotropic response to activity. Another sign of activity intolerance includes failure of systolic blood pressure to increase (Anderson, 2016).

Exercise in the Late Recovery Period

Most patients should be at a 3 to 4 MET level of activity by the time of discharge. When a steady state of activity is well tolerated at home, the duration may be increased in 5-minute increments each week as tolerated, up to 30 minutes per session. Activity in the patient's MET level range should be performed at least three to four times, and up to six times, per week (Anderson, 2016). Intensity may also be increased as activity progresses. Exercises should involve large muscle groups and include a warm-up and cool-down. The warm-up should be active, such as slow walking, and the cool-down should include stretching. Isometric activities should be limited because of their potential to increase afterload. Isometric exercises involve the contraction of a muscle with no movement of the joint. Driving requires only 1.5 to 3.0 METs; however, many patients do not drive after an MI until they return to work (Anderson, 2016).

Patients need to be instructed to balance myocardial oxygen supply and demand by monitoring their response to activity. Shortness of breath means overexertion. Patients should lower activity if breathing and heart rate do not return to normal within 10 minutes of stopping exercise. Activity that is well tolerated is accompanied by no adverse symptoms, dysrhythmias, or excessive tachycardia. The same heart rate guidelines are used for activity during the late and the early recovery periods.

Walking and secondary prevention have been shown to increase survival, decrease reoccurrence rates, and possibly slow progression of CHD. In addition, a regular walking program after an acute cardiac event improves the patient's perception of quality of life (O'Gara et al., 2013). Exercise, as part of cardiac rehabilitation, limits disability and improves the physical function of participants. The hemodynamic benefits of exercise include reduction of heart rate and blood pressure (O'Gara et al., 2013). Exercise stress testing is recommended before starting an exercise program after an acute cardiac event. Exercise later in recovery should be guided by a symptom-limited stress test.

Low-risk patients can implement an exercise prescription at home or in a community setting. Low-risk patients include those with absence of both ischemia and dysrhythmias on a stress test. High-risk patients, defined as those with ischemia or serious dysrhythmias on a stress test, should be in medically supervised exercise programs. The majority of patients exercising for secondary prevention are classified as low risk.

Formal Cardiac Rehabilitation

A formal cardiac rehabilitation program involves medically supervised exercise after an acute cardiac event. It usually begins 1 to 2 weeks after discharge and involves exercise three times weekly for a period of 4 to 12 weeks. The program is multidisciplinary and requires physician referral. Patients enrolled in a formal cardiac rehabilitation program must have baseline exercise testing and annual follow-up. Exercise prescription is guided by exercise physiologists, and the patient's plan of care is directed by a registered nurse. Aerobic exercise and resistive training are components of the exercise program. Risk factor counseling, patient education regarding signs and symptoms and medications, and psychosocial support are also components of a comprehensive program.

Health insurance generally covers formal cardiac rehabilitation programs during the immediate recovery period after admission for MI, percutaneous transluminal coronary angioplasty, or coronary artery bypass grafting for those with chronic stable angina. A patient copayment may be required. Many cardiac rehabilitation programs have sliding-scale fee structures to allow participation by those with financial limitations. Cardiac rehabilitation services have also been expanded to include patients with chronic heart failure and those who have undergone valve surgery or implantable cardioverter-defibrillator implantation.

Benefits of Cardiac Rehabilitation

Pooled data from a meta-analysis of studies involving cardiac rehabilitation in secondary prevention show a benefit of reduced cardiovascular mortality rate of approximately 21% to 34% (O'Gara et al., 2013). Fewer benefits may be seen in patients with uncomplicated NSTEMI or UA who have successful revascularization, compared with patients with more complicated NSTEMI or UA or those with STEMI. Participation in formal exercise training is safe, and patients benefit from increased functional capacity and increased exercise tolerance (O'Gara et al., 2013). However, exercise training needs to continue to show sustained improvement.

Patients who exercise experience decreases in low-density lipoprotein cholesterol and triglyceride levels (Eckel et al., 2013). Some patients experience a reduced need for oral hypoglycemic agents or insulin. Symptom reduction has been demonstrated in patients with angina and heart failure. Patients also experience improved psychosocial well-being and stress reduction. Patients who benefit from cardiac rehabilitation include those with angina, compensated heart failure, and decreased ejection fractions. Those with decreased exercise tolerance at baseline can benefit the most from participation but are often among those not referred for cardiac rehabilitation. Cardiac rehabilitation exercises are safe and beneficial in clinically stable patients with cardiac conditions. Unfortunately, appropriate cardiac rehabilitation is greatly underutilized across the United States (O'Gara et al., 2013).

Psychosocial Issues

During hospitalization, postdischarge follow-up, or cardiac rehabilitation, the patient's psychosocial status should be evaluated. Depression is not uncommon after an acute cardiac event. Depression after an acute MI occurs approximately three times more often than in the general population, but only about 50% of cardiologists treat depression in their patients (Lichtman et al., 2008). Patients with depression are three to four times more likely to die within the first year after an MI (O'Gara et al., 2013). Depression also impacts participation in exercise, medication compliance, response to symptoms, and ability to return to work.

Many patients with left ventricular dysfunction as a result of acute MI will experience role identity crisis (or difficulty recognizing their own usefulness) after acute events. Many patients miss large amounts of work, and many have to alter their work roles if high levels of physical exertion and stress are involved.

Altered work roles may add family and financial stresses. Patients may also experience anxiety and sleep disorders (Anderson, 2017).

An assessment of the patient's support system is an important part of the psychosocial assessment. Social isolation is a predictor of worse outcomes after an acute cardiac event such as MI (Mehta et al., 2016; O'Gara et al., 2013). Social workers, clergy, and cardiac clinical nurse specialists are interdisciplinary resources for the management of psychosocial issues in the cardiac patient. Mended Hearts is an organization for those who have survived a cardiac event. Referral to Mended Hearts is another option for social support for those who are depressed and those with limited social support.

Up to 20% of patients will meet the criteria for major depression after acute MI. After an acute MI, a two-point Patient Health Questionnaire (PHQ-2) is recommended as the minimal screening. If the patient answers yes to either question, then a full nine-point questionnaire (PHQ-9) can be administered (Lichtman et al., 2008). The minimum two questions to be asked are the following:

Have either or both of the following feelings been of concern over the past 2 weeks?

1. Little interest or pleasure in doing things

2. Feeling down, depressed, or hopeless

(Anderson, 2017)

Minor depression may respond to increased accomplishment and association with others. Exercise can also improve minor depression, so patients should be referred to formal cardiac rehabilitation programs for social support as well as the exercise component. Nurses can help with depression by providing referrals to programs that increase social support and assisting with the implementation of family-centered care to increase family support. Another effective nursing strategy is to help clarify the reality and

high incidence of depression regarding negative perceptions the patient has about his or her recovery (Anderson, 2016).

Selective serotonin reuptake inhibitors can be useful in treating depression during the first year after an acute MI or in patients who have cardiac conditions with coexisting depression. This group of medications is generally considered safer than other antidepressant medications for use in patients with cardiac conditions because they have fewer cardiotoxic side effects (Mehta et al., 2013; O'Gara et al., 2013). Two selective serotonin reuptake inhibitors (sertraline and citalopram) are considered first-line agents in treating patients with a history of ACS because of their safety and effectiveness in this population (Lichtman et al., 2008).

CASE STUDY

An 85-year-old female patient states that she awoke with heavy substernal chest pressure accompanied by epigastric distress last night. The patient further explains that the pain was reduced somewhat when she rolled onto her side, but it did not completely subside for about six hours. This morning, the patient reports she experienced the same chest pressure along with nausea and dyspnea. This time, the pressure was also felt in her left arm and neck. The pressure worsened with walking and was relieved 30-45 minutes after resting.

The nurse in the emergency department performs the patient's history and physical examination. The patient has no history of smoking or alcohol use, and she has been in good general health, with the exception of osteoarthritis of her hands, knees, and spine. Her only medications are simvastatin (Zocor), ibuprofen (Advil) as needed for bone and joint pain, and "herbs." She denies taking a baby aspirin daily or any today. She is married and is the primary caregiver of her 91-year old husband. They live alone in their private home.

Her vital signs upon presentation to the ED are blood pressure 132/84 mm HG, heart rate 88 beats/min, respiratory rate 18 breaths/min, and oral temperature 99° F (37.2° C). A 12-lead ECG is performed and reads sinus rhythm with occasional premature atrial contractions and ST depression in the lateral and anterior leads. Upon physical examination, the patient has the following cardiovascular exam findings: a soft systolic murmur, an irregularly irregular heart rhythm, normal first and second heart sounds, moderate edema of both ankles with brisk capillary refill, and 1+ peripheral pulses. The patient's lungs are clear bilaterally. The patient appears anxious and is worried about her husband, but she is cooperative. She is a good historian, without neurological deficits noted. When the ED physicians sees that the patient's cardiac troponin level is 0.14 ng/ml, the patient is admitted to the cardiology service of the hospital.

Questions

1. Which patient physical examination findings are indicative of acute myocardial infarction (AMI)?

2. Which medical therapies does the nurse anticipate the patient being prescribed in the first 24 hours after diagnosis of acute myocardial infarction (AMI)?

3. Which patient education concerning medical therapies after AMI is appropriate for the patient?

Answers

1. The 12 Lead ECG shows no ST elevation, but revealed anterolateral ST depression. Additionally, the patient's troponin level is elevated. Troponin levels are capable of diagnosing small amounts of myocardial necrosis not measured by rises in creatine kinase-myocardial band (CK-MB) levels.

Elevated cardiac troponin levels identify myocardial necrosis, but do not specifically identify ischemia or infarction as the cause of necrosis. A positive troponin level in the presence of ECG changes that are consistent with myocardial injury or ischemia confirms the diagnosis of myocardial infarction.

2. The nurse is aware that the underlying pathophysiology of a non-ST elevation myocardial infarction (NSTEMI) is a soft clot or platelet plug. The primary treatment strategy for a NSTEMI is focused heavily on antiplatelet therapy. Because the patient reported not taking aspirin the day of diagnosis, she should therefore receive one full aspirin upon diagnosis of NSTEMI. Anticoagulation therapy (e.g., heparin or low-molecular-weight heparin) is also anticipated in conjunction with antiplatelet therapy for patients with NSTEMI. Beta blockers are also initiated within 24 hours to all patients with AMI if there are no contraindications. Angiotensin converting enzyme inhibitors may also be administered within the first 24 hours to the patient with a NSTEMI.

3. The nurse should educate the patient about the improved outcomes for patients with AMI who take antiplatelet and anticoagulation therapy, as well as her increased risk for falling and bleeding when taking these medications. Given the patient has a history of osteoarthritis and joint pain, it is also important for the nurse to inform the patient not to take nonsteroidal anti-inflammatory drugs (NSAIDs) for pain after NSTEMI because of their association with an increased risk of complications.

SUMMARY

Nurses who specialize in the care of patients with cardiac conditions have made a tremendous impact on patient outcomes. The prevalence of ACSs demands nurses have the knowledge and skills necessary to continue improving patient outcomes through direct care and patient education. Differentiating the types of ACS in a timely manner upon presentation contributes to reduced morbidity and mortality rates of patients. Medical advances in the treatment of ACS offer hope in altering the course of disease progression and death rates. Nurses in all settings may care for patients with ACSs and therefore must be able to recognize the varying ACS presentations, collaborate effectively with an interdisciplinary team, and anticipate the necessary treatments to achieve timely intervention.

EXAM QUESTIONS

CHAPTER 13
Questions 67–71

Note: Choose the one option that BEST answers each question.

67. Which acute coronary syndrome is associated with transient ST-segment changes and the absence of biomarker elevation?

    a. Unstable angina
    b. Stable angina
    c. ST-elevated myocardial infarction
    d. Non-ST-elevated myocardial infarction

68. Which acute coronary syndrome is associated with nonspecific ST-segment findings on ECG and troponin I elevation?

    a. Unstable angina
    b. Stable angina
    c. ST-elevated myocardial infarction
    d. Non-ST-elevated myocardial infarction

69. Supportive pharmacological therapies that are indicated for the management of patients with a diagnosis of acute uncomplicated myocardial infarction include aspirin, an antiplatelet, and

    a. an antiarrhythmic.
    b. an anticoagulant.
    c. a calcium-channel blocker.
    d. a cyclooxygenase-2 inhibitor.

70. The nurse in a coronary care unit administers medication for pain control and anxiety to a patient with a ST-elevation myocardial infarction to increase comfort and reduce

    a. myocardial oxygen demand.
    b. thrombus formation.
    c. volume overload.
    d. left-ventricular dysfunction.

71. Which information is appropriate for patient education regarding reducing the risk for an acute coronary syndrome?

    a. "Smoking cessation is necessary if tobacco use exceeds one pack per day."
    b. "Once pharmacological therapies are initiated, diet restrictions are not indicated."
    c. "Daily low-dose aspirin use is used to reduce the risk for thrombotic events."
    d. "Statin therapy is utilized to increase the 'good cholesterol.'"

REFERENCES

Amsterdam, E. A., Wenger, N. K., Brindis, R. G., Casey, D. E., Ganiats, T. G., Holmes, D. R., … Zieman, S. J. (2014). 2014 AHA/ACC guideline for the management of patients with non–ST-elevation acute coronary syndromes: A report of the American College of Cardiology/American Heart Association Task Force on Practice Guidelines. *Circulation, 130*(25), e344-e426. doi:10.1161/CIR.0000000000000134

Anderson, K. M. (2016). *The advanced practice nurse cardiovascular clinician.* New York, NY: Springer Publishing.

Antman, E. M., & Loscalzo, J. (2017). ST-segment myocardial infarction. In S. E. Huether & K. L. McCance (Eds.), *Understanding pathophysiology* (6th ed.). St. Louis, MO: Elsevier.

Cannon, C. P., & Braunwald, E. (2017). Non-ST-segment elevation acute coronary syndrome. In S. E. Huether & K. L. McCance (Eds.), *Understanding pathophysiology* (6th ed.). St. Louis, MO: Elsevier.

Eckel, R. H., Jakicic, J. M., Ard, J. D., Hubbard, V. S., de Jesus, J. M., Lee, I. M., … Yanovski, S. Z. (2013). 2013 AHA/ACC guideline on lifestyle management to reduce cardiovascular risk: A report of the American College of Cardiology/American Heart Association Task Force on Practice Guidelines. *Circulation, 129*(25 Suppl 2):S76-S99. doi:10.1161/01.cir.0000437740.48606.d1

January, C. T., Wann, L. S., Alpert, J. S., Calkins, H., Cigarroa, J. E., Cleveland, J. C., … Yancy, C. W. (2014). 2014 AHA/ACC/HRS guideline for the management of patients with atrial fibrillation: Executive summary: Z report of the American College of Cardiology/American Heart Association Task Force on practice guidelines and the Heart Rhythm Society. *Circulation, 130*(23), 2071. doi:10.1161/CIR.0000000000000040

Lichtman, J. H., Bigger, J. T., Jr., Blumenthal, J. A., Frasure-Smith, N., Kaufmann, P. G., Lespérance, F., … Froelicher, E. S. (2008). Depression and coronary heart disease: Recommendations for screening, referral, and treatment: A science advisory from the American Heart Association Prevention Committee of the Council on Cardiovascular Nursing, Council on Clinical Cardiology, Council on Epidemiology and Prevention, and Interdisciplinary Council on Quality of Care and Outcomes Research: Endorsed by the American Psychiatric Association. *Circulation, 118*(17), 1768-1775. doi: 10.1161/CIRCULATIONAHA.108.190769

McCord, J., Jneid, H., Hollander, J. E., de Lemos, J. A., Cercek, B., Hsue, P., … Newby, K. (2008). Management of cocaine-associated chest pain and myocardial infarction: A scientific statement from the American Heart Association Acute Cardiac Care Committee of the Council on Clinical Cardiology. *Circulation, 117,* 1897-1907. doi:10.1161/CIRCULATIONAHA.107.188950

Mehta, L. S., Beckie, T. M., DeVon, H. A., Grines, C. L., Krumholz, H. M., Johnson, M. N., … Wenger, N. K. (2016). Acute myocardial infarction in women: A scientific statement from the American Heart Association. *Circulation, 133,* 916-947. doi:10.1161/CIR.0000000000000351

Mozaffarian, D., Benjamin, E. J., Go, A. S., Arnett, D. K., Blaha, M. J., Cushman, M., … Turner, M.B. (2016). Heart disease and stroke statistics – 2016 update: A report from the American Heart Association. *Circulation, 133,* e38-e360. doi:10.1161/CIR.0000000000000350

O'Gara, P. T., Kushner, F. G., Ascheim, D. D., Casey, D. E., Chung, M. K., de Lemos, J. A., … Zhao, D. X. (2013). 2013 ACCF/AHA guideline for the management of ST-elevation myocardial infarction: A report of the American College of Cardiology Foundation/American Heart Association Task Force on practice guidelines. *Journal of the American College of Cardiology, 61*(4), e78-e140. doi:10.1016/j.jacc.2012.11.019

CHAPTER 14

ACUTE HEART FAILURE

LEARNING OUTCOME

After completing this chapter, the learner will be able to describe current strategies for the management of patients with acute decompensated heart failure.

CHAPTER OBJECTIVES

After completing this chapter, the learner will be able to:

1. Identify the symptoms of patients with acute decompensated heart failure.

2. Compare pathophysiological factors with clinical symptoms and physical examination findings of acute decompensated heart failure.

3. Describe appropriate management and treatment options for the patient with acute decompensated heart failure.

INTRODUCTION

Acute exacerbation of heart failure is one of the most common reasons for hospital readmissions within the United States and is the leading cause in patients older than 65 years (Yancy et al., 2013). Estimates of patients having at least four hospital admissions for acute heart failure diagnoses are reported. The burden on healthcare costs and utilization estimates are greater than $69.7 billion annually, with projections to continually increase (Mozaffarian et al.,

2016). Nurses must apply their knowledge of comprehensive acute heart failure management in an effort to reduce this burden.

ACUTE DECOMPENSATED HEART FAILURE

Currently, no widely accepted name or definition for acute heart failure syndromes exists (Yancy et al., 2013). The nomenclature for acute heart failure has been referred to in heart failure guidelines as acute decompensated heart failure (ADHF) with wide acceptance across the United States. However, there is also criticism that the term *ADHF* does not accurately, or completely, describe whether the acute decompensation is a new onset of acute heart failure or whether the acute presentation of heart failure is related to chronic heart failure that is progressively worsening and/or refractory to treatment. Nevertheless, ADHF occurs equally between patients with a history of reduced (≤40%) ejection fraction and preserved (≥50%) ejection fraction for reasons such as uncontrolled hypertension, medication nonadherence, and acute myocardial infarction. Patients with ischemic heart disease can have chronic heart failure that chronically decompensates despite treatment (Yancy et al., 2013). This chapter discusses causes of ADHF secondary to acute cardiovascular events in patients with no chronic history of heart failure.

Acute Cardiovascular Events Leading to ADHF

Acute Valve Dysfunction

Chronic valve dysfunction is discussed in greater detail in Chapter 9. This chapter focuses on the most common causes of acute heart failure secondary to acute valve dysfunction.

Acute Aortic Regurgitation. Acute aortic valve regurgitation disrupts the forward motion of blood flow into the aorta and to the body's systems. The blood volume that does not move forward overwhelms the left ventricle and leads to pulmonary congestion and eventually left-sided heart failure. Acute aortic regurgitation is most often caused by infective endocarditis (Nishimura et al., 2014). Other causes include blunt chest trauma or an iatrogenic complication after transcutaneous aortic valve repair (Nishimura et al., 2014).

Acute Mitral Regurgitation. Acute mitral regurgitation also disrupts the forward motion of blood flow through the left side of the heart and results in acute pulmonary congestion and heart failure. Causes of the acute onset of symptoms include infective endocarditis or chordal rupture. Infective endocarditis usually results in a perforation of one (or more) of the valve's leaflets. Chordal rupture can occur spontaneously with degenerative mitral valve disease or because of papillary muscle rupture related to acute ST-elevated myocardial infarction (Nishimura et al., 2014).

Thoracic Aorta Dissection

Dissection of the thoracic aorta can cause ADHF in two ways. The most common reason is due to acute aortic valve regurgitation (Hiratzka et al., 2010). Dissection of the thoracic aorta causes an acute aortic insufficiency in three different ways: (1) acute dilation of the aortic root results in incomplete closure of the valve; (2) the dissection itself extends into the aortic root, resulting in a disruption of the valve's commissural attachments and leaflet prolapse; or (3) a portion of the dissection flap bulges back (prolapse) through the valve, resulting in incomplete closure (Hiratzka et al., 2010).

Other causes of ADHF after thoracic aorta dissection include large myocardial infarctions, dissection into the pericardial sac resulting in tamponade, or dissection of the ascending aorta causing ventricular outflow obstruction (Hiratzka et al., 2010).

Clinical Presentation

Patients with ADHF commonly present with the following clinical signs:

- Tachycardia
- Tachypnea
- Pallor
- Diaphoresis
- Inspiratory crackles or rales
- Jugular venous distention
- Peripheral edema
- Hepatomegaly
- Ascites
- Extra heart sounds (S3 and often S4)
- A possible mitral regurgitation murmur

Many clinicians classify patients with decompensated heart failure as "wet" or "dry," depending on whether the patient has elevated jugular venous distention, edema, or bibasilar rales, and "cold" or "warm," depending on whether the patient has decreased peripheral perfusion, hypotension, or narrowed pulse pressure (Yancy et al., 2013). In addition, patients may also experience an increase in the symptoms of dyspnea and fatigue. An evaluation for common disease processes that may precipitate an episode of acute heart failure is conducted for the patient presenting with an exacerbation of or new-onset heart failure (Anderson, 2016). Precipitating factors for decompensating heart failure are listed in Table 14-1.

TABLE 14-1: PRECIPITATING FACTORS FOR DECOMPENSATING HEART FAILURE

- Nonadherence to medication regimen, sodium and/or fluid restrictions

- Initiation of medications that increase salt retention (e.g. nonsteroidal anti-inflammatory drugs, steroids, etc.)

- Acute myocardial infarction or ischemia

- Uncontrolled hypertension

- Atrial fibrillation and other dysrhythmias

- Addition of negative inotropic medications (e.g. calcium-channel blockers, beta blockers)

- Pulmonary emboli

- Endocrine abnormalities

- Excessive alcohol or illicit drug use

- Concurrent infections

Note. From Yancy, C. W., Jessup, M., Bozkurt, B., Butler, J., Casey, D. E., Drazner, M. H., … Wilkoff, B. L. (2013). 2013 ACCF/AHA guideline for the management of heart failure: A report of the American College of Cardiology Foundation/American Heart Association Task Force on practice guidelines. *Circulation, 128,* e240-e327. doi:10.1161/CIR.0b013e31829e8776

Hemodynamic instability secondary to impaired contractility is another common presentation of ADHF. Normotensive and tachycardic patients may be in a compensatory stage for the decrease in cardiac output, but clinicians should recognize the patient is at high risk for further decompensation into cardiogenic shock (Yancy et al., 2013).

Diagnosis

Making the diagnosis for ADHF is not much different from diagnosing chronic heart failure. One thing to distinguish on initial evaluation of the patient is hemodynamic stability. Patients presenting in cardiogenic shock may require immediate therapies for stabilization before all diagnostics are completed. The 2013 American College of Cardiology Foundation/American Heart Association (ACCF/AHA) heart failure guidelines recommend prompt evaluation of acute patients by electrocardiogram, serum biomarkers (including plasma levels of brain natriuretic peptides and cardiac troponin), chest radiograph, and identification of the precipitating factor through a thorough history and physical (Yancy et al., 2013). Unfortunately, the collective findings of multiple diagnostic results are used to confirm the diagnosis because no one test is sensitive or specific enough alone (Yancy et al., 2013).

Brain Natriuretic Peptide Levels

Brain natriuretic peptide (BNP) levels are used as a diagnostic indicator in patients presenting with signs of ADHF. Plasma concentrations of BNP are elevated in patients with decompensated heart failure with fluid overload. This diagnostic tool is also helpful when a patient's primary complaint is shortness of breath, yet the etiology is unclear. A BNP level less than 100 pg/ml has a high negative predictive value; therefore, it can be used to eliminate heart failure as the cause of dyspnea. BNP levels greater than 500 pg/ml at the time of discharge are highly associated with readmission within 30 days. BNP levels can remain chronically elevated in end-stage heart failure but are becoming a less reliable predictive tool (Anderson, 2016; Yancy et al., 2013). BNP levels may be elevated for reasons other than heart failure, such as pulmonary hypertension (later resulting in right-sided heart failure) and pulmonary emboli. BNP levels should not be used in isolation of other available clinical information for diagnosing heart failure. A collection of correlating findings strengthens the diagnostic value of BNP (Yancy et al., 2013).

Cardiac Troponin

The serum cardiac troponin T or troponin I are other biomarkers used to trend the progression or improvement of ADHF states. Elevated cardiac troponin levels are often associated with acute myocardial infarction; however, elevated concentrations of these biomarkers are also seen in patients with chronic and acute states of heart failure. In chronic heart failure, elevated troponin levels are associated with progressive left ventricle dysfunction and impaired hemodynamics. In patients with ADHF, elevated troponin levels are associated with worse clinical outcomes and higher mortality. Patients with decreasing troponin levels over time were found to have a better prognosis than patients whose levels remain persistently high in acute and chronic heart failure. The 2013 ACCF/AHA guidelines for the management of heart failure report troponin being useful in establishing prognosis or symptom severity in heart failure (Yancy et al., 2013).

Chest Radiograph

Chest radiograph findings indicative of ADHF include a full, or congested, perihilar vasculature, enlarged heart chamber size, and a widened vascular pedicle (diameter of the superior vena cava to the midline of the mediastinum; Yancy et al., 2013). These findings reflect vascular congestion if the radiograph is taken upright. In the supine position, these findings would be unreliable. An enlarged heart size and alveolar edema can also provide evidence of pulmonary edema but are not specific to ADHF. They are variably sensitive for assessing alveolar edema; therefore, a negative chest radiograph cannot always rule out ADHF (Anderson, 2016; Yancy et al., 2013).

Treatment Options

Diuretics

A diuretic, such as furosemide (Lasix), is the first-line treatment strategy for ADHF with volume overload. If currently on diuretic therapy, an intravenous (IV) diuretic dose equal to the patient's total daily oral dose is recommended. Because early intervention may be associated with improved outcomes in patients hospitalized with heart failure, the American College of Cardiology/American Heart Association (ACC/AHA) recommends diuretic therapy begin at the earliest presentation – emergency department or outpatient clinic (Yancy et al., 2013). Decreased jugular venous distension is one of the most useful clinical findings for evaluating the effects of diuretic therapy in the patient with good diuretic response. In addition, a decrease in pulmonary congestion, peripheral edema, and body weight all demonstrate the effectiveness of diuretic therapy (Yancy et al., 2013).

Ultrafiltration

Ultrafiltration is a mechanical method of removing excess fluid through a semipermeable membrane according to a pressure gradient. The process of ultrafiltration occurs with a machine much like a dialysis machine. However, unlike dialysis, the goal is fluid removal only and excludes removing particles such as electrolytes (Yancy et al., 2013). The fluid-removal process with ultrafiltration is slow and occurs over many hours and sometimes days. When a patient is nonresponsive to diuretics or if the degree of renal dysfunction is severe, ultrafiltration is recommended to resolve the problem of fluid overload (Yancy et al., 2013).

Inotropic Therapy

Patients with ADHF may require IV administration of a positive inotrope to increase the heart's contractility and cardiac output (Yancy et al., 2013). Inotropic agents should not be used if the patient is normotensive without evidence of pulmonary vascular congestion, however. Long-term use of inotropes has been found to further impair contractility and accelerate myocardial decompensation (Yancy et al., 2013). Dobutamine, a sympathomimetic, and milrinone, a phosphodiesterase inhibitor, are the commonly used IV inotropes. Milrinone has vasodilator properties in addition to inotropic properties (Manaker, 2014).

Vasodilator Therapy

Patients with ADHF may also need vasodilator therapy to help reduce preload and/or afterload (Yancy et al., 2013). Whereas inotropes increase the force of contraction in the setting of an overdistended ventricle, vasodilators decrease venous return on the venous side and decrease systemic vascular resistance on the arterial side. The use of these medications together can decrease the heart's workload and facilitate forward blood flow to relieve the volume overload state of the heart.

Nesiritide, a synthetic BNP, is one vasodilator used for treatment of ADHF. Nesiritide is a venous and arterial vasodilator, so it reduces both preload and afterload. Other vasodilators used for ADHF include nitroglycerin and nitroprusside. IV nitroglycerin is usually given in low doses as a venous vasodilator, and nitroprusside is used predominantly as an arterial vasodilator. IV nitroglycerin in high doses can be used as an arterial vasodilator, especially in conditions in which nitroprusside is contraindicated (e.g., end-stage kidney disease). These medications should only be used in patients who have an adequate blood pressure (Yancy et al., 2013).

Patient Management and Nursing Care

Patients who are admitted with ADHF require careful observation until they are stabilized. Evaluation of the effects of treatment includes

- careful measurement of intake and output,
- frequent vital sign evaluation,
- daily weight measurement (same time each day),
- daily supine and standing blood pressures, and
- frequent assessment of perfusion and congestion status.

(Anderson, 2016)

SPECIAL CONSIDERATIONS IN HEART FAILURE

Patients presenting with signs and symptoms of ADHF may require unconventional therapies to maintain or restore their quality of life. These therapies are considered for specific clinical situations in which conventional therapies are proven to be ineffective.

Patients with advanced heart failure have special management issues. Patients with advanced heart failure include those with New York Heart Association class III or IV heart failure with severe symptoms at rest or minimal exertion. Other findings of advanced heart failure include signs of peripheral hypoperfusion, left ventricular ejection fraction less than 30%, a mean pulmonary artery wedge pressure of 16 mmHg, impaired functional capacity, and a history of one or more hospitalizations within 6 months (Yancy et al., 2013). These patients need very careful control of their extracellular fluid (ECF) volume status because many of their symptoms are related to sodium imbalances caused by ECF overload. ACE inhibitors and beta blockers are effective in patients with advanced heart failure; however, these patients may not tolerate these medications well and, therefore, lower doses may need to be prescribed. Patients should not receive these medications if their systolic blood pressure is less than 80 mmHg or if they show signs of hypoperfusion (Yancy et al., 2013). Patients should not be initiated on beta blockers if they have symptomatic ECF retention or require IV inotropic therapy.

Patients with advanced heart failure may have frequent acute decompensation that requires hospitalization for IV inotropic or vasodilator therapy. After the patient is stabilized and oral medications are resumed, the patient must be observed for a period to assure the oral regimen is sufficient to avoid further decompensation. Patients unable to be weaned from IV inotropic support may be candidates for at-home, continuous, inotropic support. This measure is a final option, used only for palliative relief in end-stage disease. Intermittent inotropic therapy at one time was an option for end-stage heart failure treatment. However, this therapy is no longer recommended for the management of advanced heart failure because it has been shown to increase mortality (Yancy et al., 2013).

Palliative Care and Hospice Referral

Clinicians should discuss end-of-life care issues with patients with advanced heart failure while they are still able to participate in the decision-making process. A palliative care referral can be made at any time after the diagnosis of a chronic medical condition for which there is no cure. The primary goal of palliative care is to provide comfort and preserve one's quality of life. A referral to palliative care does not prohibit the patient from continuing active treatment, but rather offers adjunctive resources and support to help with decision making and to address psychosocial aspects of care (Yancy et al., 2013).

Palliative care referrals are often accompanied by hospice care referrals, but they do not have to be. Hospice care services are for the patient with a prediction for death to occur within 6 months. Palliative care is just one of the services hospice care provides; thus, these referrals must be made on an individual basis. Hospice services include (but are not limited to) pastoral care, patient sitters for personal assistance and supervision, pet therapy, music therapy, condition-specific medical care, bereavement and grief care for the patient and family, and the provision of needed home medical equipment (Prochaska, Putman, Tak, Yoon, & Curlin, 2016).

Because sudden cardiac death is one of the major causes of death in patients with heart failure, the time of death is difficult to predict. Many patients with advanced heart failure have periods of good quality of life during the final 6 months. Therefore, palliative care referrals can be made without full hospice care referrals. The ACC/AHA 2013 heart failure guidelines recommend that healthcare providers who treat patients with heart failure should be more attentive to end-of-life care needs in this population, initiate more patient dialogue regarding end-of-life care options, and appropriately initiate palliative care and/or hospice referrals according to the wishes of the patient and family (Yancy et al., 2013).

Heart Transplantation

Cardiac transplantation is the only established surgical treatment for refractory heart failure. Unfortunately, each year this treatment option is available to only a select group of patients with stage IV heart failure (having severe symptoms of heart failure at rest) who meet criteria for cardiac transplantation. Transplantation is indicated only for patients with severe functional impairment who require continuous IV inotropic support or meet the criteria for ventricular assist device placement (discussed in more detail in the next section). These candidates need to be otherwise healthy. The survival rate at 1, 3, and 5 years posttransplant are 87.8%, 78.5%, and 71.1%, respectively (Yancy et al., 2013). After transplantation, patients remain on lifelong immunosuppression therapy, placing them at risk for additional complications. Nevertheless, cardiac transplantation has been shown to improve functional status and overall quality of life in this population (Yancy et al., 2013).

Left Ventricular Assist Devices

Left ventricular assist devices (VADs) can be used to provide short-term or long-term hemodynamic support to failing hearts (Dirks & Waters, 2014). Left VADs can be placed percutaneously in the cardiac catheter laboratory or via open thoracotomy in the operating room. These devices are battery-powered pumps that facilitate forward blood flow by diverting blood from the ventricle, through the device cannula, and into the aorta or system to increase cardiac output and system perfusion (Dirks & Waters, 2014).

Short-term VADs are small and are placed within the left ventricular outflow tract (see Figure 14-1). These are most often placed percutaneously but can be placed via open thoracotomy. These devices are minimally invasive and are used as a bridge to myocardial recovery after acute postoperative ventricular dysfunction, cardiogenic shock after myocardial infarction, or acute viral myocarditis (Dirks & Waters, 2014).

Long-term VADs are placed via open thoracotomy (see Figure 14-2). These devices are cannulated through the ventricle and cannot be removed after placement. Thus, the long-term VADs are used to replace ventricular function and are often referred to as a bridge to transplant therapy or destination therapy. These VADs are used for patients with advanced heart failure that is refractory to other therapies, either until transplantation can occur or indefinitely (Dirks & Waters, 2014).

Complications with left ventricular assist devices are common and can be life-threatening (e.g., stroke, infection, or adverse bleeding). For

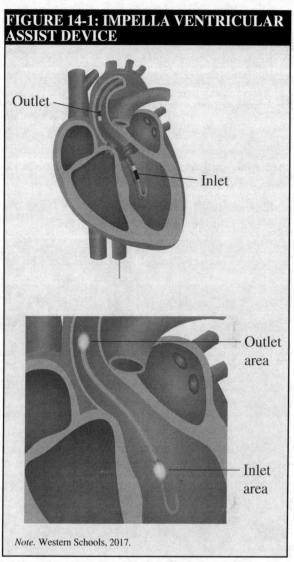

FIGURE 14-1: IMPELLA VENTRICULAR ASSIST DEVICE

Outlet

Inlet

Outlet area

Inlet area

Note. Western Schools, 2017.

this reason, the use of these devices is highly selective among patients with stage IV heart failure (i.e., severe symptoms of heart failure at rest) as well (Yancy et al., 2013).

SUMMARY

The comprehensive care of patients with ADHF events is costly. Nurses can have a significant impact on reducing hospital readmission rates and costs by providing comprehensive heart failure education and care to patients and their families. Nurses must be able to differentiate signs and symptoms of acute and chronic heart failure to aid in appropriate readmissions

FIGURE 14-2: LONG-TERM VENTRICULAR ASSIST DEVICE

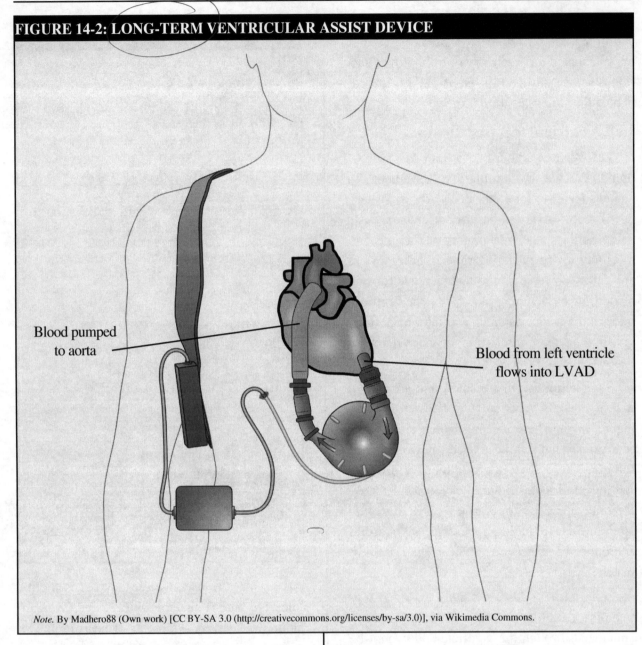

Blood pumped to aorta

Blood from left ventricle flows into LVAD

Note. By Madhero88 (Own work) [CC BY-SA 3.0 (http://creativecommons.org/licenses/by-sa/3.0)], via Wikimedia Commons.

from home. Nurses in all settings must also recognize findings of cardiogenic shock secondary to ADHF to communicate appropriate findings to medical providers, initiate appropriate treatments in a timely manner, and ultimately improve patient outcomes. Recognizing advanced heart failure refractory to therapy is also important so that end-of-life discussions can be initiated in an effort to provide comfort and preserve quality of life as much as possible in this patient population.

EXAM QUESTIONS

CHAPTER 14
Questions 72–74

Note: Choose the one option that BEST answers each question.

72. Which assessment findings are associated with acute decompensated heart failure?

    a. Mild dyspnea, clear lung sounds, 3+ pitting edema

    b. Warm skin to distal extremities, 2+ palpable distal pulses

    c. Bibasilar rales, pallor, tachycardia

    d. Hypertension, clear lung sounds, bounding distal pulses

73. What is a precipitating factor associated with acute decompensated heart failure?

    a. Medical adherence to low-to-moderate sodium intake

    b. Medical adherence to prescribed medication regimen

    c. Abstinence of alcohol or illicit drug use

    d. New addition of a calcium channel blocker to medication regimen

74. Which pharmacological therapy is most appropriate for the patient with acute decompensated heart failure?

    a. IV furosemide

    b. IV diltiazem

    c. IV metoprolol

    d. 0.9% saline challenge of 500 to 1000 ml

REFERENCES

Anderson, K. M. (2016). *The advanced practice nurse cardiovascular clinician*. New York, NY: Springer Publishing.

Dirks, J., & Waters, J. (2014). Cardiovascular therapeutic management. In L. D. Urden, K. M. Stacy, & M. E. Lough (Eds.), *Critical care nursing: Diagnosis and management* (7th ed., pp. 200-221). St. Louis, MO: Elsevier/Mosby.

Hiratzka, L. F., Bakris, G. L., Beckman, J. A., Bersin, R. M., Carr, V. F., Casey, D. E., ... Williams, D. M. (2010). 2010 ACCF/AHA/AATS/ACR/ASA/SCA/SCAI/SIR/STS/SVM guidelines for the diagnosis and management of patients with thoracic aortic disease. *Journal of the American College of Cardiology, 55*(14), e27-e129. doi:10.1016/j.jacc.2010.02.015

Manaker, S. (2014). Use of vasopressors and inotropes. *UpToDate.com*. Retrieved from http://www.uptodate.com/contents/use-of-vasopressors-and-inotropes?source=search_result&search=alpha+adrenergic+agonists+adult&selectedTitle=1%7E150

Mozaffarian, D., Benjamin, E. J., Go, A. S., Arnett, D. K., Blaha, M. J., Cushman, M., ... Turner, M.B. (2016). Heart disease and stroke statistics – 2016 update: A report from the American Heart Association. *Circulation, 133,* e38-e360. doi: 10.1161/CIR.0000000000000350

Nishimura, R. A., Otto, C. M., Sorajja, P., Sundt, T. M., Thomas, J. D., Bonow, R. O., ... Skubas, N. J. (2014). 2014 AHA/ACC guideline for the management of patients with valvular heart disease: A report of the American College of Cardiology/American Heart Association Task Force on practice guidelines. *Journal of the American College of Cardiology, 63*(22), e57-e185. doi:10.1016/j.jacc.2014.02.536

Prochaska, M. T., Putman, M. S., Tak, H. J., Yoon, J. D., & Curlin, F. A. (2016). U.S. physicians overwhelmingly endorse hospice as the better option for most patients at the end of life. *American Journal of Hospice & Palliative Care.* doi:10.1177/1049909116636344

Yancy, C. W., Jessup, M., Bozkurt, B., Butler, J., Casey, D. E., Drazner, M. H., ... Wilkoff, B. L. (2013). 2013 ACCF/AHA guideline for the management of heart failure: A report of the American College of Cardiology Foundation/American Heart Association Task Force on practice guidelines. *Circulation, 128,* e240-e327. doi:10.1161/CIR.0b013e31829e8776

CHAPTER 15

ACUTE DYSRHYTHMIAS

LEARNING OUTCOME

After completing this chapter, the learner will be able to describe common, acute dysrhythmias in the patient with cardiovascular disease.

CHAPTER OBJECTIVES

After completing this chapter, the learner will be able to:

1. Identify acute dysrhythmias that commonly occur with heart disease.

2. Summarize nursing care strategies for the management of various acute dysrhythmias.

3. Describe appropriate medical treatment for acute dysrhythmias.

4. Review special patient populations at risk for acute dysrhythmias.

INTRODUCTION

Knowledge of acute cardiac dysrhythmias (sometimes called *arrhythmias*) is necessary for the comprehensive care of the cardiovascular patient. Recognition of whether the patient is stable or unstable reduces the patient's risk for adverse outcomes secondary to the dysrhythmia. The cardiovascular nurse must be able to differentiate among acute dysrhythmias and anticipate the best and safest nursing strategies and medical therapies indicated. When there is risk for or actual history of recurrent acute dysrhythmias, the nurse must also be able

to educate patients and families on recognizing symptoms and taking required actions when an acute dysrhythmia occurs.

INITIAL EVALUATION

The initial evaluation of the patient with an acute dysrhythmia includes determining whether the patient is hemodynamically stable. This means assessing the patient's heart rate, blood pressure, and respiratory rate and checking for evidence of acute ischemia or impaired tissue perfusion (e.g., chest pain, mental status changes, and skin color changes). The patient who is symptomatic with an acute dysrhythmia is always considered hemodynamically unstable. The next step in the initial evaluation includes determining what is the underlying rhythm. Determining the primary pacemaker in an acute dysrhythmia aids the clinician in identifying the possible underlying cause and in anticipating an effective treatment. These steps should be done regardless of whether the acute dysrhythmia is fast or slow (Prutkin, 2016).

Pathophysiology of Dysrhythmias

Gaining an understanding of the processes of dysrhythmias can facilitate the nurse's application of this knowledge to his or her initial evaluation of the rhythm. Dysrhythmias generally result from a disorder of impulse formation, a disorder of impulse conduction, or both (Aehlert, 2013).

Disorders of Impulse Formation

Disorders of impulse formation involve enhanced automaticity or triggered activity of cardiac cells. Enhanced automaticity occurs either from cardiac cells generating an impulse that is not normally associated with pacemaker function or from pacemaker cells other than those in the sinoatrial (SA) node generating impulses above its intrinsic firing rate (see Figure 15-1). Enhanced automaticity is generally caused by ischemia, hypoxia, electrolyte imbalances, or toxic exposures to chemicals or medications (Aehlert, 2013).

Triggered activity is caused by abnormal electrical impulses that can occur during the repolarization phase of the cardiac cycle. This activity requires a stimulus to begin depolarization such as when pacemaker cells other than those in the SA node depolarize more than once after being stimulated by a single impulse. Triggered activity may result from hypoxia, excessive catecholamines, myocardial ischemia or injury, digitalis toxicity, and medications that prolong repolarization. Manifestations of triggered activity are atrial or ventricular beats that can occur alone, in pairs, or in "runs" (i.e., three or more beats; Aehlert, 2013).

FIGURE 15-1: CONDUCTION PATHWAYS THROUGH THE HEART

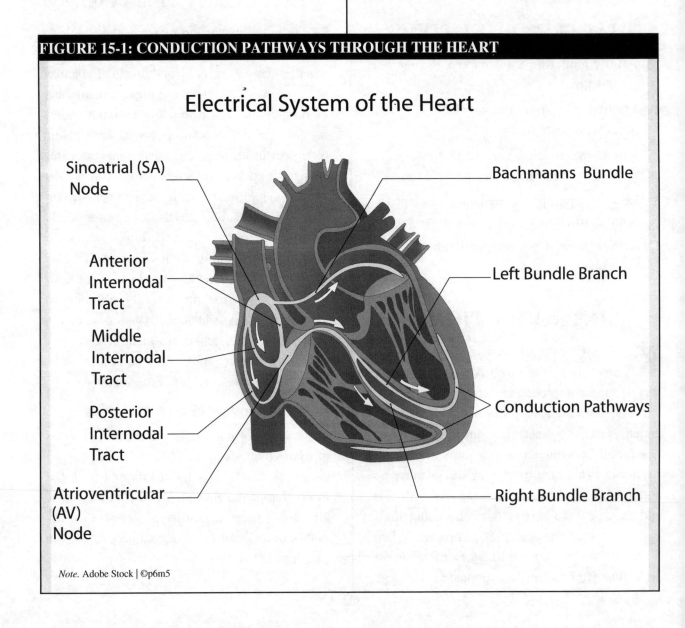

Electrical System of the Heart

Sinoatrial (SA) Node

Anterior Internodal Tract

Middle Internodal Tract

Posterior Internodal Tract

Atrioventricular (AV) Node

Bachmanns Bundle

Left Bundle Branch

Conduction Pathways

Right Bundle Branch

Note. Adobe Stock | ©p6m5

Disorders of Impulse Conduction

Disorders of impulse conduction involve conduction blocks or reentry impulses. Conduction blocks involve the slowing of impulses through pathways (intermittent or partial blocks) or when no impulses are conducted through pathways (complete block). Blocks occur because of trauma, drug toxicity, electrolyte imbalances, and most commonly, myocardial ischemia or infarction (Aehlert, 2013).

Reentry impulse disorders involve the spreading of an impulse through tissue that was already stimulated by the same impulse. This disorder occurs when one impulse is delayed or blocked, or both, in one or more areas of the conduction system while the same impulse is conducted normally through the rest of the conduction system. Reentry requires conditions that affect the conduction circuit, or cause a circular conduction pathway (see Figure 15-2) or a block within part of the circuit and delayed conduction within the remainder of the circuitry. When this reentry impulse occurs during the relative refractory period, the impulse produces a single premature beat or repetitive impulses resulting in short periods of an abnormally fast heart rate. Causes of reentry impulses include hyperkalemia, myocardial ischemia, and some antiarrhythmic medications (Aehlert, 2013).

TACHYDYSRHYTHMIAS

Tachydysrhythmias are defined as abnormal heart rhythms with a ventricular rate greater than 100 beats/min. Tachydysrhythmias that originate in the upper chambers of the heart are described as supraventricular. Ventricular tachydysrhythmias that occur can be associated with sudden cardiac death (Prutkin, 2016). It is necessary to recognize that tachydysrhythmias require urgent medical intervention to prevent cardiac decompensation and ultimately

death. Atrial fibrillation with rapid ventricular response is excluded from this chapter because it was discussed in greater detail in Chapter 10.

Clinical Approach to Acute Tachydysrhythmias

Patients presenting with symptomatic tachycardia must be evaluated for hemodynamic stability and signs or symptoms of acute ischemia. In the absence of a cardiac monitor, identifying whether the patient has a palpable pulse can assist the clinician in determining whether the patient is having a lethal ventricular dysrhythmia. If the patient is pulseless, immediate cardiopulmonary resuscitation (CPR) is warranted (Prutkin, 2016).

Identifying whether the patient is in a sinus rhythm is also important in guiding the plan of care in the hemodynamically unstable patient with a tachydysrhythmia. For instance, sinus tachycardia (ST) is usually resolved by treating its underlying cause. If the tachydysrhythmia is not a sinus rhythm, identifying whether the QRS complex is narrow or wide and whether the heart rate is regular or irregular are the next steps in guiding treatment plans. Narrow QRS complex tachydysrhythmias have QRS intervals less than 120 milliseconds, and wide QRS complex tachydysrhythmias have QRS intervals greater than 120 milliseconds (Prutkin, 2016).

Narrow Complex Tachydysrhythmias

There are many regular narrow complex tachydysrhythmias, including ST, atrial flutter, multifocal atrial tachycardia (MAT), junctional ectopic tachycardia, and the three forms of supraventricular tachycardia (SVT): focal atria tachycardia, atrioventricular nodal reentrant tachycardia (AVNRT), and atrioventricular reentrant tachycardia (AVRT; Prutkin, 2016). The most common of these dysrhythmias are ST, AVNRT, AVRT, focal atrial tachycardias and MATs, and atrial flutter.

FIGURE 15-2: REENTRY PATHWAYS THROUGH THE HEART

Conditions Required for Reentry

1. A potential circuit

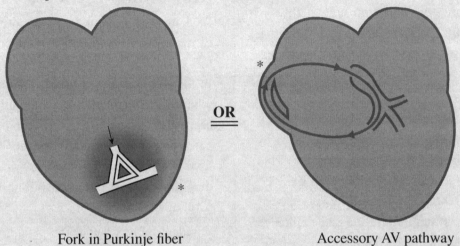

OR

Fork in Purkinje fiber   Accessory AV pathway

2. Unidirectional block within the conduction circuit

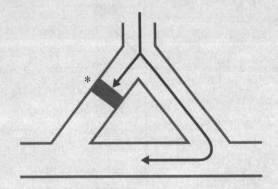

3. Delayed conduction within the circuit

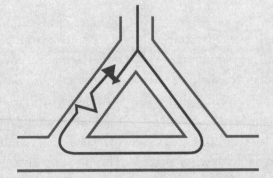

AV = atrioventricular.

Note. Western Schools, 2017.

Sinus Tachycardia

ST is the most common tachydysrhythmia and meets all the criteria for a normal sinus rhythm except for having a heart rate greater than 100 beats/min (see Figure 15-3). ST is primarily a benign finding in young, healthy adults undergoing physical exertion. However, rates greater than 150 beats/min should cue the clinician to look for triggers other than the sinus node. In the older adult, ST can decrease cerebral blood flow and cause detrimental consequences such as syncope, falls, or stroke. ST can be caused by natural and synthetic stimulants, such as amphetamine drugs; a sympathetic response associated with acute hemorrhage, shock, or heart failure; or other physiological pathologies such as fever, pain, or thyrotoxicosis. ST causes increased workload to the heart and is associated with decreased diastolic filling times resulting in a lower stroke volume. Symptoms associated with these hemodynamic changes can be responsible for patients presenting with light-headedness, dizziness, palpitations, syncope, chest pain, and dyspnea when heart rates are high enough to compromise cardiac output. Treatments are aimed at decreasing the ventricular rate to less than 100 beats/min using medications with negative chronotropic qualities such as beta blockers, calcium channel blockers, and digoxin (Anderson, 2016; Urden, Stacy, & Lough, 2015).

Atrioventricular Nodal Reentrant Tachycardia

AVNRT is the most common type of SVT and can result in a narrow complex or wide complex tachydysrhythmia (see Figure 15-4). The anatomic substrate is a dual AV node physiology (Page & Joglar, 2016). Regardless of its presentation, it requires prompt assessment of hemodynamic status. If the patient is hemodynamically compromised and has AVNRT in its narrow complex form, prompt treatment with direct current cardioversion (DCCV) is warranted. AVNRT most commonly occurs in younger healthy adults without significant structural heart disease. It is generally well tolerated and rarely leads to hemodynamic instability. In the rare occasion hemodynamic instability does occur, prompt cardioversion is warranted (Page & Joglar, 2016). When the patient maintains hemodynamic stability, vagal maneuvers are recommended as first-line treatment. When vagal maneuvers are proven ineffective, short-acting atrioventricular (AV) nodal blocking agents (i.e., adenosine, verapamil, beta blockers) should be initiated. Intravenous (IV) adenosine is the first-line recommendation over other agents due to its high efficacy rate (terminates 95% of AVNRTs) and short half-life (Page & Joglar, 2016). When adenosine is ineffective, verapamil is the second-line agent for narrow complex AVNRT (Prutkin, 2016).

FIGURE 15-3: SINUS TACHYCARDIA ELECTROCARDIOGRAPH READING

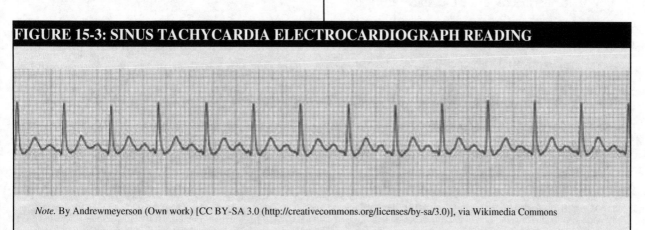

Note. By Andrewmeyerson (Own work) [CC BY-SA 3.0 (http://creativecommons.org/licenses/by-sa/3.0)], via Wikimedia Commons

FIGURE 15-4: ATRIOVENTRICULAR NODAL REENTRANT TACHYCARDIA ELECTROCARDIOGRAM READING

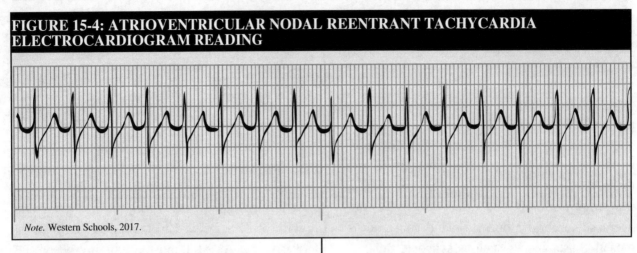

Note. Western Schools, 2017.

Atrioventricular Reentrant Tachycardia

Similar to AVNRT, AVRT is an SVT that requires assessment of hemodynamic status. It is a reentrant tachycardia with two distinct pathways: the normal AV conduction system and also an accessory pathway system (see Figure 15-5). AVRT can also be a narrow complex (orthodromic AVRT) or a wide complex (antidromic AVRT) tachydysrhythmia. AVRT is a pre-excitation syndrome that most often manifests as Wolff-Parkinson-White (WPW) syndrome, as noted in Figure 15-5. The involvement in the accessory pathway is one of the primary differences between AVRT and AVNRT (see Figure 15-6; Aehlert, 2013). Its treatment is the same as AVNRT: If hemodynamically unstable, DCCV is warranted without delay; if hemodynamically stable, first-line therapy is vagal maneuvers over pharmacological agents. However, if pharmacological therapies are necessary (meaning vagal maneuvers were ineffective), adenosine is the first-line drug followed by verapamil and an IV beta blocker. Careful attention must be paid to the ECG findings. If there is any evidence of pre-excitation and the patient is in atrial fibrillation, AV node blockade should not be given because it can enhance conduction over the accessory pathway and result in increased ventricular rates that may deteriorate into a dangerous ventricular arrhythmia (Page & Joglar, 2016). Radiofrequency catheter ablation therapy is the definitive treatment for WPW syndrome (Prutkin, 2016).

Focal Atrial Tachycardia

Focal atrial tachycardias are usually self-limiting and paroxysmal (see Figure 15-7). They are a form of SVT that arises from a single site of microreentry outside of the sinus node. Hemodynamically unstable patients require immediate DCCV. In contrast, hemodynamically stable patients with atrial tachycardia who are symptomatic should be treated with oral or IV beta blockers or nondihydropyridine calcium channel blockers (e.g., diltiazem or verapamil) to slow down the ventricular rate or terminate the tachydysrhythmia altogether. Amiodarone IV is another acceptable treatment and could benefit patients who may be borderline hypotensive (Prutkin, 2016).

Atrial Flutter

Atrial flutter should be high in the differential diagnosis for a patient presenting with a regular narrow complex tachycardia with a ventricular response greater than 150 beats/min (see Figure 15-8). Although this rhythm can sometimes present with an irregular ventricular response (in tachydysrhythmias with variable conduction), it is most often a regular tachycardic rhythm and characterized as having a "sawtooth" baseline,

WPW

FIGURE 15-5: ACCESSORY PATHWAY AND ELECTROCARDIOGRAM CHARACTERISTICS WITH THE ATRIOVENTRICULAR REENTRANT TACHYCARDIA OF WOLFF-PARKINSON-WHITE SYNDROME

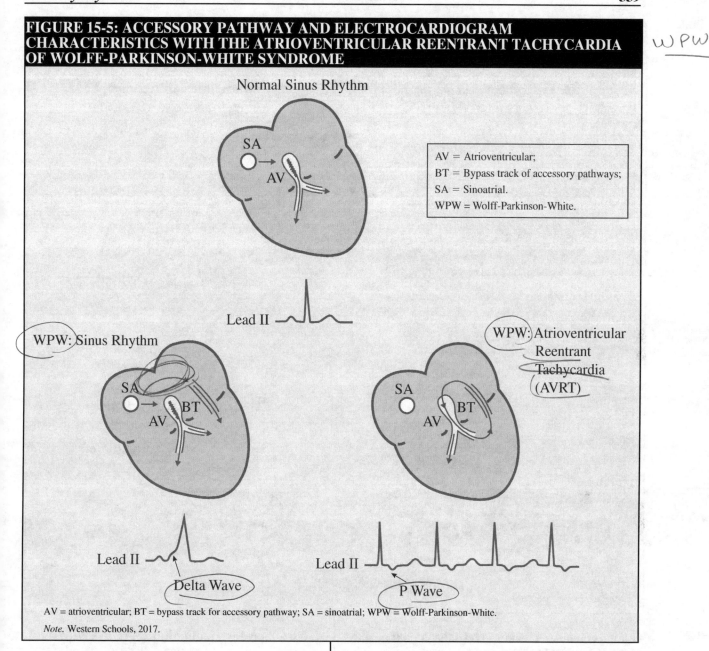

Normal Sinus Rhythm

AV = Atrioventricular;
BT = Bypass track of accessory pathways;
SA = Sinoatrial.
WPW = Wolff-Parkinson-White.

Lead II

WPW: Sinus Rhythm

WPW: Atrioventricular Reentrant Tachycardia (AVRT)

Lead II

Delta Wave

Lead II

P Wave

AV = atrioventricular; BT = bypass track for accessory pathway; SA = sinoatrial; WPW = Wolff-Parkinson-White.

Note. Western Schools, 2017.

as noted by the arrows in Figure 15-8. Similar to the treatment of atrial fibrillation discussed in Chapter 10, early steps in the management of atrial flutter involve assessing the need for cardioversion, ventricular rate control, and antithrombotic therapy (Prutkin, 2016).

Multifocal Atrial Tachycardia

MAT requires three or more consecutive P waves of different morphologies (see Figure 15-7). MAT was formerly known as a wandering atrial pacemaker (Aehlert, 2013). It is not com-

monly associated with hemodynamic instability, but it is commonly associated with electrolyte imbalances involving hypokalemia or hypomagnesemia, or an underlying pulmonary or cardiac illness. Therefore, medical therapies aim to replenish electrolytes as needed and treat the underlying disease process inciting the tachydysrhythmia. Treatment of the dysrhythmia of MAT itself is initiated only when there is a sustained ventricular response. MAT treatment for ventricular rate control includes nondihydropyridine

FIGURE 15-6: ATRIOVENTRICULAR NODAL REENTRANT TACHYCARDIA COMPARED WITH ATRIOVENTRICULAR REENTRANT TACHYCARDIA

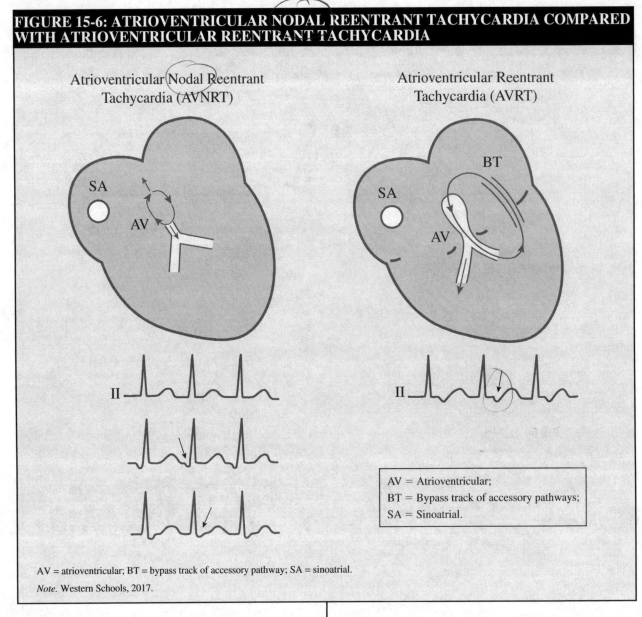

AV = atrioventricular; BT = bypass track of accessory pathway; SA = sinoatrial.

Note. Western Schools, 2017.

calcium channel blockers and beta blockers. In the absence of decompensating heart failure or bronchospasm, initial therapy should be a beta blocker such as metoprolol. However, when a beta blocker is contraindicated, initial therapy should be a nondihydropyridine calcium channel blocker such as verapamil (Prutkin, 2016).

Wide Complex Tachydysrhythmias

The most common wide complex tachydysrhythmia is monomorphic ventricular tachycardia (VT; Mozaffarian et al., 2016). Other wide complex tachydysrhythmias include SVT with aberrant conduction (e.g., AVNRT with right bundle branch block), SVT with a paced ventricular response, and antidromic AVRT. Because the most concerning of these dysrhythmias is VT, all wide complex tachydysrhythmias should be assumed as VT until proven otherwise, and immediate assessment of hemodynamic stability should take precedence over any other diagnostic evaluation (Prutkin, 2016).

Ventricular Tachycardia

The leading cause of sudden cardiac death is VT (Priori et al., 2015). VT occurs when there

FIGURE 15-7: FOCAL ATRIAL TACHYCARDIA IN COMPARISON WITH MULTIFOCAL ATRIAL TACHYCARDIA ELECTROCARDIOGRAM READINGS

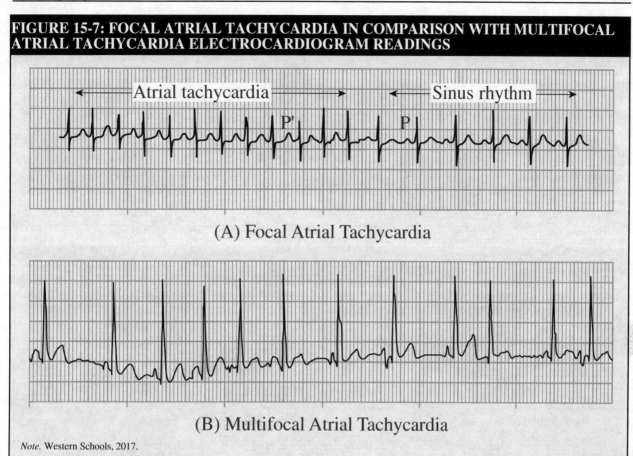

(A) Focal Atrial Tachycardia

(B) Multifocal Atrial Tachycardia

Note. Western Schools, 2017.

are three or more sequential premature ventricular contractions occurring at a rate greater than 100 beats/min (see Figure 15-9). When VT occurs temporarily (less than 30 seconds), it is referred to as *nonsustained VT.* Likewise, when VT exists for longer than 30 seconds and requires therapeutic intervention to terminate the rhythm, it is referred to as *sustained VT.* Patients experiencing runs of nonsustained VT are at high risk for sustained VT (Aehlert, 2013). All patients with VT that is sustained should be considered as having the potential to become unstable. Treating VT involves identifying whether the patient needs direct current defibrillation or has time for the underlying cause to be identified and treated (Aehlert, 2013).

Multiple morphologies of VT are related to the underlying pathophysiological and etiological factors involved with inciting the tachy-dysrhythmia. When the QRS complexes in VT are of the same shape and amplitude, the rhythm is called *monomorphic VT* and can have ventricular rates from 101 to 250 beats/min. Monomorphic VT is often caused by acid-base imbalances, myocardial ischemia, or infarction resulting in scar tissue, reentrant circuits, cardiomyopathy, cocaine abuse, digitalis toxicity, mitral valve prolapse, or electrolyte imbalances (especially hypokalemia, hyperkalemia, or hypomagnesemia; Aehlert, 2013).

Polymorphic Ventricular Tachycardia. Polymorphic VT (PMVT) manifests with QRS complexes that vary in shape and amplitude from beat to beat and appear to twist from upright to negative back to upright (see Figure 15-9). PMVT can occur with varying durations of the QT interval. PMVT involving a long QT interval (more than 500 milliseconds) is *torsades de pointes.* PMVT with a short QT interval (less than 320 milliseconds) is called *short QT*

FIGURE 15-8: ATRIAL FLUTTER WITH RAPID VENTRICULAR RESPONSE ELECTROCARDIOGRAM READINGS

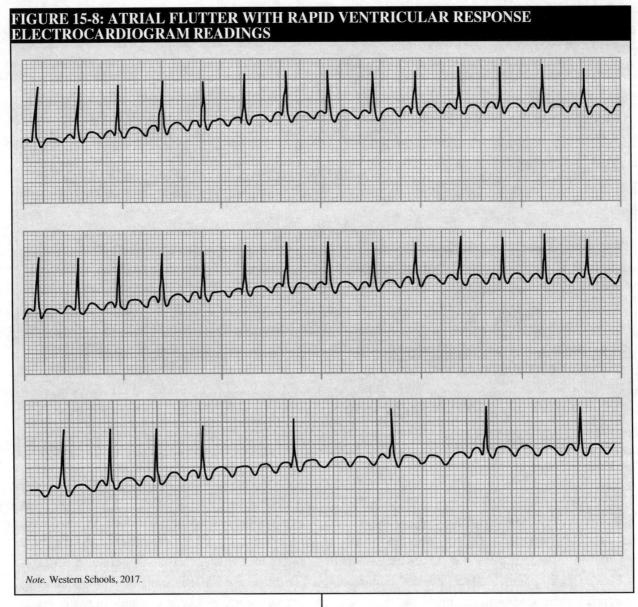

Note. Western Schools, 2017.

PMVT. PMVT triggered by exercise or stress that occurs with a normal QT interval is called *catecholaminergic PMVT.* PMVT seen with a right bundle branch block pattern and normal QT interval in a patient without a history of structural heart disease is referred to as *Brugada syndrome.* Finally, any PMVT without QT prolongation that cannot be attributed to any of these forms is called *idiopathic normal QT PMVT.* The most common causes of PMVT are electrolyte imbalances (the most common cause is hypomagnesemia), medications causing prolonged QT intervals, and ischemia (Aehlert, 2013).

Pulseless Ventricular Tachycardia. In the patient experiencing VT with no discernable central pulse (apical, carotid, or femoral pulse), CPR and defibrillation are required immediately. The initiation of antiarrhythmics such as amiodarone or lidocaine should be considered next. In PMVT, magnesium sulfate should be the first drug administered intravenously because PMVT most often occurs because of hypomagnesemia. When these steps are completed, other underlying causes must be identified and treated.

FIGURE 15-9: MONOMORPHIC VENTRICULAR TACHYCARDIA COMPARED WITH POLYMORPHIC VENTRICULAR TACHYCARDIA ELECTROCARDIOGRAM READING

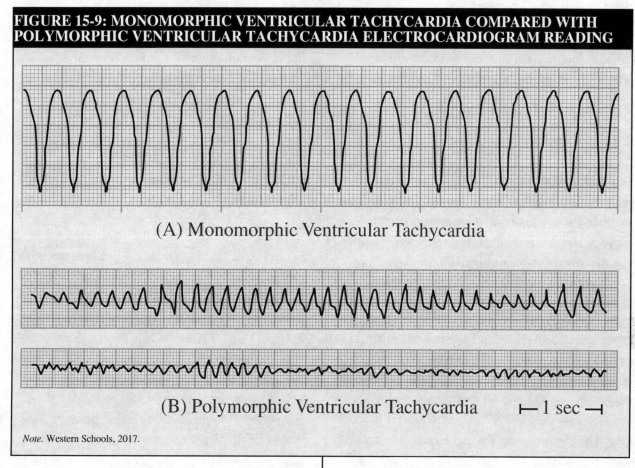

(A) Monomorphic Ventricular Tachycardia

(B) Polymorphic Ventricular Tachycardia ⊢ 1 sec ⊣

Note. Western Schools, 2017.

Ventricular Tachycardia With a Pulse. A patient with VT who has a discernable pulse is still considered unstable with a high risk for decompensation and decline. If the patient happens to be connected to a temporary pacemaker, the pacemaker rate can be increased slightly above the ventricular rate to overdrive pace the dysrhythmia. Overdrive pacing uses extrinsic electricity to capture and control the patient's intrinsic electricity for the purpose of terminating the dysrhythmia and restoring a viable rhythm. Vagal maneuvers such as asking the patient to bear down or cough can also be performed. The vagal maneuver of carotid massage has been discouraged for use by nurses because of the risk for dislodging unstable carotid plaque, but it may be provided by an advanced practice provider or physician. Antiarrhythmic infusions such as amiodarone or lidocaine can also be considered, and supplemental oxygen should be delivered (Aehlert, 2013). Blood should be collected to analyze serum electrolytes as a cause. Some hospitals may have point-of-care or bedside electrolyte analysis capabilities similar to bedside glucose monitoring that can facilitate timely identification of the cause and prevent a delay in appropriate treatments. Nurses must know the primary contraindication to antiarrhythmic infusions, such as amiodarone and lidocaine, is a QT interval greater than 0.50 second. Beta blockers can be used as an alternative to those antiarrhythmics (Aehlert, 2013).

BRADYDYSRYTHMIAS

Bradycardia is defined as a heart rate less than 60 beats/min (Mozaffarian et al., 2016). Any dysrhythmia that causes the heart rate to decrease to less than 60 beats/min is defined as a bradydysrhythmia. Bradyarrhythmias occur less frequently than other dysrhythmias within the U.S. population but are problematic when symptomatic (producing signs and symptoms of decreased tissue perfusion). *Bradydysrhythmia* is an umbrella term for a category of dysrhythmias, all of which primarily involve dysfunction of the SA or AV node. Bradydysrhythmia is one of the most common causes for implantation of devices such as permanent pacemakers (Mozaffarian et al., 2016). Common bradydysrythmias associated with SA and AV node dysfunction include symptomatic sinus bradycardia, sinus node dysfunction (SND), and AV block.

Clinical Management Strategies

It is necessary to recall the normal intrinsic rates of the heart's natural and other pacemakers. For instance, the intrinsic rate for the SA node (natural pacemaker) is 60 to 100 beats/min. The intrinsic rate for the AV node is 40 to 60 beats/min. The intrinsic rate for the bundle of His or ventricles is 20 to 40 beats/min. Thus, if a patient's rate is less than 60 beats/min, in addition to determining hemodynamic stability, it is especially important to determine which pacemaker is generating the bradydysrhythmia. Determining which pacemaker is generating the rhythm facilitates appropriate management and treatment for the bradydysrhythmia (Aehlert, 2013).

Sinus Bradycardia – Symptomatic

Sinus bradycardia meets all the criteria for a normal sinus rhythm except it has a heart rate less than 60 beats/min (see Figure 15-10). Symptomatic sinus bradycardia requires acute intervention because of the decrease in cardiac output resulting in decreased tissue perfusion. Symptoms include (but are not limited to) mental status changes, diaphoresis, chest pain, nausea, and vomiting. Causes associated with acute symptomatic bradycardia include inferior myocardial infarction (MI), increased vagal stimu-

lation (such as when straining to have a bowel movement), increased intracranial pressures, or the effects of negative chronotropic medications (e.g., beta blockers, calcium channel blockers, and digoxin). Treatments for symptomatic sinus bradycardia aim to increase the heart rate enough to produce an adequate cardiac output. This can be achieved by administering atropine (0.5 mg), starting a dopamine infusion, or using a temporary pacemaker.

Sinus Node Dysfunction

SND, formerly known as sick sinus syndrome, is any disorder that involves malfunction of the SA node. It is the leading indication for permanent pacemaker placement in the United States (Mozaffarian et al., 2016). SNDs can include SA block, sinus arrest or sinus pause, or sinus arrhythmia (see Figure 15-11). SND involving a bradydysrhythmia is caused by the SA node failing to function as the primary pacemaker of the heart. When this occurs, the lower pacemakers usually take over, which results in either a junctional rhythm (derived from the AV node) or an idioventricular rhythm (derived from the bundle of His). As is characteristic of a bradydysrhythmia, SND often manifests with a heart rate less than 60 beats/min, but it also shows the absence of or atypical look of the P wave on the ECG. The ECG may show irregular P-to-P intervals, shortened PR intervals, or notched P waves (Aehlert, 2013). SND can be caused by intrinsic (pathological conditions) or extrinsic (depression of SA function) factors (Mozaffarian et al., 2016). Specific causes include any damage to the SA node from myocardial ischemia or infarction, rheumatic heart disease, overstimulation of the parasympathetic system, mechanical trauma, obstructive sleep apnea (OSA), reactions to medications (e.g., beta blockers or calcium channel blockers), or electrophysiological changes that occur with aging (Aehlert, 2013). Degenerative changes

FIGURE 15-10: SINUS BRADYCARDIA ELECTROCARDIOGRAM READING

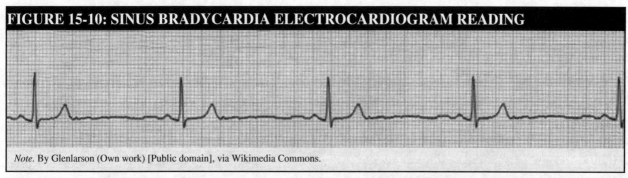

Note. By Glenlarson (Own work) [Public domain], via Wikimedia Commons.

FIGURE 15-11: SINUS NODE DYSFUNCTION PRESENTATIONS ELECTROCARDIOGRAM READINGS

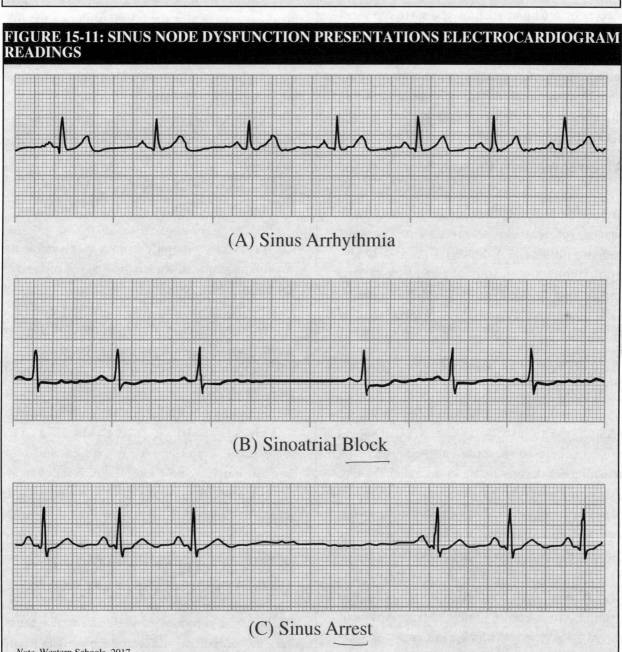

(A) Sinus Arrhythmia

(B) Sinoatrial Block

(C) Sinus Arrest

Note. Western Schools, 2017.

(such as with aging) affecting the conduction processes is the most common cause of SND, with ischemic heart disease being the next most common cause (Mozaffarian et al., 2016). When SND compromises the patient's ability to maintain hemodynamic stability, the primary treatment is extrinsic pacing by the means of a temporary or permanently implanted pacemaker. In situations such as acute MI, a patient may need a temporary pacemaker because of SND during the acute phase of myocardial injury. However, when the myocardium recovers, SA conduction can sometimes be restored and the patient no longer requires extrinsic pacing (Aehlert, 2013).

Atrioventricular Block

An AV block involves the delay or complete interruption of impulse conduction from the atria to the ventricle for any reason. The most common forms of AV block resulting in brady-dysrhythmia are complete heart block (CHB) and second-degree type II, or Mobitz type II, heart block (see Figure 15-12; Mozaffarian et al., 2016).

Second-Degree Atrioventricular Block Type II – Mobitz

The second-degree type II AV block, or Mobitz type II block (see Figure 15-12), should raise concern to the clinician because of its potential for decline into a more lethal rhythm. The Mobitz block involves two pathophysiological mechanisms: (1) a delay in impulse conduction between the AV node and bundle of His–Purkinje system, and (2) the block of impulse conduction in the bundle of His. The Mobitz block has the greatest potential to decline into a CHB (Aehlert, 2013). Although the Mobitz type AV block can occur congenitally in otherwise healthy patients, it most often occurs secondary to coronary heart disease or heart failure (Mozaffarian et al., 2016).

Complete Heart Block

CHB is also known as a third-degree AV block. CHB involves a complete block in all impulse conduction between the atria and ventricles. The site of the block is usually at the level of either the AV node or, more commonly, the level of the bundle of His–Purkinje system. This means the SA node is no longer the primary pacemaker for the heart. Although the SA node fires and produces the P wave on ECG, there is no ventricular response to SA node impulses. The heart is then led by the pacemaker within the AV node. Characteristically for CHB, the ventricular rate is about 30 beats/min and is completely disassociated from the SA rate on ECG (see Figure 15-12; Aehlert, 2013). The leading cause of CHB is MI or other forms of ischemic heart disease (Mozaffarian et al., 2016).

AV blocks generally can have reversible or irreversible causes. Reversible causes of bradycardic AV blocks include medication toxicity, electrolyte imbalances, and effects of anesthesia. Irreversible causes include those related to heart disease, such as ischemic heart disease, congestive heart failure, and degenerative electrophysiological changes (Mozaffarian et al., 2016). The primary treatment for bradycardic AV blocks is extrinsic pacing (Mozaffarian et al., 2016; Priori et al., 2015). Nurses must recognize that treating these acute dysrhythmias with atropine to increase the heart rate will be ineffective (Aehlert, 2013).

CARDIAC ARREST DYSRHYTHMIAS

The most common acute dysrhythmias causing cardiac arrest and sudden cardiac death internationally are VT, ventricular fibrillation (VF), bradydysrhythmia, and *pulseless electrical activity* (PEA; Priori et al., 2015).

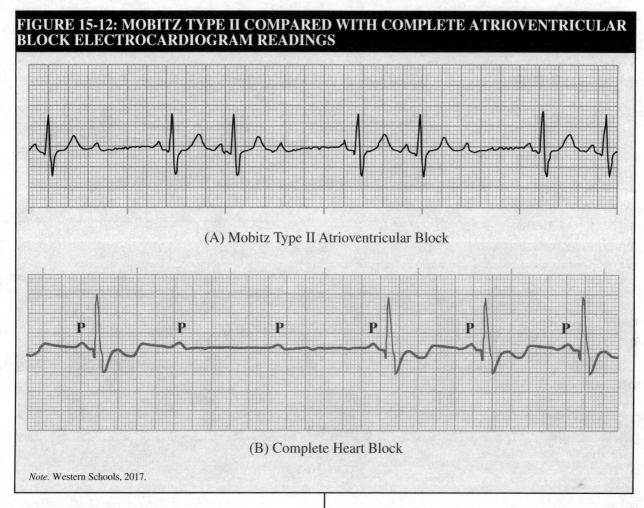

FIGURE 15-12: MOBITZ TYPE II COMPARED WITH COMPLETE ATRIOVENTRICULAR BLOCK ELECTROCARDIOGRAM READINGS

(A) Mobitz Type II Atrioventricular Block

(B) Complete Heart Block

Note. Western Schools, 2017.

Ventricular Fibrillation

VF is a chaotic rhythm generated from ventricular pacing cells that cannot produce an effective myocardial contraction, which results in cardiac arrest (Aehlert, 2013). Because of the risk for cardiac arrest, VF requires immediate chest compressions to circulate oxygen-rich blood and defibrillation to prevent decompensation to asystole (the absence of electrical impulses and rhythm). VF with waves less than 3 mm in amplitude is known as *fine VF* (see Figure 15-13). Conversely, VF with waves greater than 3 mm in amplitude is known as *coarse VF*. Characteristically, ECG readings for VF show no discernable heart rate, rhythm pattern or regularity, P wave, PR interval, or QRS duration. VF can be caused by myocardial ischemia or infarction, dysrhythmias, electro-lyte imbalances, electrocution, cardiomyopathy, increased sympathetic nervous system activity, proarrhythmic medications, severe heart failure, or vagal stimulation (Aehlert, 2013).

NURSING APPLICATION

ECG artifacts can mimic VF. The nurse must be able to differentiate between the two and assess the patient's condition before the initiation of any treatment protocols.

Pulseless Electrical Activity

PEA occurs as organized electrical activity on the ECG monitor of any heart rhythm that does not produce the mechanical function of cardiac contraction or palpable pulse (Aehlert, 2013). This dysrhythmia can manifest as a normal sinus rhythm or as tachydysrhythmia or

FIGURE 15-13: VENTRICULAR FIBRILLATION – FINE COMPARED WITH COARSE ELECTROCARDIOGRAM READINGS

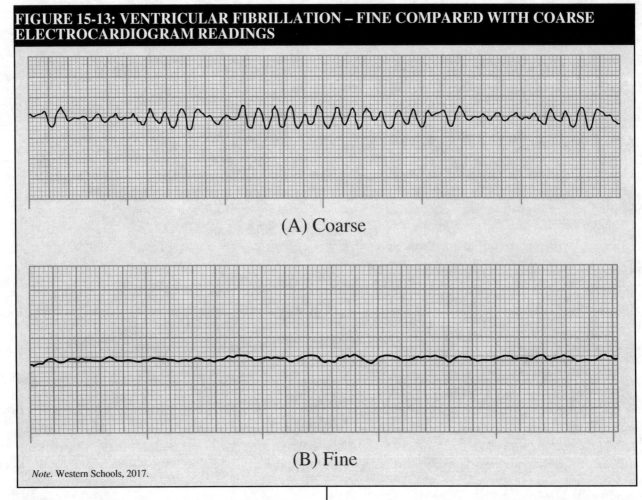

(A) Coarse

(B) Fine

Note. Western Schools, 2017.

bradydysrhythmia on the monitor. PEA is an emergency and requires immediate initiation of CPR. Causes of PEA can be remembered by the acronym of the 5 H's and 5 T's. The 5 H's of possible PEA causes are

- hypovolemia,

- hypoxia,

- hypothermia,

- hypokalemia or hyperkalemia, and/or

- hydrogen ions (or acidosis).

The 5 T's of possible PEA causes are

- tamponade (cardiac),

- tension pneumothorax,

- thrombosis of the lungs (massive pulmonary embolism),

- thrombosis of the heart (acute coronary syndromes), and/or

- tablets or toxins (drug overdose).

Reversing the underlying cause of PEA is the priority treatment for regaining cardiopulmonary function. The inability to reverse the underlying cause for PEA results in death (Aehlert, 2013).

SPECIAL POPULATIONS AT RISK FOR ACUTE DYSRHYTHMIAS

Other than patients with known heart disease, there are select populations of patients who are at high risk for acute dysrhythmias and sudden cardiac death because of the pathogenesis of noncardiac illness or the treatments for noncardiac illness (Priori et al., 2015). Awareness of these populations is important for the ability of the cardiovascular nurse to appropriately manage acute dysrhythmias.

Patients With Psychiatric Conditions

Patients with psychiatric illnesses such as anorexia nervosa, schizophrenia, or other mental health conditions have higher-than-expected risks for acute dysrhythmias and sudden death because of the effects of their psychiatric medications. Patients with schizophrenia are found to have three times higher risk for ventricular dysrhythmias and sudden cardiac death than the general population because of the number of antipsychotic medications used to treat the illness (Priori et al., 2015). The most common problem mental health medications, such as tricyclic antidepressants (TCAs), cause is the prolongation of the QT interval, which in turn increases the patient's risk for PMVT. Serotonin reuptake inhibitors also cause QT prolongation, but to a lesser degree than TCAs, and are thus preferred to TCAs when antidepressants are indicated (Priori et al., 2015).

Other problems associated with the high use of antipsychotics is hypokalemia and interactions with other medications concurrently administered for cardiac disease (e.g., digoxin). Evidence-based treatments to avoid acute dysrhythmias in this population are centered around measuring a baseline QT interval before the initiation of therapy, avoiding medications that will prolong the QT interval as much as possible, performing regular (during routine office visits) QT monitoring by 12-lead ECG, and monitoring regular serum potassium levels. Other risk factors for this group are prior history of dysrhythmia or left ventricular dysfunction before the start of antipsychotics (Priori et al., 2015). Nurses must be aware of this population's risk for acute dysrhythmias and sudden cardiac death.

Patients With Neurological Conditions

Patients with non-cardiac-involved neurological illnesses, such as seizure disorders, or with neurological illnesses that can have cardiac involvement, such as neuromuscular disorders, are at higher risk for acute dysrhythmias and sudden death (Priori et al., 2015).

Epilepsy

Patients who experience frequent seizures, regardless of adequate antiepileptic therapy, are at high risk for *sudden unexplained death in epilepsy* (SUDEP). Most cases occur with patients frequently experiencing generalized tonic-clonic seizures during sleep. Because the etiology of SUDEP is largely unknown, the treatment or prevention of this phenomenon involves maximizing seizure control (Priori et al., 2015). Nurses must recognize patients at risk for SUDEP and educate them of this potential outcome.

Neuromuscular Disorders

The neuromuscular disorders that put patients at the greatest risk for acute dysrhythmias are muscular dystrophies (MDs; Priori et al., 2015). Because MD is a group of diseases known to affect skeletal and cardiac muscle, the pathogenesis of MDs leads to conduction defects. The most common MDs with cardiac involvement include Duchenne and Becker dystrophies, which most often cause dilated cardiomyopathies. Subsequent to the development of dilated cardiomyopathies, acute dysrhythmias such as runs of VT or SVT occur (Priori et al., 2015). Other MDs responsible for acute dysrhythmias include Steinert, Emery-Dreifuss, and limb-girdle type dystrophies. These MDs can cause ventricular dysrhythmias responsible for sudden cardiac death but also conduction blocks. The pathogenesis of MDs causing acute dysrhythmias in this population involves the stretching of or fibrosis of heart muscle that interferes with conduction pathways.

Recommended treatment includes the routine monitoring of ECGs during annual clinic visits and the placement of a permanent pacemaker or automated internal cardiac defibrillator as indicated (Priori et al., 2015).

Patients Who Are Pregnant

Pregnancy can contribute to episodes of acute dysrhythmia, although mostly in patients with preexisting structural heart disease (Priori et al., 2015). This section discusses acute dysrhythmias that occur in pregnant patients in the absence of pregnancy-acquired cardiomyopathies. Women with Brugada syndrome (a congenital disorder associated with right bundle branch blocks and persistent ST elevation in the precordial leads) and congenital long QT syndrome (persistent QT prolongation since birth) are at greatest risk for acute dysrhythmias during pregnancy (Priori et al., 2015). The acute dysrhythmias most associated with this population include runs of VT and episodes of SVT. Diagnosis is generally made in this population when the patient complains of palpitations (Priori et al., 2015) or syncope. Treatment includes the avoidance of stimulants (e.g., caffeine, nicotine, and alcohol), catheter ablation, or medication blockade (e.g., beta blockers or sodium channel blockers) at low doses (Priori et al., 2015).

Patients With Obstructive Sleep Apnea

Patients diagnosed with OSA are at high risk for acute dysrhythmias and sudden death. This population can experience bradydysrhythmia or tachydysrhythmia during sleep because of episodes of hypoxia (Priori et al., 2015). The most common types of acute dysrhythmia in this population include sinus bradycardia, bradycardia related to SND, and AV blocks. Atrial dysrhythmias are highly correlated with untreated sleep apnea. Ventricular dysrhythmias and sudden cardiac death were found to occur most often within the circadian pattern of sleep from midnight to 6 a.m. Although utilizing positive airway pressure during sleep is effective for the treatment of OSA, there is limited evidence for its ability to prevent acute dysrhythmias, and it remains under investigation (Priori et al., 2015).

CASE STUDY

A 15-year-old female patient with a sudden onset of palpitations, dyspnea, and lightheadedness is accompanied by her mother to the emergency department (ED). The mother reports that the patient's symptoms started approximately 2 hours before, while her daughter was sitting in her second period high school class. The patient reports her symptoms have been off and on since they started. She denies chest pain, syncope, diaphoresis, nausea, or vomiting. The patient also denies these symptoms ever occurring before. The patient denies a medical and surgical history.

The mother reports a healthy pregnancy and delivery with her daughter and denies any congenital anomalies. The patient has no family history of sudden cardiac death or premature coronary heart disease. The patient denies the use of alcohol, tobacco, and illicit drugs. She denies taking any prescription medications or using over-the-counter medications, vitamins, herbs, and other supplements. She admits to drinking high-caffeine energy drinks mixed into protein shakes most mornings.

A review of systems was positive for a regular menstrual cycle, with the patient's last menstrual period starting 8 days ago. Upon arrival to the ED, the patient was dyspneic, anxious, clammy, and complaining of palpitations. A 12-lead ECG revealed a narrow complex tachycardia with a heart rate of 210 beats/min. The emergency medicine physician interpreted the ECG as SVT. Before the treatment of adenosine could be initiated, the patient reported her symptoms subsiding. She appeared more comfortable, and further ED evaluation was initiated.

An hour later, the patient had a follow-up 12-lead ECG, which revealed sinus tachycardia with a heart rate of 102 beats/min. The patient continued to deny that symptoms were returning. Serum labs collected upon arrival returned unremarkable results for an acute coronary syndrome or any electrolyte imbalances. The patient's chest radiograph was normal. The patient's physical examination was unremarkable for any neurological, pulmonary, or cardiovascular findings. The patient did not have peripheral edema or musculoskeletal abnormalities.

The emergency medicine physician consulted a cardiologist to further evaluate the patient. By phone, the cardiologist recommended that the patient be admitted to the hospital and to start IV fluid therapy for rehydration. Upon the cardiologist's arrival to the ED, the patient suddenly became anxious and dyspneic while complaining that her palpitations had returned. The cardiologist ordered another 12-lead ECG, which revealed the same narrow complex tachycardic rhythm with a rate of 196 beats/min. The cardiologist suspects that the patient's rhythm is the ventricular pre-excitation disorder called Wolff-Parkinson-White (WPW) syndrome.

Questions

1. Which initial medical interventions and care does the nurse anticipate the patient may need?

2. What is the definitive treatment for WPW syndrome?

Answers

1. When a patient with WPW syndrome is hemodynamically unstable, the first-line therapy is DCCV. The patient is showing signs of unstable cardiac and respiratory responses. Thus, the nurse begins to prepare the patient and family by providing education about DCCV and initiating setting up the patient for the procedure. If DCCV is required, the nurse will explain that IV medication is given to sedate the patient. The patient's heart rate and rhythm, blood pressure, breathing rate, and oxygen levels are also monitored. The nurse informs the mother and the patient that a high-energy shock will be delivered through the chest wall to the heart muscle to stop the dysrhythmia.

The first step of treatment is to identify whether the patient is in an irregular or regular rhythm and to obtain the cardiology consultation. In patients with pre-excitation, it is important to determine whether they are in atrial fibrillation versus an AVRT. In atrial fibrillation with pre-excitation, AV nodal blocking agents should be avoided. It was determined in this case that the patient was *not* found to be in atrial fibrillation. For patients who are hemodynamically stable, first-line therapy for WPW syndrome is vagal maneuvers over pharmacological agents. However, if pharmacological therapies are necessary (meaning vagal maneuvers were ineffective), adenosine is the first-line drug followed by verapamil and an IV beta blocker. The nurse prepares medication-related information to review with the patient and her mother.

2. Radiofrequency catheter ablation therapy is the definitive treatment to stop the recurrence of WPW syndrome. The etiology of the condition derives from the accessory pathway. Radiofrequency catheter ablation is used to block or disrupt conduction through the accessory pathway and terminate the dysrhythmia. The patient is given a sedative medication to reduce discomfort during this procedure.

SUMMARY

Patients who are experiencing acute dysrhythmias require urgent attention by knowledgeable and skilled clinicians. The ability to identify and distinguish between the hemodynamic consequences of bradydysrhythmias and tachydysrhythmias is necessary for the cardiovascular nurse to anticipate and initiate timely and effective therapies and management strategies. The nurse must be able to care for all populations at risk for acute dysrhythmias, articulate findings to medical providers, and educate patients and families of the disease processes, treatment plans, and necessary surveillance at home related to the potential for their recurrence. The nurse plays a vital role in reducing mortality and morbidity rates in patients experiencing acute dysrhythmias through supporting and reinforcing the patients' and families' application of knowledge, skill, and prudent vigilance.

EXAM QUESTIONS

CHAPTER 15
Questions 75–80

Note: Choose the one option that BEST answers each question.

75. What is the first-line drug for treatment of atrioventricular nodal reentrant tachycardia?

    a. Digoxin
    b. Adenosine
    c. Quinapril
    d. Atropine

76. What is another name for polymorphic ventricular tachycardia?

    a. Third-degree heart block
    b. Mobitz type II heart block
    c. Coarse ventricular fibrillation
    d. Torsades de pointes

77. If a patient's heart rate is below 60 beats/min, after determining the patient's hemodynamic stability, the nurse's next action is to

    a. administer atropine per patient protocol.
    b. determine which pacemaker is generating the bradydysrhythmia.
    c. prepare to use transcutaneous temporary pacing.
    d. prepare the patient for cardioversion.

78. Which acute dysrhythmia is often treated by administering atropine?

    a. Pulse electrical activity
    b. Sinus tachycardia
    c. Sinus bradycardia
    d. Complete heart block

79. Which bradydysrhythmia is related to the complete dissociation of electrical impulses between the atria and ventricles?

    a. Complete AV block
    b. Mobitz type II AV block
    c. Symptomatic sinus bradycardia
    d. Pulseless electrical activity

80. A patient with a neuromuscular disorder such as muscular dystrophy is more prone to acute dysrhythmias because of

    a. electrolyte imbalances.
    b. overstretch of the atria.
    c. ischemia.
    d. conduction pathway defects.

REFERENCES

Aehlert, B. (2013). *ECGs made easy* (5th ed.). St. Louis, MO: Elsevier/Mosby.

Anderson, K. M. (2016). *The advanced practice nurse cardiovascular clinician.* New York, NY: Springer Publishing.

Mozaffarian, D., Benjamin, E. J., Go, A. S., Arnett, D. K., Blaha, M. J., Cushman, M., … Turner, M.B. (2016). Heart disease and stroke statistics – 2016 update: A report from the American Heart Association. *Circulation, 133,* e38-e360. doi:10.1161/CIR.0000000000000350

Page, R. L., & Joglar, J. A. (2016). 2015 ACC/AHA/HRS guideline for the management of adult patients with supraventricular tachycardia. *Journal of the American College of Cardiology, 67*(13), e27-e115. doi:10.1016/j.jacc.2015.08.856

Priori, S. G., Lundqvist-Blomström, C., Mazzanti, A., Blom, N., Borggrefe, M., Camm, J., … Van Veldhuisen, D. J. (2015). 2015 ESC guidelines for the management of patients with ventricular arrhythmias and the prevention of sudden cardiac death. *European Heart Journal, 36*(41), 2793-2867. doi:10.1093.eurheartj.ehv316

Prutkin, J. M. (2016). Overview of the acute management of tachyarrhythmias. *UptoDate.com.* Retrieved from http://www.uptodate.com/contents/overview-of-the-acute-management-of-tachyarrhythmias

Urden, L. D., Stacy, K. M., & Lough, M. E. (2015). *Critical care nursing diagnosis and management* (7th ed.). St. Louis, MO: Elsevier/Mosby.

CHAPTER 16

SHOCK STATES

LEARNING OUTCOME

After completing this chapter, the learner will be able to describe management of the patient in shock.

CHAPTER OBJECTIVES

After completing this chapter, the learner will be able to:

1. Identify symptoms of the patient in shock.

2. Differentiate among the clinical presentations and etiologies of the varied shock states.

3. Describe appropriate treatment for the different shock states.

4. Describe nursing management of patients in shock.

INTRODUCTION

Shock is an emergent clinical syndrome resulting from inadequate tissue perfusion. Regardless of the cause of shock syndromes, a hypoperfusion-induced imbalance between the delivery of oxygen and the body tissue's requirement for oxygen leads to ischemic cellular injury and dysfunction. When hypoperfusion persists, severe and irreversible cellular injury occurs and a complex cascade of inflammatory processes is initiated throughout the entire body (systemic inflammatory response), causing the maldistribution of blood flow and worsening cellular perfusion (Brashers, 2017). The cardio-vascular nurse must recognize clinical manifestations of shock and the patients at risk for shock syndromes to improve the morbidity and mortality rates associated with shock.

TYPES OF SHOCK STATES

No matter the type of shock at presentation, the syndrome usually involves hypotension (a mean arterial blood pressure of less than 60 mmHg) in previously normotensive patients (Brashers, 2017). Recognizing the etiological factors of shock syndromes is important for initiating timely and appropriate treatment. Nurses must be able to recognize the type of shock a patient is experiencing, communicate the clinical findings to the appropriate medical provider, and anticipate safe and effective treatments to improve the patient's outcome.

Obstructive Shock

Obstructive shock does not commonly occur, but it is deadly. It occurs from any cause of compression to the thoracic cavity or any cause of increased intrathoracic pressures. This compression to the heart and great vessels within the mediastinal space tamponades the heart, resulting in less myocardial compliance, inadequate diastolic filling, and inadequate stroke volume (SV; Brashers, 2017).

Causes

The most common causes of increased intrathoracic pressures and obstructive shock are a tension pneumothorax and massive pulmonary embolus (PE). Other causes include increased positive pressure ventilation secondary to non-invasive ventilation or mechanical ventilation. Blunt abdominal trauma causing a ruptured diaphragm can also result in increased intrathoracic pressures and obstructive shock (Brashers, 2017).

Clinical Presentation

The clinical manifestations of obstructive shock are similar to those of cardiac tamponade and cardiogenic shock. When intrathoracic pressures are increased, intracardiac pressures are increased and the forward flow of blood volume is inhibited. Thus, signs and symptoms of obstructive shock will include the classic triad of cardiac tamponade: hypotension, jugular vein distension, and muffled heart tones. Depending on the cause, other findings may include tachycardia, tachypnea, tracheal deviation, mental status changes from anxiety to decreased levels of consciousness, and skin changes such as diaphoresis and pallor. Invasive hemodynamic monitoring will yield a decreased cardiac output (CO; less than 4 L/min), decreased SV (less than 50 ml), and increased central venous pressure (CVP; greater than 8 mmHg; Brashers, 2017).

Diagnosis

Diagnosis of obstructive shock is most often made from clinical findings. However, a chest radiograph may reveal a shifted mediastinum, widened mediastinum, or diaphragmatic rupture. If the patient has an arterial line in place, pulsus paradoxus (a decrease in systolic blood pressure by 15 to 30 mmHg with inspiration) will be present. If time permits for a confirmed diagnosis, an echocardiogram can reveal right atrial strain in the patient with PE and the degree of myocardial tamponade. Echocardiogram is useful in guiding decompressive treatment (Brashers, 2017).

Treatment

Treatment for an obstructive shock of any cause requires immediate decompression of what is causing the increased intrathoracic pressures. As urgent as this treatment is, it is not always easy to accomplish. For instance, thrombectomy (removal of the thrombus or clot) requires major surgery for the patient with a massive PE who is already hemodynamically compromised. The risk of performing surgery is often higher compared with no treatment. Thrombolytic therapy is an alternative to thrombectomy in the patient without contraindications to this treatment (Brashers, 2017).

Other causes of obstructive shock are not always as complicated as the treatment for a massive PE. For instance, the patient with a tension pneumothorax is treated by needle decompression of the thorax and subsequently a chest tube. The patient with a ruptured diaphragm caused by trauma would immediately go to surgery for repair and stabilization (Brashers, 2017; Rossaint et al., 2016).

Nursing Management

Nursing management of the patient in shock is prioritized to manage hemodynamic stability and evaluate the patient for adequate tissue perfusion. These patients are cared for in the critical care unit, and the condition can involve multisystem dysfunction. Nurses must be able to analyze vital signs or invasive pressure measures aimed to evaluate fluid volume and the effectiveness of heart function. Frequent physical assessments are performed to evaluate the effectiveness of therapies and report the patient's progress to the clinician managing the patient's treatment plan. Patients who are experiencing any type of shock require nursing care aimed to optimize the determinants of CO (oxygenation, preload, afterload, and contractility). For example, common nursing interventions include keeping the patient on strict bed rest to help conserve oxygen, maintaining adequate delivery of supplemental oxygen, and managing the administration of pharmacological therapies aimed to augment preload, afterload, and contractility. Nurses in the critical care unit also initiate patient and family education regarding the patient's severity of illness, plan of care, and medication education. The nurse acts as a conduit for effective communication between the patient and family members, and the clinician or other involved healthcare providers (Anderson, 2016).

Hypovolemic Shock

Hypovolemic shock syndrome is the most common type of shock in the United States (Brashers, 2017). It can occur from an absolute loss of blood volume (hemorrhage or exsanguination), the loss of plasma from the intravascular space to the extravascular (interstitial) space, or gastrointestinal (GI), urinary, or evaporative water (insensible) fluid losses.

Causes

Major trauma is the leading cause of hypovolemic shock secondary to hemorrhage (Rossaint et al., 2016). Other causes of hypovolemic shock include any reason for large amounts of bleeding, such as with the various causes of GI bleeding, coagulopathies, obstetric emergencies, or ruptured aneurysms. Causes related to interstitial or insensible fluid losses are less common (Brashers, 2017).

Clinical Presentation

The normal physiological response to hypovolemia is to maintain perfusion of the brain and heart by increasing sympathetic activity, hyperventilating in response to collapsing capacitance vessels, and releasing stress hormones. Signs and symptoms related to this normal compensatory physiological response include an increased heart rate, an initially narrowed pulse pressure that later widens as more volume is lost, mental status changes, decreased pulse amplitude, flat neck veins, oliguria, and skin changes such as pallor, diaphoresis, mottling, and decreased temperature. Invasive hemodynamic monitoring yields decreased CO, CVP, and SV. Compensatory mechanisms are effective in early hypovolemic shock – the systemic vascular resistance (SVR) measure is either normal or elevated – but in late stages this measure is decreased. Late stages of hypovolemic shock result in profound circulatory collapse that eventually results in cardiogenic shock. Late hypovolemic shock and cardiogenic shock may be indistinguishable for clinicians (Brashers, 2017).

Diagnosis

Hypovolemic shock can be easily diagnosed when compensatory mechanisms are recognized with hemodynamic instability and by considering the likely cause (e.g., trauma and GI bleeding). Diagnosis is more difficult when hemorrhage is the reason for this type of shock, such as with plasma volume depletion into the interstitial space or by insensible losses. Serum laboratory values aid in diagnosis by evaluating the patient's hemoglobin and hematocrit, albumin level, or sodium level. With severe blood loss (greater than 40% blood volume), hemoglobin and hematocrit levels are significantly lower than normal. Hypoalbuminemia (low serum albumin levels) leads to decreased intravascular colloidal osmotic pressures and the subsequent leaking of plasma into the surrounding tissues. In patients with free water loss, serum sodium levels may be increased because of hemoconcentration (Brashers, 2017).

Treatment

Initial treatment for hypovolemic shock includes the resuscitation (restoration) of circulatory blood volume. Circulatory blood volume replacement should include packed red blood cells when hemorrhage is the cause. Other colloids, such as fresh frozen plasma or platelets, can be considered as well when coagulopathies are etiological factors. In patients for whom hemorrhage is not a factor, isotonic fluids (e.g., 0.9% sodium chloride and lactated Ringer's solution) are the preferred infusions. In patients who are intravascularly depleted but cannot tolerate large volumes of fluid (e.g., end-stage kidney disease on dialysis), 5% or 25% albumin can be infused to help mobilize interstitial fluid back into the intravascular space; however, this effect is temporary and is usually used only to facilitate extravascular fluid removal and hemodynamic stability for the patient on dialysis (Brashers, 2017).

Distributive Shock

Distributive shock is the result of the maldistribution of circulating blood volume (Carlson & Fitzsimmons, 2014). This occurs when intravascular plasma volume is lost to the interstitial space (third space) secondary to a systemic inflammatory response. Such systemic inflammatory responses occur most frequently with the conditions of sepsis and anaphylaxis (Carlson & Fitzsimmons, 2014).

Septic Shock

Sepsis is estimated to be the leading cause of death and critical illness worldwide (Singer et al., 2016). To fully appreciate the urgency needed in the treatment of septic shock, one must consider the latest definitions of sepsis. According to updates added to the 2012 sepsis guidelines, sepsis is defined as "life-threatening organ dysfunction caused by a dysregulated host response to infection" (Singer et al., 2016, p. 801). The clinician must recognize that before the patient is in a discernible septic shock state, organ dysfunction (or acute injury) has already occurred because of hypoperfusion caused by the dysregulated inflammatory response to infection. Fortunately for the patient, even severe organ dysfunction does not always result in substantial cellular death. The same guidelines define septic shock as "a subset of sepsis in which underlying circulatory and cellular/metabolic abnormalities are profound enough to substantially increase mortality" (Singer et al., 2016, p. 805).

Causes. Gram-positive bacteria are the most common cause of septic shock, closely followed by gram-negative and polymicrobial bacterial infections (Dellinger et al., 2013). Fungi and other micro-organisms can also cause sepsis but do so less frequently. The immunocompromised population has a high risk for development of fungemia-related and polybacterial sepsis (Brashers, 2017).

Clinical Presentation. According to the latest updates to the sepsis guidelines, the criteria related to systemic inflammatory response syndrome are no longer specific enough for identifying sepsis or septic shock (Singer et al., 2016). As the latest definitions suggest, sepsis is recognized in a patient as signs of infection, such as fever and leukocytosis, in addition to indicators of organ dysfunction. The new guidelines suggest septic shock includes the findings associated with sepsis and a mean arterial pressure of less than 65 mmHg despite volume resuscitation (Singer et al., 2016). Other clinical findings that can manifest in the patient with septic shock (including those whose sepsis is related to organ dysfunction) include tachypnea, altered mental status, oliguria, edema, hyperglycemia, and many of the same skin changes discussed under previous types of shock.

In the early stages of septic shock, the patient has a hyperdynamic state or higher CO (greater than 7 ml/min at rest). The patient's other invasive hemodynamic measures, however, can mirror those found in hypovolemic shock (Brashers, 2017). In late septic shock, except for SVR (which is dramatically decreased because of massive systemic vasodilation), the patient's hemodynamic measures progress to mirror those found in cardiogenic shock caused by circulatory collapse (Brashers, 2017). Serum laboratory levels are measured to assess organ function and lactate level. The lactate level is a measure indicative of cellular dysfunction secondary to oxygen deprivation. An elevated lactate level is recognized as a poor tissue perfusion indicator (Dellinger et al., 2013).

Diagnosis. The diagnosis of septic shock is derived primarily from clinical criteria and serum laboratory results of organ dysfunction and lactate level. The update to the guidelines recommends the use of the Sequential Organ Failure Assessment score when serum laboratory values are available or the quick Sequential Organ Failure Assessment score before diagnostics are available (see Table 16-1 and Box 16-1). In a patient suspected of having a severe infection or sepsis, these scores and the lactate level are thought to guide the clinician in early goal-directed clinical decision making for treatment (Singer et al., 2016).

Treatment. In the first hour of having a suspicion of sepsis, early goal-directed therapy aims for timely volume resuscitation and broad-spectrum antibiotic administration for source control (Dellinger et al., 2013). Every hour that passes increases the patient's mortality risk by 10% to 30% (Singer et al., 2016). Volume resuscitation for patients in septic shock aims to achieve

- a CVP between 8 and 12 mmHg,
- a mean arterial pressure of more than 65 mmHg,
- a urine output of more than 0.5 ml/kg/hour, and
- mixed venous oxygen saturation between 65% and 80%.

(Dellinger et al., 2013)

If these parameters are met, the repeat lactate level should theoretically be decreased. The goal of volume resuscitation is to have a lactate level of less than 4 mmol/L (Dellinger et al., 2013). The patient who is not responsive to fluid resuscitation would require vasopressor therapy. Norepinephrine remains the drug of choice in septic shock; however, dopamine or epinephrine is a secondary alternative (Dellinger et al., 2013). Vasopressin can be used as an adjunctive agent to the primary or secondary vasopressor agents. If the patient requires inotropic support, dobutamine is the drug of choice despite the inotropic qualities of epinephrine and dopamine (Dellinger et al., 2013).

Anaphylactic Shock

Anaphylactic shock is a life-threatening event and an immediate response to a hypersensitivity reaction. A patient's secondary or subsequent exposure to an allergic trigger rapidly initiates a generalized shock response along with bronchial constriction. Bronchial constriction quickly complicates the body's ability to adequately deliver oxygen to the body's tissues (Carlson & Fitzsimmons, 2014).

Causes. Anaphylaxis can be triggered by the ingestion or dermatological contact with a number of allergens. Foods, food additives, environmental agents (e.g., insect stings), medications, or venoms can trigger an allergic response and later anaphylaxis. Latex was once the leading contributing factor for anaphylaxis in the hospital environment before manufacturers began to limit the use of latex in disposable supplies (Carlson & Fitzsimmons, 2014).

Clinical Presentation. Anaphylactic shock is a severe systemic reaction that affects multiple organ systems. Initial symptoms can appear within minutes to hours of exposure to the trigger. A *biphasic reaction* is a second anaphylactic reaction that occurs after resolution of the

TABLE 16-1: SEQUENTIAL ORGAN FAILURE ASSESSMENT SCORE

System	SOFA Score[a]				
	0	1	2	3	4
Respiratory					
PaO_2:FiO_2 ratio	≥400	<400	<300	<200 w/respiratory support	<100 w/respiratory support
Coagulation					
Platelets, ×103/µl	≥150	<150	<100	<50	<20
Liver					
Total bilirubin, mg/dl	<1.2	1.2-1.9	2.0-5.9	6.0-11.9	>12.0
Cardiovascular[b]					
MAP, mmHg	≥70	<70	Dop. < 5 or Dob. (any dose)	Dop. 5.1-15 OR Epi. < 0.1 OR Norepi. < 0.1	Dop. > 15 OR Epi. > 0.1 OR Norepi. > 0.1
Central nervous system					
Glasgow Coma Scale	15	13-14	10-12	6-9	<6
Renal					
Creatinine, mg/dl	<1.2	1.2-1.9	2.0-3.4	3.5-4.9	>5.0
Urine output, ml/day				<500	<200

[a]Considering the patient's baseline measures, a score greater than 2.0 is recognized with a 2- to 25-fold increased risk for dying in comparison with patients with SOFA scores of less than 2.0.

[b]All medications are in micrograms per kilogram per minute dosing for at least 1 hour.

Dob. = dobutamine; Dop. = dopamine; Epi. = epinephrine; MAP, mean arterial pressure; Norepi. = norepinephrine; SOFA = Quick Sequential Organ Function Assessment.

Note. Adapted from Singer, M., Deutschman, C. S., Seymour, C. W., Shankar-Hari, M., Annane, D., Bauer, M., ... Angus, D. C. (2016). The Third International Consensus definitions for sepsis and septic shock (sepsis-3). *JAMA, 315*(8), 801-810. doi:10.1001/jama.2016.0287

first within a 1- to 72-hour window. *Protracted anaphylaxis* is a severe form of anaphylactic shock where the symptoms can last up to 32 hours (Carlson & Fitzsimmons, 2014).

Cutaneous findings such as pruritus, generalized erythema, urticaria, and angioedema are the first signs of anaphylactic shock. The patient begins to appear restless, anxious, and uneasy while complaining of being warm all over. Effects upon the respiratory system include the development of laryngeal edema, bronchoconstriction, and mucous plugs manifesting as tachypnea, a sensation of a lump in the throat, wheezing, stridor, and

sometimes complaints of chest tightness. Findings related to the GI and genitourinary systems are the result of smooth muscle contraction and include vomiting, diarrhea, abdominal cramping, and abdominal pain (Carlson & Fitzsimmons, 2014).

Hemodynamic instability occurs quickly as the result of massive vasodilation. Consequently, mental status changes can rapidly decline to unresponsiveness, jugular veins appear flat, and, if palpable, the patient's distal pulses become weak and thready. A decreased CO, CVP, SV, and SVR are anticipated with hemodynamic monitoring (Carlson & Fitzsimmons, 2014).

BOX 16-1: QUICK SEQUENTIAL ORGAN FUNCTION ASSESSMENT (SOFA) SCORE

Quick SOFA Criteria[a]

- Respiratory rate ≥22 breaths/min

- Altered mentation

- Systolic blood pressure ≤ 100 mmHg

[a]If all criteria are present, this should prompt consideration of possible infection and sepsis.

Note. Adapted from Singer, M., Deutschman, C. S., Seymour, C. W., Shankar-Hari, M., Annane, D., Bauer, M., … Angus, D. C. (2016). The Third International Consensus definitions for sepsis and septic shock (sepsis-3). *JAMA, 315*(8), 801-810. doi:10.1001/jama.2016.0287

Diagnosis. Because of the urgency of this type of shock, diagnosis is made from clinical findings and the patient history. Clinical presentations of angioedema and other cutaneous manifestations, accompanied by hemodynamic instability, yield highly specific findings for the anaphylactic shock diagnosis (Carlson & Fitzsimmons, 2014).

Treatment. The first line of treatment for anaphylactic shock is intramuscular or intravenous injection of epinephrine. Epinephrine reverses cardiovascular and pulmonary responses to the trigger by causing vasoconstriction, increased myocardial contractility, and bronchodilation. Removal of the antigen or trigger is also warranted after epinephrine is initiated to discontinue the patient's exposure to the underlying cause of anaphylaxis. When patients do not respond to injected doses of epinephrine, a continuous infusion is initiated. Patients with a history of using beta blockers may require administration of glucagon to improve the patient's response to epinephrine. Second-line medications indicated in anaphylactic shock include inhaled beta-adrenergic agents to treat bronchospasm unresponsive to epinephrine, diphenhydramine to block the systemic histamine response, and an H_2 agonist (combined with diphenhydramine) such as ranitidine to combat GI responses to anaphy-

laxis. Patients with persistent shock states may require additional vasopressor therapy to support end organ perfusion, and tracheal intubation and mechanical ventilation to facilitate adequate oxygen delivery (Carlson & Fitzsimmons, 2014).

Cardiogenic Shock

Cardiogenic shock is also known as pump failure. This type of shock is characterized by systemic hypoperfusion caused by severe depression of the contractile force of the heart. Cardiogenic shock is defined as a patient having a cardiac index of less than 2.2 L/min/m² or a pulmonary capillary wedge pressure of greater than 18 mmHg (Brashers, 2017; Yancy et al., 2013).

Causes

The leading cause (approximately 80% of all cases) of cardiogenic shock involves left ventricular failure (Brashers, 2017; Yancy et al., 2013). The causes of left ventricular failure may include heart failure, ventricular aneurysm, myocardial tumors, ventricular septal rupture, predominant right ventricular failure, and myocardial infarction (Brashers, 2017).

Clinical Presentation

The clinical findings associated with cardiogenic shock include those common to other types of shock states (e.g., hypotension, tachypnea, mental status, and skin changes). However, findings in cardiac tamponade and obstructive shock mimic those of cardiogenic shock. Thus, a patient in cardiogenic shock also has the classic symptom triad of hypotension, jugular vein distension, and muffled heart tones, in addition to an S3 or S4 extra heart sound or murmurs related to severe valve dysfunction (Brashers, 2017). In addition to a decreased cardiac index and increased pulmonary capillary wedge pressure, an elevated CVP, decreased SV, and increased SVR are also common hemodynamic measures.

Diagnosis

Because of hemodynamic stability associated with cardiogenic shock, diagnostic evaluation often occurs concurrently with therapeutic interventions. The patient's cardiac history is important in the diagnostic evaluation, along with physical examination findings that narrow differential diagnoses. Recognizing pump failure is the relatively easy part of the diagnostic process, especially in the patient with a history of heart failure or acute myocardial infarction. Recognizing the cause of the pump failure, which may include less common infectious or inflammatory conditions, can pose multiple challenges but is necessary for appropriate treatment. Echocardiography, 12-lead electrocardiogram, and intracardiac pressure monitoring aid in confirmation of a diagnosis. When these measures fail, myocardial biopsy may be able to identify histological changes associated with inflammatory disorders such as amyloidosis, rheumatic heart disease, or myocarditis (Anderson, 2016; Brashers, 2017).

Treatment

All therapeutic interventions for the patient with cardiogenic shock aim to support myocardial contractility and maintain forward blood flow, as in the patient with acute decompensating heart failure. Fluid overload surveillance and renal function monitoring are performed when diuretics are used. Loop diuretics are preferred in acute heart failure (Yancy et al., 2013). Temporary IV inotropic therapy is recommended to support end organ perfusion or as a bridge therapy to heart transplantation. In contrast, long-term IV inotropic support can be offered as palliative therapy for symptom control, as in the patient with end-stage heart failure (Yancy et al. 2013). In patients for whom cardiac transplantation is planned or myocardial recovery is anticipated, the use of mechanical circulatory devices can be used to decrease the workload of heart muscle and facilitate forward blood flow. These devices include intra-aortic balloon pumps and ventricular assist devices (Brashers, 2017; Yancy et al., 2013). Evaluation for cardiac transplantation can be considered for a select group of patients who are in cardiogenic shock secondary to end-stage heart failure (Yancy et al., 2013).

CASE STUDY

A 36-year-old transgender male patient goes to the emergency department (ED) because of a sudden onset of dyspnea last night before going to bed. The patient states his symptoms have progressively worsened overnight and he could not lie flat and breathe. The patient's partner reports the patient having to sleep in an upright recliner to rest without distress. The patient states that today he passed out when attempting to get up and walk to the bathroom. The patient also reports mild chest tightening, diaphoresis, and palpitations. His partner stated the patient did seem to lose consciousness, which lasted only a few seconds. The patient denies fever or cough, but reports right lower-extremity calf pain. The patient denies a medical history of hypertension, myocardial infarction, or heart failure. He also denies diabetes, cancer, or autoimmune disease. He denies recent surgeries, but he had an appendectomy more than 10 years ago. He does not know his family history because he is adopted. He smokes one pack of cigarettes daily and occasionally drinks alcohol. He does not use illicit or intravenous drug recreationally. The patient's home medications include Premarin (conjugated estrogens) and multivitamins.

Upon arrival to the ED, the nurse noted the patient was anxious with labored respirations and in distress. He was lethargic but answered questions weakly. The nurse documents that the patient was afebrile with a heart rate of 118 beats/min and blood pressure of 80/55 mmHg. Upon physical examination, the patient revealed no focal neurological deficits. The patient was lethargic, awake, and oriented to self, place, time, and situation. The patient's lung sounds were clear, and heart sounds were distant with a questionable gallop. The nurse also notes bilateral jugular vein distention. His abdominal examination revealed a normal contour and color with decreased bowel sounds. Upon palpation, his abdomen was soft and nontender without the appreciation of organ borders or a pulsatile mass. His right lower calf was tender upon palpation and mildly erythematous without cellulitis or evidence of thrombophlebitis.

The nurse initiates intravenous hydration therapy for the patient while other diagnostic tests are being completed. The ED physician evaluates the patient and suspects an acute pulmonary embolus with right heart strain, and orders the necessary diagnostic evaluation studies.

Questions

1. Which historical and assessment patient data support a diagnosis of obstructive shock?

2. Which nursing considerations are applicable for a patient with obstructive shock?

Answers

1. Right lower-extremity pain and findings are consistent with deep vein thrombosis. Use of hormone replacement therapy (Premarin) places the patient at risk for thrombosis. The patient's report of sudden-onset dyspnea, orthopnea, jugular vein distension, distant heart sounds, and hemodynamic instability are consistent with obstructive shock secondary to a large or massive PE.

2. Nurses must support the medical plan of care for a patient with obstructive shock caused by acute pulmonary embolism, which includes administering thrombolytic therapy, facilitat-

ing transport to surgery for thrombectomy, and facilitating achievement of hemodynamic stability via the administration of pharmacological therapies aimed to augment preload, afterload, and contractility. In addition, patient and family education is initiated in the critical care unit regarding the patient's severity of illness, plan of care, and medication education. The nurse should also act as a conduit for effective communication between the patient and his partner and all involved healthcare providers.

SUMMARY

Clinical shock syndromes vary in presentation, but all result in impaired tissue perfusion and a life-threatening state. The cardiovascular nurse must be able to quickly differentiate and anticipate appropriate therapies aimed at hemodynamic optimization of patients with different types of shock. Nurses who effectively manage patients with shock syndrome can directly improve the patient's morbidity and mortality rates. Nurses also optimize patient outcomes by providing effective communication among all healthcare providers, patients, and families.

EXAM QUESTIONS

CHAPTER 16
Questions 81–84

Note: Choose the one option that BEST answers each question.

81. The clinical finding most associated with any shock syndrome is

    a. heart rate of 120 beats/min.

    b. cardiac output of 4 L/min.

    c. mean arterial blood pressure of less than 60 mmHg.

    d. respiratory rate of 18 beats/min.

82. Nursing care interventions for the patient in shock are aimed to optimize the determinants of

    a. cardiac output.

    b. functional status.

    c. maintaining physical activity.

    d. serum electrolyte levels.

83. Which type of shock is most associated with a hyperdynamic cardiac output?

    a. Septic shock

    b. Anaphylactic shock

    c. Hypovolemic shock

    d. Cardiogenic shock

84. What is the first-line therapy for anaphylactic shock?

    a. Ranitidine injection

    b. Epinephrine injection

    c. Diphenhydramine injection

    d. Beta-adrenergic nebulization

REFERENCES

Brashers, V. L. (2017). Alterations of cardio-vascular function. In S. E. Huether & K. L. McCance (Eds.), *Understanding pathophysiology* (6th ed., pp. 598-646). St. Louis, MO: Elsevier.

Carlson, B., & Fitzsimmons, L. (2014). Shock, sepsis, and multiple organ dysfunction syndrome. In L. D. Urden, K. M. Stacy, & M. E. Lough (Eds.), *Critical care nursing: Diagnosis and management* (7th ed., pp. 887-925). St. Louis, MO: Elsevier/Mosby.

Dellinger, R. P., Levy, M. M., Rhodes, A., Annane, D., Gerlach, H., Opal, S. M., … Moreno, R. (2013). Surviving sepsis campaign: International guidelines for management of severe sepsis and septic shock: 2012. *Critical Care Medicine, 41*(2), 580-637. doi:10.1097/CCM.0b013e31827e83af

Rossaint, R., Bouillon, B., Cerny, V., Coats, T. J., Duranteau, J., Duranteau, J., … Spahn, E. R. (2016). The European guideline on management of major bleeding and coagulopathy following trauma: Fourth edition. *Critical Care, 20,* 100. doi:10.1186.s13054-016-1265-x

Singer, M., Deutschman, C. S., Seymour, C. W., Shankar-Hari, M., Annane, D., Bauer, M., … Angus, D. C. (2016). The Third International Consensus definitions for sepsis and septic shock (sepsis-3). *JAMA, 315*(8), 801-810. doi:10.1001/jama.2016.0287

Yancy, C. W., Jessup, M., Bozkurt, B., Butler, J., Casey, D. E., Drazner, M. H., … Wilkoff, B. L. (2013). 2013 ACCF/AHA guideline for the management of heart failure: A report of the American College of Cardiology Foundation/American Heart Association Task Force on Practice Guidelines. *Circulation, 128*(16), e240-e327. doi:10.1161/CIR.0b013e31829e8776

CHAPTER 17

COMMON ACUTE CARDIAC EMERGENCIES

LEARNING OUTCOME

After completing this chapter, the learner will be able to discuss the comprehensive management of patients with common acute cardiac emergencies.

CHAPTER OBJECTIVES

After completing this chapter, the learner will be able to:

1. Identify patient symptoms associated with syncope, hypertensive emergency, and acute infectious or inflammatory cardiac disease.

2. Identify the appropriate treatment plans for patients with syncope, hypertensive emergency, and acute infectious or inflammatory cardiac disease.

3. Describe nursing care strategies for the management of patients with syncope, hypertensive emergency, and acute infectious or inflammatory cardiac disease.

INTRODUCTION

The cardiovascular nurse must be able to apply knowledge to common acute cardiac emergencies to provide quality care. Regardless of the setting in which patients with these conditions present, the nurse must be ready to pivot the plan of care toward the appropriate treatment regimen through effective communication and collaboration with the patient, family, and medical team.

SYNCOPE

Syncope is defined as a transient, self-limited loss of consciousness that occurs because of decreased cerebral blood flow and usually results in a fall (Bashore, Granger, Jackson, & Patel, 2016). Syncope is the symptom or result of an underlying condition or physiological response characterized by a loss of consciousness of rapid onset, short duration, and complete spontaneous recovery. The patients at greatest risk for syncope are patients older than 75 years and those with underlying arrhythmogenic disease or cardiomyopathy (Mozaffarian et al., 2015).

Causes

Syncope can occur secondary to a neurological, autonomic, or cardiac factor. Large studies conducted in the United States since the 1990s report that most causes (36.6%) for syncope are unknown. The second-leading cause (21.2%) of syncope is vasovagal (Freeman, 2015; Moya et al., 2009). It is vital to approach the patient with the intent to differentiate the causes of syncope to facilitate the appropriate diagnostic evaluation and initiate the appropriate treatment plan.

Neurological Causes

Neurological-derived syncope is most commonly known as vasovagal, or vasodepressor, syncope (Bashore et al., 2016). It is the most common known cause of syncope in the United States (Freeman, 2015). Vasovagal syncope can occur with emotional stress, fear, invasive procedures, or pain. Other situational causes of this type of syncope are coughing, sneezing, gastrointestinal stimulation (e.g., swallowing, defecation, and visceral pain), postexercise, and weightlifting. A common experience reported by patients, especially young men, is fainting after feeling claustrophobic (Bashore et al., 2016). The mechanisms are not fully understood but are thought to be related to increased intrathoracic pressures triggering baroreceptors or other mechanisms triggering the parasympathetic nervous system, such as excessive vagal tone or impaired reflex control of the peripheral circulation.

Autonomic Causes

Autonomic causes of syncope can overlap into neurogenic and cardiogenic causes. This syncope is also known as orthostatic (postural) syncope. Autonomic syncope occurs secondary to the loss of blood volume from the thorax to the lower extremities, resulting in a decreased venous return with standing or changing into a more upright position. Primary or secondary autonomic dysfunction can be the cause of this type of syncope when the sympathetic nervous system is impaired. However, other causes include hemorrhage or other types of intravascular volume losses (Bashore et al., 2016). The older adult is at risk for this type of syncope because of the loss of total body water with age and predisposition for intravascular volume deficits (Flaherty & Resnick, 2014).

Cardiogenic Causes

Cardiogenic causes of syncope are most commonly related to dysrhythmias (Mozaffarian et al., 2015). Paroxysmal ventricular dysrhythmias, more than atrial dysrhythmias, are the culprit in the general population. However, in the older adult (older than 65 years), atrial dysrhythmias with a rapid ventricular response are more common because of the decrease in cerebral blood flow and loss of sympathetic responses (Flaherty & Resnick, 2014; Hogarth, Graham, Baig, & Tayebjee, 2012). Other cardiogenic causes of syncope include heart failure, cardiomyopathy, or other forms of structural or ischemic heart disease (Bashore et al., 2016).

Presentation

Regardless of its cause, patients describe syncope as an abrupt but transient loss of consciousness for a few seconds followed by prompt recovery. However, identifying presyncopal symptoms can lead the clinician to its etiology. For instance, patients experiencing a neurogenic syncope describe presyncopal symptoms of nausea, dizziness or light-headedness, diaphoresis, palpitations, and pallor. During a neurogenic syncopal event, the possibility of epilepsy can occur, with bystanders observing the patient's eyes remaining open and deviating upward (rolled back), accompanied by urinary incontinence (Freeman, 2015).

Patients found to have an orthostatic syncope describe feeling dizzy upon standing or with sudden position changes. The most concerning presyncopal prodrome is the patient reporting, "I just passed out with no warning signs." A patient with a "no warning signs" history is most associated with cardiogenic syncope. In addition, patient descriptions of palpations, chest pain, shortness of breath, and diaphoresis upon exertion can be related to structural or ischemic cardiogenic syncope (Bashore et al., 2016).

Physical Assessment Findings

Upon examination of the patient, the clinician should make an effort to differentiate findings common to the causes of syncope. For instance, the patient with neurological causes for syncope may demonstrate nystagmus, pupillary changes, or focal neurological sensory or motor deficits. The patient with autonomic syncope can demonstrate pallor and diaphoresis with position changes. The patient with cardiogenic syncope may have the signs associated with heart failure, such as an S3 heart sound, murmur, edema, dyspnea, and anxiety. However, many patients do not have abnormal physical assessment findings (Brashers, 2017; Freeman, 2015).

Diagnosis

Diagnosis of syncope can fall anywhere within a spectrum from simple to complex. Considering the multiple causes of syncope, the process to diagnose benign to potentially life-threatening causes must be feasible, timely, and sufficient (Benditt, 2013). Upon patient presentation, and if the patient is not hypotensive, a simple diagnostic test the clinician can perform is taking orthostatic vital signs. A 20-mmHg or greater drop in systolic blood pressure with or without tachycardia is suggestive of an autonomic cause of syncope (Bashore et al., 2016). Another simple test to complete is an electrocardiogram (ECG). A 12-lead ECG may show multiple premature atrial or ventricular contractions, which can be a clue to whether the patient had a paroxysmal arrhythmia. The ECG can also show bradyarrhythmias such as atrioventricular blocks, QT interval anomalies, or congenital electrophysiological anomalies such as Brugada syndrome or Wolff-Parkinson-White syndrome (Freeman, 2015). Measuring a capillary glucose level is another simple test to identify potential causes of syncope.

More extensive studies may be needed when the point-of-care tests are inconclusive. For instance, patients with suspected neurological causes for syncope may require a computed tomography (CT) scan of the head to exclude a tumor or large bleed as the reason for syncope, especially if the patient presents with a headache presyncope or postsyncope (Bashore et al., 2016). Patients suspected to have had a seizure will require an electroencephalogram and neurology consult for identification of seizures, further evaluation, and treatment (Freeman, 2015). A test that can identify autonomic causes of syncope is the head up-tilt table test. The test involves the patient being placed at a 70-degree angle for 10 to 40 minutes, in conjunction with an isoproterenol infusion or sublingual nitroglycerin, if necessary. If the patient has an autonomic dysfunction, bradycardia, hypotension, or both will result (Bashore et al., 2016). Clinicians performing the tilt test in the older adult must account for this population's vasoconstrictor abnormalities and autonomic insufficiency being a leading cause for syncope and the possibility that evoking an autonomic response via the tilt test may result in another syncopal episode (Flaherty & Resnick, 2014). Patients with known dysrhythmias and an internal pacemaker or defibrillator must undergo device interrogation to investigate and identify the cause of syncope (Freeman, 2015).

Treatment

Treating syncope is dependent on identifying and aiming therapies toward the underlying cause. Withholding certain medications (e.g., beta blockers and arterial vasodilators) should be considered if their effects are suspected to be involved (Freeman, 2015). If autonomic causes of syncope were due to intravascular depletion, hydration is the treatment of choice. However, if the cause is found to be due to autonomic failure, the treatment may include medications able to provide cardiovascular support such as midodrine hydrochloride (Orvaten) or steroids (e.g., fludrocortisone; Bashore et al., 2016).

Treatment for the patient with cardiogenic syncope secondary to dysrhythmias often involves the use of antiarrhythmics and/or the placement and use of a permanent pacemaker or automatic internal cardiac defibrillator. Patients with ischemic or structural heart disease can also be treated with a permanent pacemaker or automatic internal cardiac defibrillator as needed to increase cardiac output (heart failure) or eliminate ventricular dysrhythmia (Bashore et al., 2016). If the syncope is a symptom of a decompensatory heart failure state, inotropic medication may also be indicated – not so much for the treatment of syncope, but for the underlying cause of acute heart failure exacerbation (Anderson, 2016).

Nursing Management

Nursing care for patients with syncope includes educating the patient and family about the condition, helping them to recognize its symptoms early, reviewing how to prevent injuries from a fall, and explaining to notify medical personnel immediately if syncope occurs. Primary prevention education is conducted for patients with conditions that place them at risk for syncope (e.g., hypertrophic cardiomyopathy, heart failure, autonomic dysfunction, among others). Nurses must also consider the multiple causes of syncope to better anticipate medical treatments and the patient's priorities. For instance, patients reporting syncope that is absent of warning signs before blacking out is recognized to be most associated with dysrhythmia-related cardiogenic syncope. The nurse understands the importance of monitoring a patient with this type of syncope on telemetry while in the emergency department (ED), or with a bedside monitor in the critical care unit.

The nurse also understands this patient is at risk for sudden cardiac death.

The nurse anticipates the need to check orthostatic vital signs to differentiate autonomic syncope from other types of syncope. Routine nursing management for a patient with autonomic syncope includes hourly neurological assessments for the amount of time prescribed by the clinician when the cause is suspected to be neurological.

All patients diagnosed with syncope should be placed on bed rest with fall precautions until the cause is fully examined and identified. The patient's home medications should be verified carefully with the patient and/or family because they could contribute to the cause of syncope (e.g., positional changes with blood pressure medications) or complications from the fall (e.g., bleeding secondary to the use of anticoagulants or antiplatelets). The nurse recognizes the medications that may contribute to syncope and communicates this vital information to the medical provider.

Patients with syncope in whom a cause is not known, or older adult patients who experience frequent falls and cannot provide a reliable history (e.g., dementia, stroke, no family support, or unwitnessed fall), may require other assessments to help determine a cause. For instance, a functional screening to identify a reason for frequent falls may be performed by a physical therapist, occupational therapist, or nurse. Another screening instrument is portable cardiac monitoring with a Holter monitor or loop recorder for a prescribed amount of time to determine whether dysrhythmias are a potential cause of syncope. The nurse should educate the patient and family about the reasons and procedures for such screenings.

HYPERTENSIVE EMERGENCY

Hypertensive emergency is a life-threatening condition defined as the presence of elevated systolic and diastolic blood pressure (usually more than 180 and 120 mmHg, respectively) associated with ischemic organ damage (e.g., retina, kidney, heart, or brain; Mancia et al., 2013). Hypertensive emergency was formerly known as hypertensive crisis or malignant hypertension (Scruth & Haynes, 2014). Hypertensive urgency is a blood pressure greater than 180/120 mmHg but without evidence of end organ damage (Mancia et al., 2013). Nurses must be able to recognize the necessity of differentiating the patient with hypertensive urgency from the patient with a hypertensive emergency and the respective treatment regimens for each condition.

Pathophysiology

As discussed in Chapter 5, the pathophysiology of hypertension is complex and not completely understood. However, many patients presenting with hypertensive emergency were unaware of having hypertension, were being treated with ineffective medications, or were found to be noncompliant with disease management regimens (Scruth & Haynes, 2014). This means these patients experience a rapid elevation in blood pressure superimposed upon a chronic history of hypertension (Johnson, Nguyen, & Patel, 2012). Cases of hypertensive emergency can occur secondary to other pathophysiological mechanisms in patients with no known history of hypertension (Scruth & Haynes, 2014).

Causes

Patients without a known history of hypertension experience hypertensive emergencies secondary to acute kidney injury, acute neurological events (e.g., subarachnoid hemorrhage, intracerebral hemorrhage, and traumatic brain injury), acute aortic dissection, pregnancy-induced eclampsia, pheochromocytoma, illicit drug use, or drug–drug or drug–food interactions (Scruth & Haynes, 2014).

Presentation

The most common clinical presentations of hypertensive emergency include pulmonary edema (about 23%) and heart failure (about 12%; Papadopoulos et al., 2015). Nevertheless, patient presentations with hypertensive emergency can manifest in a variety of ways. Patients often have neurological complaints of headache, blurred vision, and/or mental status changes. Cardiovascular complaints include chest pain consistent with angina or aortic dissection. Other complaints include fatigue, focal neurological deficits, palpitations, diaphoresis, shortness of breath, or sudden absence of urine output (Scruth & Haynes, 2014).

Physical Assessment Findings

Clinicians should approach the examination of the patient with hypertensive emergency systematically. Blood pressure should be confirmed and compared in both arms to evaluate the potential for aortic dissection. A funduscopic (back part of the eye) examination can reveal hemorrhages, exudate, and papilledema. Neurological assessment may reveal stupor, seizures, delirium, agitation, or any findings associated with encephalopathy. Lateralized deficits with hypertensive emergency are rare but if present can indicate a focal vascular event (Papadopoulos et al., 2015). Examination of the heart can reveal murmurs or extra heart sounds associated with heart failure. Auscultating the lungs can reveal symptoms of pulmonary edema, such as rales or wheezes. The abdominal examination should assess for bruits suggestive of renal artery stenosis or an abdominal aortic aneurysm. Unequal distal pulses can also indicate aortic dissection.

Diagnosis

The diagnosis for hypertensive emergency requires both a blood pressure greater than 180/120 mmHg and evidence of end organ damage (Mancia et al., 2013). The physical examination can provide findings indicative of end organ damage if papilledema, findings of encephalopathy, or rales are found (Papadopoulos et al., 2015). A 12-lead ECG may reveal evidence of ischemia, injury, or infarction or left ventricular hypertrophy (Scruth & Haynes, 2014). A chest radiograph or CT can reveal a widened mediastinum or dissecting aneurysm (Papadopoulos et al., 2015).

End organ damage can also be detected through laboratory results. Urinalysis may reveal proteinuria, and serum laboratory specimens can reveal abnormalities associated with target organs (e.g., elevated creatinine, elevated liver enzymes, and elevated troponin; Scruth & Haynes, 2014).

Treatment

Unlike uncontrolled or accelerated hypertension, treatment for a hypertensive emergency is aimed at reducing blood pressure by no more than 25% over minutes to hours, because lowering the pressure too quickly can result in ischemic damage to the vascular beds, which may have been compensating for prolonged periods of hypertension. Treatment aims to limit further end organ damage while maintaining adequate cerebral blood flow. Intravenous (IV) medications are used for this emergent condition; thus, placement of an arterial line should be performed to facilitate the most accurate point-of-care blood pressure measures and to facilitate the evaluation of treatment (Scruth & Haynes, 2014).

IV medications such as sodium nitroprusside can be used to reduce the blood pressure to the goal, but should be avoided in end-stage kidney disease and used with great caution in the patient with an acute kidney injury because of the potential for cyanide-like toxicity (Scruth & Haynes, 2014). Other medications include those that will result in arterial vasodilation such as angiotensin-converting enzyme inhibitors, short-acting beta blockers (labetalol or esmolol), nitroglycerin, and fenoldopam. Beta blockers are preferred in the treatment of hypertensive emergency in the setting of a dissecting aortic dissection (Mancia et al., 2013).

Nursing Management

Nursing care for patients with hypertensive emergencies includes working with other healthcare professionals toward reaching a goal for targeted blood pressure. Caution is taken to lower the patient's blood pressure gradually to avoid ischemic damage and organ hypoperfusion. The nurse helps to identify any patient comorbidities that can affect reaching the targeted blood pressure range. Nurses practice strict adherence to following blood pressure protocols, using the monitoring equipment safely, and reporting changes in clinical symptoms or presentation to clinicians to assist in implementing the most appropriate treatment plan for the patient.

INFECTIOUS AND INFLAMMATORY DISORDERS

Acute infectious or inflammatory disorders of the heart can negatively impact cardiac function and require aggressive restorative treatments. Although there are several inflammatory or infectious conditions of the heart, this chapter discusses the two most common in the United States: pericarditis and endocarditis. The nurse must apply knowledge of these conditions to the evaluation of patients seeking medical care with complaints of chest pain.

Pericarditis

Acute pericarditis is defined simply as inflammation of the pericardium. Although pericarditis can have an infectious causative agent, it is most commonly associated with inflammatory causative factors (Brashers, 2017).

Pathophysiology

The pathophysiology of pericarditis involves an immune response to an injury of the pericardial membranes. The response initiates the accumulation of fluid (transudative or exudative) within the pericardial sac known as a pericardial effusion (Brashers, 2017).

Causes

Any injury to the pericardial membranes can evoke an inflammatory response. Pericarditis can be infectious or inflammatory in etiology. Viral infections caused by coxsackie, influenza, hepatitis, measles, mumps, or varicella can be the result of injury to the pericardial membranes and, consequently, pericarditis. The most common causes of acute pericarditis are idiopathic or due to viral infection factors (Brashers, 2017). Tuberculosis is the leading cause of infectious pericarditis associated with a bacterial infection.

Noninfectious causes can be associated with myocardial infarction, trauma, neoplasm, uremia, surgery that involves penetration of the pericardial sac, or systemic inflammatory diseases (e.g., rheumatoid arthritis, systemic lupus erythematous, and connective tissue diseases). Uremic pericarditis is a common complication of chronic kidney disease in dialysis patients. Dressler's syndrome involves an inflammatory manifestation of pericarditis occurring 2 to 5 days after myocardial infarction or postcardiotomy. A patient undergoing radiation treatments can initiate a fibrotic process within the pericardium, resulting in a constrictive pericarditis (Bashore et al., 2016).

Presentation

Patients most often complain of precordial, sharp, persistent, and nonradiating chest pain that can be worsened with cough or deep breaths. Patients can also report the pain being greater when supine than in an upright position. Pericardial pain generally has a progressive onset and is not usually ischemic (Brashers, 2017).

Physical Assessment Findings

The patient's examination findings may be the only clinical manifestations used for a diagnosis in some cases. The first steps of assessing the urgency in which the medical team must respond are dependent on these findings. The cardiac examination can have physical examination findings ranging from signs of acute coronary syndrome to heart failure such as S3 or S4 gallop, to pulmonary rales, to an elevated jugular venous pressure. Cardiac findings specific to pericarditis include listening for a pericardial friction rub that may get louder at end expiration when the patient is in an upright position leaning forward. Pulsus paradoxus (a 10- to 15-mmHg decrease in blood pressure with inspiration) can be found on an arterial line or pulse oximetry tracing in patients with pericarditis who are also threatening cardiac tamponade. Finding subcutaneous emphysema on examination is not associated with pericarditis and could lead the clinician toward findings consistent with an esophageal rupture, which includes symptoms similar to those of pericarditis (Brashers, 2017).

Diagnosis

The 12-lead ECG for the patient with pericarditis usually shows generalized, or diffuse, ST- and/or T-wave changes, characteristically beginning with ST elevation followed by a return to baseline and then a shift to T-wave inversion. The chest radiograph can show an enlarged cardiac silhouette if an effusion is present, and other imaging (e.g., CT and magnetic resonance imaging) could allow visualization for mass lesions or enlarged lymph nodes to aid in diagnosis (Bashore et al., 2016).

If pericarditis is secondary to a neoplastic (tissue proliferation) process, the effusion increases in size over a long period and can include as much as 2 L of hemorrhagic and exudative pericardial fluid (Bashore et al., 2016). In patients with uremia, pericardial fluid analysis is hemorrhagic and exudative as well. Myxedema pericardial effusions caused by hypothyroidism are usually characterized by the presence of cholesterol crystals within the fluid.

Serum laboratory levels of blood urea nitrogen and the sedimentation rate can be markedly elevated with pericarditis. The white blood cell count can also be a marker of inflammation (Bashore et al., 2016).

Treatment

Nonsteroidal anti-inflammatory drugs (NSAIDs; e.g., aspirin and ibuprofen) are first-line agents for pericarditis in general. Colchicine is recommended for refractory or recurrent cases of pericarditis for as long as 6 months. For patients diagnosed with Dressler's syndrome, the mainstay of therapy should be aspirin and colchicine in lieu of NSAIDs because of the negative effect NSAIDs and steroids have on myocardial healing. For patients with severe symptoms in refractory cases, systemic corticosteroids can be used in addition to colchicine. For rare occasions when colchicine therapy fails, more significant immunosuppression with cyclophosphamide or methotrexate may be required. For the patients with infectious pericarditis, support therapies are initiated for viral causative agents and antimicrobials for other causes (Bashore et al., 2016).

When medications fail to adequately treat pericarditis, pericardial stripping may be required in recurrent cases. Other invasive therapies include pericardiocentesis for cytology and placement of a pericardial window for the draining of recurrent effusions. In the patient with neoplastic pericarditis, the instillation of chemotherapeutic agents or tetracycline is used to effectively reduce the recurrence rate (Bashore et al., 2016).

Nursing Management

The nurse assists patients with pericarditis to achieve their treatment goals, which include relief of pain and resolution of inflammation and effusion. The nurse provides patient education about medications that may be ordered for the patient, such as pain medication, antibiotics, and anti-inflammatory agents. If pericardiocentesis is recommended, the nurse helps to educate the patient about what to expect during the procedure and any possible risks (e.g., bleeding or infection) associated with the procedure. The nurse reassures the patient that these risks are minimized with an experienced clinician performing the procedure.

Endocarditis

Endocarditis can be infection and/or inflammation of the endocardium and especially the cardiac valves (Brashers, 2017). Although there are purely inflammatory forms of this type of endocarditis, this chapter discusses its most common cause: infection (Bashore et al., 2016).

Pathophysiology

Micro-organisms gain entry to the bloodstream via traumatic injuries, dental procedures, or injectable drug abuse. When the endocardium is injured, organisms such as streptococcal bacteria adhere to the damaged areas of endocardium, resulting in adhesions. The progression in growth of those adhesions then leads to the development of vegetations that can form at the site of injury or on the valves. Embolization of the vegetations or their related debris can occur (Bashore et al., 2016).

Causes

A bacterial infection is the most common cause of endocarditis. Streptococci, staphylococci, and enterococci account for approximately 80% of all cases (Bashore et al., 2016). Other causes include viruses, fungi, rickettsia, and parasites. Noninfectious causes include IV drug abuse associated with an embolic lesion.

Presentation

Patients with acute endocarditis commonly report fatigue, fever, night sweats, weight loss, back pain, petechial lesions, and painful red nodes on their fingers or toes. Patient systems can widely vary because of the systemic nature of this disease. Clinical features common to valve dysfunction may also be present; see listing of clinical features in the following section (Bashore et al., 2016).

Physical Assessment Findings

Two characteristic findings of acute endocarditis are Osler nodes (painful erythematous nodules on the pads of fingers and toes) and Janeway lesions (nonpainful hemorrhagic lesions on the palms and soles). These findings aid in the complex identification of endocarditis. Findings common to valve dysfunction or heart failure can be found upon examination. For instance, S3 or S4 gallops, new murmurs, dyspnea, rales, anxiety, and diaphoresis can be found. Neurological findings with endocarditis can include signs of stroke, abscess, or meningitis. Other findings include weight loss, back pain, night sweats, or signs of an embolic event of the vegetations involved (Brashers, 2017).

Diagnosis

Current clinical guidelines for the diagnosis and management of endocarditis recommend the use of the modified Duke criteria. These modified Duke criteria are based on the use of the original (major and minor) Duke criteria.

The two major Duke criteria are positive blood culture results for endocarditis and evidence of endocardial involvement from echocardiography. Both two-dimensional transthoracic echocardiography and transesophageal echocardiography may be utilized. The minor Duke criteria include fever, a predisposing cardiac condition, histological evidence (vegetation or intracardiac abscess present), and microbiological evidence (culture or histology in a vegetation; Sexton & Fowler, 2016). Adopting the Duke criteria for diagnosis of endocarditis involves daily blood culture surveillance for bacteria. Serum measures of C-reactive protein also show elevation caused by acute inflammation and infection (Bashore et al., 2016). Correct and prompt diagnosis of endocarditis is crucial to optimize treatment outcomes in patients with endocarditis.

Treatment

IV antimicrobial therapy is administered for several weeks until the presence of the bacteria in the bloodstream is eliminated. Antimicrobial therapies must continue beyond the first negative culture. Supportive therapy for fever and pain is also warranted. Prophylactic antimicrobial therapy for high-risk patients (e.g., unrepaired congenital heart disease and after prosthetic heart valve replacement) is indicated before dental procedures (Brashers, 2017).

Surgical options for treatment include the excision of the infected tissue. When the affected valve is severely stenotic, valvuloplasty can be performed to facilitate forward blood flow (Bashore et al., 2016).

Nursing Management

The nurse informs any patient who is at high risk for development of endocarditis to practice careful mouth and tooth care. This includes a professional tooth cleaning twice yearly, thorough brushing of the teeth twice daily, and flossing daily. Such a program can prevent the buildup of plaque and bacteria in the mouth. The nurse can also reinforce antibiotic prophylaxis education for patients who are at risk for endocarditis. Before undergoing dental and medical procedures, the nurse must address this education with the patient.

CASE STUDY

A 35-year-old male patient is brought to the ED after a sudden loss of consciousness while playing soccer with friends. His friends stated he was only unconscious for a few seconds. The patient reports remembering suddenly feeling light-headed and dizzy, along with a tingling sensation across his forehead, before blacking out. The patient denies head trauma, chest pain, palpitations, diaphoresis, dyspnea, anxiety, nausea, or vomiting. He also denies having urinary incontinence during or following the episode, a headache before the episode, or a history of seizures. His friends also report that they did not witness seizure-like activities from the patient during the episode. Upon awakening, the patient stated that he did feel as though he had injured himself. He described falling forward to his hands and knees from a standing position when fainting.

The patient has no significant medical or surgical history. He takes no home medications. He is married, is employed as a school teacher, and does not use tobacco or illicit drugs. He drinks alcohol socially. He reports no known history of heart disease or sudden death in his immediate family.

Upon physical examination, the patient's temperature is 99.6°F, blood pressure is 100/70 mmHg, heart rate is 110 beats/min, and respiratory rate is 22 breaths/min. The nurse in the ED documents positive orthostatic vital signs when the patient changes from a sitting to a standing position. The patient is oriented with no neurological deficits. His skin is warm, normal in color for his ethnicity, and sweaty. His lung and heart sounds are normal, and there is no evidence of trauma from the fall.

The nurse prepares the patient for bedside echocardiography, which reveals no significant structural heart disease, normal left ventricular size and function, and no significant valvular disease. A 12-lead ECG is also obtained and shows a sinus tachycardia, with a heart rate of 109 beats/min, and no evidence of ischemia or other abnormalities. While in the ED, the patient's heart monitor initially showed a sinus tachycardia rhythm that became a normal sinus rhythm after receiving IV fluid therapy. The patient's laboratory results are unremarkable for electrolyte imbalances or a decreased blood count, and his cardiac enzymes are within normal limits. The patient's chest radiograph is without evidence of acute problems or a widened mediastinum.

The nurse infuses 1 L of 0.9% normal saline IV to the patient. After the IV fluid administration, the nurse rechecks the patient's orthostatic vital signs, which show improvement. The ED physician diagnoses the patient with syncope secondary to dehydration and orthostatic hypotension.

Questions

1. Which information in the patient's history and physical examination supports his diagnosis?

2. How does the nurse educate the patient before he is discharged?

Answers

1. The patient's activity during the event supports a diagnosis of dehydration. He and his friends denied evidence of seizure activity, and the patient denied cardiac symptoms. His vital signs in the ED revealed orthostatic hypotension, and his ECG showed

mild tachycardia, which are both consistent with dehydration. The patient's baseline echocardiogram also revealed a structurally normal heart. His physical examination was unremarkable for murmurs, gallops, or rubs that would be found in patients with a cardiomyopathy or pericarditis leading to the suspicion for tamponade, outflow obstructed cardiomyopathy, or heart failure. The patient's neurological examination was also negative for physical findings that indicate neurogenic causes.

2. The nurse instructs the patient to rest and hydrate for the next 24 to 48 hours with limited physical activity until he is cleared by his physician. General patient education for patients with syncope and their families includes educating the patient and family about the condition, recognizing symptoms early, preventing injuries from a fall, and notifying medical personnel immediately. All of this information was carefully explained and reviewed with both the patient and his family members before discharge. If this type of episode should occur again, the patient is informed that he may need portable cardiac monitoring (Holter or loop recorder) for further investigation of his condition.

SUMMARY

Knowledge and comprehension of common acute cardiac conditions can be applied to patients within multiple healthcare settings. The cardiovascular nurse has the opportunity to positively affect outcomes for patients with common acute cardiac emergencies through high-quality care and patient education. The cardiovascular nurse's role is to address awareness of such conditions and the appropriate actions patients can take during a cardiac emergency.

EXAM QUESTIONS

CHAPTER 17
Questions 85–87

Note: Choose the one option that BEST answers each question.

85. Which patient history is most congruent with cardiogenic syncope caused by a paroxysmal ventricular dysrhythmia?

    a. "I was nauseated and felt hot."

    b. "I had no warning signs."

    c. "I became diaphoretic with palpitations."

    d. "I think I urinated on myself."

86. Nurses care management for patients with syncope of unknown origin includes

    a. placing them on bed rest with fall precautions.

    b. preparing them for implantable cardioverter defibrillator placement.

    c. following the Duke criteria.

    d. initiating physical and occupational therapy.

87. Which treatment intervention is appropriate for a patient with endocarditis and severe mitral valve stenosis?

    a. Beta-blocker therapy

    b. Head up-tilt table testing

    c. Colchicine plus aspirin

    d. Valvuloplasty

REFERENCES

Anderson, K. M. (2016). *The advanced practice nurse cardiovascular clinician*. New York, NY: Springer.

Bashore, T. M., Granger, C. B., Jackson, K. P., & Patel, M. R. (2016). Heart disease. In M. Papadakis, S. J. McPhee, & M. W. Rabow (Eds.), *Current medical diagnosis and treatment 2016* (55th ed., pp. 321-434). New York, NY: McGraw-Hill.

Benditt, D. G. (2013). Syncope risk assessment in the emergency department and clinic. *Progress in Cardiovascular Diseases, 55*(4), 376-381. doi:10.1016/j.pcad.2012.10.010

Brashers, V. L. (2017). Alterations in cardiovascular function. In S. E. Huether & K. L. McCance (Eds.), *Understanding pathophysiology* (6th ed., pp. 600-637). St. Louis, MO: Elsevier.

Flaherty, E., & Resnick, B. (2014). *Geriatric nursing review syllabus: A core curriculum in advanced practice geriatric nursing* (4th ed.). New York, NY: American Geriatric Society.

Freeman, R. (2015). Syncope. In D. Kasper, A. Fauci, S. Hauser, D. Long, J. L. Jameson, & J. Loscalzo (Eds.), *Harrison's principles of internal medicine* (19th ed., pp. 142-151). New York, NY: McGraw-Hill.

Hogarth, A., Graham, L., Baig, W., & Tayebjee, M. (2012). Syncope: A rare manifestation of a common condition. *Lancet, 379*(9818), 866. doi:10.1016/S0140-6736(11)61787-X

Johnson, W., Nguyen, M. L., & Patel, R. (2012). Hypertension crisis in the emergency department. *Cardiology Clinics, 30*(4), 533-543. doi:10.1016/j.ccl.2012.07.011

Mancia, G., Fagard, R., Narkiewicz, K., Redon, J., Zanchetti, A., Bohm, M., ... Zannad, F. (2013). 2013 ESH/ESC guidelines for the management of arterial hypertension. *Journal of Hypertension, 31*(7), 1281-1357. doi:10.1097/01.hjh.0000431740.32696.cc

Moya, A., Sutton, R., Ammirati, F., Blanc, J. J., Brignole, M., Dahm, J. B., ... Wieling, W. (2009). Guidelines for the diagnosis and management of syncope (version 2009). *European Heart Journal, 30*(21), 2631-2671. doi:10.1093/eurheartj/ehp298

Mozaffarian, D., Benjamin, E. J., Go, A. S., Arnett, D. K., Blaha, M. J., Cushman, M., ... Turner, M. B. (2015). Heart disease and stroke statistics – 2015 update: A report from the American Heart Association. *Circulation, 133*(4), e39-e358. doi:10.1161/CIR.0000000000000350

Papadopoulos, D. P., Sanidas, E. A., Viniou, N. A., Gennimata, V., Chantziara, V., Barbetsease, I., & Makris, T. K. (2015). Cardiovascular hypertensive emergencies. *Current Hypertension Reports, 17*(2), 5. doi:10.1007/s11906-014-0515-z

Scruth, E., & Haynes, A. (2014). Cardiovascular disorders. In L. D. Urden, K. M. Stacy, & M. E. Lough (Eds.), *Critical care nursing: Diagnosis and management* (7th ed., pp. 338-411). St. Louis, MO: Mosby-Elsevier.

Sexton, D. J., & Fowler, V. G. (2016). Clinical manifestations and evaluation of adults with suspected native valve endocarditis. *UpToDate*. Retrieved from www.uptodate. com

CHAPTER 18

CARDIAC REVASCULARIZATION THERAPIES

LEARNING OUTCOME

After completing this chapter, the learner will be able to discuss the indications for, and the benefits and potential complications of, cardiac revascularization.

CHAPTER OBJECTIVES

After completing this chapter, the learner will be able to:

1. Describe general cardiac revascularization strategy options and considerations.

2. Describe indications for revascularization therapies in patients with coronary artery disease.

3. Summarize current coronary artery bypass graft procedures.

4. Identify risks of coronary artery bypass grafting in special patient populations.

5. Explain nursing interventions for patients before and after both coronary artery bypass graft surgery and percutaneous coronary intervention.

INTRODUCTION

Revascularization therapies in patients with coronary artery disease (CAD) serve the purpose of redirecting or facilitating the delivery of oxygen-rich blood to an area of oxygen-deprived myocardium via the use of a conduit, or channel. Revascularization procedures provide vital treatment options for patients with acute or chronic ischemic heart disease (Bonow, 2013). Approaches to myocardial revascularization are limited to what many people know as "open-heart surgery" (coronary artery bypass graft/grafting [CABG]) or "having a stent placed in the heart" (stenting or percutaneous coronary intervention [PCI]). The decision of which approach to take is largely dependent on the patient and the cardiologist. However, the cardiovascular nurse must have knowledge about the indications and considerations for both revascularization approaches, goals of therapy, routine postoperative management, and the complications that may occur. The cardiovascular nurse plays an integral role in facilitating the patient's full recovery and maintenance of health through comprehensive patient education. This chapter provides a comprehensive review of caring for patients with indications for either revascularization approach.

GENERAL REVASCULARIZATION STRATEGY OPTIONS AND CONSIDERATIONS

Myocardial revascularization therapy began in the 1960s with CABG surgery. Although this procedure was proven to be safe and effective, technology evolved to allow a less invasive procedure to be developed as an alternative to CABG. PCI became a more accessible and less invasive revascularization therapy option with the introduction of percutaneous transluminal coronary angioplasty (PTCA) in the 1970s. PTCA is sometimes referred to today as a *balloon angioplasty* (Dirks & Waters, 2014). Specific details about CABG and PCI will be discussed further later in this chapter.

In patients with CAD who do not have symptoms, revascularization is performed only if there is an expected survival advantage. Several factors must be considered in making a decision about cardiac revascularization. These factors include suitable coronary anatomy for the procedure, left ventricular function and amount of viable myocardium, symptoms of disease and impact on functional capacity, and other comorbid conditions and factors that influence life expectancy. Patients who have coronary anatomy unsuitable for revascularization are not candidates. Other conditions that limit the option for revascularization include advanced or metastatic cancer with a life expectancy of less than 1 year, end-stage cirrhosis with severe portal hypertension, and intracranial disorders that limit the ability to anticoagulate or cause substantial cognitive impairment (Bonow, 2013).

It is often difficult to adequately compare CABG and PCI today because there have been so many advances with both procedures, as well as with medical therapy used in conjunction with these revascularization techniques. There has not been sufficient time to evaluate the long-term effects of these many recent advances. In addition, because of the length of time needed to obtain long-term results, published research studies often do not reflect the most current practices in either type of revascularization, and many early studies that evaluated revascularization

did not include large numbers of women, older adults, or patients presenting for repeat revascularization. However, although limitations exist, the most recent research has shown comparable survival outcomes with either type of interventional treatment. Because of durability and the need for repeat revascularization procedures, CABG remains the preferred reperfusion strategy for most patients with multivessel disease, especially if the proximal left anterior descending (LAD) coronary artery is involved, the patient has diabetes, or left ventricular dysfunction is present (Bonow, 2013; Hillis et al., 2011). Due to the association between diffuse CAD and diabetes, the 2014 ACC/AHA/AATS/PCNA/SCAI/STS focused update of the guideline for the diagnosis and management of patients with stable ischemic heart disease recommends a CABG over PCI for patients with concurrent diabetes (Fihn et al., 2014).

CORONARY ARTERY BYPASS GRAFTING

CABG involves the use of graft material from the patient's arteries or veins to reroute blood around areas of long stenosis in coronary arteries. This surgical revascularization has demonstrated better survival rates than medical therapy alone or medical therapy in conjunction with PCI (Bonow, 2013; Fihn et al., 2014). Although PCI provides quick access to coronary arteries during acute ischemic events, CABG allows for more complete revascularization because of the direct visualization of the coronaries and myocardium (Bonow, 2013; Hillis et al., 2011). Cardiovascular nurses must understand the significance of this therapy for patients with chronic ischemic heart disease.

Indications for Coronary Artery Bypass Graft Surgery

CABG surgery is costly; thus, it is performed only in those patients with proven survival and symptomatic benefits. CABG surgery costs approximately $149,480, in comparison with PCI costs, which are approximately $70,000 (Mozaffarian et al., 2015). However, when performed in patients with proven substantial benefit, CABG is then considered a cost-effective intervention. As technologies advance and continue to evolve, increased use of less-invasive CABG approaches along with the increased use of drug-eluting stents may contribute to cost differences narrowing between CABG and PCI (Bonow, 2013).

CABG increases the chance of survival in patients with reduced left ventricular function, severe ischemia, or potential for severe ischemia. CABG also allows revascularization to occluded small-diameter vessels that are not accessible by catheter-based techniques (Fihn et al., 2014). Other indications for CABG are noted in Box 18-1.

In patients with impaired left ventricular function, there appears to be a mortality benefit with CABG (Fihn et al., 2014). This benefit is less clear the more severe the left ventricular dysfunction, and studies comparing PCI with CABG for this group are lacking. For this reason, in patients with severe left ventricular dysfunction, other variables should be considered to assist with decision making regarding CABG, such as cardiac anatomy, presence of other comorbid conditions like diabetes and chronic kidney disease, and functional capacity (Hillis et al., 2011). Reduced left ventricular function can be a result of chronic hypoperfusion, in addition to past myocardial infarction (MI). Areas with chronic hypoperfusion can be assessed for viability using noninvasive cardiac testing. Patients with large areas of viable

---

BOX 18-1: INDICATIONS FOR CORONARY ARTERY BYPASS GRAFT SURGERY

- Triple-vessel or multivessel disease

- Multivessel disease with reduced left ventricular function

- Left main equivalent disease with significant left anterior descending coronary artery and left circumflex artery blockages

- Proximal left anterior descending coronary artery disease with greater than 75% occlusion, coronary artery disease in another vessel, plus a very positive stress test and an abnormal electrocardiogram

- Coronary heart disease in patients who have survived an episode of sudden cardiac death

Note. From Western Schools.

---

myocardium can benefit from revascularization. Compared with patients with a high risk for mortality, patients with lower risk receive only a modest survival benefit with CABG. Patients with a low risk for mortality are considered for CABG only when their symptoms have been unresponsive to medical treatment and are limiting their quality of life or functional capacity (Dirks & Waters, 2014). CABG has the greatest survival benefit for patients with the greatest mortality risk without surgery (Bonow, 2013; Fihn et al., 2014).

In addition to increasing survival, CABG is indicated to relieve symptoms and improve other outcomes. Angina is initially relieved in the majority of patients undergoing CABG; however, angina can gradually reoccur over time as atherosclerotic disease develops within the graft stenosis or progresses within the patient's native vessels (Fihn et al., 2014). These results are superior to medical treatment alone for patients with angina. The indications for CABG are very similar for patients with stable angina and unstable angina. However, there is a greater sense of urgency for those with unstable angina.

Contraindications

Patients who have inadequate native conduits are not ideal candidates for CABG. Very small coronary arteries distal to the site of stenosis are also a limiting factor in performing CABG. Patients with severe atherosclerosis of the aorta are at very high risk for intraoperative thromboembolic neurological complications (e.g., ischemic stroke) and may not be able to undergo the traditional CABG surgical approach that requires the cross-clamping of the aorta.

Traditional Coronary Artery Bypass Grafting

The traditional approach to CABG involves a median sternotomy and the use of a cardiopulmonary (heart and lung) bypass machine (see Figure 18-1). The cardiopulmonary bypass (CPB) machine allows the surgeon to operate on a still and bloodless heart while at the same time providing perfusion via a nonpulsatile flow to the other organs of the body. When the patient goes on the CPB circuit, venous blood is drained from the right side of the heart. The blood then passes through a pump, which mimics the heart, and then an oxygenator, which mimics the lungs. Blood then travels through a filter before it is returned to systemic circulation via an arterial cannula in the ascending aorta. The aorta is clamped during surgery to prevent coronary blood flow (see Figure 18-2). The CPB machine also allows the temperature of the patient's blood to be controlled and has a vent to decompress the left ventricle when the aorta is cross-clamped. A perfusionist is responsible for the complex management of the CPB circuit.

Myocardial protection is required when the aorta is clamped to prevent myocardial ischemia and injury. Myocardial protection is accomplished by the use of cardioplegia to arrest the heart. Cardioplegic solutions are rich in potassium, magnesium, and procainamide to produce cardiac arrest (Hillis et al., 2011). A cardioplegic solution is typically infused antegrade through the coronary arteries and retrograde through the coronary veins. Solutions for cardioplegia can be either crystalloid or crystalloid and blood mixtures, and are typically infused at hypothermic temperatures to aid in myocardial protection. Cardioplegic solutions that contain blood help provide additional cardiac protection because of the increased oxygen-carrying capacity of blood. Blood can be mixed with a cardioplegic solution through the CPB machine (Dirks & Waters, 2014).

Prophylactic use of an intra-aortic balloon pump (IABP) 2 or more hours before CPB can also increase myocardial protection in high-risk patients (Fihn et al., 2014; Hillis et al., 2011). IABP counterpulsation involves the placement of a balloon catheter in the descending aorta. The balloon is inflated during diastole and deflated during systole, delivering counterpulsation therapy. During balloon inflation (in diastole), myocardial perfusion is increased. During balloon deflation, just before systole, a vacuum is created to reduce afterload, thereby reducing the work of the left ventricle. IABP counterpulsation can also be used to help support left ventricular function in patients who have a difficult time being weaned from the CPB circuit (Dirks & Waters, 2014).

Graft Material

One of the historical limiting factors of CABG has been the failure of saphenous vein grafts. Up to half of all vein grafts close within 10 years after surgery (Dirks & Waters, 2014).

FIGURE 18-1: HEART AND LUNG BYPASS MACHINE

© Shutterstock

Vein grafts are not as durable as arterial grafts. Antiplatelet therapy with aspirin and lipid-lowering therapy with statins improve the short- and long-term patency of saphenous vein grafts. Aspirin is given in the early postoperative period and continued indefinitely after discharge. Aspirin, 81 to 325 mg daily, is recommended postoperatively for a minimum of 1 year, and usually indefinitely in patients who have had a saphenous vein used as a graft during CABG (Amsterdam et al., 2014; Hillis et al., 2011). Antithrombotic therapy preoperatively and postoperatively has demonstrated better saphenous vein graft patency rates in comparison with patients who were not able to receive antithrombotics such as aspirin and/or clopidogrel before and after CABG (Hillis et al., 2011).

When CABG surgery began, vein grafts were the only graft material used. The most common vein graft is taken from the greater saphenous vein of the leg. Vein grafts can be harvested using standard incisions or endoscopically. Today, most saphenous veins are harvested endoscopically (see Figure 18-3), which results in an improved cosmetic effect and a decreased risk for infection (Dirks & Waters, 2014). After harvest, the vein graft is turned inside out because veins have one-way valves. It is then attached at one end to the ascending aorta and at the other end to the coronary artery distal to the blockage. Flow through vein grafts depends on pressure (Dirks & Waters, 2014). Figure 18-3 also shows a saphenous vein graft sutured to the aorta and the coronary artery.

FIGURE 18-2: HEART CANNULATION FOR CARDIOPULMONARY BYPASS

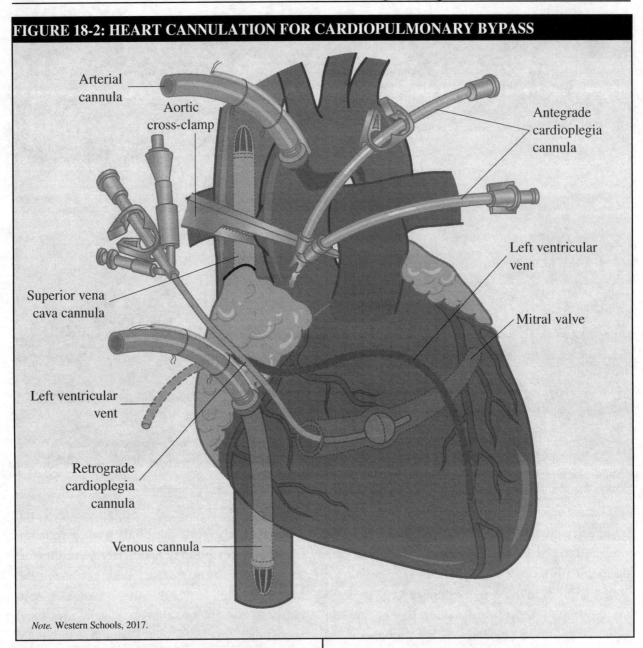

Note. Western Schools, 2017.

NURSING APPLICATION

Patients with hypotension or poor left ventricular function require diligent assessment because they are at increased risk for acute vein graft closure caused by low pressures and resultant poor flow through the vein graft.

A very important CABG surgery advancement has been the success of internal mammary artery grafts. These grafts have shown major improvement in late patency rates, with more than 90% patency at 10 years. Internal mammary artery grafts have also improved long-term survival rates and reduced postoperative mortality (Fihn et al., 2014; Hillis et al., 2011). However, harvesting of the internal mammary arteries is technically more difficult than harvesting of saphenous vein grafts. The left internal mammary artery (LIMA) is most commonly used to bypass the LAD coronary artery (Hillis et al., 2011; see Figure 18-4). Patients have shown improved long-term outcomes with the standard

FIGURE 18-3: SAPHENOUS VEIN GRAFT BYPASSING CORONARY LESION

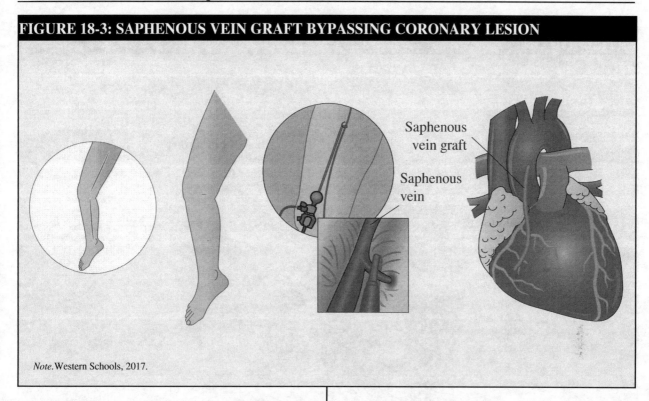

Saphenous
vein graft

Saphenous
vein

*Note.*Western Schools, 2017.

practice of using the LIMA to bypass the LAD coronary artery (Dirks & Waters, 2014).

When used as a pedicle graft (a graft left attached to the original site), the proximal end of the internal mammary artery is left intact and the distal end is sutured beyond the site of stenosis. Most CABG surgeries involve a combination of a LIMA graft and saphenous vein grafts. The right internal mammary artery (RIMA) can be used in addition to the LIMA. The decision to use both internal mammary arteries is surgeon and facility specific. The advantage of using both the RIMA and the LIMA is that the patient has the benefit of two very durable arterial grafts. The disadvantage is that the sternal wall is left with a decreased blood supply, thereby predisposing the patient to an increased risk for sternal wound infection, especially in the patient with diabetes (Anderson, 2016).

In some young patients, revascularization with all-arterial grafts may be considered, with the hope of achieving longer-term patency and avoiding the need for repeat operation. The need for one or more repeat procedures is a concern in younger patients because of increased risk for graft closure or failure. Lack of an acceptable conduit is also a concern if the procedure must be performed more than once. The radial artery also can be used as graft material; however, it is prone to spasm because of its thick muscular nature. The risk for spasm can be decreased with the use of nitrates and calcium channel blockers, both intraoperatively and postoperatively (Fihn et al., 2014; Hillis et al., 2011). The advantage of the radial artery is its length, which enables it to be used to reach most distal targets. The radial artery is not used unless the patient has adequate patency of the ulnar artery. In addition, the radial artery is most often harvested from the patient's nondominant hand (Hillis et al., 2011).

FIGURE 18-4: SAPHENOUS VEIN GRAFT AND INTERNAL MAMMARY ARTERY GRAFT

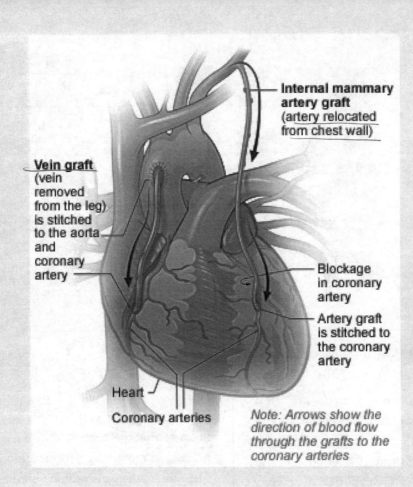

This figure shows how vein and artery bypass grafts are attached to the heart.

Note. From National Heart Lung and Blood Institute (NIH) (National Heart Lung and Blood Institute (NIH)) [Public domain], via Wikimedia Commons.

NURSING APPLICATION

The ulnar pulse and distal circulation should be checked postoperatively if the radial artery was harvested for graft material during surgery.

The right gastroepiploic artery supplies blood to the greater curvature of the stomach. When this artery is used as graft material in CABG, a more extensive surgery results because abdominal entry is also required, and this is the reason it is not a preferred conduit. This artery can be used as a pedicle graft or a free graft. A pedicle graft remains connected to its original source at one end but is rerouted to bypass the coronary lesion with the other end. A free graft is one that is harvested from its original location and reanastomosed at both ends to bypass the coronary lesion (Anderson, 2016).

For patients with limited options for use of their own vessels as grafts (such as diabetics), cryopreserved saphenous vein grafts or umbilical vein grafts that have been treated with glutaraldehyde can be used. Unfortunately, these grafts have poor long-term patency, so they are used only when no other options are available. Other nonhomologous grafts have been used but also have poor patency. These grafts include bovine internal mammary arteries and synthetic grafts (Dirks & Waters, 2014).

Minimally Invasive Techniques in Cardiac Surgery

Minimally Invasive Direct Coronary Artery Bypass Grafting

Minimally invasive direct coronary artery bypass grafting (MIDCAB) is performed on a beating heart without CPB and without the use of a full median sternotomy to gain access. Access to the heart is usually achieved through a left lateral thoracotomy or through a ministernotomy. The ministernotomy approach is cosmetically appealing to many patients. However, this procedure is technically challenging because visibility is not the same as with a full sternotomy. In addition, if a thoracotomy approach is chosen, the intercostal nerves can be irritated, resulting in increased postoperative pain (Dirks & Waters, 2014).

A ministernotomy allows the LAD and right coronary arteries to be visualized and bypassed using the same incision. A left thoracotomy approach provides direct visualization of the LAD and access to the LIMA. A right thoracotomy approach is needed to provide visualization of the right coronary artery and access to the RIMA. Access to both internal mammary arteries is improved with the ministernotomy approach (Dirks & Waters, 2014).

To allow for suturing, medications such as beta blockers or adenosine can be given to slow

or temporarily stop the heart. Mechanical stabilizers are also used to hold the coronary artery still while suturing occurs.

The advantages of MIDCAB are associated with its avoidance of the full sternotomy and CPB circuit. MIDCAB decreases the need for blood transfusions and minimizes the risk for other complications associated with the CPB circuit (such as coagulopathy, thrombocytopenia, anemia, among others). Patients who have MIDCAB have shorter lengths of hospital stay and fewer postoperative complications compared with those who have traditional CABG (Cremer, Schoettler, Thiem, Grothusen, & Hoffman, 2011). MIDCAB procedures are not performed often because the number of lesions that can be bypassed is limited. With improvements in interventional cardiology treatments, particularly with the addition of drug-eluting stents, patients needing only one or two bypass grafts are often treated with an interventional procedure (Dirks & Waters, 2014).

Off-Pump Coronary Artery Bypass Grafting

Off-pump coronary artery bypass grafting (OPCAB) is another less-invasive form of CABG. This surgery is done without CPB but involves a full median sternotomy. A full sternotomy offers better access to bypass the vessels that supply the heart's lateral and posterior walls. Intraoperative techniques are used to lower heart rate, stabilize the coronary arteries, and clear the operative field of blood. As with MIDCAB, there are technical challenges for the surgeon when suturing on a moving heart that remains full of blood. In addition, when performing OPCAB on more complex patients, there are intraoperative hemodynamic challenges that can typically be controlled by the perfusionist when the patient is on the CPB circuit. Many cardiothoracic surgeons in the United States reported they preferred to perform CABG on-pump if the patient is hemodynamically compromised, to have circulatory support from the CPB pump (Hillis et al., 2011).

The avoidance of CPB with the use of the LIMA and RIMA eliminates the need to clamp the aorta in patients with high-risk aortic atherosclerosis. All patients undergoing CABG have their aortas imaged with transesophageal echocardiography or epiaortic imaging before surgery. If an aorta is atherosclerotic, it cannot be cross-clamped as done in traditional CABG. Even with OPCAB, if a saphenous vein graft is used, the aorta is often clamped at least partially to allow for suturing of the proximal end.

Several potential advantages to OPCAB are similar to the advantages of MIDCAB. Many of the advantages are associated with avoidance of the CPB circuit, including a reduced need for blood transfusion that results in less coagulopathy, less hemodilution, and decreased heparin therapy. OPCAB may also reduce complications such as atrial fibrillation and infection (Cremer et al., 2011).

The number of OPCAB procedures performed each year has increased since the late 1990s. However, the majority of CABG surgeries done in the United States are still traditional CABG procedures (Cremer et al., 2011; Miller, 2010). OPCAB is a relatively newer technique, and the results of these techniques are expected to improve over time. With increased surgeon experience, the number of OPCAB surgeries is expected to continue to increase, which will result in shorter lengths of stay associated with CABG. Patients receiving OPCAB may be extubated in the operating room and transferred from intensive care to step-down care as soon as 12 hours after surgery (Miller, 2010).

Robotics and Other Techniques

Additional CABG techniques using robotics are also being performed. With robotic surgery, the robot's manipulators receive transmitted instructions from a remote, but interfaced, computer. The surgeon remains at the computer console, where he or she is able to visualize a three-dimensional view. The surgeon uses hand grips at the console, and the movements made by the surgeon are duplicated by the robot. Any extraneous movement from the surgeon, such as tremors, is filtered out by system software (Hughes & Platt, 2010). A major advantage of robotic technology is the ability of the robot to manipulate in small spaces where human hands are too large for optimal maneuvering. The cost of this technology, as well as the need for extensive surgeon training, has limited its widespread use. Robotic technology can also be used with endoscopic techniques. During endoscopic techniques, small incisions are made in the intercostal spaces. This technology can be used on beating hearts as well as on arrested hearts (Hughes & Platt, 2010). Without a full sternotomy, CPB cannulation and cardioplegic solution administration can occur through the femoral artery and vein (Dirks & Waters, 2014).

The Risk for Complications With Coronary Artery Bypass Grafting

Patients undergoing CABG today are older and have more comorbidities than in the past. In addition, more high-risk patients are undergoing CABG because of technological advances that allow for improved outcomes. The nurse should consider the patient's risk factors when providing education to the patient and family about the possible complications of CABG surgery. Education about possible complications can also help the patient understand the postoperative care routine and significance of postoperative activities such as deep breathing, sitting in the chair, and ambulating.

Low Cardiac Output State

The most common reason for all-cause mortality after CABG is a low cardiac output state, which is especially prevalent in patients who require emergency CABG secondary to ST-elevated myocardial infarction (STEMI) or in patients experiencing perioperative or postoperative MI (Hillis et al., 2011). Perioperative MI can occur because of graft spasm or embolization into the graft, or as a complication of CPB if myocardial protection is not adequate. Patients with perioperative MI are at increased risk for adverse outcomes. These patients are treated with maximal medical therapy, including antiplatelet agents, beta blockers, and angiotensin-converting enzyme inhibitors. Low cardiac output after CABG can also be caused by reversible conditions after surgery, including acidosis and hypoxemia (Dirks & Waters, 2014).

Neurological Complications

The second most common cause of postoperative mortality, with an incidence very close to low cardiac output state and perioperative or postoperative MI, is postoperative stroke (Hillis et al., 2011; Mozaffarian et al., 2015). Other neurological complications associated with CABG surgery include embolic ophthalmological injuries and deficits, neurocognitive dysfunction, delirium, seizures, and peripheral neuropathy (Selnes et al., 2012). Neurological complications can be caused by intraoperative or postoperative hypoxia, emboli from CPB, hemorrhage, or metabolic abnormalities (Anderson, 2016). Risk factors for neurological complications include advanced age, atherosclerotic cardiovascular disease, and hypertension. Additional risk factors include previous history of neurological disease, unstable angina or diabetes, and intraoperative use of an IABP (Fihn et al., 2014).

Complications may be related to the brain's own microcirculation, in addition to microemboli during CPB. Sophisticated arterial line filters within the CPB circuit help protect against microemboli. Complications have been associated with periods of hypotension or hypoperfusion and may be reversible. Minimizing complications is critical because stroke is the second leading cause of mortality. The use of ultrasound via transesophageal echocardiography or epiaortic imaging to assess the aorta for the presence of atherosclerotic plaque is a technique to help minimize complications (Hillis et al., 2011).

When atherosclerotic plaque is identified in the ascending aorta, the patient is at high risk for an adverse neurovascular outcome. Embolization of atherosclerotic plaque during clamping and/or unclamping of the aorta is the most common cause of perioperative stroke. Atherosclerotic emboli can be dislodged from the aortic arch during cannulation for CPB or during clamping of the aorta. In very high-risk patients, a no-clamp strategy may be used (Hillis et al., 2011).

Other factors that contribute to postoperative stroke are recent anterior wall MI with left ventricular thrombus and recent stroke. Patients with a recent stroke should not have CABG for at least 4 weeks (Hillis et al., 2011). If CABG is done within 4 weeks of a stroke, then the patient is at high risk for hemorrhagic complications of stroke. Patients who also have symptomatic or severe carotid stenosis should be treated with carotid endarterectomy before CABG. Patients routinely have carotid ultrasound examinations before surgery to assess for significant carotid stenosis. Carotid endarterectomy is generally not performed in asymptomatic carotid disease unless stenosis is 80% or greater (Hillis et al., 2011). Other risks for neurovascular complications involve increased time ($\geq$90 minutes) spent on CPB and hyperglycemia (blood glucose $\geq$ 200 mg/dl). Maintaining a blood glucose level less than 140 mg/dl was associated with fewer neurological complications postoperatively (Hillis et al., 2011).

Although stroke is the most common neurological injury associated with CABG via CPB pump, there are others that occur less frequently but also pose a threat to the patient's quality of life postoperatively. For instance, cognitive deficits, neurobehavioral changes, and ophthalmological injuries can occur. Peripheral neurovascular complications, including brachial plexus injury and ulnar nerve injury, can also occur as complications of CABG surgery.

Systemic Inflammatory Response

The use of a CPB pump during CABG surgery causes a systemic inflammatory response. This response can result in transient, multiorgan dysfunction when severe and can delay recovery after surgery (Hillis et al., 2011). Strategies used to limit the immune response associated with CPB include the use of steroids and leukocyte-poor blood transfusions. Steroids should be avoided in patients with diabetes, but in other patients they can blunt the inflammatory response by inhibiting complement activation and reducing the levels of pro-inflammatory cytokines (Hillis et al., 2011). The administration of leukocyte-poor blood or using a leukocyte-depletion filter during the perioperative period has been shown to be beneficial in improving myocardial performance during acute or chronic ischemia (Anderson, 2016; Hillis et al., 2011).

Atrial Fibrillation

Another complication of CABG is the development of atrial fibrillation postoperatively. Atrial fibrillation occurs in 20% to 50% of postoperative patients within 5 days after surgery (Hillis et al., 2011), but the incidence was found to peak on postoperative day 2 (Hillis et al., 2014; January et al., 2014). If atrial fibrillation persists for more than 24 hours, heparin or warfarin can be initiated to prevent stroke. Post-CABG atrial fibrillation

increases the patient risk for stroke 4-fold and is associated with a 3-fold increased risk for death (Hillis et al., 2011).

Patient factors that contribute to atrial fibrillation occurrence include chronic pulmonary disease, advanced age, increased time on the CPB pump during surgery, and the cessation of or the absence of beta-blocker treatment before surgery (Hillis et al., 2011). Increased circulating catecholamines, volume overload, hypoxia, and electrolyte disturbances in the postoperative state can also contribute to the development of atrial fibrillation. Atrial fibrillation extends the length of stay and also greatly increases the risk for postoperative stroke (Dirks & Waters, 2014).

The standard therapy for the reduction of postoperative atrial fibrillation is the initiation of beta blockers preoperatively and/or very early postoperatively. Patients who were taking beta blockers preoperatively and have them withdrawn perioperatively are at increased risk for development of atrial fibrillation as a complication of CABG (Hillis et al., 2011). If beta blockers are contraindicated, calcium channel blockers or amiodarone can be used as prophylactic post-CABG-related atrial fibrillation (Hillis et al., 2011).

Wound Infection

Nosocomial infections occur in 10% to 20% of all cardiac surgery patients (Hillis et al., 2011). Preoperative antibiotic administration is routinely used to help prevent postoperative infection. Cephalosporins are the class of choice. Because an adequate tissue level of antibiotics is required at the time of incision, timing of preoperative antibiotics is important. Preoperative antibiotics should be administered within 30 minutes of incision time (Hillis et al., 2011). Additional antibiotic dosing may be required for longer surgeries. Postoperative intravenous (IV) antibiotics are continued prophylactically for 1 to 2 days or while mediastinal lines, tubes, or drains remain in place (Hillis et al., 2011).

Mediastinitis, or deep sternal wound infection, occurs in 0.45% to 5% of post-CABG patients; it is a serious complication that results in a mortality rate as high as 47% (Hillis et al., 2011). Sternal wound infections typically manifest several days to 2 weeks after surgery. Skin and nasopharyngeal gram-positive organisms (e.g., *Staphylococcal aureus*) are the leading cause of postoperative deep sternal wound infections (Hillis et al., 2011). Obesity, diabetes, or hyperglycemia, repeat surgery, and excessive use of electrocautery are risk factors. In addition, the use of both internal mammary arteries increases the risk for mediastinitis because the sternum receives less blood flow. For this reason, bilateral internal mammary artery use is recommended only if the overall benefits of this procedure outweigh the patient's risks (Hillis et al., 2011). Superficial wounds are treated with antibiotics and drainage, whereas deep sternal wounds require aggressive surgical debridement and closure with a muscle flap (Hillis et al., 2011). Several strategies are used during surgery to decrease the risk for mediastinitis and sternal wound infection (see Box 18-2).

Renal Dysfunction

Renal dysfunction is another potential complication after CABG because CPB decreases the glomerular filtration rate. The following characteristics place a patient at risk for development of renal dysfunction after bypass: advanced age, heart failure, type 1 diabetes, preexisting chronic kidney disease, and prior CABG (Hillis et al., 2011). Mortality is high for those who experience development of renal dysfunction perioperatively and is especially high for those who require dialysis. Early recognition of renal insufficiency and assurance of adequate volume administration are key nursing interventions in preventing postoperative renal failure (Dirks & Waters, 2014).

NURSING APPLICATION

The administration of nephrotoxic medications, including nonsteroidal anti-inflammatory drugs and aminoglycoside antibiotics, should be avoided in patients at high risk for renal dysfunction.

Patients with end-stage renal disease are at very high risk for mortality and morbidity if they undergo CABG. However, their risk for mortality may be even higher if they do not undergo revascularization; therefore, CABG may be considered for some of these patients. Patients with end-stage renal disease are at a particularly high risk for development of postoperative infection and sepsis (Hillis et al., 2011).

Pulmonary Complications

Mild pulmonary complications can occur simply as a result of CPB. During CPB, capillary permeability and pulmonary vascular resistance increase, and acute respiratory distress syndrome, also known as noncardiac pulmonary edema, can occur. Acute respiratory distress syndrome is a serious potential complication. Acute respiratory distress syndrome is an acute inflammatory response at the alveolar-capillary unit that significantly decreases the delivery of oxygen (Dirks & Waters, 2014). Patients undergoing repeat CABG and those who require blood transfusions are at higher risk for development of acute respiratory distress syndrome. Preoperative pulmonary edema should be resolved before surgery because pulmonary edema is exacerbated with the use of CPB (Hillis et al., 2011). Most patients experience postoperative atelectasis secondary to general anesthesia effects, pain, and/or pain medication. Postoperative thoracic and abdominal surgery patients are especially prone

BOX 18-2: STRATEGIES TO DECREASE STERNAL WOUND INFECTIONS

1. Preoperative *Staphylococcal aureus* screening and decolonization of patients found to have methicillin-resistant or -sensitive *S. aureus*

2. Preoperative patient bathing in antiseptic skin cleansers

3. Hair removal by electric clippers or depilatory agents (avoid razors)

4. Identification of patients at high risk for postoperative infection

5. Administration of prophylactic antibiotic within 30 minutes of first incision time

   a. Second-generation cephalosporin is preferred in patients without methicillin-resistant *S. aureus* colonization (MRSA)

   b. Vancomycin alone or in combination with other antibiotics is recommended for patients with proven or suspected MRSA colonization

6. Use of meticulous sterile operative technique

   a. Double-gloving for operating room team

   b. Reducing operating room traffic

   c. Minimizing flash sterilization of surgical instruments

   d. Minimizing electrocautery and use of bone wax

   e. Minimizing operating time

7. Maintenance of tight perioperative and postoperative glycemic control to keep blood glucose concentration <140 mg/dl while avoiding hypoglycemia

8. Administration of leukocyte-filtered blood transfusions as needed

Note. Adapted from Hillis, L. D., Smith, P. K., Anderson, J. L., Bittl, J. A., Bridges, C. R., Gyrne, J. G., ... Winniford, M. D. (2011). 2011 ACCF/AHA guideline for coronary artery bypass graft surgery: A report of the American College of Cardiology Foundation/American Heart Association Task Force on Practice Guidelines. *Circulation, 124*(23), e652-e735. doi:10.1161/CIR.0b013e31823c074e

to hypoventilation because of postoperative pain (Dirks & Waters, 2011).

NURSING APPLICATION

Postoperative pain control is an effective intervention in preventing atelectasis by promoting adequate ventilation. Encouraging patients to use their incentive spirometers is another effective strategy to encourage deep breathing, lung expansion, and prevention of postoperative pulmonary complications (Dirks & Waters, 2014).

The most common preoperative pulmonary problem is chronic obstructive pulmonary disease (Hillis et al., 2011). Those with moderate-to-severe chronic obstructive pulmonary disease, including those with elevated partial pressure of carbon dioxide levels and those who use home oxygen, are at increased risk for postoperative complications. These patients are likely to remain on ventilators longer, which places them at risk for development of ventilator-associated or hospital-acquired pneumonia. In addition to their risk for pulmonary complications, these patients also experience an increased risk for ventricular dysrhythmias postoperatively (Dirks & Waters, 2014).

NURSING APPLICATION

Reviewing the importance of smoking cessation is another important intervention to decrease the risk for pulmonary complications in patients electively undergoing CABG.

All pulmonary infectious processes should also be resolved before surgery. Before surgery, it is important for patients to receive incentive spirometry and to perform coughing and deep-breathing exercises. This preoperative treatment also provides the instruction for postoperative exercises. If time allows, weight loss should be achieved in obese patients electively undergoing CABG because it can help to decrease the risk for adverse pulmonary effects and other complications.

NURSING APPLICATION

It is important to accomplish preoperative respiratory teaching (incentive spirometry and coughing and deep breathing), even in patients without preexisting lung disease, because postoperative sedation and pain interfere with the patient's ability to learn during the early postoperative period.

Patients who are unable to be extubated in a timely fashion because of pulmonary complications are usually ventilated using low tidal volume. The use of low tidal volume is one lung-protective strategy to limit damage to pulmonary tissue caused by mechanical ventilation (Hillis et al., 2011). Pneumothorax can also occur as a postoperative complication and can happen at the time of removal of pleural chest tubes (Dirks & Waters, 2014).

Postoperative Bleeding

Postoperative bleeding is usually venous in nature and originates from the site of sutures. Bleeding can also occur from pericardial adhesions during a repeat procedure. Blood loss measured through chest tubes should be less than 300 ml/hr during the first several hours and then should begin to taper with a total blood loss of approximately 1 L (Hillis et al., 2011). Patients who experience prolonged CPB time are at risk for development of coagulopathies postoperatively. A series of coagulation profiles is drawn in the first 24 hours postoperatively to determine clotting factor deficiencies. Recognized deficiencies are replaced by transfusion as needed. Platelet count should be kept greater than $100,000/mm^3$ (Hillis et al., 2011).

Patients who are at high risk for bleeding preoperatively, including those undergoing repeat CABG and those with expected long CPB time, may receive antifibrinolytic drugs to reduce the risk for bleeding. If postoperative bleeding cannot be adequately controlled, then mediastinal re-exploration may be needed to reduce the risk for cardiac tamponade, a life-threatening postoperative emergency (Hillis et al., 2011).

Transfusion

Patients undergoing CABG account for approximately 10% of all allogenic (blood from a compatible human donor) blood transfusions in the United States (Hillis et al., 2011). Blood transfusions produce immunomodulatory effects, thereby increasing the risk for nosocomial infection, particularly nosocomial pneumonia. Therefore, the goal is to avoid the need for perioperative transfusion whenever possible. However, when blood transfusions are needed, leukocyte-depleted blood has demonstrated lower rates of perioperative and postoperative infections and in-hospital deaths (Hollis et al., 2011). Post-CABG patients who are placed on CPB and require blood transfusions are at high risk for pulmonary complications because of the proinflammatory substances that accumulate during the storage of blood (Hillis et al., 2011).

Patients can donate their own blood during the 30 days before surgery to be used as an autologous transfusion if needed during or after surgery. Patients who have adequate hemoglobin levels and do not have unstable or potentially unstable ischemic disease are the best candidates. In other candidates, the use of recombinant human erythropoietin preoperatively to restore red blood cell volume has been shown to minimize blood loss, need for transfusion, and ischemic injuries postoperatively (Hillis et al., 2011). Other strategies for post-CABG blood volume resuscitation involve reinfusing the blood taken from the patient before CPB immediately after discontinuing CPB intraoperatively.

Anticoagulation and Antiplatelet Therapy Before Surgery

Preoperative anticoagulation can be done with unfractionated heparin (UFH) or low-molecular-weight heparin. The 2011 American College of Cardiology Foundation/American Heart Association guidelines for the management of patients undergoing CABG reported no associated increase in perioperative blood loss with the use of UFH and reported low-molecular-weight heparin can be administered less than 12 hours preoperatively without excessive perioperative blood loss (Hillis et al., 2011). Warfarin and clopidogrel should be held at least 5 days before surgery and prasugrel 7 days before surgery. If urgent CABG is needed, surgery should wait at least 24 hours after clopidogrel discontinuation to reduce major bleeding (Hillis et al., 2011).

Aspirin, 100 to 325 mg, should be administered to CABG patients preoperatively. The benefits of preoperative aspirin use include continued antithrombotic therapy for acute coronary syndrome patients, a low risk for perioperative bleeding, increased postoperative vein graft patency, and reduced operative morbidity and/or mortality rates (Hillis et al., 2011).

The glycoprotein IIb/IIIa inhibitors tirofiban and eptifibatide should be discontinued 4 to 6 hours before CABG, and abciximab should be discontinued 12 to 24 hours before surgery (Hillis et al., 2011). Special precautions to limit perioperative and postoperative bleeding can be taken in the population of patients who require emergent or urgent CABG who were not able to discontinue antithrombotic medications as recommended. For instance, lower doses of intraoperative heparin and minimizing hemodilution can be done intraoperatively to lower the risk for bleeding. Platelet transfusions and/or the use of antifibrinolytics (e.g., ε-aminocaproic acid or tranexamic acid) are other prophylactic interventions that can be ordered (Hillis et al., 2011).

Special Populations

Patients Who Require Emergency Coronary Artery Bypass Grafting

Any emergent or urgent surgery carries an increased risk for mortality and morbidity. Whenever possible, PCI, an IABP, and/or medical treatment should be maximized to stabilize the patient before CABG surgery in an effort to improve morbidity and mortality risks. Emergency CABG surgery has demonstrated good outcomes for patients with acute MI

- who underwent a failed PCI,
- in whom PCI is contradicted,
- who have suitable coronary anatomy for CABG, and
- who have persistent ischemia to a significant amount of myocardium at rest and/or hemodynamic instability that is unresponsive to nonsurgical therapies.

(Hillis et al. 2011)

Other indications and contraindications for emergency CABG surgery are listed in Box 18-3.

BOX 18-3: EMERGENCY CORONARY ARTERY BYPASS GRAFT SURGERY RECOMMENDATIONS

Emergency CABG *is* recommended in patients who

- must undergo surgical repair of a postinfarction mechanical complication of MI (ventricular septal rupture, mitral valve insufficiency caused by papillary muscle infarction and/or rupture, or free wall rupture);
- are in cardiogenic shock with suitable anatomy for CABG;
- have life-threatening ventricular arrhythmias caused by ischemia in the presence of left main artery stenosis ≥50% and/or triple-vessel CAD;
- have multivessel CAD with recurrent angina or MI within the first 48 hours of STEMI as an alternative to a delayed strategy; or
- have ST-segment elevation or left bundle branch block and are older than 75 years.

Emergency CABG *is not* recommended in patients who

- have persistent angina and a small area of viable myocardium and are hemodynamically stable, or
- have adequate epicardial reperfusion but inadequate microvascular reperfusion.

CABG = coronary artery bypass graft; CAD = coronary artery disease; MI = myocardial infarction; STEMI = ST-segment elevation myocardial infarction.

Note. Adapted from Hillis, L. D., Smith, P. K., Anderson, J. L., Bittl, J. A., Bridges, C. R., Gyrne, J. G., … Winniford, M. D. (2011). 2011 ACCF/AHA guideline for coronary artery bypass graft surgery: A report of the American College of Cardiology Foundation/American Heart Association Task Force on Practice Guidelines. *Circulation, 124*(23), e652-e735. doi:10.1161/CIR.0b013e31823c074e

Patients Who Have Had an Acute Myocardial Infarction

Patients who have had acute MIs have higher mortality with CABG for the first several days after the infarction. For patients with large MIs who are stabilized, surgery should be delayed to allow the myocardium to recover. However, some patients with acute MIs are unable to wait to have CABG, including those with left main or triple-vessel disease and those with symptomatic valve disease. The longer the patient remains unstable before surgery, the higher the mortality rate. CABG mortality is elevated for the first 3 to 7 days after an MI (Hillis et al., 2011).

Older Adult Patients

CABG surgery poses multiple risks for patients aged 80 years or older because of increased severity of CAD, left ventricular dysfunction with concomitant valvular disease, and multiple other comorbidities. Although this population has an increased risk for mortal-ity and morbidity, improvement in functional capacity and quality of life can be achieved (Hillis et al., 2011).

Women

Limited data are available on the influence that gender has on CABG outcomes. However, although there are many reasons for this, women have been found to have higher complication rates than men post-CABG despite having better overall long-term outcomes (Hillis et al., 2011).

Patients With Diabetes

Patients with diabetes have increased mortality and morbidity risks with CABG compared with patients who do not have diabetes (Hillis et al., 2011). Patients with diabetes who are post-CABG have higher rates of mediastinitis and lower long-term patency rates for saphenous vein grafts. Post-CABG outcomes are better in this population with the use of an internal mammary artery, when possible. Despite these findings, CABG provides greater survival benefits to appropriate patients with diabetes than does PCI (Hillis et al., 2011).

In addition to diabetes, any hyperglycemia during the perioperative period increases risk, especially for sternal wound infections (Hillis et al., 2011). Hyperglycemia can occur in patients without diabetes because of surgical stress, hypothermia, commonly used postoperative medications, and other complex metabolic changes that occur during CABG (Anderson, 2016). Maintaining the blood glucose level at less than 140 mg/dl during the perioperative and postoperative periods improves the patient's overall outcomes (Hillis et al., 2011).

Patients With Low Ejection Fractions

Patients with low ejection fractions (≤50%) or clinical heart failure also have an increased risk for operative mortality. However, this group of patients, when revascularized by CABG surgery, also have the greatest survival benefit compared with treatment with medical therapy. In addition, this population can benefit from symptom relief and improvement in functional capacity (Hillis et al., 2011).

Patients With Valve Disease

Patients with coexisting moderate-to-severe aortic stenosis commonly undergo aortic valve replacement at the time of CABG. In addition, patients who have clinically symptomatic mitral valve regurgitation with structural abnormalities undergo mitral valve repair at the time of CABG (Hillis et al., 2011). If the mitral valve is structurally normal and regurgitation is not severe, the regurgitation may be caused by reversible ischemia that will be corrected with the revascularization procedure. Combined procedures increase the operative risk for complications and mortality, but are reasonable risks in comparison with not performing both procedures (Hillis et al., 2011).

Patients With End-Stage Kidney Disease

Chronic kidney disease is another illness that places patients at an increased risk for morbidity and mortality compared with those who do not have it. However, CABG can improve the survival rate for patients with end-stage kidney disease and one of the following (Hillis et al., 2011):

- a left main coronary stenosis ≥50%,
- ≥70% stenosis in three major vessels, or
- ≥70% stenosis in the LAD artery plus one other major artery.

When CABG is performed for this population, clinicians must take measures to prevent and be vigilant for signs of perioperative and postoperative complications such as prolonged ventilation, the need for blood transfusion, mediastinitis, and prolonged hospital stay (Hillis et al., 2011).

Patients Undergoing Transmyocardial Laser Revascularization

Patients who are candidates for transmyocardial laser revascularization, but not other forms of revascularization, usually have very diffuse small-vessel disease. Transmyocardial laser revascularization is limited to patients who have angina that is refractory to maximal medical treatment and who are not candidates for other forms of revascularization (Hillis et al., 2011).

During this procedure, a series of transmural endomyocardial channels are created with lasers to improve myocardial blood supply. These channels are created on the epicardial surface and go through to the endocardium. The typical number of channels ranges from 20 to 40, with the size of the channels approximately 1 mm wide. The physiology behind the treatment is more complex than simply creating channels for oxygenated blood to flow from the endocardium up through the myocardium to the epicardium. Two theories are proposed regarding the mechanism of action: The laser treatment stimulates angiogenesis and causes improvement in regional blood flow to the ischemic area of myocardium, and the laser treatment creates denervation of the myocardium and an improvement of symptoms (Levine et al., 2011).

Transmyocardial laser revascularization has been effective in improving anginal symptoms, functional capacity, and quality of life. This procedure is typically done in the cardiac surgery suite as a standalone surgery, or it can be done with CABG, when not all ischemic areas can be reached by grafting. Percutaneous options for this revascularization surgery are currently being investigated.

Postoperative Nursing Care

All patients who have undergone open-heart surgery are cared for in a similar fashion, regardless of the exact operation performed. They receive care in an intensive care unit for the immediate postoperative period. During this period, patients are placed on a cardiac monitor and are usually mechanically ventilated for the next 2 to 4 hours, or until intraoperative anesthetics have worn off and the patient has spontaneous respirations with adequate gas exchange (Dirks & Waters, 2014). In addition, patients have an arterial line and pulmonary artery catheter in place for invasive monitoring of systemic and intracardiac pressures. The arterial line allows for continuous monitoring of blood pressure, which can be unstable during the early postoperative period. Hypertension or hypotension can occur after surgery. Hypotension frequently occurs in the early postoperative period as the patient is warmed. The patient can also experience hypovolemia caused by fluid volume alterations associated with CPB. The pulmonary artery catheter allows for assessment of preload, afterload, and contractility. Poor cardiac output can occur secondary to decreased pre-

load and/or decreased contractility associated with intraoperative cardioplegia and blood loss. Having a pulmonary artery catheter in place allows point-of-care hemodynamic measures to identify which component of cardiac output is abnormal and timely initiation of the appropriate treatment (Dirks & Waters, 2014).

Pulmonary artery catheters with the capability of continuous cardiac output and venous oxygen saturation monitoring are commonly used. Venous oxygen saturation levels give an assessment of the amount of oxygen left over after the patient has used a portion of what was delivered. This is called *venous reserve*. The body normally uses approximately 25% of the oxygen that is delivered to the tissues. This leaves an average venous reserve of approximately 75%. When the venous oxygen saturation level (venous reserve) drops, it is because delivery has dropped, consumption needs have increased, or both. Venous oxygen saturation levels provide a good assessment of the delivery and consumption of oxygen because they measure the patient's venous reserve. Postoperative CABG patients also have temporary epicardial pacing wires in place (Dirks & Waters, 2014).

Bradycardiac dysrhythmias (bradydysrhythmias) can occur postoperatively, especially in patients who have received valve repair or replacement. The suture lines from valve surgery are close to the conduction system, and postoperative edema can cause temporary heart block. Patients can require a temporary pacemaker when coming from the operating room or at any time during the first 24 hours postoperatively. It is the responsibility of the critical care nurse to identify and initiate temporary pacing as needed (Dirks & Waters, 2014).

Pleural and mediastinal chest tubes connected to water-seal chambers and at least 20 cm of suction are also used. Stripping of chest tubes postoperatively should be avoided because of the risk for damaging and/or rupturing bypass grafts. Blood loss should be measured in the chest tube containers no more than hourly. Blood loss more than 200 ml/hr for 2 consecutive hours should be reported to the cardiothoracic surgeon immediately (Dirks & Waters, 2014).

Postoperative anemia can occur for a number of reasons (e.g., blood loss, dilution, or cell damage by the CPB). Packed red blood cell transfusions are ordered if the hemoglobin level falls to less than 8 g/dl (Hillis et al., 2011). Maintaining a systolic blood pressure less than 130 mmHg is important during the postoperative period to reduce the risk for bleeding (Dirks & Waters, 2014).

Early postoperative aspirin administration – within the first 6 hours if none taken preoperatively, otherwise within the first 24 hours – is important to prevent saphenous vein graft closure. Continuing aspirin use also reduces postoperative complications and decreases postoperative mortality (Hillis et al., 2011).

Fast Tracking

Low- to moderate-risk patients can be selected for "fast tracking" after CABG (Hillis et al., 2011). These patients are targeted for early extubation, early ambulation, and early discharge. Special pathways are used to guide care in patients being fast tracked. Patients who are fast tracked are sedated postoperatively with short-acting agents and receive lower doses of opioids to allow for earlier extubation. Patients can be extubated postoperatively when they are awake, respond appropriately, and are able to have pain controlled without using medications that interfere with extubation. Before extubation, patients must also have no serious postoperative bleeding and have stable vital signs. Pharmacological strategies to prevent atrial fibrillation are also a key component of fast tracking (Hillis et al., 2011).

Early ambulation and phase I cardiac rehabilitation exercises are also a part of the fast-track program. Patients who undergo traditional CABG and who are fast tracked are generally discharged 3 to 5 days postoperatively (Hillis et al., 2011). Older adult patients are commonly more difficult to fast-track because of higher numbers of preoperative comorbidities. Patients who receive less invasive forms of surgery generally advance more quickly to extubation, step-down care, and discharge.

Postdischarge Care

Administration of postoperative aspirin is continued indefinitely. All patients also receive statin therapy to reduce the progression of vein graft disease. After CABG, patients are placed on a short-term 20- to 25-lb lifting restriction, with no more than 10 lb over the head for 6 to 8 weeks after discharge (Dirks & Waters, 2014).

A formal cardiac rehabilitation program referral should be made for all patients before discharge. Patients usually begin participation in outpatient cardiac rehabilitation 4 to 8 weeks after surgery. Patients participating in cardiac rehabilitation after CABG have reported increased physical mobility, ability to work, perception of better health, and perception of better overall life situations (Hillis et al., 2011).

Assessment of depression and presence of psychosocial support are important nursing interventions in the postdischarge period. Depression occurs in up to 33% of patients at 1 year after CABG (Hillis et al., 2011). Cognitive behavioral therapy or collaborative care for these patients improves symptoms (Hillis et al., 2011).

NURSING APPLICATION

Facilitating participation in cardiac rehabilitation is a key nursing intervention in the prevention and treatment of postoperative depression and social isolation.

Many patients and their caregivers experience major psychosocial adjustments after discharge. Adapting to postoperative pain, changes in body image, activity limitations, and financial burdens are a few of the areas for which nurses need to provide psychosocial support during the discharge transition. For instance, explaining that these adjustments are common after CABG can help the patient and family recognize them early. Another strategy involves telephone follow-up programs to ensure that patients who were fast tracked underwent a smooth home transition (Dirks & Waters, 2014).

Angina After Coronary Artery Bypass Grafting

Patients who present with acute coronary syndrome or other symptoms suggestive of ischemia after having CABG are generally candidates for percutaneous cardiac catheterization. It is difficult to distinguish between graft closure and progression of native vessel disease using only noninvasive testing. Most patients who present with ischemia within 30 days of surgery have graft failure caused by thrombosis. This acute graft closure can occur in vein grafts and arterial conduits. These patients are usually candidates for PCI to treat the focal stenosis. If multiple vein grafts are stenosed, or if the stenotic graft is supplying the LAD coronary artery, then repeat CABG is often indicated (Hillis et al., 2011). Mortality and morbidity risks are higher for patients who undergo repeat CABG. These patients may also have limited available graft options. Long-term results are not as successful with repeat operations as with initial operations. However, repeat CABG is

reasonable in patients to improve survival, especially with LAD coronary artery stenosis ≥50% (Hillis et al., 2011).

PERCUTANEOUS CORONARY INTERVENTION

PCI refers to a group of catheter-based technologies used to treat coronary stenosis. PTCA was the first of these catheter-based techniques. Intracoronary stents are now used in the vast majority of PCI procedures (Levine et al., 2011).

Before the use of intracoronary stenting, coronary interventional technique was primarily limited to PTCA. Sometimes referred to as *plain old balloon angioplasty,* PTCA is a catheter-based procedure in which a balloon is inflated at the site of coronary stenosis to increase the vessel lumen diameter. Balloon inflation causes plaque rupture and disruption of the endothelium (see Figure 18-5). PTCA has two primary limitations: acute vessel closure and restenosis. The risk for acute vessel closure made it necessary for standby of a CABG team in case emergency CABG was needed. Restenosis occurs through different processes, including vessel recoil and remodeling, as well as neointimal hyperplasia, which occurs in response to vessel injury. Smooth muscle cells from the media of the vessel migrate through tears to reach the luminal surface. Also, myofibrils from the adventitia transform into smooth muscle cells and migrate to the site of injury. This collection of smooth muscle cells can result in restenosis (Dirks & Waters, 2014).

Indications for Percutaneous Coronary Intervention

PCI is performed in a wide range of patients, from stable to unstable, with a varying amount of myocardium at risk. PCI is more

FIGURE 18-5: BALLOON INFLATION CAUSING PLAQUE DISRUPTION DURING PERCUTANEOUS TRANSLUMINAL CORONARY ANGIOPLASTY

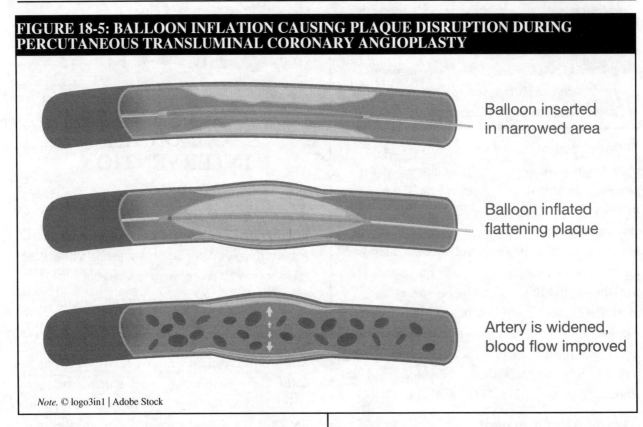

Balloon inserted in narrowed area

Balloon inflated flattening plaque

Artery is widened, blood flow improved

Note. © logo3in1 | Adobe Stock

effective than medical treatment in relieving angina (Levine et al., 2011). PCI was historically limited to single-vessel proximal coronary heart disease; however, with newer techniques, the scope of interventional cardiology has expanded. For patients with two-vessel disease, PCI is routinely considered an acceptable alternative to surgery. PCI may even be considered in three-vessel disease if left ventricular function is normal and the patient does not have diabetes; however, CABG still offers better revascularization and long-term outcomes than PCI for this patient (Hillis et al., 2011; Levine et al., 2011).

Insufficient evidence is available regarding the mortality benefits of PCI in high-risk patients. Elective PCI is an option for revascularization in patients with normal left ventricular function. However, CABG is recommended for patients with abnormal left ventricular function who have severe symptoms (Hillis et al., 2011). Some evidence shows that CABG improves survival in patients with diabetes who have three-vessel disease (Hillis et al., 2011). However, abciximab, a glycoprotein IIb/IIIa inhibitor, has been shown to improve the outcomes of PCI in patients with diabetes (Levine et al., 2011). Continued advances in PCI may open the door for more PCI procedures in groups of patients who are currently recommended for CABG only.

PCI is not indicated in non-LAD CAD, except if ischemia is found on noninvasive testing. PCI is also not performed on lesions with less than 60% stenosis, unless ischemia is found on noninvasive testing (Levine et al., 2011). Many patients with chronic angina undergo PCI for control of symptoms, even though there may be no associated survival benefit. As with all healthcare options, physician judgment and patient preferences play important roles in treatment decisions.

Interventional Revascularization and Adjunct Procedures

Intracoronary Stenting (Bare Metal)

The first U.S. Food and Drug Administration (FDA) approval for an intracoronary stent occurred in 1993 (Deelstra, 2010). Stent design and the associated pharmacology with stent use have improved significantly since that time. Bare metal and drug-eluting stenting, glycoprotein IIb/IIIa inhibitors and clopidogrel antiplatelet therapy, and newer anticoagulants (such as bivalirudin) have made PCI a safer procedure and have contributed to substantially improved outcomes.

Stenting involves the placement of a metal scaffold-type structure to help prevent elastic recoil and to keep open the lumen of the vessel. Stents can be made from various metals and have different structural designs. Most stents are delivered and expanded with the use of a balloon system (see Figure 18-6). Self-expanding stents are also available. After a stent is deployed and expanded, a high-pressure balloon is typically used to assure that the stent is fully deployed.

Stenting reduces the risk for acute vessel closure, which can lead to STEMI. Intracoronary stents have also reduced the need for emergency CABG by preventing and treating dissections caused by balloon inflation. Stenting also reduces the percentage of late vessel restenosis. Stents impact restenosis by decreasing the elastic recoil of the vessel and also by decreasing the remodeling that occurs after vessel injury associated with PTCA. Stenting with bare metal stents reduces restenosis rates to approximately 20% to 30% (Deelstra, 2010). Bare metal stents decrease restenosis by impacting vessel remodeling. With the use of intracoronary stenting, patients older than 75 years have similar outcomes with PCI to those of younger patients (Levine et al., 2011). Intracoronary stenting is usually done in conjunction with balloon angioplasty, but it can also be performed without balloon dilatation.

FIGURE 18-6: CORONARY STENT DEPLOYMENT

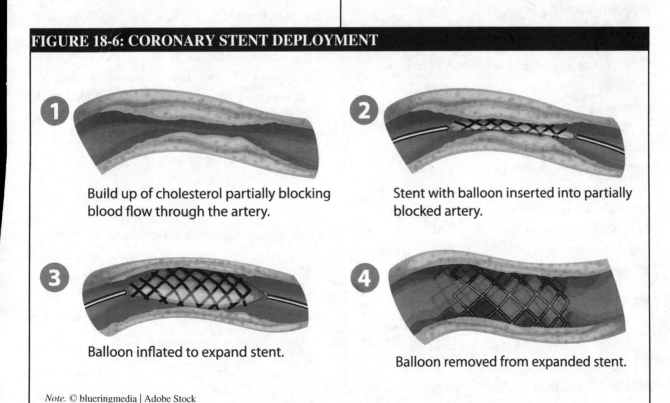

1 Build up of cholesterol partially blocking blood flow through the artery.

2 Stent with balloon inserted into partially blocked artery.

3 Balloon inflated to expand stent.

4 Balloon removed from expanded stent.

Note. © blueringmedia | Adobe Stock

Drug-Eluting Stents

Stents coated with pharmacological agents aimed at decreasing restenosis have been FDA approved since 2003 (Deelstra, 2010). Drug-eluting stents impact restenosis by both preventing vessel remodeling and inhibiting neointimal hyperplasia. The stents are coated with immuno-suppressant agents often used for organ transplant rejection prevention (Dirks & Waters, 2014).

Drug-eluting stents have shown improved restenosis rates compared with bare metal stents. With the use of drug-eluting stents in conjunction with contemporary antiplatelet therapy, restenosis rates with PCI are often in the single digits (Levine et al., 2011). Drug-eluting stents include partially bioabsorbable stents, where a bare metal stent remains after the drug is absorbed to prevent vessel recoil and remodeling. In June 2016, the FDA approved the first fully absorbable stent to treat CAD. The stent releases medication to limit the growth of scar tissue and is completely absorbed by the body in approximately 3 years.

Directional Atherectomy

Directional atherectomy can be used to cut and remove plaque in native vessels or in saphenous vein grafts. A rotating cutter is directed toward the plaque to be removed. Both directional and rotational atherectomy "debulk" coronary arteries containing a large amount of atherosclerotic plaque. Directional atherectomy can be used in calcified lesions. Figure 18-7 displays a picture of a device used for directional coronary atherectomy (Dirks & Waters, 2014).

Rotational Atherectomy

Rotational atherectomy involves the use of high-speed rotating blades or burs to remove components of the atherosclerotic plaque (see Figure 18-8). This technique is not used in the presence of acute thrombus. It is used to

help prepare for a more successful PTCA and stent procedure when a hard, calcified lesion is present. Rotational atherectomy has permitted intervention in some lesions that previously could only be treated with CABG. Creatine kinase-MB enzymes can be released during this procedure because microparticles are embolized distally. This distal embolization causes platelet activation. The use of glycoprotein IIb/IIIa inhibitors can reduce platelet aggregation and limit the release of creatine kinase-MB enzymes. Atherectomy procedures have higher rates of complications when performed alone and are typically performed in conjunction with intracoronary stent placement (Dirks & Waters, 2014; Levine et al., 2011).

Extraction Techniques

Other atherectomy techniques, such as AngioJet thrombectomy and transluminal extraction atherectomy, are used for the extraction of visible thrombi within the coronary artery. An AngioJet thrombectomy device works by delivering high-velocity saline jets. The jets are also given retrograde to assist in removal of thrombotic material (Deelstra, 2010). When thrombi are removed before intervention, the risk for postprocedure complications may be decreased. These techniques are also proposed to remove degenerative graft material and thrombi commonly seen with saphenous vein graft stenosis.

Laser

With laser techniques, tissue is ablated using a combination of photochemical, thermal, and mechanical effects. These techniques are not widely used. Early results demonstrated increased dissection and perforation with ablative techniques (Deelstra, 2010).

Cutting Balloons

Special cutting balloons are now available that can be used to make incisions into the

FIGURE 18-7: DIRECTIONAL CORONARY ATHERECTOMY DEVICE

Note. By Blausen Medical Communications, Inc. (Donated via OTRS, see ticket for details) [CC BY 3.0 (http://creativecommons.org/licenses/by/3.0)], via Wikimedia Commons.

plaque before dilatation. This technique allows for greater plaque compression in lesions resistant to balloon dilatation (Deelstra, 2010).

Radiation (Brachytherapy)

Locally delivered ionizing radiation has been used to treat in-stent restenosis. Radiation decreases the intimal hyperplasia associated with in-stent restenosis by interfering with smooth cell proliferation. Both gamma and beta radiation have been used. Patients who have undergone radiation treatment need to be on clopidogrel for an extended period because a reduction in neointimal hyperplasia increases the risk for contact between blood and stent material, as well as thrombus formation. Drug-eluting stents have

significantly reduced in-stent restenosis over bare metal stent use and brachytherapy. Therefore, brachytherapy is no longer a routinely used treatment option (Levine et al., 2011).

Intravascular Ultrasound

Intravascular ultrasound, a miniature ultrasound transducer on the end of a catheter, provides a cross-sectional image of the coronary artery that can be used to evaluate results in high-risk procedures. This technology can guide assessment of lesions that are difficult to visualize with angiography. Intravascular ultrasound can also be used to assess the quality of lesions, including those that are calcific. It can also be used to guide atherectomy procedures and to assure that intra-

FIGURE 18-8: ROTATIONAL ATHERECTOMY

Note. By Blausen Medical Communications, Inc. (Donated via OTRS, see ticket for details) [CC BY 3.0 (http://creativecommons.org/licenses/by/3.0)], via Wikimedia Commons.

coronary stents are optimally deployed. Optimally deployed stents reduce the risk for in-stent thrombosis (Dirks & Waters, 2014).

Coronary Pressure Measurements

Fractional flow reserve measurements are used to assess the maximal coronary blood flow at the area of stenosis. Flow is measured using a pressure wire. The result represents a fraction of what is normally expected with no stenosis. A result of less than 0.75 represents a significant coronary stenosis (Levine et al., 2011).

Advantages of Interventional Treatment

Advantages of PCI include low rates of procedure mortality and morbidity. These pro-cedures also take less time to perform and are easier to repeat if needed than is CABG. No general anesthesia, thoracotomy, or CPB time is required. Patients experience much shorter hospital stays and are able to return to work sooner. Central nervous system complications are also decreased. However, patients must have suitable anatomy to be candidates for PCI. Not all lesions can be reached by a catheter-based technique (Dirks & Waters, 2014).

Success Rates

Success of PCI procedures is typically defined in four different ways: angiographic success, pro-cedural success, clinical success, and long-term success. These definitions are listed in Table 18-1.

TABLE 18-1: PERCUTANEOUS CATHETER INTERVENTION SUCCESS

Term	Definition
Angiographic success	Substantial enlargement of the vessel lumen at the site of intervention; less than 20% residual stenosis
Procedural success	Angiographic success + Freedom from major hospital complications
Clinical success	Angiographic success + Procedural success + Relief from signs and symptoms of ischemia
Long-term success	Clinical success for longer than 6 months

Note. Adapted from Levine, G. N., Bates, E. R., Blankenship, J. C., Bailey, S. R., Bittle, J. A., Cercek, B., ... Ting, H. H. (2011). 2011 ACCF/AHA/SCAI guideline for percutaneous coronary intervention: A report of the American College of Cardiology Foundation/American Heart Association Task Force on Practice Guidelines and the Society for Cardiovascular Angiography and Interventions. *Circulation, 124*(23), e574-e651. doi:10.1161/CIR.0b013e31823ba622

With the use of stents and glycoprotein IIb/IIIa inhibitors, angiographic success rates with PCI are as high as 99% (Levine et al., 2011). Results of PCI are similar in patients presenting with either stable angina or unstable angina. The limiting factor for long-term success with PCI continues to be restenosis. The majority of restenosis procedures occur during the 3- to 6-month period after the procedure.

Bare metal stents help eliminate the elastic recoil associated with restenosis, and drug-eluting stents show promise of greatly impacting the neointimal hyperplasia that still limits long-term success. However, the use of drug-eluting stents is new, and long-term outcomes have not yet been evaluated. Other patient factors that affect long-term success include age, left ventricular function, diabetes, and the presence of diffuse vessel, small-vessel, or multivessel disease. Many patients with these factors are referred for CABG (Hillis et al., 2011; Levine et al., 2011).

Complications

Major hospital complications from PCI include death, periprocedural MI, the need for emergency CABG, stroke, renal failure, significant bleeding, and/or major vascular complications. Significant bleeding is defined as a greater than 3.0-g/dl decrease in hemoglobin level or bleeding that results in transfusion or extended length of stay (Levine et al., 2011). Nurses play an important role in assessing for vascular complications after PCI.

Vascular Complications

Vascular complications can include

- occlusion of the artery at the site of access,
- vessel dissection (splitting and separation of arterial layers) at the site of entry,
- arteriovenous fistula (connection between artery and vein) at the site of entry, and
- pseudoaneurysm at the site of entry.

(Levine et al. 2011)

Another vascular complication can involve a retroperitoneal bleed (resulting from a large hematoma in the retroperitoneum), which can be life-threatening. Patients typically experience lumbar pain, hypotension, and a drop in hematocrit. A computed tomography scan is performed to confirm the diagnosis. The patient is treated with IV fluids and blood transfusion, and surgical repair of the artery may also be needed. Arterial punctures made above the inguinal ligament place the patient at increased risk for retroperitoneal bleed (Levine et al., 2011).

Patients who are treated with interventional procedures are at increased risk for hemorrhagic and ischemic embolic stroke. Hemorrhagic stroke results from the anticoagulation therapy used during the procedure. A more common complication, however, is ischemic stroke, which is caused by plaque embolization during the procedure.

Distal microembolization during an intervention can result in postprocedure chest pain and a small rise in cardiac enzymes. Chest pain from embolization of microparticles is usually transient and lessens with time. There is an increased risk for embolization from larger debris during PCI with acute thrombus, saphenous vein graft PCI, and rotational atherectomy (Deelstra, 2010). Stent thrombosis most frequently occurs acutely (within 24 hours) or subacutely (within 30 days). The risk for acute and subacute stent thrombosis has been reduced with improved techniques for stent deployment and aggressive use of antiplatelet therapy. Although these remain very serious complications, they occur in only approximately 1% of patients (Deelstra, 2010). The biggest risk factor for late stent thrombosis is premature discontinuation of dual-antiplatelet therapy (Levine et al., 2011).

Additional complications that can occur during the procedure include spasm and vessel perforation. Spasm is most common during rotational atherectomy and is treated with intracoronary nitroglycerin. Vessel perforation is rare but can be a very serious complication (Levine et al., 2011). When perforation occurs, a balloon is inflated in an attempt to stop blood leakage from the perforated site. Specially coated stents are also used to tack up the vessel wall. If too much blood is lost, tamponade can occur. Pericardiocentesis may be indicated (Dirks & Waters, 2014).

Renal Complications

The use of contrast agents during PCI increases the risk for renal insufficiency and renal failure after the procedure. Renal dysfunction as a result of contrast is referred to as *contrast-induced nephropathy.* Patients with existing renal insufficiency, older adults, and those with diabetes are at highest risk for renal complications with PCI. It is important that high-risk patients are well hydrated with normal saline solution before, during, and after PCI (Levine et al., 2011). Careful use of contrast agents (to avoid any overuse during the procedure) is also important in preventing renal complications. Patients with diabetes who are taking metformin need to have the agent held before and after the procedure (Levine et al., 2011). Contrast-induced nephropathy can produce temporary or permanent renal dysfunction.

Special Circumstances

Emergency Percutaneous Catheter Intervention

Emergency PCI can usually be performed without additional cardiac assistive devices. If a patient shows signs of hemodynamic instability, has ongoing ischemia, or is in cardiogenic shock, an IABP is inserted to provide cardiac support and improve outcomes. Patients who are in cardiogenic shock and have severely depressed left ventricular function may be placed on full cardiopulmonary support during emergency PCI. Emergency PCI is ideally performed in a setting with onsite cardiothoracic surgical backup. If performed in a facility with no onsite surgical backup, there should be the ability to transfer the patient to a cardiac operating room within 1 hour (Levine et al., 2011). Emergency PCI as a reperfusion strategy during an acute MI should be done within 90 minutes from contact with Emergency Medical Services (Levine et al., 2011). Primary PCI is superior to fibrinolytic therapy when reperfusion can be achieved within 90 minutes by an experienced operator. If a fibrinolytic is given and is not successful, then PCI is indicated. PCI is termed *rescue* or *salvage* when it is performed after failed fibrinolytic therapy in a patient who is actively ischemic.

Emergency PCI is also beneficial in reducing mortality in patients who experience cardiogenic shock as an early complication of acute MI. PCI is not beneficial when cardiogenic shock is the result of a mechanical complication, such as papillary muscle or septal rupture (Dirks & Waters, 2014; Levine et al., 2011).

Vein Graft Stenosis After Coronary Artery Bypass Grafting

Patients with acute graft closure (vein graft or arterial conduit) within 30 days of surgery usually can safely undergo successful PCI to the focal area of stenosis. PCI across suture lines has been accomplished safely within 10 days of surgery (Levine et al., 2011).

Vein graft disease can produce very serious and unstable lesions. It can be caused by hyperplasia or atherosclerosis. Vein grafts are at a particularly high risk for development of brittle plaques and thrombotic occlusions. These lesions are very complex (Levine et al., 2011).

Patients with late vein graft stenosis (longer than 5 years after surgery) in a graft supplying the LAD coronary artery and patients with more than one stenotic vein graft generally need repeat CABG (Hillis et al., 2011; Levine et al., 2011). Vein graft stenosis that occurs within 5 years of the time of surgery may be able to be effectively treated with PCI. Unfortunately, the use of glycoprotein IIb/IIIa inhibitors has failed to substantially improve results of PCI for vein graft stenosis (Levine et al., 2011). Ischemia that occurs more than 1 year after CABG can represent new stenosis within the graft or new native vessel disease.

One of the challenges of PCI for vein graft stenosis is the unique brittle nature of the plaques, which can cause embolization of graft material. Extraction devices to remove

thrombi before intervention have been helpful in preventing distal embolization. In addition, devices have been developed to catch this debris and protect the patient from distal embolization. Distal protection devices include balloons or filters that are deployed distal to the site of intervention to collect debris that dislodges during the procedure. The goal is to prevent small amounts of myocardial damage that can occur because of distal embolization.

Medications Before, During, and After Percutaneous Catheter Intervention

Oral hypoglycemic agents are usually withheld the morning of PCI procedures because of the patient's nothing by mouth status. Metformin should be held for 24 to 48 hours before the procedure and should continue to be held for 48 hours after the procedure because of the potential for renal toxicity (Levine et al., 2011).

Aspirin should be given before PCI. Patients coming in for elective procedures should be instructed to take aspirin at home. If the patient is on clopidogrel at home, it is also continued and taken before the procedure. If the patient is receiving low-molecular-weight heparin before the procedure, it is typically held the morning of the procedure. If the patient is going to have the procedure done more than 8 hours from the holding of the dose, UFH can be started to maintain adequate anticoagulation before the procedure.

UFH is the anticoagulant of choice during PCI. A glycoprotein IIb/IIIa inhibitor is also typically initiated during the procedure and continued for several hours after the procedure. If a glycoprotein IIb/IIIa is used during the procedure, then UFH dosages are lowered. UFH is not routinely continued postprocedure in uncomplicated patients, and this has helped reduce the number of vascular complications (Levine et al., 2011). Bivalirudin is an alternative anticoagulant that can be used during interventional procedures. When bivalirudin is used as the anticoagulant, a glycoprotein IIb/IIIa inhibitor is not needed in low-risk patients.

Additional antiplatelet therapy is initiated before or during the procedure and continued afterward. Typically, ≥300 mg clopidogrel (or 60 mg prasugrel) is given as a loading dose before, during, or immediately after the procedure (Levine et al., 2011). Patients with non-STEMI who are at high risk and are receiving an invasive strategy should have both clopidogrel (or prasugrel) and a glycoprotein IIb/IIIa inhibitor initiated before procedure, preferably as soon as possible. Clopidogrel (75 mg) or prasugrel (10 mg) daily is continued for a recommended 12 months in patients with bare metal stents. The absolute minimum time of 1 month in patients with bare metal stents can be used in patients at high risk for bleeding. The minimum duration of therapy for daily clopidogrel or prasugrel is 12 months for all drug-eluting stents. Many patients with drug-eluting stents will remain on clopidogrel or prasugrel indefinitely. In addition to taking clopidogrel or prasugrel after stenting procedures, patients will go home on aspirin dosages of 100 to 325 mg daily for a period of time, before having the dose lowered to a maintenance level of 75 to 162 mg daily (Levine et al., 2011).

The administration of aspirin and clopidogrel after stenting procedures is referred to as dual-antiplatelet therapy. Dual-antiplatelet therapy must be continued until the stent is completely endothelialized and no longer thrombogenic. Drug-eluting stents take longer to endothelialize than bare metal stents because the eluting drug is inhibiting tissue growth. Premature discontinuation of dual-antiplatelet therapy can result in the serious complication of late in-stent thrombosis, which most often results in MI. It is recommended that the interventional cardiologist discuss the patient's abil-

ity to comply with dual-antiplatelet therapy for the recommended time frame before implanting a drug-eluting stent. If there are any concerns, a bare metal stent can be used instead (Levine et al., 2011).

NURSING APPLICATION

Many patients have financial barriers to medication compliance. This is of particular concern with patients who have clopidogrel requirements after stenting procedures. In addition, many patients see multiple physicians and may be scheduled for procedures during which the physician would prefer the patient stop clopidogrel. Therefore, it is important for the nurse to specifically ask patients about their ability to afford clopidogrel therapy and to refer patients as appropriate to manufacturer assistance programs and other available resources. In addition, patients must know that only their interventional cardiologist can give permission for them to discontinue their clopidogrel. Any request by another physician must be cleared by the cardiologist.

Before PCI, it is important to assess for allergy to iodine-based contrast agents. If a patient has never been exposed to an iodine-based contrast agent, assess for an allergy to shellfish because many contain organic iodine. If a patient has an iodine allergy, he or she will be premedicated with steroids and antihistamines to avoid an anaphylactic reaction.

Intraprocedure Considerations

Patients normally receive conscious sedation during PCI. Arterial access is achieved with sheath insertion, most typically via the femoral artery or radial artery. If the femoral or radial artery cannot be accessed, then the brachial artery can be used, but this is rare. Radial access is now being used more frequently to minimize the postprocedure vascular complications. Common procedure technique involves the threading of a guidewire across the lesion, followed by the advancement of the interventional device over the guidewire. Heparin is typically the anticoagulant used during the procedure to avoid thrombotic complications associated with the insertion of foreign devices. Bedside activated clotting times are monitored during the procedure to assure the appropriate level of anticoagulation. Ischemia from balloon inflation may cause or increase dysrhythmias during the procedure. Isotonic crystalloid agents are recommended in patients with chronic kidney disease to protect renal function. For those patients with any renal dysfunction, doses of renally cleared drugs should be adjusted (Levine et al., 2011).

Postprocedure Nursing Care

A major focus of postprocedure nursing care is the prevention of complications related to the vascular access site. The arterial sheath is generally removed 4 to 6 hours after the procedure, or as soon as clotting times allow, unless a vascular closure device is used. Upon return to the nursing unit, bedside activated clotting times are drawn until they return to acceptable levels and the arterial sheath can be safely removed.

After the arterial access sheath is removed, hemostasis is a priority. Hemostasis can be achieved with manual pressure, the use of a C-clamp, or the use of a commercial compression device. Pressure is applied for a minimum of 20 minutes to achieve hemostasis. An increasing number of interventional cardiologists are using the radial artery as an access site to minimize the bleeding complications often associated with groin access. Use of the radial artery allows for increased patient comfort and mobility, as well as easier access for holding pressure during sheath removal (Dirks & Waters, 2014).

If a vascular closure device is used, the arterial sheath is removed in the interventional laboratory. The most common vascular closure devices and their mechanisms of action are described in Table 18-2. The benefits of vascular closure devices include improved patient comfort and earlier ambulation. Associated risks of these devices include

- infection,
- bleeding from the site,
- leg ischemia (which can potentially result in the need for vascular surgery),
- vasovagal response (with or after arterial sheath removal),
- hypotension,
- bradycardia,
- diaphoresis, and nausea and vomiting.

(Deelstra, 2010)

These responses are often triggered by pain and anxiety associated with the sheath removal process. If the patient is hypovolemic, the response is exaggerated. Treatment involves fluids, atropine, and whenever possible, the elimination of pain and anxiety.

After arterial sheath removal, the access site should be frequently assessed for external bleeding or development of a hematoma. A hematoma occurs when there is a collection of blood in the soft tissue.

NURSING APPLICATION

Nurses should instruct patients who are post-PCI to immediately report any feeling of warmth or moisture, which may indicate bleeding, and any new burning at the insertion site, which commonly accompanies the development of a hematoma.

TABLE 18-2: COMMON VASCULAR CLOSURE DEVICES AND MECHANISMS OF ACTION

Closure Device	Mechanism of Action
VasoSeal	• Collagen delivered to surface of femoral artery (extravascular) • Platelets attracted to collagen and seal is formed • Collagen reabsorbs in 6 weeks
Angio-Seal	• Seals the puncture site between two absorbable structures: suture anchor below and collagen plug above • Structures dissolve within 90 days
Perclose	• Arteriotomy is sutured for immediate hemostasis
StarClose	• Staples are used to create a purse-string closure
Duett	• Liquid mixture of thrombin and collagen is delivered to puncture site

Note. Adapted from Dirks J., & Waters, J. (2014). Cardiovascular therapeutic management. In L. D. Urden, K. M. Stacy, & M. E. Lough (Eds.), *Critical care nursing: Diagnosis and management* (7th ed., pp. 200-221). St. Louis, MO: Elsevier/Mosby.

Pressure is applied to treat bleeding or hematoma formation that occurs after arterial sheath removal. Most hematomas are self-limiting and resolve without further treatment. Hematomas can result in femoral nerve compression (Levine et al., 2011). Any large hematoma should be assessed for a pulsatile mass or the presence of a bruit. These assessment findings can indicate the presence of a pseudoaneurysm. A pseudoaneurysm occurs when hemostasis does not produce an adequate amount of thrombus formation at the puncture site. This lack of thrombus leaves a communicating track between the artery and surrounding tissue. Ultrasound can confirm the presence of a pseudoaneurysm. Large pseudoaneurysms will require treatment with either ultrasound-guided compression or ultrasound-guided thrombin injection. Surgical intervention may be required if these treatments are not successful.

In addition, nurses must frequently assess for other potential neurovascular complications. Nursing assessment includes frequent pulse, pain, and sensation checks to the area distal to the insertion site. After sheath removal, these assessments are typically done every 15 minutes for the first hour and then with decreasing frequency if the patient remains free from complications.

The clinical nursing trial Standards of Angioplasty Nursing Techniques to Diminish Bleeding Around the Groin found effective nursing interventions in preventing postprocedure groin bleeding (see Box 18-4; Deelstra, 2010).

Adequate hydration is not only an important postprocedure consideration but also a preprocedure component to prevent renal complications related to contrast administration. Nothing by mouth status before the procedure increases the importance of IV hydration. Hydration with 0.9% normal saline solution is considered the gold standard in preventing contrast-induced nephropathy. Other strategies that are sometimes used to prevent contrast-induced nephropathy include hydration with a sodium bicarbonate drip (154 mEq sodium bicarbonate/L) and pretreatment with *N*-acetylcysteine. These treatments have been the subject of some research but are not yet included in evidence-based practice guidelines. Evidence-based practice guidelines support the use of isosmolar contrast agents in patients with chronic kidney disease (Levine et al., 2011).

BOX 18-4: SHEATH REMOVAL STANDARDS TO REDUCE BLEEDING

- Nurse-to-patient ratio of 1:1.5 or less during the sheath removal process

- Prompt removal of the sheath within 4 to 6 hours of the procedure

- Patient comfort measures, including pain medication and head of bed elevation to 30 degrees

- Avoidance of a sandbag, which has been shown not to decrease bleeding but to increase discomfort

- Patient ambulation 8 hours after sheath removal

Note. Adapted from Deelstra, M. H. (2010). Interventional cardiology techniques: Percutaneous coronary intervention. In S. L. Woods, E. S. S. Froelicher, S. U. Motzer, & E. J. Bridges (Eds.), *Cardiac nursing* (6th ed., pp. 537-554). Philadelphia, PA: Lippincott Williams & Wilkins.

Assessment of blood urea nitrogen and creatinine levels is important in the postprocedure evaluation. Whenever possible, nephrotoxic drugs should be held for 48 hours before and after PCI. Examples of common nephrotoxic drugs include metformin, NSAIDs, and some antibiotics. Metformin is important because patients with diabetes have an increased risk for development of postprocedure nephropathy.

Patients should also be monitored for recurrent ischemia after PCI. The ST-segment should be monitored in the leads evaluating the vessel receiving intervention. Any chest pain postprocedure should be evaluated with a 12-lead electrocardiogram. There are several causes of chest pain after an interventional procedure (Levine et al., 2011), including

- sensation from the presence of the stent, which is benign;

- transient spasm of a vessel;

- occlusion of the side branch;

- distal embolization of microemboli; and

- acute vessel closure or acute thrombosis.

Chest pain as a result of acute vessel closure or acute thrombosis warrants a return visit to the interventional laboratory.

Many patients are cared for in specialized postinterventional units. Patients without complications who undergo elective procedures are discharged within 24 hours. Some institutions have same-day discharges for uncomplicated interventions. Patients undergoing PCI during an acute MI have extended stays that vary based on the amount of myocardial damage.

Patients who underwent elective PCI are generally discharged the day after the procedure or even the same day, limiting time during the inpatient hospital stay for patient education regarding risk-factor reduction. Nurses should encourage these patients to participate in outpatient cardiac rehabilitation programs so they can receive the same education and support for risk-factor modification as those who have had CABG. Nurses should place special emphasis on the importance of addressing risk reduction (see Box 18-5) to manage disease progression in patients undergoing PCI procedures (Dirks & Waters, 2014).

NURSING APPLICATION

Because PCI has a shorter recovery period than CABG and does not provide the long-term reminder of a midsternal scar, patients may minimize the importance of their coronary heart disease and their future risks. It is important to help patients fully understand that PCI does not treat their underlying disease process and that aggressive risk reduction is critical in managing underlying cardiac disease.

BOX 18-5: CARDIOVASCULAR DISEASE RISK REDUCTION

- Smoking cessation
- Reduce salt intake
- Reduce daily fat intake to less than 30% of total calories
- Reduce total serum cholesterol to less than 200 mg/dl
- Reduce low-density lipoprotein (LDL) cholesterol to less than 70 mg/dl
- Increase physical activity to at least 30 minutes per day, 5 days per week
- Control hypertension to recommended parameters
- Control diabetes to hemoglobin A1C less than 7 mg/dl
- Achieve ideal body weight
- Reduce emotional stress and anger
- Continue regular annual and follow-up clinician appointments

Note. Adapted from Dirks, J., & Waters, J. (2014). Cardiovascular therapeutic management. In L. D. Urden, K. M. Stacy, & M. E. Lough (Eds.), *Critical care nursing: Diagnosis and management* (7th ed., pp. 200-221). St. Louis, MO: Elsevier/Mosby.

CASE STUDY

A 57-year-old male patient visits the cardiology clinic reporting a 3-month history of worsening anginal chest pain, which he describes as a heaviness in his chest when he exerts himself. The pain is promptly relieved with rest but is associated with diaphoresis and dyspnea. He goes to the cardiology clinic because these symptoms have been lasting longer after rest, and yesterday, he had the pain while at rest after a heavy meal.

The patient is moderately obese with a history of hypertension that is controlled with an angiotensin-converting enzyme inhibitor. He takes pantoprazole for a history of gastric esophageal reflux disease and simvastatin for a history of dyslipidemia. He includes a baby aspirin, vitamin D, and melatonin in his daily home medications as well. His surgical history includes bilateral inguinal hernia repair, cholecystectomy, and an arthroscopic right knee surgery. He was a social smoker and quit smoking "several years ago." He drinks alcohol once or twice a month when he and his wife eat out for dinner. He is employed with an information technology firm as a security analyst.

A 12-lead electrocardiogram is performed in the clinic and is unchanged from his prior electrocardiogram on file. Nevertheless, because of the progression of his symptoms, the cardiology nurse practitioner refers him to the cardiologist for evaluation of the need for a coronary angiogram.

The cardiologist agrees the patient needs an angiogram, and it is conducted on the same day as his cardiology appointment. The angiogram reveals severe triple-vessel CAD with 70% left main coronary artery stenosis, 90% obstructive lesions in the LAD and right coronary arteries, and an 80% obstructive lesion in the first obtuse marginal ramus. The cardiologist also evaluates the patient's heart valves, finding a normally functioning aortic valve and a moderately stenotic mitral valve with vegetative debris. The cardiologist consults cardiothoracic surgery to evaluate the patient for CABG and mitral valve repair.

Questions

1. What are the patient's indications for CABG? Why did the cardiologist consult the cardiothoracic surgeon and not attempt PCI for the patient?

2. Which preoperative patient education will the nurse provide to the patient if heart surgery is scheduled?

Answers

1. The patient has three-vessel disease and left main CAD, which are indications for CABG over PCI. CABG also allows revascularization to occlude small-diameter vessels that are not accessible by catheter-based techniques. Because of its durability and the lower need for repeat revascularization procedures, CABG remains the preferred reperfusion strategy for most patients with multivessel CAD.

2. The nurse will educate the patient and his family about the possible complications that can occur during or after cardiac surgery (i.e., low cardiac output state, neurological complications, systemic inflammatory response, etc.) and the postoperative strategies that are ordered to prevent some of these complications. The nurse will explain any medications that the patient may need to take after surgery and will review the need for CAD risk-factor modification and follow-up visits with the clinician after surgery.

   Providing patient and family education related to possible complications can help the patient understand the postoperative routine of care and significance of postoperative activities such as deep breathing, sitting in the chair, and ambulating as directed. The family can help support the patient during these activities and, by doing so, will be familiar with what the patient may need at home after discharge.

SUMMARY

Advancements continue to improve the safety and outcomes associated with CABG and PCI revascularization options. These advancements improve treatment options and outcomes for patients with CAD.

With the increasing older adult population, the number of revascularization procedures continues to increase. The impact of nursing care for patients before, during, and after revascularization procedures is critical to good patient outcomes. Revascularization does not alter the underlying disease process; therefore, patient education and risk-factor reduction remain key nursing elements in all settings.

EXAM QUESTIONS

CHAPTER 18
Questions 88–94

Note: Choose the one option that BEST answers each question.

88. Which revascularization strategy reroutes blood around areas of long stenosis in coronary arteries?

    a. Rotational atherectomy

    b. Transmyocardial laser revascularization

    c. Percutaneous coronary intervention (PCI) procedures

    d. Coronary artery bypass graft (CABG) surgery

89. An indication for CABG surgery is

    a. single-vessel disease with greater than 50% occlusion.

    b. multivessel disease with decreasing left ventricular function.

    c. permanently eliminating all occurrences of angina.

    d. needing a less costly intervention compared with PCI.

90. Which medication should be continued throughout preoperative and postoperative CABG care?

    a. Nitroglycerin

    b. Aspirin

    c. Ibuprofen

    d. Warfarin

91. Which revascularization conduit has the best long-term patency outcome when bypassed to the left anterior descending artery?

    a. Saphenous vein graft

    b. Radial artery graft

    c. Gastroepiploic artery graft

    d. Left internal mammary graft

92. Which patient has the highest risk for mediastinitis after CABG surgery?

    a. A patient with reduced left ventricular function

    b. An older adult patient

    c. A patient with diabetes

    d. A patient with heart failure

93. Which drug education information is most appropriate for the post-PCI patient before discharge?

    a. "Continue metformin while in the hospital."

    b. "Stop prasugrel in 2 weeks."

    c. "Continue aspirin indefinitely."

    d. "Stop clopidogrel on postop day 5."

94. What is considered the gold standard for preventing contrast-induced nephropathy in patients undergoing PCI?

    a. 0.9% Sodium chloride

    b. Metformin

    c. Aspirin

    d. Acetylcysteine

REFERENCES

Amsterdam, E. A., Wenger, N. K., Brindis, R. G., Casey, D. E., Ganiats, T. G., Holmes, D. R., ... Zieman, S. J. (2014). 2014 AHA/ACC guideline for the management of patients with non-ST-elevation acute coronary syndromes: A report of the American College of Cardiology/American Heart Association Task Force on Practice Guidelines. *Circulation, 130*(25), e344-e426. doi:10.1161/CIR.0000000000000134

Anderson, K. M. (2016). *The advanced practice nurse cardiovascular clinician.* New York, NY: Springer Publishing.

Bonow, R. O. (2013). Guidelines for revascularization: The evidence base matures. *Global Cardiology Science & Practice, 2012*(2), 29-35. doi:10.5339/gcsp.2012.21

Cremer, J., Schoettler, J., Thiem, A., Grothusen, C., & Hoffman, G. (2011). The MIDCAB approach in its various dimensions. *HSR Proceedings in Intensive Care & Cardiovascular Anesthesia, 3*(4), 249-253.

Deelstra, M. H. (2010). Interventional cardiology techniques: Percutaneous coronary intervention. In S. L. Woods, E. S. S. Froelicher, S. U. Motzer, & E. J. Bridges (Eds.), *Cardiac nursing* (6th ed., pp. 537-554). Philadelphia, PA: Lippincott Williams & Wilkins.

Dirks, J. (2009). Cardiac surgery. In K. K. Carlson (Ed.), *Advanced critical care nursing.* Bellevue, WA: Saunders-Elsevier.

Dirks, J., & Waters, J. (2014). Cardiovascular therapeutic management. In L. D. Urden, K. M. Stacy, & M. E. Lough (Eds.), *Critical care nursing: Diagnosis and management* (7th ed., pp. 200-221). St. Louis, MO: Elsevier/Mosby.

Fihn, S. D., Blankenship, J. C., Alexander, K. P., Bittl, J. A., Byrne, J. G., Fletcher, B. J., ... Smith, P. K. (2014). 2014 ACC/AHA/AATS/PCNA/SCAI/STS focused update of the guideline for the diagnosis and management of patients with stable ischemic heart disease: A report of the American College of Cardiology/American Heart Association Task Force on Practice Guidelines, and the American Association for Thoracic Surgery, Preventive Cardiovascular Nurses Association, Society for Cardiovascular Angiography and Interventions, and Society of Thoracic Surgeons. *Circulation, 130*(19), 1749-1767. doi:10.1161/CIR.0000000000000095

Hillis, L. D., Smith, P. K., Anderson, J. L., Bittl, J. A., Bridges, C. R., Gyrne, J. G., ... Winniford, M. D. (2011). 2011 ACCF/AHA guideline for coronary artery bypass graft surgery: A report of the American College of Cardiology Foundation/American Heart Association Task Force on Practice Guidelines. *Circulation, 124*(23), e652-e735. doi:10.1161/CIR.0b013e31823c074e

Hughes, J., & Platt, K. (2010). Minimally invasive cardiac surgery. In S. R. Hardin & R. Kaplow (Eds.), *Cardiac surgery essentials for critical care nursing* (pp. 93-114). Sudbury, MA: Jones & Bartlett Publishers, LLC.

January, C. T., Wann, L. S., Alpert, J. S., Calkins, H., Cigarroa, J. E., Cleveland, J. C., ... Yancy, C. W. (2014). 2014 AHA/ACC/HRS guideline for the management of patients with atrial fibrillation: Executive summary: A report of the American College of Cardiology/ American Heart Association Task Force on Practice Guidelines and the Heart Rhythm Society. *Circulation, 130*(23), 2071-2104. doi:10.1161/CIR.0000000000000040

Levine, G. N., Bates, E. R., Blankenship, J. C., Bailey, S. R., Bittle, J. A., Cercek, B., ... Ting, H. H. (2011). 2011 ACCF/AHA/ SCAI guideline for percutaneous coronary intervention: A report of the American College of Cardiology Foundation/American Heart Association Task Force on Practice Guidelines and the Society for Cardiovascular Angiography and Interventions. *Circulation, 124*(23), e574-e651. doi:10.1161/CIR.0b01 3e31823ba622

Miller, J. (2010). Cardiopulmonary bypass and off-pump coronary artery bypass. In S. R. Hardin & R. Kaplow (Eds.), *Cardiac surgery essentials for critical care nursing* (pp. 115-126). Sudbury, MA: Jones & Bartlett Publishers, LLC.

Mozaffarian, D., Benjamin, E. J., Go, A. S., Arnett, D. K., Blaha, M. J., Cushman, M., ... Turner, M. B. (2015). Heart disease and stroke statistics – 2015 update: A report from the American Heart Association. *Circulation, 131*(4), e29-e322. doi:10.1161/ CIR.0000000000000152

Selnes, O. A., Gottesman, R. F., Grega, M. A., Baumgartner, W. A., Zeger, S. L., & McKhann, G. M. (2012). Cognitive and neurologic outcomes after coronary-artery bypass surgery. *New England Journal of Medicine, 366*(3), 250-257. doi:10.1056/ NEJMra1100109

CHAPTER 19

CARDIOVASCULAR HISTORY, HEALTH ASSESSMENT, AND PHYSICAL EXAMINATION

LEARNING OUTCOME

After completing this chapter, the learner will be able to identify the components of a comprehensive history and physical examination of the cardiovascular system.

CHAPTER OBJECTIVES

After completing this chapter, the learner will be able to:

1. Identify subjective data pertinent to obtaining a thorough health history.

2. Identify risk factors for cardiovascular disease from a patient's health history.

3. Recognize the multiple risk factors used to calculate a validated cardiovascular disease risk score.

4. Differentiate cardiovascular physical examination findings as healthy or pathological.

INTRODUCTION

Cardiovascular disease places large health and financial burdens on patients and healthcare systems within the United States and globally (Mozaffarian et al., 2016). The cardiovascular nurse must conduct a thorough health history and physical examination utilizing fundamental knowledge of anatomy, physiology, pathophysiology, and epidemiology. Utilizing this knowledge and the knowledge gained from the health history and examination should facilitate the stratification (prioritization) of risk factors in the effort to reduce the burdens of cardiovascular disease.

PATIENT HEALTH HISTORY: SUBJECTIVE AND OBJECTIVE MEASURES

Identification of the patient's primary reason for seeking health care is the key element in conducting an adequate clinical evaluation and developing a management plan. The chief complaint should be documented as a very brief statement, such as "I felt dizzy when standing and thought I would pass out." The nurse should identify whether the complaint is an acute or a chronic symptom. To do this, the nurse should use the described symptoms to apply a prioritized line of questioning to gain historical data to help differentiate symptoms of an acute or chronic problem. If the symptoms are aligned with an acute problem, the registered nurse (RN) should communicate these findings to a medical provider (e.g., nurse practitioner, physician, or physician's assistant) to initiate a timely and focused examination and diagnostic and management plan.

Patients also seek care for routine screenings or annual checkups. During these encounters, it is important that the clinician still completes a very thorough health history and physical examination to evaluate the patient's risk for cardiovascular illness. Health-promotion visits provide the nurse an opportunity to apply primary prevention counseling to prevent or delay the onset of cardiovascular disease.

The patient's history is very important to the clinical evaluation and management of cardiovascular illness. Careful and thorough questioning during the interview requires the clinician's use of good listening and communication skills.

Patient Demographics

The person providing the history is known as the historian. Preferably, the historian is the patient. However, there are circumstances in which the patient cannot provide the history, and it is given by accompanying family, friends, or passersby or witnesses to a cardiac event. In addition, some patients are not capable of providing a reliable history because of cognitive disorders such as encephalopathy or dementia. It is important for the clinician to identify the individual who provides the history and to determine whether the individual is a reliable source when documenting the history. Details about the historian are useful when conflicting information is present in the health history (Anderson, 2016).

Age

The patient's age is a nonbehavioral (or nonmodifiable) risk factor, but age can be a risk factor for particular cardiac illnesses across the lifespan. For instance, when a child presents with signs or symptoms of cardiovascular disease, they are usually related to congenital anomalies, acquired infectious illness, or developing autoimmune illness, whereas an older adult (>65 years old) is expected to have sys-

tolic hypertension as a result of the physiological changes that occur with aging. Noting the patient's age can help the clinician differentiate common cardiovascular pathologies that occur across the lifespan (Anderson, 2016).

Gender

The patient's gender is another nonbehavioral risk factor the clinician can utilize when applying knowledge of the epidemiological prevalence of disease. For instance, hypertension is more prevalent in male individuals at younger ages than female individuals (Mozaffarian et al., 2016).

Ethnicity

Ethnicity is another nonbehavioral risk factor. Clinicians must feel comfortable enough to ask what the patient's ethnicity is because it should not be assumed from the patient's appearance. Identification of the patient's ethnicity will help the clinician to identify associated risks the patient may have for cardiovascular disease. For instance, (non-Hispanic) African Americans have a higher prevalence of hypertension at younger ages than their White, Asian or Pacific Islander, and Hispanic counterparts (Anderson, 2016; Mozaffarian et al., 2016).

Common Chief Cardiovascular Complaints

Chest Pain. Clinicians must differentiate cardiac from noncardiac chest pain. Noncardiac chest pain can be caused by pulmonary, gastrointestinal (GI), musculoskeletal, psychiatric, or other systemic illnesses that increase oxygen demand (Amsterdam et al., 2014). This chapter's discussion focuses on angina. When the patient identifies angina, the clinician must then determine whether the symptoms are related to acute ischemia or stable ischemic heart disease. Factors to consider when determining whether the angina is related to acute ischemia include age, history of symptoms, gender, prior history of coronary artery disease (CAD), and the number of traditional cardiovascular disease risk factors (Amsterdam et al., 2014).

The most common presentation of angina is poorly localized chest pain or arm pain that is reproducible with exertion or emotional stress. Angina associated with non-ST-segment elevation acute coronary syndrome (ACS) involves a pressure-type pain that occurs at rest or with minimal exertion and lasting more than 10 minutes. The pain characteristically starts in the retrosternal area and radiates to one or both arms, the neck, or the jaw. The pain can also occur in any one or more of these areas independent from chest pain. Patients most often report associated symptoms of diaphoresis, dyspnea, nausea, syncope, and abdominal pain. Exertional dyspnea that is unexplainable and increasingly worsens is the most common anginal equivalent. Other presentations that less commonly occur include complaints of unexplainable fatigue, nausea and vomiting, and diaphoresis. Clinicians must recognize that women, older adults, and patients with dementia, impaired renal function, or diabetes can present with atypical symptoms of epigastric pain, indigestion, pleuritic pain, or increasing dyspnea in the absence of chest pain (Amsterdam et al., 2014).

It is important for the clinician to note factors that relieve the chest pain. Clinicians must acknowledge that the relief of chest pain with nitroglycerin is not predictive of ACS. Also, pain relieved by GI medications (e.g., GI cocktails, antacids, or viscous lidocaine) is not predictive of the absence of ACS (Amsterdam et al., 2014).

Patients most often describe angina associated with aortic dissection as a severe tearing or ripping pain originating in the back between the scapulae and radiating to the chest. Associated symptoms often include anxiety and/or the feeling of impending doom, diaphoresis, dyspnea, and syncope (Amsterdam et al., 2014).

Shortness of Breath. As mentioned earlier, shortness of breath can manifest as an anginal equivalent, and the clinician should correlate this finding with other clinical findings (e.g., examination findings and diagnostic studies) to differentiate possible diagnoses (Amsterdam et al., 2014). When probing the complaint of dyspnea, clinicians should inquire about the onset, duration, timing, and associated aggravating and temporal factors. For example, the onset of dyspnea with acute pulmonary embolism is most often sudden, whereas the onset of pulmonary edema related to decompensating heart failure is insidious with progressive worsening (Anderson, 2016).

Palpitations. Patients with palpitations often describe them as a fast heartbeat, an erratic heartbeat, or a pounding in the chest that may or may not be fast. Patients often say that their heart was "racing" or "skipped a beat." Clinicians should ask about the onset, duration, and timing of this symptom to help narrow the possible causes. Clinicians should also inquire about specific triggers of palpitations, such as caffeine intake, fatigue, stimulant use (e.g., medications, marijuana, or over-the-counter decongestants), and alcohol use (Anderson, 2016; Anderson et al., 2013; Priori et al., 2015).

Syncope. Syncope is a transient loss of consciousness in which patients report passing out or "blacking out." This condition is often preceded by symptoms such as sudden weakness, diaphoresis, light-headedness, dyspnea, chest pain, and nausea and/or vomiting. Because of these presyncopal symptoms, many patients sit or lie down before falling to the ground. When driving, patients may even have a chance to pull over. These symptoms are most often related to a decrease in cerebral blood flow caused by tachyarrhythmias or bradyarrhythmias, or a vasovagal reaction (e.g., such as when straining to have a bowel movement). These symptoms can also occur with postural changes secondary to hypovolemia or medications (e.g., beta blockers).

Syncope can also occur with no warning. Patients may describe standing at the kitchen counter one minute and waking up on the floor the next. When such events are unwitnessed, there may be vital pieces of the history that the patient cannot remember. These types of syncope events are most often related to nonsustained ventricular tachyarrhythmias. Because patients often injure themselves during the fall (Anderson, 2016; Priori et al., 2015), clinicians must inquire whether the patient injured his or her head during the fall and whether the patient's home medications include an anticoagulant or antiplatelet to mitigate the patient's risks for stroke or other bleeding injuries.

Leg Pain Related to Cardiovascular Problems

Peripheral arterial disease (PAD) is associated with acute leg pain, often in the calf, that occurs with ambulation and is relieved with rest within 10 minutes. Pain associated with PAD or peripheral artery insufficiency is known as claudication (Anderson et al., 2013). Clinicians must recognize that the patient with PAD can experience acute arterial occlusion, with the accompanying risk of losing the tissue distal to the occlusion if surgical intervention is not initiated in a timely manner. Clinicians can ask the patient whether the pain is perceived at rest (ischemic rest pain) or only with walking. The clinician should also ask the patient about the presence of nonhealing wounds.

The pain associated with peripheral venous disease most often has an insidious onset that progressively worsens. Patients describe the leg pain associated with this condition as dull or as discomfort. Patients also complain about having varicose veins and not liking the appearance of the affected extremity (Anderson, 2016). Clinicians must recognize that this condition is not urgent but reduces the patient's quality of life.

History of Present Illness

The clinician can use open-ended questions to help the patient articulate a comprehensive reason for seeking care. For instance, the clinician may ask, "Why did you come to the hospital today?" In response, the patient will attempt to explain the reason and may provide many of the details the clinician needs, such as the onset, duration, and severity of the problem. Clinicians can use the acronym OLD CARTS (onset, location, duration, character, aggravating/associated factors, relieving factors, temporal factors/timing, severity) to ensure that they have documented the details needed for a comprehensive history of present illness (Anderson, 2016).

Onset

The exact time or date when the patient began to experience the illness or health issue is key information for the history, but patient recollections are sometimes vague. The clinician can probe for more specific details regarding the onset by asking questions such as the following: Did this start while you were at rest or during exertion or exercise? Were you eating? Were you sleeping when it occurred? Did this start all of a sudden or gradually? Probing questions can help the clinician differentiate acute and chronic cardiac problems (Anderson, 2016).

Location

The clinician must recognize that the location of the complaint is another important factor of the history. In some cases, the patient may not be able to provide anatomical references but can help the clinician by pointing to the problem area or region. Location is a factor of the history of present illness that can become more complex when the complaint involves multiple regions of the body. For instance, if the patient complains of diffuse pain, it is important for the clinician to document not only where the pain started but also the path along which it moved, or radiated, to another body part (Anderson, 2016).

Duration

Inquiring about the time frame of the patient's complaint helps the clinician in further differentiating the characteristics of acute or chronic cardiac problems. Clinicians should determine the duration of the complaint and whether it is constant or intermittent. Clinicians can assist the patient in providing this information by asking whether the complaint lasts for minutes, hours, or days (Anderson, 2016).

Character

The character of the problem refers to the nature of its development and how it feels to the patient. Clinicians can probe this component of the history by asking whether the complaint involves a sharp, dull, heavy, achy, tearing, or ripping sensation (Anderson, 2016).

Aggravating/Associated Factors

Aggravating and associated factors of the complaint can be key information for the clinician's problem identification or diagnosis. Asking the patient what makes the complaint worse and what other problems occur secondary to the chief complaint addresses this part of the history of present illness. For instance, patient complaints of chest pain that is worsened with exertion and associated with diaphoresis and dyspnea are highly associated with an ACS (Mozaffarian et al., 2016).

Relieving Factors

Asking the patient if anything has made the complaint better also aids the clinician in making a diagnosis. For example, the clinician can ask whether the symptoms improve with rest, over-the-counter medications, or application of heat or cold to the affected area (Anderson, 2016).

Temporal Findings/Timing

The temporal findings/timing component of OLD CARTS is often confused with the duration component. The timing of the complaint involves the frequency with which it occurs and other factors surrounding the onset of the complaint, such as shortness of breath that the patient experiences daily when climbing steps and walking to the mailbox, or shortness of breath that the patient has experienced every night after lying down for the past week but was not present a month ago (Anderson, 2016).

Severity

Clinicians often measure the severity of the complaint as mild, moderate, or severe or with a score on a scale from 1 to 10. The severity or intensity of a symptom is subjective, but establishing a baseline by utilizing a scale or point of reference for a later comparison can help the clinician guide the diagnostic and treatment plan (Anderson, 2016).

Review of Systems

The clinician should use a systematic approach that addresses each organ system when conducting a thorough review of systems (ROS). Table 19-1 illustrates components from each organ system that the clinician should address during the ROS. If clinicians cannot complete a comprehensive ROS involving 10 or more organ systems, they should review a minimum of 3 organ systems that can be affected by the patient's cardiovascular complaint. Information that the clinician and patient have already discussed in the history of present illness does not need to be repeated in this section of the interview (Anderson, 2016). The Centers for Medicare and Medicaid Services (CMS) agency provides specific guidelines for the number of systems that the clinician must review for a problem-focused ROS and a comprehensive ROS

TABLE 19-1: COMPREHENSIVE REVIEW OF SYSTEMS

Organ System	Subjective Data
Constitutional (health in general)	Lack of energy, unexplained weight gain or weight loss, loss of appetite, fever, night sweats, pain in jaw when eating, scalp tenderness, prior diagnosis of cancer
Ears, nose, mouth, and throat	Difficulty with hearing, sinus problems, runny nose, postnasal drip, ringing in ears, mouth sores, loose teeth, ear pain, nosebleeds, sore throat, facial pain or numbness
Heart and blood vessels	Irregular heartbeat, racing heart, chest pain, swelling of feet or legs, pain in legs with walking
Lungs and breathing	Shortness of breath, night sweats, prolonged cough, wheezing, sputum production, prior tuberculosis, pleurisy, oxygen at home, coughing up blood, abnormal chest radiograph
Stomach and intestines	Heartburn, constipation, intolerance of certain foods, diarrhea, abdominal pain, difficulty swallowing, nausea, vomiting, blood in stool, unexplained change in bowel habits, incontinence
Kidney and bladder	Painful urination, frequent urination, urgency, prostate problems, bladder problems, impotence
Muscles, bones, and joints	Joint pain, aching muscles, shoulder pain, swelling of joints, joint deformities, back pain
Skin, hair, and breast	Persistent rash, itching, new skin lesion, change in existing skin lesion, hair loss or increase, breast changes
Brain and nerves	Frequent headaches, double vision, weakness, change in sensation, problems with walking or balance, dizziness, tremor, loss of consciousness, uncontrolled motions, episodes of visual loss
Mood and thinking (psychiatric)	Insomnia, irritability, depression, anxiety, recurrent bad thoughts, mood swings, hallucinations, compulsions
Endocrinological (glands)	Intolerance of heat or cold, menstrual irregularities, frequent hunger/urination/thirst, changes in sex drive
Hematological (blood/lymph)	Easy bleeding, easy bruising, anemia, abnormal blood tests, leukemia, unexplained swollen areas
Allergic/ Immunological	Seasonal allergies, hay-fever symptoms, itching, frequent infections, exposure to HIV

Note. Adapted from Anderson, K. M. (2016). *The advanced practice nurse cardiovascular clinician.* New York, NY: Springer.

(CMS, 2015). CMS guidelines for documentation are not in the purview of this chapter.

Allergies

Clinicians must identify the patient's allergy history, including any allergies to medications, latex, environmental allergens, and foods. In addition, the clinician must document the patient's reaction to the allergen to determine whether the patient's experience was a true allergic reaction or an intolerance. A true allergic reaction involves an immune response that results in hives, redness, itching, fever, chills, joint pain, rash, swollen glands, or anaphylaxis. When patients experience nausea or drowsiness from medications, the clinician should classify these reactions as mild adverse side effects or an intolerance (Anderson, 2016).

Medication History: Current Medications

The clinician should document all current medications that the patient takes (prescribed and nonprescribed) by listing the name of the drug, dose, route, frequency, indication, start date, and stop date (if applicable).

NURSING APPLICATION

Clinicians should educate patients to keep a current list of medications in their wallets at all times that includes this information.

With every visit, clinicians should verify the list of current medications; inquire about compliance, intolerance, and missed doses; and check for interactions. If patients report that they have stopped taking a medication or have missed doses, clinicians must identify the reason – intolerance, cost, misunderstanding, and so forth. Clinicians must also verify medication regimens when patients are discharged from the hospital because regular medications may be held until the patient attends a follow-up office visit (Anderson, 2016).

NURSING APPLICATION

Clinicians should educate patients to bring all hospital discharge paperwork to the follow-up office visit. This paperwork should include discharge medications that are new, resumed, or held.

During the cardiovascular history, inquiring about specific cardiovascular medications can also facilitate the collection of an accurate or complete medication list when the patient does not have a list of his or her own. Inquiring about antihypertensive classes such as beta blockers or angiotensin-converting enzyme inhibitors by name can assist the patient or family member's memory.

Medication History: Recently Used Medications

Patients may use some medications only intermittently, such as melatonin, acetaminophen, ibuprofen, or Maalox. Nevertheless, clinicians should inquire about all recently used medications because there is the potential for drug–drug interactions to occur (Anderson, 2016).

Antibiotics. Identifying whether the patient has taken antibiotics in the last 3 months is important when considering drug therapy for acute infectious illness (Anderson, 2016).

Over-the-Counter and Alternative Therapies. Identifying whether patients are taking over-the-counter medication is important when evaluating the patient's risk for drug–drug interactions. For instance, herbal substances such as ginger, ginkgo, or alfalfa can interact with anticoagulants and cause increased bleeding risks. Ibuprofen, which patients commonly take for mild pain, can interact with prednisone and cause GI bleeding and an increased risk for nephrotoxicity (Anderson, 2016).

Complementary/Alternative Therapies. Many patients today try to avoid conventional medicine regimens to reduce the amount of medications taken for health problems. In doing so, patients often seek care from homeopathists, naturopathists, and chiropractors. Other alternative strategies include the use of guided imagery or other meditation therapies. Health providers with expertise in these alternative therapies may prescribe herbal supplements and treatments or perform procedures that have the potential to cause injury to the patient. Thus, clinicians should also inquire about use of these therapies.

Social/Lifestyle History

Many of the following behavioral and nonbehavioral risk factors were discussed in Chapter 3. They are repeated in this chapter in the context of data collection during the patient history.

Smoking/Tobacco Use. Smoking is one of the leading risk factors for the development of cardiovascular disease (Anderson, 2016; Ford, Greenlund, & Hong, 2012). Approximately one third of all coronary heart disease deaths are attributable to smoking or secondhand smoke exposure (Mozaffarian et al., 2016). Clinicians must inquire about exposure to tobacco smoke directly (personal use of tobacco) or indirectly (from secondhand smoke exposure). This includes the use of chewing tobacco, cigarettes, cigars, and pipes. When inquiring about cigarette smoking, the clinician should document the amount of use in pack-years. For instance, if a patient reports smoking two packs per day for 20 years, the clinician can either document exactly what was reported or record the pack-years. Calculating pack-years involves multiplying the number of cigarettes smoked per day times the number of years that the patient has smoked. For instance, the patient who smokes two packs per day (which is 40 cigarettes per day, 20 per each pack) for 20 years has a tobacco exposure of 40 pack-years (Anderson, 2016). Research has shown a direct correlation between tobacco exposure in pack-years and the risk for lung disease such as lung cancer.

Alcohol or Illicit Drug Use. Moderate-to-heavy alcohol consumption causes an increase in blood pressure and a decrease in the production of high-density lipoprotein cholesterol (Anderson, 2016; Mozaffarian et al., 2016). Moderate alcohol consumption is defined by the American Heart Association (AHA) as one drink per day for women and two drinks per day for men (AHA, 2015). The AHA further defines one drink by specific amounts related to the type of alcohol consumed. Clinicians should inquire about the frequency, amount, and type of alcohol consumed to identify risks for cardiovascular disease. Patient education should focus on encouraging the patient to consume alcohol in moderation and manage behavioral risk factors to reduce risks for cardiovascular disease (Anderson, 2016).

Illicit drug use includes the recreational or prescription use of marijuana; the use of cocaine, crack, heroin, and other illegal drugs;

and the nonprescribed use of opioids, benzodiazepines, and methamphetamines. Screening patients for present or past use of these drugs informs the clinician of the potential for drug-related diseases and conditions, such as ischemic myocardial disease related to coronary vasospasms or endocarditis related to intravenous drug abuse. Patients should also be informed of the potential for complications related to drug–drug interactions when the history includes drug use (Anderson, 2016).

Physical Inactivity. Physical inactivity is defined as engaging in less than 150 minutes of moderate exercise per week (Mozaffarian et al., 2016). Multiple studies report that higher levels of physical activity are correlated with lower rates of multiple chronic diseases, including cardiovascular disease, and longer lifespans (Amsterdam et al., 2014; Eckel et al., 2014; Levine et al., 2016; Mozaffarian et al., 2016). Nurses should inquire specifically about the amount and type of physical activity the patient engages in each week. Primary and secondary risk-reduction strategies should include physical activity recommendations.

Nutrition. Research has shown that diets high in fruits and vegetable are associated with a decreased risk for cardiovascular disease. Patients who report diets that are high in salt, fat, and sugar are at high risk for developing or exacerbating cardiovascular disease (Eckel et al., 2014). Nurses should inquire about the amount of fruits and vegetables, caffeine, and salt the patient consumes each day to capture whether the patient is meeting the dietary recommendations for cardiovascular risk reduction (Anderson, 2016).

Overweight/Obesity. The clinician should use objective measures to calculate body mass index (BMI) to evaluate the patient for obesity. Clinicians must also recognize that the location of body fat also plays a significant role in the calculation of cardiovascular disease risk factors. For instance, some patients may be overweight and have a body type in which a large proportion of the body fat is distributed in the hips, thighs, and buttocks. Body types with large proportions of body fat distributed in the abdomen carry the greatest risk for cardiovascular disease (Eckel et al., 2014; Mozaffarian et al., 2016).

Spiritual Considerations. Patients often integrate a spiritual framework into healthcare decision making. Therefore, in the effort to enhance the patient-centered approach, clinicians should inquire about spiritual influences in the patient's lifestyle that may affect cardiovascular health. For instance, patients may avoid specific foods because of their religious beliefs, which can narrow the clinician's choices for dietary recommendations. Thus, to facilitate a patient-centered regimen that the patient can comply with, the clinician should consider spiritual influences on the patient's health care (Anderson, 2016).

Sleep Patterns. Sleep patterns can be an indicator of the patient's physical and/or psychological health. Patients who do not get enough rest experience an increased amount of mental and physiological stress throughout the day. Manifestations of this stress can include hypertension, agitation or anger, and/or the use of addictive stimulants or sleep aids. When evaluating the patient's sleep patterns, the clinician should also determine whether patients have obstructive sleep apnea or other conditions that can disrupt sleep (e.g., orthopnea or nocturia). Clinicians can also inquire about adequate rest when evaluating risk factors for cardiovascular disease.

Sexual Health. Information about the patient's sexual history can inform the clinician about certain aspects of cardiovascular health, such as stress reduction or exercise tolerance. This information is to evaluate risks in patients without known cardiovascular disease, but is especially important for patients with cardiovas-

cular disease. For example, patients with cardiovascular disease who are able to undertake 5 metabolic equivalents of energy expenditure during exercise without experiencing ischemia have a very low risk for experiencing ischemia during sexual activity (Levine et al., 2016).

Prevention Activities

The clinician also inquires about screening and prevention activities to learn more about the patient's risk for future illness and to identify opportunities to educate and review resources with the patient.

Immunizations. The clinician should determine whether the patient is up to date on the age-appropriate vaccinations recommended by the Centers for Disease Control and Prevention. Contracting an illness that could be preventable increases the amount of undue physiological stress on the patient with cardiac disease (Anderson, 2016).

Screenings. Clinicians should also inquire about whether the patient has had the age- and gender-appropriate recommended screenings put forth by the U.S. Preventative Services Task Force for the primary prevention of illnesses such as different types of cancer, osteoporosis, diabetes, and dyslipidemia.

Collaboration of Medical Providers. Obtaining the names of and contact information for the patient's other healthcare providers (e.g., primary care provider, pulmonologist, and endocrinologist) can facilitate communication among the interprofessional team. Many offices and hospitals automatically send provider notes to all listed medical providers on file via the electronic health record. The secure sharing of information allows for all providers to be aware of current medication lists and any changes that may have been made to the regimen. Patients must grant their consent for the exchange of information among providers (Anderson, 2016).

Medical History

Cardiovascular Conditions

Clinicians should ask whether the patient has any known history of cardiac conditions. Because most patients are not aware of all cardiovascular diseases, clinicians should ask specific questions such as the following: Do you have a history of high blood pressure? Heart attack? Heart failure? Valve dysfunction, such as prolapse or hardening of the valve? Stroke? Chest pain? Atrial fibrillation or other rhythm disorders? The clinician should use lay terminology so that patients can understand the questions and answer them appropriately (Anderson, 2016).

Extracardiac Conditions

The patient with diabetes, chronic kidney disease, obesity, dyslipidemia, or metabolic syndrome is at high risk for development of cardiovascular disease if he or she does not already have it. When the patient already has a known history of cardiovascular disease, controlling these extracardiac conditions is an important aspect of reducing risks for acute cardiovascular events such as myocardial infarction, stroke, or other thromboembolic events (Mozaffarian et al., 2016).

It is also important to inquire about other recent or remote major illnesses. For instance, infectious illnesses such as recurring skin infections (especially staphylococcal and streptococcal species), pneumonia, and influenza can be temporarily disabling and require extended therapies. The clinician should also document malignancies such as skin lesions that had to be removed or other cancers and their treatments in the patient's record (Anderson, 2016).

Congenital or Childhood History

The parents of children with major congenital cardiac defects can often provide very thorough histories because they have been involved with the healthcare system on multiple levels. It is important for the clinician to note the defect and any interventions to repair the defect. Some genetic defects (e.g., Down syndrome, Turner's syndrome, and Marfan's syndrome) may not require interventions but are associated with a high incidence for the development of future cardiovascular disease (Anderson, 2016).

Other systemic illnesses, such as measles, scarlet fever, rheumatic fever, diphtheria, and Lyme disease, are associated with risk for the development of heart valve disease. Untreated Lyme disease, for example, is associated with conduction disorders and arrhythmias (Anderson, 2016).

Hospitalizations

When giving information for the health history, patients may not always volunteer hospital stays or think that a brief hospitalization is significant information. Therefore, the clinician should directly ask the patient whether there were any recent hospitalizations and determine the duration of and reason for any hospital visits. Prolonged hospitalization places the patient at risk for immobility, loss of functional status (in the older adult), and nosocomial infections (Flaherty & Resnick, 2014; Mozaffarian et al., 2016).

Mental Health History

Clinicians must consider the effects of mental health disorders and medications on the cardiovascular system. Many mental health disorders include components of depression and anxiety, which can adversely affect the patient's lifestyle choices related to substance use or abuse, diet, and physical activity. Another consideration is the use of psychotropic medications to treat mental health disorders. Psychotropic medications can have side effects such as QT interval prolongation, tachycardia, weight gain, and sedation (which limits physical activity; Anderson, 2016).

Family History and Genetics

Many cardiovascular disorders have familial patterns. Some of these patterns are genetic, and some involve adopting familial lifestyle or behavioral factors that affect cardiovascular health (e.g., diet, tobacco use; Anderson, 2016). Patients with a family history of CAD, PAD, diabetes mellitus, renal insufficiency, prior myocardial infarction, and/or prior coronary revascularization in first-degree relatives have a greater risk for development of cardiovascular disease. Patients with family members who experience sudden cardiac death or myocardial infarction before the age of 50 years also are at greater risk (Amsterdam et al., 2014; Levine et al., 2016; Anderson et al., 2013).

Surgical History

The clinician should inquire about and document the patient's past invasive and/or surgical procedures, including those that required general anesthesia and those that did not. The clinician should document the date on which the procedure took place and whether the patient experienced any complications (e.g., excessive bleeding, infection, or deep vein thrombosis) because such data can facilitate medical decision making. Clinicians may need to directly ask about cardiac-related procedures such as direct-current cardioversions or percutaneous interventions because some patients do not consider these procedures to be surgeries (Anderson, 2016).

Special Populations

Women

Special consideration must be given to women because mortality rates related to cardiovascular disease remain higher among women than men (Mehta et al., 2016). Based on the female patient's reproductive status, a gynecological and obstetric history is important in identifying the woman's risk for or severity of cardiovascular disease resulting from maternal hemodynamic changes. The risk for cardiovascular disease also increases for postmenopausal women (Mehta et al., 2016).

The pregnant female's cardiovascular volume and workload doubles, and this places her at risk for cardiovascular conditions that male individuals and female individuals who have never been pregnant do not encounter (Sanghavi & Rutherford, 2014). Complications during pregnancy (e.g., preeclampsia, gestational diabetes, pregnancy-induced hypertension) or a history of polycystic ovary syndrome predispose the female patient to greater risk for future cardiovascular disease. Because of these factors, the clinician should evaluate all women with children for postpartum cardiomyopathy (Anderson, 2016).

Aside from gynecological- or obstetric-related differences, cardiovascular illness presents differently in females as well. Women may not always have chest pain and are often referred to as having "atypical" symptoms (Amsterdam et al., 2014). Atypical symptoms that women report include epigastric pain, indigestion, pleuritic pain described as stabbing, and dyspnea that progressively increases in the absence of chest pain (Amsterdam et al., 2014). Clinicians must be sure to ask female patients whether they are experiencing atypical symptoms.

Older Adults

Older adults have an increased risk for cardiovascular disease because of the physiological changes that occur with aging in addition to behavioral and lifestyle factors (Amsterdam et al., 2014; Levine et al., 2016). Older adults also account for the majority of patients hospitalized for ACS (Flaherty & Resnick, 2014). Physiological changes that occur with aging include increased arterial stiffness, decreased autonomic/compensatory responses to hemodynamic changes, and increased conduction velocity, among others. These changes and behavioral factors such as tobacco or alcohol exposure, lack of physical activity, and obesity can increase the older adult's risk for cardiovascular disease and acute events (Flaherty & Resnick, 2014).

RISK STRATIFICATION FOR CARDIOVASCULAR DISEASE

The clinician should conduct a risk stratification during each patient visit. Risk stratification is the process of prioritizing the patient's identified risk factors by their individualized calculated probabilities for disease. Different tools are used for this process that are specific to each disease state. The tools discussed in this section are not all-inclusive; many cardiovascular risk assessment tools are available. The selected tools discussed are the more commonly used tools for risk stratification in the context of cardiovascular disease.

Framingham Criteria

Clinicians use the Framingham clinical criteria (e.g., lung rales, megalocardia, and paroxysmal nocturnal dyspnea) to calculate a score for use in the diagnosis of heart failure with reduced ejection fraction (HFrEF; formerly known as systolic heart failure). The score is highly sensitive to ruling in HFrEF, but nonspecific for ruling it out (Yancy et al., 2013).

Pooled Cohort Risk Equation

Clinicians use the American College of Cardiology/American Heart Association pooled cohort risk equation, also commonly called the atherosclerotic cardiovascular disease risk calculator, to identify patients who are at risk for experiencing an atherosclerosis-related cardiovascular

event within the next 10 years and to determine the appropriateness of cholesterol-lowering medications (Anderson, 2016; Goff et al., 2014). The equation accounts for gender, age, ethnicity, history of diabetes mellitus, treatment for hypertension, history of smoking, blood pressure, and cholesterol values (Anderson, 2016).

Thrombolysis in Myocardial Infarction Risk Score

Clinicians use the Thrombolysis in Myocardial Infarction (TIMI) risk score to predict 30-day and 1-year mortality in patients with non-ST-segment elevation ACSs. This tool has been validated for use in the early estimation of risk. For instance, a TIMI risk score of 0 and a normal high-sensitivity cardiac troponin 2 hours after the presentation of chest pain predict a very low rate of 30-day mortality or myocardial infarction. Patients with a high TIMI risk score ($\geq$3) are at moderate-to-high risk for 30-day mortality or myocardial infarction and can benefit from treatments for atherosclerosis-related cardiovascular disease (Amsterdam et al., 2014). Clinicians can utilize this tool for medical decision-making guidance, for example, regarding whether a patient with low risk for acute cardiac events should be admitted to the hospital or sent home from the emergency department with cardiology follow-up.

CHADS$_2$ Risk Score

Clinicians use the CHADS$_2$ Risk Score to predict the risk for stroke in patients with atrial fibrillation. CHADS$_2$ assigns scores as follows: chronic heart failure, hypertension, diabetes, and age older than 74 years count for one point each, and previous history of stroke or transient ischemic attack counts as two points, for a maximum of six points. This tool assigns a score of zero for low risk, one point is moderate risk, and more than one point is high risk (Chen et al., 2013).

CARDIOVASCULAR PHYSICAL EXAMINATION

The cardiovascular examination should be guided by the history. If there are symptoms indicating acute illness, a problem-focused examination may be needed to initiate timely treatment. However, a comprehensive physical examination yields the most clinical utility for identifying problems and/or establishing baseline data (Anderson, 2016).

Comprehensive Cardiovascular Assessment

General Survey

While approaching the patient, the clinician should evaluate the patient's overall general appearance: Is the patient in distress? Does the patient look comfortable? Is the patient awake, alert, and responsive to the environment? Is the patient's color normal? Is the patient diaphoretic? The clinician documents these findings to illustrate his or her overall impression of the patient (Anderson, 2016). The general survey should also note whether the patient is accompanied by family members or other individuals.

Vital Signs

Clinicians should collect vital signs when patients are at rest. The clinician should note any associated findings of distress when evaluating vital sign measures.

Pulse. The clinician evaluates the pulse for its rate, regularity, and amplitude upon examination. The pulse rate should be between 60 and 100 beats/min and in a regular rhythm (Anderson, 2016). Occasional irregularities can be benign. The clinician should palpate pulses symmetrically and compare the pulses for regularity and strength. Decreases in pulse strength can be associated with peripheral vascular disease (PVD; e.g., aortic aneurysm), or PAD or peripheral venous disease. Pulse irregularities can be associated with arrhythmias.

Blood Pressure. Arterial blood pressure should range from 100/60 mmHg to 140/90 mmHg (Anderson, 2016). Systolic blood pressure reflects cardiac output and measures blood volume and the force of blood flow against arterial walls. Diastolic blood pressure measures ventricular filling and the relaxed state of the ventricles. A difference in blood pressure between arms that is greater than 20 mmHg can indicate an aortic aneurysm, coarctation of the aorta, subclavian steal syndrome, or other vascular disorders. In hypotensive patients, measuring the blood pressure manually or with a Doppler can help confirm the value (Anderson, 2016).

Postural Vitals. Postural, or orthostatic, vital signs are useful in the evaluation of a patient's volume status or presyncopal or syncopal symptoms. Compensatory mechanisms involving the autonomic nervous system aim to compensate for the changes in cardiac output that occur with position changes. However, when volume status is low, or when the autonomic nervous system does not function effectively, patients can experience syncopal or presyncopal symptoms. Positive postural vitals are consistent with a decrease of greater than 20 mmHg in systolic pressure, a decrease of 10 mmHg in diastolic pressure, and an increase of greater than 30 beats/min in heart rate (Anderson, 2016).

Pulse Pressure. The pulse pressure is an indirect measure of cardiac output, stroke volume, and vascular resistance. It is the difference between the systolic and diastolic pressures. For instance, a blood pressure of 120/80 mmHg has a pulse pressure of 40 mmHg, determined by subtracting the diastolic pressure from the systolic pressure (Anderson, 2016). Clinicians should be aware of conditions associated with narrow and wide pulse pressures (Anderson, 2016).

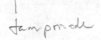
tamponade

Respirations. A normal respiratory rate is between 12 and 20 breaths/min. Tachypnea is an objective finding that can be correlated with the patient's historical data and diagnostic data such as a chest radiograph to identify the patient's problem. The clinician must differentiate between cardiac and noncardiac causes of this symptom and guide the history with this in mind (Anderson, 2016).

Temperature. A normal temperature is 98.6°F, and a fever is defined as a temperature greater than 100.4°F. Fever can indicate an acute infectious illness, an adverse reaction to a medication, or an inflammatory response. Clinicians should approach the patient with targeted interview questions to help differentiate temperature changes that might be associated with cardiovascular problems (Anderson, 2016).

Oxygen Saturation. Oxygen saturation identifies the amount of oxygen that is carried by the hemoglobin molecule. The heart is responsible for pumping blood in one direction in a coordinated effort to deliver oxygen to the body's tissues. Clinicians must connect the correlation of left ventricular (LV) dysfunction and other cardiovascular conditions to the impaired oxygenation that occurs with pulmonary edema (Anderson, 2016).

Body Size. The assessment of body size – including height, weight, BMI, and waist circumference – is a vital component of identifying the patient's risks for disease and determining the diagnostic and management plan. Obesity is defined as a BMI greater than 30 (Anderson, 2016).

Neck Vessels

Carotid Artery. Examination of the carotid artery should begin with inspection. Inspection can reveal visible pulsations in the thin-framed patient. Auscultation is the next step in the assessment sequence of the carotid. Hearing a bruit can be indicative of occluded blood flow within the carotid. The last examination technique is palpation. The carotid artery is the best pulse to palpate when evaluating systolic function. Carotid pulsations are usually strong and correlate with the apical pulse. Reduced cardiac output can be identified by palpating the carotid pulse while auscultating the apical pulse and finding a delayed pulsation. When the carotid amplitude is weak or diminished, this sign of reduced cardiac output can be related to aortic stenosis, atherosclerosis, or some type of LV impairment (Anderson, 2016).

Jugular Vein Distention. The internal jugular vein directly communicates with the right atrium, and proper examination (e.g., the head of the bed should be elevated to at least 45 degrees) of this vein by the clinician can indicate the patient's cardiac function. Ordinarily, the internal jugular vein is not visible upon examination because it lies deep within the soft tissue of the neck lateral to the carotid artery. However, when the vein is distended in the patient in an upright position, the clinician can see the vessel and its pulsations upon inspection of the neck (Anderson, 2016). Jugular vein distention (JVD) is a sign of heart failure resulting from ineffective forward blood flow. In the patient with atrial fibrillation, JVD can be an unreliable measure because of the increased pressure within the right atrium and incomplete emptying of the chamber.

Jugular vein pulsations are not as strong as carotid artery pulsations, and thus they are not ordinarily palpable. When these veins are distended, the clinician can correlate this finding with an elevated central venous pressure, indicating volume overload or increased right atrial pressures (Anderson, 2016). Medical decision making based on JVD alone can be unreliable; the clinician must correlate any JVD findings with other clinical findings.

Precordium

The precordium is the anterior portion of the anterior thorax overlaying the heart. The clinician should examine the precordium to identify abnormal movements or physical features (e.g., pectus cavitum). Clinicians should also note whether there are surgical scars in this area, which can prompt additional surgical history questions if the patient has not already provided this information. Clinicians should also inspect the precordium for retractions or pulsations. The point of maximal impulse is at the fourth intercostal space (ICS) in a child and the fifth ICS in an adult, along the midclavicular line where the apical pulse is examined. Pulsations displaced one ICS beyond the normal location are abnormal and indicative of pathology.

Palpation of the precordium can reveal a heave or lift. A heave is a vigorous or exaggerated impulse that occurs as a result of LV hypertrophy, exertion, or increased sympathetic stimulation (e.g., thyrotoxicosis). Clinicians can also palpate a thrill. A thrill is a palpable vibration produced by murmurs of at least moderate intensity. Thrills are usually palpable at the left or right ICS over the base of the heart. Thrills should not be palpable with an innocent murmur (a benign murmur) but can be associated with septal defects. Conversely, conditions such as chronic obstructive pulmonary disease (COPD) and obesity will limit the clinician's ability to palpate the point of maximal impulse. Also, when palpating this area of the chest wall, the clinician should determine whether the patient experiences pain. Costochondritis is a condition in which chest pain can be reproduced upon palpation (Anderson, 2016).

Heart

Cardiac Auscultation. Auscultation of the heart is an essential component of the cardiovascular examination. Heart sounds are created by the mechanical events in the cardiac cycle. Normal heart sounds, S_1 and S_2 (also known as "lub" and "dub," respectively), are created by the closure of valves. Open valves do not normally make a sound as blood flows through them. To better hear the S_1 and S_2 sounds, high-pitched sounds, and lung sounds, the clinician should use the bell of the stethoscope. Low-pitched sounds are best heard with the diaphragm of the stethoscope (Anderson, 2016).

The clinician should use a systematic approach when auscultating the heart. Honing these skills includes considering the general anatomical location of cardiac structures. Additionally, clinicians should evaluate their own findings and compare them with those of more experienced clinicians and diagnostic studies. During auscultation, clinicians should listen for the heart rate, rhythm, and expected heart sounds (S_1 and S_2). Clinicians should also listen closely for abnormal findings such as splitting heart sounds, clicks, murmurs, pericardial friction rubs, and gallops.

The sequence of listening to heart sounds most often follows the path of blood flow across the four cardiac valves: (1) aortic, (2) pulmonic, (3) tricuspid, and (4) mitral. The aortic valve is best heard at the base of the heart at the left parasternal border, second ICS. The pulmonic valve is best auscultated at the right parasternal border, second ICS. The tricuspid valve is best accessed at the left parasternal border, third or fourth ICS. The mitral valve is best auscultated at the left midclavicular line in the fourth ICS in children and fifth ICS in adults. In patients with dextrocardia (right-sided heart structures), the clinician's auscultation of heart sounds should mirror the sequence and process used for those with left-sided heart structures.

Cardiac Cycle. Clinicians must apply their understanding of the cardiac cycle to the physical examination of the heart. For instance, as blood flows through open valves, heart sounds should not occur. Thus, during the systolic phase of the cardiac cycle, the clinician should hear no sound because the atrioventricular valves have already closed and the semilunar valves have already opened. However, if a murmur is heard during this cardiac phase, it is called a systolic murmur.

Other sounds that the clinician may hear during systole include high-pitched clicking sounds called clicks. Clicks can occur in the mid- to late-systolic phase of the cardiac cycle. The clinician may also hear the splitting of heart sounds, indicating uncoordinated closure of the valves. A physiological split (nonpathological) can occur with inspiration when venous return to the heart is enhanced as a result of an increase in lung volume during inspiration. This process prolongs the ejection of blood from the right ventricle, causing the delayed closure of the pulmonic valve and thereby causing the splitting of the sounds of the two atrioventricular valves closing (Anderson, 2016).

Gallops. Other extra heart sounds the clinician may hear during the cardiac cycle include gallops. A gallop is also known as an S_3 or S_4 heart sound and is usually caused by a pathological condition. Gallops occur during diastolic filling of a noncompliant ventricle. Conditions that cause noncompliant ventricles include heart failure, cor pulmonale (right-sided heart failure resulting from pulmonary hypertension), and valvular insufficiency (e.g., mitral, tricuspid, or aortic insufficiency). In children and adults younger than 30 years old, an S_3 gallop can be a normal finding related to physical development. However, beyond 30 years of age and especially in older adults, this extra heart sound is usually pathological. The S_3 sound occurs early in the diastolic phase. The rhythm and sound of a gallop are similar to the pronunciation of "Ken-TUCK-y" or "lub-dub-ta" and closely follow the S_2 sound. The low-pitched sound of

a gallop is best heard with the diaphragm of the stethoscope (Anderson, 2016).

An S_4 gallop occurs during the late diastolic phase of the cardiac cycle and can be heard just before the S_1 sound. This sound occurs with the rapid filling of the ventricle associated with atrial contraction. For this reason, the S_4 gallop is also referred to as an atrial gallop. The S_4 gallop is usually associated with significant hypertension and LV hypertrophy. It can also be present in conditions such as heart failure, prior myocardial infarction, hypertrophic cardiomyopathy, or aortic stenosis. The clinician will not hear the S_4 sound during atrial fibrillation because of the lack of atrial contraction with this condition. This sound is best heard with the bell of the stethoscope at the apex of the heart, left lower sternal border (Anderson, 2016; Levine et al., 2016).

A summation gallop is the presence of all four heart sounds – S_1, S_2, S_3, and S_4. It is best heard with bradycardic rhythms and is very difficult to distinguish with normal heart rates or tachycardia. This gallop is most associated with heart failure.

Cardiac Murmurs. Not all murmurs are pathological. For instance, innocent murmurs are common in infants and children and are caused by a flow-related phenomenon that is not associated with disease. Physiological murmurs are also benign and can be caused by an increase in blood flow with changed metabolic conditions, such as fever, anemia, hyperthyroidism, exercise, or pregnancy. Such murmurs are usually systolic. Diastolic murmurs are usually pathological. Murmurs can be high-, medium-, or low-pitched blowing noises characterized by intensity, pattern, quality, and duration. Box 19-1 describes a grading system used to describe these characteristics. As murmurs become more severe, they can also become quieter as a result of a decrease in blood flow (Anderson, 2016). The characteristics of mur-

BOX 19-1: GRADING OF MURMURS

I Difficult to hear, localized (nonradiating) sound

II Quiet, but clearly heard

III Moderate intensity

IV Moderately loud with a barely palpable thrill

V Loud with a palpable thrill

VI Loud with a visible and palpable thrill

Note. Adapted from Anderson, K. M. (2016). *The advanced practice nurse cardiovascular clinician.* New York, NY: Springer.

murs specific to cardiac disease are discussed earlier in this chapter.

Pericardial Friction Rub. A pericardial friction rub occurs throughout the cardiac cycle. This uncommon condition is caused by inflammation or the infiltration of the pericardial space and is associated with pericarditis, pericardial effusion, and cardiac tamponade. Pericardial friction rubs are very specific to pericarditis but are not always indicative of an effusion or tamponade. The pericardial friction rub has a high-pitched scratching or scraping sound that can usually be heard at any auscultation location but is clearest at the apex of the heart. Clinicians can distinguish between a pleural rub and a pericardial rub by asking the patient to hold his or her breath to eliminate pleural sounds (Anderson, 2016).

Patient Positioning

The clinician can conduct most of the cardiovascular examination with the patient in the supine position and then reposition the patient to help enhance certain findings. For instance, a position in which the patient is sitting or leaning forward during auscultation can enhance high-pitched cardiac sounds. Low-pitched sounds are enhanced by the left lateral decubitus position. The clinician should place patients with dextro-

cardia in the right-lateral decubitus position to enhance low-pitched sounds (Anderson, 2016).

Dynamic Maneuvers

Clinicians can ask the patient to perform other maneuvers to increase venous return or augment intrathoracic pressures. Such maneuvers include the Valsalva maneuver and asking the patient to squat, stand, or exacerbate inspiration or exhalation. Performing these maneuvers can aid the clinician in examining pathological heart findings more closely, such as mitral valve prolapse or murmurs (Anderson, 2016).

Cardiovascular-Related Findings in Other Organ Systems

Eyes

Clinicians must identify specific examination findings of the eye related to cardiovascular disease. For instance, arcus senilis (a thin gray circle around the iris) can be normal in the older adult but can indicate dyslipidemia in younger adults. This finding is more prevalent in African Americans than in other ethnicities. Other findings associated with dyslipidemia include xanthelasmas, a yellow, raised, well-circumscribed plaque that most often appears on the nasal side of the eyelids, either unilaterally or bilaterally.

A funduscopic examination can reveal changes in the eye's vasculature and retinal changes associated with hypertension. For instance, cotton-wool spots are caused by micro-infarcts of the small retinal arterioles. Cotton-wool spots appear as pale yellow or white spots in the posterior region of the retina. A Roth spot is a cotton-wool spot with a white center surrounded by hemorrhage. Roth spots are caused by ischemic changes that rupture the arteriole. Other funduscopic findings can reveal vasculature congestion or hemorrhages and micro-aneurysms. With acute severe hypertension, papilledema occurs and presents as a blurred disc. Papilledema is indicative of increased intracranial pressure and indicates the need for urgent treatment (Anderson, 2016).

Neck

When examining the neck, the clinician should palpate the thyroid for enlargement or masses. Hypothyroidism or hyperthyroidism can influence cardiovascular risk and disease. The clinician should also palpate the neck to determine its thickness. Increased neck thickness is associated with Pickwickian syndrome and obstructive sleep apnea (Anderson, 2016).

Pulmonary

Examining the pulmonary system involves inspecting and palpating the thorax for respiratory patterns, size, shape, pain, and other abnormal findings and auscultating lung sounds. For instance, paradoxical respirations can occur in the patient with heart failure or a rib fracture. Another example is inspecting the shape of the thorax by estimating the anteroposterior diameter. Patients with an increased anteroposterior diameter often have chronic lung disease such as COPD or pulmonary fibrosis, both of which can result in right-sided heart failure (cor pulmonale; Anderson, 2016).

Abdominal

The abdominal examination should first include inspection of the size and contour of the abdomen and the presence of pulsations. Then, using the diaphragm of the stethoscope, the clinician should auscultate the abdomen for GI sounds or vascular bruits (e.g., aortic aneurysm or renal artery stenosis). Next, during expiration, the clinician should palpate the abdomen to assess for masses, organ borders, and discomfort. A patient experiencing heart failure can have palpable liver borders and a round abdomen. Percussion of the abdomen can reveal tympany (air-filled sound) or dullness. In the patient suspected to have ascites, the clinician can palpate the abdomen to assess for a fluid wave (Anderson, 2016).

Skin

A thorough examination of the skin can reveal multiple pathological cardiovascular conditions. Peripheral cyanosis is the bluish grayish appearance that occurs with hypoxia. Central cyanosis is the same discoloring but is specific to the buccal mucosa and is associated with severe right-to-left shunts, COPD, and pulmonary fibrosis.

Other findings include skin moisture and temperature related to acute conditions, such as ACSs, myocardial infarction, or other conditions associated with decreased oxygen delivery to the heart muscle. The autonomic nervous system is responsible for these fight-or-flight responses.

Acanthosis nigricans is a dark, velvety skin discoloration that occurs in the skin folds. This finding is a marker for poor glucose metabolism, which is associated with the risk for cardiovascular disease. Jaundiced skin is rarely directly associated with cardiovascular disease; however, in heart failure, the liver can become congested with blood from the lack of forward flow through the heart, exacerbating any underlying liver disease. Petechiae can occur in patients being treated with anticoagulant or antiplatelet medications. Janeway lesions and Osler's nodes can occur with infectious bacterial endocarditis (Anderson, 2016). Clinicians should assess the skin for these findings.

Peripheral Vascular

Examination of the patient's pulses usually involves the clinician's symmetric palpation of distal pulses (e.g., radial, pedal, posterior tibial) on a routine basis and central pulses (e.g., carotid, femoral) during cardiac emergencies. The characteristics of peripheral pulses can be indicative of cardiovascular disease. For instance, pulsus alternans can indicate LV failure or dysfunction, and produces a pattern of pulsations that alternates a strong pulse with a weak pulse. Pulsus paradoxus is a reduction of more than 10 mmHg in pulse amplitude during inspiration. This finding is associated with cardiac tamponade, restrictive pulmonary disease, pulmonary embolism, and cardiac amyloidosis (Anderson, 2016). The assessment findings associated with PVD are discussed earlier in this chapter.

Capillary Refill. The capillary bed reflects the joining of the venous and arterial systems with the interstitial tissue. The clinician can apply pressure to the nailbeds to evaluate capillary refill and the health of the capillary system.

Edema. Edema is the abnormal accumulation of interstitial fluid. Causes of edema specific to cardiovascular dysfunction most often produce dependent pitting edema or anasarca. Anasarca is generalized edema caused by systemic disease such as severe heart failure.

Clinical Manifestations of Cardiovascular Conditions

Clinicians should approach the physical examination by looking for the clinical manifestations (signs and symptoms) associated with cardiovascular conditions and the damage to other organs that results from cardiovascular disease (Anderson, 2016).

Acute Coronary Syndrome or Myocardial Infarction

The clinician should frequently evaluate hemodynamic stability by trending vital signs. The physical examination findings associated with ACS or acute myocardial infarction can reveal a new murmur secondary to papillary muscle rupture, an S_4 extra heart sound, and/or a paradoxical splitting S_2 heart sound. Clinicians must recognize that these findings can be associated with acute myocardial ischemia or chronic conditions resulting from prior cardiovascular events. Chest pain that is reproducible upon palpation is usually not associated with angina and can be attributed to costochondritis or a musculoskeletal cause (Amsterdam et al., 2014).

Tamponade

The examination findings most closely associated with cardiac tamponade are referred to as Beck's triad: distant heart sounds, hypotension, and a widened pulse pressure. Other objective clinical findings with tamponade can include tachycardia, an altered mental status, tachypnea, pallor, and weak distal pulses (Anderson, 2016).

Left Ventricular Dysfunction

The vital signs for patients experiencing acute decompensating LV dysfunction often reveal hypotension, tachycardia, and tachypnea. The patient's oxygenation status can be diminished as well. Physical examination findings are consistent with those of heart failure: basilar rales, S_3 gallop, and weak distal pulses. Patients with severe LV dysfunction experience cardiogenic shock (also known as pump failure; Amsterdam et al., 2014).

Hemodynamic parameters consistent with cardiogenic shock include a cardiac index less than 2.2 $L/min/m^2$, an elevated central venous pressure, and elevated pulmonary artery and wedge pressures. Physical examination findings can include dependent peripheral edema, abdominal distention and a positive fluid wave indicative of ascites, and right upper quadrant discomfort; hepatomegaly is also a possible finding (Anderson, 2016; Amsterdam et al., 2014).

Valve Dysfunction

Cardiac valve dysfunction is slow and progressive in nature. For this reason, many patients do not recognize the worsening severity of the disease until greater-than-usual exertion or later stages of dysfunction have developed (Nishimura et al., 2014). The most common physical examination findings specific to valve dysfunction are murmurs. The characteristics of different pathological murmurs are discussed later in this chapter. Other findings on examination can include a snap. If a mechanical valve was used to replace a malfunctioning native valve, the clinician can hear a click when auscultating heart sounds. The heart sounds of patients who have received a bioprosthetic valve replacement should be no different from those of patients with normal native valves. The physical examination should focus on identifying the severity of valvular dysfunction (Anderson, 2016). The different types of valve disease are discussed in greater detail in Chapter 9. The constellation findings (e.g., dyspnea, basilar rales, and peripheral edema) accompanying valve dysfunction are consistent with those that occur in the patient with heart failure.

Aortic Dissection

If the clinician suspects that the patient has an aortic dissection, the clinician should frequently trend the patient's vital signs (every 15 to 30 minutes) and take blood pressure readings in each arm. Examination findings for the patient with an aortic dissection can vary with the location of the dissection. For instance, patients with ascending aortic dissections can present with symptoms and signs of stroke to symptoms and signs of cardiac tamponade or ACS. Patients with dissections involving the descending aorta can present with signs and symptoms of mesenteric ischemia (e.g., severe nonfocal abdominal pain incongruent with the physical examination and asymmetric distal pulse amplitude).

Peripheral Arterial Disease

The physical examination associated with PAD should focus on differentiating the severity of arterial occlusion. Patients at risk for PAD include those with a heavy smoking history,

those with dyslipidemia, and those with known coronary or cerebrovascular disease. The clinician can evaluate patients suspected to be at risk for PAD by measuring the ankle-brachial index (ABI). The normal ABI is 0.91 to 1.30 (Anderson et al., 2013). Research has shown that patients with asymptomatic PAD and an abnormal ABI are at risk not only for an acute occlusive event but also for myocardial infarction; thus, the clinician must initiate appropriate treatment to reduce the risk for their occurrence (Anderson et al., 2013).

Specific physical examination findings associated with patients with PAD include cool distal extremities, the absence of hair and shiny skin distally, elevation pallor, and varying pulse amplitude.

Physical Examination Considerations for Special Populations

Pregnant Women

Pregnant women have a 40% to 50% increase in total blood volume from 12 to 34 weeks of gestation. This increase produces a 30% to 40% increase in the woman's cardiac output. The increased blood volume can produce physiological murmurs. Blood pressure should not increase with the increased blood volume during the first and second trimester because of the increased production of estrogen, which results in relaxation of the peripheral vessels (decreased afterload). However, the woman's blood pressure may increase late during the third trimester. There may be venous pooling and venous varicosities because of these changes (Anderson, 2016; Sanghavi & Rutherford, 2014).

Older Adults

Age-related changes will occur in every older adult regardless of the presence or absence of cardiovascular disease. These changes most often cause a slower heart rate as a result of aging electrophysiology, increased systolic blood pressure as a result of arterial stiffening, and decreased autonomic responsiveness to stress as a result of the decreased number of pressure and chemical receptors within the vasculature and heart. In addition, the myocardium becomes less elastic with age, and the endocardium becomes thicker, further affecting the ability of the heart to adapt to the hemodynamic changes that occur in the older adult.

CASE STUDY

A 70-year-old male patient goes to the cardiology clinic for right lower leg pain in the calf. The patient states that he first noticed this pain 2 years ago, but it has become much worse over the past 2 to 3 months. The patient reports that he can no longer walk around his yard without the pain becoming worse, but it is relieved with rest. He also feels that he has to stop and rest more often than he needed to 6 months ago.

The patient denies fever, chills, dyspnea, syncope, or chest pain. He denies redness or swelling to the right lower leg as well. He has a medical history of CAD, hypertension, PVD, COPD, and osteoarthritis. His surgical history includes a three-vessel coronary artery bypass graft more than 7 years ago and a cholecystectomy more than 15 years ago. He has smoked two packs of cigarettes per day for the past 45 years and states he is not ready to quit. He does not drink alcohol or use illicit drugs. He is married and is a retired electrician. He reports compliance to his home medications of metoprolol 50 mg twice daily, enalapril 5 mg daily, clopidogrel 75 mg daily, atorvastatin 40 mg daily, and Advair inhaler twice daily.

The patient's vital signs include a temperature of 98.4°F, blood pressure of 163/91 mmHg, heart rate of 82 beats/min, respiratory rate of 20 breaths/min, and a pulse oximetry reading of 93% on room air. He is in no acute respiratory distress but appears to be generally uncomfortable while rubbing his right calf, and he complains of pain after walking from his car to the waiting area and then to the examination room.

The patient's physical examination findings include a regular heart rate and rhythm with no murmurs, gallops, or rubs. His lung sounds are diffusely diminished with no wheezing or rales noted. A peripheral vascular examination of the patient reveals skin color on the right leg paler than the left leg, and there is less hair distribution on the right leg in comparison with the left. The right leg is cooler to touch than the left leg as well. He has weak but palpable left pedal and posterior tibial pulses, and nonpalpable but present by Doppler right pedal and posterior tibial pulses.

Questions

1. Which peripheral vascular disorder does the patient present with? Which patient symptoms support your answer?

2. Which information does the nurse review with the patient about treatment and risk-factor reduction strategies for his condition?

Answers

1. The patient's presentation and examination are most associated with peripheral arterial disease (PAD). Acute leg pain, often in the calf, that occurs with ambulation and is relieved with rest within 10 minutes are common symptoms of PAD. Examination findings of cool and pale skin with less hair distribution and weak pulse amplitude are also consistent with this condition.

2. The patient is informed about the need for further testing (i.e., ABI measurements and peripheral angiography) to verify a diagnosis of PAD. The nurse reviews the risk for acute arterial occlusion if medical or

surgical intervention is not initiated in a timely manner for PAD. The nurse also educates the patient about the effects of tobacco abuse on the peripheral vascular system. The nurse provides the patient with smoking cessation education despite his desire to continue smoking. Finally, the nurse educates the patient about the importance of medication compliance and the possible side effects of the medications he is currently taking (e.g., bleeding with antiplatelets or generalized muscle pain with statins).

SUMMARY

Cardiovascular nurses must be able to perform a focused cardiovascular and comprehensive health history and physical examination for patients who have cardiovascular conditions or are at risk for cardiovascular disease. Recognizing common complaints and symptoms of cardiovascular problems is vital and can often be the patient's first presentation to healthcare services. In addition to interpreting subjective findings, the nurse must also be able to differentiate acute from chronic physical assessment findings, which enables the nurse to facilitate a timely and most appropriate management plan. A thorough history and examination will also facilitate cardiovascular risk stratification and the patient education needed to reduce morbidity and mortality. Cardiovascular nurses are in a unique position to influence patient self-care and, ultimately, improve patient outcomes.

EXAM QUESTIONS

CHAPTER 19
Questions 95–98

Note: Choose the one option that BEST answers each question.

95. A patient reports palpitations at night before going to bed. Regarding which specific trigger for palpitations does the nurse question the patient?

    a. Low activity levels

    b. An underactive thyroid

    c. Caffeine intake

    d. Drinking plenty of fluids

96. When obtaining a patient's health history, which component is focused on obtaining subjective data from the patient?

    a. The history of present illness

    b. The nurse's observation of anatomical findings

    c. The patient's nonbehavioral risk factors

    d. The patient's current medications

97. Which risk stratification score is valid for determining a patient's risk for experiencing an atherosclerotic cardiovascular event within 10 years?

    a. The Thrombolysis in Myocardial Infarction Score

    b. Pooled cohort risk equation

    c. Heart failure with reduced ejection fraction calculation

    d. The Framingham Criteria Score

98. When the clinician has properly positioned the patient in an upright sitting position for the physical examination, which finding is most specific for poor cardiac function?

    a. Absent carotid artery pulsations

    b. Cool distal extremities

    c. A physiological murmur

    d. Jugular vein distention

REFERENCES

American Heart Association. (2015). *Alcohol and heart health*. Retrieved from http://www.heart.org/HEARTORG/HealthyLiving/HealthyEating/Nutrition/Alcohol-and-Heart-Health_UCM_305173_Article.jsp#.V_w_PvkrLIU

Amsterdam, E. A., Wenger, N. K., Brindis, R. G., Casey, D. E., Ganiats, T. G., Holmes, D. R., ... Zieman, S. J. (2014). 2014 AHA/ACC guideline for the management of patients with non–st-elevation acute coronary syndromes: A report of the American College of Cardiology/American Heart Association Task Force on Practice Guidelines. *Circulation, 130,* e344-e426. doi:10.1161/CIR.0000000000000134

Anderson, J. L., Halperin, J. L., Albert, N., Bozkurt, B., Brindis, R. G., Curtis, L. H., ... Shen, W. K. (2013). Management of patients with peripheral artery disease (compilation of 2005 and 2011 ACCF/AHA guideline recommendations): A report of the American College of Cardiology Foundation/American Heart Association Task Force on Practice Guidelines. *Journal of the American College of Cardiology, 61*(14), 1555-1570. doi:10.1016/j.jacc.2013.01.004

Anderson, K. M. (2016). *The advanced practice nurse cardiovascular clinician.* New York, NY: Springer.

Centers for Medicare and Medicaid Services. (2015). *Evaluation and management services.* Retrieved from https://www.cms.gov/Outreach-and-Education/Medicare-Learning-Network-MLN/MLNProducts/Downloads/eval-mgmt-serv-guide-ICN006764.pdf

Chen, J.-Y., Zhang, A. D., Lu, H. Y., Guo, J., Wang, F. F., & Li, Z. C. (2013). CHADS2 versus CHA2DS2-VASc score in assessing the stroke and thromboembolism risk stratification in patients with atrial fibrillation: A systematic review and meta-analysis. *Journal of Geriatric Cardiology, 10*(3), 258-266. doi:10.3969/j.issn.1671-5411.2013.03.004

Eckel, R. H., Jakicic, J. M., Ard, J. D., Miller, N. H., Hubbard, V. S., Nonas, C. A., ... Yanovski, S. Z. (2014). 2013 AHA/ACC guideline on lifestyle management to reduce cardiovascular risk: A report of the American College of Cardiology/American Heart Association Task Force on Practice Guidelines. *Circulation, 129,* S76-S99. doi:10.1161/01.cir.0000437740.48606.d1

Flaherty, E., & Resnick, B. (2014). *Geriatric nursing review syllabus: A core curriculum in advanced practice geriatric nursing* (4th ed.). New York, NY: American Geriatrics Society.

Ford, E. S., Greenlund, K. J., & Hong, Y. (2012). Ideal cardiovascular health and mortality from all causes and diseases of the circulatory system among adults in the United States. *Circulation, 125*(8), 987-995. doi:10.1161/CIRCULATIONAHA.111.049122

Goff, D. C., Lloyd-Jones, D. M., Bennett, G., Coady, S., D'Agostino, R. B., Gibbons, R., … Wilson, P. W. F. (2014). 2013 ACC/AHA guideline on the assessment of cardiovascular risk: A report of the American College of Cardiology/American Heart Association Task Force on Practice Guidelines. *Circulation, 129,* S49-S73. doi:10.1161/01.cir.0000437741.48606.98

Levine, G. N., Bates, E. R., Blankenship, J. C., Bailey, S. R., Bittl, J. A., Cercek, B., … Zhao, D. X. (2016). 2015 ACC/AHA/SCAI focused update on primary percutaneous coronary intervention for patients with ST-elevation myocardial infarction: An update of the 2011 ACCF/AHA/SCAI guideline for percutaneous coronary intervention and the 2013 ACCF/AHA guideline for the management of ST-elevation myocardial infarction: A report of the American College of Cardiology/American Heart Association Task Force on Clinical Practice Guidelines and the Society for Cardiovascular Angiography and Interventions. *Circulation, 133,* 1135-1147. doi:10.1161/CIR.0000000000000336

Mehta, L. S., Beckie, T. M., DeVon, H. A., Grines, C. L., Krumholz, H. M., Johnson, M. N., … Wenger, N. K. (2016). Acute myocardial infarction in women: A scientific statement from the American Heart Association. *Circulation, 133,* 916-947. doi:10.1161/CIR.0000000000000351

Mozaffarian, D., Benjamin, E. J., Go, A. S., Arnett, D. K., Blaha, M. J., Cushman, M. … Turner, M. B. (2016). Heart disease and stroke statistics – 2016 update: A report from the American Heart Association. *Circulation, 133,* e38-e360. doi:10.1161/CIR.0000000000000350

Nishimura, R. A., Otto, C. M., Sorajja, P., Sundt, T. M., Thomas, J. D., Bonow, R. O., … Skubas, N. J. (2014). 2014 AHA/ACC guideline for the management of patients with valvular heart disease: A report of the American College of Cardiology/American Heart Association Task Force on Practice Guidelines. *Journal of the American College of Cardiology, 63*(22), e57-e185. doi:10.1016/j.jacc.2014.02.536

Priori, S. G., Blomstrom-Lundqvist, C., Mazzanti, A., Blom, N., Borggrefe, M., Camm, J., … Van Veldhuisen, D. J. (2015). 2015 ESC guidelines for the management of patients with ventricular arrhythmias and the prevention of sudden cardiac death. *European Heart Journal, 36*(41), 2793-2867. doi:10.1093/eurheartj/ehv316

Sanghavi, M., & Rutherford, J. D. (2014). Cardiovascular physiology of pregnancy. *Circulation, 130,* 1003-1008. doi:10.1161/CIRCULATIONAHA.114.009029

Yancy, C. W., Jessup, M., Bozkurt, B., Butler, J., Casey, D. E., Drazner, M. H., … Wilkoff, B. L. (2013). 2013 ACCF/AHA guideline for the management of heart failure: A report of the American College of Cardiology Foundation/American Heart Association Task Force on Practice Guidelines. *Circulation, 128,* e240-e327. doi:10.1161/CIR.0b013e31829e8776

CHAPTER 20

COLLABORATIVE MANAGEMENT: INTERPROFESSIONAL CARDIOVASCULAR TEAM

LEARNING OUTCOME

After completing this chapter, the learner will be able to discuss the significance of interprofessional education and collaboration regarding the delivery of high-quality care to the patient with cardiovascular disease.

CHAPTER OBJECTIVES

After completing this chapter, the learner will be able to:

1. Describe the core competencies for interprofessional education and collaborative practice.

2. Identify core members of the interprofessional team for patients with cardiovascular disease.

INTRODUCTION

Since the early 2000s, the professional healthcare community has confirmed that a patient's healthcare outcomes are directly connected to the effectiveness of interprofessional teams. Evaluation of healthcare systems identified fragmented or uncoordinated care among healthcare professionals and systems. Consequently, medical errors increased, the duplication of services and/or omission of necessary services occurred too often, and overall healthcare costs increased, whereas the quality of patient care and outcomes diminished. For this reason, legislation and healthcare policy has undergone significant redesign in guiding healthcare delivery (Gandhi, Berwick, & Shojania, 2016). Multiple organizations promote the necessary adoption of interprofessional education and collaborative practice (IPECP) within educational institutions and healthcare facilities nationwide as part of the solution to these healthcare issues. To meet the high demands of today's healthcare systems and patients, IPECP competencies must be fundamental to the culture and operations of all healthcare teams, healthcare agencies, and academic curricula (Institute of Medicine [IOM; now the Health and Medicine Division of the National Academies], 2001, 2012; Interprofessional Education Collaborative Expert Panel [IPEC], 2011). The cardiovascular nurse must become knowledgeable of the competencies for interprofessional collaboration and recognize its significance in positively impacting the healthcare team's effectiveness and, ultimately, improving the delivery of high-quality patient-centered care.

CORE COMPETENCIES FOR INTERPROFESSIONAL COLLABORATIVE PRACTICE

Historically, healthcare delivery in the United States has been dependent on the physician providing the lead for all clinical and educational services that patients need. However, research has shown that this delineation of health education is far too great a burden to place upon one profession, and there were not enough physicians to meet the needs of healthcare consumers (IOM, 2001). For this reason, other professionals have assumed some of these responsibilities in an effort to reduce the burden physicians held for so long, to reduce healthcare costs, to increase preventative services and access to healthcare offered to healthcare consumers, and to improve patient outcomes (IOM, 2012; Nester, 2016). For instance, clinical pharmacists have taken the lead in providing medication education to consumers and delivering health-promotion services such as vaccinations. Another example includes the emergence of nurse practitioner (NP)-run clinical practices in professional health shortage areas or rural areas to increase access to healthcare services. Although many of the services each professional can provide overlaps, a healthcare need is being met without the demand being assumed by the physician only. Most important in the collaboration of such healthcare professionals is the recognition of each other's expertise and the application of interprofessional competencies yielding to the avoidance of duplication of services rendered and to the promotion of patient-centered, effective, efficient, safe, and equitable care (IOM, 2001, 2012; IPEC, 2011). The interprofessional team can consist of any healthcare professional, including the physician, nurse (at all levels – practical nurse, registered nurse (RN), or advanced practice nurse), pharmacist, physical therapist, dietician, dentist, optometrist, among others.

Box 20-1 lists definitions of terms common to IPECP language. These terms contribute to the fundamental knowledge of interprofessional education and interprofessional collaborative practice. From this language, models or frameworks were designed to facilitate the implementation of IPECP practices across academic and practice organizations for prelicensure through health professionals practicing at all levels (IPEC, 2011). These frameworks were integral to the development of IPECP core competencies.

Competency Domain 1: Values/Ethics for Interprofessional Practice

All professions adopt core values and ethical principles as a makeup of their professional identity. This competency focuses on the foundation of mutual respect and trust interprofessional relationships must have for effective collaboration among the team, including patients and families (IPEC, 2011).

Competency Domain 2: Roles/Responsibilities

The need to address the complexities of a patient's healthcare requirements in an efficient and cost-effective manner calls for an understanding of the expertise of all members of the healthcare team. Without understanding each team member's role and responsibilities, costly inefficiencies (both to financial resources and the patient's health outcomes) occur. Team members must recognize the diversity of expertise on the team and leverage the expertise for the benefit of the patient without conflict or disagreement eroding the trust and diversity of the team (IPEC, 2011).

Competency Domain 3: Interprofessional Communication

Using language or professional jargon can contribute to the barriers of interprofessional care. A common language is an underpinning for literacy; thus, presenting information in a way that all members of the healthcare team (including patients and families) can understand contributes to safe and effective interprofessional collaborative practice. Effective

BOX 20-1: INTERPROFESSIONAL EDUCATION AND COLLABORATIVE PRACTICE DEFINITIONS

- **Interprofessional education** – the opportunity where students from two or more health professions learn about, learn from, and learn with one another to enable effective collaboration for the purpose of improving health outcomes

- **Interprofessional collaborative practice** – the time when multiple health providers from different professional backgrounds deliberately work together with patients, families, caregivers, and communities to deliver the highest quality of care

- **Interprofessional teamwork** – the levels of cooperation, coordination, and collaboration characterizing the relationships between health professions in delivering patient-centered care

Note. Adapted from Interprofessional Education Collaborative Expert Panel. (2011). *Core competencies for interprofessional collaborative practice: Report of an expert panel.* Washington, DC: Interprofessional Education Collaborative. Retrieved from http://www.aacn.nche.edu/education-resources/ipecreport.pdf

communication within the team is also inclusive of recognizing the limitations professional hierarchies create among people of different professions. Lending higher value to one's expertise contributes to dysfunctional communication, including other members of the team not speaking up. Interprofessional communication encourages all members of the team to firmly, but respectfully, speak up, especially when their concerns are centered around the quality and safety of patient care (IPECP, 2011).

Competency Domain 4: Teams and Teamwork

Learning to work as part of an interprofessional healthcare team involves the understanding that members join a small but complex system. Sharing ideas centered on the best outcomes for patients and families will often yield conflict. However, effective teamwork behaviors include sharing the goals of coordinating the patient's care to identify and close gaps to care and services, reduce redundancies, and reduce errors. Meeting these shared goals requires all team members to participate in shared problem solving and shared decision making (IPEC, 2011).

COMMON ROLES ON THE CARDIOVASCULAR HEALTHCARE TEAM

Employing effective interprofessional teams can improve patient outcomes and lower healthcare costs. However, an additional benefit of effective teamwork is reducing provider fatigue and burnout (Anderson, 2016). An effective cardiovascular healthcare team must recognize each member's licensing scope of practice and decide for themselves how to best approach the care of the patient with cardiovascular disease. This chapter discusses core members of the cardiovascular healthcare team. Ancillary members such as exercise physiologists, registered cardiac sonographers, or vascular surgeons are not discussed.

Cardiologist/Physician

The cardiologist is a licensed physician who has completed doctoral-level education in medicine, a residency in internal medicine, and an additional fellowship in cardiology. This physician is usually board certified in both internal medicine and the specialty of cardiology. Cardiologists can choose to subspecialize in conditions such as hypertension, dyslipidemia, interventional cardiology, electrophysiology, advanced heart failure/transplant, or other forms of heart disease. The physician must be certified in both basic life support and advanced cardiac life support. The physician's scope of practice is to manage the patient's overall cardiac-specific plan of care, which includes conducting a physical examination, providing a diagnosis, and recommending treatment of disease (Anderson, 2016).

Nurse Practitioner

The nurse practitioner (NP) is an advanced practice RN with either a master's level or doctoral level of education. This professional is licensed as an RN and advanced practice RN and must be board certified in the role of NP and a population focus (e.g., primary care family, adult/gerontology primary care or acute care, psychiatric/mental health, pediatric, neonatal, among others). The NP's education, licensing, and certification changed from a general practitioner to a population-focused provider to meet population healthcare needs. For instance, primary care NPs focus on the health maintenance needs of patients, whereas acute care NPs focus on the continuum of a patient's care from stable chronic illness to health decompensation. NPs can gain additional experience and certification in clinical specialties such as diabetes, lipidology, emergency nursing, and other specialties. NPs with doctorate education can also function as academic faculty within NP or other advanced practice RN programs. The NP practicing specifically with patients who have cardiovascular disease must be certified in both basic life support and advanced cardiac life support. Their scope of practice includes examination, diagnosis, and treatment. The degree to which the NP can practice to the full extent of his or her role is dependent on the rules and regulations of each state. Some states in the United States allowing full practice authority of NPs without the supervision or collaborative practice agreement

with physicians. However, there are more states that limit the NP's scope of practice to require physician supervision or collaborative practice (Anderson, 2016).

Registered Nurse

The RN is a licensed healthcare professional who has completed either an associate's or a bachelor's degree. There are many RNs who also gain a master's level of education as a clinical specialist, educator, or nurse leader without licensure as an advanced practice RN. The scope of practice for the RN can be a bedside clinician who assesses the patient, executes medical orders, and evaluates the patient; an administrator of a clinic, hospital, or other healthcare agency; or a nurse educator to RN students in an academic setting or to healthcare staff within the healthcare agency or unit. The RN practicing specifically with cardiovascular patients must be certified in both basic life support and advanced cardiac life support (Anderson, 2016).

Unlicensed Assistive Personnel

The unlicensed assistive personnel (UAP) must be educated with at least a high school diploma or equivalent diploma (GED). It is preferred, but not required, that the UAP complete a certification program for this role as well. The use of UAPs on interprofessional cardiovascular healthcare teams can be very helpful. The UAP serves to appropriately carry out the tasks (which vary by state) delegated by medical or nursing staff. For instance, UAPs can collect vital signs, connect patients to electrocardiogram monitors, or copy medical records for patient transfers. It is preferred, but not required, that UAPs have medical terminology literacy and knowledge of some procedural protocols.

Interprofessional Cardiovascular Team Example

Utilizing the interprofessional cardiovascular team members described earlier, an example of effective collaboration between members of the interprofessional team might involve the following delineation of responsibilities:

- The NP in the cardiology practice oversees the management of a patient with chronic hypertension and dyslipidemia; in this role, the NP functions as the patient's primary care provider.

- Once a year, or as needed, the patient exchanges a follow-up visit with the NP for a visit with the practice's noninvasive/general cardiologist, who performs a full cardiac evaluation.

- The RN serves to coordinate the patient's overall in-office care and patient education about his or her cardiovascular disease; the RN may also serve as the clinic or office manager.

- The UAP serves to assist the NP or cardiologist by carrying out delegated tasks, such as taking vital signs or drawing laboratory blood tests, for the patient.

- Should the patient demonstrate the need for an electrophysiologist or interventionalist, the NP or cardiologist consults with these professionals and integrates their services and expertise in the patient's plan of care.

- Cardiac rehabilitation nurses are consulted to gradually increase the patient's activity and evaluate tolerance to these adjusted activity levels.

- Dieticians are consulted to recommend and educate the patient on customized diet plans.

SUMMARY

Interprofessional education pervades all healthcare settings to support effective interprofessional collaborative practice. All persons on the healthcare team must be respected and utilized to the full scope of their practice to optimize patient outcomes, healthcare costs, and patient or professional satisfaction. The cardiovascular clinician recognizes the significance of his or her role on the interprofessional team in reducing inefficiencies and improving overall patient and healthcare utilization outcomes.

EXAM QUESTIONS

CHAPTER 20
Questions 99–100

Note: Choose the one option that BEST answers each question.

99. Which interprofessional education and collaborative practice competency focuses on the foundation of mutual respect and trust that interprofessional relationships must have for effective collaboration?

    a. Competency Domain 1: Values/Ethics for Interprofessional Practice

    b. Competency Domain 2: Roles/Responsibilities

    c. Competency Domain 3: Interprofessional Communication

    d. Competency Domain 4: Teams and Teamwork

100. Which professional on the interprofessional cardiovascular team has the education and training to manage the patient's overall cardiac care in all states?

    a. Nurse practitioner

    b. Medical assistant

    c. Registered nurse

    d. Cardiologist

This concludes the final examination.

Please answer the evaluation questions found on page v of this course book.

REFERENCES

Anderson, K. M. (2016). *The advanced practice nurse cardiovascular clinician.* New York, NY: Springer Publishing.

Gandhi, T. K., Berwick, D. M., & Shojania, K. G. (2016). Patient safety at the crossroads. *JAMA, 315*(17), 1829-1830. doi:10.1001/jama.2016.1759

Institute of Medicine. (2001). *Crossing the quality chasm: A new health system for the 21st century.* Retrieved from http://www.nationalacademies.org/hmd/~/media/Files/Report%20Files/2001/Crossing-the-Quality-Chasm/Quality%20Chasm%202001%20%20report%20brief.pdf

Institute of Medicine. (2012). *Best care at lower cost: The path to continuously learning health care in America.* Retrieved from http://patientadherence.com/wp-content/uploads/2012/09/IOM-2012-Report-Best-care-at-lower-cost.pdf

Interprofessional Education Collaborative Expert Panel. (2011). *Core competencies for interprofessional collaborative practice: Report of an expert panel.* Washington, DC: Interprofessional Education Collaborative. Retrieved from http://www.aacn.nche.edu/education-resources/ipecreport.pdf

Nester, J. (2016). The importance of interprofessional practice and education in the era of accountable care. *North Carolina Medical Journal, 77*(2), 128-132. doi:10.18043/ncm.77.2.128

GLOSSARY

abdominal obesity: Obesity with a distribution of fat around the abdomen that produces an abnormal waist-to-hip ratio.

acetylcholine: The neurotransmitter of the parasympathetic nervous system.

acidosis: Condition characterized by an arterial blood pH less than 7.35.

activated clotting time (ACT): A test to evaluate coagulation status that can be evaluated at the bedside.

activated partial thromboplastin time (aPTT): Coagulation test used to monitor the therapeutic effectiveness and safety range of heparin.

acute coronary syndrome (ACS): The presentation of coronary artery disease in the form of unstable angina, non-ST-segment elevation MI, or ST-segment elevation MI.

acute decompensating heart failure: An acute change leading to new-onset heart failure or worsening of chronic heart failure, which causes hemodynamic instability or failure to meet the metabolic needs of the body.

acute respiratory distress syndrome (ARDS): A complex clinical syndrome resulting in acute respiratory failure from hypoxic lung injury.

adenosine: Coronary vasodilator used in chemical stress testing. Also used as an antiarrhythmic to slow conduction through the atrioventricular node during some forms of tachycardia.

adenosine diphosphate (ADP): Substance responsible for activation of glycoprotein IIb/IIIa receptors.

adenosine diphosphate (ADP) inhibitors: Medications that prevent ADP-mediated activation of platelets.

adenosine triphosphate (ATP): An enzyme in muscle cells that stores energy and produces energy when split.

adrenal cortex: Outer layer of the adrenal gland.

adrenergic receptor: Receptor of the sympathetic nervous system.

advanced heart failure: Another term for end-stage refractory heart failure; congruent with New York Heart Association (NYHA) class III or IV symptomology.

adventitia: Fibrous outer layer of an artery that is designed to protect the vessel and provide connection to other internal structures.

afferent pathway: Sensory pathways used to send signals to the vasomotor center in the brainstem with increases or decreases in cardiovascular wall tension or pressure.

afterload: Pressure the ventricle must overcome to eject its contents.

aggregation: Clustering or coming together.

albumin: A simple protein widely distributed in tissues that circulates in the blood as serum albumin.

aldosterone: A mineralocorticoid hormone that increases sodium and water reabsorption.

aldosterone antagonist: Medication that blocks the effects of aldosterone.

alkalosis: Condition characterized by a pH more than 7.45.

alpha1 adrenergic receptor: Sympathetic nervous system receptor located in the vessels of vascular smooth muscle.

alveolar membrane: Membrane of the alveoli in the lungs and the site of gas exchange.

aminophylline: Pulmonary vasodilator used as an antidote for adenosine or dipyridamole during chemical stress testing.

amiodarone: A class III antiarrhythmic with vasodilative properties that is generally well tolerated in patients with left ventricular dysfunction; used to treat atrial and ventricular dysrhythmias.

amyloidosis: Disease in which protein fibrils (amyloid) collect in body tissues and impair organ function.

anaphylactic shock: Shock caused by an allergic reaction.

anasarca: Generalized edema that occurs because of systemic disease such as severe heart failure.

androgen: Hormone that produces male characteristics.

anemia: Reduced hemoglobin level or red blood cell count.

aneurysm: A local dilation or outpouching of a vessel wall, or the walls of the heart's ventricles.

angina pectoris: The clinical symptom resulting from decreased blood flow to the myocardium.

angioedema: Allergic response in which the skin, mucous membranes, and viscera become edematous. Commonly occurs around the eyes or lips. Swelling is deep, extending beneath the skin, and can involve the airways.

angiography: Procedure in which serial radiographs of a blood vessel are taken in rapid sequence after the injection of a radiopaque substance. Used to determine the size and shape of vessels. Coronary angiography is also called *cardiac catheterization.*

angiojet thrombectomy: Atherectomy procedure used for the extraction of visible thrombi within the coronary artery.

angiotensin I: Precursor to angiotensin II.

angiotensin II: Potent vasoconstrictor and stimulator of aldosterone secretion.

angiotensin II receptor blocker (ARB): Medication that blocks the effects of angiotensin II.

angiotensin-converting enzyme (ACE): A proteolytic enzyme that converts angiotensin I to angiotensin II.

angiotensin-converting enzyme (ACE) inhibitor: Medication that prevents the conversion of angiotensin I to angiotensin II.

ankle-brachial index (ABI): Blood pressure in the ankle divided by blood pressure in the arm. A decrease in ABI during exercise is an indication that peripheral arterial disease is present.

annulus: Fibrous ring that forms the opening of the valve and joins the valve cusps (leaflets) together.

anorexia: Loss of appetite.

antagonize: To counteract.

antianginal: Medication effective in preventing or decreasing angina.

antibody: A protein substance developed in response to an antigen.

anticoagulant: Medication that interferes with clot formation by disrupting the intrinsic, extrinsic, or common pathway of the coagulation cascade.

antioxidant: An agent that protects against oxidation.

antiplatelet: An agent or medication that interferes with the action of platelets in clot formation.

antiproliferative: Blocking of rapid cell reproduction.

antitachycardia pacing: Pacemaker therapy that utilizes the pacemaker to override a fast rhythm with a higher pacemaker rate. When the pacemaker has control of the rhythm, it slows the rate to a normal range. Also known as *overdrive pacing*.

antithrombin III: An agent that opposes the action of thrombin, inhibits the coagulation of blood, and inactivates several clotting factors.

antithrombotic: Agent that counteracts clot formation.

anxiolytic: Medication given to reduce anxiety.

aorta: Main trunk of the arterial system that originates from the left ventricle.

aortic dissection: Separation of the layers of the aorta.

aortic regurgitation: Abnormal aortic valve function in which valve cusps do not close tightly, causing retrograde movement of blood through the valve during ventricular systole.

aortic root: Beginning of the aorta, where the aorta attaches to the aortic valve.

aortic stenosis: Abnormal aortic valve function, resulting in obstruction of flow from the left ventricle to incorrect or incomplete valve opening.

aortic valve: Valve between the left ventricle and the aorta.

apelin: An endogenous peptide that is important in the regulation of hypertension-induced pathology, such as myocardial hypertrophy and aortic remodeling.

apex: The bottom of the heart. Located approximately at the fifth intercostal space, at the midclavicular line.

apical impulse: The area normally near the apex of the heart where the contraction of the heart can be palpated.

apoptosis: Programmed cell death.

aprotinin: A serine protease inhibitor and hemostatic agent used to prevent bleeding in high-risk patients undergoing coronary artery bypass graft surgery. Also an anti-inflammatory agent.

arginine vasopressin: Antidiuretic hormone that can also be used as a vasopressor.

arrhythmia: No heart rhythm.

arrhythmogenic right ventricular cardiomyopathy: A genetic disorder characterized by right ventricular cardiomyopathy caused by an electrical disturbance that produces dysrhythmias.

arterioles: Small arteries with thick muscular walls.

ascites: Accumulation of serous fluid in the peritoneal cavity.

atelectasis: A condition in which a portion of the lung is unexpanded or collapsed.

atherectomy: Interventional procedure utilizing a cutting tool to cut atherosclerotic plaque away from the wall of the coronary artery.

atheroma: Extracellular lipid core of atherosclerotic plaque.

atheromatous: Pertaining to atheroma.

atherosclerosis: The deposit of lipids, calcium, fibrin, and other cellular substances within the lining of the arteries and the progressive inflammatory response that results from the effort to heal the endothelium.

atherosclerotic plaque: A buildup of the deposits of lipids, calcium, fibrin, and other cellular substances that occurs with atherosclerosis.

atrial fibrillation: Rapid chaotic activity of the atria that results in the deterioration of atrial mechanical activity and produces irregular atrial fibrillation waves with an atrial rate greater than 350 beats/min; there is also variable ventricular conduction resulting in an irregularly irregular ventricular rhythm.

atrial kick (or atrial systole): Atrial contraction, or systole.

atrial myxoma: A benign tumor located in the upper chamber of the heart on the wall that separates the left chamber from the right (the atrial septum).

atrial natriuretic peptide (ANP): Hormone released by the atria during periods of volume overload. Increased production causes vasodilation and diuresis.

atrioventricular (AV) block: Block of the impulse that normally travels from the sinoatrial node to the AV node, disrupting the normal heart rhythm and conduction of impulses through the heart.

atrioventricular (AV) junction: Tissue surrounding the AV node and bundle of His that contains pacemaker cells capable of firing at a rate of 40 to 60 beats/min.

atrioventricular (AV) node: A small mass of tissue that slows conduction from the atria to the ventricles and is located in the right atrium, just above the insertion of the tricuspid valve.

atrioventricular (AV) node ablation: Ablation of the AV node that permanently prevents any rapid ventricular response. Patients who require AV node ablation also need permanent pacemaker implantation.

atrioventricular (AV) valves: Valves located between the atria and ventricles.

autoimmune response: Process by which the body produces an immunological response against itself.

autologous transfusion: Transfusion of blood donated by the patient himself or herself.

automated external defibrillator (AED): Defibrillator designed to be used by trained laypeople in the event of cardiac arrest due to ventricular fibrillation. Rhythm recognition and defibrillation are done automatically via a hands-off approach.

automaticity: Intrinsic ability to depolarize spontaneously.

autonomic dysfunction: Dysfunction of the autonomic nervous system.

autonomic nervous system: Nervous system that controls involuntary bodily functions. Consists of the sympathetic and parasympathetic nervous systems.

autoregulation: The process of the body's structures and functions regulating blood flow according to the body's tissues' oxygen needs.

Bachmann's bundle: Conduction pathway that allows depolarization of the left atrial tissue as conduction travels from the sinoatrial node to the atrioventricular node.

balloon angioplasty: Percutaneous transluminal coronary angioplasty (PTCA) done without the placement of an intracoronary stent.

baroreceptors: Specialized nerve tissues functioning as sensors that are located in the aortic arch and carotid sinus (the origin of the internal carotid artery).

base: Top of the heart, which is located at approximately the second intercostal space.

beta1-adrenergic receptor: Sympathetic nervous system receptor located in the heart.

beta2-adrenergic receptor: Sympathetic nervous system receptor located in the lungs and periphery.

beta blocker: Medication that blocks either beta1- or beta2-adrenergic receptors.

beta radiation: Type of radiation used for in-stent restenosis with less dwell time and less scatter than gamma radiation.

beta receptor down-regulation: An attempt to protect the failing heart from chronic overstimulation of the sympathetic nervous system.

Bezold-Jarisch reflex: Cardiovascular reflex that causes a vasovagal response when triggered.

bifascicular block: A block of the normal conduction system involving simultaneous blockage of the right bundle branch and blockage of one of the two fascicles of the left bundle branch.

bile acid sequestrant: Also called a *resin,* a lipid-lowering drug that combines with bile acids in the intestine to form an insoluble complex that is excreted in feces.

bioprosthetic valve: Tissue valve from a human or animal donor.

biphasic reaction: A second anaphylactic reaction occurring after resolution of the first within a 1- to 72-hour window.

biphasic waveform defibrillator: Newer generation of defibrillators that use energy more efficiently, therefore requiring lower amounts of energy for a defibrillation or cardioversion shock.

bisferiens carotid pulse: Characteristic of a patient with hypertrophic obstructive cardiomyopathy in which the initial upstroke of the carotid pulse is brisk; however, as systole progresses, left ventricular outflow tract obstruction can occur. This obstruction results in a collapse of the pulse and then a secondary rise.

biventricular pacing: See *cardiac resynchronization therapy.*

body mass index (BMI): An index used to define overweight and obesity. Calculated by using height, weight, and a constant.

brachial plexus: Network of nerves supplying the arm, forearm, and hand.

brachiocephalic artery: Also called the *innominate artery,* the largest branch off the aortic arch that divides into the right common carotid and right subclavian arteries.

bradycardia: Heart rate below 50 beats/min.

bradydysrhythmia: A dysrhythmia characterized by a ventricular rate less than 60 beats/min.

brain natriuretic peptide (BNP): A hormone released from myocytes during heart failure that produces vasodilation. Serum BNP levels are used in the diagnosis of heart failure.

Brugada syndrome: Ventricular tachycardia seen with right bundle branch block, a normal QT interval, ST segment changes, and without a history of structural heart disease.

bruit: An adventitious sound heard on auscultation of a vessel.

bundle branch block: Block of either the right or left bundle branch.

bundle of His: Conduction pathway that divides and gives rise to the right and left bundle branches.

bupropion: Oral antidepressant used for smoking cessation.

calcium channel blocker: Medication that decreases the flux of calcium across the cell membrane.

cannulation: The placement of a tube inside a vessel to allow the escape of blood and other fluids from the body. Used in cardiopulmonary bypass surgery.

capillary: The very smallest vessel that connects the smallest arteries and veins. Also the location of oxygen and nutrient exchange.

carbon monoxide: A poisonous gas that is colorless, odorless, and tasteless.

cardiac biomarker: Substance released into the blood when necrosis occurs as a result of myocyte membrane rupture.

cardiac catheterization: An invasive diagnostic procedure, used to identify blockage of coronary arteries, whereby a catheter is threaded through an artery into the heart, a contrast agent (dye) is injected into the coronary arteries, and angiography is performed.

cardiac index: A measure of cardiac output utilizing the patient's height and weight divided by his/her own body's surface area.

cardiac myoplasty: Surgery that involves wrapping a muscle from the patient's back around the heart and stimulating it to contract via a pacemaker wire.

cardiac output: The amount of blood ejected by the left ventricle every minute.

cardiac resynchronization therapy (CRT): Pacemaker therapy aimed at eliminating dyssynchrony of the contractions of the right and left ventricles that occurs in severe heart failure. Utilizes a pacemaker lead for each ventricle (biventricular pacing).

cardiac tamponade: Accumulation of excess fluid in the pericardium that prevents ventricular filling.

cardiogenic shock: Failure of tissues to receive an adequate blood supply because of severely decreased cardiac output caused by left ventricular failure.

cardiomyopathy: A structural disorder associated with the development of heart failure; heart muscle disease.

cardioplegia: Paralysis of the heart.

cardiopulmonary bypass: Process by which the normal circulation of blood bypasses the heart and lungs during the administration of cardioplegia for coronary artery bypass graft surgery. This is accomplished by rerouting the blood through a cardiopulmonary bypass machine that functions in place of the heart and lungs.

cardioversion: Restoration of a tachydysrhythmia (atrial fibrillation, supraventricular tachycardia, ventricular tachycardia) to a normal rhythm, using electrical stimulation or pharmacotherapy.

carotid endarterectomy: A surgical procedure whereby the fatty buildup of plaque is removed from the carotid artery.

catalyze: To speed up the rate of a reaction.

catecholaminergic polymorphic ventricular tachycardia (PMVT): PMVT triggered by exercise or stress that occurs with a normal QT interval.

catecholamines: The sympathetic nervous system neurotransmitters epinephrine and norepinephrine.

cephalosporin: Class of antibiotics most frequently used to prevent postoperative infection in coronary artery bypass graft surgery.

cerebrovascular accident (CVA): Also known as *stroke*. Injury to the brain caused by inadequate oxygenated blood supply. Can be caused by thrombus or embolus (ischemic stroke) or by hemorrhage (hemorrhagic stroke).

chemoreceptors: Receptors located in the aortic arch and carotid arteries that respond to changes in blood chemistry, including arterial oxygen content, arterial carbon dioxide levels, and arterial pH.

cholinergic: Name of response of the parasympathetic nervous system.

chordae tendineae: Delicate strands of fibrous material that attach atrioventricular valve leaflets to the papillary muscles.

chronic obstructive pulmonary disease (COPD): A chronic lung disease characterized by a limitation in airflow during normal breathing.

chronic venous insufficiency: Inadequate venous return over a long period (greater than 3 to 6 months) that causes persistent ambulatory venous hypertension resulting in multiple venous pathologies such as edema, leg pain, and ulcerations.

chronotropic: Affecting the heart rate.

cirrhosis: Chronic disease of the liver involving connective tissue, fatty infiltrates, and degenerative changes.

claudication: Acute pain associated with muscle ischemia.

coagulopathy: Pathology of the coagulation system.

coarctation of the aorta: Malformation resulting in narrowing of the aorta.

coarse ventricular fibrillation (VF): VF with waves greater than 3 mm in amplitude.

collagen: Fibrous protein found in connective tissue.

commissure: Point where the cardiac valve leaflets connect.

commissurotomy: Procedure during which the valve commissures are cut apart to allow for increased movement of the leaflets.

common pathway: Final pathway in clotting cascade in which a fibrinogen is converted to fibrin and a fibrin stable clot is formed.

complete heart block: Complete failure of the atrial impulses to be conducted to the ventricles.

concentric hypertrophy: A change in the walls of the ventricle resulting in thickened walls that are stiff and noncompliant but do not increase the overall size of the ventricle.

conduit: Term used to describe a blood vessel used as a bypass graft during coronary artery bypass graft surgery.

contractility: Ability of the ventricle to pump independent of preload or afterload.

contrast-induced nephropathy: Renal dysfunction caused by the administration of contrast agents during invasive or interventional cardiac procedures.

coronary artery bypass graft (CABG) surgery: Surgery during which blood flow through a coronary artery is rerouted around a blockage or narrowing in the coronary artery utilizing a bypass graft. A variety of veins or arteries from the patient or a donor can be utilized as bypass grafts.

coronary artery disease (CAD): Disease process that results in narrowing or occlusion of the coronary artery.

coronary heart disease (CHD): Term used interchangeably with CAD.

coronary sinus: The vessel that receives blood from the cardiac veins and empties into the right atrium.

creatine kinase (CK): Biomarker present in the heart, brain, and skeletal muscle.

creatine kinase-MB: Biomarker specific to the heart that rapidly rises in the presence of myocardial damage.

cryopreservation: Preservation by subjection to very low temperatures.

cryotherapy: Therapy using cold.

crystalloid solution: Clear intravenous solution with dissolved substances that can diffuse across cell membranes. For example, normal saline solution.

cutting balloon: A device used to make incisions into the plaque before dilation during percutaneous transluminal coronary angioplasty.

cyclooxygenase: Chemical substance that performs the first step in the creation of prostaglandins.

cyclosporin: Medication used to suppress the immune system.

cytokine: Protein secreted by cells of the immune system that helps to regulate the immune system.

debridement: Removal of dead or damaged tissue from a wound.

defibrillation: Desynchronized shock delivered to patients in ventricular fibrillation or ventricular tachycardia.

depolarization: Stimulation of cardiac muscle cells.

diabetes mellitus: Insulin deficit (type I) or inappropriate response to insulin (type II), resulting in a random glucose level greater than 200 mg/dl or a fasting glucose level greater than 126 mg/dl.

diastole: Relaxation of the heart muscle that permits filling of the chamber.

diastolic dysfunction: Left ventricular dysfunction whereby the ventricle has impaired relaxation and does not fill properly.

Dietary Approaches to Stop Hypertension (DASH) diet: A diet that manipulates potassium, calcium, and magnesium while holding sodium constant.

dilatation: Expansion of an organ or a vessel.

dilated cardiomyopathy (DCM): Cardiomyopathy caused by an enlarged, dilated cardiac chamber that affects the ability of the ventricle to contract, resulting in systolic dysfunction.

dipyridamole: A coronary vasodilator used in chemical stress testing.

direct current cardioversion: Procedure in which an electrical shock is synchronized with the intrinsic activity of the heart to convert an abnormal rhythm back into a normal rhythm.

directional atherectomy: Procedure used to cut and remove plaque in native vessels or in saphenous vein grafts by directing a rotating cutter toward the plaque to be removed.

distensibility: Ability to stretch.

dobutamine: Inotropic agent used for chemical stress testing. Also used in critically ill patients in cardiogenic shock or end-stage heart failure.

dopaminergic receptor: Sympathetic nervous system receptor located in the renal, mesenteric, and coronary blood vessels.

Dressler's syndrome: Pericarditis occurring several weeks after an infarction.

dromotropic: Affecting cardiac conduction.

drug-eluting stent: Stent coated with a pharmacological agent aimed at decreasing restenosis.

dual-chamber pacemaker: Pacemaker that has an electrode for pacing in two chambers of the heart – traditionally, the right atrium and the right ventricle.

Duroziez's sign: Systolic murmur heard over the femoral artery when compressed proximally or diastolic murmur heard over the femoral artery when compressed distally.

dyslipidemia: An abnormal amount of lipids in the blood.

dysrhythmia: Abnormal heart rhythm.

dyssynergy: An increase in the energy needed for contraction resulting in a decrease in cardiac output.

eccentric hypertrophy: Hypertrophy caused by volume overload and resulting in ventricular dilation. Wall thickness is in proportion to chamber size.

echocardiogram: Cardiac ultrasound.

ectopic beat: Beat originating outside the sinus node.

efferent pathway: Motor pathways by which signals interpreted by the medulla are transmitted back to the heart and blood vessels.

ejection fraction: The percent of blood volume ejected with each heartbeat.

electrocautery: Cauterization (destruction of tissue) by means of a device heated by a current of electricity.

electromechanical interference: Electrical signals external to a pacemaker that may be sensed by the pacemaker, making it difficult for the pacemaker to sense the heart's activity in the normal manner. This can lead to a dysfunctional pacemaker.

electrophysiology: Field of cardiology dedicated to the study and treatment of disorders of the heart's electrical conduction system.

embolus: A particle of undissolved matter in the blood (can be solid, liquid, or gas; e.g., a piece of a clot or fat or an air bubble).

emergency medical system (EMS): Community response system where paramedics and other trained personnel respond to medical emergencies. Activated by dialing 911 in most parts of the country.

endocarditis: Inflammation of the endocardium (the inner lining of heart), including the heart valves.

endocardium: The inner surface of the heart chambers and valves that also covers the walls of the vessels of the entire vascular system.

endomyocardial biopsy: Tissue biopsy obtained from the septal wall of the right ventricle using an invasive catheter-based approach. Used in the diagnosis of restrictive cardiomyopathy.

endomyocardial fibrosis: Fibrosis of the ventricular endocardium and subendocardium that extends to the mitral and tricuspid valves and greatly decreases the functioning of the ventricular chambers.

endothelin: Endogenous hormonal vasoconstrictor released by the endothelium.

endothelium: Layer of epithelial cells that lines the heart, blood vessels, and other body cavities.

endovascular: Minimally invasive techniques using catheter-based treatments, as opposed to full, open surgeries.

epiaortic imaging: Ultrasound imaging directly over the aorta that is used in coronary artery bypass graft surgery.

epicardial fat: Fat tissue in the epicardial layer of the heart that increases with age and obesity, and consequently increases the patient's risk for coronary artery disease.

epicardium: The smooth outer layer of the heart that contains the network of coronary arteries and veins, the autonomic nerves, the lymphatic system, and fat tissue.

epigastric: Referring to the area over the superior portion of the stomach.

epinephrine: Also called *adrenaline,* a neurotransmitter of the sympathetic nervous system.

epistaxis: Bleeding from the nose.

ergonovine maleate: Arterial vasoconstrictor that can be given during cardiac catheterization to assist in the diagnosis of vasospastic angina.

erythropoietin: A hormone that regulates red blood cell production.

estrogen: Female sex hormone.

external counterpulsation: Nonpharmacological treatment option for debilitating angina in which a series of cuffs are wrapped around the patient's legs and compressed air is used to apply pressure in the cuffs in synchronization with the cardiac cycle, resulting in increased arterial pressure that increases retrograde aortic blood flow into the coronary arteries during diastole.

extrinsic pathway: Pathway in the clotting cascade activated by injured tissue.

extubation: Removal of an endotracheal tube.

Fabry's disease: A lipid storage disorder caused by the deficiency of an enzyme involved in the biodegradation of fats.

false aneurysms: Involve the collection of blood within the vessel walls, or hematoma, communicating with the intravascular space; most often caused by a leak between a vascular graft and a natural artery at the site of anastomosis, or cannulation of the vessel wall during catheterization.

fibric acids: A group of lipid-lowering medications most noted for their ability to lower triglycerides. Also called *fibrates.*

fibrin: Fine protein filaments formed by the action of thrombin on fibrinogen that entangle red and white blood cells and platelets and form a clot.

fibrinogen: A protein that is converted to fibrin through the action of thrombin in the presence of calcium ions.

fibrinolytic: Fibrin-specific medication used to break down clots.

fibrous atheroma: Atheroma characterized by the accumulation of fibrous connective tissue within the intima.

fibrous cap: Fibrous tissue, mainly collagen, that covers the lipid core coronary plaques; rupture of fibrous cap often appears at shoulder regions of plaques.

fibrous pericardium: External cover of the pericardium.

fine ventricular fibrillation (VF): VF with waves less than 3 mm in amplitude.

foam cell: Macrophage (scavenger cell) that is engorged with lipids.

forward flow: The concept of the mechanical function of the heart, heart valves, and blood vessels maintaining unidirectional blood flow to achieve the delivery of oxygen and nutrients to all body tissues.

free graft: Graft where both ends of the vessel are removed from their original locations and reattached elsewhere.

fusiform aneurysm: True aneurysms that develop circumferentially.

gamma radiation: Type of radiation used to treat in-stent restenosis. Has a longer dwell time than beta radiation and is used to treat more difficult lesions.

glomerular filtration rate (GFR): A calculation to determine how well the blood is filtered by the kidneys. It is calculated using a mathematical formula that compares a person's age, sex, and race with serum creatinine, albumin, and blood urea nitrogen levels. Normal GFR in adults is 120 to 125 ml/min.

glutaraldehyde: Chemical that is used as a cold sterilant and a tissue fixative.

glycoprotein (GP) IIb/IIIa receptor: Receptor site on platelet surface where platelets and fibrinogen bind to form a fibrin mesh.

graft: A portion of a vessel taken from another part of the body that is used to bypass a coronary artery blockage during coronary artery bypass graft surgery.

great vessels: The aorta, the pulmonary artery, the inferior vena cava, and the superior vena cava.

gynecomastia: Enlarged mammary glands in a male.

heart block: Condition that arises because of a cardiac conduction system disturbance, resulting in the lack of coordination of the atrial and ventricular activity of the heart.

heart failure preserved ejection fraction (HFpEF): Formerly known as diastolic heart failure; accompanied by an ejection fraction from 40% to 71%.

heart failure reduced ejection fraction (HFrEF): Formerly known as systolic heart failure; accompanied by an ejection fraction less than 40%.

heart rate: Number of times the heart beats in a minute.

hematoma: Mass of blood within the tissue caused by bleeding from a blood vessel.

hemochromatosis: Condition in which the body stores excess iron, causing organ damage.

hemodynamics: Forces influencing the circulation of blood throughout the body.

hemoglobin A$_{1c}$ (HbA$_{1c}$): Glycosylated hemoglobin, a reflection of the average blood sugar level for 2 to 3 months before the test.

hemoptysis: Coughing or spitting up blood that is the result of bleeding from the respiratory system.

hemostasis: Cessation of bleeding.

hemothorax: Collection of blood in the pleural cavity.

hepatojugular reflux: Response of jugular venous pressure when firm pressure is applied to the midepigastric region. This response is exaggerated in right-sided heart failure.

hepatomegaly: Enlargement of the liver.

high-ceiling diuretics: Diuretics with a rapid onset and short duration of action (e.g., loop diuretics).

high-degree atrioventricular (AV) block: The true block of two or more atrial impulses (not in atrial flutter). Also called *advanced AV block.*

high-density lipoprotein cholesterol (HDL-C): A high-density lipoprotein that contains small amounts of cholesterol and triglycerides. High levels of HDL are usually associated with a decreased risk for heart disease.

high-sensitivity C-reactive protein (hs-CRP): A marker of inflammation. Elevated levels increase cardiovascular risk.

hirudin: Direct thrombin inhibitor.

HMG-CoA reductase: Key enzyme in the synthesis of cholesterol.

HMG-CoA reductase inhibitor: Also called a *statin,* the most widely used lipid-lowering medication in the treatment of cardiovascular disease. Inhibits HMG-CoA reductase during cholesterol synthesis.

holosystolic murmur: A murmur that can be heard throughout systole.

homocysteine: An amino acid that has toxic effects on the endothelium when elevated.

homologous: Similar in both structure and source.

hydrogenated oil: Oil that has hydrogen added to it to make it solid at room temperature.

hydrostatic pressure: Pushing pressure inside a vessel that forces fluids and nutrients across a membrane.

hypercholesterolemia: Elevated serum cholesterol.

hyperdynamic: Increased contractility and ejection fraction (when referring to the left ventricle).

hyperhomocysteinemia: Elevated serum homocysteine.

hyperkalemia: Elevated serum potassium.

hyperlipidemia: Condition characterized by elevated total cholesterol (hypercholesterolemia), elevated low-density lipoprotein cholesterol, or elevated triglycerides.

hyperplasia: Excessive proliferation of normal cells.

hypersensitive carotid sinus: A reflex caused by increased parasympathetic tone when pressure is applied to the carotid sinus, resulting in a slowing of the heart rate.

hypertension: Condition characterized by a systolic or diastolic blood pressure above the normal range.

hyperthyroidism: Excessive secretion from the thyroid gland, resulting in increased basal metabolic rate.

hypertriglyceridemia: Elevated serum triglycerides.

hypertrophic cardiomyopathy (HCM): Cardiomyopathy characterized by hypertrophy of the myocardium, resulting in a decrease in ventricular filling and a decrease in cardiac output.

hypertrophic obstructive cardiomyopathy (HOCM): Hypertrophic cardiomyopathy with obstruction.

hypertrophy: Increased size or volume because of enlargement of the cells.

hypokalemia: Low serum potassium.

hypomagnesemia: Low serum magnesium.

hypoperfusion: Decreased perfusion.

hypotension: A systolic or diastolic blood pressure below the normal range.

hypoventilation: Decreased ventilation (amount of inhaled oxygen).

hypovolemia: Diminished blood volume.

hypoxemia: Low level of oxygen in the blood.

hypoxia: Decreased oxygenation of the tissues.

idiopathic: Having no known cause.

idiopathic hypertrophic subaortic stenosis (IHSS): Previous name for hypertrophic cardiomyopathy.

idiopathic normal QT polymorphic ventricular tachycardia: PMVT without QT prolongation that cannot be attributed to Brugada syndrome or catecholamines.

implantable cardioverter-defibrillator (ICD): Device inserted into the heart that provides a defibrillation shock and other therapies to treat rapid heart rates in a variety of patients.

incentive spirometry: Procedure designed to mimic natural sighing by encouraging the patient to take long, slow, deep breaths using a device that provides visual or other positive feedback upon inhalation of a predetermined volume and sustained inflation for a minimum of 3 seconds.

inferior vena cava: Principal vein that receives blood from below the level of the diaphragm, including the abdomen, pelvis, and lower extremities. The inferior vena cava empties into the right atrium.

innervation: Distribution of the nervous system.

inotrope: Medication used to increase the strength of the heart's contractions.

inotropic: Influencing the force of contractility.

interatrial septum: A mass of connective tissue that separates the right and left atria.

intercalated disks: Disks that form a tight junction, allowing cardiac muscle cells to function as integrated units.

internal iliac arteries: Arteries that arise from the abdominal aorta and supply blood to the lower trunk, including the reproductive organs and the legs.

internal mammary artery graft: Most common arterial graft used in coronary artery bypass grafting. Has better long-term patency rates than vein grafts.

international normalized ratio (INR): A value that relates prothrombin time to the intensity of actual coagulation. Developed to correct problems with standardization of prothrombin time.

internodal pathways: Conduction pathways in the right atrium that allow conduction between the sino-atrial and atrioventricular nodes.

interstitial pneumonitis: Lung disease characterized by marked interstitial fibrosis. Has an insidious onset with slow, but severe, progression and a poor prognosis, with most patients dying of the disease.

interventricular septum: A mass of connective tissue that separates the right and left ventricles.

intima: The innermost wall of all arteries, which consists of a thin layer of endothelium.

intraaortic balloon pump (IABP): An invasive catheter-based assistive device that uses counterpulsation therapy. The balloon, located in the descending aorta, inflates during diastole and deflates during systole. The timing of balloon deflation just before systole reduces cardiac afterload, and balloon inflation during diastole increases myocardial perfusion.

intracoronary stent: Metal scaffold-type structure that is inserted into a coronary artery to help prevent elastic recoil and keep open the lumen of the vessel.

intracoronary (intravascular) ultrasound: A tiny ultrasound device that is threaded into an artery inside a millimeter-thick catheter. Ultrasound waves measure changes in wall thickness, providing a detailed cross section of the coronary artery.

intracranial hemorrhage: Bleeding inside the skull that encloses the brain.

intrinsic pathway (coagulation cascade): Pathway in the clotting cascade that is activated by damage to the red blood cells or the platelets. The intrinsic pathway can be assessed by monitoring activated partial thromboplastin time.

intubation: Placement of an endotracheal tube.

ischemia: Temporary lack of oxygen because of insufficient blood supply to an organ, muscle, or tissue.

isolated systolic hypertension: A systolic blood pressure greater than 160 mmHg that is accompanied by a normal diastolic blood pressure.

isovolumetric contraction: Contraction of the ventricle, occurring during the first phase of cardiac systole, when all cardiac valves are closed and the volume of blood in the ventricle remains constant. Also know as *isovolumic contraction.*

jugular venous pressure: Pressure in the jugular vein that increases or decreases in response to fluid status.

kinin: Substance that produces vasodilative effects.

Kussmaul sign: When the jugular venous pulse either does not fall or rises with inspiration.

Law of Laplace: The pressure required to inflate a sphere is equal to twice the surface tension divided by the radius of the sphere.

left anterior descending artery (LAD): Coronary artery arising from the left main coronary artery that is responsible for supplying oxygenated blood to the anterior wall of the left ventricle.

left anterior hemiblock: Block of the anterior fascicle of the left bundle.

left atrial appendage: Appendage off the left atrium that is frequently the source of clot formation in atrial fibrillation.

left atrium: Chamber of the heart that receives oxygenated blood from the pulmonary veins.

left bundle branch: Conduction pathway that divides into the left posterior bundle branch and the left anterior bundle branch and carries impulses to the posterior, inferior, and anterior walls of the left ventricle.

left circumflex (LCX) artery: Coronary artery arising from the left main coronary artery that is responsible for supplying blood to the lateral wall of the left ventricle.

left common carotid artery: Artery that branches directly off the thoracic aorta and is one of two common carotid arteries that supply blood to the neck and head.

left main coronary artery: Major coronary artery arising from the left side of the aorta that supplies oxygenated blood to a major portion of the myocardium via the left anterior descending and left circumflex coronary arteries.

left subclavian artery: Artery that arises from the end of the aortic arch and is one of two subclavian arteries that supply blood to the upper extremities.

left ventricle: A thick-walled, high-pressure pump that receives oxygenated blood from the left atrium and pumps blood into the aorta.

left ventricular reduction surgery: Surgery in which a part of the left ventricle is cut out and the remaining walls are sewn together to decrease the size of the ventricle. Also called the *Batista procedure.*

leukocyte: White blood cell.

linear ablation: Catheter-based technique developed to achieve the same effect as with the surgical Maze procedure.

lipid: Fat or fatlike substance that is insoluble in water.

lipoprotein: Refers to triglycerides, cholesterol, phospholipids, and lipids bound to carrier proteins.

lipoprotein (a): A lipoprotein similar to low-density lipoprotein cholesterol.

Löffler's endocarditis: Endomyocardial disease characterized by endomyocardial fibrosis, an unusually large number of eosinophils in the blood with infiltration of the heart.

lone atrial fibrillation: Atrial fibrillation in patients with normal cardiac and pulmonary function and with no known predisposing factors.

loop diuretic: An agent that works at the loop of Henle to increase sodium and water excretion.

low-density lipoprotein cholesterol (LDL-C): A lipoprotein that is commonly referred to as the "bad" cholesterol because of its role in the development of atherosclerosis. LDL deposits cholesterol on the artery walls.

low-molecular-weight heparin (LMWH): Heparin that is lower in molecular weight and smaller in size than unfractionated heparin.

lysis: Dissolution or decomposition (as in clot lysis).

Marfan's syndrome: Disorder characterized by abnormal length of the extremities, congenital anomalies of the heart, and other associated deformities.

mast cells: Connective tissue cell that plays a key role in the initiation of inflammation.

Maze procedure: Surgical procedure in which a series of incisions are made in the atria using radiofrequency or another form of energy to block reentrant pathways within the atrial tissue and to channel conduction in a more normal fashion.

media: The middle layer of an artery, which consists of smooth muscle and elastic connective tissue.

mediastinitis: Inflammation of the tissue of the mediastinum.

mediastinum: The space near the midline of the chest between the pleural sacs of the lungs that extends from the sternum to the spine. This space contains all the organs and tissues of the chest except the lungs.

medulla: The vasomotor center of the brain that interprets all information received from the baroreceptors.

MET level: Metabolic equivalent unit used to estimate the amount of oxygen utilized by the body during physical activity.

metabolic syndrome: A grouping of lipid and nonlipid risk factors of metabolic origin.

metastatic cancer: Cancer that has spread beyond the site of origin.

metformin: Oral hypoglycemic agent that can potentially cause nephrotoxicity.

mevalonic acid: A precursor to cholesterol.

microvascular: Related to very small vessels.

microvascular complications (of diabetes): Vision loss, nephropathy, neuropathy, and amputation.

minimally invasive coronary artery bypass (MIDCAB): Procedure performed on a beating heart without cardiopulmonary bypass and without the use of a median sternotomy.

mitral facies: Pinkish purple discoloration of the cheeks that is common in patients with severe mitral stenosis.

mitral regurgitation: Inadequate closure of the mitral valve that results in backward flow of blood from the left ventricle to the left atrium during ventricular systole. Also called *mitral insufficiency.*

mitral stenosis: Condition in which the mitral valve is unable to open normally, causing an obstruction of blood flow from the left atrium to the left ventricle during ventricular diastole.

mitral valve: Valve located between the left atrium and left ventricle.

mitral valve prolapse: Condition in which one or both of the mitral valve leaflets collapse into the atrium, sometimes allowing small amounts of blood to flow back into the atrium.

monophasic waveform defibrillators: Early generation defibrillators that use energy inefficiently and require higher amounts of energy for defibrillation or cardioversion shock.

monounsaturated fat: Beneficial fat in a heart-healthy diet that derives from a plant source and is liquid at room temperature. Examples include canola oil and olive oil.

murmur: An atypical sound produced by vibrations caused by turbulent blood flow. A cardiac murmur is typically associated with cardiac valve disease that creates turbulent blood flow through a valve that does not open or close properly.

muscarinic receptor: Type of parasympathetic, or cholinergic, receptor located in the heart and smooth muscle.

Musset's sign: Bobbing of the head with each heart beat.

myocardial imaging: Noninvasive studies utilized to assess various functions of the heart. These studies include cardiac echocardiography and radionuclide imaging and can be done individually or in combination with a stress test.

myocardial infarction (MI): Damage or death (necrosis) of part of the heart muscle.

myocarditis: Inflammation of the myocardium.

myocardium: Thick middle layer of heart that contains cardiac muscle fibers.

myocyte: Contractile cardiac muscle cell.

myofibril: Small fiber that is the contractile element of muscle cells.

myoglobin: Sensitive cardiac biomarker that rises the earliest with myocardial damage.

natriuretic peptide: Hormones released by the heart during periods of volume overload. Increased production of these hormones causes vasodilation, both pulmonary and systemic, as well as diuresis. The release of these hormones is beneficial during periods of acute decompensated heart failure. Types of natriuretic peptides include atrial natriuretic peptide and brain natriuretic peptide.

necrosis: Accidental death of a portion of tissue.

nephrotoxic: Toxic to the kidneys.

nesiritide (Natrecor): A synthetic form of brain natriuretic peptide that is administered intravenously for patients in acute heart failure.

neurocardiogenic syncope: A loss of consciousness caused by overstimulation of the vagus nerve and a reduction in normal sympathetic activity resulting in hypotension, bradycardia, and peripheral vasodilation.

neurogenic atrial fibrillation: Atrial fibrillation caused by either increased vagal tone or increased adrenergic tone.

neurohormonal responses: Various hormonal and neurological responses that occur in heart failure to attempt to compensate for decreased cardiac output.

niacin: A B complex vitamin with additional dose-related pharmacological positive effects on lipid levels. Also called *nicotinic acid.*

nicotine: The physically addictive substance in tobacco.

nicotinic receptor: Type of parasympathetic, or cholinergic, receptor.

noncompliant ventricle: A ventricle that is unable to relax and fill properly during diastole.

nonhomologous graft: Grafts from another species.

non-ST-segment elevation myocardial infarction (non-STEMI): A myocardial infarction diagnosis based on elevated cardiac biomarkers or enzymes. This type of myocardial infarction does not present with ST-segment elevation on the 12-lead electrocardiogram.

nonsustained ventricular tachycardia: Less than 30 seconds of ventricular tachycardia.

nonvalvular atrial fibrillation: Atrial fibrillation in the absence of rheumatic heart disease that causes mitral stenosis or the absence of a prosthetic heart valve.

norepinephrine: A neurotransmitter of the sympathetic nervous system. Also called *nonadrenaline.*

normal muscular synergy: The inward movement occurring simultaneously among all walls of the ventricle.

nosocomial pneumonia: Pneumonia acquired in the hospital.

NPO: Nothing by mouth.

off-pump coronary artery bypass (OPCAB): Coronary artery bypass surgery done without the use of a cardiopulmonary bypass machine. This approach to surgery does require an open-chest procedure with a midline sternal incision.

omega-3 fatty acid: Nonessential fatty acid contained in oily fish, such as salmon, lake trout, tuna, and herring.

oncotic pressure: The pulling pressure inside a vessel that draws fluid and other substances into the vessel.

opening snap: Abnormal sound made by the opening of a stenotic mitral or tricuspid valve.

opioid: Drug derived from an opium alkaloid. An example is morphine.

orthopnea: Shortness of breath when in a supine position.

orthostatic: Concerning an upright position.

ostium: Small opening in the aorta that gives rise to the right and left coronary artery systems.

overdrive pacing: Involves extrinsic electricity capturing and controlling the patient's intrinsic electricity for the purpose of terminating the dysrhythmia and restoring a viable rhythm.

oxidation: The process of a substance combining with oxygen.

oxyhemoglobin: The capacity each hemoglobin molecule has to chemically bond with four oxygen molecules.

P wave: Wave on an electrocardiogram that represents atrial depolarization.

pacemaker electrode: Electrode located at the end of a pacemaker lead wire that delivers the stimulus to the heart muscle to make it contract.

pacemaker generator: Lithium battery and the electrical microcircuitry necessary to operate a pacemaker. Also referred to as the *battery* or *can*.

pacemaker lead: Wire that travels from the pacemaker generator to the wall of the heart that carries the message to contract from the generator to the heart. Houses the pacemaker electrode at the end of the wire.

pacemaker pacing: The ability of a pacemaker to send an impulse through a lead wire to an electrode and stimulate the heart to contract.

pacemaker sensing: The ability of a cardiac pacemaker to recognize native cardiac activity that is occurring in a cardiac chamber that has a cardiac pacing electrode.

paclitaxel: An antiproliferative or antineoplastic agent used on drug-eluting stents that is also used as a chemotherapeutic agent.

papillary muscles: Muscle projections from the inner surface of the ventricles that attach to the chordae tendineae of the atrioventricular valves.

parasympathetic nervous system: Branch of the autonomic nervous system that helps the body conserve and restore resources.

parasympatholytic: Medication that lyses the parasympathetic nervous system.

parietal pericardium: Inner lining of the fibrous pericardium.

paroxysmal: Coming on suddenly and terminating without intervention. Used to describe tachydysrhythmias.

paroxysmal atrial fibrillation: Atrial fibrillation that comes on spontaneously and terminates itself. Cannot last longer than 7 days and usually lasts less than 24 hours.

paroxysmal nocturnal dyspnea: Awakening from a sleep state with sudden and intense shortness of breath.

pathological Q wave: Abnormally deep or wide Q wave that indicates necrosis of myocardial tissue.

pedicle graft: Graft in which one end of an artery is left in its original position. Examples include internal mammary artery graft.

percutaneous alcohol septal ablation (PASA): Procedure performed in a cardiac catheterization laboratory during which a catheter is inserted into a septal perforator branch (provides blood flow to the septum). Ethyl alcohol is then injected to produce a controlled septal myocardial infarction.

percutaneous coronary intervention (PCI): A procedure that treats coronary artery disease without the use of surgery. Most commonly, balloon angioplasty with or without stent placement.

pericardial knock: High-frequency heart sound heard in patients with restrictive pericarditis.

pericardiocentesis: Perforation of the pericardium via a needle for the purpose of removal of fluid from the pericardial space.

pericarditis: Inflammation of the pericardium.

pericardium: Thin fibrous sac that surrounds the heart.

perioperative: Period around surgery, which can include the preoperative, intraoperative, and postoperative periods.

peripartum cardiomyopathy: Cardiomyopathy associated with the last trimester of pregnancy or the postpartum period.

peritoneum: Membrane that lines the abdominal cavity.

permanent atrial fibrillation: Atrial fibrillation that is accepted as permanent or lasts longer than 1 year.

permanent pacemaker: Artificial device implanted in the heart that consists of a battery or generator, a lead wire, and an electrode that delivers a stimulus to the heart to maintain a normal heart beat.

persistent atrial fibrillation: Atrial fibrillation that lasts longer than 7 days.

pharmacogenomics: The study of how an individual's genes affect that person's response to a drug.

pheochromocytoma: A tumor that produces catecholamines.

phrenic nerve: A motor and sensory nerve that provides innervation to the diaphragm, pericardium, and pleura.

plasmin: Fibrinolytic enzyme derived from plasminogen.

plasminogen: A protein important in preventing fibrin clot formation. The precursor to plasmin.

pleura: Membrane surrounding the lungs.

pneumothorax: Collection of air in the pleural cavity from a perforation through the chest wall or visceral pleura covering the lung.

poikilothermia: Involves an extremity with neurovascular compromise assuming the temperature of its environment.

polarization: The resting state of the cardiac muscle action potential.

polyneuropathy: Noninflammatory disorder that affects the peripheral nerves.

portal hypertension: Increased pressure in the portal vein (vein providing blood flow to the liver) caused by obstruction of blood flow through the liver.

posterior descending artery (PDA): Coronary artery arising from the right coronary artery in most people that supplies oxygenated blood to the posterior wall of the left ventricle.

postpericardiotomy syndrome: Inflammation of the pericardium late after coronary artery bypass graft surgery due to autoimmune response.

precapillary sphincter: The smooth muscle at the arteriole level of the capillaries that help to regulate blood flow.

precordial leads: Chest leads on a 12-lead electrocardiogram; V_1 to V_6 or V_{1R} to V_{6R}.

preload: Stretch on the ventricular myocardial fibers caused by the volume in the ventricle at the end of ventricular diastole.

pressure gradient: Difference in pressure from one side of a valve to the other side of that valve.

prevalence: An epidemiological term meaning the number of cases of a disease at a specified period.

primary aldosteronism: Excessive excretion of aldosterone by the adrenal cortex.

primary prevention: Reducing cardiovascular risk in people without known coronary heart disease to prevent the development of disease.

proarrhythmic: Causing dysrhythmias.

procainamide: A potent class Ia antiarrhythmic agent used in the treatment of several cardiac dysrhythmias, including atrial fibrillation and ventricular tachycardia. A derivative of the local anesthetic procaine.

progesterone: A steroid hormone responsible for changes in the endometrium during the second half of the menstrual cycle, development of the maternal placenta, and development of the mammary glands.

progestin: Hormone that prepares the endometrium to receive a fertilized egg. Also a synthetic drug that has a progesterone-like effect on the uterus.

prolonged QT syndrome: A condition characterized by a prolonged QT interval on an electrocardiogram that predisposes a person to torsades de pointes.

prostaglandin I2: A chemical substance that produces vasodilation and inhibits platelet aggregation.

protease: A protein-splitting enzyme.

prothrombin: A circulating chemical substance that interacts with calcium salts to produce thrombin.

prothrombin time (PT): Coagulation test used to monitor the safety and effectiveness of warfarin.

protracted anaphylaxis: A severe form of anaphylactic shock where the symptoms can last up to 32 hours.

pruritus: Severe itching.

pseudo: False.

pseudoclaudication: Nonarterial claudication.

pseudohypertension: Increased blood pressure resulting from the incompressibility of blood vessels that happens in older adults because of excessive vascular stiffness.

pulmonary artery catheter: Catheter that is threaded through right heart and placed in the pulmonary artery. Has various ports that allow for measurement of various heart pressures and cardiac output.

pulmonary edema: Fluid in the pulmonary alveoli that interferes with gas exchange.

pulmonary embolus: Embolus in the pulmonary artery system that increases pulmonary pressure that can cause pulmonary infarction.

pulmonary vascular resistance: Resistance in the pulmonary system that the right ventricle must pump against. Also called *right-sided afterload.*

pulmonary vein ectopic foci ablation: Catheter-based procedure in which areas around the four pulmonary veins are isolated with radiofrequency energy to create a block and eliminate the ability of the foci to enter the left atrium.

pulmonary veins: Veins that carry oxygenated blood from the lungs to the left atrium.

pulmonic valve: Valve between the right ventricle and the pulmonary artery.

pulse pressure: Difference between systolic and diastolic blood pressure.

pulseless electrical activity: Organized electrical activity on the ECG monitor of any heart rhythm that does not produce the mechanical function of cardiac contraction or a palpable pulse.

pulsus alternans: An alternation between weak and strong heart beats, with weak beats occurring every other beat.

Pulsus paradoxus: A 10- to 15-mmHg decrease in blood pressure with inspiration.

Purkinje fibers: Conduction fibers located in the ventricles. Serve as the third option as a pacemaker for the heart, with the ability to pace at a rate of 20 to 40 beats/min.

Purkinje network: The location of the heart's third group of pacemaker cells.

Q wave: First negative deflection of the QRS complex.

QRS complex: Complex on an electrocardiogram that represents ventricular depolarization.

radial artery: Artery along the thumb side of the wrist, which is used as a conduit for coronary artery bypass graft surgery.

recombinant deoxyribonucleic acid (DNA): DNA that has been artificially manipulated to combine DNA from one organism with DNA of another organism.

red clot: The stable fibrin clot.

reentrant mechanism: Mechanism of a dysrhythmia whereby a wave of depolarization turns upon itself and reenters the tissue it just activated.

reflex tachycardia: Increased heart rate that occurs in response to a lowered blood pressure.

remodeling: A process of pathological growth whereby a ventricle hypertrophies and then dilates.

renin: An enzyme produced by the kidneys that, when released, stimulates activation of the renin-angiotensin-aldosterone system.

renin-angiotensin-aldosterone system (RAAS): Neurohormonal system that is activated in response to low cardiac output or low blood pressure. The end result is angiotensin II, a potent vasoconstrictor, and aldosterone, which causes sodium and water reabsorption.

renovascular disease: Disease of the renal arteries.

reperfusion: Restoration of oxygen to ischemic tissue.

repolarization: Return of a cardiac cell to a resting state.

resin: Another name for bile acid sequestrant medications; used to lower cholesterol level.

resistant hypertension: Continued hypertension on full-dose therapy, including a diuretic.

restenosis: Renarrowing of the vessel lumen after a primary coronary intervention.

restrictive cardiomyopathy (RCM): Cardiomyopathy characterized by rigidity of the myocardial wall with decreased ability of the chamber walls to expand during cardiac filling.

retroperitoneal bleed: Bleeding into the space behind the peritoneum.

revascularization: Restoration, to the extent possible, of normal blood flow to the myocardium by surgical or percutaneous means.

rhabdomyolysis: Breakdown of muscle fibers with leakage of potentially toxic cellular contents into the systemic circulation.

rheumatic fever: A hemolytic streptococcal infection.

rheumatic heart disease: Damage to the heart that is the result of rheumatic fever. Normal cardiac complications include bacterial endocarditis with damage to the cardiac valves.

right atrium: Chamber of the heart that receives deoxygenated blood from the venous system.

right bundle branch: Conduction pathway that carries impulses to the right ventricle.

right coronary artery (RCA): Major coronary artery arising from the right side of the aorta that supplies blood to the inferior wall of the left ventricle.

right gastroepiploic artery: Artery that supplies blood to the greater curvature of the stomach and can be used as a conduit in coronary artery bypass graft surgery.

right ventricle: A thin-walled, low-pressure pump that receives deoxygenated blood from the right atrium and pumps blood into the pulmonary artery.

risk equivalent: Same risk as someone diagnosed with a disease, such as coronary heart disease.

risk factor: A characteristic found in a healthy person that is independently related to the future development of a disease, such as coronary heart disease.

Ross procedure: Procedure in which the pulmonic valve is placed in the aortic valve position and a tissue valve is placed in the pulmonic valve location.

rotational atherectomy: Use of high-speed rotating blades or burs to remove components of atherosclerotic plaque.

S_1: First heart sound; heard with contraction of the ventricles; an indication of the onset of ventricular systole.

S₂: Second heart sound; heard immediately after closure of the aortic and pulmonic valves; an indication of the onset of ventricular diastole.

S₃: Third heart sound; heard immediately after the second heart sound; an indication of fluid overload.

S₄: Fourth heart sound; heard just before the first heart sound; an indication of a noncompliant ventricle.

saphenous vein graft: Vein graft taken from the greater saphenous vein of the leg. Most common vein graft material used in coronary artery bypass graft surgery.

sarcoidosis: Disease that causes inflammation or small lumps (also called *nodules* or *granulomas*) in the tissues.

sarcomere: A portion of the myofibril that contains protein units.

saturated fats: Fats that are usually solid at room temperature and typically come from animals.

secondary prevention: Method of reducing risk in people with known coronary heart disease to prevent future events.

second-degree heart block: A cardiac dysrhythmia that results when atrial impulses are not conducted normally through the AV node to the ventricle. Also referred to as *second-degree AV block.*

selective serotonin reuptake inhibitors (SSRIs): Class of antidepressant medications commonly used to treat depression in cardiac patients.

semilunar valves: The valves located between the ventricles and great vessels.

senile degenerative calcification: Progressive calcification of the valve leaflets.

serine: An amino acid found in many proteins.

sheath: Small, flexible catheter in a vascular access site. Guidewires and diagnostic and interventional devices are thread through the sheath during invasive and interventional procedures.

sick sinus syndrome (SSS): Rhythm marked by sinus node dysfunction (bradycardia or sinus arrest) alternating with periods of rapid atrial dysrhythmias. Also called *tachy-brady syndrome.*

single-chamber pacemaker: A pacemaker that has an electrode for pacing in one chamber of the heart; traditionally, a ventricular pacemaker.

sinoatrial (SA) node: Natural pacemaker of the heart, which is located in the right atrium near the junction of the superior vena cava.

sirolimus: An immunosuppressive agent used on drug-eluting stents that is also used to prevent organ rejection during kidney transplantation.

ST-segment elevation myocardial infarction (STEMI): A myocardial infarction that produces ST-segment elevation on an electrocardiogram.

stable angina pectoris: Angina with a stable pattern that is brought on by exertion and relieved by rest or sublingual nitroglycerin.

stanol: A sterol that has been saturated.

statins (HMG-CoA reductase inhibitors): Another name for HMG-CoA reductase inhibitors; all drugs in this class end with the letters "statin."

stenosis: Narrowing of a passage.

sternotomy: The act of cutting through the sternum.

sternum: Flat bone in the middle of the thorax, or chest.

sterol: Compound found in the cell membranes of plants and animals. Plant sterols are used in the treatment of high cholesterol.

stress testing: Noninvasive assessment tool for coronary artery diseases that uses exercise or chemicals to stress the heart. May be done with or without myocardial imaging.

stroke volume: Volume of blood ejected by the left ventricle with each beat.

subendocardium: Middle myocardium.

substernal: Below the sternum.

sudden unexplained death in epilepsy (SUDEP): Patients with known epilepsy who experience frequent generalized tonic-clonic seizures despite adequate therapy and die without any other explanation for death.

superior vena cava: A principal vein that receives venous blood returning from the head, neck, upper extremities, and thorax and empties into the right atrium.

supraventricular dysrhythmia: Dysrhythmia originating above the ventricles. Called *supraventricular tachycardia* when the heart rate is more than 100 beats/min.

sustained ventricular tachycardia: When ventricular tachycardia exists longer than 30 seconds and requires therapeutic intervention to terminate the rhythm.

sympathetic nervous system (SNS): Branch of the autonomic nervous system that allows the body to function under stress.

sympathomimetic: A medication that mimics the sympathetic nervous system.

syncope: Transient lack of consciousness due to inadequate blood flow to the brain.

systemic lupus erythematosus (SLE): An autoimmune disease characterized by fever, skin rash, and arthritis, often with small hemorrhages in the skin and mucous membranes and inflammation of the pericardium.

systemic vascular resistance: The overall resistance the left ventricle must pump against.

systole: Contraction of the heart muscle that results in ejection of blood from the chamber.

systolic dysfunction: Left ventricular dysfunction involving a problem with ejection.

systolic ejection murmur: A murmur that occurs as blood is ejected through a stenotic aortic or pulmonic valve during early systole.

T lymphocyte: Lymphocyte cell that differentiates in the thymus and is responsible for cellular immunity.

T wave: Wave on an electrocardiogram that represents ventricular repolarization.

tachycardia: Heart rate greater than 100 beats/min.

tachydysrhythmia: Cardiac dysrhythmias with a ventricular rate more than 100 beats/min.

tachyphylaxis: The body's decreased responsiveness to a drug over time. Avoided by weaning or titrating medications.

tachypnea: Increased respiratory rate.

tacrolimus: A potent immunosuppressant medication used to prevent and treat organ rejection.

Takotsubo cardiomyopathy (TCM): An acute and transient cardiac syndrome (not disease) involving akinesis of the apex of the left ventricle; takotsubo is a Japanese word for "octopus pot."

thiazide diuretic: Diuretic that inhibits sodium and water reabsorption. Works in the ascending loop of Henle and the early distal tubule.

thiocyanate: Cyanide ions released into the system are converted to thiocyanate in the liver. Thiocyanate level should be monitored during infusions of nitroprusside because nitroprusside releases cyanide ions into the system.

thoracic aorta: Portion of aorta located in the thoracic cavity that contains the ascending aorta, the aortic arch, and the descending thoracic aorta.

thoracotomy: Surgical incision of the chest wall.

thrombin: An enzyme formed from prothrombin that converts fibrinogen to fibrin.

thrombocytopenia: Abnormal decrease in platelet number.

thromboembolus: Embolus that has broken away from a thrombus.

thrombolytic: Nonfibrin medication used to break down clots.

thrombophlebitis: Inflammation of a vein in conjunction with the formation of a thrombus.

thrombosis: Formation or existence of a blood clot.

thrombotic stroke: Ischemic stroke caused by a thrombus or an embolus from a thrombus.

thromboxane A2: Substance released with vascular injury that is a potent vasoconstrictor and platelet agonist.

thrombus: A blood clot that causes obstruction.

tissue factor: A protein released after injury within the subendothelial layer of the vessel; the protein reacts with factor VII to facilitate the formation of a clot.

tissue plasminogen activator (t-PA): A fibrin-specific lytic agent; a serine protease produced by vascular endothelial cells.

torsades de pointes: A special ventricular tachycardia associated with a prolonged QT interval.

transesophageal echocardiography (TEE): Placement of an ultrasound probe into the esophagus to view the aorta and cardiac structures. Eliminates the need to image through the chest wall.

transluminal extraction atherectomy: Procedure used for the extraction of visible thrombi within the coronary artery.

transmural: Full thickness of myocardium.

transmyocardial laser revascularization (TMLR): Form of revascularization whereby a series of transmural endomyocardial channels are created with lasers to improve myocardial blood supply.

transverse (T) tubules: Extensions of cell membranes in the cardiac muscle that allow calcium to enter the cells.

Traube's sign: Booming systolic and diastolic sounds heard over the femoral artery. Also called *pistol-shot sounds.*

tricuspid valve: Valve located between the right atrium and right ventricle.

trifascicular block: A block of the normal conduction system involving simultaneous blockage of the right bundle branch, one of the two fascicles of the left bundle branch, and AV block.

triglyceride: Chemical compound of glycerol and three fatty acids that is a component of most animal and vegetable fats.

troponin: Biomarker found only in cardiac muscle. The most sensitive indicator of myocardial damage.

true aneurysm: Involves all three layers of the artery wall and is described as a weakening of the vessel.

ulnar artery: Artery alongside the wrist, opposite the thumb.

unfractionated heparin (UFH): A commercially available anticoagulant produced from porcine or bovine tissue. Heparin prevents the extension of thrombus but does not lyse clots.

unstable angina pectoris: Angina at rest or with minimal exertion or an increased need for nitroglycerin.

urticaria: A vascular skin rash that produces papules or wheals and causes severe itching.

vagal response: Related to the stimulation of the parasympathetic nervous system, specifically the vagus nerve; characterized by a low heart rate, low blood pressure, light-headedness, and nausea.

Valsalva maneuver: A maneuver that increases intrathoracic pressure, elicits the parasympathetic response, and decreases venous return to the heart.

valvuloplasty: Procedure in which a balloon is inflated in the cardiac valve orifice to fracture calcium deposits in the leaflets and stretch the annulus to return the valve to normal functioning.

vasoconstriction: Constriction of vessels.

vasodilation: Dilation of vessels.

vasopressor: Medication used to increase blood pressure and afterload.

vasospastic angina: Angina caused by spasm of a coronary artery. Also called *Prinzmetal's angina.*

vasovagal response: Response of the parasympathetic nervous system that produces hypotension, bradycardia, diaphoresis, nausea, and vomiting.

Vaughan Williams classification system: Classification system for antiarrhythmic pharmacology that contains four classes.

venous oxygen saturation: The percent of oxygen saturation of venous blood after the tissues have extracted oxygen from the arterial blood. Normal range is 60% to 80%.

ventricular aneurysm: Localized dilation of the left ventricle at the site of infarction.

ventricular dysrhythmia: Dysrhythmia originating from the ventricles. Called *ventricular tachycardia* when the heart rate is more than 100 beats/min.

ventricular dyssynchrony: Occurs when the right and left ventricles do not contract at the same time.

ventricular ectopy: Abnormal heartbeats that originate from a ventricle rather than from the sinus node.

ventricular fibrillation: A quivering of the ventricles that results in a pulseless rhythm and cardiac arrest and is treated with immediate defibrillation.

ventricular outflow tract: The path the blood in a ventricle must follow when ejected from the ventricle.

ventricular septal myectomy: Surgical removal of a portion of a hypertrophied septum that is contributing to outflow obstruction.

viable: Capable of living.

visceral pericardium: Inner lining of the pericardium and outer lining of the heart and great vessels. Also called the *epicardium.*

vulnerable plaque: Atherosclerotic plaque that is prone to ulceration and rupture.

wall motion abnormality: Abnormal movement of a wall of the left ventricle. Can be seen on echocardiogram.

warfarin: An oral anticoagulant agent that works indirectly through the liver by altering vitamin K-dependent clotting factors.

water-hammer pulse: A rapid rise and collapse of the pulse that can be felt upon palpation. Also called *Corrigan's pulse.*

Wolff-Parkinson-White (WPW) syndrome: Syndrome in which one or more accessory pathways connect the atria to the ventricles. Conduction over the accessory pathways causes preexcitation of the ventricles, predisposing the patient to tachydysrhythmias.

INDEX

Page numbers followed by an italicized *f* indicate figures; *t*, tables; and *b*, boxes.

A

abciximab (ReoPro), 80, 402, 408
abdominal aorta, 12, 13*f*, 238*f*
abdominal aortic aneurysm, 239, 241, 256. *See also* aortic aneurysms
abdominal examination, 444
ABI (ankle-brachial index), 253, 254, 446
acanthosis nigricans, 444
ACEIs. *See* angiotensin-converting enzyme inhibitors (ACEIs)
acetaminophen, 309
acetylcholine, 22
N-acetylcysteine, 419
action potential, 17, 223*f*, 266
activated partial thromboplastin time (aPTT), 75-76, 78-79
Actos (pioglitazone), 169, 174
acute coronary syndromes (ACSs), 289, 290*f. See also* angina; myocardial infarction (MI)
    angina in, 122, 429
    atherosclerotic plaque in, 120-121
    cardiac rehabilitation for, 310, 311-313, 314
    case study for, 314-315
    clinical manifestations of, 445-446
    high-risk features of, 302*t*
    long-term management of, 308-314
    pathogenesis of, 291*f*
    patient education for, 309-311
    psychosocial issues for, 313-314
    special considerations for, 307-308
    supportive therapy for, 303-305
    TIMI risk score for, 438
acute respiratory distress syndrome, 399
adenosine, 87*t*, 125-126, 230
adenosine diphosphate, 81
adenosine diphosphate inhibitors, 80-82
adenosine triphosphate, 20
adrenaline. *See* epinephrine
adrenergic antagonists. *See* beta blockers
adrenergic receptors, 21, 21*t*
afferent pathways, 22
afterload, 9, 34*t*
    aortic stenosis and, 193-194

    drugs altering, 58, 83-84, 84*t*-85*t*
    measurement of, 39
    stroke volume and, 32, 33*f*, 34*f*, 35
age, cardiovascular disease and, 50, 428. *See also* older adults
Aggrastat (tirofiban), 80, 402
albumin infusion, 360
alcohol use, 434
aldosterone, 63-64
    effects of, 23, 65, 66
    heart failure and, 160, 161, 161*f*, 162*f*, 163*t*
    in pregnancy, 24, 25
    for tricuspid regurgitation, 207
aldosterone antagonists, 63-64
    for acute coronary syndromes, 308
    for heart failure, 167-168
    for hypertension, 100*t*, 101-102
    preload and, 84*t*
alirocumab, 110
allergies
    anaphylactic reaction in, 361-363
    history of, 432
    iodine, 417
    latex, 361
alpha1 receptors, 21, 21*t*
    drugs stimulating, 58
    heart failure and, 160, 162*f*
alpha blockers, 68, 85*t*
alteplase, 73-74, 74*t*
alternative therapies, 433
alveolar-capillary membrane, 38, 38*f*
ambulatory blood pressure monitoring, 98
American College of Cardiology (ACC)
    CardioSmart website of, 311
    guidelines of
        for aortic valve replacement, 199*b*
        for cardiac catheterization, 127
        for cardiovascular risk reduction, 48
        for coronary artery bypass, 402
        for diuretics, 324
        for heart failure, 164-165, 166*t*, 323, 324, 326
        for hypertension, 100*t*
    pooled cohort risk equation of, 438
American Diabetes Association (ADA), 100*t*

American Heart Association (AHA)
     guidelines of
         for alcohol use, 434
         for aortic valve replacement, 199*b*
         for cardiac catheterization, 127
         for cardiovascular risk reduction, 48
         for coronary artery bypass, 402
         for diuretics, 324
         for heart failure, 164-165, 166*t*, 323, 324, 326
         for hypertension, 100*t*
         for physical activity, 49
     Life's Simple 7 campaign of, 48
     pacemaker information from, 280
     pooled cohort risk equation of, 438
American Society of Hypertension (ASH), 100*t*
aminoglycosides, 399
aminophylline, 126
amiodarone, 71
     for atrial fibrillation, 220, 223-224, 230, 398
     cardioverter-defibrillators and, 276
     digoxin and, 72
     for heart failure, 169
amlodipine, 69, 129, 169
amyloidosis, 141
anaphylactic shock, 361-363
anasarca, 445
anemia, 406
aneurysms, 237-239, 239*f. See also* aortic aneurysms
     left ventricular, 306
     true *vs.* false, 237-238, 239*f*, 306, 418
angina, 121-122. *See also* acute coronary syndromes (ACSs);
   chest pain
     aortic stenosis and, 194, 199
     after coronary artery bypass, 407
     drugs for, 69, 129
     features of, 122-123
     history of, 428-429
     myocardial infarction and, 292, 293*t*, 295, 300
     revascularization therapies for, 389-390, 404-405, 408
     stable, 37, 122, 289, 290*f*
     subpopulations with, 123-124
     unstable, 122, 123, 289, 290*f*, 291*f*, 300-303
     variant (Prinzmetal's), 307
angioedema, 66, 67
angiography. *See also* cardiac catheterization
     for coronary heart disease, 127
     for peripheral arterial disease, 253-254
angioplasty
     percutaneous transluminal coronary, 388, 407, 408*f*
     for peripheral arterial disease, 255
angiotensin II, 23
     drugs blocking, 65, 66
     heart failure and, 161, 161*f*, 163*t*

angiotensin-converting enzyme, 23, 75
angiotensin-converting enzyme inhibitors (ACEIs), 65-66
     for acute coronary syndromes, 299, 305, 308, 315
     afterload and, 85*t*
     aldosterone and, 64
     for aortic aneurysm, 246-247
     for aortic valve conditions, 198, 204, 205
     for atrial fibrillation prophylaxis, 229
     cardiac resynchronization and, 281
     for heart failure, 161, 165, 167, 168, 169, 172, 174,
         325-326
     for hypertension, 100*t*, 101, 112
     for mitral regurgitation, 191
     for peripheral arterial disease, 254
     preload and, 84*t*
angiotensin receptor blockers (ARBs), 66-67
     for acute coronary syndromes, 308
     afterload and, 85*t*
     for aortic regurgitation, 204
     for atrial fibrillation prophylaxis, 229
     for heart failure, 167, 168
     for hypertension, 100*t*, 101
angiotensin receptor-neprilysin inhibitor (ARNI), 168
anistreplase, 73, 74*t*, 75
ankle-brachial index (ABI), 253, 254, 446
annulus, 7
antiarrhythmics, 69-71
     action potential and, 223*f*
     for atrial fibrillation, 221-224, 222*t*
     cardioverter-defibrillators and, 276
     classification of, 70
     digoxin and, 72
     for heart failure, 169
     heart rate and, 87*t*
     for mitral valve conditions, 184, 190
     for sinus rhythm maintenance, 226, 226*b*, 227*t*
     for syncope, 374
     for ventricular tachycardia, 343
antibiotic prophylaxis
     for aortic valve conditions, 198, 201, 205
     for coronary artery bypass, 398-399, 400*b*
     for endocarditis, 379, 380
     for mitral valve conditions, 185, 186, 191, 192
antibiotics
     for endocarditis, 379
     history of recently used, 433
     nephrotoxic, 399, 419
anticoagulants, 75-80, 77*t*
     for acute coronary syndromes, 302, 303-304, 315
     for aortic valve conditions, 200, 205
     for atrial fibrillation, 218-219
     for coronary artery bypass, 402
     herbal remedies and, 433

for mitral valve conditions, 184, 185, 190
    pacemaker insertion and, 273
    for percutaneous coronary intervention, 409, 416
    pre-cardioversion, 224-225, 230
antidepressants, 349
antidiabetic drugs
    heart failure and, 169
    percutaneous coronary intervention and, 414, 415, 419
antidiuretic hormone. *See* vasopressin
antifibrinolytic drugs, 401, 402
antiplatelet drugs, 80-82
    for acute coronary syndromes, 302-303, 315
    for atrial fibrillation, 219
    for coronary artery bypass, 391, 402
    for coronary heart disease, 128
    for percutaneous coronary intervention, 409, 416
    for peripheral arterial disease, 254
antipsychotic drugs, 349
antithrombin III, 75, 76
anxiety, 299, 310, 436
aorta, 3, 3*f*, 7*f*, 8*f*, 237, 238*f*
    atherosclerosis of, 390, 396, 397
    divisions of, 12, 13*f*
    expansion and relaxation of, 201, 202*f*
aortic aneurysms, 237-247
    case study for, 255-256
    causes of, 240
    clinical presentation of, 242
    diagnosis of, 245, 246*f*
    ischemic injuries related to, 243-245
    location of, 242
    medical/surgical therapy for, 246-247
    nursing management of, 245
    pathophysiology of, 240-241
    physical examination of, 242-243, 243*t*
    prevalence of, 239-240
    types of, 237-239, 239*f*
aortic arch, 12, 13*f*, 238*f*
aortic dissections, 239*f*, 241-242
    cardiac tamponade and, 6
    classification of, 239, 240*f*, 241
    clinical findings for, 242-243, 243*t*, 446
    complications of, 243-245
    heart failure and, 322
    hemodynamic monitoring for, 244
    hypertensive emergency and, 375, 376
    myocardial infarction *vs.*, 295, 303
    signs and symptoms of, 429
aortic valve, 6, 7-9, 8*f*, 193*f*
    auscultation of, 441
    function of, 9, 10*f*, 13, 19, 192

aortic valve regurgitation, 9, 201-205
    aortic aneurysm and, 243
    causes of, 201
    clinical presentation of, 202-203
    diagnosis and management of, 203-204, 204*t*
    heart failure in, 322
    medical/surgical therapy for, 204-205
    outcomes management for, 205
    pathophysiology of, 201-202
    physical examination of, 203, 203*t*
    after valvuloplasty, 199
aortic valve replacement, 199-200, 199*b*, 205
aortic valve stenosis, 9, 179, 192-201
    afterload and, 35
    causes of, 192-193, 194*f*
    clinical presentation of, 194-196
    coronary artery bypass and, 404
    diagnosis and management of, 196-197
    hypertrophic cardiomyopathy and, 143
    medical therapy for, 197-198
    outcomes management for, 200-201
    pathophysiology of, 193-194, 194*f*
    physical examination of, 196
    surgical interventions for, 199-200, 199*b*
aortogram, 245
apelin, 88
apex of heart, 2, 3*f*
    akinesis of, 146
    murmur over, 183
apical pulse, 441
apixaban (Eliquis), 78, 79
aPTT (activated partial thromboplastin time), 75-76,
    78-79
ARBs. *See* angiotensin receptor blockers (ARBs)
arcus senilis, 443
argatroban, 76, 78
arginine vasopressin. *See* vasopressin
arm movement, pacemakers and, 272, 281, 283
ARNI (angiotensin receptor-neprilysin inhibitor), 168
arrhythmias. *See* dysrhythmias
arrhythmogenic right ventricular cardiomyopathy, 145-146
arterial disease, peripheral. *See* peripheral arterial disease
    (PAD)
arterial grafts, 391, 392-395, 394*f*, 399
arterial sheath, 417-418, 419*b*
arteries, 9-11, 11*f*
    coronary, 12, 13*f*, 15-17, 16*f*, 16*t*
    hypertension effect on, 98
    layers of, 10, 11*f*
    in older adults, 25-26
arterioles, 11, 16, 35
ascending aorta, 12, 13*f*, 238*f*

ascending aortic aneurysm, 241, 242. *See also* aortic aneurysms
aspirin, 81, 82
    for acute coronary syndromes, 302, 303, 308, 309, 315
    for aortic valve conditions, 200, 201, 205
    for atrial fibrillation, 219
    for coronary artery bypass, 391, 402, 406
    for coronary heart disease, 128
    for mitral valve conditions, 186, 192
    nicotinic acid and, 107
    for percutaneous coronary intervention, 415-416
    for pericarditis, 378
    for peripheral arterial disease, 254
    for venous disease, 251
    warfarin and, 80
atelectasis, 399-400
atenolol, 89-90
atherectomy, 409-412
    directional, 409, 411*f*
    rotational, 409-410, 412*f*
atheroma, 120, 290
atherosclerosis
    acute coronary syndromes and, 290, 300
    aortic, 390, 396, 397
    cholesterol and, 49
    cocaine and, 307
    coronary heart disease and, 119-121, 121*f*
    heart failure and, 157
    hyperlipidemia and, 102-103, 104*f*
    myocardial infarction and, 290
    peripheral arterial disease and, 251, 252
    venous insufficiency and, 248
atorvastatin (Lipitor), 105, 108, 109, 110
atria, 2, 3*f*, 7*f*, 8*f*
atrial fibrillation, 213-215, 214*f*
    acute, hemodynamically unstable, 230
    aortic stenosis with, 194, 197-198
    atrial kick in, 19
    atrioventricular reentrant tachycardia *vs.,* 351
    cardioversion for, 224-225, 226*b*
    case study for, 230-231
    catheter ablation for, 228-229
    causes of, 215, 216*f*
    classification of, 215-217
    complications of, 218-219
    after coronary artery bypass, 398
    defibrillators for, 227-228
    drugs for, 184, 220-224, 222*t*, 223*f*, 226, 226*b*, 227*t*, 230
    idiopathic, 216-217, 218, 219, 227*t*
    jugular vein distension in, 440
    Maze surgical procedure for, 228
    mitral valve conditions with, 182, 184, 189, 190
    neurogenic, 216, 227*t*
    nonvalvular, 215-216, 218-219
    pacemakers for, 227, 269
    pathophysiology of, 217
    primary prevention of, 229
    right ventricular infarction and, 298
    special populations with, 25, 227*t*, 229-230, 230*b*
    stroke risk score for, 218, 229, 231, 438
    symptoms of, 217-218
    treatment considerations for, 219-220
    tricuspid regurgitation and, 206
atrial flutter, 338-339
    drugs for, 219, 223
    electrocardiogram for, 342*f*
atrial gallop, 442
atrial kick, 19
    atrial fibrillation and, 217, 219
    loss of, 19, 25
    right ventricular infarction and, 298
    single-chamber pacing and, 268
atrial natriuretic peptide, 162, 163*t*, 218
atrial tachycardia
    focal, 338, 341*f*
    multifocal, 339-340, 341*f*, 342*f*
atrioventricular block, 263-264, 335, 346, 347*f*
    atropine and, 22, 346
    complete, 296, 346, 347*f*
    after coronary artery bypass, 405
    myocardial infarction and, 296
    pacing for, 263
    rate-control drugs and, 220
atrioventricular junction, 18, 18*f*
atrioventricular nodal reentrant tachycardia (AVNRT), 337, 338*f*, 340*f*
atrioventricular node, 18, 18*f*, 213, 262, 262*f*, 334*f*
    ablation of, 220, 227, 228
    blood supply to, 15, 17
    intrinsic rate for, 18, 344
    rhythm derived from, 344, 346
atrioventricular reentrant tachycardia (AVRT), 338, 339*f*, 340*f*, 350-351
atrioventricular valves, 6-7, 8-9, 8*f*, 10*f*. *See also* mitral valve; tricuspid valve
Atromid-S (clofibrate), 105, 107
atropine, 22, 86*t*, 346
Austin Flint murmur, 203
automaticity, enhanced, 334
autonomic nervous system, 20, 32, 35*f*
autoregulation, 11
AV node. *See* atrioventricular node

B

Bachmann bundle, 18, 334*f*

balloon angioplasty, 388, 407, 408*f*

baroreceptors, 22-23

base of heart, 2, 3*f*

batteries, pacemaker, 266, 267
    replacement of, 271, 278, 279

behavioral factors. *See* lifestyle factors

beta1 and beta2 receptors, 21, 21*t*, 58
    blockade of, 67
    heart failure and, 160, 162*f*

beta-adrenergic agents, 363

beta blockers, 67-68
    for acute coronary syndromes, 299, 304-305, 308, 315
    for angina, 129
    antiarrhythmic action of, 70
    for aortic aneurysm, 246, 247
    for aortic valve conditions, 198, 204-205
    for atrial fibrillation, 220, 221, 222*t*, 398
    calcium channel blockers with, 69
    cardiac resynchronization and, 281
    cardioselective, 67
    cardioverter-defibrillators and, 276
    catecholamines and, 307
    digoxin and, 72
    exercise stress testing and, 126
    for heart failure, 161, 165, 167, 169, 325-326
    heart rate and, 86*t*, 87*t*
    for hypertension, 89-90, 100*t*, 101, 376
    for mitral valve conditions, 184, 190
    noncardioselective, 67, 68
    ophthalmic, 68
    for peripheral arterial disease, 254

beta-receptor down-regulation, 160

bifascicular block. *See* bundle branch block

bile acid sequestrants, 105, 105*t*, 106-107, 106*t*

biofilm, 273

biomarkers
    for acute coronary syndromes, 289, 293, 300, 301, 302*t*
    for heart failure, 323-324
    for inflammation, 120

biopsy, myocardial
    for cardiogenic shock, 364
    for cardiomyopathy, 139, 142, 145, 146-147
    for heart failure, 167

bisoprolol, 101

bivalirudin, 76, 78
    for percutaneous coronary intervention, 409, 416

bleeding
    after coronary artery bypass, 401, 406
    gastrointestinal, 245

hypovolemic shock and, 359-360
    intracranial, 294
    after percutaneous coronary intervention, 413, 414, 417, 418, 418*t*, 419*b*

blood culture for endocarditis, 379

blood glucose. *See also* diabetes mellitus
    cardiovascular disease and, 49
    coronary artery bypass and, 397-398, 404
    syncope and, 373

blood pressure, 48-49, 439. *See also* hypertension; hypotension
    age and, 97
    aortic aneurysm and, 241, 244, 246, 256
    aortic regurgitation and, 203
    after coronary artery bypass, 406
    goals for, 99, 100*t*
    in hypertensive emergency, 375, 376
    intraarterial, 39
    monitoring, 10, 98
    in older adults, 25, 447
    peripheral arterial disease and, 254
    in pregnancy, 24, 446
    regulation of, 20-23, 96
    smoking cessation and, 101
    systemic vascular resistance *vs.*, 35

blood transfusion
    for coronary artery bypass, 398, 401-402, 406
    for hypovolemic shock, 359-360

blood vessels, 11*f*, 14*f*
    arterial, 9-11
    capillary, 11-12
    collateral, 16-17, 291
    coronary, 12, 13*f*, 15-17, 16*f*, 16*t*
    forward flow through, 6, 9
    venous, 12

body fat, 434-435

body mass index (BMI), 434, 440

brachytherapy, 411-412

bradycardia, 343
    atrioventricular block and, 263
    cardiac output and, 32
    myocardial infarction and, 292, 296
    rate-control drugs and, 220
    reflex, 22
    sinus, 263, 344, 345*f*

bradydysrhythmias, 343-346
    after coronary artery bypass, 405
    syncope in, 429

bradykinin, 65, 66, 163*t*

brain, hypertension effect on, 98

brain natriuretic peptide
    acute coronary syndromes and, 301

heart failure and, 162, 163*t*, 323
    synthetic, 325
Bruce protocol for exercise testing, 125, 125*t*
Brugada syndrome, 342, 350
bundle branch block, 264
    heart failure with, 170
    myocardial infarction and, 293, 294, 296
    resynchronization therapy for, 274, 275*t*
bundle branches, 18, 18*f*, 262*f*, 334*f*
    blood supply to, 15
    impulse conduction via, 213, 262
bundle of His, 18, 18*f*, 262, 262*f*, 334*f*
    intrinsic rate for, 344
    rhythm derived from, 344
bypass grafting, peripheral, 255. *See also* coronary artery
    bypass graft (CABG)

C

CABG. *See* coronary artery bypass graft (CABG)
CAD. *See* coronary heart disease (CHD)
caffeine, 189
calcification, degenerative, 193, 194*f*, 196
calcium, serum
    cardiac function and, 17, 20
    drugs altering, 64, 72
calcium channel blockers (CCBs), 68-69, 69*t*
    action potential and, 223*f*
    afterload and, 85*t*
    for angina, 129, 307
    antiarrhythmic action of, 70
    for aortic aneurysm, 246
    for aortic regurgitation, 204
    for atrial fibrillation, 220, 221, 222*t*, 230, 398
    digoxin and, 72
    dihydropyridine, 68, 69*t*
    diuretics with, 64
    for heart failure, 169
    heart rate and, 86*t*, 87*t*
    for hypertension, 99, 100*t*, 102
    for mitral stenosis, 184
calf muscle pump dysfunction, 248, 250
cancer, history of, 436
capillaries, 11-12, 11*f*
    coronary, 16
    pulmonary, 13, 14*f*, 38, 38*f*
    systemic, 14*f*
capillary refill, 445
cardiac arrest
    aortic aneurysm and, 242
    cardiomyopathy and, 143, 145, 146
    dysrhythmias causing, 335, 340, 346-348, 348*f*
    heart failure and, 326
    induction of, 390

cardiac catheterization
    for acute coronary syndromes, 294, 302
    for aortic valve conditions, 197, 204
    for cardiomyopathy, 144, 147, 148*f*
    for coronary heart disease, 120, 121, 127-128
    for mitral valve conditions, 183, 190
cardiac cycle, 19-20, 441-442
cardiac glycosides, 71-72, 85*t*, 87*t*. *See also* digoxin
cardiac index, 32, 363
cardiac monitoring, 405
cardiac output, 9, 31, 34*t*
    aortic valve and, 192
    atrial fibrillation and, 219
    calculation of, 86
    components of, 31-37, 33*f*-35*f*
    coronary artery bypass and, 397
    drugs altering, 58, 83-86, 83*t*-87*t*
    normal range for, 32
    in older adults, 25
    oxygen delivery and, 37
    in pregnancy, 446
    regulation of, 20
    shock states and, 358-359, 360-361
cardiac pacemakers. *See* pacemakers
cardiac rehabilitation
    for acute coronary syndromes, 310, 311-313, 314
    after coronary artery bypass, 406-407
    for heart failure, 172
    after percutaneous coronary intervention, 419
cardiac resynchronization therapy (CRT), 274-275
    for heart failure, 170
    indications for, 275*t*
    pacemaker for, 268
    patient education for, 281
    postoperative care for, 279
cardiac syndrome X, 308
cardiac tamponade, 445
    aortic aneurysm and, 6, 244
    Beck's triad for, 358, 363, 445
    friction rub in, 443
    obstructive shock and, 358
    pacemaker insertion and, 273
cardiogenic shock, 363-364
    heart failure and, 323, 445
    hypovolemic shock and, 359
    myocardial infarction and, 305
    percutaneous coronary intervention and, 415
cardiologists, 455-456, 457
cardiomyopathy, 5, 137, 138*f*
    arrhythmogenic right ventricular, 145-146
    dilated, 37, 137-140, 138*f*, 157-158, 164*f*, 349
    heart failure and, 156, 157-158, 159, 159*f*, 164*f*

hypertrophic, 69, 138*f*, 142-145, 143*f*, 159, 159*f*,
    164*f*, 229
postpartum, 437
restrictive, 138*f*, 140-142
tachycardia-induced, 219, 220
takotsubo, 146-148, 147*f*, 148*f*
cardioplegia, 390
cardiopulmonary bypass machine
    complications of, 395, 397-402
    for coronary artery bypass, 390, 391*f*, 392*f*
cardiovascular disease (CVD), 47, 427
    clinical manifestations of, 445-446
    history of, 436
    nursing considerations for, 51
    older adults and, 25
    pharmacogenomics in, 88
    prevention of, 51, 420*b*
    risk factors for, 48-50, 428, 433-435, 437
    risk stratification for, 50-51, 427, 438
    trends in, 47-48
cardiovascular system, 1. *See also* circulatory system;
heart
    assessment of, 439-443, 443*b*
    neurohormonal regulation of, 20-23
    in special populations, 23-26
cardioversion. *See also* implantable cardioverter-defibrillators (ICDs)
    for atrial fibrillation, 217, 221, 224-225, 226*b*, 230
    direct current, 225
    for mitral valve conditions, 184, 190
    pharmacological, 224, 225, 226*b*
    shock in, 227, 277, 282
    for tachydysrhythmias, 337, 338, 351
carotid artery, examination of, 440
carotid endarterectomy, 397
carotid pulse, 196, 440
carotid sinus massage, 23, 264, 343
carvedilol, 101
catecholamines, 20-21, 306-307
catheter ablation
    for atrial fibrillation, 220, 227, 228-229
    for Wolff-Parkinson-White syndrome, 338, 351
CCTA (coronary computed tomography angiogram), 127
cellulitis, 250
central nervous system depressants, 10
central venous pressure (CVP), 41
CHA2DS2-VASc risk score for stroke, 218, 229, 231, 438
CHD. *See* coronary heart disease (CHD)
chemical stress testing, 125-126
chemoreceptors, 23
chest pain. *See also* angina
    assessment of, 441, 445

cocaine-induced, 307
history of, 428-429
in myocardial infarction, 292, 293*t*, 295
after percutaneous coronary intervention, 414, 419
in pericarditis, 306, 377
in women, 437
chest radiograph
    for aortic aneurysm, 245
    for aortic valve conditions, 197, 204
    for cardiomyopathy, 139, 144
    for heart failure, 323, 324
    for hypertensive emergency, 376
    for mitral valve conditions, 183-184, 186, 190
    for obstructive shock, 358
    for pericarditis, 377
chest tubes, 405-406
chief complaint, 427, 428-430
children
    cardiovascular disease in, 428
    medical history for, 436
cholesterol, 49, 102-103. *See also* high-density lipoproteins (HDLs); low-density lipoproteins (LDLs)
    bile acid formation from, 106
    biosynthesis of, 109
    reducing total, 105
cholestyramine (Questran), 106
cholinergic receptors, 22
chordae tendineae, 6, 8*f*, 187*f*
    lengthening of, 186, 188
chronic obstructive pulmonary disease, 400
chronotropic response, 263, 270
chylomicrons, 102
cilostazol, 254
circulation, 12-13, 13*f*
    collateral, 16-17, 291
    systemic, 14*f*
    through heart, 13, 15
circulatory system, 1, 9-15
    coronary, 15-17, 16*f*, 16*t*
    in older adults, 25-26
    vessels of, 9-12, 11*f*
citalopram, 314
CK (creatine kinase), 109, 301
CK-MB (creatine kinase-MB), 301, 302*t*
claudication, 252, 253
    history of, 430
    therapies for, 254-255
clicks, systolic, 442, 446
Clinical, Etiology, Anatomic, Pathophysiology (CEAP)
    classification of venous disease, 248, 250
clofibrate (Atromid-S), 105, 107
clopidogrel (Plavix), 80-82

for acute coronary syndromes, 302-303, 308
for atrial fibrillation, 219
coronary artery bypass and, 391, 402
for coronary heart disease, 128
cost of, 416-417
for percutaneous coronary intervention, 409, 412, 416
for peripheral arterial disease, 254
pharmacogenomics of, 88
coagulation, 72-73
drugs affecting, 73-82, 74*t*
postoperative monitoring of, 401, 417
cocaine, chest pain induced by, 307
colchicine, 378
colesevelam (Welchol), 106
colestipol (Colestid), 106
collaborative practice, interprofessional, 435, 453-455, 455*b*
collateral circulation, coronary, 16-17, 291
commissurotomy, mitral, 185
communication, interprofessional, 435, 454-455
complementary and alternative therapies, 433
compression stockings, 249, 250, 251
computed tomography (CT)
for aortic aneurysm, 245, 246*f*
for coronary heart disease, 127
for hypertensive emergency, 376
for pericarditis, 377-378
for peripheral arterial disease, 253
for syncope, 373
for venous disease, 250
concentric hypertrophy, 163, 164*f*, 194, 197
conduction pathways, cardiac, 17-18, 18*f*, 262, 262*f*, 334*f*
congenital disease, 192, 350, 436
congestive heart failure. *See* heart failure
contraceptives, oral, 96, 97
contractility, 9, 20, 34*t*
drugs altering, 48, 83, 84-85, 85*t*-86*t*
estimation of, 39
in older adults, 20
stroke volume and, 32, 33, 33*f*, 34*f*, 35-36, 36*f*
contrast agents, 414, 417, 419
coronary arteries, 12, 13*f*, 15-17, 16*f*, 16*t*
occlusion of, 17
in older adults, 25-26
coronary artery bypass graft (CABG), 387, 388-407
angina after, 407
anticoagulation before, 402
case study for, 420-421
complications of, 396-402, 421
considerations for, 387-388
contraindications for, 390

for coronary heart disease, 128, 130
emergency, 397, 402, 403*b*, 407
grafts for, 390-395, 393*f*, 394*f*, 406, 415
indications for, 389-390, 389*b*, 408, 421
minimally invasive direct, 395
nursing care after, 405-407, 421
off-pump, 395-396
robotics in, 396
special populations and, 402-405
traditional approach to, 390, 391*f*, 392*f*
coronary circulation, 5, 5*f*, 15-17, 16*f*, 16*t*
collateral, 16-17, 291
dominance in, 16
coronary computed tomography angiogram (CCTA), 127
coronary heart disease (CHD), 119
angina in, 37, 121-124
aortic valve conditions with, 194, 197, 198, 203, 204, 205
atrial fibrillation in, 227*t*
diagnosis of, 124-128, 125*t*
hyperlipidemia and, 102
mortality rates for, 47-48
pathophysiology of, 119-121, 121*f*
revascularization therapies for, 387, 408
risk factors for, 49-50
treatment considerations for, 128-130
coronary veins, 13, 17
Corrigan's pulse, 203*t*
corticosteroids, 374, 378, 398
costochondritis, 441, 445
cotton-wool spots, 443
cough, 66, 401
Coumadin. *See* warfarin (Coumadin)
coumarins, 250
counterpulsation therapy, 130
C-reactive protein, 379
creatine kinase (CK), 109, 301
creatine kinase-MB (CK-MB), 301, 302*t*
CRT. *See* cardiac resynchronization therapy (CRT)
CT. *See* computed tomography (CT)
cutting balloons, 411
CVD. *See* cardiovascular disease (CVD)
cyanosis, 444
cyclooxygenase-2 inhibitors, 309
cyclophosphamide, 378
cytokines, 160, 162, 163*t*

D

dabigatran (Pradaxa), 76, 78, 79
for atrial fibrillation, 218-219
contraindications to, 80
DASH diet, 99, 100-101
DCCV. *See* direct current cardioversion (DCCV)

DDD pacing mode, 269*t,* 270

DDDR pacemaker codes, 283

DDI pacing mode, 269

DeBakey aneurysm classification, 239, 240*f,* 241

deep vein thrombosis (DVT), 26, 248

defibrillation, 277. *See also* implantable cardioverter-
   defibrillators (ICDs)
     atrial, 227-228
     cardioversion *vs.,* 225
     shock in, 277, 282

de Musset's sign, 203*t*

dental care, endocarditis and, 379-380

depolarization, 17, 266

depression
     acute coronary syndromes and, 313, 314
     coronary artery bypass and, 406-407
     history of, 436

dermatitis, 250

dextrocardia, 441, 443

diabetes mellitus
     angina in, 124
     coronary artery bypass and, 403-404
     heart failure and, 157
     history of, 436
     percutaneous coronary intervention and, 414, 415,
       419
     peripheral arterial disease in, 254
     revascularization therapy for, 388, 408
     risk factors for, 49

diaphragm, 1, 2*f*
     ruptured, 358

diastole, 19
     aortic function in, 202*f*
     coronary circulation in, 15
     murmurs during, 442
     valve function in, 7, 8, 9, 13
     ventricular, 19

diastolic heart failure, 156

diet
     for heart failure, 172
     history of, 434
     for hypertension, 99, 100-101, 112
     for mitral valve conditions, 184, 191

dieticians, 457

digoxin, 71-72
     for atrial fibrillation, 220, 230
     cardioversion and, 225
     contractility and, 85*t*
     for heart failure, 169
     heart rate and, 87*t*
     for hypertrophic cardiomyopathy, 144
     for mitral valve conditions, 184, 190

     toxicity of, 72, 207

dilated cardiomyopathy, 137-140, 138*f*
     contractility in, 37
     dysrhythmias in, 349
     eccentric hypertrophy in, 164*f*
     heart failure in, 157-158

diltiazem, 68-69, 69*t*
     for atrial fibrillation, 220-221
     digoxin and, 72
     for mitral stenosis, 184

diphenhydramine, 363

dipyridamole stress testing, 125-126

direct current cardioversion (DCCV)
     for atrial fibrillation, 224, 225, 230
     for narrow complex tachydysrhythmias, 337, 338,
       351

direct thrombin inhibitors, 76, 78, 79
     for acute coronary syndromes, 303
     contraindications to, 80

distributive shock, 360-363, 362*t,* 363*b*

diuretics, 63-65
     for aortic stenosis, 197
     for cardiogenic shock, 364
     for heart failure, 168-169, 172, 324
     high- *vs.* low-ceiling, 63
     for hypertension, 99, 100*t,* 101
     for mitral valve conditions, 184
     preload and, 84*t*
     for tricuspid regurgitation, 207

dobutamine, 58, 59, 60*t*
     contractility and, 85*t*
     for heart failure, 325
     for septic shock, 361
     stress testing with, 125, 126, 197

dofetilide, 71, 169, 223

dominance, coronary artery, 16

dopamine, 58, 59, 60*t,* 361

dopaminergic receptors, 21, 21*t,* 58

Dressler's syndrome, 306, 377, 378

driving
     acute coronary syndromes and, 310, 312
     pacemakers and, 274

dronedarone, 224

drugs, illicit, 434. *See also* medications

Duke criteria for endocarditis, 379

Duroziez's sign, 203*t*

DVT (deep vein thrombosis), 26, 248

dyslipidemia. *See* hyperlipidemia

dyspnea
     exertional, 156-157, 429
     history of, 429

dysrhythmias, 333. *See also* atrial fibrillation; cardiac
   resynchronization therapy (CRT); defibrillation;
   implantable cardioverter-defibrillators (ICDs); pacemakers
     antiarrhythmics for, 69-71
     bradydysrhythmias, 343-346
     cardiac arrest, 346-348, 348*f*
     case study for, 350-351
     digoxin toxicity-induced, 72
     initial evaluation of, 333
     pathophysiology of, 333-335, 336*f*
     populations at risk for, 348-350
     sympathomimetics and, 58-59
     syncope related to, 372, 373, 374
     tachydysrhythmias, 335, 337-343
dyssynchrony, ventricular, 37, 170, 274
dyssynergy, ventricular, 37

E
eccentric hypertrophy, 163, 164*f*
ECG. *See* electrocardiogram (ECG)
echocardiography
     for aortic aneurysm, 245
     for aortic valve conditions, 196, 198, 203, 204, 205
     for cardiomyopathy, 139, 141-142, 144
     for coronary heart disease, 126
     for endocarditis, 379
     for heart failure, 164, 165-167
     for mitral valve conditions, 183, 186, 190
     for myocardial infarction, 294
     pre-cardioversion, 224
     for shock states, 358, 364
     for tricuspid regurgitation, 206
edema. *See also* pulmonary edema
     angioedema, 66, 67
     examination of, 445
     fluid overload and, 206
     in older adults, 26
     papilledema, 443-444
     venous disease and, 249
education, interprofessional, 453-455, 455*b*
efferent pathways, 23
ejection fraction, 33, 34*t*
     coronary artery bypass and, 404
     heart failure with preserved, 156, 158-159, 159*f*,
       160*t*, 321
     heart failure with reduced, 139, 156, 158, 160*t*, 321,
       438
elderly. *See* older adults
electrocardiogram (ECG)
     for acute coronary syndromes, 289, 292-293, 294,
       295-298, 296*f*, 297*f*, 300-301, 315
     for aortic aneurysm, 245
     for aortic valve conditions, 197, 204

artifacts on, 347
     for atrial fibrillation, 214*f*, 215, 219
     for atrial flutter, 342*f*
     for atrioventricular block, 347*f*
     for atrioventricular nodal reentrant tachycardia, 338*f*
     for atrioventricular reentrant tachycardia, 339*f*
     for cardiogenic shock, 364
     for cardiomyopathy, 144, 147
     for cocaine-induced chest pain, 307
     for coronary heart disease, 124
     for focal atrial tachycardia, 341*f*
     for hypertensive emergency, 376
     for mitral valve conditions, 184, 186, 190
     for monomorphic ventricular tachycardia, 343*f*
     for multifocal atrial tachycardia, 341*f*
     normal, 213, 214*f*, 297*f*
     for pacemakers, 278
     after percutaneous coronary intervention, 419
     for pericarditis, 295, 303, 377
     for polymorphic ventricular tachycardia, 343*f*
     for sinus bradycardia, 345*f*
     for sinus node dysfunction, 344, 345*f*
     for sinus tachycardia, 337*f*
     for syncope, 373, 380-381
     for ventricular fibrillation, 348*f*
electrodes, pacemaker, 267-268, 267*f*
electroencephalogram, 373
electrolyte imbalances
     drug-related, 64, 72, 207, 349
     ventricular dysrhythmias and, 305, 342
electromagnetic interference, 282
electrophysiology
     cardiac, 17-18, 18*f*, 262, 262*f*, 334*f*
     field of, 261
Eliquis (apixaban), 78, 79
embolism. *See* thromboembolism
Emery-Dreifuss muscular dystrophy, 139
EMS activation, 309, 310
enalapril, 168
endarterectomy, 255, 397
endocarditis, 4, 376, 378-380
     mitral regurgitation and, 188, 322
     skin lesions in, 444
endocarditis prophylaxis, 379, 380
     for aortic valve conditions, 198, 201, 205
     for mitral valve conditions, 185, 186, 191, 192
endocardium, 3, 4, 5*f*, 8*f*
endothelin, 160, 161, 161*f*, 163*t*
enoxaparin, 78
ephedrine, 97
epicardium, 3, 5-6, 5*f*, 7*f*
epilepsy, 349, 372, 373

epinephrine, 58, 59*t*
    endogenous, 20-21
    for shock states, 361, 363
eplerenone, 64, 101-102, 167-168
eptifibatide (Integrilin), 80, 82, 402
ergonovine maleate, 127
erythropoietin, 24, 402
estrogen, 24, 26
ethics, professional, 454
ethnicity. *See* race/ethnicity
evidence-based guidelines for hypertension, 99, 100*t*
evolocumab, 110
exercise. *See also* physical activity
    in cardiac rehabilitation, 311-313
    for claudication, 254
    for depression, 314
    for heart failure, 169, 172
    for mitral stenosis, 182
exercise stress test, 124-125, 125*t*
    after acute cardiac event, 312, 313
    for aortic valve conditions, 197, 198, 204
    contraindications to, 126-127
    for peripheral arterial disease, 253
    for tricuspid regurgitation, 206
extracellular fluid (ECF)
    overload of, 157, 168, 206, 325
    third-spacing of, 360
eyes
    examination of, 443-444
    hypertension effect on, 98
ezetimibe, 110

F
factor Xa inhibitors, 76, 78
    for acute coronary syndromes, 303, 304
    contraindications to, 79
family history, 437. *See also* genetics
fascicles, bundle branch, 264
fat
    body, 434-435
    epicardial, 3, 5-6
felodipine, 72, 129
fenofibrate (Tricor), 105, 107, 108
fever, 440
fibrates, 107-108, 112
    lipid-lowering effects of, 105, 105*t*, 106*t*
    for peripheral arterial disease, 254
    statins combined with, 108, 109-110, 109*b*
fibrin, 73, 78
fibrinogen, 73, 80
fibrinolytics, 73-75, 74*t*
    for myocardial infarction, 293, 294-295, 295*t*, 304
    percutaneous coronary intervention *vs.,* 415

fibrous atheroma, 120
fibrous pericardium, 5*f*, 6, 7*f*
flavonoids, 250
flecainide, 223
fluid therapy
    for percutaneous coronary intervention, 418-419
    for right ventricular infarction, 298
    for shock states, 359-360, 361
    for syncope, 373
fluid volume status
    for aortic stenosis, 194
    for heart failure, 157, 168, 325-326
    for mitral valve conditions, 184, 191
    preload and, 34
    for tricuspid regurgitation, 206-207
fluvastatin (Lescol), 108, 109
focal atrial tachycardia, 338, 341*f*
fondaparinux, 78, 79, 304
food labels, reading, 172
forward flow concept, 6, 9
fractional flow reserve, 412-413
Framingham criteria for heart failure, 438
free graft, 394-395
funduscopic examination, 443-444
fusiform aneurysm, 238, 239*f*

G
gallops, 442
gastrointestinal bleeding, 245
gemfibrozil (Lopid), 105, 107, 108
gender, cardiovascular disease and, 50, 97, 428. *See also*
  women
general survey, 439
generators, cardioverter-defibrillator, 276
generators, pacemaker, 266, 271
    migration of, 273-274
    permanent, 267*f*
    temporary, 265*f*
genetics, 50, 436, 437
    cardiomyopathy and, 139, 142, 143, 144
    drug response and, 87-88
    hyperlipidemia and, 102
    hypertension and, 96
Glucophage (metformin), 169, 414, 415, 419
glycoprotein IIb/IIIa inhibitors, 80, 82
    for acute coronary syndromes, 302, 303
    coronary artery bypass and, 402
    for percutaneous coronary intervention, 408, 409,
        410, 413, 416
    for vein graft stenosis, 415
grafts, peripheral bypass, 255. *See also* coronary artery
  bypass graft (CABG)
grapefruit juice, 110, 129

gynecological history, 437
gynecomastia, 64

H

HDL. *See* high-density lipoproteins (HDLs)
headache, nitrate-induced, 62, 129
head up-tilt table test, 373
healthcare literacy, 171
health history, 427-428
    allergies in, 432
    case study for, 447-448
    chief complaint in, 427, 428-430
    medical, 436-437
    medications in, 432-433
    patient demographics in, 428
    present illness in, 430-431
    prevention activities in, 435
    review of systems in, 431-432, 432*t*
    social/lifestyle factors in, 433-435
    for special populations, 437-438
health insurance, 313
health promotion activities, 51, 428, 435
health-related quality of life (HRQOL), 156
heart, 1-2, 2*f*
    aortic aneurysm effect on, 243
    cardiac cycle of, 19-20, 441-442
    chambers of, 2-3, 3*f*, 4*f*
    circulation through, 13-15, 14*f*
    conduction system of, 17-18, 18*f*, 262, 262*f*, 334*f*
    congenital defects of, 192, 436
    coronary vessels of, 15-17, 16*f*, 16*t*
    electrical stimulation of, 261
    examination of, 441-443, 443*b*
    hypertension effect on, 98
    infectious and inflammatory disorders of, 376-380
    layers of, 3-6, 5*f*, 7*f*
    mechanical physiology of, 18-20
    neurohormonal regulation of, 20-23
    in older adults, 25
    in pregnancy, 24, 24*f*
    reentry pathways through, 335, 336*f*
    valves of, 6-9, 8*f*, 10*f*
heart block. *See* atrioventricular block
heart failure
    acute decompensated, 321
        clinical presentation of, 322-323
        diagnosis of, 323-324
        events leading to, 322
        precipitating factors for, 323*t*
        special considerations for, 325-327, 327*f*, 328*f*
        treatment options for, 324-325
    aortic aneurysm and, 244
    aortic stenosis and, 194, 195-196, 197, 199

atrial fibrillation in, 221, 224, 227*t*
    cardiogenic shock and, 363, 364
    cardiomyopathy and, 137, 139, 140, 141
    chronic, 155-156
        assessment of, 164-167, 166*t*
        case study for, 173-174
        classification systems for, 165, 166*t*, 275*t*, 325
        clinical presentation of, 156-157
        epidemiology of, 155
        etiology of, 157-158
        follow-up for, 173
        left ventricular remodeling in, 162-164, 162*f*, 164*f*
        medications for, 161, 165, 167-169, 171-172, 174
        neurohormonal responses in, 160-162, 161*f*, 162*f*, 163*t*
        nonpharmacologic treatment for, 169-170
        pathophysiology of, 158-164
        patient education for, 170-173
        with preserved ejection fraction, 156, 158-159, 159*f*, 160*t*, 321
        with reduced ejection fraction, 139, 156, 158, 160*t*, 321, 438
        risk factors for, 157
    coronary artery bypass and, 404
    hypertension and, 35
    jugular vein distension in, 440
    mitral regurgitation and, 191
    mortality rates for, 48
    pulmonary hypertension and, 3
    resynchronization therapy for, 274-275, 275*t*
    right ventricular infarction and, 298
    syncope related to, 372, 374
    tricuspid regurgitation and, 206, 207
    troponin levels in, 324
    valvular heart disease and, 179
    venous valves in, 12
Heart Failure Society of America (HFSA), 173
heart rate, 32. *See also* bradycardia; pulses; tachycardia
    activity tolerance and, 312
    aortic aneurysm and, 246
    assessment of, 441
    cardiac output and, 32, 33*f*, 34*f*
    chronotropic response by, 263, 270
    coronary artery perfusion and, 15
    drugs altering, 22, 58, 83, 86, 86*t*-87*t*
    mitral stenosis and, 181-182, 184, 185
    in older adults, 447
    in pregnancy, 24
    regulation of, 21, 22, 23, 32, 35*f*
    ventricular diastole and, 19-20
heart rate recovery score, 126
heart sounds, 8-9, 441-443, 443*b*. *See also* murmurs

in acute coronary syndromes, 292, 445
in aortic valve conditions, 196, 203, 203t
in cardiac tamponade, 358, 445
in cardiogenic shock, 363
in heart failure, 157
in mitral valve conditions, 183, 189
for prosthetic valves, 446
heart transplantation
for cardiomyopathy, 140, 142
for heart failure, 326-327, 364
parasympathetic innervation after, 22
hematoma
intramural, 242, 245, 246f, 247
after percutaneous coronary intervention, 418
hemodynamic monitoring, 39, 41-42, 41f
for aortic dissection, 244
for coronary artery bypass, 405
for percutaneous coronary intervention, 412-413
for shock states, 358, 359, 360-361, 362, 364
for venous disease, 250
hemodynamics, 31-37
in atrial fibrillation, 218, 219, 230
in cardiogenic shock, 363, 445
drugs altering, 83-86, 83t-87t
evaluation of, 333
in myocardial infarction, 305
hemoglobin, 37, 38, 39, 40f
hemoglobin A1c, 49, 254
hemorrhage. *See* bleeding
hemothorax, 272
heparin, 75-76, 77-79
for acute coronary syndromes, 302, 303, 315
for cardioversion, 224
for coronary artery bypass, 402
low-molecular-weight, 76, 78, 79
for mitral stenosis, 184
for percutaneous coronary intervention, 416, 417
herbal remedies, 433
high-density lipoproteins (HDLs), 49, 102, 103
alcohol use and, 434
drugs for increasing, 105, 106t
histamine, 107, 363
histamine2 agonists, 363
history of present illness, 430-431. *See also* health history
HIV, 50
HMG-coenzyme A reductase inhibitors, 108-110
for acute coronary syndromes, 308
for aortic aneurysm, 246
for aortic stenosis, 197
for coronary artery bypass, 391, 406
fibrates combined with, 108, 109-110, 109b
lipoproteins, triglycerides, and, 105, 105t, 106t

for peripheral arterial disease, 254
side effects of, 110b
hormone replacement therapy, 123-124
hospice care, 326
hospitalization, history of, 436
HRQOL (health-related quality of life), 156
hydralazine, 168
hydrostatic pressure, 11
hypercalcemia, 64, 72
hyperglycemia, coronary artery bypass and, 397-398, 404. *See also* diabetes mellitus
hyperkalemia, 64, 65-66, 72, 207
hyperlipidemia, 95, 102-110
case study for, 111-112
causes of, 102
cholesterol levels in, 49
complications of, 103
diagnosis of, 103
drugs for, 105-110, 105t, 106t, 109b, 110b
familial, 102, 103
history of, 436
nonpharmacologic treatment of, 105
ocular signs of, 443
pathophysiology of, 102-103, 104f
symptoms of, 103
treatment considerations for, 103
hypersensitive carotid sinus syndrome, 264
hypertension, 48-49, 95-102
afterload in, 35
aortic aneurysm and, 240
aortic stenosis and, 198
atrial fibrillation and, 227t
case study for, 111-112
causes of, 95-96
complications of, 98
diagnosis of, 98
drugs for, 100t, 101-102
epidemiology of, 97
heart failure and, 157, 158
hypertrophic cardiomyopathy and, 143
isolated systolic, 99
malignant, 22, 375-376
nonpharmacologic treatment of, 99-101
ocular signs of, 443-444
pathophysiology of, 96-97
peripheral arterial disease and, 252
primary and secondary, 96
pulmonary, 3, 181, 182, 186, 189
symptoms of, 97
treatment considerations for, 98-99, 100t
hypertensive emergency, 22, 375-376
hypertrophic cardiomyopathy, 138f, 142-145, 143f

atrial fibrillation in, 229
calcium channel blockers for, 69
concentric hypertrophy in, 164*f*
heart failure in, 159, 159*f*
hyperuricemia, 64
hypokalemia
drug-related, 64, 72, 207, 349
ventricular fibrillation and, 305
hypomagnesemia
drug-related, 64, 72
ventricular dysrhythmias and, 305, 342
hyponatremia, 64
hypotension
cardiac tamponade and, 358, 445
coronary artery bypass and, 392, 405
drug-related, 62, 65, 304
shock states and, 357, 363
hypovolemic shock, 359-360

I

IAPB. *See* intra-aortic balloon pump (IAPB)
ibuprofen, 80, 433
ICDs. *See* implantable cardioverter-defibrillators (ICDs)
idarucizumab, 80
idioventricular rhythm, 344
immunizations, 435
immunosuppressants, 326-327, 378, 409
implantable cardioverter-defibrillators (ICDs), 276-277
for arrhythmogenic right ventricular cardiomyopathy, 145-146
for atrial fibrillation, 225
biventricular pacing with, 275
implantation of, 277
indications for, 262
magnet function with, 280
patient education for, 281-282
postoperative follow-up for, 279-280
subcutaneous, 277
inamrinone, 61
incentive spirometry, 400, 401
infections. *See also* endocarditis; pericarditis
after coronary artery bypass, 398-399, 400*b,* 401
history of, 436
pacemaker-site, 273
septic shock and, 360-361
inferior vena cava, 2, 3*f,* 8*f,* 12-13
inflammatory response. *See also* endocarditis; pericarditis
in acute coronary syndromes, 120
after coronary artery bypass, 398
in heart failure, 162
in peripheral arterial disease, 252
in shock, 357, 360
ventricular remodeling and, 306-307

inotropes, 58, 85, 85*t*
for cardiogenic shock, 364
for heart failure, 169, 324-325, 326
for right ventricular infarction, 298
insulin resistance, myocardial, 88
Integrilin (eptifibatide), 80, 82, 402
interatrial septum, 2
INTERHEART study, 48
internal mammary artery grafts, 392-393, 394*f,* 395, 399
International Normalized Ratio (INR)
for atrial fibrillation, 219
for cardioversion, 224
for heparin, 75-76, 79
for mitral regurgitation, 192
for warfarin, 77, 78
interprofessional education and collaborative practice (IPECP), 453-455, 455*b*
information sharing in, 435
team for, 455-457
intestinal absorption inhibitors, 105*t,* 106*t,* 110
intra-aortic balloon pump (IAPB)
for coronary artery bypass, 390
for coronary heart disease, 130
for percutaneous coronary intervention, 415
for takotsubo cardiomyopathy, 148
intracranial hemorrhage, 294
iodine allergy, 417
ischemia. *See also* myocardial ischemia
end-organ, 243-245
limb, 251, 252-253
isosorbide, 61, 62, 168
ivabradine, 168

J

Janeway lesions, 379, 444
jaundice, 444
Joint National Committee-8 guidelines, 100*t*
jugular vein distension, 358, 363, 440
junctional rhythm, 344

K

Kite, Charles, 261
Kussmaul sign, 141

L

labetalol, 85*t*
laboratory tests
for coronary heart disease, 124
for endocarditis, 379
for heart failure, 164
for hypertensive emergency, 376
after percutaneous coronary intervention, 419
for pericarditis, 378
for shock states, 359, 361, 362*t*

for tricuspid regurgitation, 207
lactate, serum, 361
lanoteplase (n-PA), 73
Laplace, law of, 241
laser therapy
    for coronary revascularization, 404-405, 411
    for venous disease, 251
latex allergy, 361
LDL. *See* low-density lipoproteins (LDLs)
leads, pacemaker, 266-267, 267*f*
    insertion of, 271-272
    migration of, 274
left anterior descending artery (LAD), 15, 16*f,* 16*t*
    bypass of, 388, 389*b,* 392, 394*f*
    occlusion of, 17, 296
left circumflex artery, 15, 16*f,* 16*t*
    dominance of, 16
    occlusion of, 297-298
left coronary artery, 13*f,* 15, 16*f,* 16*t*
left ventricle
    aneurysm of, 306
    failure of, 159-160, 363
    infarctions of, 295-298, 296*f,* 297*f*
    remodeling of, 162-164, 162*f,* 164*f*
left ventricular assist devices (LVADs)
    for heart failure, 327, 327*f,* 328*f*
    for restrictive cardiomyopathy, 142
left ventricular dysfunction
    clinical manifestations of, 445
    coronary artery bypass for, 388, 389, 392, 408
left ventricular hypertrophy, 138*f,* 159, 159*f*
    aortic stenosis and, 194, 195-196, 197, 200
    atrial fibrillation in, 227*t*
    concentric *vs.* eccentric, 163, 164*f*
Lescol (fluvastatin), 108, 109
Life's Simple 7, 48
lifestyle factors
    for cardiovascular disease, 48-49, 433-435
    history of, 433-435
    for pacemaker insertion, 266
lifestyle modifications
    for aortic aneurysm, 245
    for coronary heart disease, 128
    for hyperlipidemia, 105
    for hypertension, 99-101
    for hypertrophic cardiomyopathy, 144
    for peripheral arterial disease, 254
lipid metabolism, 102. *See also* hyperlipidemia
lipid panel, 103
Lipitor (atorvastatin), 105, 108, 109, 110
lipodermatosclerosis, 249

lipoproteins, 50, 102. *See also* high-density lipoproteins
    (HDLs); low-density lipoproteins (LDLs)
liver function studies, 109
long QT syndrome, congenital, 350
loop diuretics, 63, 64
    for cardiogenic shock, 364
    for heart failure, 168
    preload and, 84*t*
    for tricuspid regurgitation, 207
Lopid (gemfibrozil), 105, 107, 108
lovastatin (Mevacor), 108
low-density lipoproteins (LDLs), 49, 102
    drugs for lowering, 105, 105*t,* 246
    peripheral arterial disease and, 254
lungs, auscultation of, 444
LVADs. *See* left ventricular assist devices (LVADs)
lymphedema, 249

M

magnesium, serum
    drugs altering, 64, 72
    ventricular dysrhythmias and, 305, 342
magnesium sulfate, 305
magnetic resonance imaging (MRI), 283
    pacemakers and, 280
    for pericarditis, 377-378
    for peripheral arterial disease, 253
    for takotsubo cardiomyopathy, 147-148
    for venous disease, 250
magnets, pacemakers and, 280, 281, 282
Marfan's syndrome, 242
MAT (multifocal atrial tachycardia), 339-340, 341*f,* 342*f*
Maze surgical procedure, 228
mean arterial pressure, 39
mechanical ventilation, 400, 401, 405
mechanoreceptors, 22-23
mediastinitis, 399
mediastinum, 1, 3*f*
medical history, 436-437
medical providers, collaboration of, 435
medications, 57-58. *See also specific drug and drug class*
    for acute coronary syndromes, 303-305, 308, 310
        non-ST-segment elevation, 302-303, 315
        ST-segment elevation, 293, 294-295, 295*t,* 299
    allergies to, 432
    for aortic aneurysms, 246-247
    for aortic valve conditions, 197-198, 204-205
    for atrial fibrillation, 184, 219-224, 222*t,* 223*f,* 226,
        226*b,* 227*t,* 230*b*
    atrioventricular block and, 263
    bile acid sequestrants and other, 106, 107
    for cardiomyopathy, 139, 142, 144, 145, 148
    for cardioversion, 225, 226*b*

case study for, 88-90
classes of, 58-72
    angiotensin-converting enzyme inhibitors, 65-66
    angiotensin receptor blockers, 66-67
    antiarrhythmics, 69-71
    beta blockers, 67-68
    calcium channel blockers, 68-69, 69*t*
    cardiac glycosides, 71-72
    coagulation-affecting, 72-82, 74*t*
    diuretics, 63-65
    nitrates, 61-63
    nonsympathomimetics, 60-61
    sympathomimetics, 58-60, 59*t*-61*t*
for coronary artery bypass, 391, 402, 406
for coronary heart disease, 128-130
discharge, 433
emerging science for, 87-88
financial concerns about, 416-417
for heart failure
    acute decompensated, 324-326
    chronic, 161, 165, 167-169, 171-172, 174
hemodynamic alterations and, 83-86, 83*t*-87*t*
history of, 432-433
for hyperlipidemia, 105-110, 105*t*, 106*t*, 109*b*, 110*b*
hyperlipidemia-promoting, 102
for hypertension, 100*t*, 101-102
hypertension-promoting, 96, 97
for hypertensive emergency, 376
for mitral valve conditions, 184, 190-191
nephrotoxic, 399, 419
older adults and, 87
over-the-counter, 80, 433
for percutaneous coronary intervention, 409, 415-417
for pericarditis, 378
for peripheral arterial disease, 254-255
pregnancy and, 80, 87
proarrhythmic, 223
psychotropic, 349, 436
for shock states, 361, 363, 364
for sinus rhythm maintenance, 226, 226*b*, 227*t*
sodium retention due to, 323*t*
statins and other, 109-110
for stroke prophylaxis, 218-219
for syncope, 373-374
syncope due to, 374
for tricuspid regurgitation, 207
for venous disease, 250-251
medulla, 32, 35*f*
Mended Hearts, 314
mental health history, 436
mesenteric ischemia, 244-245
metabolic risk factors, 49-50, 428

metabolic syndrome, 436
metal detectors, pacemakers and, 280, 282
metformin (Glucophage), 169, 414, 415, 419
methotrexate, 378
metoprolol succinate, 101
Mevacor (lovastatin), 108
MI. *See* myocardial infarction (MI)
Micra pacing device, 268-269
microangiopathy, 249
microcirculation, coronary, 16
midodrine hydrochloride (Orvaten), 374
milrinone, 61, 85*t*, 325
mitral valve, 6-7, 8*f*
    function of, 9, 10*f*, 13, 19, 180
    normal, 181*f*, 187*f*
mitral valve prolapse, 186, 188*f*, 189
mitral valve regurgitation, 186-192
    aortic stenosis with, 199
    causes of, 186-188, 188*f*
    clinical presentation of, 189
    coronary artery bypass and, 404
    diagnosis and management of, 190
    heart failure and, 322
    medical/surgical therapy for, 190-191
    myocardial infarction and, 306
    outcomes management for, 191-192
    pathophysiology of, 188-189
    physical examination of, 189
mitral valve repair/replacement
    for regurgitation, 190, 191, 199
    for stenosis, 185, 186
mitral valve stenosis, 179, 180-186, 182*f*
    causes of, 180
    clinical presentation of, 181-182
    diagnosis and management of, 183-184, 183*t*
    medical/surgical therapy for, 184-185
    outcomes management for, 185-186
    pathophysiology of, 180-181
    physical examination of, 183
Mobitz type II block, 346, 347*f*
monoamine oxidase inhibitors, 60
monomorphic ventricular tachycardia, 340, 341, 343*f*
morphine sulfate, 83*t*, 84*t*, 304
MRI. *See* magnetic resonance imaging (MRI)
multifocal atrial tachycardia (MAT), 339-340, 341*f*, 342*f*
murmurs, 9, 442-443, 443*b*
    in aortic valve conditions, 196, 197, 203
    in mitral valve conditions, 183, 189
    in myocardial infarction, 296, 306
    papillary muscle rupture and, 445
    pregnancy and, 446
    thrills produced by, 441, 443*b*

in tricuspid regurgitation, 206
valve dysfunction and, 446
muscarinic receptors, 22
muscles, electrical stimulation of, 261
muscular dystrophies, 139, 349-350
myocardial infarction (MI), 5, 289. *See also* acute coronary syndromes (ACSs)
    anterior wall, 296, 297*f*, 306
    aortic aneurysm and, 243
    atherosclerotic plaque in, 120-121, 290, 300
    atrial fibrillation in, 229
    clinical manifestations of, 445-446
    complications of, 305-307
    coronary artery bypass and, 403
    coronary circulation and, 15
    inferior wall, 295-296, 296*f*, 298
    lateral wall, 297-298
    non-ST-segment elevation, 289, 290*f*, 300-303
        angina in, 122
        diagnosis of, 300-301, 302*t*
        pathogenesis of, 291*f*
        TIMI risk score for, 438
        treatment strategies for, 302-303
    papillary muscle rupture in, 7, 186-187, 188*f*
    percutaneous coronary intervention for, 415
    perioperative or postoperative, 397
    posterior wall, 294, 296*f*, 298, 300
    right ventricular, 298
    ST-segment elevation, 289-299, 290*f*
        angina in, 122
        clinical presentation of, 291-292, 293*t*
        coronary artery bypass for, 397
        diagnosis of, 292-293
        location of, 295-298, 296*f*, 297*f*
        nursing care for, 298-299, 299*t*
        pathophysiology of, 290-291, 291*f*
        treatment strategy for, 293-295, 295*t*, 303-304
    transmural, 291
myocardial ischemia
    aortic aneurysm and, 243
    conditions involving, 289, 290*f*, 291*f*
    coronary circulation and, 15
myocarditis, 5, 138
myocardium, 3, 4-5, 5*f*, 8*f*
    hypertrophy of, 15
    oxygen supply to, 37, 86, 122-123
    perforation of, 272-273
myocytes, 20
    death of, 162*f*, 163
    hypertrophy of, 162-163, 307
myofibrils, 20
myoglobin, 301, 302*t*

N
naproxen, 80
natriuretic peptides
    acute coronary syndromes and, 301
    atrial fibrillation and, 218
    heart failure and, 162, 163*t*, 323
    N-terminal pro-B-type, 301
    synthetic, 325
neck, examination of, 440, 444
nephropathy, contrast-induced, 414, 419. *See also* renal dysfunction
neprilysin, 168
nesiritide, 83*t*, 84*t*, 325
neurohormonal regulation
    of heart, 20-23
    heart failure and, 160-162, 161*f*, 162*f*, 163*t*
neurological complications of coronary artery bypass, 397
neuromuscular disorders, 139, 349-350
neurotransmitters, 20, 22
New York Heart Association (NYHA) heart failure classification, 165, 166*t*, 275*t*, 325
nicotinic acid, 50, 105, 105*t*, 106*t*, 107
nicotinic receptors, 22
nifedipine, 69
nitrates, 61-63, 69, 129
nitric oxide, 163*t*
nitroglycerin, 61, 62, 89
    for acute coronary syndromes, 299, 304, 307, 308, 309-310
    for angina, 122, 129
    for aortic stenosis, 198
    chest pain relieved by, 429
    for heart failure, 325
    preload and, 83*t*, 84*t*
nitroprusside. *See* sodium nitroprusside
nonsteroidal anti-inflammatory drugs (NSAIDs). *See also* aspirin
    acute coronary syndromes and, 309, 315
    heart failure and, 169, 172
    for pericarditis, 378
    renal dysfunction and, 399, 419
    warfarin and, 80
nonsympathomimetic agents, 60-61
norepinephrine, 58, 59*t*
    endogenous, 20, 21
    for septic shock, 361
nosocomial infections, 398-399, 400*b*, 401
NSTEMI. *See* myocardial infarction (MI), non-ST-segment elevation
nurses and nurse practitioners, 454, 456, 457
nutrition. *See* diet

O

obesity, 434-435, 440
    cardiovascular disease and, 49, 436
        epicardial fat in, 5-6
        heart failure and, 157
obstetric history, 437
obstructive shock, 357-359, 364-365
obstructive sleep apnea, 350
OLD CARTS assessment of present illness, 430-431
older adults, 25-26
    angina in, 124, 429
    aortic stenosis in, 193
    aortic valve replacement in, 200
    atrial fibrillation in, 217, 219
    cardiovascular disease in, 47, 50, 428
    coronary artery bypass and, 403
    digoxin toxicity in, 72
    drug therapy for, 87
    health history for, 437-438
    heart failure in, 155, 156, 159
    hyperlipidemia in, 103
    hypertension in, 97, 99
    myocardial infarction in, 290
    myocyte loss in, 20
    physical examination of, 446-447
    sinus tachycardia in, 337
    syncope in, 372, 373, 374
omeprazole (Prilosec), 82
oncotic pressure, 11
opening snap, 183, 446
organ systems
    cardiovascular-related findings in, 443-445
    review of, 431-432, 432*t*
orthostatic syncope, 372, 380-381, 430
orthostatic vital signs, 373, 374, 439
Orvaten (midodrine hydrochloride), 374
Osler's nodes, 379, 444
oxygen
    for acute coronary syndromes, 303
    delivery and consumption of, 37-39, 38*f*, 40*f*
    myocardial demand for, 86, 122-123
oxygen saturation, 440
    oxygen delivery and, 37, 38
    venous, 42, 405
oxyhemoglobin, 38, 39
oxyhemoglobin dissociation curve, 39, 40*f*

P

pacemakers, 262-274. *See also* sinoatrial node
    cardioverter-defibrillator, 277
    development of, 261
    evaluating function of, 271
    indications for, 262-264, 263*b*

    permanent
        for atrial fibrillation, 220, 225, 227, 229
        atrial fibrillation with, 215
        for bradydysrhythmias, 263-264, 344, 346
        case study for, 283
        complications of, 272-274
        components of, 266-268, 267*f*
        concepts of, 266
        CRT-D, 282
        follow-up for, 277-279
        for heart failure, 170
        insertion of, 271-272
        modes and codes for, 269-270, 269*t*
        paradigm shift in, 270-271
        patient education for, 280-281
        for restrictive cardiomyopathy, 142
        types of, 268-269
    reprogramming, 279
    temporary, 264-266, 265*f*, 346
pacing
    antitachycardia or overdrive, 276, 343
    biventricular, 170, 268, 275 (*See also* cardiac resyn-
        chronization therapy (CRT))
    dual-chamber, 268, 269, 270-271
    epicardial, 264, 266, 405
    single-chamber or right ventricular, 268-269, 271
    transcutaneous, 264, 265-266
    transvenous, 264, 266
PAD. *See* peripheral arterial disease (PAD)
pain, claudication, 252, 430. *See also* angina; chest pain
pain control
    for acute coronary syndromes, 309
    for aortic aneurysm, 247
    for coronary artery bypass, 400
    for myocardial infarction, 299
palliative care, 197, 326, 364
palpitations, 429
papillary muscles, 7, 8*f*, 187*f*
    impairment or rupture of, 186-188, 188*f*, 306, 445
papilledema, 443-444
paraplegia, 244
parasympathetic nervous system
    function of, 20, 22
    heart rate and, 32, 35*f*
parasympatholytics, 86*t*
parietal pericardium, 5*f*, 6, 7*f*
Partnership for Prescription Assistance, 81
patient demographics, 428
Patient Health Questionnaire (PHQ-2), 314
PCI. *See* percutaneous coronary intervention (PCI)
PCSK9 inhibitors, 110
PDEIs (phosphodiesterase inhibitors), 61, 63, 85*t*

PEA (pulseless electrical activity), 347-348
pedicle graft, 393, 394
pentoxifylline, 251, 254
percutaneous balloon valvuloplasty, 199
percutaneous coronary intervention (PCI), 387, 407-420
    for acute coronary syndromes, 293-294, 302, 303-304
    advantages of, 413
    complications of, 413-414
    considerations for, 388
    for coronary heart disease, 128, 130
    drugs for, 409, 415-417
    emergency, 414-415
    indications for, 407-408
    nursing care after, 417-420
    procedures for, 408-413, 417
    rescue or salvage, 415
    restenosis after, 407, 409, 411-412, 413
    risk reduction after, 420, 420*b*
    success rates for, 413, 413*t*
    troponin level after, 301
    for vein graft stenosis, 415
percutaneous left atrial appendage transcatheter occlusion, 228-229
percutaneous mitral balloon commissurotomy, 185
percutaneous transluminal coronary angioplasty (PTCA), 388, 407, 408*f*
pericardial effusion, 6
    friction rub in, 443
    pericarditis and, 377, 378
pericardial friction rub, 292, 306, 377, 443
pericardiocentesis, 378
pericarditis, 6, 376, 377-378
    constrictive, 140, 141, 377
    electrocardiogram for, 377
    friction rub in, 292, 306, 443
    myocardial infarction and, 292, 295, 303, 306
    uremic, 377, 378
pericardium, 3, 5*f,* 6, 7*f,* 8*f*
peripheral arterial disease (PAD), 237, 251-255
    case study for, 447-448
    diagnosis and management of, 253-255
    leg pain in, 430
    pathophysiology of, 252
    physical examination of, 252-253, 446
peripheral vascular assessment, 444-445
peripheral vascular disease, 237
    arterial, 251-255, 430, 446, 447-448
    beta blockers and, 67
    venous, 247-251, 430
petechiae, 444
pharmacists, 454
pharmacogenomics, 87-88

pharmacotherapeutics. *See* medications
phenylephrine, 58, 61*t*
phosphodiesterase inhibitors (PDEIs), 61, 63, 85*t*
physical activity, 49. *See also* exercise
    acute coronary syndromes and, 310
    aortic valve conditions and, 195, 198, 204
    assessment of, 165, 434
    heart failure and, 165, 172
    hypertension and, 100
    intolerance to, 171, 312
    mitral valve conditions and, 185, 191
physical examination, 427, 439
    cardiovascular, 439-443, 443*b*
    of cardiovascular clinical manifestations, 445-446
    case study for, 447-448
    of other organ systems, 443-445
    of special populations, 446-447
physicians, 454, 455-456, 457
pioglitazone (Actos), 169, 174
platelet count, 79, 401
platelets
    coagulation and, 73, 75, 80
    inhibition of, 75, 80-82
Plavix. *See* clopidogrel (Plavix)
pleural effusion, 244
pneumothorax, 272, 358, 401
poikilothermia, 252-253
point of maximum impulse, 441
polarization, 17, 266
polymorphic ventricular tachycardia (PMVT), 341-342, 343*f*
polypharmacy, 87
pooled cohort risk equation, 438
posterior descending artery, 16, 298
postural syncope, 372, 380-381, 430
postural vital signs, 373, 374, 439
potassium, serum
    cardiac function and, 17, 71
    cardioversion and, 225
    drugs altering, 64, 65-66, 72, 207, 349
    ventricular fibrillation and, 305
potassium channel blockers, 70
    action potential and, 223*f*
    for atrial fibrillation, 221, 222*t,* 223
potassium-sparing diuretics, 63-64
Pradaxa. *See* dabigatran (Pradaxa)
prasugrel, 81, 82
    for acute coronary syndromes, 302, 303, 308
    coronary artery bypass and, 402
    for coronary heart disease, 128
    for percutaneous coronary intervention, 416
precapillary sphincter, 11
precordium, examination of, 441

prednisone, 433
preeclampsia, 25
pregnancy, 23-25, 24*f*
    angiotensin-converting enzyme inhibitors and, 66
    aortic valve replacement and, 200
    dilated cardiomyopathy in, 137
    dysrhythmias in, 350
    health history for, 437
    hyperlipidemia in, 103
    hypertension in, 99
    medications and, 80, 87
    physical examination during, 446
preload, 9, 34*t*
    drugs altering, 58, 83, 83*t*-84*t*
    fluid status and, 34
    measurement of, 39
    stroke volume and, 32, 33-34, 34*f*, 36*f*
premature atrial contractions, 217
pressure receptors, 22-23
Prilosec (omeprazole), 82
primary prevention, 51, 428, 435
Prinzmetal's angina, 307
progesterone, 24-25
propafenone, 72, 223
prostaglandin I2, 81
protamine, 79
prothrombin, 73
prothrombin time (PT)
    for heparin, 75-76, 79
    for warfarin, 77
pseudoaneurysms, 238, 239*f*
    after percutaneous coronary intervention, 418
    ventricular, 306
pseudoclaudication, 253
pseudohypertension, 99
psychotropic medications, 349, 436
PTCA (percutaneous transluminal coronary angioplasty),
    388, 407, 408*f*
pulmonary arteries, 3, 3*f*, 8*f*, 13, 14*f*
    compression of, 244
pulmonary artery catheter, 405
pulmonary artery pressures, 41, 41*f*, 363
pulmonary edema
    alveolar-capillary membrane in, 38
    after coronary artery bypass, 399
    dyspnea in, 429
    heart failure and, 324
    mitral stenosis and, 182, 185
pulmonary embolism, 358, 365, 429
pulmonary hypertension
    heart failure and, 3
    mitral valve conditions and, 181, 182, 186, 189

pulmonary system
    examination of, 444
    postoperative complications of, 399-401
pulmonary veins, 2, 8*f*, 13, 14*f*
pulmonic valve, 6, 7-9, 8*f*
    auscultation of, 441
    function of, 9, 10*f*, 13, 19
    stenosis of, 35
pulseless electrical activity (PEA), 347-348
pulse pressure, 97, 203, 439
pulses, 439, 444-445. *See also* heart rate
    apical, 441
    arterial occlusion and, 253
    atrial fibrillation and, 213, 215
    pacemakers and, 281
pulsus alternans, 445
pulsus paradoxus, 358, 377, 445
Purkinje fibers, 18, 18*f*, 213, 262, 262*f*, 334*f*

Q
QRS complex, 214*f*
    narrow, 335
    wide, 170, 223, 274, 275*t*, 335
QT interval, 214*f*
    prolonged, 223, 224, 341, 343, 349
    short, 341-342
Questran (cholestyramine), 106
quinidine, 72

R
RAAS. *See* renin-angiotensin-aldosterone system (RAAS)
race/ethnicity
    cardiovascular disease and, 50, 428
    heart failure and, 155, 156
    hypertension and, 97
radial artery graft, 393
radiation therapy
    for in-stent restenosis, 411-412
    pacemakers and, 280-281
    restrictive cardiomyopathy due to, 141
radiofrequency ablation, 228, 338, 351
radionuclide imaging, 126
ramipril, 101
ranolazine, 129
rate responsiveness, pacemaker, 269*t*, 270
red clot, 73
reentry impulse disorders, 335, 336*f*, 337-338, 338*f*-340*f*
reflux, venous, 248, 250
regadenoson stress testing, 125-126
registered nurses, 456, 457
religious beliefs, 435
renal dysfunction
    cardiac troponins and, 301

coronary artery bypass and, 399, 404
    drugs causing, 66, 399, 414, 419
    history of, 436
    hypertension and, 98
    percutaneous coronary intervention and, 414
renin-angiotensin-aldosterone system (RAAS), 23
    heart failure and, 160, 161, 161*f*, 162*f*, 163*t*
    pregnancy and, 24
ReoPro (abciximab), 80, 402, 408
reperfusion therapy, 293-295, 295*t*. *See also* fibrinolytics;
    percutaneous coronary intervention (PCI)
repolarization, 17, 266
respiratory rate, 312, 440
restrictive cardiomyopathy, 138*f*, 140-142
resynchronization. *See* cardiac resynchronization therapy
    (CRT)
reteplase (r-PA), 73, 74, 74*t*
retinopathy, hypertensive, 98
retroperitoneal bleeding, 414
revascularization therapy, 387-388. *See also* coronary
    artery bypass graft (CABG); percutaneous coronary
    intervention (PCI); stents
Revatio, 63
review of systems (ROS), 431-432, 432*t*
rhabdomyolysis, 108, 109-110
rheumatic fever, 180, 181
rheumatic heart disease, 186, 192, 218
right coronary artery (RCA), 13*f*, 15, 16*f*, 16*t*
    dominance of, 16
    occlusion of, 17, 295-296
right gastroepiploic artery graft, 394
right ventricle
    failure of, 159-160, 181, 183
    infarction of, 298
risk stratification
    for aortic aneurysms, 245
    for cardiovascular disease, 50-51, 427, 438
rivaroxaban (Xarelto), 78, 79
robotic surgery, 396
role identity crisis, 313-314
Ross procedure for aortic stenosis, 200
rosuvastatin, 108
Roth spot, 443
rubor, 253

S

saccular aneurysm, 238, 239*f*
sacubitril, 168
SA node. *See* sinoatrial node
saphenous vein grafts, 390-395, 393*f*, 394*f*, 406
saponosides, 250
sarcomeres, 20
screenings, 428, 435

secondary prevention, 51
seizures, 349, 372, 373
selective serotonin reuptake inhibitors, 314
semilunar valves, 6, 7-9, 8*f*, 10*f*. *See also* aortic valve;
    pulmonic valve
sepsis, 360
septal rupture, 296, 306
septic shock, 360-361, 362*t*, 363*b*
Sequential Organ Failure Assessment (SOFA) score, 361,
    362*t*, 363*b*
serotonin reuptake inhibitors, 349
serous pericardium, 5*f*, 6, 7*f*
sertraline, 314
sexual activity, 310
sexual history, 435
shock, 357
    anaphylactic, 361-363
    aortic aneurysm and, 244
    cardiogenic, 305, 323, 359, 363-364, 415, 445
    cardioversion and defibrillation, 227, 277, 282
    case study for, 364-365
    distributive, 360-363, 362*t*, 363*b*
    hypovolemic, 359-360
    obstructive, 357-359
sick sinus syndrome, 263, 344-346, 345*f*
sildenafil (Viagra), 63, 304
simvastatin (Zocor), 105, 108, 110
sinoatrial block, 263, 344, 345*f*
sinoatrial node, 17-18, 18*f*, 213, 262, 262*f*, 334*f*
    blood supply to, 15, 17
    dysfunction of, 263, 344-346, 345*f*
    intrinsic rate for, 17, 344
    modulator of, 168
sinus arrest, 263, 344, 345*f*
sinus arrhythmia, 344, 345*f*
sinus bradycardia, 263, 344, 345*f*
sinus rhythm
    drugs maintaining, 226, 226*b*, 227*t*
    normal, 213, 214*f*
sinus tachycardia, 337, 337*f*
skin
    examination of, 444
    venous disease signs in, 249-250
sleep apnea, obstructive, 350
sleep patterns, 435
smoking
    aortic aneurysms and, 240, 245
    blood pressure and, 101
    cessation of, 51, 101, 401
    history of, 433-434
    peripheral arterial disease and, 251, 252
    variant angina and, 307

smooth muscle relaxants, 85*t*
social history, 433-435
social support, 172, 314, 406-407
sodium, serum
    cardiac function and, 17, 71
    drugs altering, 64, 323*t*
sodium bicarbonate, 419
sodium channel blockers, 70
    action potential and, 223*f*
    for atrial fibrillation, 221, 222*t,* 223
sodium nitroprusside, 61, 62
    contraindications for, 63
    for heart failure, 325
    for hypertensive emergency, 376
sodium-potassium-adenosine triphosphatase system, 71
sodium restriction
    for heart failure, 172
    for hypertension, 100
    for mitral valve conditions, 184, 191
SOFA (Sequential Organ Failure Assessment) score, 361,
    362*t*, 363*b*
sotalol, 71
spiritual considerations, 435
spironolactone, 64, 101-102, 167-168
Stanford aneurysm classification, 239, 240*f*, 241
Staphylococcal infections, 273, 399, 400*b*
Starling's law, 33, 36*f*
statins. *See* HMG-coenzyme A reductase inhibitors
STEMI. *See* myocardial infarction (MI), ST-segment
    elevation
stents
    anticoagulant therapy for, 416
    aortic valve prosthesis with, 200
    drug-eluting, 409, 412, 413, 416
    intracoronary, 387, 407, 408-409, 410*f*
    for peripheral arterial disease, 255
    restenosis and, 409, 411-412, 413
    thrombosis of, 414
sternotomy, median, 390, 395
stimulant agents, mitral prolapse and, 189
streptokinase, 73, 74, 74*t*, 75
stress, 146, 310, 435
stress testing, 121, 124-127, 125*t*. *See also* exercise stress test
    for aortic valve conditions, 197, 198, 204
    contraindications to, 126-127
stroke
    aortic aneurysm and, 244
    atrial fibrillation and, 218-219, 228
    cardioversion and, 224
    CHA2DS2-VASc risk score for, 218, 229, 231, 438
    coronary artery bypass and, 397, 398
    mitral stenosis and, 182, 184

mortality rates for, 48
    percutaneous coronary intervention and, 414
stroke volume
    aortic stenosis and, 194
    cardiac output and, 32-36, 33*f,* 34*f,* 34*t*
    components of, 9, 18, 32
    measurement of, 39
    in older adults, 25
    tachycardia and, 305
ST segment. *See also* myocardial infarction (MI),
    ST-segment elevation
    elevation of, 289, 292-293, 296*f,* 297*f,* 307
    non-elevation or depression of, 298, 300-301
subcutaneous emphysema, 377
sudden cardiac death. *See* cardiac arrest
summation gallop, 442
superior vena cava, 2, 3*f,* 7*f,* 8*f,* 12-13
supraventricular tachydysrhythmias, 335. *See also* atrial
    fibrillation
    narrow complex, 335, 337-340, 338*f*-342*f*
    wide complex, 340
surgical history, 437
SVR (systemic vascular resistance), 33*f,* 35, 39
sympathetic nervous system, 20-21
    heart failure and, 160, 161*f,* 162*f,* 163*t*
    heart rate and, 32, 33*f,* 35*f*
    receptors of, 21*t*
sympathomimetics, 58-60, 59*t*-61*t*
    afterload and, 84*t*
    contractility and, 85*t*
    heart rate and, 86*t*
syncope, 371-374
    aortic aneurysm and, 244
    aortic stenosis and, 194, 199
    atrial fibrillation and, 218
    case study for, 380-381
    causes of, 371-372
    history of, 429-430
    neurocardiogenic, 264
    treatment of, 373-374
synergy, normal muscular, 36-37
systemic vascular resistance (SVR), 33*f,* 35, 39
systole, 19-20, 214*f*
    aortic function in, 202*f*
    coronary circulation in, 15
    heart sounds in, 442
    valve function in, 7, 8, 9
systolic heart failure, 156

T
tachybrady syndrome, 263
tachycardia, 335. *See also* ventricular tachycardia
    atrioventricular nodal reentrant, 337, 338*f,* 340*f*

atrioventricular reentrant, 338, 339*f*, 340*f*, 350-351

beta blockers to prevent, 68, 69

cardiac output and, 32

cardiomyopathy and, 219, 220

drugs causing, 58, 62, 63, 89, 247

focal atrial, 338, 341*f*

multifocal atrial, 339-340, 341*f*, 342*f*

myocardial infarction and, 292, 305

reflex, 22

sinus, 335, 337, 337*f*

tachydysrhythmias, 335, 337-343

cardioversion for, 276-277, 351

clinical approach to, 335

narrow complex, 335, 337-340, 337*f*-342*f*

syncope in, 429, 430

wide complex, 340-343, 343*f*

tachyphylaxis, 58

tachypnea, 440

tadalafil, 304

takotsubo cardiomyopathy, 146-148, 147*f*, 148*f*

team, interprofessional, 455-457, 455*b*

temperature, body, 440

tenecteplase (TNK-t-PA), 73, 74, 74*t*

tension pneumothorax, 358

thiazide diuretics, 63, 64

for heart failure, 168

for hypertension, 99, 100*t*, 101

thiazolidinediones, 169

thoracic aorta, 12, 13*f*, 238*f*

thoracic aortic aneurysm, 239, 241. *See also* aortic aneurysms

heart failure and, 322

signs and symptoms of, 256

thoracic cavity, 1-2, 2*f*

thorax, examination of, 444

thrill, precordial, 441

thrombectomy

AngioJet, 410-411

pulmonary, 358, 365

thrombin, 73

direct inhibitors of, 76, 78, 79, 80

heparin and, 75

thrombocytopenia, heparin-induced, 78, 79

thromboembolism

atrial fibrillation and, 218, 228-229, 231

cardioversion and, 224-225

coronary artery bypass and, 397

percutaneous coronary intervention and, 414

peripheral arterial disease and, 252

pulmonary, 358, 362, 429

vein graft and, 415

thrombolysis, catheter-based, 255

Thrombolysis in Myocardial Infarction (TIMI) risk score, 438

thrombolytics, 73-75, 74*t*

for pulmonary embolism, 358, 365

thrombophlebitis, 249-250

thrombosis

acute coronary syndromes and, 290-291, 300

deep vein, 26, 248

incomplete, 300

thromboxane A2, 81

thyroid gland, palpation of, 444

thyroid hormone, 207

ticagrelor, 81, 82

for acute coronary syndromes, 302, 303, 308

tilt test, 373

tirofiban (Aggrastat), 80, 402

tissue factor, 73

tissue plasminogen activator (t-PA), 73-74, 74*t*

tobacco use, 433-434. *See also* smoking

toe-brachial index, 253

torsades de pointes, 341

drugs causing, 223, 224

magnesium sulfate for, 305

transmyocardial laser revascularization, 404-405

transtelephonic monitoring of pacemaker, 277-278

Traube's sign, 203*t*

Tricor (fenofibrate), 105, 107, 108

tricuspid valve, 6-7, 8*f*

auscultation of, 441

function of, 9, 10*f*, 13, 19, 205

tricuspid valve regurgitation, 205-208

tricuspid valve repair/replacement, 207-208, 208*b*

tricyclic antidepressants, 349

triggered activity, cardiac, 334

triglycerides, 49, 102

bile acid sequestrants and, 106

drugs for lowering, 105, 106*t*

troponins, cardiac

acute coronary syndromes and, 293, 301, 302*t*, 315

heart failure and, 323, 324

T tubules, 20

tuberculosis, 377

tunicae, vascular, 10, 11*f*

T wave inversion, 300

twiddler's syndrome, 273

U

ulcers, 249, 251

ultrafiltration, 324

ultrasound

duplex, 250, 253

intravascular, 412

umbilical vein grafts, 395

unlicensed assistive personnel, 456, 457

uremia, pericarditis in, 377, 378

V

vaccinations, 435
vagal maneuvers, 337, 338, 343
vagal response, 22, 23
Valsalva maneuver, 443
valsartan, 168
values, professional, 454
valves. *See also* aortic valve; mitral valve; pulmonic
  valve; tricuspid valve
    atrioventricular, 6-7, 8-9, 8*f*, 10*f*
    prosthetic, 446
    semilunar, 6, 7-9, 8*f*, 10*f*
    venous, 12, 248
valvular heart disease, 179-180
    acute, 322
    aortic, 192-205, 243
    clinical manifestations of, 445-446
    coronary artery bypass and, 404
    endocarditis and, 378, 379
    hypertrophic cardiomyopathy and, 143
    mitral, 180-192, 306
    regurgitation in, 9, 179, 180
    risk factors for, 436
    stenosis in, 9, 35, 179
    tricuspid, 205-208
valvuloplasty, percutaneous balloon, 199
varicose veins, 12, 248, 251, 430
vascular closure devices, 417, 418*t*
vascular complications of percutaneous coronary intervention, 413-414, 418
vasodilators, 58. *See also* nitrates
    afterload and, 84, 85*t*
    for aortic aneurysm, 247
    for aortic valve conditions, 198, 204
    for heart failure, 325, 326
    for hypertensive emergency, 376
    preload and, 83, 83*t*, 84*t*
vasopressin, 60-61
    afterload and, 84*t*
    angiotensin II and, 65
    heart failure and, 160, 161, 161*f*, 163*t*
    in pregnancy, 24
    for septic shock, 361
vasopressors, 58
    afterload and, 83, 84*t*
    for shock, 361, 363
vasovagal syncope, 371, 372, 429
Vaughan Williams antiarrhythmic drug classification,
  221, 222*t*
veins, 11*f*, 12
    cardiac, 17
    in older adults, 25
    varicose, 12, 248, 251, 430

vena cava, compression of, 24
venography, 250
venous disease, chronic, 237, 247-251
    diagnosis and management of, 250-251
    leg pain in, 430
    pathophysiology of, 248-249
    physical examination of, 249-250
venous grafts
    for coronary artery bypass, 390-392, 393, 393*f*, 394*f*,
      395
    preventing closure of, 406
    stenosis of, 415
venous insufficiency, chronic, 247-248
venous pressure monitoring, ambulatory, 250
venous reserve, 405
ventricles, 2-3, 3*f*, 7*f*, 8*f*. *See also* left ventricle; right ventricle
    myocardium of, 4, 4*f*
    normal muscular synergy of, 36-37
ventricular dysrhythmias
    drugs causing, 222*t*, 223
    myocardial infarction and, 305
    tachycardic, 335
ventricular fibrillation, 347, 348*f*
    cardioverter-defibrillators for, 276-277
    myocardial infarction and, 305
ventricular remodeling, 306-307
ventricular septal rupture, 296, 306
ventricular tachycardia, 340-343, 343*f*
    cardioverter-defibrillator for, 276-277
    monomorphic, 340, 341, 343*f*
    polymorphic, 341-342, 343*f*
    with pulse, 343
    pulseless, 342
    sustained *vs.* nonsustained, 341
ventriculography, 147, 148*f*, 206
verapamil, 68-69, 69*t*
    for atrial fibrillation, 184, 220
    for atrioventricular nodal reentrant tachycardia, 337
    digoxin and, 72
very low-density lipoproteins (VLDL), 102
Viagra (sildenafil), 63, 304
visceral pericardium, 5*f*, 6, 7*f*
vital signs, 439-440
    orthostatic, 373, 374, 439
    trending, 445, 446
vitamin K, 76-77, 77*t*
vitamins, fat-soluble, 106, 107
VVI pacing mode, 269, 269*t*

W

waist circumference, 440
walking program, 310, 312
warfarin (Coumadin), 76-77, 78

for aortic valve conditions, 200, 201, 205
for atrial fibrillation, 219
contraindications to, 80
coronary artery bypass and, 402
for mitral valve conditions, 184, 186, 192
for peripheral arterial disease, 254
pharmacogenomics of, 88
pre-cardioversion, 224
side effects of, 79
vitamin K and, 77, 77*t*
water-hammer pulse, 203*t*
weight, 434-435, 440. *See also* obesity
daily monitoring of, 171, 174, 206-207
reduction of, 99-100, 250
Welchol (colesevelam), 106
white clot, 73
Wolff-Parkinson-White (WPW) syndrome, 338, 339*f*
atrial fibrillation with, 220, 229-230, 230*b*
case study for, 350-351
women. *See also* pregnancy
acute coronary syndromes in, 292, 300, 302
angina in, 123-124, 429
cardiac syndrome X in, 308
cardiovascular disease in, 50
coronary artery bypass and, 403
health history for, 437
heart failure in, 156, 159
mitral regurgitation in, 186
takotsubo cardiomyopathy in, 146
World Health Organization, 51
wound infection, sternal, 398-399, 400*b*

X

xanthelasmas, 443
Xarelto (rivaroxaban), 78, 79

Z

Zocor (simvastatin), 105, 108, 110